DATE DUE

DEC 1 7 2002	
FEB 1 4 2003	
MAR 1 9 2003	
APR 3 - 2003	
MAY 2 5 2003	
JUN 2 5 2003	
JAN 2 1 2005	
MAY 3 1 2005	
3/1/09	

GAYLORD   PRINTED IN U.S.A.

CUBA CONFIDENTIAL

CUBA CONFIDENTIAL

LOVE AND VENGEANCE IN MIAMI AND HAVANA

ANN LOUISE BARDACH

RANDOM HOUSE | NEW YORK

Library of Congress Cataloging-in-Publication Data

Bardach, Ann Louise.
Cuba confidential : love and vengeance in Miami and Havana / Ann Louise
Bardach.
p. cm.
Includes bibliographical references and index.
ISBN 0-375-50489-3
1. United States—Foreign relations—Cuba. 2. Cuba—Foreign relations—United
States. 3. Exiles—Florida—Miami—Political activity. 4. Cuban Americans—
Florida—Miami—Politics and government. 5. Political corruption—United
States—History—20th century. 6. González, Elián, 1993– 7. Refugee children—
Cuba—Biography. 8. Castro, Fidel, 1927– 9. Castro, Fidel, 1927– —Family.
10. Castro, Fidel, 1927– —Friends and associates. I. Title.

E183.8.C9 B35 2002
972.9106'4—dc21
2002017887

Printed in the United States of America on acid-free paper
Random House website address: www.atrandom.com

24689753

FIRST EDITION

Book design by Barbara M. Bachman

In grateful memory of José Rodríguez Feo,

who inspired this adventure, and

José Luis Llovio-Menéndez, who was my guide

ACKNOWLEDGMENTS

THIS BOOK HAS HAD MANY MUSES AND MENTORS. Its origin was in my first meeting with Joŝe Rodríguez Feo, the great essayist, critic, former aristocrat and onetime libertine, at his crumbling Vedado apartment in Havana. During our brief friendship—cut short by his death in 1994— Rodríguez Feo transmitted to me his passion for Cuban culture, politics and intrigue. The following year, I met Joŝe Luis Llovio-Menéndez, a Cuban official who defected in 1986. It was Llovio who steered and guided me along the slippery shoals of the Cuba-Miami showdown, brainstorming interviews and trips to Cuba, and who escorted me on several trips to Union City, New Jersey. The influence of these two men on my work is incalculable, their loss immeasurable.

The void has been filled, to a large degree, by many Cubans on both sides of the Florida Straits who have extended their support and friendship to me. They include Salvador Lew, Lilia Medina, Rosario Moreno, Uva de Aragón, Sonia Báez, Jorge Tabio, Achy Obejas, Rosa Lowinger, Richard Alexander, John Padilla, MariTeri Vichot, Anibal Quevedo, Al Arias and Natália Bolívar. Special thanks go to Jorge Munero and his wife, María, who shared the story of their family with me.

This work would have been impossible had it not been for the dozens of scholars, writers, analysts and historians who trailblazed the path. The most influential and useful in my research have been Hugh Thomas, the late great Tad Szulc, Louis A. Pérez, María de los Angeles Torres, Guillermo Cabrera Infante, Luis Conte Agüero for his *Cartas del Presidio,* Carlos Franqui, Nelson Valdés and Ruth Behar for her collection *Bridges to Cuba.*

I have been blessed over the years by many superb and good-humored assistants who have toiled in the trenches with me—fact-checking, researching, transcribing, translating. They are Luis Prat, Joanne Wright, Gina Becchetti, Lupe Corona, Robert Figueroa, Libby Báez, Lochy Le Riverend and Ana Fresquette. Invaluable insights and suggestions have come from many people, including David Rieff; George Volsky; Lou Cannon, who urged me to write this book; Constance Penley; Frank and Nita Manitzas; Beryl Kreisel; and Reinaldo Herrera. My friends Holly Palance, Anton Vonk and Diane Boss saw to it that I had some restorative breaks from writing, and my computer whiz, Serge Espinosa, saved many a day for me. The indefatigable Jan Miller guided me through an earlier foray into publishing. Special thanks go to a small army of lawyers who scrubbed down this manuscript, most notably the terrific media attorney Tom Julin, who vetted the manuscript with his trademark conscientiousness; Richard Ovelmen, who has been a continuous source of wisdom; and Random House's wise Amelia Zalcman. I also want to extend thanks to Steve Messina, who faced a formidable task as the book's production editor.

Thanks go to my editors at *Vanity Fair,* the *New York Times* and the late *Talk* magazine for supporting and underwriting much of this research, along with Jonathan Clarke and the American Journalism Foundation. Photographer Cindy Karp and CORBIS went the extra mile to assemble the photographs for this book.

My greatest and ongoing debts are to my literary agent, the remarkably gifted and diligent Tina Bennett, and to the sagacious Ann Godoff, who steered this project to Random House. One would be hard-pressed to find a more dedicated and intelligent editor than Joy de Menil, who brought her own scholarship and superb judgment to bear on the manuscript. Her assistant, Robin Rolewicz, facilitated and simplified the most daunting logistics.

I have also benefited immeasurably over the years from the assistance, advice and friendship of several reporters in Miami, most notably Andrés Oppenheimer, Meg Laughlin, Jane Bussey, Karl Ross, Kerry Gruson and Lucia Newman, and I thank my parents, Ruth and Emil Bardach, who set the gold standard for taking the road less traveled.

Regrettably, there are many others I would like to credit in both Cuba and Miami, but I must refrain from doing so in the interests of their personal well-being and serenity.

Last but most crucial is my husband, Robert Lesser, who made this— and most all else in my life—possible.

CONTENTS

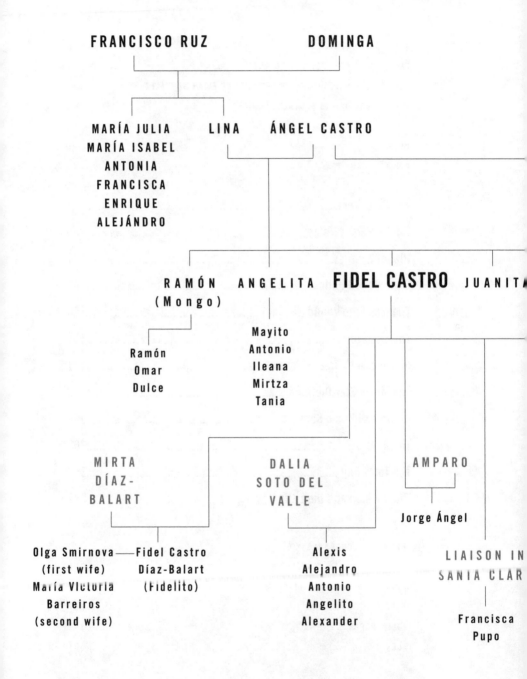

FAMILY TREE OF
FIDEL CASTRO RUZ

FRANCISCO RUZ — DOMINGA

MARÍA JULIA
MARÍA ISABEL
ANTONIA
FRANCISCA
ENRIQUE
ALEJÁNDRO

LINA — ÁNGEL CASTRO

RAMÓN
(Mongo)

ANGELITA

FIDEL CASTRO

JUANITA

Ramón
Omar
Dulce

Mayito
Antonio
Ileana
Mirtza
Tania

MIRTA
DÍAZ-
BALART

DALIA
SOTO DEL
VALLE

AMPARO

Jorge Ángel

Olga Smirnova
(first wife)
María Victoria
Barreiros
(second wife)

Fidel Castro
Díaz-Balart
(Fidelito)

Alexis
Alejandro
Antonio
Angelito
Alexander

LIAISON IN
SANTA CLARA

Francisca
Pupo

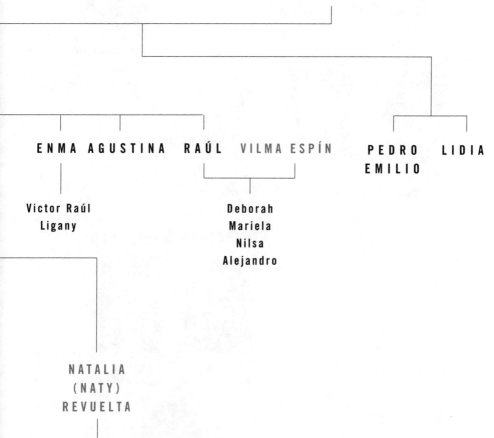

MARÍA LUISA ARGOTA

ENMA   AGUSTINA   RAÚL   VILMA ESPÍN   PEDRO   LIDIA
                                            EMILIO

Victor Raúl   Deborah
Ligany   Mariela
                             Nilsa
                             Alejandro

NATALIA
(NATY)
REVUELTA

Alina Fernández

THE RODRÍGUEZ FAMILY

Manolo
Rodríguez

Mérida Loreto
Barrios

Lirka Guillermo,
neighbor
of the Rodríguezes

Juan Carlos
Rodríguez

Nelson
Rodríguez

Nelson's wife,
Zenaida Santos

THE OTHER SURVIVORS

Nivaldo
Fernández

his girlfriend,
Arianne Horta

Estefany Herrera Horta
(Arianne's daughter,
who returned to shore)

THE BOAT OF ELIÁN GONZÁLEZ

THE MUNERO FAMILY

Rafael Munero

María Elena
García

Jikary Munero

Lázaro (Rafa)
Munero

Lázaro's fiancée,
Elizabet Brotón

Elián González

FAMILY TREE OF
THE GONZÁLEZ FAMILY

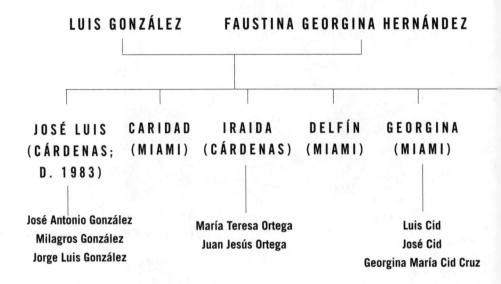

LUIS GONZÁLEZ   FAUSTINA GEORGINA HERNÁNDEZ

JOSÉ LUIS
(CÁRDENAS;
D. 1983)

CARIDAD
(MIAMI)

IRAIDA
(CÁRDENAS)

DELFÍN
(MIAMI)

GEORGINA
(MIAMI)

José Antonio González
Milagros González
Jorge Luis González

María Teresa Ortega
Juan Jesús Ortega

Luis Cid
José Cid
Georgina María Cid Cruz

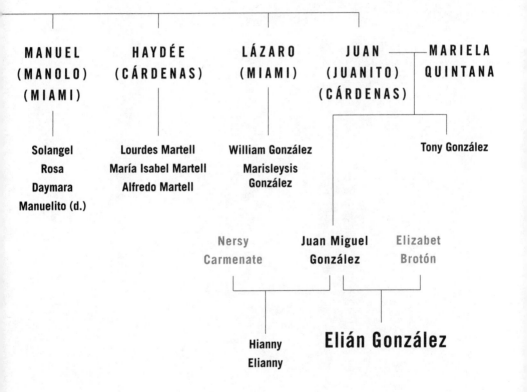

MANUEL
(MANOLO)
(MIAMI)

HAYDÉE
(CÁRDENAS)

LÁZARO
(MIAMI)

JUAN ———— MARIELA
(JUANITO)   QUINTANA
(CÁRDENAS)

Solangel
Rosa
Daymara
Manuelito (d.)

Lourdes Martell
María Isabel Martell
Alfredo Martell

William González
Marisleysis
González

Tony González

Nersy
Carmenate

Juan Miguel
González

Elizabet
Brotón

Hianny
Elianny

Elián González

PREFACE

*C*UBA CONFIDENTIAL is the outcome of my ten years of reporting on Cuba and its exiles. It is a chronicle of that ever-simmering standoff between Miami and Havana that seems to ignite each year with the clockwork precision of a hardy perennial, animating the parties with hope and, inevitably, disappointment. I have struggled to write a history of this high-stakes showdown through the stories of the central personalities and events that dominate it. However, this is not a history of Cuba. Nor is it a Fidel Castro biography. For the former I would recommend Hugh Thomas's opus *Cuba; or, The Pursuit of Freedom,* and Tad Szulc's *Fidel: A Critical Portrait* for the latter. Both have invaluably informed this work.

The foremost challenge in writing about Cuba and the exile world is finding fresh and useful perspectives—dodging the swirl of stale rhetoric and hyperbolic propaganda that envelops the subject. One prism through which I have chosen to view this forty-three-year-old quagmire is that of the broken family. The Cuban Revolution has ravaged the Cuban family much as the Civil War in the United States ravaged American families, with cousins, aunts and uncles often facing off against brothers, sisters and parents. The trope of the shattered family has infused the Cuban conflict with an emotionality that is the stuff of Greek drama, with plotlines borrowed from Shakespeare and afternoon *telenovelas.* From the family of Fidel Castro, who rages against his former in-laws, to that of the most recent rafter washed up on the shores of Florida, it is the rare Cuban family that has not faced wrenching separation and loss. Lincoln and Mario Díaz-Balart, congressional and state representatives from Miami, are also the cousins of Fidelito Castro Díaz-Balart, the eldest son of the Cuban leader. Even Luis Posada Carriles, Castro's lifelong would-be assassin, unhappily confronts the fact that most of his family have remained stalwart *fidelistas* in Cuba. Puzzled and impatient observers will often ask why this conflict has proven so intractable, so immune to resolution. The answer, in part, with no diminishment intended, is that it is a huge family feud, filled with the corresponding heartbreak, rancor and bitterness.

The second prism through which I have chosen to tell this story is the parallel universes of the Two Cubas: that of the largest island in the Caribbean, home to more than eleven million inhabitants, and the one in

Miami, to which one and a half million exiles have fled. Contrary to expectations, the most salient feature of the warring parties is *not* how different they are, but how similar. Exiles may have escaped Fidel Castro, but they have not left him behind. Nor have they eluded the Cuban predilection, spanning centuries, for *caudillos*—political bosses. In Miami, the controversial Jorge Mas Canosa led the charge against Castro for almost twenty years. Like his nemesis, Mas Canosa was a belligerent *oriental* from Santiago de Cuba who never won an election and adopted a scorched-earth policy toward those who opposed him. This book seeks to chronicle two parallel tragedies: the hijacking of the Cuban Revolution by Fidel Castro and a similar phenomenon in Miami—as exiles seeking freedom have been shunted into silence by hard-liners bent on revenge, retribution and power.

In Cuba, one used to be either a *revolucionario* or a *contrarevolucionario,* while those who decided to leave were *gusanos* (worms) or *escoria* (scum). In Miami, the rhetoric has been equally harsh. Exiles who do not endorse a confrontational policy with Cuba, seeking instead a negotiated settlement, are typically excoriated as *traidores* (traitors) and sometimes *espías* (spies). Cubans, notably cultural stars, who visit Miami but choose to return to their homeland are routinely denounced. One either defects or is repudiated.

But there has been a slow but steady shift in the last decade—a nod to the clear majority of Cubans *en exilio* and on the island who crave family reunification. Since 1978, more than one million airline tickets have been sold for flights from Miami to Havana. Faced with the brisk and continuous traffic between Miami and Havana, hard-liners on both sides have opted to deny the new reality. Anomalies such as the phenomenon of reverse *balseros,* Cubans who, unable to adapt to the pressures and bustle of entrepreneurial Miami, return to the island, or *gusañeros,* expatriates who send a portion of their earnings home in exchange for unfettered travel back and forth to Cuba (the term is a curious Cuban hybrid of *gusano* and *compañero,* or comrade), are unacknowledged by both sides, as are those who live in *semi-exilio,* returning home to Cuba for long holidays.

This is also the story of another bad marriage—Havana and Washington. Despite their small numbers (Cuban-Americans make up 0.4 percent of the U.S. population), the influence and clout of Cuban exiles in Washington is almost without equal. This is all the more remarkable given that there is perhaps only one point of consensus among all the players in the Cuban debate: that the U.S. Embargo has failed to achieve its stated goals—it has yet to displace Fidel Castro and Cuba has yet to see open elections and a free press.

Nevertheless, for four weary decades Washington has promulgated this transparently disastrous policy, trading off sensible and enduring solutions for short-term electoral gains in one or two counties in South Florida and in Union City, New Jersey.

The family politics of this story are not limited to Cubans. To a surprising extent, the fortunes of the Bush family, from former President George H.W. Bush to the current President, George W. Bush, and, most notably, his brother the governor of Florida, Jeb Bush, have ebbed and flowed in relation to their dealings with Cuban exiles. Indeed, the Miami exile leadership often and proudly takes credit for George W. Bush's presidency while doing its part in maintaining the vitriolic, take-no-prisoners political dynamic. A typical volley came in March 2002, when Secretary of the Treasury Paul O'Neill said he favored loosening travel restrictions on Cuba, musing aloud what most law enforcement officials have been muttering for some time, that he would prefer to spend Treasury resources on tracking terrorists and their covert funds instead of stalking geriatric retirees who visit Cuba. Immediately, both of Miami's exile congressional representatives, Ileana Ros-Lehtinen and Lincoln Díaz-Balart, demanded that President Bush fire O'Neill for his heresy. And they were heard. O'Neill quickly backpedaled and the White House offered a message of appeasement.

Several points need to be made clearly upfront and cannot be overstated. Cuban exiles are not a monolith; they have the diversity and multifacetedness of every other ethnic group. When I speak of and refer to the exile leadership, I mean those who have occupied the seat of power—elected or not—in Miami since 1959. This group is commonly described as right-wingers or hard-liners, but even this is misleading. Exiles are not, as a rule, conservatives. More often than not, they champion a political platform commonly ascribed to Democrats or liberals: they favor generous social benefits, including increases in Social Security, Medicare, aid for prescription drugs and bilingual education. More often than not, they are pro-choice and concerned about environmental issues. Their commitment to the Republican Party hangs on one issue: its hard-line nonengagement policy with Cuba, which goes back to Eisenhower, and a lingering bitterness at President John F. Kennedy's refusal to provide air cover during the Bay of Pigs invasion. A current member of the exile organization the 2506 Brigade points out this irony: "Many of us were social progressives in Cuba—left-wingers fighting Batista," he said. "Now we're right-wingers fighting Castro."

The playing field of the Cuban debate has shifted considerably in recent years. Hard-line exiles—*duros*—are being challenged not only by free-trade

Republicans, farmers and businessmen eyeing a stake in a future Cuba, but also by their own offspring. Scores of U.S.-born Cuban-Americans, unfettered by their parents' rage, have sought to engage with Cuba. They travel regularly to the island, often without notifying their families. An unlikely but compelling parallel is with the Chinese in New York and San Francisco. For decades, these successful and prosperous communities, bound by bitter memories of Mao's brutal rule, swore unyielding allegiance to the Kuomintang and vowed never to engage with China until the end of communist rule. But in the late 1970s, their American-born children became interested in their roots and began to establish new ties with mainland China.

And young Cuban-Americans are not the only ones gazing southward. Even as an embargoed Third World country, Cuba bristles with allure. The story of Cuba, this extraordinary country, has ceaselessly engaged our most extreme passions and dominated the American imagination, from our foreign policy to our fantasies. "So far from God and so close to the United States," goes the lament, lifted from former Mexican President Porfirio Díaz's ironic quip about his country but cited more often, and more aptly, about Cuba.

Cuba has always had a special, insistent hold on Americans—from its gambling casinos to its sugarcane fields to the siren song of its infectious music. Every year, America's fascination with Cuba bursts into the headlines. In the last year, the U.S. military base in Guantánamo, Cuba, became the unlikely holding cell for Al Qaeda terrorists, refocusing the world on the peculiar U.S.-Cuba relationship. In May 2002, Jimmy Carter made history by becoming the first American President to go to Cuba since 1928; he visited the island's leading dissidents, addressed the Cuban people on live television and denounced the U.S. Embargo from Havana. In 1999 and 2000, the country was held spellbound by the saga of Elián González for more than seven months. In 1999, the dizzying success of the movie *Buena Vista Social Club* introduced Main Street USA to *vieja trova* music. In 1996, pilots from the exile group Brothers to the Rescue were shot down by the Cuban government, precipitating the passage of the Helms-Burton Act, which vastly tightened the Embargo—and on through the Mariel refugee crisis of 1980 and going back to the Cuban Missile Crisis and beyond.

My decade of reporting on this conflict took me on eleven trips to Cuba, where I visited every province and major city on the island. To meet a diverse sampling of exiles, I made more than a dozen extended trips to Miami, Union City, Puerto Rico and Venezuela. I have interviewed hundreds of Cubans, including Fidel Casto in Havana, his sister Juanita in Miami, the family of Elián González in Cárdenas and supporters of his relatives in Miami, the family of Robert Vesco, family members of Fulgencio Batista and the Díaz-Balarts. Covering Cuba and Miami is not without its hazards, and has prompted recriminations against me at various times from both sides. It has cost me my press visa for travel to Cuba on several occasions—notably after I reported on Robert Vesco (I did not get another visa for almost two years) and more recently after I compiled an oral history of Castro for his seventy-fifth birthday. In the best of circumstances, traveling to Cuba for reporters involves a grueling ritual of begging for a visa for each expedition. One's work is thoroughly scrutinized and press visas are dispensed accordingly, or withheld. I have always been keenly aware that some of my comings and goings have been duly noted. Likewise, I have been denounced in Miami on more than one occasion.

I have used the Elián González affair as a starting point through which to tell this story, as it has proven to be the single most transforming event for Cuba-U.S. relations since the Bay of Pigs. For seven months, Miami convulsed with a frenzy that transformed a five-year-old boy from Cárdenas into the poster child of the U.S.-Cuban Cold War and wrought profound political repercussions in Washington. But I have never been interested as much in the charismatic boy-child as in his fellow passengers on that doomed voyage and why they left. The searingly tragic shipwreck and what it came to represent, coupled with the rhetoric and politics of demonization that followed in its wake, offered another prism through which to look again at Miami and Havana and how their feud played out in Washington.

The central personality in the Cuban conversation is, of course, Fidel Castro, the movie star dictator, the ham actor who has steadfastly refused to leave the stage. But as his rule comes to its inevitable close, we are faced with a new challenge—that of seeing Cuba without his bearded visage. And that may prove to be the most daunting task to date: to develop an approach to Cuba that is not merely a reaction to an aging *comandante* who cannot admit that he has made a mistake.

The origin of this book was an assignment ten years ago from my editor at *Vanity Fair*—to find and interview Fidel Castro. Cuba would become an obsession, and later an adventure and, at times, a crucible—but one I would not have missed for all the world.

ANN LOUISE BARDACH
June 15, 2002

A NOTE ON THE TEXT

IN DEFERENCE TO THE ENGLISH LANGUAGE READER, I have sought to streamline the many names in this book. The conventional Cuban last name or *apellido* includes the last names of both the father and mother, often appended to several middle names. For example, the full name of the Cuban president is Fidel Alejandro Castro Ruz and that of his nemesis is Luis Clemente Posada Carriles. In the interest of clarity, I have generally dropped the second part of the *apellido,* usually after an initial identification. In some cases I have used the name of the subject's preference: therefore, Eloy Gutiérrez Menoyo is referred to as Menoyo.

In the chapters dealing with the many members of the González, Munero and Rodríguez families of Miami and Cárdenas, I have chosen to use mostly first names—Juan Miguel, Lázaro, Marisleysis and so on. This seemed necessary to avoid confusion. In identifying the mother of Elián González, I have used the spelling Elizabet Brotón, along with her nickname, Elisa, deferring to her mother as the ultimate authority. Elisa's boyfriend, Rafael Lázaro Munero, is referred to by his nickname, Rafa, to avoid confusion with his father and with the great-uncle of Elián González.

CUBA CONFIDENTIAL

CHAPTER 1

THE SHIPWRECK

Dos patrias tengo yo—Cuba y la noche.
I have two countries—Cuba and the night.

JOSÉ MARTÍ

O N SATURDAY, NOVEMBER 20, 1999, fifteen Cubans ranging in age from
five to sixty-five straggled through a cluster of mangrove trees to the marshy
shoreline of Cárdenas, Cuba. There they huddled around a seventeen-foot
aluminum handcrafted boat with a fifty-horsepower outboard motor, camou-
flaged by knee-high *pangola* grass. Swiftly and quietly they loaded the small
craft with everything that they would be taking: cheese and crackers, hot
dogs, water and some blankets. All the money they had in the world was
stuffed in their pockets.

The group was made up of two extended families, friends of long standing. There was the Rodríguez clan with their two sons, a daughter-in-law,
and a next-door neighbor. And there was the Munero family—Rafael, forty-
nine, his wife, María Elena, forty-eight, and their two sons. One of their
sons, twenty-four-year-old Lázaro Munero, called Rafa by his family, was the
mastermind, boat builder and driving force behind the escape. Accompanying him was his girlfriend, Elizabet Brotón, a shy, sweet-faced woman with
long, dark hair and bangs running along her broad forehead, who was
known as Elisa. With her was her five-year-old son, Elián González.

Then there was another couple in their early twenties—two fleeing
lovers and the young woman's five-year-old daughter. The couple, unknown
to most of the others, were the only ones who had paid Rafa for passage on
the boat.

All of the fifteen aboard had their own reasons for leaving, their own expectations, their own dreams. Some were seeking more opportunity, some
were fleeing a spouse or family in Cárdenas, some loathed Fidel Castro and
communism, and some wanted better clothes and a better house. But the

glue that bound the group together was love and family: the love of a spouse or a sibling waiting for them in America—the dream of family reunification.

More than half of the group could not swim and several had a dread of the sea. María Elena, Rafael Munero's wife, was recovering from recent heart problems and, like many working-class women from the country's provinces, had never learned to swim. For her, the splendid waters that enveloped Cuba's crocodile-shaped form were to be admired from the shoreline but never entered. María Elena had not been feeling well and had had an ominous presentiment about the crossing. But family was the cornerstone of her existence, and if her husband and sons were leaving, so would she.

Earlier in the evening, Rafael Munero had gone out alone to inspect the boat. Suddenly, he heard footsteps coming from behind him and, alarmed, swung around. Seeing that it was his brother Dagoberto who had secretly followed him to the boat, Rafael sighed with nervous relief.

Five days before, Rafael had confided to his younger brother that he and his family planned to flee the country and asked him to come. Dagoberto refused. He had had other opportunities to defect—when two other brothers had done so—but leaving was not for him. He lacked the ambition and energy of his siblings, and Cuba's socialism provided for his basic needs whether he worked or not. To prove his point, he boasted of having had laparoscopic surgery on his knee. "How much would that cost in the U.S.?" he asked knowingly. For days, the two argued and bickered. At times, Rafael would change his mind and say he wouldn't go, but after a pep talk from his son, he would recommit to the trip. On and off it went, even through their farewell dinner of roast pork in their cramped apartment, with Juan Gabriel crooning on the tape deck. Dagoberto had swung by around 9:30 in the evening. "The group was all gathered there," he would later recall. "I saw the couple there with her daughter. She was asking if the sea was rough. I asked her: 'You're going with that little girl?' And she told me yes. I told her: 'Here the waves are a meter high but out there they are four or five times more, up to ten meters high.' "

Dagoberto would not give up. He could not bear to lose Rafael, who had raised him like a son after their father had died when Dagoberto was still a teenager. "I was crying because when someone goes over there you always think the worst. My brother ate his dinner, then he left his place alone. I thought this was my last opportunity to talk to him again. I saw that he went for the brush that is all along the shore and I followed him. And when I got there I saw the boat."

Circling the narrow homemade boat, Dagoberto could see that parts of it were rusty and that holes in its bottom had been patched with packing materials. "I can't believe you're leaving on this piece of shit," Dagoberto bellowed to his brother. "This is not a boat. It's garbage! You're crazy." But, Rafael had made up his mind and didn't want to hear any more from him. "We're leaving on it," he said, his voice pitched with anger, "and if you're not coming with us, get out of here and leave me alone!"

There was nothing more to say or do. Angry and wounded, Dagoberto shuffled back to the main road, then made his way home. "I didn't say goodbye to him. I left him there alone maybe 10:30 that night," Dagoberto mumbled. "I left and I never saw him again."

AROUND 6:00 A.M. on Thanksgiving Day, Juan Ruiz and his friend Reniel Carmenate were coming ashore after an evening of fishing off Miami's Key Biscayne. Ruiz said that as they docked they could make out the forms of two people huddling and shivering on the shore by the water's edge. Nearby was an oversized Russian-made black truck tire. "They were in really bad, bad condition," said Ruiz. "Their skin was a sickly purple color, all ripply with wrinkles and covered in blisters. I wanted to help them take their clothes off because the material was welded into their skin but I was afraid that their skin would tear. The man was in the worse shape, almost going in and out of consciousness. They kept asking for water but I knew from experience that water could really hurt them unless it was given to them through an IV drip. We called the police and I ran to my truck and got some dry clothes."

The man was almost delirious; the woman's bones had decalcified from days of ocean immersion. Their bodies were latticed with the bite marks of fish. "The lady was the one who spoke and told us what had happened," said Ruiz. "She said they left Cuba with twelve others but that everyone had drowned—including a little boy." The young couple were the fleeing lovers—thirty-three-year-old Nivaldo Fernández and his twenty-two-year-old girlfriend, Arianne Horta.

Thirty miles farther north off Fort Lauderdale, Sam Ciancio was out in his cabin cruiser. With him was his cousin Donato Dalrymple, a housecleaner, out for the first time on his cousin's boat. Ciancio spied a large black inner tube bobbing in the Atlantic and thought he saw the outlines of a large doll inside the tire. But as they steered closer to the tire, they saw it was not a doll but rather a small child tied to the inner tube. Ciancio dove into the water and brought the boy aboard. The trembling child was five-year-old Elián González, who, in a matter of hours, would become the poster boy for both sides of America's forty-year-old Cold War with Cuba.

The three were the sole survivors of the group that had left Cárdenas in the wee hours of November 22. Elián's mother, Elisa, and her boyfriend, Rafa Munero, were among the eleven who had drowned—along with his brother, mother, and father. Not far from Elián's inner tube, the body of sixty-one-year-old Mérida Loreto Barrios, the matriarch of the Rodríguez clan, tethered to the end of a long rope, was found floating over the surface of the waves like bait. Stuffed in her undergarments was $210 in twenty- and ten-dollar bills. She had been the last of her family to die—after witnessing the drowning of her two sons, her husband and her daughter-in-law. Some of the bodies were found a hundred miles away from one another—swept by the driving currents of the Gulf Stream to Key West and as far north as Fort Pierce.

But the bodies of Elisa and her lover, his younger brother and Mérida's husband were never found. They would join the thousands of others, failed seekers of a better life, in that immense aquatic graveyard—the Florida Straits.

SEEKING TO PUT FACES on those who died, I went to Cárdenas, Havana and Miami several times over the next two years. There were scores of pieces to find, identify and jiggle into the puzzle. There were two extended families, eleven dead, two adult survivors and two five-year-old children who would become estranged from their grieving parents. But clinging to the bare facts were conflicting stories to reconcile, and personal ambitions and political agendas to sort out amidst a surfeit of grief, rage and shame.

In Key Biscayne's Crandon Park Marina, the shipwreck survivors Nivaldo and Arianne, wrapped and shivering in blankets, told police detectives the saga of their deadly journey. Then they were whisked away to Jackson Memorial Hospital and later to Arianne's aunt in Hialeah—where they shut themselves in, rarely speaking about their ordeal. I first met Arianne and Nivaldo in early February 2000 at her aunt's small home on a torn-up and pot-holed street in Hialeah, the working-class Cuban community that borders Miami. The strains of their ordeal and their new lives were painfully evident. At the time, they had no money, no jobs, no clothes and did not speak English.

Arianne is a small, dark-haired beauty with a sultry beauty mark on her chin. Outwardly, she seemed to have emerged from her ordeal entirely unscathed, her gaze riveted on the present and the future. Phoenix-like, she promptly enrolled in an English school in a Hialeah shopping mall, attending class every night from six to nine and charting out her new life. Soon after her miraculous rescue, she made an appointment at the local *peluquería* in Hialeah and had dagger-length acrylic nails applied to her fingertips.

At our first meeting, Nivaldo seemed particularly stressed—his legs bobbing nervously, his face drawn and wounded. A light-skinned black man with translucent hazel eyes, he was still unable to sleep. Every evening, he said, he awoke over and over again—revisiting the shipwreck and the days they spent drifting in the water. "When we remember everything that happened, we feel it deeply," he said softly, "having seen so many people drown."

Nivaldo was besotted with Arianne, his eyes rarely leaving her. Although he too would like to learn English, he said that one of them had to sacrifice and he was willing to do so. And for the love of Arianne, he was willing to make many sacrifices. It was Nivaldo who had paid the entire fee for the two. He had left behind a wife, a good job and a new house in Cárdenas. He rattled off the fine appliances he had in his home on Calle San José. "I lived a lot better in Cuba," he told me, "than I'm living here now." And while he thinks he would like Chicago, where his mother and other relatives live, he has contented himself in Miami because Arianne loves it so.

After surviving a perilous shipwreck and an excruciating ordeal in the raging Atlantic, Nivaldo found himself in a home feeling unwelcome. Indeed, when I spoke with her weeks later, Arianne's aunt couldn't have been more candid about her feelings. Repeatedly tapping her forearm with two fingers—Cuban for signifying that someone is black—she found my eyes and sighed. Racial prejudice is not uncommon in Miami's exile community, which is roughly 95 percent white. Local talk radio speculated that had Elián González been black—as are 65 to 70 percent of Cubans on the island—"he would have been tossed back into the sea." A close friend of the couple said that Arianne's aunt was uncomfortable with Nivaldo in her home. "Supposedly one room is for them but the aunt doesn't want Nivaldo sleeping with Arianne. So he has to sleep in the living room." Pushing back her red-blond hair, the aunt told me that Nivaldo's arrival had been difficult for her. "For us, it is a very big thing. He is the first black person in our family. We grew up in a time when parents brought us up right. We accept him," she said with another, deeper sigh, "because he is a good, hardworking man. What can we do?"

SITTING IN A HIALEAH coffee shop where he was unable to eat or drink anything, Nivaldo said that talking about his ordeal only seemed to make it worse. The voyage was ill fated from the beginning, he said. "The most difficult thing was the trip. It was four days long but we were in the water for three days." By the time the group left shore it was almost 2:30 in the morning of November 21. Under the shield of darkness on a moonless night, they hoped to evade detection from the Cuban Coast Guard. There were two five-year-olds in tow when they left: Arianne's beautiful, curly-haired daughter, Estefany, named after Princess Stephanie of Monaco, and Elián, Elisa's son. While Estefany cried and cowered fearfully from the huge, dark waves, Elián delighted in the adventure. He teased passengers who he said were eating too many of their crackers. Everyone giggled at his precocity; his mother glowed.

The mood on the boat darkened abruptly less than two hours after they took off, when the motor clacked and sputtered, then died. "We could still see land," recalled Nivaldo. Using oars, they paddled back to the nearest key off Cárdenas. There they hid out for fourteen hours until sunset, then paddled back to Cárdenas at 6:00 P.M.

Although it was clearly a poor omen, Nivaldo said no one was deterred from going except Arianne, who was having second thoughts about bringing Estefany, who was crying and fretting. Elisa had unwavering confidence in Rafa—after all, he had made the trip twice before, with even less of a boat than they had. And she could not bear to be parted from Elián.

While the men repaired the engine, Arianne walked her daughter back to her mother's home on Calle Vives and returned to the boat alone. It was a fateful, prescient decision that she is certain saved their lives. Had they struggled to save or calm her daughter as the others had done for one another, they too would have drowned.

Rafa repaired the boat by inserting "a piece of scrap metal in the engine from another part of the boat," according to Nivaldo. "They fixed the engine, it was fine, we left, everything was perfect." Having lost a full day, they finally motored off at 3:00 A.M. on November 22, a Monday. Arianne said she would never forget the date, because it happened to be her twenty-second birthday "and I spent it in the water." In lieu of life jackets, they took along three *gomas*—the large black inner tubes used on Russian-made trucks. The plan was to have seven, but Rafa decided that they could make do with three.

A few hours later, in the glare of daylight, they were spotted by two cruisers from Cuba's Guardia Frontera, who ordered them to return and threatened to use a water cannon on them. Nivaldo claimed that he seized Elián and held him high over his shoulders. "We have kids in here!" he called out, bluffing them. "There's five, maybe six children aboard." Arianne had no memory of the event; Nivaldo said that the guardsmen backed down but continued to trail them for another hour. Before turning back, they would radio the American Coast Guard and pass on the position of the boat and its direction. The U.S. Coast Guard confirmed that they had been alerted but never located the craft.

The group was relieved that they didn't encounter the U.S. Coast Guard, which, under current policy, would have immediately returned them to Cuba. They knew they had to make it to shore to qualify for residency under what is known as the "wet foot/dry foot" policy. A peculiar confection of U.S. policy that was created in 1994, it grants any Cuban who makes it to land the right to stay. Haitians, Dominicans, Mexicans and everyone else get tossed back whence they came.

Notwithstanding its heavy human cargo, the boat zipped across the Florida Straits, making excellent time. In roughly nineteen hours they had come within thirty-five miles of U.S. shores—two thirds of their journey. To reach the U.S. in thirty hours or less was their goal. But suddenly the sky blackened and the ocean roiled furiously beneath them. They had steered directly into a storm, a nasty Northeaster. Bitter cold winds and relentless rain lashed at them. "It was a bad time, there was a cold front with very big waves," recalled Nivaldo. "A lot of water getting into the boat. Then the engine stopped and it wouldn't start. We were nervous and afraid."

The flailing winds jostled one fuel tank loose, spilling gasoline that burnt a hole in one of the inner tubes. And then, said Nivaldo, "a huge wave hit and flipped the boat over." All fourteen were thrown into the churning Atlantic. Through the night, they clung to the edges of the boat calling out to the few passing ships, which didn't hear their cries. "The first day we were all together holding on to the boat," said Nivaldo. When the sun rose again, they expended their strength trying to flip the boat back over—but the craft capsized and sank along with the damaged inner tube—leaving fourteen people at the mercy of only two tires in the pitch-dark Atlantic. What few possessions they had—clothes, food, blankets—and all their water had tumbled into the sea. Arianne could feel the spilled gasoline burning her back.

The group split into two—the men huddled on one inner tube, the women and Elián on the other, some clinging to the sides of the tires, others, the nonswimmers, tethered to them with rope. They had succeeded in tying the two tubes together, thus keeping the group together. But hunger and dehydration quickly took their toll. The first casualty was seventeen-year-old Jikary Munero, Rafa's younger brother. "Look, land, there's land, an island. I can see lights," he shouted to the others, then dove into the sea, swimming off to find it. Rafa immediately dove in to rescue his brother. Soon after, the group heard calls of "*Ayúdame!* Help!" and Nelson Rodríguez swam to the aid of the brothers.

It was an unforgiving, starless stormy night, without moonlight, and no one could see what was happening. After fifteen minutes, when none of the three young men had returned, the group feared the worst. Elisa began to mumble over and over again: "I think they drowned. . . . I think they drowned." Silently, their helpless families realized that Nelson, Jikary and Rafa, the architect of the trip, had drowned. Worse was to come.

Lirka Guillermo, a pretty twenty-five-year-old medical student who lived across the street from the Rodríguez family, was the next casualty. She had planned to reunite with her boyfriend, who had made the voyage successfully a year earlier with Rafa. "I want black beans and rice," she cried aloud, then suddenly released the inner tube and swam off toward the other tire. Nelson's brother Juan Carlos, a thirty-five-year-old maintenance man who lived in Havana, tried to save her. Juan Carlos had left his family behind—his nine-year-old daughter and his wife, who was too ill to come following a failed kidney transplant. Nivaldo said that he tried to rescue Lirka in the dark sea but could barely see anything. He swam toward them, he said, but both she and Juan Carlos had gone under.

Fatigue soon brought down Rafael Munero, and his wife, María Elena, having seen her two sons and husband perish, no longer had the strength or will to hang on.

The following day, as sunlight broke through at dawn, Manolo Rodríguez, who had witnessed the drowning of his sons, disappeared from the inner tube. Next, Nelson's wife, Zenaida, who had a lifelong fear of the ocean and couldn't swim, slipped into the sea.

Mérida, Manolo's wife, having watched her entire family drown, barely clung to the tire with Nivaldo and Arianne. Delirious, she kept asking for her family. "Mérida kept trying to drown herself, sliding down into the water. She was saying, 'I want to die. I want to die,'" recalled Arianne. Nivaldo would push her back up and comfort her, telling her that they would be rescued. "Leave me alone I want to die," she mumbled like a chant. Nivaldo dozed off, and when he awoke, Mérida was no longer crying. She had slipped away. The coroner said she died of a heart attack and then drowned.

"People were drowning from fatigue," said Nivaldo, "until it was just Arianne, me, Elián and Elisa." Strangely, Elián seemed removed from the entire drama. He was gaily dressed in an orange jacket selected by his mother, who had heard that the bright color deflected sharks. Draped across the tire, he dozed much of the time. "He was just sleeping and when he was awake it was like an adventure for him. He wasn't panicked at all. And he would wake up and say, 'I'm hungry.' " Elisa comforted him but said nothing. "She couldn't say anything because there was no food." But she covered him in her jacket—protecting him from the grilling sun and nipping fish. Before the shipwreck, Elián seemed excited by the journey. "He knew we were coming here because Rafa would say, 'Where are you going?' And Elián would say, *'Me voy pa' La Yuma'*—'I'm going to the U.S.' " (*La Yuma* is Cuban slang for America, adapted from the title of a 1957 Glenn Ford movie, *3:10 to Yuma*, which was based on an Elmore Leonard short story.)

Arianne found a bottle of water floating in the sea. She said she offered it to Elisa, telling her, "This is for Elián." And before they drowned, Rafa and the other men would throw their bodies over Elián, protecting him from the immense waves and keeping the salt spray out of his mouth.

By now Elisa's strength was ebbing. She had seen Rafa, the great passion of her life, die, and now she struggled to live only to protect her son. She had nothing to offer him when he cried for milk. "I want to die," she mumbled. "All I want is for my son to live. If there's one here who has to die, let it be me, not him."

The following morning, Nivaldo and Arianne awoke and found themselves bobbing alone in the immense Atlantic. Sometime during the night, the rope securing the two inner tubes together had torn apart. Nivaldo and Arianne said they had no idea what had happened to Elián and Elisa, but they knew one thing: Elisa could not swim. "In the morning we couldn't see them anymore," said Nivaldo. "I don't know what could have happened to her. She could have lost her strength because of the current or a shark ate her. Something big must have happened because her body never turned up."

Two more nights would pass and Arianne and Nivaldo would feel fish nipping and biting their legs and arms. They saw dolphins everywhere, which they prayed would keep the sharks at bay. On their third night in the water, Nivaldo became delirious, ranting, "We're going to die! We're going to die!" Arianne grabbed him fiercely and talked him down until he snapped out of it.

That night, they could finally see the glimmer of lights from the Florida shoreline. Exultant, they put all their energy into swimming but the current was against them and they eventually dozed off on their inner tube. At daybreak, they could see that they were even closer. They swam and paddled exhaustedly—their arms and legs thrashing at the water until they made it to shore. Two early-morning fishermen, Juan Ruiz and Reniel Carmenate, in Key Biscayne's yacht harbor watched them, startled, then ran to help them. They had made it to land. They could stay. They were "dry footers."

CÁRDENAS, ONCE A BUSTLING Spanish colonial seaport, has a unique L-shaped geography: ninety miles east of Havana, ninety miles south of the tip of Key West, Florida. Notwithstanding a population of 100,000, it has a small-town feel, where people meet and greet one another with affection and embraces. Despite a polluting plume of black smoke from the Havana Club rum refinery, Cárdenas has certain charms not found in Havana. Locals do their errands in horse-drawn carriages for a peso a trip and street vendors on bicycles sell paper cones filled with peanuts for even less.

Sustained by Varadero, Cuba's most lucrative tourist resort, a half hour away, Cárdenas enjoys one of the highest standards of living on the island. But that hasn't lessened its appeal for *balseros*—rafters who favor its coastline with its ocean currents that glide cleanly toward Miami. Most everyone here has family "over there" in La Yuma. Thousands have chosen Cárdenas as their point of departure, where smugglers charge anywhere from $500 to $10,000 per person depending on the seaworthiness of the craft. It is estimated that only about half of those who attempt the crossing make it alive.

As the Elián hullabaloo hit critical mass, *balsero* departures dropped off dramatically, the result of a government crackdown. By February 2000, they had resumed, and more stories of death and dying at sea were whispered about. Everyone in Cárdenas, it seemed, knew someone who had perished on one crossing or another. All the blather about Elián only underscored the official silence about the thousands who have drowned. For Elián's ship mates there were no memorials, no services, no funerals. The only government action involved seizing the homes of those who left—to be quickly assigned to other Cuban families to fill the country's desperate need for housing.

The grief was still palpable at the Hotel Paradiso–Punta Arenas in Varadero in early February, where Elián's mother, Elisa, and Zenaida and Nelson Rodríguez had worked. While suntanned Canadian and German tourists buzzed about sipping tropical drinks, the staff seemed almost listless—stunned by the loss of three of their own. Unlike *habaneros*, who love to gossip, people in Cárdenas seem to avoid mean-spirited *chisme* (gossip), and lean toward understatement. For six months, street banners proclaiming the town's adoration for Elián were hung across a half dozen streets and the locals had grown weary of the perpetual Elián Show. One of Elián's school chums told me that the "all Elián, all the time" activities in school were "very boring," adding, "We want Elián to come home so we can do something else."

Lisbeth García was Elisa Brotón's good friend. I found her on the fourth floor of the hotel cleaning a room. "We were always together," she said softly. "Elisa was my best friend and we worked together. Zenaida worked on the seventh floor and was the godmother of my five-year-old daughter." Lisbeth's eyes welled up with tears, which she wiped away on her white maid's uniform. Nelson, Zenaida's handsome and sweet-humored husband, worked in the maintenance department.

Lisbeth had been close with Elisa for more than ten years, since her marriage to Juan Miguel. She said that Juan Miguel was "a very good man, simple, *simpático*," adding with a smile, "though not necessarily an intellectual. But he's from a good family." Elisa, she said, was remarkably similar to Juan Miguel in that both were quiet, unassuming people with modest ambitions. Both had quit school in the tenth grade and had received their high school diplomas by attending night school. "She didn't love sports or dressing up, but she was exceptional," said Lisbeth. "She had a great passion for her son. All her heart was for her son." Though only thirty, Lisbeth looked very tired, her skin pale and strained by grief. We agreed to meet later when she wasn't working.

The next day I found her at her home in Cárdenas. Like most Cubans, Lisbeth lives with an extended family—her mother, daughter, some in-laws. Her home is typical of Cárdenas—something like a roomy New York City railroad flat of five rooms but with a front porch and a small, scraggly backyard. As in most Cuban homes, there is no hot water. Water for cooking or bathing has to be boiled.

Wearing cheap black patent leather shoes and loose plaid slacks with a black sweater, Lisbeth glanced glumly at her nails and chipped fingernail polish. She had given up on Cuban men, she said, and was resigned to raise her daughter alone just as her mother had raised her. "Divorce here is normal," she noted. So is going to Miami. "I have five paternal uncles in Miami." Many are less fortunate, she says. Before the Elián saga, she said, "people left every day." She paused and surveyed her ragged fingernails, then said quietly, "The sea is a cemetery of people."

Lisbeth learned the bad news the way Cubans learn everything—by *la bola en la calle,* street gossip. "A neighbor found out because she had seen Zenaida's daughter moving her stuff from their apartment. 'I have bad news to give you. The godmother of your daughter is gone,' she told me. I told her, 'That's a lie!' Then I changed clothes and went over to the daughter's house. I found her crying with all of Zenaida's things around the house. Zenaida had left her a note telling her that she was leaving and to come and get her things. They left Saturday and I found out on Monday. On Thursday, they found Elián. It was days of uncertainty, not knowing if they arrived or not. At the hotel, everyone knew about it, everyone was crying."

Juan Miguel found out through a mutual friend, she said, who went to his house and told him what had happened. "I did not want to go myself because I did not have the strength to tell him the news," she said. "On Monday night I went to Elisa's house to see if her mother, Raquel, knew. That's when she tells me that Elisa had sent her a letter saying that she had had problems with Munero and she was in Havana and that when she returned she would move back and live with her again. I told Raquel that Elisa had left with Nelson, Zenaida, with the parents and all. Then she started to cry because she still believed what Elisa wrote in her note."

Moments later, Juan Miguel raced up the stairs. Elisa had told him that she was taking Elián to Havana for the weekend and would return on Tuesday. Now, he said, everyone is saying that she has left the country. He had been to Elisa's small apartment and found it empty and locked and ran over to Rafa's parents' place and found the same thing. "I was on my way to your house," he told Lisbeth, his face flushed with emotion. "I want you to confirm the whole story to me." "Then I told him that it is all true," continued Lisbeth. "That Elisa left and took the boy. He started to cry— inconsolably—for both of them. He loved Elisa—she was the mother of his child, and because they were good friends who had known each other for twenty years."

Juan Miguel raced home and spoke with his mother, Mariela Quintana, a woman of uncommon fortitude, who worked for the Ministry of Justice. Immediately she picked up the phone, then charged about town, pulling every string available to her. She would lobby her boss and his chief, who was one of the town's top politicos, Ricardo Chapelín, first secretary of the

Communist Party for Cárdenas. But to no avail. No one knew anything other than that the group had left for La Yuma.

On Thursday, November 25, when Elián was discovered bobbing in the sea, an exultant Juan Miguel rushed about putting his papers in order: Elián's birth certificate, his wedding decree and his divorce papers—knowing he would need them to claim his child. Soon he would be reunited with his son, he told friends.

Elisa and Juan Miguel had met at a friend's *quinceañera,* a fifteenth-birthday party celebration, and began dating when she was fourteen years old. The couple abandoned school to marry when she was sixteen. With both of them working in tourism, the newlyweds prospered enough for Juan Miguel to buy a 1956 Nash Rambler station wagon and to raise a family. For years they tried unsuccessfully to have children. Prior to Elián's birth, Elisa had miscarried seven times. In 1989, she lost a seven-month pregnancy, leaving the couple devastated. "She had everything prepared for the birth," said Lisbeth. The couple divorced in 1991 but continued seeing each other and redoubled their efforts to have a child, even seeking out obstetric care and counseling. In 1993, they finally had a child, Elián. His birth came at the same time that Elisa's father was battling terminal stomach cancer and leavened her sadness. "Elián was a child very much wanted by her and Juan Miguel," said Lisbeth. His name, in fact, was an elision of their two names with an accent over the fourth letter. Eliding names or creating fanciful confections of nomenclature is as popular in the provinces of Cuba as it is in the inner cities of the U.S. Elián was an exceptional child, "very alive and intelligent," who loved mango juice and the little cones of peanuts hawked by street vendors on bicycles.

Neither Elisa nor Juan Miguel was known to be interested in politics, nor did either have a rebellious streak. They both had been members of UJC—the Young Communist League—and both later joined the Party, assuming roles like their parents, who had always been active members. They participated in the local CDR (Committee for the Defense of the Revolution), the neighborhood watchdog group that monitored the community, and Elisa held a fairly important position in the local Communist Party. "She was second secretary of the nucleus of the Party in our department," explained Lisbeth, a "very responsible" position, and she attended meetings up until the time she left.

A few years after Elián's birth, the couple drifted apart. Juan Miguel's philandering, which had dogged their marriage from the beginning, was at the root of the breakup. Lisbeth García didn't mention it during my first interviews with her, but when I returned to Cárdenas some months later, she confirmed my suspicions. The marriage had two significant stresses: the frustration of having lost seven pregnancies before Elián's birth and the fact that Juan Miguel was what Cubans called a *mujeriego*—a skirt-chaser. "Here in Cuba, the men are like that," Lisbeth said ruefully. "He was a little *salsero*. He tried to make it so Elisa would not find out because he was never going to leave her . . . but she was never sure he wasn't with another woman. Mariela [Juan Miguel's mother] always defended Elisa, not Juan Miguel. And despite all this, Raquel [Elisa's mother] adored him. She never wanted Elisa to have another husband."

But after years of coping with his infidelities, Elisa left for good. "She didn't trust him anymore," Lisbeth said with a shrug, adding that Juan Miguel was shattered when she finally left and he begged her to return. "Elisa was the love of his life."

At a Varadero nightclub in August 1997, Elisa met and fell headlong in love with Lázaro Munero, known to his family and intimates as Rafa, a high school dropout six years her junior. Bold, impulsive and entrepreneurial, Rafa couldn't have been more different from Juan Miguel. "He was fun and liked to party," says Lisbeth. "We went out a lot. He liked discos. He enjoyed life. Rafa had lots of spirit, lots of ideas, he was quick-witted. He wouldn't think things through, though. He was very wild. He was called El Loco," and, at times, he could be "a spoiled brat." Two months later, he moved in with Elisa at her mother and stepfather's comfortable apartment above a pharmacy on Calle Coronel Verdugo.

Elisa, said Lisbeth, "was lost in love" for Rafa, "too much in love."

ONE THING WAS CLEAR early on: the decision of the Miami relatives of Elián González to keep the five-year-old and not return him to his father was a gift from God for Fidel Castro. To the horror of his critics, Castro claimed the moral high ground. He had grasped immediately that no matter the outcome, the situation would be a win-win for him and a black eye for the Miami exiles.

Castro immersed himself in the Elián drama with the same obsessive zeal with which he had attended to the Cuban Missile Crisis. Virtually daily there was a *tribuna abierta*—open town meeting—or government-organized demonstrations on behalf of Elián, often rallying as many as 100,000 Cubans.

By the time I got to Havana in February, Elián Fatigue was a nationwide epidemic. On television, even cartoons and children's programming were preempted for Elián updates. A popular newscaster who dared to use a mildly sarcastic tone when providing the schedule of more Elián coverage vanished from the screen for several months. A noted intellectual greeted me, hollering aloud, "I hate Elián González," and even a high-level government official confided with a weary shrug, *"Ya basta!"*—it's enough already. Dissidents and intellectuals puzzled and groaned over why and how the Miami exile leadership picked such a loser of a cause to champion.

Once the Elián Show became the centerpiece of Castro's foreign policy, Cárdenas was treated to a quick makeover. The entire block on Cossio Street where Elián lived was completely repainted, as was his schoolhouse. Even a hole in his desk had been repaired. Although everyone was dismissive of the propaganda sweepstakes at work, no one believed the government was on the wrong side. Most cringed at the thought of being in Juan Miguel's shoes: having their child snatched by angry Miami relatives who wanted to get even with Fidel Castro. Neighbors howled about how Juan Miguel had even given up his bed for his Uncle Lázaro when he visited from Miami and slept in his car during his 1998 visit—only to be repaid with him stealing his son! *"Qué desgracia!"* they scolded.

In Cárdenas, Juan Miguel and his family were well known and well liked. Even Elisa's boyfriend, Rafa Munero, had maintained an amicable relationship with him. Vivian, a neighbor whose children played with Elián, said that Juan Miguel was an unusually dutiful dad. "He was always fretting about the boy. Always bringing him gifts, toys, taking him out for visits and spending the weekend with him."

On January 30, Elián's grandmothers, who had been dispatched to the States to plead their case for the return of their grandson, had completed "their triumphant tour" and were greeted at the airport as heroes of the Revolution. They were installed in a swank Havana protocol house in El Laguito to be on call for government-organized events. Cubans were chagrined to hear the two grandmothers had been elevated to Che-hood and compared to Mariana Gragales, the iconized mother of Cuban revolutionary heroes Antonio and José Maceo.

On February 4, as I was chatting with some of Elián's classmates outside his house, a van pulled up. Out popped Juan Miguel, Elián's grandmothers and their spouses. As I would later learn, they too were sick to death of the Elián Show and craved a little privacy in their own homes. A small crowd of neighbors gathered to greet them—it being their first day home since their whirlwind U.S. tour. Everyone headed inside Mariela and Juan González's home at 170 Cossio Street, which is directly next to Juan Miguel's house and had previously been the home of Juan's parents. I decided to tag along and get a look at the González family without any handlers around.

Raquel Rodríguez, Elisa's mother, is a small, thin woman with a face etched with grief and worry. Prone to tears, she seemed fragile. As there had been no funeral for her daughter, some friends had suggested that she place a large photograph of Elisa in her living room. "She asked me for my opinion," said a close friend. "I told her no. She has always been a woman with a nervous condition, taking little pills. I told her that if she did it, every time she would look toward that corner of the living room, she would remember." Out back on the patio, an elderly neighbor bounced a baby in her arms, coaching it to chant, *"Que venga Elián . . ."*—"Let Elián come. Let Elián come"—which had become the national mantra.

The González men, described by one friend as being "like a family of state troopers," have all held low-level jobs in the Ministry of the Interior—which is basically spies and cops. Juanito—the father—is retired. Tony did police work at the dock, and Juan Miguel worked as a guide and cashier at Parque Retiro Josone, a twenty-five-acre nature resort in the center of Varadero, popular with tourists. All the men are chain smokers. They're uncomfortable with making small talk. The most amiable is Tony, who once applied for an American visa until he was talked out of leaving by his family. Tony cheerfully dissected his father's complex family tree for me: three brothers and two sisters live in Miami, while two sisters and his father stayed on in Cárdenas. One of the nine siblings, José Luis, had died in 1983.

Juan González, the patriarch, a slight, dark-haired man partial to *guayaberas,* the traditional short-sleeved tailored shirt of Cuba, was wary of chitchat. He declined to bash his brothers, Lázaro and Delfín, for keeping Elián in Miami, saying only, "Myself, I am convinced that they have been pressured to behave like this. Otherwise they would not do this to me." On another occasion, after the *New York Times* broke the story of his brother's troubled history with alcohol and repeated drunk driving arrests, he stressed that Manuel, who supported reuniting Elián with his father, is "the one who doesn't drink." He confirmed that "Delfín and Lázaro have always liked to drink. This has always been so." Asked if there was a family history of alcoholism, he seemed to take offense. "They are not alcoholics. They just like to drink."

A FEW BLOCKS AWAY on Calle Vives, I met the other estranged six-year-old, Estefany Herrera Horta, Arianne's daughter. Estefany, whose features have a dusky, exquisite beauty, is a child of mercurial moods. During my first visit, she charged around the house like a renegade train, pausing only to grasp at her grandmother as she flew by.

Estefany, who was hyperactive, was receiving psychiatric help. Her grandmother said that her condition was exacerbated by the loss of her mother. "She needs to be with her. I don't know if it's today or tomorrow but it is her only daughter," said Arianne's mother, Elsa Alfonso. "I miss my daughter, I love her. How must she feel about this one that is here. No matter how much I love her I am not her mother."

However, under American law, Arianne could not apply for her daughter's visa until one year after her arrival. There was another impediment at that time: Estefany's father, Victor Herrera. I caught up with Herrera, a drop-dead stunning man with bronzed skin and black hair, who works as a bartender at the Hotel Internacional in Varadero. "I am not worried about Estefany because she's not going anywhere," he said. "She has her grandmothers, her father, her friends, her school and her neighbors. Maybe when she's fifteen or older—that would be okay."

Arianne claimed that Victor had been somewhat of an absent dad until the celebrity of the shipwreck. "He was the richest man in Cárdenas but he didn't pay for anything," she fumed. "I can't say that he smokes or takes drugs, but saying that he takes care of the girl is a lie." Nivaldo chimed in, also claiming a paternal role: "I bought everything for her. When Arianne speaks with her, she always wants to talk with me. I took her out and would buy her ice cream."

But however belatedly, Victor had discovered the joys of fatherhood. Now he was visiting his daughter regularly, keenly involved in her affairs. Even Arianne's mother nodded in approval. Victor, who described himself as "a revolutionary," seemed nervous at our first visit. He reluctantly acknowledged that he had had several visits from government officials. Six months later, he was considerably more relaxed. He spoke of Estefany's vivid memories of her near-death boat trip. "She remembers everything that happened on the boat that night and everybody who was on it," he said while tending bar at the Internacional. "When she saw a photograph of Elián, she told me, 'Look Daddy, look Daddy, that's Elián.' She said that she and Elián were playing together on the boat. And that one of the women, I think it was Lirka Guillermo, was eating a lot of cookies and Elián had said, 'Let's throw her in the water because she's eating too many cookies.' He was joking around. She remembered everybody and everything on the boat."

ACCORDING TO THE Cuban government, Rafa Munero was a career petty criminal. According to his relatives in Miami, he was a conscientious, hard-working young man. Friends and family in Cárdenas say he was a bit of both: a disaffected, hot-tempered natural entrepreneur who often fell afoul of the law. But after he met Elisa Brotón in 1997 at a local dance haunt, the Havana Club, he became another man. He even wanted children. "She wanted to get pregnant with him," said Lisbeth, "but never could."

Rafa's Aunt Milagros in Miami said that he had been arrested for going AWOL from the Cuban army and spent fourteen months in a prison in Matanzas in 1992. His uncle and a half-brother told one reporter that Rafa was sent to prison following a bar fight in which he sliced off three fingers of his adversary's hand. After his release, according to Lisbeth, "he sold cigarettes and liquor at a kiosk in Varadero for a short time and also used his car as a *botero*," an illegal taxi service. After being arrested for driving a *botero*, he was so seriously beaten, said his aunt, that he needed to be hospitalized. His mother filed a complaint concerning the incident. Cuban authorities also claimed that Rafa spent a year in prison for breaking into the hotel room of a tourist and stealing his cash.

In June 1998, after he was arrested again—this time for black market activity—he decided that he had to leave the country. On June 15, 1998, he fled with his close friend Humberto Pérez Castro, his uncle José García and an older friend they called El Guajiro, a nickname loosely meaning "the hill-billy." The four men made the trip in under twenty-four hours in an aluminum boat with an outboard motor similar to the one he used on his final trip. It was an arduous crossing and Humberto became delirious from sunstroke. For a time, he hallucinated that sharks were attacking them until Rafa slapped him back to consciousness.

Around the same time, Elisa's niece, twenty-one-year-old Carmita Brotón, fled with her boyfriend, Orlando Rodríguez, and six others. Owing to a glitch in U.S.-Cuban law at the time, all were assigned "deportable" status, which meant that their fate was at the whim of INS authorities.

———

ON FEBRUARY 8, 2000, *Granma,* the official publication of the Cuban Communist Party, ran a six-page special investigative report on the shipwreck entitled "Threats and Violence Lead to Tragedy." The heroine of the report was Elisa Brotón, depicted as a sweet, submissive, hardworking woman bullied into leaving by her hectoring, no-good boyfriend: "Munero, with his dominating and violent personality, exerted a strange and fatal influence over Elizabet." The two survivors, Arianne and Nivaldo, who by this time had begun to campaign with the Miami relatives to keep Elián in the States, were also tarred. Arianne, it was suggested, was a prostitute who had married at twelve. Nivaldo was an unstable "womanizer" who couldn't hold a job. The report's villain was Lázaro Munero, Rafa, described as a bully and rogue—who forced Elisa and Elián onto the boat and who was to blame for the entire tragedy.

But his relatives in Miami, with whom he stayed for five months in 1998, knew another Rafa and another version of events. He was an intense young man, they said, who had a single-minded focus and was utterly fearless. Every day he worked—from seven in the morning to seven at night scrubbing cars at a car wash. In his spare time, he scrounged around for other jobs.

Rafa's aunt, Milagros García, whom I spoke with at her home in Kendall, a suburb of Miami, told me he had lived most of his time with her and her family. Concerned that he had no other interests besides work, she said she had tried to play matchmaker. "There was a young girl staying at his Uncle Jorge's house and we wanted him to start a relationship," she said. "But he wasn't interested. He spoke about Elisa obsessively. He was really in love. It was incredible."

Jorge Munero said that his nephew had made a decision early on to go back and get Elisa. "I'm going to be frank," he said in his West Miami home facing a large photograph of his deceased brother. "He was always talking about leaving and I was concerned that he was going to go back. He never wanted to discuss it with me because if I told him no, it would be a disaster. But he kept talking about going back to get Elisa and the boy. He didn't really want to admit that it was because of her. He started making excuses—like he missed his family. He made a huge mistake. He got desperate because he missed Elisa."

Rafa's mother, María Elena, suspected he was planning to return. With a prescient dread, she wrote Jorge begging him to keep her son, whom she called Rafelito, in Miami.

Dear Jorge,

    After writing to Rafelito and trying to make him understand, we appeal to you. You can imagine the fear we have that Rafelito is going to commit a huge mistake that will weigh heavy on him for the rest of his life. We cannot endure life knowing that he is going to injure himself in a dangerous adventure. It's worse to think that he could never go back, if in fact, he arrived. . . . Martyrdom and prison [await him here] and I'm certain that he could not tolerate it. It seems that he doesn't understand this because he only thinks about himself and the woman that fills his life. Well Jorge, I'm grateful for whatever you can do for Rafelito. Talk to him. Make him realize that life is this way.

Love Mari

But her pleas went unheeded. "Every day it was the same thing, arguing why it was that he wanted to leave," recalls Jorge. "María Elena tells me: 'Jorge, please, you better not help him return. If he wants to come back let him do it on his own. Don't involve yourself.' So I didn't help him because my sister-in-law told me that if I helped him she would never speak to me again. So, I left it alone. I told him that what he was doing was a mistake, but he wanted to do it. He preferred dying in the sea or jail because he told me, 'I don't care if I have to do five years in jail.' "

Rafa's pal Humberto was also lonely for his girlfriend, Lirka Guillermo. Likewise, Orlando Rodríguez pined away for his family, who lived across the street from Lirka and who were friends of Rafa's parents. By the time he left, Rafa had a pretty good idea that he would come back with all of them.

In October 1998, Rafa headed for Key West, where he bought an inflatable raft with a small motor and boldly set sail for Cuba by himself. Miraculously, he nearly made the entire trip without a mishap. But just short of land, his motor died. He was picked up by the Cuban Coast Guard near Cádiz Bay in Villa Clara on October 26. As he feared, he was arrested and jailed for illegal entry. He was taken to a prison in Santa Clara, several hours from Cárdenas, where, he told his aunt, he was often beaten. "At first he was not allowed visitors," said their friend Lisbeth, "but then, Elisa went many times—four, maybe six times."

Dagoberto remembers the day that his brother came to his apartment and told him the news of his nephew's return. "I need you to come to Santa Clara with me. Rafaelito came back and he is in prison." "I said, 'He's crazy.' And he told me these words: 'He will disgrace my life.' Just like that, sitting in that chair that you're sitting in. And, in fact, he did disgrace their lives."

Three months later, on New Year's Eve, he was released. Initially, Rafa moved back with Elisa at her parents' place—but the situation soon became untenable. Among other issues, Elisa's mother and stepfather were unhappy with Rafa's checkered past and status as an "undesirable." In a matter of days, he had become a wedge between mother and daughter, who had always been very close.

One family friend suggested that part of Raquel's subsequent distress stemmed from having asked Rafa to leave her home, knowing that her daughter would soon follow him. The young couple moved into a small place rented with money Rafa had made in Miami, and the relationship between Raquel and Elisa, her only child, was strained further. Raquel was blunt on the subject. "I would rather not talk about that person," she said, her eyes welling up. "I don't want to know anything about him."

AFTER THE SHIPWRECK, Jorge Munero and his wife, María, came upon some of Rafa's belongings in the room he had lived in some of the time during his stay in Miami. Bundled in with clothes and papers, they discovered a five-page letter from Elisa written in exquisite penmanship on both sides of yellow legal paper with green ink. Tucked inside were three photographs of her and Elián. "It was a love letter. She was giving him a rundown about everything going on in Cárdenas—about how close she had become with his mother and family," said María Munero. "And how sad she was with Rafaelito gone and that she was often in bed crying like she was dying. Her mother would tell her, 'Think about your son and not about Rafa,' and was not especially sympathetic to her suffering. She said she didn't come the first time because she didn't want to leave her mother and she didn't want to risk Elián's life on the sea."

I read the letter, dated August 14, 1998, at the Munero home on SW 3rd Street. It began, *"Mi amor espero que al recibo de estas líneas te encuentro bien y te alegren tanto como alegran tus llamadas. . . ."* Milagros said that after they read the letter, "we realized that Elisa had planned to leave at an earlier date with the other [Rodríguez] family. Then we realized that while Rafa was here he was already plotting the trip to get Elisa. She asked him what he was going to do. Would he return with them? He told her to wait for him." The letter was signed "Ely" and underneath was girlishly written "Ely y Rafa."

Milagros gave the letter to the Gonzálezes' lawyers, but it was hardly the smoking gun they needed. It only proved that Rafa had not forced Elisa to leave. The central argument of the Miami lawyers was that Elisa had died to bring her son to freedom, but they never offered any evidence to support their claim. Elisa was a small-town girl—closely bound to her family and community—with little curiosity about the world. She had never learned to swim, never tried to learn English and rarely ventured outside Cárdenas.

Indeed, the letter seemed to undermine the lawyers' case that Elisa had given her life to bring her son to freedom. It made no mention of such a desire or even a passing reference to any troubles in Cuba: only that she wanted to be with her boyfriend, wherever he might be. In fact, the letter supported the contention of Elisa's friends and family—namely that she had risked and lost her life for love. And as she had arranged to have the letter hand-delivered, she would not have written it with self-censorship. The Miami lawyers were grateful to have the letter in their hands and, not surprisingly, they never released or revealed its contents.

As Milagros pushed tears from her face, her husband, Ricardo, stared morosely at the white tile floor of their living room. "Rafa took $1,000 with him, with which he bought a raft. Then we wired him another $1,800, from earnings he made here. He left his clothes and stuff here," she said. "My brother, who came with Rafa the first time, always said that the worst thing is to cross the Florida Straits with family. If my husband sees me drowning, he's going to try to help and so on. And that's exactly what happened. Everyone was trying to help someone and at the same time they were drowning. The survivors didn't bring anyone. They were not beholden to anyone."

THE FLIGHT OF ELISA and her lover left many stunned. Rafa, upon his return, had convinced many that he loathed Miami. And Elisa was hardly an adventuress. "She was always very timid," said Lisbeth, "scared." Elisa never expressed an interest in visiting Cuba's other cities or provinces such as historic Santiago de Cuba or the cobblestone streets of Trinidad. She rarely even visited Havana, only two hours away. Once she had a job only an hour away and quit because she didn't like to be so far from her family. "She never had ideas to leave the country," Lisbeth said emphatically.

Still, Lisbeth doesn't believe that anyone forced Elisa onto that boat, contrary to the Cuban government's report. "First of all, when she got on the boat, she knew where she was going. She was not lied to. She was timid but she was not dumb. She decided to leave because she was in love," she said, adding that if Rafa had wanted to move halfway around the world, Elisa would have followed.

Nor does Lisbeth believe that Elisa wanted to bring her son to America so that he could have more opportunity. "That is a bunch of lies that 'the boy should go to the land of liberty,' " she huffed, "because those thoughts were never expressed by Elisa. They were never her ideals nor her thoughts. I can say that for sure." And she was certain that her friend told no one of her plans—not a friend, a relative, not her mother and certainly not Juan Miguel, who she says would have taken immediate action to stop her.

We drove over to an immense Soviet-built housing project in Cárdenas that locals have come to call El Pulmón. Literally, it means the Lung, but the epithet is too kind. El Pulmón is rows of concrete buildings—four stories high and unforgivably ugly. We climbed to the top and knocked on what was once Zenaida and Nelson's apartment. A man opened the door and explained that he and his family now lived there. Less than two months after the couple had left, the apartment had been reassigned by the government to another family.

A few blocks away, we found Zenaida's aunt, who rocked in her chair, holding tears in check. She had seen her niece only the day before she had left. It had been Zenaida's thirty-eighth birthday. "There was no indication," she said. "If she had talked with me, she wouldn't have left." But she was certain that Zenaida's daughter, Yusleidys, who was almost eight months pregnant, knew. "They saw each other every day. She knew her mother's plans. They were very close. When I saw Yusleidys, she was in very bad shape. She gave birth after she found out her mother was dead."

Twenty minutes away, Zenaida's mother, Sara Sanabries, lives on the outskirts of Cárdenas. Her home is austere, without running water in the kitchen. A small woman with sad, leathery skin, Sara was listless. She showed us some photos of her daughter—a slim, pretty, light-skinned *mulata* with a shy smile. "I don't know why she left. I found out two days after she had gone. I went to the in-laws [the Rodríguez home] and when I arrived I saw all the people and they told me that the boat had turned over. I started to cry so much that I became ill. I couldn't function."

Sara said that her daughter had been married for seven years to Nelson Rodríguez, who at twenty-nine was nine years her junior, and was very close with his family, especially her mother-in-law, Mérida. "He was a very good man," Sara said. "He helped her when she had a spinal column operation. I loved him very much.

"I had a bad feeling because I had already lost a son over there," Sara continued. "My son did not leave, he was thrown out of here. He has the same life span as the Revolution. Born the same year, in 1959. In 1980 he was

twenty-one. There were many street demonstrations because of Mariel.*
And he had a placard. A policeman arrived and put him in the motorcycle's
sidecar. I pleaded and I cried. But my son was told he had to leave." In 1998,
her son was killed in a car accident in Miami. "That happened to me with my
son and now my daughter. I want to say that I do not like it 'over there.' To
me, over there doesn't exist because every time one of my children arrives
there, something bad happens to them. What hope do I have?"

Sara said there was no official notification from the government about
her daughter's death, only what she learned on the street or on pirate radio.
"No one said anything to me," she said bitterly. "I turned on the radio until I
heard it. Her name was the second one and that's when I knew it was true.
Then they asked for records to identify her body. I don't sleep at night." She
wiped at her face with a wad of Kleenex. She looked up at me, her eyes dark-
ening. "You know that Zenaida always had a tremendous fear of the sea. She
never bathed at the beach. She couldn't swim. Her birthday was on Friday
and they left on Saturday. I didn't go because I was sick and the next day she
left. She enjoyed herself at the party very much. She was saying goodbye to
everybody without anyone knowing it."

RAFAEL MUNERO AND HIS WIFE, MARÍA ELENA, lived in a particularly
funky part of the Pulmón in a ground-floor apartment looking out on a
scruffy lawn littered with odd bits of garbage. After they left, their apartment
was locked up awaiting disposition by the government. Housing is so scarce
in Cuba that any property is valuable, even a dreary Pulmón apartment filled
with the ghosts of your dead family. So it was not entirely surprising that
Rafaelito Munero, thirty-two, Rafael's eldest son from his first marriage who
lives in Caibarién with his own family, was coping with both the grief of his
loss and his desperation to lay claim to his father's home.

Upstairs I chatted with the neighbors, the Díazes, whose small, grim
quarters had nothing but a color TV and a slim wooden bench to sit on in the
living room. There was no bedding on the beds and only a few bare light-
bulbs to illuminate the apartment. Blacks suffer more in Cuba because they
are less likely than whites to have family in the U.S. and therefore do not share
in the estimated $1 billion of remittances sent every year. And although Cuba
has made incontestable strides in dismantling racism, dark-skinned blacks
are not often employed in Cuba's cash cow, the hotel industry.

*The flight of 125,000 Cubans to the United States from the coastal town of Mariel in 1980.

The Díazes spoke effusively of their former neighbors. Ricardo Díaz, a car mechanic, said that when their father died a year ago, Rafael and María Elena stayed up comforting them from four in the afternoon until six in the morning. Rafa, who bore a notable resemblance to his father, they said, was also a stand-up guy. "I would work on his car. He was a good person. He would commit himself to people. He didn't care if you had money, position, status—he treated everyone the same." His sister said that they often saw Elián at the Muneros' and that Rafa seemed especially fond of him. "He was very good with the boy," said Ricardo. "Elián called Rafa 'Pipo,' " which is Cuban for Daddy.

His sister stepped into the darkened room and joined the conversation. When the news leaked out, she said, "everyone was crying, worried and feeling the pain. But we don't talk about [the deaths] here. The only thing that is talked about is Elián." Emboldened by his sister, Ricardo chimed in, disputing the news in that day's *Granma:* "I don't believe that Rafa put a knife to the mother so she'd leave."

Ricardo took me a few blocks away in the Pulmón and up four flights of unlit cement stairs to the apartment of Rafael's youngest brother, Dagoberto Munero, a disabled petroleum worker. Four cramped rooms accommodate Dagoberto, his wife, a son and his pregnant wife and another young son, an asthmatic with an alarming cough.

Despite the passage of three months, Dagoberto was still in bad shape and there was plenty in the apartment to remind him of his loss. Virtually every amenity—a color TV, a stereo system, a new refrigerator, a washing machine, a stove—had been given to him by his brother the night he left, luxuries he was able to afford by having once worked as a bartender in a Varadero hotel.

Holding a framed photograph of his brother in his hands, Dagoberto described their last days in Cuba, roughly wiping the tears from his face with the back of his hand. "When someone decides to leave, they don't tell anybody. It was a secret but he told me because I am his brother. My brother didn't have that much desire to leave but he was going because of the family—his wife, sons. On Saturday, the day of the departure, at 9:30 P.M., I was at his house with him. There were my sister-in-law, Elisa, the boy, my nephew and Nelson. The Rodríguez family were friends. Rafael and Manolo Rodríguez were friends. They were eating pork and had music on the tape player."

Tears rushed down his face as he spoke of his brother. "Rafael knew three other languages, English, Italian and German. He was really talented and smart. My brother had been a fisherman in the Bahamas, in international waters for ten years, he was a diving sea turtle fisherman. My nephews and my brother were like three fish in the water. I don't know how they drowned so easily like that. My brother had worked twenty years in the petroleum industry and ten years in Varadero at the Kawama Hotel. He was never in jail, never had problems."

Which was not exactly true. Rafael Munero had had his own share of run-ins with the government. As a teenager, he had done some stints in jail "for stupid things and pranks and such," Dagoberto conceded during my second visit six months later. In fact, his brother had lost his job in Varadero several years earlier, after being accused of bartering with dollars when the American dollar was still illegal.

At the time of his escape, Rafael had been selling "bread and ham sandwiches" to get by. And he also had a bit of a temper. Dagoberto recalls a fistfight his brother got into at the Petroleum Social Club. "This was in the cantina for the workers," he said. "I was there with my brother in the cantina and a drunken co-worker came in and he was being annoying. Rafael took him outside and he turned on him. And he let him have it."

Dagoberto took out a photo of Rafa at the baptism of his son, a three-year-old from a previous liaison, according to Dagoberto, "but he never took care of the boy and he had no relationship with the boy." Rafa's Aunt Milagros agreed. "He had his own son in Cuba, but he would say that the boy was not really the one. That Elián was the one."

Dagoberto felt sure that his hotheaded nephew had talked his mother into going along, who in turn convinced her husband. Rafa and María Elena were similar in temperament and closely bonded, he said. Her other son, Jikary, was easygoing like her husband. "María Elena had a strong character and she dominated Rafael," Dagoberto explained. "She was stronger than Rafael. He would have stayed here, but since Rafa came back it was nothing but 'Let's get out of here,' and then my sister-in-law became the same way. Imagine, they had him crazy."

Six months later, Dagoberto mentioned something to me he had omitted previously. Less than forty-eight hours after the group had left, he was awakened at one in the morning by a series of loud, insistent knocks. "I was afraid," said Dagoberto, "and I asked: 'Who is it?' and [a voice] said: 'It's me, Rafaelito' "—as Rafa sometimes called himself. "He said to me: 'Uncle, do you have blankets for the cold? I need a little water and two blankets.' They were all wet from a storm during the night. It was a riveted boat with a very powerful outboard motor and the vibration of the motor loosened the rivets.

And it seems that as it loosened, water started coming in. They were fixing the boat on the shore and they were cold, so he came looking for blankets to warm themselves. I told him I didn't have [extra] blankets and to go to his house. And then I went back to the bedroom and [my wife, Regina] asked me: 'Who was it?' And I told her: 'Rafaelito came.' When I looked out the window, it seemed like he came in a car. I never saw him again. . . . The only thing that I told him was, 'Are you crazy? Everyone knows that you already went.' Because everyone finds out everything quickly here. A house closed up. Well, then everyone knew that they had gone. If they came back here, they had a problem. Then they had to go."

Dagoberto was certain about one thing: the whole debacle was due to a terminal case of lovesickness. He described a voyage that could well have been dubbed *The Love Boat.* "The first time Rafa left, he was with Humberto, Lirka's boyfriend. In Miami, they both missed their girlfriends. He missed Elisa and Humberto missed Lirka. Humberto said to him, 'Go back to Cuba and bring Lirka and Elizabet.' Rafa made this trip in order to get his girlfriend, her son and his friend's girlfriend, Lirka. It was all about love."

A FEW BLOCKS AWAY in the Pulmón, I heard a similar story from Nivaldo's family. His sister Marta, who shares the apartment with their father and her son, said that her brother was blinded by love. "He was struck by a *golpe de amor,*" said Marta—a thunderbolt of love. And his family was still reeling from the shock of his leaving.

At the time of his departure, the family was planning a sumptuous party to celebrate Nivaldo and Rosita's tenth wedding anniversary on December 13. Marta shook her head, smiled and looked heavenward. She said she was grateful and amazed that her brother lived—"*Se salvaron en tablitas,*" she said, saved by the skin of their teeth. "It was a phenomenon of God. It makes you believe."

Only a year earlier, Nivaldo and Rosita, a pretty, freckled, light-skinned *mulata,* had bought themselves one of the nicest homes in Cárdenas with wrought iron gates and a small pillared porch. It even boasted air-conditioning. Both had high-paying jobs as chefs in Varadero hotels and were able to afford most everything they desired—including a spiffy motorcycle for Nivaldo. Marta says she was as clueless as Nivaldo's wife about his romance. "We met her [Arianne] for the first time on TV," she said, with some amusement. Although Nivaldo would say in Miami that he left "for freedom," Marta disagreed. "He was very happy here," she said softly. "He went only for her."

Arianne's mother, Elsa Alfonso, agreed with Marta: "They met on March 26, 1999, and it was love at first sight." Although Arianne indicated that her mother knew of her plans, Elsa denied it. She said that on that Saturday night, Nivaldo came for Arianne and the two went out for a walk and then came back and picked up Estefany, telling her only that they were going on a camping trip. "That was all. She left wearing the same clothes. It happened without me knowing about it," said Elsa. "I feel sad for the others who died. I thank God my daughter is alive. She survived the 22nd, 23rd, 24th, 25th before they made it. For that, I thank God."

LIRKA GUILLERMO'S GRANDMOTHER Rosa Betancourt, with her sheet-white hair and wobbly gait, looks older than her sixty-eight years. A framed Technicolor-enhanced print of Jesus over the television set rivets one's attention in her comfortable living room. The coffee table has been made into a shrine to Lirka, with a large framed portrait of her, a pretty girl with long soft brown curls. Underneath the glass of the coffee table are her diplomas, recommendations and several photos of her—as a Young Pioneer in the uniform of Cuban youth, and in a bathing suit and a Halloween costume.

In 1994, Lirka's mother, Silvia Lluis, fled to the States, settling in Phoenix, leaving her daughter behind because she wanted to finish her studies and become a pharmacist. But government officials seized their home and evicted Lirka. The spacious house, they argued, was needed to house a medical clinic. Lirka was told she would get another place but never did and was forced to move into her grandmother's home on Calle Spriu, joining her father, stepmother and uncle, a well-known doctor in Cárdenas.

For five years Lirka campaigned to get a place for herself—even writing Raúl Castro, Fidel Castro's brother and the chief of Cuba's armed forces, in 1997: "I think my situation should have an immediate solution. Return my house or get me another because I cannot pay for my mother's mistakes. My mother left her country. I stayed. So why should I pay? What message is there in that?"

Holding a flimsy plastic produce bag on her lap, Rosa pulled out a front-page obituary from Miami's *El Nuevo Herald* and pointed to a photo of Lirka's mother weeping at her funeral in Miami watched over by Lirka's boyfriend, Humberto. "She died for a house," Rosa said angrily, a handkerchief clutched in her fingers. "She died because they took her house away."

But more than just a home, Lirka died for love. Her boyfriend, Humberto, had fled with Rafa in 1998. Each year, she had tried and failed to win a lottery slot to emigrate to the States. Without a home or a job, she fretted and pined to be reunited with Humberto. For the last year, she had been plotting with her neighbors and friends, the Rodríguez family, across the street. They would all leave together with the Rodríguez sons, their daughter-in-law, Zenaida, and her friend Elisa. But Rafa had written Elisa and told her it was too dangerous to try to come without him. Wait, he told her after consulting with Humberto, I will come and get all of you. So they waited.

Every Sunday, Lirka's mother would call and the two would speak. On November 22, she learned from Rosa that Lirka had tried her luck on the sea. "How could you let my daughter do that?" she cried into the phone at her former mother-in-law.

"Her dog is very sad because he misses her," said Rosa, fingering a handkerchief in her palm. "Her mother worked in Varadero so I brought her up. I gave her everything she wanted. I had a mass for her at the church. Me and the neighbors. We have not played any music since she left. We always used to listen to music. She was my only granddaughter."

ACROSS THE STREET AT the boarded-up house of Mérida and Manolo Rodríguez, the tragedy took on a searing dimension. The entire family of five had drowned. Their twenty-two-year-old son, Orlando, with whom they planned to reunite in Miami, was now an orphan.

The family had lived in Cárdenas for twelve years, but they were country people from Máximo Gómez. Manolo, sixty-five, was retired, a serious but friendly man who sat out front talking with the neighbors every afternoon. "He farmed rice and would bring sacks of rice for the whole year. He raised pigs. He didn't need to leave," Rosa said glumly.

On Saturday, November 20, Lirka told Rosa, " 'Grandma, I'm going to the country with Mérida because all the sisters [from the States] are coming.' There, all the *guajiros* kill pigs." In December, Manolo's mother would turn ninety-three and a family reunion was planned for her birthday—so it seemed inconceivable that he would leave before then.

"They were very good, decent people," said Rosa, standing in her doorway. "He should have waited a little. His family [from the States] were coming with the visa forms to fill out. They left on Sunday, and on Friday his sisters and their husbands arrived from Miami for the mother's birthday." Rosa shook her head and looked toward the ceiling. "They came here and left the dead there."

Across the street, I chatted with Norma, a heavyset woman in her mid-sixties, who speaks too boldly to use her real name. Norma is a rare breed—a woman who vents her rage at the government with the same effortless passion as exiles sipping coffee on Calle Ocho in Miami. *"Todo el mundo tiene cinco caras!"* she said loud enough for all the neighbors to hear—*"Everyone has five faces!* They are hypocrites. Not me. I am against everything here. Everyone partied and danced at a government party on the 28th—even the ones who left and died. Everyone danced except me. I'm not afraid. I don't care. If the gates were opened everyone would leave, even Elián's father would leave. I know that whole family. They are all good people—the ones over there too. The uncle [Delfín] too—we called him Pino, because he was a prisoner at Isla de Pinos for a long time. He was a friend of mine.

"The Rodríguez family were very nice, decent, honest, sincere people. They were from the country. Manolo was a political prisoner and so was my husband. Jailed two years. The whole family left. Their son Juan Carlos lived in Havana. They left a small granddaughter there. The mother was sick—dying with bad kidneys. They gave her a transplant and she rejected it." As much as she needed a new kidney, Juan Carlos's widow, Estrella, needed a better place to live and was willing to make the trek to Cárdenas in hopes of winning her in-laws' home. But to no avail. The government had its lists of who was to receive a new home, explained Norma with a gesture of disgust.

Another neighbor approached me and furtively handed me a large black-and-white photograph of the family. About ten years old, it showed Manolo and Mérida with their young granddaughter. I promised to return it promptly. "Don't mail it back to me," the woman said with a nervous laugh. "My husband is an official in the Party. Send it to Norma."

SEVERAL WEEKS LATER, in mid-February, I visited with Arianne and Nivaldo again. The two had moved out of her aunt's house into a cozy one-bedroom place of their own a few blocks away. They were doing better financially but were bickering with each other. Both were working at a Metro Ford dealership owned by a director of the Cuban American National Foundation; Arianne was doing clerical work, Nivaldo maintenance on the cars. Nivaldo, wearing a blue pin-striped Metro Ford dealership uniform with a matching blue cap, sat next to Arianne, sifting through photos of their families I had brought back from Cárdenas.

The fissures and ill will between the couple and the relatives of those who died had deepened. Nivaldo, said Munero family members, was only an acquaintance who learned that Rafa was leaving and insisted on coming. "Nivaldo would follow Rafa about—even sleeping outside his house for the last week begging to leave with them," said Dagoberto Munero. "Arianne had waited outside Rafa's home the night before they left. Rafa told me that he had agreed to take them for $700."

Nivaldo protested that Rafa was a friend of his and the two shared a passion for music, discotheques and motorcycle races. He insisted that they didn't pay for the trip, contradicting what he had told the Miami-Dade police on his first day. He added that when Rafa traveled to Jagüey to purchase the boat and motor, he went with him. Arianne even disputed Dagoberto's account, saying he did not have a fight with his brother but stayed at the shoreline and waved them off.

María Díaz, a cousin of the Rodríguez family who lives in Miami, recalled that after the disaster neither Arianne nor Nivaldo could identify the others when shown photos by the police. "She didn't know Lirka's name and would just say, 'The one in the flowered bathing suit.' It was clear they didn't know the others." Some of the relatives had darker suspicions. Why were the two outsiders the only ones to survive? Milagros García and her husband, Ricardo Sardinas, say that the Coast Guard also had suspicions and did a thorough investigation and autopsy of the recovered bodies. Their conclusion: a seriously overloaded boat but no evidence of foul play.

Still, Ricardo personally viewed the bodies to assure himself. He felt that Arianne and Nivaldo badgered Rafa into letting them come along—further overloading the boat. The relatives also said that the Coast Guard told them it was impossible for them to come ashore the way they did with currents going the other direction that day.

Border Patrol anti-smuggling agent Verne Eastwood said that he has seen many "staged landings" but there was no hard evidence that this was the case with Arianne and Nivaldo. He said that the two were interviewed separately for several hours after their arrival at Jackson Memorial Hospital. "They looked pretty good for what they had been through," said Eastwood. "They're pretty tough." He said that the two independently confirmed that they had paid $2,000 for their fare. The couple also told the Border Patrol that Rafa and his father, Rafael, were the co-captains of the trip but said that they were unfamiliar with most of the others on board. They identified Elián only by a photograph, not by name.

Sometimes Arianne's version would be at odds with Nivaldo's and sometimes with what they told investigators and with what they told reporters. On

November 28, while still in the hospital, Arianne told reporters that they swam "against the current to get to a boat that rescued them." Later, the couple insisted that they had swum all the way to shore.

By May 2000, questions emerged as to whether the couple and their rescuers were entirely telling the truth. In a *Miami Herald* story, air-conditioning installer Reniel Carmenate, who had been out fishing with his friend, said that he had not found Arianne and Nivaldo on shore as he had previously stated. "I guess I'll have to tell you what really happened," he was quoted as saying. "The real story is that we found them several miles off Key Biscayne," possibly as much as seven miles from shore. Carmenate said he took Nivaldo and Arianne to shore at Crandon Park Marina before calling authorities so the couple would not be automatically returned to Cuba. Carmenate knew the drill: he had been a *balsero* only two years earlier. By his account, it was a staged landing.

A young businessman who leases boats near the dock at Crandon Park where the couple said they swam ashore said he did not believe their story. "Hundreds of Cuban rafters land here every month," he said. "They get to the sandbar out there and then the smugglers go out and get them and bring them ashore. Everyone knows but no one talks about it because [the local authorities] could shut us down if we complained about it. You cannot mess with the Cubans in Miami."

After being told Carmenate's story, Arianne still insisted that they had swum ashore, and Nivaldo refused to comment at all. "He is saying that so he can be famous," she protested. The conflicting stories only darkened the misgivings of the relatives of those who had perished in the shipwreck.

Whatever happened on that boat, Arianne and Nivaldo paid a far steeper price than they could ever have imagined. Within the year, strains in their own relationship were evident. Nivaldo, she confirmed, was "too possessive," and he seemed uncertain and nervous around her. Two years later, they had separated and Arianne started seeing someone else.

One evening, Arianne read me her night-school homework, a long essay she had written in English: "I want to speak about my life. I am not very happy because I don't feel complete. I am twenty-two years old. I am from Cuba. I am been [sic] in United States from three month [sic]. I live in Hialeah. I have a daughter that is five years old. She lives in Cuba and her name is Estefany. She is beautiful. I am very sad. I am not completed [sic] because I miss her and need her in my life. . . . I am going to the school. When I finish my school I am going to my house and sleep. I clean my house on Saturday. On Sunday I go out. My life is not what I want because I miss my daughter. She is not here with me. I am very sad."

In May, Arianne said she had made efforts to visit Estefany in Cárdenas, but she had been defeated by the bureaucratic struggle to obtain a visa and a new passport and, of course, by the problem of raising the money. Despite the passage of more than two years, it is unlikely that Arianne will see her daughter any time soon. As students of exile politics well know, the most enduring legacy of the Cuban Revolution is the shattered family.

CHAPTER 2

CASTRO FAMILY VALUES

One day I'll be out of here and I'll get my son and my honor back—
even if the earth should be destroyed in the process.

FIDEL CASTRO IN A LETTER TO HIS HALF-SISTER, LIDIA, IN 1954

S OME TIME AGO, a Cuban in exile contacted his divorced wife, who had
left for the United States with their six-year-old son. He asked that their son
be allowed to visit him, arguing that as he was about to undertake a perilous
excursion, it might well be the last time for him to see his cherished son. Although his former wife was wary and wounded from a protracted divorce and
custody suit, she relented, accepting his promise "as a gentleman," as he put
it, to return the boy in two weeks' time.

But when the two weeks elapsed, the boy was not sent home. And two
months later, when the father embarked on his dangerous mission, he did not
return the son to his mother but rather turned him over to the care of his relatives and close friends.

The kidnapped six-year-old boy was not Elián González but six-year-old
Fidelito Castro, the firstborn son of Fidel Castro by his first wife, Mirta Díaz-
Balart. Nor would this be the final round in their bruising custody battle.

For those who were baffled by the passion and tenacity of the battle
waged by Fidel Castro for the return of Elián González, or, indeed, his half
century of railing against the United States, many of the answers lie in Castro's own family history. For Fidel Castro, and many Cubans, the personal *is*
the political. For them, the four-decade stalemate between Miami and Havana is the natural outcome of an extended broken family. In certain respects,
it is a huge family feud.

The shattered family is manifest in Cuban society from the top to the bottom. Indeed, the Castro–Díaz-Balart relationship can be viewed as the
Cuban equivalent of the Hatfields and the McCoys. But in blood ties and po-

litical ambition, the relationship withstands analogy to the House of Atreus. Castro sees himself as the absolute patriarch not only of his family but also of his country. In a 1993 interview, when asked what his greatest mistake was, Castro told me, "We may have been guilty of excessive paternalism." The most tragic casualty of the Cuban Revolution has been the Cuban family. As in the American Civil War, thousands of Cuban families have been driven by politics, geography and conflicting convictions: siblings pitted against each other or their parents or grandparents. And Castro's own family has been no exception.

In 1948, twenty-two-year-old Fidel Castro married Mirta Díaz-Balart, an exceedingly pretty philosophy student. The two were introduced by her brother, Rafael Díaz-Balart, who at the time was one of Castro's most trusted friends and is today one of his most aggrieved enemies. "Mirta was very beautiful but like a Nordic girl, not the typical Cuban woman," recalled Max Lesnik, a classmate of both young men at the University of Havana's law school. "Rafael was very, very close to Fidel Castro. Rafael recognized in Fidel a very important figure but Rafael was also a great speaker and he was a restless, ambitious man."

Both were from small towns in what used to be called Oriente—about a half hour's drive from each other—and the sons of powerful, strong-willed fathers. Díaz-Balart's father, also named Rafael, was a representative in Cuba's Congress and the mayor of Banes, a small, prosperous town that was thought of almost as a colony of the United Fruit Company. "Our town was about fifteen blocks long," said Rafael Díaz-Balart, reminiscing about his family over dinner in Coral Gables in 2001. "My father loved to walk from our house on Cárdenas Avenue to the end of town where the headquarters of the United Fruit Company were located." The elder Díaz-Balart was a friend and close ally of Fulgencio Batista, Cuba's president in the 1940s, who hailed from Banes as well.

Rafael Díaz-Balart, an intelligent and dapper man, his nails neatly buffed, splits his time between his residences in Madrid and Key Biscayne. Like many Cubans of his background and generation, he knows English fairly well but speaks only Spanish. Over a dinner of paella, he held forth for several hours on his former best friend and brother-in-law.

His long relationship with Fidel Castro and the fact that it was he who had introduced Castro to his sister still clearly haunted him. With each pass-ing year Castro has stayed in power, his malevolence has grown in the mind of Rafael. "Fidel is a psycho-paranoid," he told me, his hands gesticulating sharply to punctuate each phrase. "When Mirta told me, 'We are in love and I believe we are going to get married,' I told her, 'You know very well Fidel is a brilliant man, he has exceptional qualities, but you know he is a psycho-paranoid! In the same manner he gives you a fur coat today, tomorrow he might push you off the stairs from the ninth floor!'

Castro's father, Ángel, was a *guajiro* (a country rustic) who through his ceaseless labor became one of the wealthiest *latifundistas* in the region. "He was very cagey and started out working for United Fruit and then buying land from them," said a former neighbor. "There used to be a joke among the United Fruit Company people that when they all went to bed at night, Ángel Castro moved the fence posts to his advantage." By the time Fidel Castro was born, his father was the lord of Finca Manacas, a sprawling estate in Birán.

Jack Skelly, a neighbor and family friend of the Díaz-Balarts, has known Mirta since he was five years old. "My father was in charge of the railroad for United Fruit, which is today Chiquita Banana," he said, referring to the company then viewed as a symbol of American exploitation of Latin America. "Batista was Banes's best-known citizen, then the Díaz-Balarts. They lived in a company home and paid no rent. It was a big house even by American standards. They were powerful, but they weren't wealthy. The father was the main lawyer for the United Fruit Company. They were not rich but they had clout. The Castros had a lot of land but they were not a class thing. Fidel's father made a lot of money.

"When I came back from the army in the summer of '44, Mirta was fifteen and suddenly gorgeous," said Skelly over coffee at a Denny's in Fort Lauderdale. "Dirty blond with green eyes, about five foot seven. And she was the most lovely person. Mirta was *el alma de Dios* [the soul of God]. She was absolutely saintly. Her laugh was sunshine. I still can hear her laughing. And she just loved to dance!" Rafael Díaz-Balart said that Fidel was not the only friend to whom he introduced his sister. "I had introduced her to a lot of other friends of mine," he said, somewhat defensively, about his role in bringing the two together. "Mirta was a gorgeous woman, one of the most beautiful at the university. I introduced her also to Rogelio Cequeira, a very handsome engineer, who later became a multimillionaire in Venezuela. But I think she fell in love with Fidel because he was very handsome with many unusual qualities and he had personality. But I believe the main thing she saw in him was someone to challenge our stepmother. Our mother had died when I was five years old when she was only twenty-eight years old. It was not a great loss or shock because we had our grandmother, and she lived with us like a mother. My father was a wonderful person but he did not share with us, he was an introvert, and he traveled a lot. And our stepmother, Angelica Franco, was a horrible stepmother."

Marjorie Skelly Lord, Jack's sister and Mirta's English teacher at the Friends School in Banes—a Quaker school—first met Castro at the Díaz-Balarts' home. "He was a very good-looking man," she said. "And he was very attentive to her but he was indifferent to us. He didn't like Americans and he hated the United Fruit Company because his father had some bad dealings with them. He had a lot of complexes and always had a chip on his shoulder. I remember once we drove down to the beach and we had to go through some private land and gates which kept the cattle from eating the sugarcane. Well, he didn't know that and he was giving this big speech in the car about how he objected to the gates."

Barbara Walker Gordon, whose father was the manager of the United Fruit Company division in Banes, was a close friend of Mirta's and spent time with the young Castro over two summers. "We thought he was a great guy," she said. "He was very handsome and a very Cuban macho type. He impressed a lot of us, in a teenage kind of fashion, as a big guy on campus, which he was at the University of Havana. He was a very good friend of Rafael." Gordon saw similarities between the two young men. "Rafael was also a political guy—believe you me, and I don't think he was above corruption either. A different kind, different degree shall we say. I was crazy about Rafael."

From the start, Mirta's parents had doubts about her beau. "Her father was very opposed to him," said Gordon, "because he knew what kind of person he was and how he acted at the university and what happened when he visited Colombia [in 1948, Castro attended the Anti-Imperialist Student Congress in Bogotá, which ended in riots] and he thought he was a dangerous young man."

But Castro was a persistent suitor who "kept hammering at the door," said Gordon. To woo Mirta, Castro stepped into her social world, one very different from his own. "We had dances that rotated at these three clubs—the American Club, the Spanish Club and the Cuban Club," Gordon reminisced. "Of course, it was all a family affair. Fidel came to the dances but he couldn't dance. I think he would do one trip around the dance floor with Mirta and that would be the end of it. He would end up chatting politics to the men. He didn't like dancing. He loved to talk and he'd go around talking while we were all dancing with Mirta by his side listening."

Fidel and Mirta married on October 12, 1948, at the Díaz-Balart home in Banes. Marjorie Lord attended both the civil and church weddings and hosted a shower for Mirta at the American Club of the United Fruit Company. "It was a very big reception at her parents' home," said Lord, with the house overflowing with people. "I remember seeing Fidel's mother and brother there. Most of us did not like Fidel, nor did her parents, but they tried to get along."

Indeed, Castro had several agendas at the time of his nuptials. One was that he was hiding out from the paramilitary gangster Rolando Masferrer, for reportedly killing one of Masferrer's Tigres at the university. "There were about three groups, and Fidel was in one of them," said Skelly. "They were called the Happy Trigger Groups. The man who was in charge of what they called the Banes Barracks sent word to Masferrer that if he put one foot toward Banes he would shoot him on sight. So Masferrer never came to Banes looking for him."

Lieutenant Felipe Mirabal was the chief of the army in Banes, said Rafael Díaz-Balart, "and a close friend of my father." Following Castro's wedding to Mirta, it was Mirabal who escorted the young couple to the Camagüey airport to fly off to Miami for their honeymoon. "It was Fidel's idea because he knew that Masferrer's people could be waiting to kill him at the airports in Havana or Santiago," said Rafael. "Because of my father, Lieutenant Mirabal and another soldier toting a machine gun" drove the newly married couple to the airport. "Mirabal could have been dismissed from his military position by consenting to my father's request," said Rafael. "And Fidel became very good friends with Lieutenant Mirabal, who became one of the Secret Service bodyguards to President [Carlos] Prío and second in command of the Military Intelligence Services. Fidel and I would have lunch with Mirabal regularly at his house in Havana, because his wife, Inés, was a wonderful cook. Later Fidel would repay him by throwing him in prison for twenty years until he died there."

Rafael also married around the same time and met up with his sister and brother-in-law in New York. "We then drove to Miami in a car that Fidel bought, a Lincoln Continental, from the $20,000 he brought on his honeymoon," said Rafael. The couple's extravagant honeymoon in Miami and New York was paid for by Ángel Castro and included hotel accommodations at the Waldorf-Astoria. "The money did not come from Batista because Batista was cheap and he gave them a table lamp for their wedding gift," said Rafael disdainfully. "They stayed in a very luxurious hotel in Miami, where the Shah of Iran would stay. Fidel called me from Miami and told me all about it."

"How she married Fidel is a mystery to all of us," said Skelly. "A guy who has two left feet and no sense of humor. His whole thing was politics. He wasn't Cuban because Cubans have an incredible sense of humor. And he didn't dance or like music and Cubans live for music and dance. And he was a *zurdo* [a klutz]." But few doubted her ardor for him. Some felt that Castro had married up—garnering crucial and tangible benefits for his future. "He's an opportunist and being married to the sister of the [future] Deputy Minister of the Interior was a good move," observed the late Tad Szulc, Castro's principal biographer. However, Skelly remembers Mirta as a long-suffering spouse, though he concedes a bias. "We had a pretty good puppy love before Fidel. I was what is known as *un medionovio*—a half of a boyfriend." "I don't think he ever mistreated her," said Marjorie Skelly Lord, "but he was only interested in politics."

Back in Havana, the couple settled into an apartment in front of the Tropical Stadium in the Havana suburb of Marianao. Skelly recalled a memorable first meeting with Castro in the summer of 1949. "Mirta was about seven months pregnant and United Fruit had a regular picnic at the beach on the Fourth of July," said Skelly. "It was a full-moon night and we had a nine-piece combo, Cole Porter songs, down by the beach. And lo and behold, who approaches wearing a white *guayabera* but Fidel, walking toward me with Mirta. So Mirta came over and gave me a big hug and kiss. And that was my introduction to him. He spent a week at the beach there with us. We had no electricity—just windmills—and running water that you got from the rain, coming in barrels. Every night we played canasta by hurricane lights, drank beer, smoked cigars and argued politics. And also dominoes. There was a group of eight or ten that gathered in different homes every night on the beach. We laughed a lot. Drank mostly beer, and everybody smoked cigars. Fidel was always yelling and lecturing everybody—although Rafael was right up there with him."

In 1949, the young couple's son was born and christened Fidel Castro Díaz-Balart, an *apellido* (last name) that would soon become an oxymoron, uniting two warring families in one name. "Mirta was not the type to get involved in her husband's affairs; she was a homemaker," said Lesnik. "I remember we used to go to the Orthodox Party meetings when Fidel was campaigning for representative. Fidel was traveling throughout the provinces, speaking at meetings, and Mirta would remain in the car alone, sleeping, and waiting for him to finish. Everyone says that Rafael was always a *batistiano*, but I remember when he was in the Orthodox Party with myself and Fidel," said Lesnik. "He switched in 1949 when Batista named him the head of his

Youth Party." In 1933, Batista had risen out of the ranks of the army and assumed the presidency in a questionable but accepted election.

Rafael Díaz-Balart had tried to forge an alliance between his ambitious brother-in-law and Batista, arranging a meeting at Batista's palatial estate, Finca Kuquine, famous for its solid-gold telephone, a gift from the American Telephone and Telegraph Company. "Fidel told Batista, who was angling to get back into power, that he should implement a coup at that time," said Díaz-Balart. "He said that Prío was ready to flee the country and Batista should make his move immediately. I also remember that he looked over the books in Batista's library and said to him, 'You have many books here but you don't have a very important book, Curzio Malaparte's *The Technique of the Coup d'État*.' He said, 'I'll send you a copy,' and Batista broke with laughter. He loved to laugh."

In the spring of 1952, Castro was an Orthodox Party candidate in the upcoming election. But his chance of winning a seat as a congressman, as well as the dream of democracy for Cuba, evaporated when Batista, realizing he would not win the scheduled election, seized control of the country with a military coup on March 10, 1952. The historian Hugh Thomas likened the impact of Batista's treachery on Cuba to an individual struck by a "a nervous breakdown after years of chronic illness." Although the coup was accepted and validated by the U.S., which saw Batista as a reliable ally to safeguard its interests, Cuba's intelligentsia and democracy proponents were shattered. The Díaz-Balarts, however, emerged as winners and their friendship and loyalty to Batista were well rewarded. "The Díaz-Balart family were always *batistianos*," said Juanita Castro, Fidel's younger sister, with undisguised contempt. "Rafael ran Batista's Ministry of the Interior and Batista created a ministry—Secretary of Communications and Transportation—for Rafael's father." The powerful Interior Ministry, a Cuban amalgam of the FBI and CIA and Batista's dreaded secret police, was charged with maintaining "public order." In fact, Díaz-Balart was its deputy minister under Ramón Hermida.

Barbara Gordon visited her old friend Mirta in August 1952. "They had a funny little apartment in Marianao," she recalled. "Rafael took me around in his car and he was carrying a gun in the car. He was with Batista by then and Fidel was already a guerrilla. Fidelito was still crawling," she said. "I remember I was sort of horrified by the way she was living. I said I want to see Fidel and she said, 'He's gonna drive by and wave at you.' And he did. He waved and that was it. She was separated from her family because she didn't think that Batista should have come back. She was very supportive of Fidel."

Batista had spent much of the late 1940s at his mansion in Daytona Beach, where he amassed a sizable art collection and became pals with his neighbor the gangster Meyer Lansky.

On July 26, 1953, Castro declared war on Batista—and his in-laws—with an audacious and disastrous attack on the Moncada military garrison in Santiago de Cuba. Castro believed that if he seized control of the garrison, he could arm his civilian supporters in Santiago de Cuba and capture the backing of many in Batista's army. A week before the assault, Castro had stopped by to visit his brother-in-law Rafael at his office in the Ministry of the Interior to suss out whether the police were wise to his plans. Castro left confident that word had not leaked out. Nevertheless his grand assault was doomed. Outnumbered ten to one by Batista's soldiers, 31 of Castro's 134 guerrillas were captured and killed, some brutally tortured.

Luis Ortega, the editor of *La Prensa,* one of Cuba's most popular newspapers, didn't think that the attack on the military garrison was as harebrained as many thought. "He attacked the Moncada because he had the idea that if he took control of Santiago de Cuba, he could spread the revolution to the rest of the country. He was not crazy. It was not the first time that someone had attacked the Moncada. Nationalism is the most important aspect of Castro, that and his opposition to the United States. Before Castro, Cuba was like a state of the United States. I believe that he liberated the country from the United States at a high cost. Too high. But he has profound roots in Cuban history." Castro also had a keen appreciation for Cuban memory. José Martí, the revered poet, muse and champion of Cuban independence, had been born one hundred years earlier in 1853, and the *fidelistas* took to calling themselves the "Generation of 100 Years."

Fidel and his brother Raúl, who also participated in the assault, were among those who emerged unscathed—in no small part owing to the influence of his wife's powerful family. Castro owed his life to his father's good friend Archbishop Pérez Serantes, who negotiated his surrender after the catastrophic assault. But according to one Díaz-Balart relation, family ties also played a role in keeping the young revolutionary and his brother alive. "One reason Fidel was not tortured and killed after Moncada was because my cousin's husband, who became the patriarch of the Díaz-Balart cousins, paid off the guards. So much for ideology." But Rafael Díaz-Balart maintains that neither he nor his father gave any special treatment to their revolutionary in-law. "I never saved his life in prison," he said. "Those are stories. We saved his life when he married my sister because my father asked Mirabal to do him a favor—that one time only." However, most observers from that period agree with Gordon's appraisal: "He never would have gotten out of prison—alive—if it had not been for the Díaz-Balart family," she said. They also noted that the tug-of-war between the Castro and Díaz-Balart families took a toll on young Fidelito. Castro's confidant, the writer Luis Conte Agüero, recalled the precocious young Fidelito declaring, "When Batista falls, my dad is going to cut off the heads of the *batistianos*, except for my uncle and grandfather because they are good."

The Moncada assault made Castro a national hero, a stature that bloomed exponentially during his trial, in which he defended himself and gave his famous 1953 courtroom oration, "History Will Absolve Me." But it was also an irreparable wounding to his wife's family—from which bad blood has flowed ceaselessly ever since. Castro was now directly at odds with his brother-in-law, who felt conflicted by a need to protect his only sister and by his rage against her ungrateful husband. Rafael Díaz-Balart got one measure of revenge when Castro and his brother Raúl were sentenced to fifteen years in prison on Isla de Pinos. But more was to come.

Castro had been conducting a relationship with a stunning, green-eyed beauty named Natalia Revuelta, known as Naty. Revuelta, a wealthy married socialite-turned-revolutionary, offered her Miramar mansion to Castro and his conspirators and was a valiant and reliable courier during the plotting of the Moncada assault. Her ardor for the indefatigable revolutionary was unabated throughout his imprisonment.

In Castro, Naty had found the ideal antidote for her ennui with society life, her marriage to a doctor named Orlando Fernández and motherhood. "Naty was raised to marry well. She had gone to prep school in Philadelphia and then went to the equivalent of a finishing school," said her biographer, Wendy Gimbel. "When Fidel met Naty she looked like a movie star who had been dipped by the gods into a golden oil like Ava Gardner and Rita Hayworth. She had wide green eyes and a beautiful mouth and raven hair. She always juxtaposed herself against Mirta. She was the cosmopolitan, well-traveled, educated woman, and Mirta was a provincial little girl with no sort of worldliness to her. Part of Naty's self-vindication was her belief that Mirta was incapable of being the kind of wife that a young revolutionary leader needed."

Castro had both his wife and Naty running operations for him. Lesnik remembers that "a friend of mine, using my car, took Mirta to the airport to fly to Isla de Pinos to see Fidel and get this very important document he had written in prison. Mirta smuggled it out of the jail in her bra. She took it to this lawyer belonging to the Orthodox Party named José Manuel Gutiérrez.

That document, which Castro [also] called 'History Will Absolve Me,' was rewritten by the great Cuban intellectual Jorge Manach and became the 'Manifesto of the 26th of July Revolution.' "

Salvador Lew, a lawyer and Orthodox Party activist, was close to the future brothers-in-law at the university, and remembered clearly the escalating drama between the two families. "Mirta loved Fidel very much but Rafael never liked that marriage and he was always pushing for their breakup. As the deputy head of the Ministry of the Interior in Cuba when Fidel was in jail, he could see their correspondence because all prison mail was censored. And he got a letter for Naty and put it in the envelope for Mirta. And he put Mirta's letter in the envelope to Naty. Of course, Mirta was very hurt when she read the letter that Fidel wrote to Naty. That was the key to the whole divorce. She wouldn't have left the marriage except for the letter Castro wrote to Naty." A humiliated Mirta phoned Naty to inform her of the letter she had received and request her own letter, which Naty claimed not to have opened. Although some biographers have attributed the letter exchange to a mid-level clerical mistake, Lesnik and Juanita Castro concur with Lew's version that there was nothing accidental about the letter mix-up. Certainly, Mirta came to resent her brother's role. "Mirta and Rafael are not on great terms at all," said Gordon, who traced the breach back to their differences over Castro fifty years ago.

While Mirta was devastated by the letter mix-up, Naty was hopeful that it would enliven her prospects to succeed Mirta. "Naty said that Mirta called her up and accused her of all manner of things," explained Gimbel. "At one point, she thought maybe the prison censor was responsible, but the censor had been so kind to them previously that she doubted it. So she became suspicious of Mirta's family's role." The final blow to the marriage was Castro's discovery in prison that the Díaz-Balarts had put Mirta on the government payroll, which Castro saw as an irrevocable affront to his honor. "Tell Rafael that I am going to kill him myself," a fuming Castro told a journalist friend at the time.

In July 1954, Mirta Díaz-Balart announced that she wanted a divorce from her husband and soon left for the United States with their five-year-old son, Fidelito. Learning that his child had been taken to the land of Yankee imperialism by his hated *batistiano* in-laws, Castro flew into a rage: "I refuse even to think that my son may sleep a single night under the same roof sheltering my most repulsive enemies and receive on his innocent cheeks the kisses of those miserable Judases," Castro wrote his half-sister, Lidia, in 1954. "To take this child away from me . . . they would have to kill me. . . . I lose my head when I think about these things." Should the courts rule against him, he vowed "to fight until death." Castro, facing a long prison term, was hardly in a position to be issuing orders, much less making unprecedented paternity demands. But he did just that. Instructing his lawyers to seek custody of his son, he flat-out refused his wife a divorce unless Fidelito was returned and enrolled in a school in Havana.

By year's end, Castro had lost the first battle. Mirta got her divorce and retained custody. Castro fumed in his letters to his sister: "One day I'll be out of here and I'll get my son and my honor back—even if the earth should be destroyed in the process. . . . I don't give a tinker's damn if this suit lasts until the end of time. If they think they can wear me down and that I'll give up the fight, they're going to find out . . . that I'm disposed to reenact the famous Hundred Years' War. And I'll win it." And he did just that.

Fidel Castro's prison letters leave no doubt that he was and is a scorched-earth warrior. Indeed, his belligerent intractability is a point of honor. In another letter, he boasted of being "a man of iron," then reminded his sister that "you know I have a steel heart. And I shall be dignified until the last day of my life."

Castro and his brother were sprung from jail in 1955 after Batista made the mistake of his life and granted a general amnesty to political prisoners. Castro stayed briefly in Havana, where he threw himself into reorganizing his followers and mulled over the possibility of running for mayor. But fearing for his life, he fled to Mexico in July 1955. There he relentlessly plotted dual strategies: his triumphant return to Cuba and getting custody of his cherished son "by any means necessary." In the end, he negotiated custody of Fidelito for himself for one month of every year.

With her son in tow and her divorce final, Mirta moved to Fort Lauderdale. "We got her and Fidelito an apartment about a block from my father's," said Jack Skelly. "She spent a lot of time with us. Every Sunday, she would cook a meal for my mother. This is where our *medionovio* started up again. But she was also a very good Catholic. I should have married her." His sister Marjorie recalls this period as being a "very tough time for Mirta. She lived alone in an apartment with Fidelito. My mother would baby-sit for her sometimes." She recalls that Mirta held down two jobs, hostessing at Creighton's restaurant, an upscale eatery in Fort Lauderdale, and teaching part-time at a private school. In 1956, Mirta abruptly decided to return to Cuba. "She didn't tell us why," said Marjorie.

Within the year Mirta met and married Emilio Núñez Blanco, the son of Batista's ambassador to the U.N. The new family went to New York, where

Fidelito attended school in Queens, registered under his own name: Fidel Castro Díaz-Balart. It seemed that Mirta had gained the upper hand. But not for long.

In 1999, Castro described Elián González's situation as a "kidnapping" and an "abduction." Again, there are personal parallels. In September 1956, Castro placed an arranged phone call from Mexico to his ex-wife at the office of his father-in-law, then Batista's Minister of Communications. Present for the speakerphone conversation were Mirta, her brother Rafael, their father and Mirta's new husband. The estranged couple agreed to a fifteen-day visit for Fidelito with his father, the dates of which coincided with Mirta's honeymoon to Paris with her husband. Castro would send his sister Lidia to Havana to pick up Fidelito and travel with him to Mexico and return him two weeks later. Instead, Castro promptly installed his son in the walled Mexico City mansion of his allies and patrons, a Cuban singer named Orquídea Pino and her wealthy Mexican husband. One month and then two went by without Fidelito's return.

In what amounted to a will, Castro bequeathed his son to the couple, in the event of his death. Using arguments not unlike those that Elián's relatives would employ forty-five years later, Castro wrote that "because my wife has proven to be incapable of breaking away from the influence of her family, my son could be educated with the detestable ideas that I now fight. . . . I am leaving him with those who can give him a better education, to a good and generous couple who have been, as well, our best friends in exile. . . . And I leave my son also to Mexico, to grow and be educated here in this free and hospitable land. . . . He should not return to Cuba until it is free or he can fight for its freedom." Castro defended his actions in a November 24, 1956, letter to the couple, writing that "I am making this decision because I do not want, in my absence, to see my son Fidelito fall into the hands of my most ferocious enemies and detractors, who in an extreme act of villainy . . . disgraced my home and sacrificed it to the blood tyranny they serve." Castro protested disingenuously that he had not acted out of anger but in his son's best interests: "I do not make this decision through resentment of any kind, but only thinking of my son's future."

With that, Castro and his *barbudos*—bearded followers—sailed back to Cuba on the catastrophically overburdened *Granma* to burrow themselves in the Sierra Maestra mountain range above Santiago de Cuba, from which Castro would wage his guerrilla war. A distraught Mirta repeatedly called Lidia concerning the boy's whereabouts. Rafael Díaz-Balart recalled the traumatic event. "Lidia told Mirta, 'I'm really sorry but Fidel says that the boy cannot be sent home to you because your family are *batistianos.*' Mirta became hysterical. She came to see me and we prepared a trip with her husband, Emilio, who was quite helpful. Mirta and Emilio went with two of my men from the secret police and an arrangement was made for Mexican policemen to be with my people during the operation. We figured out that Fidelito and Lidia were staying at Orquídea Pino's house near Chapultepec Park. We had two cars at opposite ends of the street: in one car was Mirta with Emilio, the Mexican policemen and my men. We were lucky it was daytime because Mirta was able to spot the child in the car with Lidia, when it drove up with Castro's militiamen. We followed them into a busy street and Mirta's car pulled up right next to the car. Immediately we jumped from our cars and the Mexican police aimed their firearms toward Castro's armed men. Fidelito saw his mother, and ran directly toward her."

When Enma Castro, Fidel's younger sister who lived in Mexico, protested to the police that the men had "seized my nephew," the Cuban Foreign Minister responded coolly, "The child is with his mother, which excludes the possibility of a kidnapping."

Two years later, when Castro toppled Batista, he promptly took charge of his son. Salvador Lew was on the plane that brought Fidelito and dozens of jubilant exiles waiting out the war in New York back to Havana on January 6, 1959. The plane was delayed twelve hours because of poor weather. On the plane, Fidelito, traveling with his stepfather's sister, was playing with the son of Raúl Chibás, the brother of Eddy Chibás, the dynamic leader of the Orthodox Party. "They were having a very adult conversation," said Lew. "They were joking about [Colonel Esteban] Ventura, the police chief who had tortured Chibás."

A patient Mirta waited at Havana's José Martí Airport for her son. But it was Castro who would be calling the shots from the minute their son stepped off the plane. Two days later, Fidelito accompanied his father atop a Sherman tank for his triumphant march through Havana to the cheers of a million Cubans. Mirta watched the event on television at her home in Tarara Beach, outside Havana, with a half dozen of her friends. She now had two young daughters with her second husband. An old friend of Mirta's, who requested anonymity, was also at her house watching the great event. "We were watching it on live TV," he said. "Fidel was standing on this tank with Huber Matos [a revolutionary hero] and Fidelito. And Mirta said, 'Ah, poor Cuba. If he's as good a leader as he was a father, then poor Cuba!' That's what she said because he was a terrible father and husband."

As Cuba's *máximo líder,* Castro reversed her custody order and refused to allow Fidelito to leave with her. A plainly outwitted Mirta was forced to remain in Cuba for another eight years. "She had hated her stepmother so much that she didn't want Fidelito to go through the same thing," opined her friend Barbara Gordon. "She wasn't going to leave the country and let her son disappear. There was a mutual agreement that she would stay. I asked her, 'What does Fidel do with Fidelito?' And she said he would send the car every so often and take him out to baseball games and things like that." Later, Fidelito would attend school in the Soviet Union, earn a doctorate in physics and marry a Russian woman. Today, he lives with his second wife, the daughter of the Cuban General Germán Barreiro (the former chief of Cuban counterintelligence who fell into disgrace because of a political scandal in 1989), and three children in Havana.

In early 1959, Castro gave a television interview to Edward R. Murrow for his *Person to Person* series from his suite at the Habana Libre hotel, which a month earlier had been the famous Havana Hilton. Turned out in stylish white pajamas, Castro spoke in strained but understandable English. Asked if he would soon cut his beard, the guerrilla leader seemed amused, and responded, "When we fulfill our promise of good government, I will cut my beard." Then he summoned his son to join him. The fair-haired Fidelito, clutching a black Labrador puppy and looking not unlike the 1950s American television child character Beaver Cleaver, rushed on camera to kiss his adoring father. "Hello, Fidel Jr.," boomed Murrow. "Is that your puppy?" Speaking as fluently as a kid in a Peoria playground, Fidelito grinned winningly and responded, "No. Someone gave it to my father as a present."

Not long after, Castro was being interviewed on *Meet the Press* in Havana when he learned that Fidelito had been in a very serious automobile accident and was rushed to the hospital. Jack Skelly recalled the events vividly. "The TV moderator said, '*Comandante,* thank you for your time tonight, but we understand that you will want to go to the hospital.' And he said, 'No, no,' and Fidelito was almost dying. I went to the hospital. His brother Raúl was there with Mirta. Raúl was the one that came to comfort her."

By all reports, Fidelito, who has his mother's light eyes and his father's visage and beard, is said to be a thoughtful man, a devoted father and a less-devoted husband who enjoys Havana's disco scene. Mirta has lived in Madrid with her second husband and two grown daughters since the mid-1960s. In late 2001, Mirta told friends that she had filed for divorce. "It was a very sad marriage," said Skelly. "Emilio is a very jealous, possessive guy. She has had terrible luck with men." Mirta has resumed her relationships with the Castro family in Cuba, notably with Raúl Castro. She has never spoken publicly about her former husband.

For years, Mirta would visit with her son in Europe—on his various trips to conferences in Belgium, Geneva, Amsterdam and Madrid. In the early 1990s, Fidelito was dismissed from his job running Cuba's atomic power industry and supervising the now defunct nuclear reactor in Cienfuegos amid a corruption scandal. Gordon and Rafael Díaz-Balart believe that Fidelito was put under house arrest—a charge denied by the Cuban government. But he was indisputably *en desgracia* for a period, during which relations with his father were said to be frosty. Barbara Gordon saw Mirta in 2000 in Madrid at a time when she had not seen her son for about eight years. "Mirta worried about when she would see him again and she did not look well but gave the impression of being very fraught and anxious," said Gordon. Fidelito resumed his duties in full in late 2000, although the nuclear reactor remains mothballed.

Mirta's nephew Lincoln Díaz-Balart, born five years after his cousin Fidelito, would become the first Cuban-American member of the U.S. House of Representatives. His brother, Mario, is an outspoken Republican state senator who headed up the Florida Legislature's redistricting committee in 2001 and is now running for the congressional seat he created. Lincoln is among Castro's most implacable and bellicose enemies and led the crusade to keep Elián González in the U.S. During his political career, he has called for a naval blockade of Cuba and for military force to be used against his former uncle. In a stunning but seemingly unconscious parallel, Lincoln Díaz-Balart gave Elián González a black Labrador puppy soon after his Miami relatives laid claim to him. "What's happening today with Rafael and Lincoln and Fidel is a family quarrel," observed Lesnik. "It has less to do with ideology than opportunism. It is a nasty family quarrel in a divided family."

IT WAS IN THE Sierra Maestra in February 1956 that Castro met the most significant woman in his life. Celia Sánchez, a doctor's daughter from Manzanillo, was already a committed revolutionary with an impressive and courageous track record. At thirty-six, she was six years Castro's senior, dark-haired, dark-eyed, flinty and lean in an attractive way. She was a natural strategist of incisive intellect with unstinting devotion to Castro and the Revolution. Like Castro, she was forged from waging battle, and she soon became his comrade, lover and confidante.

"I'd say Celia Sánchez was the great love of his life," said Tad Szulc, who spent considerable time with Castro and his inner circle. "Celia was the only person in my experience who had any kind of sway over Fidel, the only person who could say, 'You're full of it and you shouldn't be doing this.' I went to their hideout at the top of the Sierra Maestra with some of his close friends and they showed me the bed and the desk where she worked. This was their way of saying that they were everything to each other. She ran the logistics of his whole operation, and then when they came down to Havana, she was absolutely vital to him."

Huber Matos, an early revolutionary hero, was introduced to Castro through Sánchez. "She was a Catholic activist. We were friends from long before Fidel appeared on the scene." Both belonged to Chibás's Orthodox Party, and Sánchez's father lived in El Pilón, in the south of Oriente. "We had worked together in another conspiracy in 1952 after Batista's coup. After the Moncada assault, she told me, 'We have to join these people.' Celia had already organized a 26th of July cell and the majority of the boys in it had been students of mine. She even came to my house in Yara with some of those boys to see if she could talk me into joining the 26th of July Movement. I committed myself to help. I gave them a rifle and I told them they could discreetly practice shooting on a small farm that we had. She asked me for some money, which I gave to her, not very much. When I arrived in the Sierra, she had become a very important person. Neither of them told me they were lovers, but I spent some nights in the hideout where they lived. Fidel had a hammock and Celia had a big bed. Fidel would sleep with me on the floor, all night telling me stories. Celia had great influence over Fidel. I never saw them argue. Many times she would say, 'Fidel, you have to do this and that,' but she wasn't ordering him about. Celia was a woman of character who was almost religious in her dedication. She wore a little chain around her ankle. She was easygoing, very loyal to her friends. She was a full-time guerrilla fighter who had realized herself in the struggle."

After the Revolution, Sánchez's apartment on Calle 11 in the Vedado district of Havana became Castro's second home. The apartment served as auxiliary headquarters for Castro, where she often cooked his meals and watched over his food. She even set up a dentist's chair for Castro to have his teeth fixed. Sánchez died from lung cancer in 1980. "It was probably the most tragic loss in Fidel's life," said Szulc. "She smoked Camels like a chimney, just like he used to."

Lee Lockwood, a *Life* reporter who traveled with Castro in the early 1960s, said her death marked the end of an era. "She and René Vallejo [Castro's doctor and close friend, who died in 1967] were the two most important people of his life," he said, "but Celia was the most important." Interestingly, both Vallejo and Sánchez were adherents of Santería, the syncretic Afro-Cuban religion of the country, and both were believed to be *santeros*. While Castro cracked down hard on the Catholic Church, he adopted a laissez-faire attitude toward Santería, and even dabbled himself.

When Lockwood visited Castro at his home in Isla de Pinos and again in Pinar del Río, Sánchez and Castro "would return to their room together after dinner. She had no ego and he is all ego, so that was the key. He trusted her totally. She was a warm person, funny person, tough *oriental*. She was attractive, in kind of a tough, stringy way—not voluptuous or sexually noticeable. In the Sierra, she was indispensable, and when they got to Havana, she ran interference, she was the troubleshooter. Her answering machine announcement—and three or four million people had her private number—gave you this long message, giving tips for just about everything imaginable. And she was much more worldly than Fidel. She had homosexual friends for example, painters, artist friends."

But Sánchez was unyielding in her devotion to Castro. After the Revolution, Huber Matos, feeling that Castro had betrayed its original ideals, sent a letter of resignation. Consumed with paranoia and rage, Castro had Matos tried for treason and sentenced to twenty years in jail. "I was always treated very well by Celia, until I fell in disgrace," said Matos. "When that happened I didn't hear from her anymore. I imagine that her loyalty to Fidel made her swallow whatever affection might be between us. She subordinated everything to her unconditional loyalty to Fidel, even abandoning her Catholicism and her convictions as a person. I imagine that before she died she must have felt a little frustrated and sorry about her role."

"Cuba has never been the same since Celia died," said Alfredo Guevara, Castro's closest friend going back to their university days. "She kept Fidel in touch with the people. She was a thousand times more effective than any intelligence organization and she was one of the few people who could tell Fidel news he didn't want to hear." When I asked Castro about Sánchez, he betrayed little emotion and responded with the formality of a eulogy. "She was like a guardian angel for all the revolutionary fighters whose problems she took care of. She died prematurely"—he paused—"so she never knew these difficult times." He was referring to the early 1990s after Cuba lost its Russian patron.

Celia Sánchez undoubtedly knew that Castro had his share of paramours. As his grip on his island tightened, Castro assumed more and more of the role of the Cuban Romeo—albeit in his own discreet, almost prudish fashion. Unlike many in his inner circle, he loathes pornography and discourages its circulation in Cuba. Despite the multiplicity of his conquests, said to include the Italian film siren Gina Lollobrigida, Castro has engendered loyalty and discretion. Never have tawdry photographs or tell-all memoirs surfaced about Castro. Like many Cuban men, he is a dedicated womanizer but he does not take chances. Any woman who captures his fancy is first checked out by security to ensure that she is not a CIA or hostile plant. After her screening, unbeknownst to her, a third party would invite her on an excursion such as a picnic or reception, at which point Castro would make his move.

Graciela, who now lives in Miami and requested a pseudonym, said she began seeing Castro in 1963, when she was a teenager, although, she hastens to add, "at fourteen, I looked eighteen and was already working as a dancer at the Tropicana." She said introductions were done by Castro's close aide José Abrantes, who she said was designated to handle the delicate negotiations between Castro and women. Graciela began her three-year affair with Castro when she was fifteen and said that most of their trysts took place at his suite at the Habana Libre. She remembered him "as the most tender of lovers," quietly adding that she was deeply in love with him. Beside his bed, she said, was a book that keenly engaged him at the time, *The Psychology of the Masses,* written by Gustave Le Bon. She recalled with amusement how on one occasion in the mid-1960s she stepped out on the balcony of his suite with him overlooking the Malecón, the broad boulevard of Havana that borders the sea. "Fidel was looking down at the hundreds of people below strolling and milling about and he said to me, 'One day very soon, Graciela, every Cuban will have a car!' " She laughed. "And they still don't have bicycles."

Marita Lorenz, another of Castro's conquests, is one of the few who have sought to profit from a fling with Fidel Castro. Lorenz claims that after Castro spurned her, she turned CIA operative and his would-be assassin. Having first met Castro in 1958, when her father's ship docked in Havana harbor, Lorenz said she returned to Havana in 1960 to kill her former lover. Although she says she was spurred on by his rejection of her after she became pregnant, there is ample evidence that an aide of Castro's was the actual father of her terminated pregnancy.

Lorenz offered an account of one of her counterrevolutionary capers, which unfolded like a 1950s noir thriller. "I was given two botulism toxin pills that looked like white gelatin capsules to drop in Castro's drink. Just one would do the trick, I was told, killing within thirty seconds. When you swallow it, right away your throat would be paralyzed. You can't even scream," Lorenz said, clutching her throat dramatically. "I knew the minute I saw the outline of Havana I couldn't do it. Too many memories. I hopped in a jeep and went to the Hilton [Habana Libre]. Just simply walked in, said hi to the personnel at the desk, went upstairs to the suite. Room 2048. I went in and waited. I was scared to death. I had stashed the capsules in a jar of cold cream. And when I looked for them, they were all gunked up. I fished them out and flushed them down the bidet even before Fidel got to the room. Why did I leave so suddenly? was his first question, then, 'Are you running around with those counterrevolutionaries in Miami?' I said yes. I tried to play it cool. The most nervous I have ever been was in that room because I had agents on standby and I had to watch my timing. I had enough hours to stay with him, order a meal, kill him and prevent him from making a speech that night, which was already announced. He was very tired and wanted to sleep. . . . He was chewing a cigar and he lay down on the bed and said, 'Did you come here to kill me?' Just like that. I was standing at the edge of the bed. I said, 'Yes. I wanted to see you.' Then he leaned over, with his eyes closed, and pulled out his .45 and handed it to me. A beautiful hand-carved gun with a pearl handle. I flipped the chamber out and hit it back. He didn't even flinch. And he said, 'You can't kill me. Nobody can kill me.' And he kind of smiled and chewed on his cigar."

FOLLOWING THE REVOLUTION, Naty Revuelta sought to renew her relationship with Castro, but with little success. Notwithstanding Revuelta's considerable allure and usefulness, her dream of succeeding Mirta was never realized. "She was useful while he was in jail because she got him books, and because she was beautiful, and she could be a fantasy for a moment," said Wendy Gimbel. "But by the time he got out of jail, he didn't really care about her. He was in the business of revolution. Celia was the most important. Naty and the others had walk-on parts."

Naty continued to see him during his three-month stay in Havana in 1956 before he fled to Mexico. And it was during one of these rendezvous—at his sister Lidia's apartment—that Naty has said her daughter, Alina, was conceived. The Castro family has harbored some doubts about Alina's paternity but Castro saw to it that Naty and her family were provided for—if not quite in the manner she was accustomed to. "Castro chose to behave decently to her later," said Szulc, "seeing to it she had a good car, not a Cuban Lada, and that she kept her beautiful house." Gimbel disagrees. "I don't think Castro looks after her at all. If she were down and out, he probably would take care of her. Naty is a real survivor. It helped having Alina as her daughter."

According to a memoir penned by Alina Fernández, there was persistent tension between Naty and Celia. On more than one occasion Celia met with Alina, who led a troubled life in Cuba, including four marriages, and "tried to straighten her out," said Gimbel. Alina was not appreciative and would refer to Celia as *La Venenosa* (the poisonous one) and "Fidel's personal witchcraft counselor." The latter was no doubt a reference to Sánchez's lifelong interest in Santería, but it is difficult to find anyone—on either side of the political divide—who didn't respect Celia Sánchez. Celia, for her part, was capable of coping with Castro's infidelity and subsuming her own romantic ambitions. "It was a bit of a class war. Women like Celia and Haydée [Santamaría, another guerrilla leader] viewed Naty as a country club socialite who happened to sleep with Castro. And she looked down on them as *guajiras.*"

With her privileges and ability to travel, Naty Revuelta has had countless opportunities to defect. She has chosen to remain in Havana, and notwithstanding difficult times and a recent bout of illness, seems to be without bitterness. She can often be found at parties at the elegant residence of the head of the U.S. Interests Section, holding court. "Naty was part of history from her own point of view. And she had a good part," reasons Gimbel. "If she left, she'd just be another middle-class Cuban in Miami."

IN THE EARLY 1990s, word began to circulate among the Cuban *nomenklatura* that Castro had married a second woman, Dalia Soto del Valle, a beauty from the southern port city of Trinidad, sometime in the mid-1960s. The couple have five grown sons, all curiously given names beginning with the letter A: Ángel, Antonio, Alejandro, Alexander and Alexis. But unlike her predecessor, Soto del Valle has never been publicly acknowledged as Castro's wife nor is she seen at official functions by his side. (Days after I wrote about their peculiar lifestyle in a national magazine in July 2001, Cuban television beelined on Dalia at a public reception for several minutes, as if to announce her to the world.) An accomplished gardener, Dalia cultivates exotic roses at her home in Jaimanitas, a posh suburb in western Havana that borders the sea. The same ideological schism that has divided the Díaz-Balarts runs through Soto del Valle's extended family. She has a cousin and a granddaughter living in Miami and, according to a memoir of a political prisoner, Dalia's father, Fernando Soto del Valle, wrote a lengthy letter—in essence a political screed—filled with fury and despair at his son-in-law. Although it is clear that Dalia's father, who died a decade ago, was deeply embittered by Castro, the letter has questionable authenticity.

There are two versions of how Castro met Dalia. Former guerrilla leader Lázaro Asencio ties the meeting of the two to the disappearance of the beloved revolutionary idol Camilo Cienfuegos, whose plane was lost in 1960. "Camilo had gone down in Macio Bay near Casilda in Trinidad. We saw an oil slick on the water and a fisherman told me, 'That oil spot is a sign that a boat or a plane went down.' We went back to Casilda and talked with Commander Peña, who was the uncle of this girl Dalia, who was a very good underwater swimmer. She was tall, thin with very white skin and very beautiful. We took Dalia with us in the boat to have her dive and see if she could find the plane, but she didn't find anything. Later we found a small pillow from Camilo's Cessna. When Fidel came to Trinidad, he was introduced to this girl and he fell in love and he took her back to Havana and nobody has ever seen her since."

But Nancy Pérez-Crespo, born and raised in Trinidad and now living in Miami, was told that the couple had met in Havana. "Dalia's father, who was called Quique, came from a very wealthy family who owned a cigarette factory in Trinidad. Quique married this woman Blanca, who was low-class in comparison with Quique's family, who were opposed to the marriage. They had two daughters and a son, Fernando, who was my good friend. When they were divorced, Blanca left for Havana with the two girls; Fernando lived with his father, grandmother and Aunt Gloria in Trinidad. But the girls would come in the summer to Trinidad and for vacations. I remember Dalia as beautiful and blond. She was dating a guy in my neighborhood, Tony Muñoz, a doctor's son who lives in New Jersey now."

In 1964, prior to leaving Cuba, Pérez-Crespo met with her friend Fernando, who confided an extraordinary secret. "On a recent trip to Havana, his mother had told him, 'Your sister has a lover who is a very important figure in the Revolution and they have children, and Dalia wants you to see her sons,'" recounted Pérez-Crespo. "So he went to see Dalia but the street where she lived had what they called a frozen zone and nobody could pass by. And he got very suspicious. He finally made it into the house and Dalia told him that her boyfriend was Fidel Castro. He was in shock."

Although Dalia's status remains a state secret, her existence has long been known among Castro's inner circle. The late José Luis Llovio-Menéndez, a high-ranking Cuban official who defected in 1982, recalled seeing Dalia often at Castro's house, actually a compound, on 166th Street in Siboney. "We went to his home often for state meetings and sometimes to watch movies in his screening room with a big screen," he said. "The security was always around but you couldn't see them. There were three gates and it was well protected. I saw Dalia there but she and the children lived in another house nearby. I saw her there many times. We went there for meetings that were very confidential. Dalia was very polite but Fidel never introduced her as his wife, only as 'compañera' [comrade]. He treated her like everyone else, no show of affection, nothing. But I knew that she was his wife just like everybody knew."

SOME CASTRO CRITICS CONTEND that the peculiar personal lifestyle of Fidel Castro has had deleterious consequences for the formerly cherished institution of the Cuban family. Indeed, Castro haters routinely point to Castro as a role model for the island's moral woes. The counterargument is that adultery is the norm for much of the hemisphere, hardly abated by the Catholic Church's position on divorce. Nevertheless, the Cuban family has seen a dramatic breakdown since the Revolution. More than half of all couples divorce, many never marry, and infidelity is the national sport.

The fact that eight out of ten Cubans who defect are men has only augmented the staggering number of single mothers. If the Maximum Leader never created a role for a First Lady or introduced his brood of children to the public, argue his critics, why should the ordinary Cuban be any more deferential to women? Castro defends his position as a refusal to indulge in the celebritization of his family. "I've always been opposed to mixing politics and my personal life," he told the documentary filmmaker Estela Bravo. But having no family model has had undeniable costs for the Cuban people. The coup de grâce of this familial disaster has been the one million Cubans who have fled. It is the rare Cuban family that has emerged intact—on either side of the Florida Straits.

JUANITA CASTRO HAS LIVED in Miami since October 1964. A month earlier, she convinced her brothers that she wanted to visit their sister Enma and her family in Mexico City. Raúl Castro, who has served as the family patriarch since their father's death, arranged an exit visa for her. Once in Mexico, however, she denounced the Revolution and—implicitly—her brothers. Salvador Lew, a former classmate of Castro's who had fled Havana two years earlier, handled her subsequent trip to Miami and public relations. "Juanita was a revolutionary. She fought Batista and she bought weapons for Castro," said Lew, "but she felt betrayed because she saw that the communists were taking over the government. Fidel didn't want her to leave Cuba but they believed her story that she was going to live in Mexico with Enma."

Lew waited at the Miami airport for Juanita's plane, expecting a somewhat dowdy woman, based on photographs she had sent him. He was shocked when she stepped off the plane. "She was young and beautiful with dark hair, wearing sunglasses and beautiful legs," he said. "I told her right away that we had already won. And she said, 'Why?' And I said, 'Because you're very beautiful.' She's tough too. Just like her brothers. She has to be."

I first met Juanita Castro at the pharmacy she owns on Miami's Calle Ocho. She is a woman with the carriage and bearing of her brother Fidel but the somewhat softer facial features of her younger brother, Raúl. At sixty-nine, she has been twice engaged but never married. In her narrow but tidy office in the rear of the drugstore are photographs of her family and the Pope. She bears the same devout faith of her mother, Lina, and wears a small gold cross. Her life has been difficult but she says she has no regrets. "If the same thing were to happen again," she told me, "I would do it the same way." Eight years earlier, her brother had expressed to me, almost word for word, the same belief.

Juanita Castro's bustling pharmacy is very successful and has made her a woman of means. But although she was born to considerable wealth, there is nothing flamboyant about her or her Coral Gables home. A no-nonsense trim woman with gold-rimmed glasses and auburn-tinted hair, she greeted me in slacks and a black blazer adorned with a handsome, understated gold pin. A trace of whimsy was evident in her leopard-skin slipper shoes, which she extolled for their comfort. She drove us to a Coral Gables restaurant in her taupe Mercedes sedan.

Despite all the estrangements and byzantine complexity of her family, it remains the cornerstone of her existence. She is close to all her sisters, Enma in Mexico and Agustina and Angelita in Havana. Although she has not spoken with her brothers since she left, she said she found the conventional wisdom about them baffling. "Everybody says Raúl is the bad guy and Fidel is the good guy. But these are roles they took at the beginning of the Revolution. It's not true—maybe the opposite. Raúl was the favorite of my mother, and the favorite of mine, because, as I have said, he was very tender-hearted. With the family he is very, very good."

Like her older brother, Juanita is not moved easily to forgiveness or surrender. Forty years have not cooled her ire for some intemperate comments he made about their father. "When the Revolution triumphed, Fidel said on a TV program that he was the son of a landowner, an exploiter," she said with evident injury. "At the beginning he said that 'all family ties are produced by virtue of pure animal instinct.' He said this in regards to the family ties. Animal instinct, not love! This is something that has troubled me."

Juanita feels that her brother was less than a dutiful son to her beloved parents. "My father was very badly treated by Fidel at the very beginning of the Revolution. I never could forget this. Later, he wrote very well of my father. But what Fidel said about my father was not fair because my father was a very good man, a very generous person. He supported Fidel all the time, when he was in school and after school and when he got married to Mirta. If Fidel wanted a car, my father bought a car. Whatever Fidel wanted, he got. I remember once Fidel drove from Havana to Matanzas and crashed his car. And our father bought him another car."

The Castro clan was a large one: three brothers, four sisters plus two half-siblings, Lidia and Pedro Emilio, who were raised by the first wife but visited often. "When we were young, we all got along well and there were no problems," recalled Juanita. "During vacations we were always together, we would go to the beach together with our mom. It was very pleasant. I have no bad memories from my childhood with respect to my brothers. The problems came later. Before the Revolution, Fidel was normal." Juanita described her parents as caring without being effusive. "They were affectionate but nothing extraordinary outwardly," she said. "Raúl was closer to my mother and my father than Fidel, but Fidel was close too. Fidel was different—he didn't show his feelings easily, he was very reserved. The personalities of Fidel and my father are very similar. I remember my father as an austere, reserved, strong character and personality, and not especially expressive. Very *gallego*. My mother was more affectionate. My mother had more of a sense of humor and she liked to joke, to tell stories. But Fidel was distant from everybody. Fidel did everything on his own. He had his own ideas."

Their father, Ángel Castro, hailed from an impoverished family in Galicia, Spain, and had come to the backwoods of Oriente at the turn of the century seeking a better life. Juanita denies the claim of the Díaz-Balarts that her father had been a cavalry soldier for the Spanish, but her brother Ramón has contradicted her and said their father came to Cuba as a conscript for the Spanish. What is certain is that Ángel Castro worked ceaselessly and established one of the largest estates in Oriente. "Our father was very dedicated to his work—a formidable worker. He never rested," recalled Juanita. "Every year he said he was going back to visit Galicia but he never did. He had a nephew and niece there and he helped them with money. My oldest sister, Angelita, took charge of writing letters and sending money to the relatives in Spain."

Her mother's family of seven children had hailed from the westernmost province of Pinar del Río but had resettled in Oriente, at the eastern end of the island, seeking better jobs. One maternal Castro aunt, María Isabel, now in her late eighties, today lives in Camagüey, according to Juanita. Seeking to help her family make ends meet, a teenage Lina took work as a housekeeper at the Castro *finca* in Birán, about a hundred miles farther west. Fidel Castro often notes that his mother came from an impoverished, illiterate family and did not learn to read until she taught herself as an adult. It was not long before she attracted the interest of Ángel Castro.

Ángel had an earlier wife, María Argota, a schoolteacher and the mother of his first two children, Lidia and Pedro Emilio. When and how he married Lina (who was several decades his junior), and how he disposed of María Argota, is a subject of dispute. It is commonly believed that Fidel, his brother Raúl and his sister Angela were born out of wedlock and that it was some years later before Lina was able to convince her stubborn lover to submit to a church wedding. Some claim that María Argota died; others say Ángel divorced her.

Some observers and historians contend that Castro's illegitimacy marked him irrevocably. "Fidel Castro is the son of a servant with his father," said Father Amado Llorente, Castro's favorite high school teacher at the Belén School. "It is important to know this because in Spain and in Cuba they were too tough with these cases. So he hated society. He spoke to me about his mother not being the mother of the first two children of his father and this was difficult and complicated for him. Apparently, the first wife died from a psychological illness and that's how Fidel's mother and father began living together. But he is not completely illegitimate because later the Archbishop of Santiago de Cuba married his parents and baptized the children. Still, this was always a shadow over his life; he never could overcome it completely. More than once he said to me, 'If I had not found you, I would say that I have no family.' "

However, the rough-and-tumble Mayarí region where the Castro clan was raised had an elastic and unconventional moral code. Common-law marriage was not unusual and often married couples would separate but never bother to divorce. Some of this is attributable to the iconic individualism found in the countryside but certainly the strictures of the Catholic Church played a part as well. Infidelity is as Cuban as sugarcane and, for a period, Ángel Castro juggled two families. Left to his druthers it is unlikely that the hardheaded Ángel would have bothered with a church wedding or the baptism of his children.

Llorente agrees with Juanita Castro that Fidel was the father's favorite: "His father was cold and tough, but was very proud of him because he knew he was the most intelligent of the children." José Ignacio Rasco, a school friend from Belén, takes another view. "Don Ángel was an old-fashioned Spaniard, a *gallego,* who was a harsh man with rude manners and very hard on his most rebellious son, Fidel." Rasco and Llorente contend that Castro had a troubled relationship with his father. "He and his father had a bad time of it," said Rasco. "He had a duel with his father on horseback because he said that he was defending the workers from his despotic father."

But Juanita Castro asserts that such a rift never existed until after the Revolution. "No, he never fought with my father and was never upset with my father. They had good relations. My father was a straight shooter and good guy with very good feelings toward Fidel. My father financially supported Fidel all the time, when he was in school, after school and when he got married to Mirta." Indeed, Luis Conte Agüero recalled meeting Ángel Castro in Havana shortly before his death. "Fidel is my favorite son," he said as his wife, Lina, looked on and smiled.

Unlike their older brother, Ramón, nicknamed Mongo, a renowned *mujeriego* (skirt-chaser), Juanita contends that Fidel was far more subdued. "I remember Fidel as being always very private. He didn't brag and he was always very reserved about his personal issues. Mongo was the most amorous. It didn't matter if they were married or single, Mongo went after them. Fidel was Mirta's boyfriend and then they married very quickly."

All the Castro siblings remained close through childhood and all were active in the Revolution. And with the exception of Juanita, who speaks only with her sisters, the family members maintain ties to one another, however strained at times. "Fidel sees and visits with my sisters—but on a totally familial level. They don't get into politics," Juanita explained. "The only one who stood against them and could not take what was happening was me. At the beginning, my mother supported the Revolution, of course. Later she had problems, but she was their mother also. She used to joke about the situation. She was a woman with a great sense of humor and she would take things lightly. She worried about what was going on, but she always kept it to herself." Juanita believes that her father, who dedicated his life to building an estate and a legacy for his children, would have taken an even dimmer view of his son's Revolution.

Like her brother, Juanita can hold a grudge indefinitely. In 1955, when her brothers were released from prison, only Raúl returned home for a week-long visit with their parents in Birán. "My father had wanted Fidel to study, to begin his career as a lawyer, to become a good man. He always worried about him. When Fidel was a prisoner, Dad suffered much during those two years. He never saw Fidel again. When Fidel got out of prison, Fidel didn't go back to see my father but stayed in Havana. He promised to go, but Fidel never went home. Then my father died one month before Fidel returned to Cuba in 1956." The fact that her father never saw his favorite son before he died still troubles her.

However, Juanita disputes those who claim that Castro did not visit their mother on her deathbed. "My mother died in my house in Miramar on 7th Avenue in 1963. It was a massive heart attack. She had circulation problems and already had suffered a heart attack before. One afternoon around 5:00 P.M., when she was finishing her bath she had a strong pain in her chest. We sent word immediately to Fidel and Raúl and they came to my house as soon as they found out. There are people who say that Fidel didn't come, but he was immediately at the house."

Juanita felt, however, that her brother gave short shrift to her mother's burial. "The whole family came to the burial except my sister Enma, who was in Mexico and could not get a plane. She came two days later. I can't say how sad Fidel was but Raúl was very affected by her death. He had been her favorite because he was so caring. From the moment Raúl came to my house in Miramar, he was with us the whole time and traveled with us to Oriente by train. Fidel flew and met us at the train station." His cursory visit to their home in Birán, where their mother was laid out, only worsened matters in her view.

Juanita's view of Fidel as a less than dutiful son is confirmed by Castro's former comrade Lázaro Asencio, who saw Lina Castro and her famous son at the end of 1959 at a rally outside the famous church near Santiago de Cuba, the triple-tiered Basílica del Cobre, where a shrine of Cuba's patron saint, La Virgen de la Caridad (the Virgin of Charity), is kept. "Lina was a great lady, a peasant woman, and she was very religious," said Asencio. "It was raining cats and dogs and Fidel didn't take off his coat to give it to his mother. I had to take off my coat and give it to his mother."

Asencio noted that Castro family members had little immunity from the actions of their brother. Ramón Castro, who had always tended to the family *finca* and who took charge after their father's death, found out quickly that his younger brother would be calling the shots. "Fidel called for Mongo to come and see him," said Asencio. "We were friends and I saw him on the way in. I was there to see Juan Orca, Fidel's secretary. When Ramón came out of his meeting with Fidel he told me, 'Lázaro, I went in a rich man and I came out a poor man.' Fidel had taken the family farm away from him."

Asencio related another anecdote about Castro and his half-brother, Pedro Emilio, in early 1959. Following a television interview in Havana, Castro and Asencio went out for coffee at Calle 12 and 23rd. "We sat down for our coffee and a soldier, the type of guy we called an *alcahuete,* a fawning type, said, 'Fidel, look, Pedro Emilio is over there drinking,' " related Asencio. "Fidel stood up and went over to him and said, 'Pedro Emilio, why are you wearing a 26th of July captain's uniform when you never fought against Batista? And there's an order that those in uniform cannot be out drinking?' Pedro Emilio said, 'So what! I'm not doing what you want.' Right then and there they took Pedro Emilio off to jail. That was astonishing to see." Asencio quips that the only Cuban to get a measure of revenge on Fidel Castro has been his infant son in 1952. "We used to live in Santa Clara by this highway on the outskirts, and Lazarito was about a year old and some months, and every time Fidel went by Santa Clara he would come to my house and eat with us. Back then we had cloth diapers and Lazarito was hot so he took off his diaper, and Fidel goes, 'Ay, Lázaro, how beautiful is your son' and he picks up Lazarito over his head, who suddenly pisses all over Fidel."

LIKE MOST EXILES, Juanita Castro copes with the complexities, secrets and anguish of being separated from her homeland and family. Nevertheless she remains generous and available to all visiting relatives and is especially close with her three sisters, Agustina and Angelita, the eldest, in Havana, and Enma. "My sister Enma is very much like Fidel, physically. She has always gotten along well with Fidel and visits him a few times a year. She's not political and leads a very private life in Mexico City with her husband, her daughter and son." "Enma likes Fidel very much," says Lew. "Enma is not a communist but she feels that he's a great person." Enma's daughter visits Juanita often and always spends Christmas with her. Ramón's son has also visited Miami and his Aunt Juanita. But unlike many visiting Cubans, he chose to return home.

Two of Agustina's sons have lived quietly and privately in central Florida since the mid-1990s, their identity unknown outside the family. Juanita bemoaned the fact that Agustina had been unable to get a visa to visit them for so long. "She's a woman who really loves her sons and worries about them," says Juanita, her voice rising, "but she has to wait for a special permit to be allowed to travel here. You only see this in Cuba. If I want to go to China I go without having to ask for anybody's permission. In Cuba, you have to wait till they do you the charity."

In January 2001, Agustina, after nearly a year's wait, finally received her travel visa. The Miami Castro clan, with Juanita as their matriarch, celebrated at her house. As expected, Agustina returned to Havana six weeks later, bearing the conflict of many Cuban families. "She will miss her sons but she doesn't want to leave her relatives in Cuba," explained one friend. Unlike Enma, Agustina is not especially close with Fidel.

The only relative whom Juanita has shut her doors to is Alina Fernández, the illegitimate offspring of her brother and Naty Revuelta. When Alina fled Cuba in a theatrical exit—first to Madrid, then Miami—she availed herself of Juanita's generosity. But after she penned her memoir, which Juanita felt misrepresented and slandered her family, Juanita filed a lawsuit against her and her publisher. She even questions whether they share a bloodline. "Alina is not a good person. If you have a chance, ask Fidel if he is her father," she says, "because he tells people that he is not." It is true that Castro has never said that she was his daughter, but the special treatment she received in Cuba belies the fact that he thinks otherwise. Juanita's friends warned her that such a lawsuit could bankrupt her, to which Juanita responded, "Then so be it. I will serve my parents." In December 2001, Juanita informed her friends that she had finally prevailed.

Prior to her defection, Fernández had endured a position in Cuba not unlike Billy Carter's during his brother's presidency. In a country at war with glitz and glamour, she had chosen to be a fashion model and had a series of sensational quickie marriages. One Castro insider said there had been little contact between Alina and Castro. "He never spoke to her," she said wryly. "That's why *she* became a dissident."

Among the issues in Fernández's irreverent and bitter memoir that disturbed Juanita Castro was her claim that Lina Ruz de Castro was descended from Turkish Jews. Fernández offers neither evidence nor sources to support her claim; however, it is not unlikely that the ancestors of Castro's father were Jewish. Ángel Castro hailed from the northern town of Lugo in Galicia, an area in Spain where Jews traditionally lived, and the Castro *apellido* is regarded as a Jewish name in Sephardic circles. Armando Castro, who says he is a distant cousin of Fidel's, asserts that "all the Castros in Oriente were

Jews." And in an interview with the exile banker Bernardo Benes in the mid-1980s, Castro confided that the rumors were true. "He said to me, 'As you know, I have Jewish ancestors,' " remembered Benes, who is a Cuban Jew. "I think it was on his father's side. And he said he wanted Cuba to be a second Israel." Castro's rhetoric has been, on occasion, anti-Israel and within his inner circle, according to José Luis Llovio-Menéndez, Castro derided Israel and what he saw as the excessive influence of Jews in America. But his policies have been notably benign toward Jews. In 1993 he returned a synagogue in Santiago de Cuba to its congregation and in 1998 he attended Hannukah services at the Patronato, the historic synagogue of Havana.

Fernández's book makes reference to other illegitimate offspring of Fidel Castro. One, hatched from a three-day liaison on a train trip to Oriente in 1949, is named Jorge Ángel Castro. All of Castro's children, legitimate or not, have been provided with good homes, schools and jobs. But Castro is not known for being much of a father. In a conversation in 1993, Castro declined to say how many children he had, but conceded, half in jest, "almost a tribe." Lázaro Asencio claims Castro told him in 1961 that he had fathered more than fifteen children. Asked in 1993 how many children he has, Castro replied, "Not that much. Less than a dozen." He paused, adding coyly, "I think."

Contrary to Alina Fernández's account, she is not the only daughter of Fidel Castro. There is at least one other. Her name is Francisca Pupo, known to her friends as Panchita, and she was born in 1953. She has lived quietly in Miami with her husband since 1998, when she won a lottery visa to leave Cuba and her father granted her an exit visa.

Lázaro Asencio remembered Francisca's inauspicious beginnings. "After Batista's coup, we all mobilized. I was president of the Las Villas University and Fidel was into the students' struggle. He went to a rally in Cienfuegos in mid-1952 and they arrested him and took him to the jail in Santa Clara. Fidel sent for me and said, 'Look, Lázaro, I want your brother Pepe to defend me.' Fidel was already a lawyer but could not practice because he had not yet been sworn in."

After his dismissal, Castro asked his friend if he could borrow his car, explaining that he wanted to go out with another friend and two pretty local girls. Asencio agreed and turned over the keys. "I had a 1950 bluish-gray aerodynamic Buick that my father had given me. This was about four in the afternoon and I walked home," he said. "I was already married to my wife of fifty-three years then. About 6:00 A.M. the next day, Fidel called me from the Santa Clara train station and said, 'Lázaro, I have to take the train back to Havana. Where should I park the car?' " Asencio instructed his friend to park the car in front of the Hotel Santa Clara with the keys on top of the tire.

After the Revolution, Asencio went back to work in his family's notary office in Santa Clara. One day in 1960, a young woman, with a seven-year-old little girl in tow, asked to speak with him. "I saw the same young lady from that day and she tells me, 'Do you know who this little girl is?' And she said, 'This is my daughter. And she is Fidel Castro's daughter. And our relationship began in your car.' "

The woman asked him for a small favor and then passed on a stunning piece of news. "When you see Fidel, would you tell him that I had a daughter with him?" Asencio assured her that he would and did so at his next meeting with Castro. "I met Fidel in Havana and I said, 'Look, that girl who went out with you years ago came to see me and told me she had a daughter with you. She said that she had been unable to contact you about it so she asked me to do so.' And Fidel said, 'Yes, it's true.' I learned that later he put Raúl in charge of the little girl and he organized birthday parties for her. He also gave her mother a good house in Santa Clara."

Upon her arrival in Miami in 1998, Francisca Pupo contacted Juanita Castro, who assumed the role of the dutiful aunt and helped her out financially. "She's a nice girl and a private person," said Juanita. "Her mother married a man who raised her, but Fidel took care of her support in Cuba. She is not bitter. She does not speak against Fidel and I don't blame her. After all, he is her father."

Max Lesnik believes that parenting is not in Castro's nature. "I think that as a father Fidel may have been like his father was to him, that is, paternally protective, but I don't think there's much closeness." Like his father who also had children with two wives, Castro seems uncomfortable in the construct of a family. "Fidel's a man who imposes distance. He is not a homebody. Just the fact that he never appears with his wife in public tells one that," remarked Lesnik. "One evening when we were dining a few years ago, he told my wife, Miriam, 'Whoever gets married again after a divorce must be crazy.' " Another time, Castro told Miriam Lesnik about a dream he had and said, "I was married to a princess and we were going on this ship." Max Lesnik offered an interpretation of the dream. "I think he was saying that the love of his life has always been Mirta," said Lesnik. "She was the love of his youth."

These days, Mirta visits her son and grandchildren often in Havana. "Mirta gets anything she wants and sometimes she calls Fidel directly," said Lew, a trusted friend of Juanita Castro. "Today, Mirta is the only person who has some influence over Fidel. When they used to send people to the wall for execution, she saved the lives of a few people and some others from going to Angola. When she goes to Cuba, Raúl is waiting for her at the airport." Mirta has also had medical treatment and an operation in CIMEC, the hospital for VIPs. One knowledgeable source claims that Mirta returned to Cuba in early 2002 and is now living with Fidelito and his family.

Contrary to popular opinion, the sentimental Castro is actually Raúl Castro, head of the armed forces and the heir apparent. Although Fidel portrayed himself as the country's patriarch during the Elián saga, he has ceded that role to his brother in his own family. It is Raúl who untangles family snafus, who remembers everyone's birthday and attends the weddings and graduations, according to Juanita and others close to the family. Indeed, Castro did not make it on time to the wedding of his favorite sister, Enma, in 1960. Despite the fact that he was her best man and was charged with giving her away, Castro arrived twenty minutes after a family friend was recruited to fill in for him.

It was Raúl who arranged for Juanita to leave for Mexico in 1964 and Enma's trips back and forth to Havana. And it is Raúl who stays in close contact with Mirta—expediting her various visits to Cuba and seeing to her medical care—and who resolved differences between Fidelito and his father.

Although Raúl has been separated for more than twenty years from his wife, Vilma Espín, who was among the original cadre of revolutionaries, she retains First Lady status. Raúl, who fathered four children with Vilma, is said to be happiest when surrounded by family. "I have seen him with children and he loves them," concedes Natália Bolívar, often a government critic. "He is very good with them and no one can deny this. Remember it was Raúl who is responsible for keeping Fidelito involved with his mother after their divorce. It was Raúl who negotiated the peace between the three of them."

Deborah Andollo, who holds the world's record for women's depth diving, spent much of her childhood around Raúl Castro. Her father, Leonardo Andollo, is one of the country's top generals and one of Raúl Castro's most trusted friends. Andollo's own brother defected to Miami in the early 1990s—a move that caused considerable consternation among the ruling elite and their offspring, known as *"los hijos de Papá,"* something along the lines of a Cuban "brat pack." Since then a rapprochement between her brother and father has been achieved, with her brother visiting the family again in Havana. Andollo says that the forbidding image of Raúl is dead wrong. "He's not like that at all," she said. "He's funny and clowns around.

He loves being a grandfather." However, no one disputes the fact that Raúl Castro runs the army with an iron fist and zero tolerance for disloyalty and dissent.

Outside the family, aggrieved parties often appeal to Raúl's familial side. When the relatives of the imprisoned Patricio de la Guardia, a former colonel in the Interior Ministry, sought "home leave" for him, they appealed to Raúl, not Fidel, and were successful. And when Castro's former chief of staff, José Abrantes, was imprisoned in 1989, Raúl granted him connubial rights. When a child was born to Abrantes's young wife, "Raúl sent a huge cake with yellow and white icing—the same as he sent to all the officers," said a relative. The cheerless irony is that Raúl Castro plays both roles to equal effect: good cop and bad cop. After all, he directed the purge that led to the executions of four of his top officers and was the one who imprisoned Abrantes.

For decades, gossip has swirled around the fact that the two brothers do not physically resemble each other. Raúl is markedly shorter than Fidel and their older brother, Ramón, and his features have an almost *chino-cubano* cast. (There is a large Chinese population in Cuba. Batista, for example, was part Chinese and part black.)

Moreover, detractors of Raúl Castro have long circulated the rumor that he is gay—even dubbing him *La China,* "the Chinese girl," in his early days. But Castro insiders have always scoffed at the charge. In 1991, a decorated Cuban colonel who was among Raúl Castro's closest aides defected and was thoroughly debriefed by the CIA. The colonel dismissed the rumors, adding that his boss was a committed ladies' man—although, unlike his brother, he pursued one dalliance at a time, and generally for a long period. The only vice that got the better of the younger Castro, said the colonel, was booze—a weakness shared by all his brothers. Over the years, Raúl Castro has entered alcohol treatment centers in Cuba on several occasions.

One story has it that Raúl's actual father was a counterrevolutionary or a *batistiano* whom Raúl saved from execution in 1959, at the request of his mother. Another variant comes from an unlikely source, Ricardo Mas Canosa, the brother of Jorge Mas Canosa, Castro's most formidable exile antagonist until his death in 1997. Mas Canosa's father, an army veterinarian, sometimes tended to the animals on the Castro farm. Ricardo said that his father had told the family that Lina Ruz de Castro had become estranged from her hardheaded, hard-drinking husband and was having an affair with a man who ran the general store, who happened to be Chinese. Raúl Castro, he said, was the offspring of that relationship.

But the story has some glaring holes. Raúl is almost a mirror image of Juanita and both resemble their mother, whereas Fidel, Ramón and Enma look like their father. Many Cubans, however, believe that Raúl and Fidel are half-brothers.

Seeking insight into the hermetically protected Castro clan, I drove out to their family home in the heart of what used to be called Oriente, the eastern end of this lush island. In the two-horse town of Birán, about ten miles southwest of Mayarí, Castro's father acquired a vast amount of property that included 26,000 acres of sugar plantations, streams, forests and mountains. Curiously, the road to this vast property is unpaved and unmarked and never appears on tourist maps. And no one can enter without a permission visa from the authorities in Holguín. The grounds, however, are maintained and guarded, and the property is said to be slated soon for historical landmark status.

The original structures remain: assorted barns and stables, the two-story main house (built on wood pilings, over a cattle barn), repair shop, a private schoolhouse for the Castro children, even living quarters for their instructor. The property's sturdy wood structures were designed to be functional, not beautiful. Simplicity, even austerity, is its signature. In the center of the property is a handsome tombstone under the inscrutable gaze of a vivid Virgin Mary. The gravesite holds the bodies of Castro's mother, Lina, his father, Ángel, and his maternal grandparents, Dominga and Francisco Ruz. Fresh flowers adorning the graves are, according to a guard, brought daily by an orphan whom Lina adopted and baptized as a young boy. Juanita Castro said she had no knowledge of such an orphan.

According to the guards and the "historian," who needed a ride home, the most frequent visitor to the home is Ramón Castro, "usually two or three times a year with his wife, and he puts flowers on the grave," the guard said. "And if he doesn't have flowers he goes and he picks wildflowers." Fidel rarely visits, they say, but Raúl comes occasionally, when he visits nearby Santiago de Cuba. The historian pointed out the swimming hole on the property where Fidel, a fearless daredevil, would dive in from the embankment. He said that Fidel's wife Dalia had visited with some of their sons in 1995 and had made quite an impression. "She is very pretty, tall with red hair, how do you say it—*esvelta*—svelte, with a lot of dignity and personality. And most of all, she was very nice."

Juanita Castro said that even her siblings have faced privations in Cuba. "I send my brother Ramón's wife medicine for her blood pressure. They ask me for it and I send anything she needs. And I help Agustina, my youngest sister, because otherwise she'll starve to death. She doesn't have a job, she can't work. So I send her medicines and I send her money, like thousands of Cubans do."

Longevity runs in the Castro family. Ángel Castro, who rarely saw a doctor, was felled by a fluke of a hernia at the age of eighty-two. Diehards who declare that they would rather wait until the seventy-six-year-old Castro leaves the scene before negotiating with his government had best be prepared for quite a long wait. A maternal aunt in her mid-eighties who lives in Camagüey is thriving. Both of Castro's older siblings, Angela, seventy-nine, and Ramón, eighty, are said to be quite fit. Another Castro relation who lives in Los Angeles returned to Santiago de Cuba in 1999 for his mother's 105th birthday. That would indicate roughly thirty years of more of the same.

"Here in Miami, even the cat has gone back to Cuba," quips Juanita. "It is the exiled Cubans who keep up the kingdom with their currency and all their trips back and forth to Cuba. Now we are at the end of our road—Fidel with his power. If I could talk to Fidel again, I would say, 'Leave it alone already. It is enough. Forty-three years.' "

CHAPTER 3

PLANET ELIÁN

Le zumba el mango!
This takes the cake!

CUBAN SAYING (UNTRANSLATABLE)

THE MYTH-MAKING OF ELIÁN GONZÁLEZ began within hours of his rescue. The fact that he was fished out of the sea on Thanksgiving Day of the pre-millennium year of 1999 was taken as an auspicious omen. It was said that "the miracle child" had been saved by dolphins who encircled him and kept away the sharks, although the "fishermen" who found him turned out not to be fishermen and no one saw any dolphins near him. There were the inevitable comparisons to the Virgin of Charity, the patron saint of Cuba, and to the legend of the three desperate sailors in the storm-tossed waters of Oriente who miraculously coasted to safety after an icon of the Virgin washed into their foundering vessel. Some began to speak of Elián as their Moses; others invoked the Jesus child. "The daughter of the pharaoh took in Moses and this changed the history of the Hebrews," wrote *El Nuevo Herald* columnist José Mármol. "Moses lived to lead his people out of slavery in Egypt to the promised land of Israel, an exodus that lasted 40 years—about the same as our exile from Cuba." Surely, Elián, *"el niño milagro,"* was their Moses.

The tug-of-war between Elián's father, Juan Miguel, and his relatives began not long after Elián was admitted to the Joe DiMaggio Children's Hospital in Hollywood, Florida. One version had it that a remarkably cogent Elián gave doctors his father's phone number and address in Cuba and asked that they call him. Elián's grandfather, Juan González, said that he received a phone call from the hospital soon after Elián's admission. "They asked for Juan Miguel and I said he was at work," he recalled. "They told me they had Elián. So I called my sister Georgina and asked her if she could check on him for us." Georgina in turn contacted their brother Lázaro González, Juan Miguel's uncle, who hurried over to the hospital.

In an incomprehensible act of haste, the INS released Elián into the care and temporary custody of Lázaro González on November 26, without first checking with the boy's father. It did so despite the fact that a staffer had been in contact with the family in Cuba. This colossal blunder set in motion the six-month-long *telenovela*—soap opera—that would follow. INS officials, who were understaffed over the holiday weekend, would argue that they acted out of the best of intentions and that it was inconceivable to them that the child's great-uncle would not cooperate in returning him to his father. They would quickly learn otherwise.

The González family's small two-bedroom stucco house at 2319 NW 2nd Street, a $600-a-month rental, sat in the heart of Little Havana. Not far away is Calle Ocho, formerly SW 8th Street, the bustling main artery of Cuban life in Miami, where rapid-fire, high-pitched Caribbean Spanish is the idiom and nary a word of English is mumbled. At the center of Calle Ocho's sprawl of boxy buildings and strip malls is Woodlawn Cemetery, a gated and bucolic final resting place, where four former Cuban presidents have been buried. It is also the eternal abode of Nicaraguan strongman Anastasio Somoza, whose mausoleum faces the massive white marble grave of Jorge Mas Canosa, the *jefe* of the exiles' government-in-waiting until his death in 1997.

Lázaro González shared his modest home with his forty-seven-year-old wife, Angela, a quiet, hardworking woman who toiled at a factory as a seamstress, and their pretty twenty-one-year-old daughter, Marisleysis, who worked as an assistant loan officer in a bank but hoped to become a beautician. A son, William, in his late twenties, lived a stone's throw away in a garage apartment. Like most of their relatives in Cárdenas, Lázaro's family are working-class people whose children ended their education with high school. Marisleysis enrolled in but quickly dropped out of Miami-Dade Community College. "Academics are not her thing," one of her high school teachers told the *Herald*.

Like the majority of Cuban families, the Gonzálezes are a family divided by the Florida Straits and by irreconcilable politics. In April 1966, Lázaro's sister Caridad, a thirty-five-year-old seamstress, left for Miami. One of nine siblings, she was the first González to leave their homeland. "It was very sad, very emotional for me," Caridad told the *Los Angeles Times*. Her husband had left in 1961, and she nursed hopes for a reconciliation. But the marriage foundered and ended in divorce. In time, Caridad began her own business,

Cary Gold Fashions, and established herself as the matriarch of the González Miami clan. Over the next thirty-four years, more than two dozen relatives spanning three generations would follow her to Miami. Although it was Caridad's most fervent wish that the entire family be united in Miami, it was not to be. At least a dozen relatives stayed. Even her parents would be separated by the political divide. Her mother died in Cárdenas in 1980, too ill to make the trip by the time she was granted a visa; her father died years later in Miami, at the age of ninety-two.

Caridad's younger brother Delfín, a dockworker, had been arrested in their hometown as a counterrevolutionary in 1962 and spent ten years in prison. The lost years spent in harsh confinement deeply embittered Delfín and, seven years after his release, in 1979, he left Cuba. Upon his arrival in Miami, he started a successful lobster and lumber business in the Florida Keys.

Jailed along with Delfín was his brother-in-law Joaquín Cid, who served two years. Sponsored by Caridad, Joaquín and his wife, Georgina, left Cuba in 1983, hoping to avoid draft notices that would send their fifteen-year-old twin sons, Luis and José Cid, to Angola. They were also deeply resentful about the prevailing prejudice against practicing Catholics like themselves. Accompanying them was their eight-year-old daughter, Georgina María, who would grow up to be an attractive young woman and would serve as a spokesperson for the family.

Two other brothers, Manuel and Lázaro, made the trip with their families in 1984, by way of Costa Rica. Owing to an INS snafu, Manuel was forced to leave his wife and three children behind in Costa Rica while he established residency in the U.S., a process that took more than two years. The ordeal indelibly marked Manuel and his family. Later, his only son would die of cancer. The two events were the basis of Manuel's unflinching and unpopular vote that Elián be returned to his father. Lázaro, a former gymnast and coach who had briefly worked as a police officer, would have less success than his brothers in the States, achieving only an erratic employment history as an auto mechanic.

Left behind in Cárdenas was their younger brother Juan and his family, along with two sisters, Haydée and Iraida. In the late 1990s, Haydée's children and their families left without visas and made the dangerous crossing in a barely seaworthy boat.

With the exception of Delfín, who settled in the Keys, most of the Gonzálezes live close to one another in or near Little Havana, just as they had in Cárdenas. Although Caridad never stopped trying to get her brother Juan and his family to join them in Miami, Juan never had any serious quarrel with the Cuban government and had no interest in leaving. Nevertheless, the Gonzálezes were a notably close-knit family. Relations were always amicable and affectionate—with the proviso that politics not be discussed. That changed within hours of Elián's rescue. Once the shipwrecked tot from Cárdenas was adopted as the mascot of *la causa,* there was no keeping politics out of family conversation.

ON NOVEMBER 26, the day that Elián was released to his great-uncle's home, he spoke by phone with his father. "Papá, my mamá got lost in the sea," he told Juan Miguel. It was the last time he would speak of the shipwreck or the loss of his mother to his father for five months. Later that night, Juan Miguel received calls from his Aunt Caridad and his Uncles Lázaro and Delfín, pleading with him to leave his son in their care until he could join them in Miami.

On November 27, Juan Miguel González, sensing a change of heart from his relatives, spoke with American authorities in Havana and told them that he expected his son to be returned to him immediately. The following day, he formally petitioned the U.S. government for his son's return to Cuba. That same day, the Cuban American National Foundation (CANF) put out a poster of Elián describing him as a "child victim" of Fidel Castro.

It soon became clear that more than just family members had stepped into the decision-making process on both sides of the Florida Straits. On the day before Elián's release from the hospital, CANF spokeswoman Ninoska Pérez-Castellón, in the first salvo of the Elián War, declared on her radio show, *Ninoska a la Una,* that Elián's tragedy was the personification of Castro's tyranny. Elián was not just a little boy who had survived an unimaginable trauma: he was a symbol on his way to becoming a weapon. On Elián's first day at his relatives' home, the traumatized five-year-old met with Miami congresswoman Ileana Ros-Lehtinen—the first of what would prove to be a veritable soup line of Miami VIPs queuing up for photo ops. Once Elián was ensconced in the González home, his life soon became a 24/7 *Truman Show* spectacle.

From the earliest days of the Elián War, both sides of the González family were surrounded by a platoon of counselors and wise men. And whatever their respective passions, ideals and beliefs, neither side had the wherewithal or resources to resist the pressures upon them. Indeed, it seemed that within twenty-four hours, the Gonzálezes of Little Havana and the Gonzálezes of Cárdenas had signed on as the willing proxies of their handlers to square off against each other. The Cuban side claimed that Lázaro had assured them he would return Elián to his father immediately—quoting him as saying, "even if I have to take him back to Cuba myself." But the goodwill between the branches of the family quickly evaporated as the battle lines were carved in stone. Elián's great-aunt, Georgina Cid, would produce her phone bill showing a collect call from her brother Juan on Sunday, November 22, at 9:01 P.M. She claimed that her brother had called to warn her that Elián was en route to live there with his mother. Juan vehemently denied such a conversation, saying that he was only imploring his sister to be on the lookout for Elián and his mother, after he learned that the two had vanished from Cárdenas.

ARMANDO GUTIÉRREZ, ARGUABLY Miami's most influential political consultant and rainmaker, said he saw Elián on the news on the morning he was rescued. "I said to my wife, 'I'm going over there and I'm going to try to help them,'" he explained to me in a series of interviews conducted over his cell phone as he zipped about Miami. He said he had showed up the same day Elián was brought back to Lázaro's house and returned later in the day with Miami Beach city commissioner Bruno Barreiro and State Representative Carlos Valdéz. The three chatted with Ros-Lehtinen, who was already discussing Elián's future with the Gonzálezes. "I told the family that they're going to need a lawyer, a good lawyer," said Gutiérrez, who became the principal adviser, spokesman and traffic cop for the family for the next six months. The next day, he brought by Spencer Eig, a former INS lawyer, the first of what would build to a small legal army that would diligently work on the case.

To achieve their goal of keeping Elián, the family upended their own lives and became full-time caretakers of their new charge. They, in turn, were adopted by the most powerful and influential cadre in Miami politics, the exile leadership. Although Cuban exiles are not a monolith and have all manner of politics and allegiances, since 1959, anti-Castro hard-liners have dominated exile life in business, media and politics. By the mid-1980s, exile hard-liners dominated Miami, occupying the seat of power in both the political and cultural life of the county.

Ileana Ros-Lehtinen, who left Cuba as a child, was elected to represent Miami-Dade's central Eighteenth District in 1989, the first Hispanic woman to win a seat in Congress. Her campaign manager was none other than Jeb

Bush, who saw to it that her Cuba-related concerns got the ear of his father, President George H. W. Bush. Her mentor was and is her own father, Enrique Ros, a businessman, author and dedicated anti-Castro activist who advocates a harsh, restrictive policy on Cuba. Her ties to her parents (who live across the street from her) and *la causa* of Cuba are the backbone of her life and political career. Ros-Lehtinen, an attractive, friendly woman with a blowsy bob of blond hair, is the mother of two teenage daughters. She is known for her hands-on constituent services. She succeeded the legendary Miami congressman Claude Pepper, winning a special election held after his death, and represents a district that is now more than 70 percent Hispanic. Her seat on the House Foreign Affairs Committee has enabled her to advance her strongly felt hard-line views on Cuba and to block attempts to weaken the Embargo. The congresswoman and her husband, Dexter Lehtinen, a hard-driving man who had served as U.S. Attorney, were close friends and allies of Jorge Mas Canosa, who served almost as a godfather to her candidacy.

Miami elected a second Cuban in 1989, Lincoln Díaz-Balart, to represent the western sector of the county. Like his colleague, Díaz-Balart is an ardent Republican with a fulsome desire to see the end of Fidel Castro, fueled in part by a family vendetta. He too is the son of a powerful father, Rafael Díaz-Balart, former Deputy Minister of the Interior under Batista, the grandson of Batista's Minister of Transportation and the brother of Fidel Castro's first wife. Lincoln was four years old and visiting Paris with his father and family when Batista fled Havana on New Year's Day, in the first hours of 1959. "I lost all respect for Batista when he left Cuba," his father, Rafael, told me over dinner at a Coral Gables restaurant in the summer of 2001. He waved his right hand disparagingly by the side of his head, Cuban style. "The captain should go down with his ship."

Like his former brother-in-law, Rafael is a canny politician and cagey strategist who has never lost his taste for politics. He has remained a behind-the-scenes player in the rough-and-rude body politic of Miami and is very much the power behind his son's throne. There is no decision or appointment made by Lincoln relating to Cuba that Rafael does not sign off on.

Lincoln Díaz-Balart was educated in Madrid before attending college in Sarasota, Florida, and getting his law degree from Case Western Reserve University. From 1979 through 1989, prior to his congressional bid, he served as a state representative and state senator. Both Díaz-Balart and Ros-Lehtinen are known for bringing home the bacon to Miami by fashioning legislation to generously aid their exile constituents. They also serve as the standard-bearers of the U.S. Embargo against Cuba, ever vigilant and quickly reactive in slashing back any initiative or opponent who wants it gone. It has been Lincoln's ironic fate, and burden, to share his birthday with his despised Uncle Fidel—August 13.

ON DECEMBER 6, TEN DAYS after his arrival in Little Havana, Elián celebrated his sixth birthday with a party held at his relatives' home on NW 2nd Street. Gifts, toys and goodies poured in and Marisleysis trotted Elián out on the front lawn for an extended photo op. Congressman Díaz-Balart, trailed by cameras, arrived at the small house with a black Labrador in his arms for the six-year-old. It would be the first of many visits. The puppy was named Dolphin, a tribute to the proliferating legend that dolphins had encircled and saved Elián from sharks while he drifted in the ocean. Four days later, the Miami legal team filed papers on behalf of Lázaro González seeking political asylum for Elián, over the howls of protest from the child's father in Cuba.

The Miami relatives soon made the claim that they were speaking on behalf of Elián's mother—despite the fact that none had an acquaintance with her. "Elián's mother died for his freedom," became the mantra of the family and the exile leadership. Only one day after Elián's release from the hospital, Marisleysis, Elián's second cousin, who had appointed herself his "surrogate mother," threw down the gauntlet. Addressing reporters outside the Little Havana home, she said she was distressed to learn that Elián's father wanted his son back. "His mother lost her life for him to be here. He needs his freedom and we're his family," she said, speaking about a woman whom she had never met and a child whom she had known for twenty-four hours. "He should be with us."

In May 1998, Lázaro and Delfín González had visited their brother Juan in Cárdenas. Delfín bought Juan's grandson Elián a goat to have as a pet and Juan Miguel gave up his bed and slept in his car so that his uncles could have his bedroom during their visit. Now Juan Miguel would even question his Uncle Lázaro's acquaintance with Elián. "He would spend his nights drinking in the hotel bars in Varadero, then sleep all day," he said. The uncles never got around to meeting Elián's mother, according to the family in Cárdenas. Indeed, Elián's mother and her boyfriend had no intention of contacting the Miami Gonzálezes, whom they did not know. They were, after all, her ex-husband's distant relatives. Their plan had always been to stay with an aunt of Rafa's who lived in Kendall, a suburb in Miami-Dade County.

Ros-Lehtinen and Díaz-Balart were soon joined by Miami-Dade's mayor,

Alex Penelas, and Joe Carollo, the bulldog mayor of the city of Miami. This political quartet, along with the powerful Spanish language radio hosts, were the armchair generals of Miami, commanding the front lines in the war against Fidel Castro. All have impeccable anti-Castro credentials. Penelas's father, an imprisoned labor organizer in Cuba, escaped with his family to Florida, where his son was born. Penelas, who was elected to the Hialeah City Council at twenty-five, was one of the rare Democrats in the exile pantheon.

Carollo had arrived as a six-year-old child, one of nearly fourteen thousand "Pedro Pan" children sent by their parents to America through the Catholic Church in the early 1960s to save them from being raised in a communist country. He was eventually reunited with his parents in Chicago, where he was raised in an Irish neighborhood. In 1970, the family moved to Miami, by which time Carollo's Spanish had become audibly rusty. A former police officer, Carollo was elected a Miami city commissioner at twenty-four. He briefly flirted with being a Democrat before returning to the Republican fold. His tempestuous outbursts—he once claimed that his adversaries were part of a communist conspiracy against him—won him the designation "Crazy Joe." Unlike Penelas, whose politics were shaped in backroom deals, Carollo was a populist who governed with his gut. In the early 1980s, he had even taken on the formidable Jorge Mas Canosa. Although tactless, and often bombastic, Carollo came across as the genuine article.

THE CORE BELIEF OF *la comunidad* was that to return a child to Cuba was immoral and a heresy. Once in Cuba, Elián would become a prop and puppet of Fidel Castro, they maintained. Driving the emotional riptide was their belief that Elián's return would mean that Fidel Castro had won. This was unbearable, and they swore it must never come to pass.

Over the ensuing days and weeks, the exile leadership huddled with the family, rolling up their sleeves and plotting political and legal strategies to keep Elián from being returned home. The family's team of advisers and lawyers settled on a three-track strategy. First was their battle in the courts—to convert Lázaro González's temporary custody into permanent custody. The lawyers knew from the start that they were on legal thin ice: Elián had a devoted father, and Lázaro, as a great-uncle, was generally not recognized as close enough kin to challenge guardianship in either state or federal court. Nevertheless, they decided to pursue every legal option and maneuver—if only to slow the clock and buy time. Spencer Eig brought on two more immigration attorneys, Roger Bernstein and Linda Osberg Braun, who were soon joined by José García Pedrosa, a veteran Miami lawyer and politician. In January, the team recruited another two INS and family law specialists, attorneys Laura Fabar and Barbara Lagoa. All the family's lawyers agreed to work the case pro bono. A two-day fund-raiser over Spanish language radio, orchestrated by Armando Gutiérrez, brought in over $200,000 to cover legal costs and fees to third parties.

The family's second front was the political arena—working closely with their traditional allies in Congress to devise legislation that could supersede the courts. Over the next five months, their political stalwarts would propose three bills regarding Elián: for permanent residency, political asylum and citizenship. They would also invoke their committee privilege to subpoena Elián to seek to keep the child from leaving the country. The third offensive was public relations, selling America with two talking points: first, that they needed to save Elián González from the clutches of Fidel Castro, who they insisted was the one calling the shots—not his father—and second, that simply living in Cuba was a form of child abuse.

At the heart of the Elián command center was the Cuban American National Foundation, the powerful exile lobbying group, and its new chairman, Jorge Mas Santos. Having assumed the position of his late father, the legendary and controversial Jorge Mas Canosa, Mas Santos was eager for a crusade that would enhance his own profile and advance the cause of exiles. Certain that Elián's sad story and pixie face would engender a groundswell of sympathy, Mas Santos bet the bank on the shipwrecked tot from Cárdenas. CANF picked up the tab for much of the family's expenses and found what other employees termed a virtual no-show job for Lázaro at a Metro Ford dealership owned by a CANF director, Lombardo Pérez, the same dealership that provided jobs for the boat survivors Arianne Horta and Nivaldo Fernández. Mas Santos, who became a fixture in the Gonzálezes' Little Havana home, also came up with the brainstorm of injecting Elián as an issue into the upcoming World Trade Organization conference in Seattle, which, rumor had it (incorrectly), Fidel Castro would attend. It would be the first of many missteps. Dozens of protesters wearing "Save Elián" T-shirts were upstaged by the thousands of anti-globalization demonstrators who laid siege to the conference in the last days of November.

This gesture was not lost on Fidel Castro, who, up until that point, had largely ignored the flap over Elián. Now Castro felt challenged, quickly sized up the odds and stepped into the fray. A chess player extraordinaire, Castro realized that win or lose the boy, he would emerge as a winner. If he got Elián back to Cuba with his father, he would have an international victory to lord over his enemies. If he failed to bring him home, world opinion would lash against Miami exiles and award him with a blistering propaganda triumph.

On December 5, Castro took center stage and issued a seventy-two-hour ultimatum for the return of the "kidnapped" Elián to his father. The U.S. had until December 9 to resolve the situation, said Castro, or else Cuba would boycott immigration talks with the U.S. scheduled for a week later. The threat of disrupting the negotiations, and potentially setting off another refugee exodus, galvanized the attention of Washington. Suddenly an INS misstep over a five-year-old boy had taken on the furor and vengeance of the Hundred Years' War.

IT'S UNLIKELY THAT Fidel Castro or any of the counterintelligence sleuths at Cuba's Ministry of the Interior could have conjured up a more successful or satisfying scenario for themselves—one that would garner international support and the sympathy of 70 percent of Americans and divert all attention from Cuba's crushing domestic woes. Its human rights abuses, economic insolvency and ever growing ranks of dissidents quickly faded from view. While the Miami family's campaign generated the support of an estimated 75 percent of Cuban exiles in Miami, it bombed in the heartland. In fact, it was even bombing in South Florida among all other ethnic groups.

And a grand opera it would turn out to be: a Miami family decides to keep the child of a loving father only to have it alleged that they and some of their advisers had a shabby history of moral and ethical problems, drunk driving arrests and multiple felony arrests for violent crimes. The *New York Times* ran a page-one story chronicling Lázaro's and Delfín's long-standing battles with alcoholism. Both men had multiple arrests for drunk driving and were each twice convicted of driving under the influence. Both had had their driving licenses suspended at different times.

Not long after the *Times* exposé, it came to light that Luis and José Cid, Georgina's sons, who were frequent visitors to the house, had extensive criminal records. José Cid had been arrested more than five times since 1986 on felony charges including robbery with force, grand theft and petty larceny and had been sentenced to two years' probation for burglary. His twin, Luis, had last been arrested in September 1999 for assault and robbery of a tourist in Little Havana. In 1994, Luis Cid was sentenced to six months' probation for carrying a concealed weapon and his ex-wife sought a restraining order against him, charging domestic violence. In 1998 he was again arrested for felony firearms possession and for prowling. The presence of the Cid brothers around Elián was more than just an embarrassment for the family, as Florida law prohibits felons from consorting with foster care minors. Asked about his troubled nephews, Delfín suggested that reporters focus on the other cousins: "Lázaro's kids have turned out good," he shrugged.

Soon after Elián's Miami residence began, questions were raised about the power brokers who championed the family. Armando Gutiérrez, the family's spokesman, who masterminded the All Elián, All the Time Show, is one of the most wily politicos in South Florida. An impressive kingmaker who is lauded by his clients and feared by adversaries, Gutiérrez is renowned for his ability to get out the Cuban vote. He has handled the campaigns of scores of politicians and judges in Miami and was described by the *Herald* as having "a reputation for hardball tactics." A former colleague described him as one who "goes after your throat. He believes he must destroy you." Gutiérrez insisted that he was acting out of compassion for the boy, saying, "I saw his little sad eyes and had to help him."

Jorge Mas Santos's business integrity and ethics were also questioned. After the Miami *Daily Business Review* raised serious questions about the contracts of his company, Church & Tower, with the county, the company became the focus of a criminal investigation. In a hugely damaging scandal, Church & Tower was found to have billed the county $58 million for asphalt and road striping that was never done or improperly done. The county froze payments to the company and barred it from further contracts with Miami-Dade.

Even the choice of Elián's education ignited controversy. The family accepted a full scholarship from Demetrio Pérez, a school board member, to attend his privately run Lincoln-Martí School in Little Havana. Pérez wrote the school's primary textbook, which teaches, according to the *Herald*, that "Richard Nixon got a raw deal when he was forced to resign as President" and that "Americans now regret this and honor him." Elián's curriculum included instruction explaining that "he lives in a Christian society and should support school prayer in public and private schools. He should oppose abortion, homosexuality and racism . . . and we in no way support Cuba or people in Cuba who believe in that system." (In 2001, Pérez would be found guilty of bilking a tenant in a state-subsidized apartment and forced to resign his position on Miami's school board. In 2002, it was learned that Pérez was under investigation yet again for having "pocketed more than $1 million in rent payments from public funds," according to the *Herald*, "money meant to benefit a program for at-risk children.")

Another early star in the Miami drama was family court judge Rosa Rodríguez, who had thirteen months' experience on the bench when she decided that she, and not the U.S. Immigration and Naturalization Service or federal court, had jurisdiction over the case. In her ruling of January 10, 2000, Rodríguez swiftly awarded custody of Elián to Lázaro González—writing that the boy faced "imminent and irreparable harm ... to his physical and mental health and emotional well-being" if reunited with his father. No evidence was offered in support of her ruling. She also ordered Elián to stay with his relatives and forbade his leaving Miami-Dade County. As her decision was read aloud in the courtroom, Jorge Mas Santos and Lázaro González leapt to their feet and hugged each other.

The following day it was learned that Rodríguez had failed to disclose that she had paid more than $63,000 in fees to the family of Armando Gutiérrez, her political consultant and, not incidentally, the public relations wizard representing the Miami relatives. Additionally, the young judge had been under investigation since her 1998 election for campaign finance violations, for exceeding the $500 cap on contributions with a whopping $200,000 undisclosed loan to herself that the Judicial Qualifications Commission found raised a "serious question of personal and professional integrity." (In 2001, the Florida Supreme Court would reject a proposed settlement concerning Rodríguez, arguing that it did not sufficiently punish her for such wrongdoing, which could have prompted her removal from the bench.)

BY JANUARY, AS THE two sides hardened their positions, the principals decided to have a makeover. Marisleysis, who had been a dyed blonde partial to the Madonna look of halter tops and miniskirts, now sported a demure brunette do and conservative clothes. Her father and uncle, both chain-smokers who favored sleeveless muscle shirts, jeans and gold chains, were now wearing short-sleeved shirts and less jewelry and not smoking on camera. Marisleysis would give occasional press interviews outside their house, in which she would invariably weep as she spoke of Elián's desire to live in America. But in Camp Elián, as the massive press corps parked outside their home was known, Marisleysis was dubbed "the actress," for her dramatic transitions from laughter to tears when the cameras rolled.

Often her role as "surrogate mother" was interrupted by mysterious trips to the hospital. The *Miami Herald*'s Meg Laughlin reported that she had visited the hospital on at least twelve occasions for "panic attacks" and "vomiting" over a ten-month period. Rumors and speculation ran rampant: Marisleysis was suffering from colitis, a breakdown, a romantic breakup with a powerful Cuban exile, bulimia, even a pregnancy. The family steadfastly refused to comment, offering only vague explanations such as "emotional anxiety." Their refusal to account for Marisleysis's maladies prompted snide twitters from critics, but it played well on Calle Ocho, where she was beatified as a long-suffering Camille.

Donato Dalrymple, the housecleaner who had been out boating for the first time with his cousin when they came upon Elián in the sea, crafted a new identity. No longer an unemployed housecleaner, he became El Pescador, the Fisherman, with the attendant biblical halo. Dalrymple's cousin, Sam Ciancio, who had spotted Elián and had dived into the ocean to rescue the boy, dismissed his relative as "an opportunist who's never fished in his life." Not content with fifteen minutes of fame, Dalrymple became Velcro to the camera lens. In ceaseless television interviews, he suggested that he had been divinely summoned to rescue Elián. Proceeding from being Elián's messiah, he sought the role of Elián's mascot, attaching himself to the six-year-old whenever possible. Notwithstanding the fact that he spoke and understood no Spanish and Elián spoke no English, Dalrymple said that he understood what Elián wanted in his heart—to live and grow up in Miami.

After the Rosa Rodríguez debacle, Armando Gutiérrez approached Kendall Coffey, a highly regarded prosecutor, to spearhead the legal effort to secure custody of Elián by his great-uncle Lázaro. Coffey had served as Clinton's U.S. Attorney in Miami from 1993 until 1996, when he had resigned following a scandal generated by a *Miami Herald* exposé. Following a courtroom loss in February 1996, Coffey had gone to a Miami strip bar called Lipstik to console himself, where, evidently under the influence of excessive alcohol, he had bitten a stripper on her arm. The dancer, a woman with a forgiving nature, never pressed charges, but Coffey acceded to the public clamor for his resignation.

"Armando Gutiérrez contacted me in mid-February as it became clear that the case was heading into federal court," said Coffey. "Armando was the CEO of the whole Elián case because he was the liaison with the family. I was asked to come in to take the lead in the federal litigation—and I argued the right of Lázaro to represent Elián as his 'next friend,' " the court's term for guardian. Coffey was later joined by his law partner Manny Díaz, a corporate attorney who generally negotiated rather than litigated cases. As a fellow exile, however, he developed closer ties with the family than the other lawyers. Díaz would take on a prominent role as a negotiator with the INS in the final weeks of the crisis.

On January 5, some forty days after Elián was found bobbing in the sea, the INS ruled that the child should be reunited with his father and returned to Cuba. The family and its advisers reacted with fury. Two days later, exiles staged street demonstrations in Miami, blocking off roads. Less than a week later, on January 11, a firestorm erupted in Miami over four seconds of videotape in which Elián González made a casual comment as an airplane flew over the Little Havana house. Channel 10—station WPLG—had broadcast the brief videotape, in which Elián was reported as saying, *"Yo quiero que tú me regreses pa' Cuba"* (I want you to take me back to Cuba). An acrimonious dispute ensued as partisans of the family insisted that Elián would never say such a thing. Linguists and translators were retained to resolve the issue. Some backed the station's version and some said that Elián had said just the opposite: "I don't want you to take me back to Cuba." But most agreed that it was impossible to hear precisely what he said because of the noise of the passing plane.

The station was soon surrounded by outraged pickets and demonstrators who found the broadcast offensive and heretical. One protester nailed a wooden sign to a telephone pole next to the Little Havana house, reading, "We don't want Channel 10 here." With Miami radio calling for a boycott, the station's general manager, John Garwood, read an unusual on-air statement: "We carefully consulted trusted associates as to the accuracy of what was said before airing that story last night," Garwood said. "Even now, due to the quality of the audio, there remains confusion, controversy and differences of opinion on precisely what was said or what Elián really meant." But such uncertainty was unacceptable to the family. "What he said on the tape is, 'I don't want to be sent back to Cuba,'" insisted Lázaro González. Two days later, the child was asked to clarify his comments in a car with his greatuncle, Gutiérrez and AP photographer Alan Díaz. Lázaro González said that he asked the boy, "So what is it that you said last night?" And Elián replied: "That I don't want to go to Cuba," Gutiérrez assured reporters. Lázaro's message to Channel 10 was loud and clear: it did not matter whether or not their report was accurate, it was unconscionable and disloyal of them to broadcast it.

In the decathlon of grandstanding, exiles had plenty of Anglo company. There was the relatives' most vocal advocate, Representative Dan Burton of Indiana, whose eponymous legislation, the Helms-Burton bill, had significantly tightened and codified the U.S. Embargo against Cuba. It was suggested that Burton's zeal to please the Miami family was fueled by an eye-popping treasure chest from the exile lobby, whose contributions exceeded those of his Indiana constituents by 600 percent. The wiry, combative Hoosier congressman, who fancied himself an expert on Cuba, threw himself into the Elián drama with great fanfare and expectations. After discussions with the family and their advisers, Burton issued a subpoena to Elián to testify before Congress—at a hearing that never came to pass seeking to prevent him from leaving the country. As it turned out, Burton was uniquely qualified in paternity and custody matters. Although a staunch and relentless advocate of so-called family values, he had fathered a child sixteen years earlier with a woman other than his wife. He had no relationship with his illegitimate son and had declined to put his name on his son's birth certificate.

Burton was joined by a Republican colleague in the Senate, Robert Smith of New Hampshire. At a press conference early in the drama, Smith said that he had asked Elián if he wanted to return to Cuba and that the boy had assured him that he did not. There was one problem: Smith neither spoke nor understood Spanish. On January 14, Florida's Republican senator, Connie Mack, backed by Burton and Smith, announced that he would seek U.S. citizenship for Elián—on the presumption that a six-year-old was mature enough to grasp the concept of citizenship. That same week, Lázaro's lawyers filed a federal lawsuit to block Elián's return to Cuba and sought a political asylum hearing.

MANUEL GONZÁLEZ, ELIÁN'S GREAT-UNCLE, had been on a family trip to Spain when his brothers laid claim to the young rafter. Upon returning, he declared that the boy should be reunited with his father. Manuel, who lived about eight blocks from Lázaro, had the closest relationship on the Miami side with Elián, having visited his family in Cárdenas annually since Elián's birth. Manuel was ostracized by his Little Havana relatives for his position, pilloried as a pariah and trashed on Miami radio. His attempts to mediate a solution between the two sides of the family were rebuffed. Following one family meeting in which his brothers refused to speak with him, he was rushed to the emergency room with chest pains. No one in the family escorted him to the hospital.

On March 2, 2000, a hearing on Elián González was conducted before the Senate Judiciary Committee, called by Senator Connie Mack and held over the objections of ranking Democrat Patrick Leahy, who protested what

he called its "partisan" nature. Marisleysis, Alina Fernández (Castro's illegitimate daughter, who had defected in 1993) and others exhorted members to
keep Elián in America, charging that all Cuban children were the property of
Fidel Castro. Marisleysis told the senators that although the boy's father had
repeatedly said otherwise, she believed that he, in fact, wanted Elián to stay
in Miami but was under the gun of the Cuban government. Marisleysis also
said that it would be traumatic for Elián to be separated from her. "He asked
me to promise him I would never leave his side and would always protect
him," she said.

Manuel González disagreed and spoke passionately on behalf of Juan
Miguel. "Every child needs his father, regardless of where he is, in order that
the child might follow the right path," he said. "When I was in Cuba, I had
rights as a father, and I knew how to fight for my children." Manuel said he
found the boy not to be himself and expressed concern about his well-being,
adding, "He doesn't know where he is." Later Manuel would file a petition
to be temporary guardian of Elián at Juan Miguel's request. As he entered
and exited the courthouse, he was jeered as a "traitor" and a "sellout" by
protesters—the same exiles who were demanding that Elián stay in the U.S.
because there was no freedom of speech in Cuba.

IT WAS PERHAPS INEVITABLE that one of the television divas, in their quest
to "get the get" and lay hands on the precious tot, would become part of the
opéra bouffe. After all, Elián had supplanted the murdered five-year-old Jon-
Benét Ramsey as the celebrity fix for sensation-addicted Americans. Diane
Sawyer swooped in to grab the honor—running footage for two nights of her
frolicking on the floor with young Elián, under the watchful gaze of Marisleysis. To the dismay of legal ethicists, Sawyer did not seek the permission of
the child's father before putting his son on television.

After hours of taped inanities, Sawyer elicited from Elián his belief that
his mother was still alive and his statement that he did not want to return
home to his father in Cuba. The six-year-old described how the boat that was
bringing him and his mother from Cuba had sunk and said that he didn't believe that his mother was dead. "My mother is not in heaven, not lost," he
said in Spanish translated by Marisleysis. "She must have been picked up
here in Miami somewhere. She must have lost her memory, and just doesn't
know I'm here." The camera hovered over the boy as he drew crayon pictures
of the voyage in which his mother and ten other people drowned.

While Sawyer spoke of Marisleysis with a hushed reverence, the TV star seemed to impugn the motives of Juan Miguel for wanting his son back. In her three-part interview, she never broached the possibility that the six-year-old might be echoing the sentiments of his caretakers or the hundreds of anti-Castro protesters chanting outside his home for months. Nor did she ask Elián whether he wanted to return to Cuba. As it turned out, Sawyer had been exploring several alternative leads. Two days prior to filming her interview with Marisleysis, Sawyer had been in Havana, where she was the guest of honor at a dinner hosted by Ricardo Alarcón, the president of Cuba's National Assembly and his country's lead negotiator on Elián. But as Alarcón had not delivered on either an interview with Juan Miguel González or Fidel Castro, Sawyer beelined for Miami.

She was hardly alone in profiting from the young boy. The neighbors of Lázaro González also made out quite well. According to newspaper reports, some homeowners on Lázaro's street were charging $500 to $1,500 a day to media outlets to park on their lawns on NW 2nd Street—the precious real estate that made up Camp Elián.

IN THE END, the coup de grâce for self-aggrandizement went to Sister Jeanne O'Laughlin, who volunteered a neutral site to facilitate a meeting between Elián and his visiting grandmothers, Mariela Quintana de González and Raquel Rodríguez. On January 21, 2000, the grandmothers had arrived in New York City, escorted by the Reverend Joan Brown Campbell, the former head of the National Council of Churches, who sponsored their trip. Campbell, who had plenty of good capital with Fidel Castro from her years of running church-sponsored programs in Cuba, went to Havana in early January 2000 to see if she could break the logjam. She said she got the call from her church counterpart in Havana about four days after Elián's arrival in Miami, asking for help on behalf of Elián's father. "Sandy Berger's office put me in touch with María Echavistes, Clinton's deputy chief of staff, who was their point person on Elián." Echavistes had evidently not been reading the tea leaves in Miami. Two weeks after the child's rescue she told Campbell, "This will not last very long because we're just going to turn around and send that boy back."

Once in Havana, Campbell said she found Juan Miguel González "too fragile" and stressed to come to the States. Juan Miguel had made one appearance on American television, and it was not a success. In December, the young father appeared on *Nightline*, where he was questioned by newsman Chris Bury. He seemed like a man in a smoldering rage, which did not advance his cause. When asked what he would like to do to his relatives holding his son, he answered that it made him want "to take a rifle and strafe the SOBs who had kidnapped" his son.

"I thought the grandmothers might be more appealing," said Campbell, a formidable politician in her own right. "There was a full complement of grandparents with a wonderful great-grandmother who said to me, 'I don't know about the rest of them but I pray. Would you pray for us?' And she wanted me to know that Elián is a baptized Catholic, which surprised me because not every child in Cuba is baptized." Campbell responded by removing her Jerusalem cross from her neck and giving it to the great-grandmother. "She draped it over Fidel's photograph," Campbell said dryly. "What really got to me was when Raquel said to me, 'Elizabet was my only child and Elián will be the only grandchild I will ever have. And I want Juan Miguel to raise him.' "

Campbell said she was deeply moved by Raquel's grief and came up with the idea of bringing Elián's grandmothers to America, then sold it to Fidel Castro. Her sales pitch that two distraught and grieving grandmothers, one of whom had lost her one and only child in the shipwreck, would be irresistible to the American public scored well with the Maximum Leader.

Campbell had traveled to Havana with her successor at the council, Robert Edgar, who was anxious, she said, not to appear pro-Castro. Consequently, when they were invited to dine with El Comandante, Edgar declined, tartly telling one of Castro's aides, " 'I came to pick up the grandmothers, not to have dinner with the President.' And it had the effect I knew it would have," said Campbell. "Castro got very mad. That was the first time I had seen him angry and it's not a pretty picture. Castro said, 'They are not a bag of groceries. You don't come down here to pick them up and take them back.' They were worried all along that they were going to get sucked into the Miami scene." Late that night Campbell got a call that Castro wanted to see her right away. "I went there at 1:30 in the morning to the palace . . . and I stayed until five in the morning. I knew very well if I didn't go, the grandmothers would never come to the States."

Campbell struck a deal with Castro: "I told him they could stay at my place in New York and we would do everything we could to keep them safe." The two would be free to come and go from the spacious Riverside Drive apartment, but there was a doorman to keep out uninvited visitors."

Upon their arrival at JFK Airport on January 21, 2000, the grandmothers gave a short press conference. Raquel said little but Mariela was fired up, which surprised everyone, not least the Immigration and Naturalization Service officials who had met her in Havana. At Juan Miguel's second INS interview, he was accompanied by his parents. "Mariela was crying and was very upset and I told my superiors in Washington that this is a very distressed grandmother," recalled an American diplomat who was present for the interview. "And then she showed up in New York and gives this press conference, denouncing the Miami Mafia. They called me and said, 'Hey, what happened to the timid grandmother?' " The metamorphosis of Mariela to a fiery activist had happened under their noses and did not play especially well with the general public in the States.

"Castro was very worried about Miami, and just didn't feel there was any way for them to go there," Campbell said. "He wanted them to see Janet Reno"—which they did on January 22. The grandmothers had a very good meeting with Reno and INS commissioner Doris Meissner together. "Janet Reno cried," said Campbell. "She was very moved by what they had to say."

Attorney General Janet Reno, who was ultimately responsible for the disposition of Elián González, felt that someone needed to make the case to the country, and who better than two doting grandmothers? With the shadow of the deadly Waco assault of 1993 forever haunting her tenure, she would make each Elián decision with excruciating caution and circumspection. And as a native Floridian and former State Attorney for Miami-Dade, Reno understood the depths of the troubled waters into which she was about to wade. She told the grandmothers that she would arrange for them to see their grandson, but with one caveat: they would have to go to Miami. Lázaro González had refused to allow them to visit with Elián outside Miami.

It was not what they wanted to hear. "The key thing was that they did not want to encounter Lázaro and his family," Campbell explained. Reno told them that they would be well advised to go. With considerable misgivings, the two women flew to Miami on January 24. Upon arrival, they learned that the González clan had raised the bar yet another notch. Now they were told that the visit would have to take place in the home of Lázaro, whom the grandmothers by now detested.

Sensing that they were losing the propaganda war, the Miami family announced that they would welcome the grandmothers with a grand roast pig dinner. The welcoming committee would be the hundreds of protesters surrounding the house chanting anti-Castro slogans. As negotiations continued, the two women idled in the airport—hoping and waiting for their promised visit with their grandson. It never happened: they returned to New York that evening in tears.

The next day, Reno spoke with Campbell and told her the bad news: the grandmothers would have to go back to Miami. "We cannot move this boy out of Miami," Reno told Campbell, "but we will try to find a neutral site." Reno said she had an old friend who could offer a neutral site and be trusted to defuse the escalating standoff. That person was Sister Jeanne O'Laughlin, president of Barry University, a large Catholic campus in North Miami. The two women had become friends during Reno's long tenure as State Attorney from 1978 until early 1993, often socializing together. On January 25, the Attorney General ordered that Elián be made available for a visit, and the following day the grandmothers were flown by Learjet to Florida and then helicoptered to Sister Jeanne's Miami Beach estate.

The choice of Sister Jeanne, a seventy-year-old nun, would prove disastrous and embarrassing to Reno. Sister Jeanne, who is partial to stylish clothes and sports a crown of well-coifed curls, has long been a colorful player in the Miami political firmament. A celebrated fund-raiser who evidently did not take the vow of poverty, she lives in a thirteen-bedroom, seven-bathroom gated mansion on Pine Tree Drive, the toniest neighborhood of Miami Beach. The home, one of the loveliest in the area, was donated to Barry University by a wealthy Catholic patron, but according to its caretaker, Sister Jeanne lives there alone.

Wearing a conspicuously large gold cross outside a plaid shirt, Elián arrived in the car of CANF's Jorge Mas Santos, who was described as "the official driver of the González family," and was greeted by several dozen anti-Castro pickets outside the long circular drive leading to the house. One sign read "3 Kings, 3 Children—Moses, Jesus & Elián," reflecting the quasi-religious frenzy in Miami that surrounded him. Also in Elián's entourage were spokesman Armando Gutiérrez, Marisleysis, Lázaro and Raquel Rodríguez's half-sister, Doris. Several pickets chanted *"Traidores!"* (Traitors!) and *"Quédate!"* (Stay here!) as the grandmothers entered the house.

Strict conditions were imposed at the insistence of Elián's relatives, who remained in the house throughout the visit. The boy was not allowed to be alone with his grandmothers at any time. Sister Jeanne or other nuns remained in the room—keeping a watchful eye on the proceedings. At one point a phone call was placed between Elián and his father on his grandmother Mariela's cell phone. Juan Miguel had been complaining for some time that he had been unable to speak with his son. Either his calls went unanswered, he charged, or when he did get Elián on the line, other relatives would listen in or interrupt their conversations. It would be his first private conversation with his son in over two months. But moments after Mariela passed her cell phone to Elián, one of the nuns rushed over and admonished her that phone conversations were not allowed. In fact, no such restrictions had been agreed to.

The grandmothers said they left feeling more heartbroken than they had before the visit. "It was supposed to be a neutral place where no one would interrupt us and where we would be all alone with just him, but it was not like that," Raquel Rodríguez told me upon her return to Cuba. "The room we were in did not even have doors, it was an area of open entry. To one side was Marisleysis, which is why the boy could not develop communication with us. The boy knew that Marisleysis was on the other side and we were aware that Marisleysis *le leyó la cartilla*—read him the riot act—before his visit with us."

The grandmothers were so troubled by their grandson's listlessness that they began to charge that the boy was "drugged" or placed under some medications before they arrived. "This was not the same boy," Rodríguez said repeatedly. "This is not the Elián we know. Afterward we showed him the small books, the photo album, the notes his schoolmates had sent him," she continued. "I read him the messages that each child sent and then I showed him the book of Elpidio Valdés [a beloved Cuban cartoon character] and asked him: Would you like me to read it to you? And he said yes, and I read him the book. But there were always interruptions from the nuns and the business with the telephone was hard. Elián's conversation with his dad was ended right away. The nun told the officer, who came and told us that we had to give him the telephone. When it came time to leave, it was sadder yet, because we were told it would be two to three hours but it was not even an hour and a half. The nun came in and said that the visit was over."

The following day, Sister Jeanne became a vocal partisan for the Miami relatives and even trooped off to Washington to lobby on their behalf. Asked if she was seeking favor with powerful exiles, she countered, "If I wanted to curry favor, I would have gone with the poll that said that 63 percent of Miami wants to send Elián back home." She felt the need to add that "CANF doesn't approve of me and hasn't given me a cent."

Unquestionably, Sister Jeanne had had firsthand experience with exile fury. In 1998, she signed up to go to Havana for the Pope's historic visit on a cruise offered by Bishop Thomas Wenski. But when the exile leadership threatened to halt all donations to the local church, the cruise was canceled. Representative Ileana Ros-Lehtinen did not mince words on the subject. "If you want to see the Pope," she admonished exiles, "go to Rome!"

Following the Pope's visit, Sister Jeanne went to Havana as part of a religious delegation organized by the Center for International Policy—but only after considerable arm-twisting.

Sister Jeanne countered that she had taken plenty of flak because "one of my biggest benefactors, Archer Daniels Midland, wants to lift the Embargo." But she was too shrewd to go against the exile leadership on Elián. When she and her home were first named as the site for the grandmothers' visit, exile radio blasted the nun for her trip to Cuba and urged listeners to remove their children from Barry University. A not inconsiderable number of its students were Cuban-Americans and a boycott of the college would have been a devastating blow.

Over the ensuing months, Sister Jeanne would chat up reporters and dangle damning allegations against Elián's Cuban family. Several reporters noted that these were the very same stories floated by Armando Gutiérrez, the family's handler. In late February, Sister Jeanne landed on the front page of the *Miami Herald* when she claimed that one of the grandmothers had told her she wanted to defect and that Juan Miguel had abused Elián's mother. When she was asked how she had garnered this information, she claimed that she was sufficiently fluent in Spanish to communicate with the grandmothers directly.

The problem was that Sister Leonor Esnard, the Cuban-born nun present throughout the grandmothers' visit, said that she was there expressly "to translate for Sister Jeanne because she doesn't understand Spanish." Asked about Sister Jeanne's allegations, Sister Leonor said, "I have no idea where she gained that information." The grandmothers were incensed. "She only saw us when we came in and left the house," said Raquel Rodríguez. "We never had a conversation with her."

Later that day, Sister Jeanne would say that the *Herald* had misquoted her. Martin Baron, the editor of the *Miami Herald,* issued a statement refuting her: "We can say without hesitation that our story was an accurate account of what Sister Jeanne told us." The *Herald*'s reporter, Meg Laughlin, said that Sister Jeanne had made the allegations on several occasions. "I asked who her sources were because we had all heard these stories from the Miami family," recalled Laughlin. "I told her that we could not run the story without firsthand sources. My feeling was that she wanted us to run these rumors on background and felt we should just take her word for it. Finally, she told me that she heard it from the grandmothers. She said, 'The light-haired grandmother told me this and the dark-haired grandmother told me that' . . . and she said that they were horribly afraid of their Cuban handlers."

Within a day, Sister Jeanne retracted her story, admitting that she had never met alone with the grandmothers, nor was she fluent in Spanish. But two weeks later she would make similar allegations in a notarized affidavit—this time citing "independent sources including INS officials, American family members and persons present at the university president's home." The INS and Justice Department denied being her sources, stating they were unaware of any of her allegations—leaving only the González clan and their advisers.

But the damage had been done. She had floated her sizzling allegations, which were promptly vacuumed up by Miami's Spanish language media and ceaselessly repeated in the loony echo chamber that envelops the Miami media—until they became articles of faith in every exile home in South Florida: the grandmothers would defect, Juan Miguel wanted to defect and Elián's family was part of some notorious smuggling ring.

The grandmothers' visit had a secondary plotline. Raquel Rodríguez, Elisa's mother, said that she was well aware that her half-sister, Doris, who lives in Miami, had tagged along with Jorge Mas Santos to Sister Jeanne's. Indeed, the Miami team of advisers felt that Doris was their best shot at getting at least one of the grandmothers to defect. But Raquel surprised both sides with her resoluteness. She had deeply bonded with Mariela and her family and, having lost her daughter, was determined not to lose her grandson. During her visit with Elián, Sister Leonor Esnard handed her a note from Doris. "It was at the same time as Elián was being taken away and I was crying. I read it but I don't even remember what it said. I gave it back to the nun that handed it to me."

Sister Jeanne offered another explanation to me. "Doris just wanted to embrace her sister and give her sympathy for losing her daughter. That's why Sister Esnard tried to bring them together. I thought the visit went very well but there's a lot of anti–Miami exile feeling out there."

In Cuba, anti-Catholic, anti-Church sentiment blossomed. Church leaders lamented that whatever good the Pope had done toward improving relations with Cuba over the last ten years was undone in a fortnight by Sister Jeanne.

Asked about her relationship with her sister, Raquel said only, "We get along." But she told friends that she was unhappy because a year earlier Doris had come to Cuba and hadn't called or visited her. The final straw was that Doris had allied herself with the Miami relatives and was said to be the source of the rumor that Raquel wanted to defect. The defection rumors had pursued Raquel Rodríguez throughout her U.S. visit. Joan Campbell said that the two women, who stayed in her Manhattan apartment for five days, had "had plenty of opportunities to go down to the lobby and defect if they had wanted." Raquel finally decided to give a spontaneous mini–press conference in D.C. Speaking clearly and emphatically, she said she had no intention or desire to defect.

When Raquel and Mariela returned to Cuba, having not defected as prophesied, Miami's Spanish language media began a campaign of demonization. At her home in Cárdenas, Mariela chatted and giggled with the neighbors. But the ordeal had transformed her into a warrior—a pariah in Miami but a heroine in Cuba. She said she was dumbstruck by the comments of Sister Jeanne O'Laughlin. "I don't know why she said what she said," Mariela told me. Raquel was even more distraught about her treatment at the hands of Sister Jeanne. She kept repeating how unlike himself Elián had seemed to her. She was convinced he had been drugged. "That woman," she said, referring to Sister Jeanne, "that is not a nun. That is a devil."

Days after the grandmothers' "triumphant return," as it was dubbed by Cuba's government-controlled media, *Pingagate* erupted in Miami. During an interview on Cuban television, Mariela had regaled viewers with details about her visit with Elián and her attempts to cheer up her grandson by biting his tongue and peering down his pants to see "if it had grown." Although bizarre to some, the behavior is not unfamiliar in many Cuban families, particularly in the provinces. Indeed it is not uncommon in Hispanic families, where the *machista* ethic rules the roost.

Almost immediately, the Miami team suggested that the grandmothers had been guilty of sexual molestation, and went so far as to threaten a lawsuit. Miami radio sizzled with attacks and epithets for days, which lost steam after Uva de Aragón, a writer and assistant director of Florida International University's Cuban Research Center, wrote that Mariela's behavior was the custom in many families. For several days the professor withstood a fiery attack for breaking rank. Others pointed out that a ninety-minute reunion with three nuns buzzing about would hardly be the ideal setting for child molestation, much less chatting about it on live TV. No one on either side of the debate was willing to say the obvious: that these were two *guajiras,* two unsophisticated, provincial women.

IRONICALLY, THE FINAL BATTLE of the Castro-Clinton years found the two adversaries on the same side. Joan Brown Campbell returned to Havana two months later with Washington power lawyer Gregory Craig, who had represented, among others, the President of the United States. The two endured the de rigueur wait for an audience with Castro. "We went out to dinner and cooled our heels for a day or so," she said. "As is always the case, you get a phone call late at night saying, 'We can't see you right now. How about tomorrow?' which meant staying another day." The meeting was held in the conference room at the Palace of the Revolution, where Castro has his office. Campbell and Craig and the sponsor from the Methodist Church, which was picking up the tab for Juan Miguel's U.S. legal bills, arrived with Ricardo Alarcón. They were met by Castro; his famed virtuoso translator, Juanita Vera; and some other aides. Craig brought along his own translator—an attorney with his firm. The meeting began at 5:00 P.M. and ended shortly before midnight.

"In the beginning, the interaction between Greg Craig and Fidel was like a duel between two brilliant lawyers," said Campbell. "Castro took Craig through every single step of the case without any notes at all and he knew every date, every name, every detail. And then Castro said, 'In forty-one years, we have never won a case with the United States. What makes you think we will win this one?' And I said, 'I don't know whether you'll win or not, but you won't get this boy back without a good lawyer.' He asked why and I said, 'Listen, you have one now and it's the U.S. government.' And that really stopped him. Castro didn't make the deal [to have Craig represent Juan Miguel and, in essence, Cuba's case], he refused to sign anything and he said that Juan Miguel will make the final decision. Then Greg said to Castro very clearly, 'I want you to understand that I will be representing Juan Miguel—not the Cuban government.' Fidel said, 'I have great respect for this young man and of course you'll be his lawyer and you will do whatever he asks you to do.' " The following morning, Juan Miguel met with Greg Craig.

FOR FIVE MONTHS THERE would be obsessive near-twenty-four-hour media attention on Elián, whose every move seemed choreographed and filmed for optimum impact. One day he would wave a congressional subpoena he could not read, another day he would flash a victory sign he didn't understand—serving as an all-around prop in the Miami political circus. There were constant breathless announcements about all the gifts bestowed on the boy, suggesting that the quantity and quality of toys was as important as parental love. There was the family outing to Disney World on December 12, sponsored by Orlando's Republican Party chief, Mel Martínez, and accompanied by the requisite media entourage. The event backfired when

Elián was urged to take Disney World's "It's a Small World" ride in a simulated ocean—just four weeks after having been shipwrecked and witnessing the drowning of his mother. The six-year-old nervously asked if the boat was going to sink and then declined the invitation.

At the Little Havana house, the gifts were piling up, mostly sent from exiles in Miami but some from as far away as California and Puerto Rico. Elián slept in a small bed the shape of a hot rod in the room he shared with Marisleysis. His closet was crammed with crisp new clothes: six pairs of identical white tennis shoes, school uniforms of blue pants and white shirts and what the family said was his favorite outfit—a white karate suit. The decidedly modest home began to resemble a Toys "R" Us showroom. Outside there was a brand-new swing set and a motorized car that Elián skidded wildly around the small yard as television cameras recorded his frolicking. Favorite gifts included collections of remote-controlled toy vehicles and giant stuffed Tweety Birds. Behind the house, four spanking-new bicycles were parked.

As the mythology surrounding Elián blossomed with each passing day, hordes of exile pilgrims descended upon the boxlike Little Havana home as if it were Lourdes. Some called it the Shrine House and left flowers and prayers in the chain link fence surrounding it. Throughout the saga, the family's advisers kept the drumbeat pounding behind their justification for keeping Elián González—namely that to live in Cuba was in itself child abuse. But their critics claimed that Elián's new life making the rounds of television shows was a more credible form of child abuse. They noted that on some days, the six-year-old would appear on the 7:00 A.M. news and again on the 11:00 P.M. news. Some armchair psychologists said it was clear that the boy was exhausted and stressed, a charge dismissed by the family, who said it was obvious from Elián's smiling face that he was enjoying himself.

Local celebrities like singer Gloria Estefan and actor Andy Garcia made the pilgrimage to the Shrine House, paid their respects to the family and kissed Elián on his cheeks. But VIPs and celebrities were not the only visitors to the house on NW 2nd Street. Some claimed that the Virgin Mary herself had paid a visit. The first sighting of the Virgin was on January 9, across the windows of TotalBank on NW 27th Avenue, a few blocks from Lázaro's home. What appeared to most passersby to be a smudged window, they said, was in fact the Blessed Virgin, a diaphanous, iridescent visage of gold, green and purple. Not all Cuban-Americans agreed. "It looks like when you get Windex and then you have that rainbow," said a young woman who stopped to examine the image. But some exiles said there had been other sightings of the Virgin Mary, including one miraculous appearance in a mirror inside the

Little Havana home. "All signs are good signs," averred Armando Gutiérrez, who described the González family as "very religious." Surely God was on their side and meant for Elián to live with them.

AS THE ELIÁN WAR progressed, some observers began to note that many of the broadsides launched from Miami radio against Havana were virtually identical to what *Granma*, the Communist Party daily, was saying about Miami. Exiles insisted that Juan Miguel was under the steely thumb of Fidel Castro, unable to speak his mind, while *Granma* claimed that the Miami Gonzálezes were simply puppets of the "Miami Mafia." "My brothers would not be doing this to us," said Juan González, Elián's grandfather, at the peak of the crisis, "if they were not under pressure from the others in Miami." Each side produced psychiatrists and experts who testified that the boy had been damaged and subjected to "psychological brainwashing and indoctrination."

A fount of scurrilous rumors floated through Miami, passed along as fact. From the radio stations they would be passed on to Spanish language television in Miami—Telemundo and Univisión—where news and opinion on Cuban issues are often one and the same. From TV, the rumors would often slip into *El Diario de las Américas* and *El Nuevo Herald*, the *Miami Herald*'s Spanish language paper, which is run primarily by Cuban-American editors and staff. At a Miami party a Cuban intellectual and former Marxist asked me whether it was true that the Gonzálezes in Cárdenas were "part of a smuggling ring."

Havana responded in kind. It launched its own "investigative report," published in *Granma* in February 2000, depicting some of those who fled with Elián as scoundrels and worse. A later *Granma* story sought to discredit Lázaro González by reporting that he had consorted with "homosexual elements," which Lázaro decried as libel.

The charges and countercharges between Havana and Miami conjured up a dizzying mirrored universe. More often than not, the same words and rhetoric were invoked by both sides. The Cuban government repeatedly referred to Elián's caretakers as "kidnappers," the same epithet that was later invoked by Delfín González against those who took Elián from Miami. After the grandmothers' brief visit with Elián in Miami, they repeatedly claimed that their grandson had been "drugged," which quickly became the party line of the Cuban government. Drugging rumors reached an incendiary pitch in mid-May, when a sleeping Elián was carried from a Washington party in the arms of a policeman. Certainly the boy was not simply tired, hollered Miami radio, he had been drugged!

While Fidel Castro relentlessly harped on the "kidnappers" in Miami, he had a hand in keeping more than one child separated from its parents. A Miami-based exile group calling itself Mission Elián claimed to have documented more than two dozen such cases. The plight of José Cohen, who defected in 1994, was among the most notable. Since 1996, when he became a U.S. resident, Cohen has ceaselessly petitioned for his wife and three children to join him. But the family has been inexplicably denied visas—while being harassed in Cuba for wanting to leave. "My wife and three children are hostages of the regime," Cohen told the *Wall Street Journal.* Perhaps the most celebrated case was that of Orestes Lorenzo, the Cuban Air Force fighter pilot who flew his MiG-27 to the Boca Chica Naval Air Station in the Florida Keys in 1991. Following his defection, his wife and two sons were told directly by Raúl Castro that they would not be able to leave; he insisted that Lorenzo would have to return. In 1993, Lorenzo did in fact return in a plane with a dramatic and audacious rescue, swooping up his waiting family on a rural road.

Even the most quotidian and banal matters were treated with near religious intensity by both Havana and Miami. Both sides consecrated Elián's school desk. The wobbly, knotholed *pupitre* remained untouched in his classroom at the Marcelo Salado School in Cárdenas during his absence and, following Elián's departure from Miami, the Lincoln-Martí School memorialized Elián's former desk as a monument to Cuban suffering. Official landmarks celebrating the life of Elián and his mother were designated. Hialeah, the densely populated ghetto of mostly working-class Cubans north of Miami, created the Parque de Elisa, while Havana settled on Parque Elián. And when the final act of the melodrama had concluded, both sides had established Elián museums: Miami consecrated the small González home as a shrine house for Elián and Cuba converted a former firehouse into a hall of tribute to its "victorious fight," rechristening the building with the bloated name Museum for the Battle of Ideas. Not exempted was Radio Martí—funded by U.S. taxpayers to disseminate neutral information and news to Cuba—which listeners noted was sounding not unlike its Cuban counterpart, Radio Rebelde, in its hyperbolic stridency and transparent propaganda.

AS HIS SON WAS BEING trooped about Miami, Juan Miguel González began a series of interviews with the INS at the U.S. Interests Section in Havana to determine his eligibility to retrieve his son. "I found him to be honest, sincere and that he really loved and missed his son," said one of the State Department officials present at his interviews. "We were convinced that he had had no prior notice that his son was leaving with the mother. What I found most compelling is that as soon as he found out that Elián was gone, he went the very next day to the Municipal Courthouse and started to get the papers of Elián's birth and everything to do with Elián." As to why Juan Miguel did not immediately take off for the States to retrieve his son, the official responded: "Cubans do not run to the airport and jump on airplanes. He would have to get a Cuban visa, then an American visa, and he would need to have $1,000 in cash lying around. By the time he figured it all out, he realized that [his relatives] were not going to return his son to him."

There was also the danger that once Juan Miguel González landed in the United States, he would be slapped with a subpoena. Congressman Dan Burton had made clear his determination to keep Elián in the country and had voiced his intention to compel Juan Miguel to testify before his House Committee on International Relations. Burton hoped such a venue would lead to the father's defection. At the very least, it could delay his return to Cuba. Also on the agenda was legislation proposed by Florida Senator Connie Mack and Representatives Ileana Ros-Lehtinen and Lincoln Díaz-Balart that would grant Elián citizenship or legal residency, thereby cutting the INS out of the process. But the bills sparked scant enthusiasm among politicians, and even less among the public, and never made it to a vote.

Caridad González said she was flabbergasted at her nephew's insistence that Elián be sent back to Cárdenas. "After Elián came here, I called Juan Miguel twelve times," she told a *Los Angeles Times* reporter. "I told him that I could get visas for him and his family and child. . . . But he said that within twenty-four hours, someone will be there to pick him up. . . . I couldn't believe he would take him back to that hellhole." One of her nephews tried to explain his aunt's mind-set. "The obsession of her life has been to have the whole family here," he told the *New York Times*. "That has been her reason for living. The idea was to use the boy to bring the others here." Caridad herself made this clear to Juan Miguel. "I came to this country to bring Cubans here," she told her nephew incredulously, "not to send them back."

Both sides took to taping the phone calls between the boy and his father, which in the state of Florida is illegal. One conversation, taped from Cuba, included an exchange of harsh words between Juan Miguel and his cousin Marisleysis and was published in *Granma*. "I want that child to be next to me," Juan Miguel told Marisleysis. She replied that Elián did not want to go back to Cuba. "Before the Virgin of Charity and the Sacred Heart of Jesus, I swear to you, that I asked him if he wanted to go back there with his father, and you know what he said to me? 'Let him come here if he wants.' "

Juan Miguel would tell U.S. officials in Havana that his Miami kin were so desperate that they were offering him bribes. "They called," he said, "and that is when they started offering me $2 million, a house, a car. Also, a church had offered $4 million to Elián so he would be set for life." Armando Gutiérrez was dumbfounded by the young father's intransigence. Pointing out the offers that were pouring in, he told reporters, "Juan Miguel could be a very rich man if he came here."

With each passing week, polls expressing disapproval of the Miami relatives swelled. *Time* magazine would run a cover story on the Internet entitled "Miami Cubans: The Big Losers." *The New Yorker* featured a cartoon of tourists driving on a Miami freeway ogling a sign that read "Welcome to Miami: Home of the Miami Relatives." On the *New York Times*'s editorial page, David Rieff, who had written empathetically of the community in his book *The Exile*, now spoke of "an out-of-control banana republic within the American body politic." Virtually every editorial page around the globe, with the exception of those in the *Miami Herald* and the *Wall Street Journal*, penned salvos of outrage against the Miami body politic and the relatives. The family became fodder almost nightly for Leno, Letterman and Bill Maher, after getting it all day from Howard Stern and talk radio America. Fidel Castro predictably denounced the "Miami Mafia" and the "kidnapping" of Elián on a weekly basis, and the Cuban Harvard scholar Jorge Domínguez seemed to have been a prophet when he wrote earlier of the exile community's relationship with Fidel Castro: "With an enemy like this one, he may not need friends."

But the Gonzálezes, their advisers and their supporters were unfazed. No one understood them. Betrayed by Castro, betrayed by the U.S., which had failed to back them in the disastrous Bay of Pigs invasion, betrayed by leaders of Latin America, even betrayed by the Pope's visit to Cuba, they simply didn't care what anyone else said or thought. What did the Anglos know of their suffering? "I could care less what the American public thinks about the Cuban exile community," José Basulto, an exile leader, huffed in the pages of the *New York Times*. If Fidel Castro wanted the boy returned, then they were damn well going to keep him.

CHAPTER 4

CALLE OCHO POLITICS

El mundo y yo—estamos en guerra.
The world and I are at war.

REINALDO ARENAS

"**W**E ARE THE JEWS of the Caribbean," goes a cheeky Cuban adage heard on both sides of the Florida Straits. Some argue it is a disparagement, but most say it is a tribute. One friend living in Havana, with barely a blush of embarrassment, explained her interpretation: "It means that we are sharper, faster and shrewder than our neighbors," she said, adding, "and really we are the most successful." The irony that these naturally savvy entrepreneurs have been condemned to a forty-three-year-old socialist experiment seemed to elude her. Indeed, the stake through the heart of many exiles was the killing of entrepreneurialism by Castro—eliminating private enterprise and a thriving middle class almost overnight. Suddenly, Cuba, renowned for its all-night cafés, its frenzied intellectualism and a plethora of newspapers and magazines, was without a coffee shop or a decent broadsheet. No doubt my friend in Havana would be the first to say that Cuban ingenuity to *resolver* (resolve), *conseguir* (get) and *inventar* (invent) is *how* they have survived.

Cuban culture has long dazzled the Southern and Northern Hemispheres and beyond: its writers, intellectuals, musicians, artists and poets are among the most gifted, while its athletes and business titans have achieved renown around the world. The influence of Cubans is even more remarkable in light of their insignificant numbers. Cuba is an island of fewer than 12 million people, while Cubans in the U.S. make up less than .05 percent of the population. However, a whopping 58 percent of Cuban-Americans own their homes in the U.S., a greater percentage than for any other Hispanic group. In Broward County, just north of Miami, 77 percent of Cuban-Americans are homeowners, according to the new census. Jaime Suchlicki, director of the Institute for Cuban and Cuban-American Studies at the University of Miami, told the *Miami Herald* that he attributed the phenomenon to an established infrastructure of Cuban and Hispanic banks and mortgage companies that "nurtures this kind of upward mobility." Dario Moreno, a Florida International University political science professor, added, "It points to the continuation of the Cuban success story."

Indeed, the breadth of their successes has made Cubans the object of envy. Following the Cuban Revolution, exiles streamed into Puerto Rico, Venezuela, Costa Rica and the Dominican Republic, quickly making a name for themselves and not infrequently dominating their fields. "The Cubans are the Chosen People," intones the title character of Luis Aguilar León's classic monograph, "The Prophet," "chosen by themselves. And they pass through other people like a ghost over water." As such, they are not popular in Latin America—where they are not infrequently derided as being egotistical and arrogant. Some Hispanics bristle at the refusal of Cubans to be identified as immigrants—as well as their insistence on calling themselves *exiliados,* with the implication that the persecution they fled was worse than, say, the death squads of Guatemala, Argentina, El Salvador or Chile.

Tony Suárez of Orlando, who became the first Puerto Rican elected to Florida's House of Representatives, joked edgily about Cuban exiles. "Everyone talks about the Florida Hispanic population as Cuban Republicans," Suárez told the *Miami Herald.* "When Cubans open a restaurant, it's called a Cuban restaurant. Puerto Ricans would just call it a Spanish restaurant. . . . They ask me if I want some Cuban coffee. I say, 'I didn't know we were importing coffee from Cuba!' I say, 'It's Colombian coffee, not Cuban.' They like to appropriate everything."

Aside from geographical expediency and cultural history, it is perhaps fitting that Cubans would settle in large numbers in South Florida side by side with one of the world's largest Jewish communities. Both Cuba and Israel have been pariah countries among many of their neighbors for roughly the same period of time. However, in Miami the two groups have had a singularly successful cohabitation—notwithstanding a durable strain of anti-Semitism, as well as racism, among a segment of Cubans. Indeed, exiles rallied for Israel in resounding numbers and with passion in the wake of the siege of suicide bombings in 2002. One radio personality, Agustín Tamargo, even penned a column entitled "Yo Soy un Sionista Cubano" (I Am a Zionist Cuban). Jews and Cubans are renowned for their intellectualism as well as their emotionalism—and both have a keen sense of victimization. In fact, one of the rare instances of friction between Cubans and Jews in Miami involved the relative merits of their respective persecution.

When Jews erected a Holocaust Memorial in Miami Beach in 1990, Cuban exile leaders announced that they too wanted their own Holocaust tribute. When their plans were received with a firestorm of howls, denouncing the hubris of comparing their plight with the murder of six million Jews, the exile leadership reluctantly, and with no particular grace, backed down. In 2001, they would establish a more fitting memorial by restoring the Freedom Tower on Biscayne Boulevard, port of call for most Cuban exiles in the United States. The building was purchased by the family of Jorge Mas Canosa to honor the sacrifices and losses of exiles.

The inappropriate analogies with Nazi Germany reappeared during the Elián drama. "My husband and I saw a disturbing billboard when driving out of Miami International Airport," a resident wrote in the *Miami Herald*. "The billboard shows three photos. . . . A Nazi youth with a swastika . . . Joseph Stalin and a child . . . and the third is of Elián González with this message: 'A crime against a child is a crime against humanity.' Who is responsible for this billboard, and does this group or individual really equate a child's return to a loving father with the atrocities perpetrated against children during the Nazi regime and in communist Russia during the Stalin era?"

But there is a clarion distinction between Jews and Cuban exiles, which has made all the difference in their success and acceptance. American Jews subscribe to a multitude of ideologies (liberal, conservative, Democrat, Republican, hawk, dove and so on), but the golden rule is to protect the unity of the community and one another. Cubans, on the other hand, on both sides of the Florida Straits, seemingly revel in self-demonization. Doubters need only tune in to Miami Spanish language radio for a dose of withering denunciations and character assassinations of those who dare to disagree with the views of the exile leadership.

Over the last forty years, a good deal of Miami Spanish language radio has operated as the Big Brother of the community. "Miami radio stations are the most inquisitorial and *lengüeteras* [long-tongued] of the entire world," observes the Cuban writer René Vázquez Díaz. "There is gossip, persecution, lies and the lowest politicking at a rhetorical level." The most successful broadcaster is Armando Pérez-Roura, the director general of Radio Mambí, the number one station among exiles. A man with an interesting past, Pérez-Roura was closely allied in the 1950s with the dictator Batista, working as his official radio announcer. When Fidel Castro trounced Batista, Pérez-Roura promptly switched sides and became Castro's choice to head up Cuba's National College of Broadcasters. Exile activist and author Bernardo Benes, who fearlessly calls the Mambí broadcaster "the cancer of Miami," remembers Pérez-Roura's broadsides against "Yankee imperialists" during his days as a zealot *fidelista* and his role in closing down and confiscating the CMQ radio and television station in Havana as part of Cuba's nationalization of all media. Pérez-Roura had a relatively long career under Castro and did not arrive in Miami until 1968, when he once again reinvented himself— setting up shop as the premier anti-Castro propagandist of Calle Ocho.

Over the years, Pérez-Roura has offered a hospitable welcome to some of the most notorious characters in the exile community. Convicted terrorists such as Orlando Bosch and disgraced politicians like Demetrio Pérez Jr. are often heard on Mambí. "No cloud of criminal—or even terrorist— suspicion has kept any connected figure off the air," charges the *Herald* columnist Liz Balmaseda. "It doesn't matter if you repeatedly rip off the tax-payers.... It doesn't matter if you have been suspected, or even convicted, of setting off bombs ... or if you're wearing a convict anklet."

Pérez-Roura's clout at Mambí, which bills itself as La Grande, has made him a kingmaker in exile politics, sort of the Walter Winchell of Calle Ocho. And anyone nurturing political ambitions dares not get on his wrong side. Borrowing a page from Senator Joseph McCarthy, Pérez-Roura seems to consider it his mission to identify and oppose those who are insufficiently anti-Castro. In his book, *Tome Nota* (which means "Take Note" and is also the name of his talk show), he calls two of Cuba's most renowned dissidents "mercenaries": Elizardo Sánchez, who spent eleven years in jail, much of it in solitary confinement, and Vladimiro Roca, who was released from prison in April 2002. Listeners recall a 1994 program on the topic of "what to do with the leftover communists" once a new government is installed in Cuba. "Burn them alive," said one caller. Another suggested that they "open the in-cinerators and throw them all in—men, women and children." The affable Pérez-Roura, in his well-honed basso, thanked his callers for their com-ments. Nor have family troubles slowed his ascent. His eldest son has had his share of tangles with the law and his wife has passed on. In August 1984, Ar-mando Pérez-Roura Jr. was arrested, and later convicted, on narcotics charges following a bust in which more than a ton of cocaine was confis-cated. Federal agents at the time ranked the raid as the second-largest cocaine seizure in U.S. history. The radio king would lose his wife in 1998, an event that prompted the city elders of Miami to recommend that a portion of Coral Way be renamed in her honor—as it is today, as Ofelia Pérez-Roura Memorial Way.

The radio host is also regarded by many as the power behind the throne at Radio Martí, the taxpayer-funded radio station that beams news to Cuba.

He has long had his own show on Martí and has recently begun doing five-minute commentaries once a week. Some in Miami believe him to have been responsible for the dismissal of Hermenio San Román, Martí's former director. Furious that San Román had invited Elizardo Sánchez to participate in a long interview at the station in 2000, Martí staffers say that Pérez-Roura lobbied his friend Governor Jeb Bush, who saw to it that the director was replaced. As for Jeb Bush, who "doesn't do national media," according to his communications director, he is unstintingly generous with his time for live interviews with Pérez-Roura.

In 1993, a crowd said to be spurred on by the oratory of Pérez-Roura physically attacked demonstrators protesting the U.S. Embargo. Two police officers were injured and sixteen arrests were made. But Miami's leadership defended the assailants, and Miriam Alonso, then the Miami City Commissioner, remarked casually, "We have to look at the legalities of whether the city of Miami can prevent them [the protesters] from expressing themselves." During the Elián saga, Pérez-Roura's glass-enclosed sound booth was often ground zero for the exile leadership. The broadcaster, who frequently participated in strategy talks, took to calling Marisleysis "Elián's spiritual mother" while deriding Juan Miguel as merely a "biological father."

Pérez-Roura shares the Mambí pulpit with other *emisora* stars such as Marta Flores, Raquel Regalado and Agustín Tamargo—all of whom can make or break one's life in Miami. Radio Mambí, while the most powerful, is hardly the only game in town. Also stoking the airwaves over Miami are La Cubanisma (WQBA—1140 AM, also owned by Mambí) and its superstar Ninoska Pérez-Castellón, La Poderosa (WWFE—670 AM), La Cadena Azul (WRHC—1560 AM) and, formerly, WCMQ (1210 AM) and its host, Tomás García Fusté, who went on to other shows.

Non-Cubans also come in for attack—as was the case in 1990 for Nelson Mandela. The South African leader had been scheduled to receive the key to the city of Miami. But after an appearance on *Nightline* in which he credited Cuba for its assistance to South Africa, the honor was withdrawn and he was snubbed by hard-line exiles and leaders during his U.S. visit. Miami Spanish language radio daily derided Mandela as an enemy of the community, invoking one of its most virulent epithets, *"un marijuanero maricón"*—a pot-smoking faggot—because of his cordial relations with Fidel Castro. The vitriol unleashed against Mandela led him to curtail his visit in Miami, and prompted an African-American boycott against the city, exacerbating the already frosty relations between Miami blacks and Cubans. The Mandela brouhaha augmented the unspoken and glaring racial divide among exiles.

Miami is a segregated city and there are no black or mulatto exile leaders, despite the fact that Cuba today is 70 percent black or what's called *una mezcla* (mixed race). More often than not, when black Cubans emigrate to Miami, they relocate to black Overtown or Allapattah, home to many black Dominicans, feeling unwelcome in Little Havana and other neighborhoods popular with Cubans.

While the exile leadership denounces the government-controlled media of Cuba, it has turned a blind eye to an array of conflicts of interest that permeate local media. In Miami, it is not uncommon for talk radio hosts to accept contributions from local politicians, especially during election cycles. According to a *Herald* investigation, the practice has drawn "complaints that favorable coverage is for sale on the airwaves of Miami." Those cited include Radio Mambí's opinionated Marta Flores, WMBM's Ricky Thomas, the late Carlos D'Mant of La Poderosa and Matías Farías, all of whom "earn money during election season while also commenting on campaigns." In the 2000 elections, Flores accepted a total of $10,000 from Miami-Dade Commissioners Bruno Barreiro, Natacha Seijas and Jimmy Morales. But the payoffs are hardly the worst of their sins.

In 1994, Human Rights Watch/Americas Group issued a report on human rights violations in Miami, which concluded what the community had long known: that the exile leadership did not tolerate dissident opinions, that Spanish language radio fomented aggression and intimidation, and that local government leaders and law enforcement refused to act against the perpetrators. "Denunciation over the airwaves as a 'traitor,' a 'communist' or a Castro agent is often followed by a telephone threat, an act of vandalism or a physical assault," concluded the report. At the time, a CANF spokesman downplayed the charges, commenting that he "prefer[red] to think of Miami radio as a sort of a catharsis for Cubans."

For most Americans, indeed most of the world, the tug-of-war over Elián González was their first peek into the roiling ecosystem of Miami. As the polls duly registered, they did not like what they saw. And while exiles chanted in Miami that keeping Elián from his father was a protest against the communist dictatorship of Fidel Castro, the rest of the world took note of another dictatorship, albeit a modified one—the one in Miami.

In January 2000, a protester outside the home of Sister Jeanne O'Laughlin carrying a sign that read "Stop the deaths at sea. Repeal the Cuban Adjustment Act" was attacked physically by a nearby exile crowd before police came to the rescue. Four months later, a visitor from Portland, Oregon, wearing a T-shirt reading, "Send the boy home" and "A father's rights," was physically assaulted by exiles before the police showed up.

After the Elián affair, PBS television interviewed a group of former Pedro Pans for a documentary on *Frontline* called "Saving Elián." Because of their painful experiences, such a group would have been expected to support the hard-liners. However, none of those interviewed did so. Citing the wrenching estrangement that they had experienced, they felt that the sooner Elián was reunited with his father, the better. But they dared not speak publicly about it at the time: "All along, I thought if I walked down south of Eighth Street and said [that], I would have been lynched," said Frank Avellant, a Pedro Pan child. The show's award-winning producer said she was blindsided by the quota of fear in the exile culture in Miami. "This is the only show that I've ever done where people said, 'I'd love to talk to you, but I can't on camera. We live here. You wouldn't understand,' [and] more people in Miami said it than said it in Cuba."

DENUNCIATION HAS A LONG and venerated tradition in Cuba. In postrevolutionary Cuba, the Committees for the Defense of the Revolution (CDRs), neighborhood watchdog groups, specialize in snitching on and denouncing their neighbors. Often the offenses involve the pettiest of infractions, such as buying food on the black market, and result from the basest of motives, such as envy and jealousy.

When Castro took power, he systematically eliminated freedom of the press, imposing a steely, airless net over the lives of Cubans. Close rein is maintained over all incoming and outgoing information on the island. Presently, there are two skinny government-issued newspapers, *Granma* and *Juventud Rebelde*, of a few pages each, available five days a week, and two primary radio stations, Radio Rebelde and Radio Reloj. Cuban state television offers several channels of news, entertainment and educational programming, but all news is carefully sifted by government censors. Exiles are rarely mentioned in the Cuban media without the accompanying epithets of "the Miami Mafia" or *gusanos* (worms) or *escoria* (scum). Raúl Rivero, an independent journalist living in Havana, derides Cuba's TV shows, referring to the "daily opinion carnivals of character assassination and verbal throat slashing in Cuba's state-run *Mesa Redonda* TV show." Only those who work in hotels or have homemade satellite dishes are able to watch CNN or other non-Cuban stations. Some professionals and intellectuals have access to the

Internet, but all communications on the island—phone, fax and Internet—are monitored. "There is no opposition in Cuba," said commentator Saul Landau. "Opponents are either in jail or in Miami."

One of the whiplashing ironies of the Havana-Miami divide is that the Cubans who fled to escape a dictatorship and the tyranny of the CDRs instituted almost a mirror system in Miami. In South Florida, "CDR consciousness" flourishes: neighbors, acquaintances and enemies are not uncommonly reported to the police, FBI and, most particularly, Customs or the Treasury Department's Office of Foreign Assets Control (OFAC) for suspected illegal travel or purchases in Cuba or for exceeding the permitted limit on remittances to Cuba. On not a few occasions at Miami airport, weeping elderly women en route to their loved ones in Cuba have been detained and divested of cash hidden on their bodies. Some suspected offenders have been denounced on the radio, pilloried as *traidores* (traitors) or *espías* (spies), borrowing a page from the experts of denunciation at Castro's Ministry of the Interior.

Certainly, the Cuban government has done its best to augment the brew of suspicion and mistrust. Jack Devine, a thirty-two-year veteran of the CIA who ran the Latin America desk for many of those years, was impressed by Castro's thoroughness in infiltrating the exile community. "Cuban intelligence has always been very effective," he explained. "Much more effective than even the Russians in Latin America. The Cuban spy world is doubly shadowy. I suspect that all of the exile groups have been infiltrated. In the mid-1970s, we tried to recruit some [exile] agents. They were all bad," he said—meaning they were Cuban double agents.

In June 2001, Devine predicted that a Cuban operative would eventually be uncovered high up in the U.S. intelligence infrastructure. "The Cubans turn out very good agents—they are very dedicated. We had a lot of respect for them. I am waiting for the other shoe to drop—a scandal at the high end of the scale. Like [FBI spy Robert] Hanssen." Devine's prophecy proved true on September 28, 2001, when Ana Belén Montés, forty-four, a senior Defense Intelligence Agency analyst, was arrested on alleged charges of "conspiracy to deliver U.S. national defense information," a charge for which she could have received the death penalty. Born to Puerto Rican parents of a progressive political disposition and educated at Johns Hopkins University, the attractive and highly regarded Montés began working at the DIA in 1985. Seven years later, she was assigned to analyze Cuban affairs and rose through the ranks to be the agency's senior analyst on Cuba. As such, she had access to classified information within the entire intelligence community. In March

2002, she admitted in a plea bargain that she had been spying for sixteen years—not for money, but out of her moral outrage against U.S. policy toward Cuba. She could serve as much as twenty-five years in prison.

In 2001, the trial of the so-called Wasp Network mesmerized Miami for months and resulted in life sentences for several of the defendants for espionage of exile groups and U.S. military facilities. Cuba admitted that the five were part of a state-sponsored undercover operation but maintained that they had not spied on the U.S. but had only infiltrated militant exile groups in Miami to protect Cuba, claiming that Cuba has had 3,400 casualties since 1959 from exile terrorism.

Since 1998, more than a dozen alleged operatives of the Cuban government have been arrested. Exiles are inveterate conspiracy theorists, and now they had proof. In September 2001, the FBI arrested two Cuban intelligence agents in Florida, husband and wife George and Marisol Gari, who were sentenced to five and three years respectively for trying to infiltrate the military facility of the U.S. Southern Command in Miami, which oversees military operations in Latin America, and conducting surveillance of the Cuban American National Foundation offices. A particularly memorable case was that of Mariano Faget, an INS agent, who was convicted of spying in 2000. Faget's case was a shock and a harsh blow for exiles of the *batistiano* persuasion: his father, also named Mariano Faget, had long been held in high esteem, having distinguished himself as a torturer for Batista's secret police.

Bernardo Benes maintains that in 1978 José Abrantes, a former Castro aide, confirmed for him that Cuba had about three hundred operatives working undercover in Miami. Cuba, of course, insists that the spies are necessary to protect the country from exile plots, and that the United States has its share of spies in Havana.

While it is certainly true that Miami Cubans have enemies in their midst, those they denounce are not spies: they are most often exiles who advocate a negotiated settlement to the Cuban stalemate—people known as *dialogueros*. In Miami, *dialogue* is a famously dirty and dangerous word. Because of the inherent perils of espousing diplomacy with Cuba, *dialogueros* are more likely to emigrate to New York or California or other states where there is far greater tolerance within the exile community. But even in Miami there has always been a sizable minority of exiles who believe in ending the Embargo and negotiating with Castro. Miami even boasts a pro-Cuba party, the Antonio Maceo Brigade, formed in the fall of 1977 and headed today by Andrés Gómez. (The Antonio Maceo Brigade came out of *Areito*, a magazine published by New York–based exiles who supported the Cuban Revolution.) Still, exiles who go public with their beliefs pay a price. Being denounced can lead to losing one's job or being harshly ostracized, which was the fate of Magda Montiel-Davis, who was captured on videotape in 1994 calling Castro "a great teacher." Soon after she was reviled on Spanish language radio, her law office received a bomb threat, all of her Cuban employees resigned and family members were repeatedly heckled on the street and at public events.

"I AM EL CAPITÁN DREYFUS OF MIAMI," Bernardo Benes, a former banker, is fond of telling visitors. "I was *the* number one activist of this community before it happened. I was the *good* Jorge Mas Canosa," said Benes, a hyperactive septuagenarian, over a noisy lunch at La Malaga on Calle Ocho. "It" was a reference to Benes's near fatal brush with his fellow exiles when he spearheaded a nongovernmental diplomatic initiative, known as *El Diálogo*—The Dialogue—in 1977 and 1978, under the auspices of President Jimmy Carter. His efforts produced two exile conferences in Havana and the release of 3,600 political prisoners from Cuban jails. But Benes paid a huge price for his statesmanship and learned that for some in Miami, dialogue is a criminal act. Miami's three exile radio stations trashed him around the clock, denouncing him as a "traitor" and a "communist." His bank was bombed, then picketed for three weeks. For a year, he wore a bulletproof vest. Friends and even relatives were frightened of being seen with him, and his children were ostracized by other children, whose parents were fearful of reprisals. Within the year, two conference participants were murdered—one assassinated in Puerto Rico in 1979 and another gunned down in New Jersey. *El Diario-La Prensa* was bombed after running an editorial endorsing exile visits to Cuba. "You see, no one is interested in free speech in Dade County," said Benes. "Only in Havana."

I asked Benes, who refers to Miami radio as "radio terrorism," about one local poll in the mid-1990s which indicated that the majority of Miami exiles support the Embargo. "You can't trust polls here," he said. "People are very fearful and they say only what they think the caller wants to hear. Miami is like Guatemala. We are talking about uncontrollable fear." One day after my first meeting with Benes, the Little Havana office of *Réplica*, a Spanish language entertainment magazine published since 1967, was bombed for the seventh time, and several Miami businesses, citing threats against them, stopped selling the magazine. *Réplica*'s editor is Max Lesnik, a left-leaning Cuban exile, who has advocated dialogue with Cuba and lifting the Embargo. Seeking to deflect responsibility from the obvious culprits, Metro-Dade Commissioner Pedro Reboredo said, "It could be anybody on any side trying to promote chaos," and asked that the incident "not be blown out of proportion."

One FBI agent based in Miami said there have been other close calls that Lesnik does not know about. "I cannot tell you how many times we have rescued Lesnik in the nick of time," he said, with a whistle of awe.

Over the years, those denounced as insufficiently anti-Castro in Miami have paid dearly. In 1996, a beloved dinner and music club, El Centro Vasco, was bombed because a Cuban entertainer, Rosita Fornés, had been invited to perform. To hard-liners, Cuban performers—or, indeed, any Cubans offered the chance—who do not defect are regarded as traitors. Run by Juan Saizarbitoria and his wife, Totty, Centro Vasco had been a cultural institution in Havana before the family fled in 1960 and reestablished the venue on Calle Ocho.

Curiously, the club had often been the mecca for the right-wing leadership of Miami's exiles—hosting countless fund-raisers and political events. But when the Saizarbitorias decided that the time had come to allow an artist who actually lived in Cuba to perform, they found themselves castigated as traitors and communists. According to Juan Saizarbitoria, call-in shows on Radio Mambí hosted by Armando Pérez-Roura and Marta Flores conducted a relentless campaign of vilification against them. "Every day, Pérez-Roura and Flores encouraged attacks on us," said Saizarbitoria. "They would say the most horrible things about us—passing out personal information—which were all lies. We tried to get the tapes of the show so we could sue—but they said they made no tapes. We asked a friend who we know taped the shows, but she was too afraid to give them to us. We heard that *El Nuevo Herald* kept tapes but we couldn't get copies."

It wasn't long after the Radio Mambí campaign that the Saizarbitorias began receiving death threats. Chanting protesters picketed outside the club, culminating in a Molotov cocktail being tossed inside. The bombing caused enough damage to force the temporary closure of the club. In a matter of two months, the fifty-three-year-old family business was plunged into ruin. Blacklisted in Miami, the Saizarbitorias realized they would be unable to continue with their popular music hall and were forced to sell. The buyer, Felipe Valls, owner of the famed Cuban restaurant Versailles, was a close ally of Jorge Mas Canosa, who had blasted the owners for inviting Rosita Fornés.

Despite the number of prominent performers who had been showcased at Centro Vasco, not one spoke out in support of the besieged couple, according to the club's owners. Gloria Estefan and her husband, Emilio, the royal couple of Miami, were notably mute, as were Jon Secada, Albita (who made her name and fame at the club), Arturo Sandoval and Julio Iglesias. After all, they had their own careers to think about. Back in 1972, Iglesias had commented in passing while performing at a local nightclub that he wouldn't mind "singing in front of Cubans." The audience erupted in fury and Iglesias needed a police escort to get him out of the club. In the ensuing weeks, many radio stations promptly stopped playing his music. One station that did not, Radio Alegre, was deluged with bomb threats. In 1994, Jon Secada was called on the carpet over Miami radio and compelled to explain and repudiate an interview in which he allegedly credited the Cuban Revolution with "a lot of achievements."

In the steamy, overcaffeinated body politic of Miami, city employees are compelled to sign an Oath of Allegiance pledging that they do not belong to the Communist Party, stating: "I am not a member nor have I knowingly ever been a member." No matter that such an oath is patently unconstitutional. Miami has conducted its own domestic and foreign policy for decades. Until 2000, when a U.S. Supreme Court ruling declared the policy unconstitutional, Miami-Dade prohibited companies that do business with Cuban nationals or Cuban companies from working in Miami. Under a de facto Cultural Revolution, Cuban artists and performers had been banned from appearing in its public facilities.

Hard-liners in the exile leadership put a high premium on keeping culture in Miami stringently, indeed antiseptically, anti-Castro. Cuban nationals who dare to perform in Miami's private venues are often met with threats and violence. In 1996, after receiving threatening calls, promoters canceled a local appearance by Cuba's La Orquesta Aragón. The same year, patrons attending a concert by Cuban jazz pianist Gonzalo Rubalcaba were physically assaulted and jeered by two hundred exile protesters whose transportation was arranged by Dade County Commissioner Javier Souto. A year later, bomb and death threats poured into radio station WRTO-FM following its short-lived decision to include songs by Cuban musicians. And in 1998, a bomb threat emptied the concert hall at the MIDEM music conference during a performance by ninety-one-year-old Cuban musician Compay Segundo, the award-winning star of *Buena Vista Social Club*. Bomb threats have also plagued the Amnesia nightclub in Miami Beach, which allows Cuban artists to perform. The violence was captured on film at the 1999 concert of the popular Cuban band Los Van Van, at which one person was injured and eleven were arrested. One Radio Mambí commentator had urged that concertgoers be videotaped as they entered the club and that the tape be aired later on television so that "Fidel Castro sympathizers" could be identified. The message was clear: Cuban artists who dare to perform in Miami—and those who patronize them—do so at their own risk.

Perhaps the apex of Miami's Cultural Revolution was the case of Veronica Castro. A Mexican actress popular with Cubans, Castro (no relation to Cuba's ruler) was awarded a star on Calle Ocho's "Walk of Fame." After she traveled to Cuba in 1991, she was denounced on the radio and singled out by civic leaders like César Odio, Miami's powerful City Manager—prior to his sojourn in prison for corruption. Soon after, a mob of exiles armed with crowbars and hammers urinated on her star on Calle Ocho and then began to tear it out of the sidewalk with pickaxes, lest her name degrade the honor of the community.

City Manager Carlos Jiménez asked that the Caribbean soccer tournament be denied permission to be held in Miami's Orange Bowl. He argued that it would be intolerable for exiles to witness a possible win by the Cuban team—adding that he could not guarantee that the tournament would be without incident. Citing a fear of violence against performers and patrons, the producers of the Latin Grammys yanked them from Miami in the summer of 2001.

THE POLITICAL AND CULTURAL universe of Miami is the product of four decades of seething betrayal, suspicion and conspiracies directed to and from Havana. For a fringe of hard-line exiles, conspiracy is the very oxygen of their existence. Virtually any misfortune or ill omen they will attribute to Fidel Castro—whether an upsurge in flu statistics in Miami or the attack on the World Trade Center on September 11. It was out of such thinking that the boundaries of the Castro War were drawn: any individual or business viewed as sympathetic to Havana became fair game for vigilante justice.

The war to silence the opposition in Miami and Havana began in 1959, the year Fidel Castro toppled Batista. By 1989, Miami was named "the capital of U.S. terrorism," according to Cuban-American sociologist María de los Angeles Torres, after eighteen bombs exploded at the homes and businesses of exiles seeking improved relations with Cuba. "The difference here is that the dissidents in Miami don't get sent to jail like they do in Cuba," says columnist Andrés Oppenheimer. "There is intolerance and repression. It is undeniable but it is not state-sponsored." But while it is not sponsored by the state, it is studiously overlooked by the state, according to a report by

Human Rights Watch, which concluded that Miami-Dade officials routinely turned a blind eye and, charged their critics, were complicit as well.

Although Miami is geographically part of the United States and ostensibly subject to its laws, a sampling of some of the politically motivated crimes over the last forty years suggests otherwise. According to federal investigators, between 1973 and 1976 alone there were more than one hundred politically motivated attacks in South Florida directed by anti-Castro groups.

In 1968, Orlando Bosch, a pediatrician turned terrorist, fired a bazooka from Miami's MacArthur Causeway into a Polish freighter that had traveled to Cuba. Around the same time, a close associate of Bosch's, Hector Cornillot, staged attacks against Cuba-friendly firms in Los Angeles and Miami, blowing up Mexican tourism offices, a Shell Oil office and three airline offices—Air France, Japan Airlines and Air Canada. In one two-hour period in July 1968, he set off five bombs. It would be another five years before Cornillot was finally convicted of a crime—bombing an Air Canada office in Miami Beach.

Even militant anti-Castro exiles were not safe. Among those murdered in internecine exile power struggles were Héctor Díaz Limonta, Arturo Rodríguez Vives, Ramón Donestevez, José Elías de la Torriente (murdered in his Coral Gables home while watching TV after allegedly failing to carry out a planned invasion of Cuba) and Rolando Masferrer, who was blown up in his home by a remote-control bomb.

Among the most notorious killers of the period were Valentín Hernández and Jesús Lazo, who gunned down Luciano Nieves in February 1975 for speaking out in support of dialogue with the Cuban government. Nieves was ambushed by Hernández in a hospital parking lot after visiting his eleven-year-old son. Two years earlier, Hernández had been charged with aggravated assault for beating Nieves over the head with a restaurant stool. Hernández fled during a bathroom break during his trial and was a fugitive when he killed Nieves. He remained a fugitive for two years after Nieves's murder, protected by sympathetic exiles. Less than a year later, Hernández and Lazo murdered a former president of the Bay of Pigs Association, Juan José Peruyero, outside his home in a power struggle. Hernández was finally captured in Puerto Rico in July 1977 and sentenced to life in prison. His accomplice, Jesús Lazo, has never been brought to justice.

In 1985, Miami-Dade Commissioner Javier Souto, then a state representative, sought clemency for Hernández, writing that Hernández "tried to do something to stop the agents of Soviet Imperialism to take over this nation, and the whole Western Hemisphere." Representative Ileana Ros-

Lehtinen appealed to Governor Bob Graham's "high sense of compassion for the plight of anti-communists" in a bid to have him pardon Hernández, as did numerous other local mayors, city commissioners and state legislators. In March 2001, an exile group exhorted listeners on Radio Mambí to petition Jeb Bush for Hernández's early release. Lincoln Díaz-Balart and Ileana Ros-Lehtinen urged George W. Bush to release both Hernández and Cornillot. The new President obliged in one case and allowed Cornillot out of prison.

The complicity of the Miami political establishment manifests itself on several levels—from pressuring local law enforcement to strategic neglect. In 1976, a car bomb blew off the legs of WQBA-AM news director Emilio Milián, who had condemned the ongoing wave of exile violence, very nearly killing him. Milián spent six months in a hospital riddled with shrapnel. He required major reconstructive surgery and had to learn to walk with artificial legs. U.S. Attorney Atlee Wampler obtained a four-count grand jury indictment in April 1981, hours before a five-year statute of limitations was to elapse. But the suspects, exiles Gaspar Jiménez and Gustavo Castillo (also suspects in the 1976 murder of a Cuban diplomat's bodyguard in Mexico), and a third unnamed exile, were never arrested. Wampler's successor, Stanley Marcus, dismissed the indictments without explanation. Janet Reno, who was State Attorney at the time and was expected to prosecute the case, chose to do nothing.

Between 1975 and 1983, Eduardo Arocena and his comrades from Omega 7, one of the deadliest anti-Castro vigilante groups, detonated bombs in Miami and New York, according to the FBI, killing Cuban attaché Félix García Rodríguez in New York. Upon Arocena's arrest for a second attempted murder, the chief of the 2506 Brigade of Bay of Pigs veterans told reporters, "Anyone who fights communism has my sympathy. The best communist is a dead communist." Arocena also is credited with the murder of Eulalio José Negrín, an exile who supported diplomatic relations with Cuba; Negrín was machine-gunned down as he stepped into a car with his thirteen-year-old son.

Xavier Suárez, a Harvard-educated lawyer who served as Mayor of Miami from 1985 to 1993 and again in 2000, said he "preferred to think of Arocena as a freedom fighter, not a terrorist." Along with most of the exile leadership, Suárez lobbied to have March 25, 1983, named Orlando Bosch Day, in honor of Miami's most notorious terrorist, and contributed to Bosch's defense fund. Another Miami Mayor, Maurice Ferré, defended a $10,000 grant to exile commando group Alpha 66 during his tenure in 1982, saying that the organization "has never been accused of terrorist activities inside the United States." Ferré traveled to Caracas so that he could visit Bosch during his incarceration.

Violence in Miami reached peak levels during the Reagan-Bush years, 1981–1989, when the Contra war in Nicaragua was being waged. In 1985, the FBI cited Miami as the murder capital of America, in part because of the drug traffic, in part owing to exile violence. Four bombs went off at Padrón Cigars, whose owner, Orlando Padrón, helped negotiate the release of Cuban political prisoners as part of the 1979 Dialogue. Bombs also exploded at American Airways Charter and the Nicaraguan, Mexican and Venezuelan consulates because of their relations with Cuba. In 1983, bombs exploded at five Little Havana companies and banks that did business with Cuba and at more than a dozen businesses that shipped parcels or medical aid to Cuba. In the late 1980s, South Florida Peace Coalition members were physically attacked with eggs and rocks in downtown Miami while demonstrating against U.S. aid to the Nicaraguan Contras and one couple was beaten up. A bomb was also placed in the garage of María Cristina Herrera, a Catholic activist and organizer of a conference on U.S.-Cuba relations, and another exploded at the home of Griselda Hidalgo, who supports unrestricted travel to Cuba.

Lee Tucker, the coordinator of the 1994 Americas Watch report on Miami, said at the time that she was stunned by the unwillingness of any agency to prosecute threats and intimidation in Miami. "There is no public defense of the right to free speech or the right to dissent," said Tucker. "No one at the local, state or federal level has spoken out against the violence or threats against moderates."

According to several members of the Metro-Dade police force and the FBI office in Miami who spoke on the condition of anonymity, the situation has only worsened in the last two years. They described both the FBI and local police as "paralyzed" by conflicts of interest and by unrelenting pressure from the exile leadership.

One veteran FBI agent described what he felt was the history of Miami's unique crime cycle. "To some extent, the *gangsterismo* of Havana was transported to Miami by a handful of early *batistiano* arrivals," he said, "guys like Rolando Masferrer, Havana's former police chief [Colonel Esteban] Ventura, José Miguel Battle, Orlando Piedra. And they set up shop here just like they did in Havana—running protection rackets and illegal gambling, primarily *bolita,* which flourished until the lottery became legal."

Another agent in the FBI's Miami office said that when Hector M. Pesquera, formerly the tough-talking special agent in charge of the FBI's San

Juan bureau, was transferred to Miami, spirits soared. But the hopes of the agents and police officers were quickly dashed. Pesquera, they said, began to socialize with key members of the exile leadership like Alberto Hernández (formerly of CANF), Ileana Ros-Lehtinen, Domingo Otero (another former CANF hard-liner) and Roberto Martín Pérez, a former Cuban political prisoner whose father was a Batista police captain in Havana. Pesquera, said one agent in his office, soon made a hard right turn, abandoning all investigations into exile terrorism. Instead, he decided to make his name with the Wasp network, rounding up Cuban agents in Miami and throwing the book at them. "It made him a hero to the exile honchos," complained the agent, "but we could have saved millions of dollars by picking those guys up and deporting them back to Cuba. Or we could've done a trade with Joanne Chesimard [a Black Panther fugitive living in Havana] or some fugitives we really want back from Cuba." Of particular concern was Pesquera's relationship with broadcaster Armando Pérez-Roura, who is not averse to hosting fund-raisers on his station for "freedom fighters" convicted of terrorism or murder, or in support of paramilitary operatives.

There is a long history of such fund-raising throughout Miami radio. But some of these fund-raising campaigns were little more than protection rackets, according to the FBI. " 'If you don't give X number of dollars to the Cause,' " explained radio commentator and former Broward County Assistant District Attorney Alberto Milián, Emilio's son, " 'we're going to firebomb you.' My father received many complaints about that and talked about that on his show." Although the rackets proliferated mostly in the 1970s and 1980s, misuse of funds continued through the 1990s. One Miami-Dade police officer spoke of a 1993 fund-raiser on Radio Mambí that hauled in more than half a million dollars for *la guerra*. However, not all the money found its way to the promised recipients fighting *la lucha*. "Most of it was stolen," said the detective. "We had dozens of complaints about the money, which just went into the pockets of certain people."

The agent described Orlando Bosch, who lives in Westchester, outside Miami, as "the godfather of the paramilitary groups," along with Rubén Darío and López Castro, other renowned militants. "But we cannot get the bureau to okay a wiretap on him, even though we know he's in the thick of it," he said. "We chased López Castro out of Miami and he's in Ramrod Key, but it's a perennial thing: we chase them out, they come back and go at it again. Every day we have a Neutrality Act violation because people leave from Miami to do runs on Cuba. But no one will allow us to do our job."

IN 1980, MIAMI UNDERWENT an irreversible transformation as 125,000 Cuban refugees came ashore during the Mariel Boat Lift. Although it has become an article of faith that many of the *marielitos* came from Cuban prisons or insane asylums, an investigation by a Miami-Dade grand jury found that, in fact, less than 10 percent had criminal backgrounds. Still, Miami was coping badly with even that number. They were joined by thousands of fleeing Haitians who took to the seas in the flimsiest of crafts. The same year, Miami boiled over into riots as blacks took to the streets protesting the city's history of police brutality and other excesses and the lack of prosecution. By now, Miami was awash in narcotics. "By the beginning of 1981, federal officials estimated that 70 percent of all cocaine and marijuana smuggled into the United States passed through the Miami area," reported journalist T. D. Allman. "The municipal morgue was so overcrowded that the bodies of murder victims now had to be stored in refrigerated trucks." Soon a TV series, *Miami Vice,* forever linked the city with crime and corruption.

Compounding Miami's unique history of exile violence is the fact that prosecution has been exceedingly rare or limp-wristed. The perpetrators and murderers mingle openly in the community, quietly feared by their enemies while applauded and protected by their supporters. Some have been honored and financially supported for years.

In 1990, Francisco Aruca, the head of Marazul Charters, which has been flying exiles back and forth to Cuba since 1979, started Radio Progreso as an alternative to Miami's right-wing radio. Aruca, who supports normalizing relations with Cuba, has been blasted on the radio as "a spy of Castro," a "communist" and a "traitor." Following his denunciation, three exiles broke into the station, vandalized it and beat up an employee. Twice Aruca's Marazul offices were bombed. "Initially we had many companies that signed up as sponsors for our station," says Aruca, "but they would call and say they had received bomb threats, death threats against employees and threatened product boycotts." Although his station has proven to be a success with listeners, Aruca was forced to bankroll it himself for a period. "The *batistiano* element here is very small in their numbers," charged the provocative and pint-sized Aruca, "but they control the media and the political machinery and just about all business contracts handed out in Dade County."

Following the September 11 attacks on the World Trade Center and the Pentagon, Francisco Aruca wrote an open letter to President Bush: "The events of Tuesday, September 11, 2001, cannot be overlooked and will remain with us for the rest of our lives. . . . Terrorism, political assassinations, intimidation and violence are a fact of life that many of us in South Florida have come to know for decades. . . . On the streets of Miami some of these perpetrators walk freely and with impunity." However, Aruca's entreaty fell on deaf ears. In fact, the Bush administration continued to release from prison several of the most notorious exile criminals.

Side by side with its violent history, corruption has been a growth industry in Miami, where not a few civil servants seem to spend much of their time keeping themselves out of jail. The depth and breadth of corruption in Miami is unparalleled in the U.S. More often than not, it has been the intervention of state or federal prosecutors, not local authorities, that has brought local politicians into court. Jessica Reilly, a former corruption prosecutor in the office of Katharine Fernández Rundle, the State Attorney of Miami-Dade, said the office was riddled with conflicts of interest and "paralyzed by an unwillingness to make waves politically."

Critics of Rundle, such as Alberto Milián, who ran against her in 2000, point out that she has rarely pursued a corruption case and never an instance of exile violence. "Kathy Rundle is the best thing that ever happened to public corruption," declares the outspoken Milián, who calls himself "a law-and-order Republican" and who hammers Rundle and most of Miami's leadership regularly on his radio show. "Her number one priority is protecting her friends who put her in office," Milián charges in his trademark rapid-fire delivery. "I'll give you a case: Church & Tower [now MasTec], owned by the Mas Canosa family, with seventeen million dollars of fraudulent billing to the county, she spends five years investigating and doesn't hand out a single indictment to anybody linked to the Mas Canosa operation." Rundle did charge a subcontractor employed by Church & Tower, Antonio Reyes, with swindling the county, but many viewed Reyes merely as a scapegoat for the scam. Even the presiding judge left no doubt that he concurred with Milián. "I'm not going to get into my personal opinions about who might have been charged," declared a sarcastic Judge Sanford Blake during sentencing, "but that contract was a relief act for anyone who could get a piece of it."

Nor does Milián have kind words for Rundle's predecessor, Janet Reno, whom he blames, along with the former U.S. Attorney, for not prosecuting his father's alleged assailants, Gaspar Jiménez and Gustavo Castillo. "One of the reasons that Miami became a banana republic is because Janet Reno created an environment where prosecutors simply would not investigate, [or,] when confronted with overwhelming evidence, would find a way *not* to prosecute."

The fact that judges in the state of Florida are elected, leaving them more vulnerable to corruption, has deepened the taint of South Florida's judiciary. In April 1993, Operation Court Broom, conducted by the U.S. Attorney, investigated a half dozen judges for bribery and kickbacks. Two judges pleaded guilty, two were convicted, and one was acquitted. Another state judge resigned rather than face charges.

In the last decade there have been dozens of indictments of Miami-Dade's ruling elite. In defiance of satire, politicians charged with and convicted of vote fraud, embezzlement and larceny often get second and third acts—a veritable revolving door in what is called the "pay to play" arena of Miami political theater. "Miami has a prevalence of petty crooks that run for office for the sole purpose of stealing," observed the *Herald*'s salty columnist Carl Hiaasen. "The list is endless. And, all you can do is laugh, put them in jail and wait for the next one to come along."

In 1996, a federal sting aptly named Operation Greenpalm brought down several key players in Miami's political firmament. Miami City Commissioner Miller Dawkins was sentenced to twenty-seven months in prison after entering a guilty plea on charges of taking bribes to influence a city contract. The biggest catch, however, was Miami's powerful City Manager, César Odio, who was sentenced to a year in prison after pleading guilty to charges of obstructing a federal probe. Odio's prosecution sent a chill through Miami's elite. A close friend and ally of Jorge Mas Canosa, he was regarded as untouchable. But Miami takes care of its own, and city commissioners rewarded Odio, *while* he was serving his jail sentence, with a lifetime pension of $58,000 a year.

The following years were banner ones for indictments of county and city commissioners. Another Miami city commissioner, the flamboyant Humberto Hernández, pleaded guilty to money laundering and mortgage fraud charges and is serving a four-year prison sentence. Hernández, who was reelected as commissioner while under indictment, was also sentenced to a year in prison for his role in trying to cover up the vote fraud in the 1997 mayoral election and was disbarred from practicing law. He appealed the rulings on the grounds that his lawyer was having an affair with his wife at the time of the prosecution, but lost.

One of the city's most stellar graft and corruption scandals in recent years centered on the Port of Miami, whose director, Carmen Lunetta, was indicted along with two port contractors for misusing public funds in 1998. Those charges were eventually dropped, but Lunetta was found guilty of funneling $20,000 in illegal political campaign contributions to dozens of politicians and sentenced to six months of house arrest. One of the politicos on his payroll, Hialcah councilwoman Marie Rovira, was indicted on federal charges of taking a salary from the Port of Miami for a phantom job and sentenced to twelve months' probation. Another was Pedro Reboredo, one of Miami-Dade's most colorful commissioners and an indefatigable anti-Castro activist. The previous year, he had paid a fine to settle campaign finance violations, and in February 2001 a grand jury indicted him for hiring two close friends for no-show jobs at County Hall. The geriatric pair, ninety-year-old Adelfa Pérez-Cruz and seventy-eight-year-old Benito Mongeotti, had been on the county's payroll for almost eight years.

State Senator Alberto Gutman and his wife were both indicted in 1998 on federal charges of Medicare fraud, money laundering and witness tampering. Gutman pleaded guilty and was sentenced to five years in federal prison, his wife to six months of house arrest. While Gutman was under indictment, Miami voters reelected him.

On April 22, 2002, Miami-Dade Commissioner Miriam Alonso, along with her husband and an aide, were arrested and charged with misusing public funds, unlawful compensation and exploitation of her political office.

Even when corruption is prosecuted in Miami, it may not be so much in the interests of the public as in the interests of certain members of the ruling elite. No case in Miami revealed this duality with greater clarity than the prosecution of Hialeah's colorful mayor Raúl Martínez on federal racketeering and extortion charges in a ballot-tampering case in 1990. Martínez's conviction was reversed on appeal in 1996.

One cannot get the full measure of Raúl Martínez from photographs or television video. Few contemporary politicians press the flesh as deeply and well as Martínez, who has presided over Hialeah for twenty-two years, through seven terms. Although lacking the telegenic looks of fellow Democrat Alex Penelas, Martínez commands any room he steps into. A pothole populist, Martínez typically works a fourteen-hour day and rules his Cuban-American enclave with the aplomb of Fiorello La Guardia and the pork-barrel politics of Huey Long.

The Martínez office dispenses cradle-to-grave constituent services, and seemingly twenty-four-hour-a-day hand-holding. Consequently, Hialeans have elected him to office continuously since 1977, first as their state representative, then as Mayor, and appear willing to continue to do so—whether he's indicted again or not. While waiting for Martínez, I listened to one of his secretaries field calls from constituents seeking everything from advice to directions to favors. Each is accorded the courtesy of royals. One man called hoping to recover his car without a fee—which was towed, he admitted, for good reason. Nevertheless, he was patiently directed to the appropriate person in the police department by name for assistance.

Martínez is a large, strapping man who likes to dress well. His mostly silver hair is carefully coiffed. He is partial to monogrammed shirts with broad cuffs and black onyx cufflinks and his left hand sports a glittering 18 karat gold watch. But what really sets him off in the world of Miami exile politics is his allegiance to the Democratic Party.

In 1989, a special election was held for the congressional seat held by Claude Pepper, the veteran Democratic congressman, who had died at the age of eighty-nine, having held the seat since 1962. Martínez claimed to be Pepper's presumed successor. "Claude and I had been good friends for years," he said, "so in 1982, when they were redrawing the districts, I asked Claude Pepper to include my house in the district, which he did. So I know how the system can be manipulated." But just as Martínez was planning his run, he was told that he would be indicted on federal racketeering and extortion charges brought by the office of the acting U.S. Attorney, Dexter Lehtinen, the husband of Ileana Ros-Lehtinen. "It was a politically motivated indictment," Martínez said, slapping his broad desk, "because that way he could enhance his wife's political career."

Dexter Lehtinen countered with several salient points. "One, I recused myself from that case because I knew he would say things like that," said Lehtinen. "Raúl Martínez's problems preceded me and succeeded me into a Democratic administration. Raúl is always trying to divert the issue."

Nevertheless, ever since the indictment was brought, Martínez has ceaselessly charged on the radio, and to anyone who will listen, that he was the victim of backstabbing exile politicos who wanted Pepper's seat to become Republican. At the hub of the scheme, claimed Martínez, were Enrique Ros, Ileana's father, a savvy but low-profile Miami kingmaker; her husband, Dexter Lehtinen; the late Jorge Mas Canosa; and Ros-Lehtinen's campaign manager, Jeb Bush. "I have witnesses who saw me [talking to] Enrique," Martínez charged, "and I say, 'Enrique, why is Dexter doing this to me?' And Enrique says, 'Nothing's going to happen to you because you're like a son to me and Amanda [his wife].' " And a surprising number of both Democrats and Republicans say they believe him. "There is no question that Dexter went after Raúl so that his wife, Ileana, could get that seat," echoed Alberto Milián, who reminded me that he was a Republican. Sensitive observers see some truth on both sides. "Every Miami politician has been enriched, and it's doubtful that Martínez was an exception," said a veteran

Herald reporter, "but since when has corruption been investigated in Miami-Dade?"

Selective prosecution is not the only tool for influencing elections in South Florida. Vote fraud in Miami-Dade is a resilient perennial. In 1997 the results of the mayoral race for the city of Miami were invalidated after an investigation found all manner of irregularities, including ballots signed by dead people. Mayor Xavier Suárez was forced to step down in a matter of months, replaced by his opponent, Joe Carollo, who was represented by Kendall Coffey. "I don't think any other place in the United States has comparable voter fraud," said Coffey. "Miami has a legacy of lawlessness going back to the 1920s. It's part a function of geography, and wave after wave of immigration. Plus it's a debtor's paradise, because of the bankruptcy laws that allow scofflaws to keep their homes and assets, and finally, the judges here run for office."

The 1997 tainted-election scandal did nothing to dampen the political ambitions of Ángel González, who admitted he had taken part in the vote fraud and was sentenced to an $800 fine and one year's probation. In November 2001, González ran for Miami city commissioner from District 1 and won, proving the irrelevance of corruption in Miami. There were doubts as to whether González even lived in the district—he had listed four different addresses. One address was the residence of Guillermo Novo, one of the attempted assassins of Fidel Castro, currently in prison in Panama.

González's disreputable record was the subject of several shows by Alberto Milián. Following his father's death in 2001, Alberto took over his show *Habla El Pueblo* (The People Speak) on La Poderosa. But after repeatedly questioning González's participation in the 1997 vote fraud, Milián was fired by the station's owner, Jorge Rodríguez. Two nights before the election, Rodríguez turned over Milián's time slot to González to improvise his own infomercial. "He did what any self-respecting censor would do," wrote the *Herald*'s Liz Balmaseda, "turn the microphones over to a politician with a crooked past who had been targeted on the commentator's show." When two *Miami Herald* editorial board writers penned an editorial condemning Milián's firing, the newspaper's publisher, Alberto Ibargüen, spiked it from the paper.

SOME EXILES CLAIM that the scrutiny of the violence and corruption that has plagued Miami has been motivated by critics with an anti-exile agenda. They point out, accurately, that corruption has always been rife in South

Florida, predating the mass exodus of Cubans. They argue that there is a systemic prejudice against exiles—a charge that was amplified during the Elián affair. This may have been the case in the 1960s, but for the last decades the evidence points to the opposite conclusion. Cuban exiles are, in fact, the most privileged immigrants in the history of the United States and have been the recipients of more taxpayer generosity than any other ethnic group.

It is generally agreed that there have been three waves of Cuban immigration: a first wave who fled the Revolution, a second group who supported the Revolution but saw it hijacked by Fidel Castro, and the last who wanted better jobs, clothes and cars. The first wave of Cuban exiles—generally wealthy and highly educated and often *batistianos*—were well positioned to lobby effectively for their brethren. Aided by the agendas of ten feckless Presidents anxious to corner the Miami electorate, exiles carved out an exclusive and proprietary niche for themselves in Washington. In 1966, Congress passed the Cuban Adjustment Act, granting permanent residency to any Cuban who made it to the U.S. and stayed one year. During the Clinton years, the policy was extended to any Cuban who makes it to shore—the infamous "wet foot/dry foot" policy. All other immigrants from around the world are routinely shipped back—unless they can meet the elusive threshold of proving persecution in their home country. Cuba is the only country that is guaranteed 20,000 visas annually for its citizens to come legally to the U.S.

There are other perks awarded solely to Cuban immigrants. Nelson Valdés, who came over as one of the Pedro Pan children sent ahead by his parents to the States, said he received benefits that not even American children were entitled to. "As Pedro Pan kids, we went to private high school and the U.S. government paid for it," said Valdés, a historian of the Cuban diaspora who teaches at the University of New Mexico. "Moreover, when we finished high school and wanted to go to universities, there was the 'Cuban loan,' which basically meant that we could go to a loan office at a university and borrow whatever we wanted, which very few ever paid back. Then there is the Small Business Administration. In the mid-1960s, Cuban-Americans could get nifty loans at a rate below what anyone else could. This is also part of the Cuban exile success story."

In 2000, the *Miami Herald* published a survey concluding that although Hispanics made up 58 percent of the population of Miami-Dade County, they held only 25 percent of the top slots of government positions. But columnist Max Castro was quick to point out that not all "top jobs are equal in power," and enumerated a hefty list of power jobs held by Cubans, including the head of Miami-Dade's public university, the head of the community college system, the State Attorney, the county police chief, the fire chief, the Mayor of Miami, the publisher of the *Miami Herald* (half Cuban), the presiding partner of Miami's biggest law firm, the superintendent of the Miami-Dade County public schools and the Executive Mayor of Miami-Dade County. And only those exiles who endorse a hard line on Cuba hold these coveted and well-paid positions. Those who stray ideologically do not last long.

Each year, Miami's guardians of cultural and ideological purity redouble their efforts to keep their city free of the influence of their island brethren. But sometimes the enemy is sitting among them. In 1995, the legendary singer Celina González, who stayed behind in Cuba and embraced the Revolution, was dining at Victor's Café, an eatery favored by the exile elite that has since been shuttered. She was in Miami visiting family on one of her frequent crossings—as so many Cubans do. In 1990, González's visa to perform in the States was revoked at the behest of the Miami exile leadership. Since then she moved quietly around Miami on her visits. But on this November night, some restaurant patrons spotted the diva and beseeched her to sing. Finally, she agreed and belted out an a cappella rendering of "Guantanamera" with her trademark pipes, described by Lydia Martin of the *Herald* as "an unmistakable voice that resonates of Cuba itself, of sweet cane fields and palm-thatched *bohíos*, of rum-fueled feasts for Chango and fragrant *despojos*—cleansings, in the name of Yemayá." Before the chanteuse was finished, the entire restaurant was on its feet, cheering with tears welling in their eyes, their rancorous heartbreak and exile politics momentarily stilled.

CHAPTER 5

THE MAN WHO WOULD BE KING

Sin patria pero sin amo.
Without a country but without a master.

JOSÉ MARTÍ

"**W**E WILL NEVER FORGET our friends," Jorge Mas Canosa was wont to say, "and we will always remember our enemies." And no one ever doubted the steadfastness of his memory. On August 19, 1994, Jorge Mas Canosa sauntered out of the White House Cabinet Room following a ninety-minute meeting with the President of the United States. He was irrepressibly gleeful. The controversial tycoon, who had long dominated South Florida politics from the bully pulpit of his Cuban American National Foundation, had just pulled off another coup. A little more than three years later, Mas Canosa would be felled by cancer, but in his last years, with the acquiescence of Bill Clinton, he would reformulate America's Cuba policy, recalibrating its tone to that of the height of the Cold War.

President Clinton, dressed in jeans, cowboy boots and a western shirt, had left his own birthday party to meet with *el jefe* of the exile government-in-waiting. Aware of Clinton's vacillating nature, the fifty-five-year-old Mas Canosa made sure his would be the final word. With Vice President Al Gore, Attorney General Janet Reno, Florida Governor Lawton Chiles and a small delegation of Miami politicos in attendance, he thumped the table as he spoke, demanding that the President punish Fidel Castro for the current refugee crisis. "You must kick out the last leg of the stool," he insisted. Mas Canosa later regaled Miami's Spanish language television viewers with a dramatic reenactment of his presidential conquest. *"No tengas piedad!"*—Have no pity!—he claimed to have bellowed at Clinton. And twice, he said, he found the President "looking into my eyes."

With the exception of a naval blockade to encircle the island, which Clinton said he would reserve as a possible future option, the President signed off on almost all of Mas Canosa's wish list: severing all direct flight service between Miami and Cuba, reducing the financial remittances that could be sent to relatives in Cuba, detaining all rafters at U.S. bases at Guantánamo or the INS's South Florida Krome facility and expanding the broadcasting of TV and Radio Martí into Cuba—both under the control of Mas Canosa, who served as chairman of their advisory board.

Even Mas Canosa, long inured to the perks of being the *caudillo,* or political boss, of Miami, seemed somewhat dazed at the degree of his success. "Bill Clinton deserves our gratitude and recognition," he said with giddy excitement. And when Fidel Castro two days later charged that the U.S. policy was in the stranglehold of "the fascist Mafia of Miami," the chairman of CANF was unperturbed. "I have very good company," he purred on national television. "I stand with the President of the United States."

How a Democrat from Arkansas with little discernible interest in foreign policy got tangled up with the roughest, toughest crowd this side of the *mujihadeen* posed an interesting question. Beginning with the presidential campaign of 1992 until his death in 1997, Mas Canosa, a devout Republican, would rack up victory after victory with Clinton on issues he had been rebuffed on by his ideological soul mates, Ronald Reagan and George Bush. The savvy exile impresario had quickly sized up Clinton's willingness to trade Cuba policy for immediate political gains and adroitly played him off against Republicans.

In early 1992, George Bush declared his intention of vetoing the proposed Embargo-tightening Cuban Democracy Act. Known on Capitol Hill as the Torricelli Bill, it was sponsored by New Jersey congressman Robert Torricelli, arguably Mas Canosa's most prized disciple. Prior to the exile leader's patronage, Torricelli had opposed the Embargo and had even visited Cuba in 1988 and had praised the island country: "Living standards are not high," he had said upon his return, "but the homelessness, hunger and disease that is witnessed in much of Latin America does not appear evident." In 1989, Mas Canosa introduced himself to the congressman, then a newcomer on the House's Committee on Western Hemisphere Affairs. The two became close allies and good friends, with Torricelli enjoying sailing trips on Mas Canosa's yacht. From 1990 onward, CANF and Mas Canosa would be faithful and generous contributors to all of Torricelli's campaigns, and the congressman disavowed his former comments on Cuba.

However strong George Bush's dislike of Castro, he was at heart a free trader and knew a flawed and troubling piece of legislation when he saw one. The proposed legislation was rife with extraterritorial provisions, banning

U.S. subsidiaries abroad from trading with Cuba, introducing civil penalties of up to $50,000 for Americans violating the Trading with the Enemy Act and barring ships engaged in trade with Cuba from U.S. ports for six months after a stop in Cuba. The curious coincidence that the one exemption written into the bill allowed U.S. telecommunications firms to do business with Cuba and that Mas Canosa presided over one of the largest phone cable systems in Florida prompted Beltway wags to dub the legislation the "Jorge Mas Canosa Telecommunications Act."

Gloomy at the prospect of losing Florida, the fourth most populous state, Clinton had come to believe that Jorge Mas Canosa was just the man to avert such a destiny. Over a span of several weeks and a flurry of private conversations, the wily exile plutocrat convinced the Governor of Arkansas that a foray into exile politics would boost him just enough to put him over the goal line. It would be a tall order. After all, exiles had forged a rock-solid bond with the Republican Party since the early 1960s. There were two blots of Democratic infamy in the minds of hard-line exiles. First was April 1961, when JFK held back air support in the Bay of Pigs invasion, and the second was October 1962, when Kennedy negotiated, rather than bombed, his way out of the Cuban Missile Crisis. "There was so much rage and feelings of betrayal," recounts exile historian Nelson Valdés, "that some exiles celebrated in the streets when Kennedy was killed. No one wants to talk about that now, but it happened." Bill Clinton was well aware of the odds against him, and Mas Canosa was well aware of the risk of such an alliance. But if George Bush had the temerity to defy him on the Torricelli Bill, then, by God, he would be made to pay.

And so, following an initial meeting with the Arkansas Governor at the Tampa airport, the exile strongman assured his brethren that they "need not fear a Bill Clinton administration." Then on the afternoon of April 23, 1992, Clinton, who had been perilously short of funds, stood before three hundred of Miami's wealthiest Cubans at Victor's Café. "I think this administration has missed a big opportunity to put the hammer down on Fidel Castro and Cuba," Clinton told the rapt crowd, pausing to let the applause wash over him before delivering the goods: "I have read the Torricelli-Graham Bill and I like it!" The bill, which had been hopelessly waterlogged in the Congress for more than a year, suddenly roared to life. Moreover, Clinton's championing of the bill threatened Republican hegemony over exile voters and made Bush appear soft on Castro. Faced with the potential loss of a valued constituency, Bush backpedaled and agreed to sign the bill.

Clinton's pandering paid off in several ways. When he walked out of

Victor's restaurant, he had pledges of more than $125,000. Earlier in the day, he raked in $150,000 at another event attended primarily by CANF members and, within a month, he received another $100,000. Soon the figure from Florida would climb to well over $1 million, a good deal of it from exiles, making it the largest state contributor to the Clinton campaign. There were invaluable votes secured as well. In August 1992 Mas Canosa and Clinton dined at Versailles on Calle Ocho, the restaurant and headquarters for Miami's armchair generals.

Some attributed Clinton's cave-in to his traumatic loss of the Arkansas governor's mansion in 1980, which he blamed on the unwanted exodus of refugees into his home state from the Mariel Boat Lift. But Jeff Eller, who worked closely on Clinton's 1992 Florida campaign, felt it was more a question of character than politics. "We all knew that there was no percentage in wooing the Cuban vote. It's a Republican vote," said Eller. Hard-line exiles have made the Democratic Party pay in perpetuity for the treason of JFK's failure to supply air support for the Bay of Pigs invasion. In 1980 and 1984, more than 80 percent of Florida's Cuban-Americans voted for Ronald Reagan. In 1988, 82 percent voted for George Bush, and in 1992, 70 percent voted for him again. "But the way Clinton works is that if there are ten people in a room and nine like him but one doesn't, he becomes completely focused and hell-bent on getting that one guy to like him. And that's what happened with him and the Miami exiles. In order to get the holdouts to like him, he ended up giving them everything they wanted," Eller recounted.

Whatever his motives, Clinton had pitched an arrow into the heart of the Bush camp. He had forced a wedge among hard-line exiles, many of whom had never supported a Democrat. A checkmated George Bush was sent reeling from what he and his team regarded as an explicit betrayal by Mas Canosa, from whom they expected lockstep loyalty. Indeed, the relationship between the Bush family and the Mas Canosa family, as well as the Foundation, would never be the same. But Mas Canosa had extraordinary political instincts and invariably picked winners. In 1994, he backed Lawton Chiles over Jeb Bush in the Florida gubernatorial race, further souring relations with the Bush family. Both his political horses, Clinton and Chiles, won. Then again, exile politics are not called the "third rail" for nothing (the third rail being the rail that electrocutes one on touch). "In the exile world, vengeance trumps all," former U.S. diplomat Cresencio Arcos opined. "Revenge and vengeance are the watchwords."

Clinton persevered. In 1996, he finally carried Florida, taking 70 percent of the exile vote. The price, to a large extent, was the passage of the

Helms-Burton bill, officially known as the Cuban Liberty and Democratic Solidarity Act, which demonstrably tightened the Embargo and codified it into law. No longer would an American President simply be able to dispense with the Embargo by a stroke of the pen, as had been the case for four decades. After Helms-Burton, the Embargo can only be terminated by the agreement of the U.S. Congress.

The law allows Americans to sue foreign companies doing business in Cuba, a statute that was fiercely opposed by all U.S. allies. Although Helms-Burton entitles a President to waive the lawsuit provision every six months—and none have dared to do otherwise—it remains a contentious and burdensome dispute that Washington must revisit and endure biannually.

Helms-Burton rapidly fell victim to the "Christmas tree" syndrome—a process through which congressional legislation is freighted down by a plethora of "ornaments" awarded to special interests. There was a provision that further benefited Mas Canosa's business interests, forbidding any American from investing in Cuba's domestic telecommunications network, presumably to eliminate any competition down the road. And in a transparent quid pro pro to Clinton's friend and donor Pepe Fanjul, the bill prohibited imports not only of Cuban sugar but of any product containing sugar of Cuban origin. Bacardi Rum, which lobbied fiercely for the legislation, also did well. Helms-Burton cut U.S. aid to Russia and other former Soviet republics unless they terminated their aid to Cuba, and reduced American contributions to the World Bank and other financial institutions if they provided loans to Cuba. In short, Helms-Burton sought to internationalize the U.S. Embargo and encouraged nuisance litigation. Since Helms-Burton became law in 1996, more than eighty lawsuits have been filed, all but eight dismissed outright.

Many foreign policy wags were surprised that Clinton would sign such a retrograde piece of legislation, one that capitulated to a narrow segment of exiles while imperiling U.S. relations with its allies. Dan Fisk, one of Jesse Helms's aides who worked on the bill, was also said to be surprised. He had inserted the Embargo codification clause, planning to use it as a bargaining chip, he told one adversary, never believing that Clinton would agree to it. Until then, the Clinton administration policy had been crafted to ensure that it was not "Castro-centric" but rather "people-centric," according to Richard Feinberg, who dealt with Cuba policy on the National Security Council. Some Clinton aides blamed the bill's passage on Clinton's National Security Adviser, Sanford Berger. "People warned [Clinton] not to sign it," said the aide. "Madeleine [Albright, then ambassador to the United Nations] was against it, as were most of us. But Sandy convinced him that he needed the political cover in Florida." Peter Tarnoff, Under Secretary for Political Affairs at the State Department, argued that its passage was guaranteed once Fidel Castro shot down two planes piloted by members of the exile group Brothers to the Rescue on February 22, 1996. "Once the shoot-down occurred, it was all over," said Tarnoff. "They had the votes for a veto override. And it would have been an *even* worse bill."

In terms of U.S. public relations, the Torricelli and Helms-Burton bills have been symbolically toxic. Both are starkly reminiscent of the infamous Platt Amendment of 1901—which codified U.S. control over Cuba, allowing the U.S. to intervene militarily at any time. The two bills dictate the present and future terms of Cuba's economic, social and political systems—as if the island nation were an American colony. Under Helms-Burton, the U.S. Embargo cannot be lifted until a host of requirements are met, including the establishment of a transitional government, legalization of all political activity, release of all political prisoners and a commitment to free multiparty elections within eighteen months. Moreover, the transitional government cannot include Fidel or Raúl Castro. "These laws truly out-Platt Platt," wrote historian Jane Franklin, while ennobling Castro's revolutionary outlaw status.

But Clinton was not finished with his attempts to mollify hard-liners. Congress slipped in, and Clinton signed, Section 211 in the 1999 Omnibus Appropriations bill. It was drafted primarily by Otto Reich, an exile lobbyist for Bacardi Rum who was paid $600,000 by the distillery and was a former Reagan-Bush official allied with the Iran-Contra effort. Reich would become George W. Bush's controversial choice to run the State Department's Western Hemisphere desk—requiring a recess appointment. Known in Cuba policy circles as the Bacardi Act, Section 211 denied trademark protection to products of Cuban businesses confiscated by the Cuban government after the Revolution, a provision keenly sought by the Bacardi family. In 1973, the Arechabala family had allowed their Havana Club rum trademark to lapse. Three years later the Cuban government registered the name and in 1993 went into a joint venture with the French liquor giant Pernod Ricard to distribute the rum. The legislation was slipped into the four-thousand-page appropriations bill by Florida's retiring Senator Connie Mack as a parting gift to exile special interest groups. It promptly put the U.S. on a collision course of expensive lawsuits, almost always on the losing side, with the European Union and World Trade Organization over trademark protection for years to come.

The Torricelli Bill was said to be virtually dictated by Mas Canosa. "Anything the Foundation wants, it gets," quipped one Torricelli aide, with a re-signed shrug. Before its passage, Torricelli declared his intentions were to "wreak havoc on that island," and prophesied that Castro would fall within three months after his bill was enacted. He couldn't have been more wrong: its passage only emboldened and reinvigorated Castro, who was quick to in-voke José Martí's nationalist rallying cry: "I have lived inside the monster [the U.S.] and know its entrails." Ironically, neither law came close to achiev-ing its desired effect: foreign investment continues to come into Cuba—not at its optimum level, but at one more manageable, and thus perhaps more at-tractive to Fidel Castro.

Many Embargo critics and the majority of dissidents living in Cuba have long argued that American trade legislation against Cuba effectively keeps Fidel Castro in power. Indeed, some Cuba scholars are convinced that Fidel Castro deliberately ushered in Helms-Burton with his decision to shoot down the two Brothers to the Rescue airplanes. While Helms-Burton was being debated early on, Castro told Robert Pastor, formerly Carter's NSC point man on Latin America, that he saw its passage as an opportunity to showcase his country's victimization. "This is a chance to reinvigorate Cuban nationalism," Castro told Pastor, "and to ally with America's allies against America."

In the days prior to the shoot-down, a delegation of visiting Americans including the late Congressman Joe Moakley of Massachusetts met with Ri-cardo Alarcón, president of Cuba's National Assembly. At one point, Alar-cón took aside a prominent American businessman and asked his opinion concerning a hypothetical scenario: "What do you think would happen if we shot down the Brothers to the Rescue's planes?" The businessman told Alar-cón that it would provoke a disastrous response, according to Medea Ben-jamín, who heads Global Exchange, a San Francisco–based anti-Embargo organization, and had organized the delegation. "Alarcón just listened qui-etly." Benjamín observed that the savvy and pragmatic Alarcón seemed trou-bled by these private inquiries. Indeed, Alarcón was seeking outside opinion and counsel as he built his case, hoping to dissuade Castro from just such a course of action.

A week earlier, Alarcón had asked Congressman Moakley the very same hypothetical. And on yet another occasion, he queried retired Admiral John Stockton along the same lines. All three men concurred that any such action would have catastrophic implications for U.S.-Cuba relations.

In fact, the stage had been set for a shoot-down some months earlier. On December 26, 1995, Fidel Castro gave an especially hard-line speech to the

National Assembly in which he chastised owners of the *paladares,* the family-run restaurants, about "getting rich off the backs of the ordinary Cubans." He threatened to institute an income tax, and gave every indication that he was anxious and apprehensive that the capitalistic opening in Cuba was going too fast and needed to be slowed down.

It was a period of dark anxiety in Cuba. I remember speaking with several grim-faced owners of *paladares* who said they would have to shut down, as there would be no profit once the new taxes were imposed. But the issue that had triggered the ominous atmospherics in the Consejo de Estado, the Cuban Offices of State, was the so-called Track Two provision crafted by Clinton aide Richard Nuccío. Announced in October 1995, it sought to expand people-to-people contacts outside the Cuban government and the funding of nongovernmental organizations. The naming of the provision was, unfortunately, acutely offensive to the Cubans, who recalled that Track Two was the code name for the U.S. strategy to destabilize the Allende government in Chile in the early 1970s. Castro responded with alarm bordering on paranoia.

Juan Antonio Blanco, a distinguished intellectual who ran the Félix Varela Foundation, one of Cuba's nongovernmental organizations, worried at the time about the groups being "demonized by the government as subversive." He lowered his voice when we talked in Havana about the process of becoming a *non-persona.* "When they shut down your foundation, you become a nonperson, and then anything can happen to you," he said nervously. (Several years later, he was allowed to leave Cuba and settled in Montreal, where he now works at Human Rights Watch.) The ongoing power struggle in the Politburo had accelerated and the *históricos*—revolutionary extremists—were winning. In a moment of prescient clarity, Blanco warned that he was quite certain a Castro-generated crisis would happen *before* the next U.S. election—in order to put the brakes on change.

On February 24, 1996, Fidel Castro disregarded the pleas of Alarcón and other moderates and ordered that two planes flown by Brothers to the Rescue be shot down. Four Cuban-Americans, including three U.S. citizens, were killed by Cuban MiGs. Founded by exile José Basulto in 1991, Brothers to the Rescue's purpose was to save rafters foundering in the Florida Straits. In its first five years, the group assisted in the rescue of thousands of *balseros,* with Basulto flying hundreds of missions in his own Cessna.

Considerable debate ensued over the degree of provocation engendered by these flights. It was true that the Cuban government had repeatedly warned the U.S. to halt the flights, which had previously flown into Cuban airspace and had even buzzed over Havana dropping leaflets. Certainly, if the reverse were true, the U.S. would not have hesitated to respond militarily. Indeed, the U.S. had been told that dire consequences would result from future flights but did little to prevent the impending catastrophe. But it was also true that on this occasion, according to American intelligence, the planes had not strayed into Cuba's airspace.

Clinton declared the Cuban government to be "repressive, violent and scornful of international law." Madeleine Albright famously attacked Castro at the United Nations as not having *"cojones"* and marched off to Miami's Orange Bowl for a flamboyant show of support for the exiles. Within weeks, the Helms-Burton bill sailed through Congress and received Clinton's signature. Clinton also suspended charter travel to Havana, which primarily punished exiles wanting to visit their relatives.

The following year, the families of the four deceased pilots sued Cuba in federal court in Miami and won the largest single award against a foreign state, a whopping $187 million. Still, they had almost no chance of laying hands on Cuba's frozen funds until Bill Clinton, on the day before he left office, reversed four decades of American diplomatic policy. While dishing out pardons, Clinton agreed to tap into Cuba's assets frozen in the U.S. to pay the pilots' families. With a stroke of a pen, he jumped the four exile families ahead of six thousand Americans who had previous claims, some going back to 1959.

Brothers to the Rescue had also been infiltrated by Cuban double agents, one of whom was Juan Pablo Roque. Hours prior to the shoot-down, Roque fled Miami and returned to Cuba. His jilted wife, Ana Margarita Martínez, would later sue the government of Cuba for "rape"—an unprecedented charge—and win an astonishing award of more than $27 million in damages in a Miami courtroom, which she hopes to collect from the frozen assets.

Clinton seemed to be of two minds about Cuba. Although he signed off on the most retrograde legislation on Cuba since the Platt Amendment, he would later loosen the noose in other respects: increasing remittances, expanding people-to-people contacts, permitting more direct charter flights to Havana from the U.S., allowing food sales to independent entities and upgrading phone service and Western Union service.

Prior to Helms-Burton, Castro told me in a 1994 interview that he "respected" Clinton and called his wife, Hillary, "a beautiful woman." But as dissent growled anew, Castro played his trump card once again, opening the gates to anyone who wanted to leave in early 1994. While Mas Canosa was getting the deal he wanted from Clinton, so was Fidel Castro. In 1995, in secret negotiations conducted by his U.S. point man, Ricardo Alarcón, Castro finally secured an immigration package out of the U.S. that sanctioned twenty thousand annual visas for Cubans seeking to emigrate and instituted the practical but controversial policy of returning rafters picked up on the high seas.

It was Mas Canosa's outrage over Clinton's direct diplomacy with Cuba that led to his crusade for the Helms-Burton legislation, ensuring that no President would ever override him again. In 1996, when Clinton faced reelection, Mas Canosa allied himself with his opponent, Bob Dole.

LIKE THE MAJORITY of Cubans, Jorge Mas Canosa was industrious and hardworking, starting out as a dishwasher at the Fontainebleau hotel in Miami and later working as a milkman. At the time of his death at the age of fifty-eight, Mas Canosa was worth well in excess of $400 million. His company, MasTec Inc., formed in 1994 by acquiring a competitor, was valued at over $700 million. When he wasn't globetrotting drumming up anti-Castro support or lobbying for business contracts, he lived with his wife, Irma, behind electric gates in a large but shapeless home in Pinecrest, a suburb in southwestern Miami. Perched on the roof was a huge satellite dish, and he told friends that inside he had a state-of-the-art communications system and was ready to take over the command of Cuba at a moment's notice.

Jorge Mas Canosa was born in Santiago de Cuba in 1939, one of five children. The son of a career army officer and veterinarian, he early on developed a passion for intrigue and politics. His younger brother, Ricardo, recalled a terrifying day in 1956 in Santiago when Rolando Masferrer and his Tigres, the dreaded paramilitary group active during the Batista years, stormed and ransacked their family home. "Jorge was doing counterrevolutionary work," recounted Ricardo, who said they were probably spared a worse fate due to their father's status in the army. "My father was in the military and they told him that he had seventy-two hours to get Jorge out of the country."

Mas Canosa's father, Ramón Emilio Mas, hustled him out of Cuba and enrolled him at Presbyterian Junior College in Maxton, North Carolina, in 1956. By all accounts, Mas Canosa's father was well regarded and not averse to taking personal risks. Two unrelated men told me in Havana in the mid-1990s that Mas Canosa's father had engineered their release from the Moncada garrison, where they were certain to face torture and probable death. Mas Canosa returned to Santiago a week after Castro seized power in early

January 1959, and briefly attended law school at Oriente University. But he soon fell afoul of the new government and was arrested for plastering anti-Castro stickers on buildings. Mas Canosa often regaled friends with the story of his arrest. "God came to my rescue. I delivered a beautiful piece of oratory," he said. His fervor and loquaciousness so impressed his captors that they released him.

On July 15, 1960, Mas Canosa fled to Miami and immediately hooked up with several of the dozens of CIA-financed anti-Castro groups in South Florida. He would play a supporting role in the Bay of Pigs invasion as squad leader of a diversionary unit called El Grupo Niño Díaz, which returned to Miami once the invasion was deemed a failure. Following the Bay of Pigs debacle, Mas Canosa enlisted in the U.S. Army; he was accepted as an officer candidate and was eventually commissioned as a second lieutenant. While the majority of Cuban recruits were dispatched to Fort Knox or Fort Jackson, he was dispatched to Fort Benning, which trained the exile elite, instructing them in intelligence, clandestine operations and propaganda. At Fort Benning, he became close to two men who would remain lifelong friends and associates: Félix Rodríguez and Luis Posada Carriles, both CIA assets intermittently through the Iran-Contra affair. The former would participate in the murder of Che Guevara; the latter would be Fidel Castro's most persistent would-be assassin. When it became clear that a second invasion of Cuba would never happen, Mas Canosa returned to Miami.

In 1961, he married Irma Santos, his high school sweetheart from Santiago. The couple had three sons, all of whom would eventually work at their father's company. In the early 1960s Mas Canosa became deeply involved in another CIA-backed group, RECE (Cuban Representation in Exile), and, according to his brother, its military arm, CORU (Commandos of the United Revolutionary Organizations), an alliance of twenty men from the most extreme anti-Castro groups run by dedicated militants such as Orlando Bosch, Luis Posada Carriles and Ignacio and Guillermo Novo. "RECE was financed by Pepín Bosch [no relation to Orlando Bosch] from Bacardi and my aunt's husband, Alberto Miranda, who worked for Bacardi for thirty-seven years," said Ricardo. The idea behind RECE originated with his brother, who convinced their uncle of its merit; he, in turn, talked tycoon Pepín Bosch into financing their movement. "One was the political arm and the other one was the military arm," explained Ricardo, "and the moneys would go from RECE into CORU."

As a young man, Ricardo Mas Canosa said he "used to go all over town in my car with Jorge to deliver the monthly paper that [RECE] put out. Jorge didn't travel to Cuba. Jorge did the organization and planning." Few could compete with his ingenuity, which included refurbishing a retired B-26 bomber for launching attacks on Cuba's oil refineries and investigating the possibility of attacking Cuba with missiles launched from small boats—a topic he broached with a U.S. Army general at a country club in Orlando. He later became the group's director.

Mas Canosa also worked as a broadcaster at Radio Swan, the CIA anti-Castro propaganda station, under the tutelage of David Atlee Phillips, the urbane master spook who headed CIA operations in Latin America for almost two decades. "Mas Canosa was born and bred by the CIA and was a master of psychological warfare," said Gaeton Fonzi, a former investigator for the House Select Committee on Assassinations. And he honed his propaganda skills at the knee of the best spooks in the business. His CIA ties and friendships began with Phillips and included former covert operations chief Theodore Shackley, ex–CIA chief William Casey and Oliver North, the zealous adventurer on the NSC staff.

It was through RECE that Mas Canosa met Ignacio Iglesias and Hector Torres, two former International Telephone and Telegraph employees who had formed their own eponymous telephone cable company in Puerto Rico. In 1968, he joined their company and soon opened a Miami branch. "I was told that [the company] was originally a CIA proprietary," said a former official in the Reagan administration. In 1970, the Iglesias & Torres company began to fail mysteriously. In 1971, Mas Canosa bought the company for the bargain price of $50,000 and translated its name into English, rechristening it Church & Tower.

Alberto González, the host of a popular exile radio show, said that Torres had told him that Mas Canosa had "robbed him of his company." Salvador Lew, a former radio host and current head of Radio Martí, said that the scuttlebutt in Miami was that "Mas had deliberately mismanaged the company's billings in order to secure the price he did." Within the year, Mas Canosa was doing $1 million in business with Southern Bell. Luis Posada also recalled running into a distraught Torres, who bitterly related to him that his former friend had stolen his company. "He was a little guy with a big mustache," recalled Posada. "He had tears in his eyes. He said, 'I loved Jorge like a son. I put everything in him.' " In May 1973, Torres wrote a letter to RECE denouncing Mas Canosa.

Mas Canosa's achievements with RECE included masterminding the raids on Cuba by anti-Castro militant Tony Cuesta and his paramilitary group, the Comandos L, which sought to topple the Castro government.

Ricardo Mas Canosa, who was living with his brother at the time, recalled one raid, which left his brother and Cuesta in a state of alarm. "They were trying to hide the boat . . . which was parked in front of the house," he explained. "They were very nervous, saying, 'We have to get rid of the boat in the Keys.' " Cuesta's ill-fated final assault in 1966 resulted in the deaths of most of his commandos, while Cuesta was thrown overboard, blinded, and landed in a Cuban prison for eight years. Following his release, Cuesta received a weekly paycheck from Church & Tower through its Equipment and Personnel accounts, although he had never worked there. Over a two-year period alone, according to Ricardo, who was the company's comptroller, more than three hundred checks were paid to Cuesta, written out to his uncle. Cuesta would visit his brother Jorge at the office about twice a week, he said.

In the early 1970s, when Miami was awash in drug money, Mas Canosa had a cozy relationship with two notorious drug dealers, Rafael de Arce and Antonio Canaves. They would "visit Jorge maybe once or twice a week," recalled Ricardo, "until they got in trouble with the law because of drug trafficking. I remember them because they used to have big Cuban cigars and [drove] Cadillacs to the office. One was white and the other was a cream color. They would go in his office in the front of the trailer and close the door." Ricardo said that he was excluded from their conversations. Mas Canosa later testified that "I met them once," when he bought a condo in a building they owned in Key Largo. He had no memory of forming a company with them called "the de Arce–Mas Corporation," and said he was unaware that his partners were drug smugglers with extensive rap sheets. A Miami attorney who was well acquainted with de Arce and Canaves said the two were always looking for partners to launder their profits. De Arce was later murdered; Canaves died in prison.

Throughout the 1970s, Mas Canosa split his energies between building his business into one of Miami's most important contractors and pursuing his anti-Castro work with RECE and other militant groups. In 1978, he told a *Miami Herald* reporter: "Am I non-violent? No, I am pro-violence. I think Castro should be overthrown by a revolution." The abiding irony was that Mas Canosa was unable to keep his own family in Miami, and, like most Cuban families, his family was a divided one. Although his immediate family had fled Cuba in the early 1960s, two maternal aunts had stayed behind. According to his brother, Mas Canosa arranged visas to the States via the Nicaraguan Foreign Ministry in April 1993 at considerable pain and cost to himself. The two women lived in the southern coastal city of Cienfuegos, from which his mother hailed. Securing the visas was not easy and required a generous bribe to officials in Nicaragua, recalled Ricardo. Eventually, the aunts made the trip and settled down in Miami. But the women found the glittering modern city not to their liking. Not long after, they returned home to Cienfuegos.

BY THE LATE '70s, Mas Canosa realized that paramilitary strikes against Cuba were unlikely to topple Castro on their own. He became keenly interested in American politics and threw his explosive energy behind the 1980 Florida Senate campaign of Paula Hawkins, who coattailed to victory on the Reagan landslide. When she won, he virtually "parked himself " in her Senate office, according to a former CANF director. Using his influence with Hawkins, Mas Canosa won introductions to some of the key players in the Reagan administration—among them Richard Allen, Reagan's first National Security Adviser. It was Allen who came up with the brainstorm of forming a Cuban-American organization that would advance and popularize the administration's agenda and policies in Latin America while at the same time burnishing Cuban-Americans' own image and legitimacy. In March 1981, Mas Canosa co-founded the Cuban American National Foundation with two prominent exile businessmen and activists, Raúl Masvidal and Carlos Salman, both of whom were better known than he at the time.

CANF was modeled on the powerful Israeli lobby with the help of Washington attorney Barney Barnett, who had formed AIPAC (the American Israel Public Affairs Committee). Barnett introduced the men to Tom Dine, AIPAC's executive director, and counseled them on the mechanics of forming a nonprofit, a PAC and a lobbying entity. Fourteen Miami businessmen were the founding members. Their charter was based on a proposal drafted by Frank Calzón, who would serve as the new foundation's first executive director.

CANF moved into a Miami building that was built by Church & Tower, according to Ricardo Mas Canosa, who said he supervised its construction. Later, CANF leased tony glass offices in Washington overlooking the Potomac, eventually purchasing a landmark building off Embassy Row. Until 2000, CANF enjoyed nonprofit, tax-exempt status while securing vast sums of fungible government grants. Its various umbrellas and PACs, like the Free Cuba Committee, paid out much of its assets to favored politicians and causes. From 1981 until his death, reported Gaeton Fonzi, a Mas Canosa chronicler, more than $200 million of taxpayer money ended up financing Mas Canosa's crusade to topple Fidel Castro.

Known as "the Foundation" in Miami and Washington, CANF received between $5,000 and $50,000 in annual dues from those sitting on its board of directors and from its trustees. Virtually every Florida politician since CANF's inception has been enriched by hefty contributions, notably Ileana Ros-Lehtinen, Lincoln Díaz-Balart, former Senator Connie Mack, the late Governor Lawton Chiles, and former Congressmen Dante Fascell and the late Claude Pepper, as well as out-of-staters such as New Jersey's Robert Torricelli and Robert Menéndez and Senator Fritz Hollings of North Carolina— all of whom proved to be reliable pit bulls for CANF. "The Israeli lobby buys Democrats and rents Republicans," quipped one former Bush official. "The Cubans buy Republicans and rent Democrats."

"One of our great successes," CANF spokesman José Cárdenas told me, "was getting rid of Lowell Weicker and getting Joe Lieberman instead. Joe's been great for us." Weicker, a moderate Republican senator from Connecticut, had long been a thorn in Mas Canosa's side with his anti-Embargo stance. Mas Canosa and CANF were among Lieberman's most generous contributors and played a critical role in securing his narrow victory over Weicker. In turn, Lieberman has backed every CANF initiative—even sitting on Mas Canosa's blue ribbon panel to decide the fate of Cuba after Castro.

The hubris of forming a commission without the input of Cubans living in Cuba seemed not to trouble Mas Canosa. However, seeking to deflect charges that he was autocratic, he said in a 1992 interview, "I am a misunderstood man. I have never assimilated. I never intended to. I am a Cuban first. I live here only as an extension of Cuba." Soon after the founding of CANF, Ricardo said his brother began to speak of his plans for being the next President of Cuba. One businessman recalled being told by Mas Canosa the exact location and building in the Vedado district of Havana that would house his company once he took power in Cuba.

In return for administration support, Mas Canosa became a stalwart ally of the Reagan-Bush Latin American initiatives, notably its Contra operation. Raúl Masvidal, CANF's co-founder, complained that Mas Canosa spent an excessive amount of time at National Security Council briefings in Washington. Ricardo Mas Canosa said that soon after the founding of CANF, his brother began spending "90 percent of his time in Washington, D.C." Mas cultivated and maintained warm relations with several in the administration, including Reagan, Bush and Oliver North, but his closest relationship was with Jeane Kirkpatrick, Reagan's ambassador to the United Nations, who often came to Miami to speak at CANF events.

To galvanize support among exiles for the Contra operations, Mas Canosa coined a new mantra for Calle Ocho—"The road to Havana runs through Managua!"—and dedicated himself to assisting the illegal resupply operation. He worked closely with his old friend Félix Rodríguez, whom he proudly introduced to friends as "the guy who killed Che Guevara," describing how Rodríguez finished off the Argentine revolutionary with a shot through the heart. Rodríguez became a frequent visitor at Church & Tower's and CANF's offices when he was not in Nicaragua or El Salvador running arms for the Contras. Cresencio Arcos, the U.S. press attaché in Honduras, remembers meeting Rodríguez at the embassy in 1983. "He came and introduced himself with a card from Mr. Mas Canosa and said that he should talk to me [classified deletion]. . . . Then he spoke of his role in helping bring these physicians [deleted] . . . to attend to the FDN [Nicaraguan Democratic Force—the primary Contra organization] wounded, and also to take the more serious cases back to the United States for treatment."

Ricardo Mas Canosa said he overheard conversations between his brother and Rodríguez about how "to raise funds and keep the pipeline open to the Contras in Nicaragua . . . to get rid of the Sandinistas . . . and Jorge talked about some Cuban doctors [who were going] to treat the Contras. The checks were made out to the Cuban American National Foundation. . . . Jorge told me go pick up these checks. They are to go to the Contras." On one occasion, Mas Canosa told his brother about an afternoon meeting at Miami's Omni Hilton on Biscayne Boulevard; "he told me that high level people were coming down. He told me that Oliver North and Félix Rodríguez were going to be there. And he told me that George Bush was going to be there. . . . He told me they were going to discuss the Contras."

Mas Canosa's name and four phone numbers (including his private home line) were found in Oliver North's notebook, near notations under the name of Félix Rodríguez reading: "expedite 50K for I.R. Jorge Mas," "Domingo for Jorge Mas" (a reference to his close friend CANF director Domingo Moreira), and, on another page under Rodríguez's name, "still have not gotten $ from Jorge Mas." Other notations read, "call Jorge Mas— 305/233-6540 (Inez)," a reference to Mas's longtime faithful secretary, Inez Díaz, and "mtg. w/ Jorge Mas," in which North and Mas Canosa were said to have discussed Contra activities and support. Rodríguez confirmed at Senate hearings in 1988 that he was given $50,000 from Mas Canosa to pass on to Oliver North.

Over time, all manner of unsavory miscreants, even criminals, were seen coming and going from Mas Canosa's offices. There were the infamous Novo brothers—Guillermo and Ignacio—both of whom were tried for and the former initially convicted of the 1976 murder of Chilean ambassador Orlando Letelier and his American aide, Ronnie Moffitt, on Washington's Embassy Row. According to Saul Landau, co-author of *Assassination on Embassy Row,* Mas Canosa financed the legal defense at the second trial for the Novos in which Guillermo's conviction for murder was overturned on a technicality, although his conviction for perjury was stayed. In 1976, Mas Canosa's old nemesis from Cuba, Rolando Masferrer, was blown to pieces by a remote-control bomb in Miami. It was one of the dozens of bombings in Miami that were never prosecuted, although investigators said they believed it too was the handiwork of the Novo brothers. Mas Canosa later hired both Novos to work at CANF and their names appeared on CANF's Information Commission in 1990. "Mas led the perfect double life," said Landau. "He was running covert military raids against Cuba while publicly denouncing violence as an option."

Raúl Masvidal, in an interview with former House investigator Gaeton Fonzi, said that "between 1981 and '85, I was very involved in the Foundation while Jorge started getting closer and closer to the White House and the Washington intelligence community. . . . Jorge was in meetings with the Bush White House, with Bush people when Bush was vice-president. He was getting marching orders from the White House or the CIA. The Foundation became very much involved in the Contra effort. . . . We were involved in a number of clandestine operations which were illegal and Jorge was more involved than any of us. He had links to the Novo brothers and their terrorist organizations and it was not out of the ordinary for Jorge to be working on the fringes of these organizations. I think Jorge had links to all of these guys," he said. In a later interview, Masvidal called Mas Canosa's domination of CANF "110 percent. And his control of Radio Martí was 100 percent."

Mas Canosa also enjoyed a close relationship with Orlando Bosch, arguably the most dedicated exile terrorist, who served eleven years in a Venezuelan prison, prior to winning an acquittal, for his alleged role in blowing up a civilian Cuban airplane, killing all seventy three passengers. "I saw him a couple of times in the 1960s when I was a kid at the house talking to Jorge," said Ricardo, "and twice at the RECE office around 1968." During Bosch's imprisonment for the bombing, Mas Canosa raised funds to provide care and comfort to Bosch's family, while negotiating quietly with the Reagan-Bush administration to secure his release. In 1982, Ricardo recalled an occasion when "a gentleman came to the office with one of Orlando Bosch's paintings, the first painting that he made in jail, with this letter. Jorge told me to prepare $25,000 in cash . . . from the Panamanian bank accounts . . . [which] were given to the man to help Orlando Bosch and his family or for legal fees." Soon after, Bosch won another trial and was acquitted in a Venezuelan court, known to be among the most corrupt in the hemisphere.

Accompanying Bosch's painting was a letter of gratitude. It read, in translation: "Here is this painting, created in humility for my appreciated old friend in battle Jorge Mas Canosa, as well as his lovely wife, Irma, to serve as gratitude and testimony for your unceasing and uninterrupted efforts and sacrifices—forever trying to liberate our country of so much crime and oppression. Orlando Bosch, January of 1982, Cuartel San Carlos de Caracas, Venezuela." After Bosch's friend left their office, Ricardo was handed the painting and the letter by his brother. "He told me to keep [them], that he didn't want to be associated with the painting or letter because the guy was a known terrorist. The painting is hanging in my house."

In return for CANF's resolute support and contributions, the Reagan administration obliged Mas and CANF whenever possible. There would be a presidential pardon for convicted Watergate burglar Eugenio Martínez, a Cuban exile, on the eve of Reagan's campaign swing through Miami in May 1983, where he was the guest of the Foundation. Reagan had previously announced the formation of a Commission on Broadcasting to Cuba to create Mas Canosa's dream, Radio Martí, despite the fact that the Voice of America seemed to be getting the job done. The members of the commission included Mas Canosa, the eccentric right-wing tycoon Richard Mellon Scaife, the beer magnate Joseph Coors, the Mobil Oil executive Herbert Schmertz, former Florida senator Richard Stone, and Reagan's close friend Charles Wick.

Radio Martí went on the air in May 1985 and two years later Reagan signed off on the creation of Televisión Martí. "We will show the Cuban people how they can overthrow a government," declared Mas Canosa. He remained steadfastly indifferent to the fact that no one in Cuba has ever seen Televisión Martí, as the Cuban government successfully jams it, wasting millions of U.S. taxpayer dollars. Although Mas Canosa was appointed chairman of the President's Advisory Board on Cuba Broadcasting for a three-year term in 1984, no one—not Reagan, Bush or Clinton—was able or willing to dislodge him from Martí's chairmanship when his term expired. He would remain chairman for life—until his death in 1997.

"There are two Cubas," said Gaeton Fonzi. "There's the real Cuba and there's the Cuba that Mas Canosa created in the minds of the exiles, a volatile, dissident community in Cuba that is about to overthrow the government—a myth he sustained for years." Fueled by his determination to topple and replace Fidel Castro, he nurtured the exiles' dream of return. Wayne Smith, the head of the U.S. Interests Section in Havana from 1979 to 1988, said Mas Canosa never let go of his pipe dream of an American intervention to install himself. "It's the old 1950s school of CIA thinking about how to get rid of their guy and install our guy," said Smith.

Among Mas Canosa's role models was Anastasio Somoza, the Nicaraguan strongman who ruled the country as his private fiefdom until he was overthrown and later assassinated. Some visitors and VIPs to his office were shown a photograph of Mas Canosa and Somoza together. Another model was the Chilean dictator Augusto Pinochet, whom Mas Canosa extolled on a popular Miami TV show. In the mid-1970s, he became especially close with Pinochet's military attaché, a colonel based in the Chilean consulate in Miami. As with his heroes, people did not necessarily like Mas Canosa but they feared him, which suited him fine. Nevertheless, he took precautions and buzzed around Miami in an armored bullet- and bombproof Mercedes 560 SEL that he had purchased from Somoza, sometimes in a three-car caravan in the style of Fidel Castro. His private jet was kept in a secure location and he was reported to debug his home twice weekly. His longtime mistress contended that Mas employed bodyguards from 1975 until his death and kept a trusty .357 Magnum nearby.

By the time Clinton arrived in the White House, Mas Canosa had the power to decide who would represent Cuba policy at the State Department. In 1993, he nixed the nomination of Mario Baeza for the position of Assistant Secretary for Inter-American Affairs, fearing that he was insufficiently anti-Castro. A Cuban mulatto, Baeza was a partner in the prestigious New York law firm of Debevoise & Plimpton with an expertise in Latin American trade and economic issues. He is also a man of considerable culture and erudition, a graduate of the Harvard Law School and Cornell. According to a source close to Baeza, Mas Canosa phoned him as soon as the nomination was announced and offered to send his jet to fly him to Miami. When Baeza declined his invitation, Mas Canosa decided he could not be trusted.

Nevertheless, Mas Canosa denied having torpedoed Baeza's nomination in a letter to the *Herald*. Employing his finely honed propaganda skills, he denounced a critical column by Richard Cohen in the *Washington Post* taking him to task for Baeza's ouster as "McCarthyite guilt-by-association tactics . . . and racist." But the truth was that he had had everything to do with kiboshing Baeza's nomination and race was, indeed, a factor. In an April

1993 confidential memo written on CANF stationery and addressed to its directors and trustees, Mas Canosa boasted of "our first direct confrontation over [Clinton's] intention to name the *abogado negro* [the black lawyer] Mario Baeza." Crediting his triumph in the matter to "an early showdown," he called "the Clinton/Baeza chapter a great success."

Mas Canosa's vengeance toward those unwilling to do his bidding became legendary. When Joe Carollo was a Miami city commissioner, he was literally challenged to a gun duel in 1987 by Mas Canosa after he vetoed one of Mas's real estate deals, a $130 million development for Watson Island in which he was partnered with then U.N. Ambassador Jeane Kirkpatrick, according to papers filed with the city of Miami. Carollo lost his seat in the following election when Mas Canosa backed his opponent. Former Colorado congressman David Skaggs discovered just how rough Miami hardball gets when he vetoed Radio Martí's funding during a tight budget year. Mas retaliated and, with the help of Lincoln Díaz-Balart, targeted Skaggs's pet projects. Not long after Alberto González began satirizing Mas Canosa on *La Morgolla* in 1989, the popular radio show was canceled.

Through three administrations, Mas Canosa controlled access to the White House on Cuban issues, ensuring that only hard-liners participated in policymaking. He even boasted that he frequently rewrote White House briefings on Cuba. "We got a call today to look over another one of their speeches," he told a visiting dissident in August 1994. "We made some changes and sent it back to them."

Although the *Miami Herald* claims that it calls its own shots, it has been through too many bruisers with Mas Canosa and the exile leadership ever to be fully independent. In 1992, the *Herald* had the temerity to run an editorial opposing the Torricelli Bill. Although virtually every newspaper in the country had run a similar editorial, its airing in Mas Canosa's backyard was patently unacceptable. Very quickly, the *Herald* experienced payback. Mas Canosa jumped on his soapbox via Miami radio and blasted the *Herald* and its Spanish language twin, *El Nuevo Herald,* as "tools of the Fidel Castro regime," guilty of "conducting a continuous and systematic campaign against Cuban-Americans," and urged the paper's top leadership to resign. David Lawrence, the *Herald*'s publisher, ran a lengthy column defending the paper under the imploring headline "Please Mr. Mas, Be Fair." But to a gutter fighter like Mas Canosa, civility was the equivalent of weakness. He went in for the kill, blasting the *Herald*'s advertisers with a letter-writing campaign apprising them of the newspaper's "bias and half truths."

The *Herald* was inundated with bomb and death threats and some of its vending machines were smeared with excrement. In Little Havana, buses carried large display ads proclaiming, "YO NO CREO EL HERALD," while Anglo routes bore the English equivalent, "I DON'T BELIEVE THE HERALD." At one point, Mas Canosa threatened their top brass, saying that he had "hired private detectives to investigate them and their children." And when he learned that a senior editor at the *Herald* was having an extramarital affair with one of his female reporters, say several *Herald* staffers, he obliquely threatened the newspaper with disclosure. Moreover, they say he succeeded in tempering future coverage of himself, exiles and Cuban issues.

Mas Canosa's behavior so violated accepted norms that the Inter-American Press Association sent a delegation to investigate the harassment. Even CANF stalwarts such as former Reagan administration official Elliott Abrams publicly chastised Mas, who attributed the more vile excesses to "Castro agents" in Miami seeking to discredit exiles. The campaign raged on for months until a truce was finally called at a Miami luncheon in which Mas Canosa humiliated Lawrence one more time—cruelly mocking the publisher's strained Spanish.

In the fall of 1994, the *Herald* had another brush with CANF's chairman when it reprinted an interview with him from Spain's *El País*. Asked whether he thought Americans would take over Cuba after Castro's departure, Mas Canosa referred to Americans as *"gringos,"* adding, "That's bullshit! *Mierda!* Crap! They haven't even been able to take over Miami. If we have kicked them out of here, how could they possibly take over our own country?" When the predictable outcry blew through South Florida, he issued an irate denial. The fact that the reporter, Antonio Caño, had tape-recorded the interview did not deter him from taking out a full-page ad headlined, "Why so much hate, Mr. Lawrence?" He went on to accuse the paper of "racism and bigotry," "McCarthyism" and conducting a "witch hunt."

Among those responding to the *Herald*'s siege, one letter, written by journalist Emily Cárdenas, was remarkable for its candor on the plight of reporters in Miami: "As a former news producer at Channel 51, I can tell you that Mr. Mas and others have created an undercurrent of fear and intimidation," she wrote, "that few admit or care to discuss. Journalists who cover exile politics know the 'witch hunts' well and are careful to cover their backs. . . . Why? Fear of being blacklisted by the CANF, fear of having their journalistic integrity debated on Spanish language radio talk shows, fear of being branded a Communist and fear of losing their jobs or having their careers ruined entirely." Certainly, no one at the *Herald* could disagree.

Through the clout of CANF and Miami radio, Mas Canosa succeeded in marginalizing dozens of exiles, many with impeccable anti-Castro credentials. In the 1980s and early 1990s, his most insistent attacks were reserved for Elizardo Sánchez Santacruz, Cuba's preeminent dissident and president of the Cuban Commission on Human Rights and National Reconciliation. Sánchez was cited by Amnesty International as one of Cuba's primary targets of political repression. Mas Canosa, however, dismissed Sánchez as "Castro's puppet." His reasons were clear: Sánchez was a rival in a post-Castro Cuba and he detested Sánchez's insistence that the U.S. Embargo was counterproductive. Sánchez was targeted for derision not only on Miami's big three radio stations but also on Radio Martí and La Voz de la Fundación, CANF's private station. "We are very worried about these attacks because we have no way to respond," Sánchez said at the time.

Ramón Cernuda, who represented Sánchez's group in Miami for many years, also found himself in the crosshairs of Mas Canosa's scope. In May 1989, Cernuda, a successful publisher and art collector, saw his home invaded by fourteen armed U.S. Treasury agents who seized his collection of Cuban art. An irrepressible Mas Canosa boasted on Radio Mambí that it was he who had urged his friend U.S. Attorney Dexter Lehtinen (husband of Congresswoman Ileana Ros-Lehtinen, whose campaign he had backed) to make the bust. "We are responsible for this and other investigations. I am going to continue to press for an investigation of Cernuda, and of the twenty more Cernudas who are here in Miami," Mas warned on Miami radio, according to a tape of the broadcast. During the same broadcast, Mas denounced exile activist Alicia Torres of the moderate Cuban American Committee as "a Castro agent." A year later, the Cernuda case was tossed out of court by a judge who derided its prosecution as "arbitrary and capricious."

Events would take an even more sinister turn. Cernuda found himself targeted for exhaustive and expensive investigations by the INS, the Florida Labor Department and the IRS (none of which resulted in any charges). Likewise, the Cuban Museum of Arts and Culture, of which Cernuda was vice president, was threatened with eviction by the Miami City Commission because it showcased the work of some artists who had not publicly denounced Fidel Castro. Although the commission was harshly criticized by a judge who blocked the eviction, the museum lost $150,000 of state funding and was bombed and picketed. Soon after, a Miami police officer investigating one of the museum bombings told Cernuda he wanted to speak with Lino Sánchez, Elizardo's brother. When Lino arrived to meet with the officer, he was seized by DEA agents and arrested on drug and murder charges. Lino Sánchez was quickly released when it proved to be a mysterious case of mistaken identity. "Mas set out to create a *junta* in Miami," said Cernuda. "And he almost succeeded. My persecution ended only with the intercession of authorities at the federal level."

NOTHING IRRITATED MAS CANOSA more than when his critics pointed to the similarities between himself and his nemesis, Fidel Castro. "*Fidel, Mas Canosa—es la misma cosa* (it's the same thing)," went the chant of his critics. Like Castro, Mas Canosa established himself as leader for life. From 1981 until his death sixteen years later, he was the sole chairman of CANF, running it, its PACs, and Radio and TV Martí as his personal empire, disposing of colleagues, associates and even a handful of CANF directors at his whim. His influence in Miami extended to deciding who would run for office and who would win coveted city and county contracts. Some of Miami's most controversial and lucrative contracts—such as for its "people mover" transit system and its jail, both of which cost more than $100 million, were handled by his company.

Mas Canosa had been a prosperous businessman prior to the founding of the Cuban American National Foundation, but following his ascension to chairman, he became a mega-millionaire, perhaps a billionaire. Believing or fearing his bluster, that he would be the next president of Cuba, many American corporations believed that they could not afford not to do business with him. Others, desirous of being in his good graces, gave generously to CANF. The exile leader brilliantly and synergistically dovetailed his political ties into business contacts. Those who admired his easy access to the Reagan and Bush White Houses were anxious to offer him friendship and contracts. After awarding Argentina's Carlos Meném a CANF "Medal of the Apostle" for his support, Mas bought a troubled Argentine broadcasting company. Likewise, after a warm reception with Spain's President José María Aznar, who promised a harder line on Cuba, he purchased a large Spanish telecommunications company. In 1989, Russian President Boris Yeltsin visited Miami on a CANF-sponsored trip and Mas Canosa was said to have taken the Russian leader out for a night of "booze and broads," according to a former CANF member. By 1990, Mas Canosa viewed himself as the emperor of Miami, soon to lead the largest island state in the Caribbean.

IN 1985, CANF'S co-founder Raúl Masvidal, a prominent Miami banker, was tossed overboard by Mas Canosa. "When I protested that we were getting involved too much in issues that were not related to Cuba, Jorge called me a traitor and every name in the book," Masvidal recalled. "Jorge was a nobody but somehow he grabbed the leadership . . . and eventually pushed Salman [Carlos Salman, the other co-founder] out and eventually eased me out too. A number of times, we discussed rotating the leadership, but Jorge was so adamant about it. He'd say, 'I'm afraid of losing control.' " Masvidal quietly conferred with other CANF directors, who were equally alarmed by Mas Canosa's burgeoning megalomania. "Jorge operates very much like Castro," Masvidal explained soon after their split. "He makes personal threats to people like 'I'll destroy you,' he says to his business partners. He physically threatens people. Jorge feels he is above bipartisan politics . . . because politicians need him more than he needs them. . . . In Dade County, if he decides to rezone a piece of land, he has the vote of the County Commission. . . . He tells people, 'If you do that, you will never get a job in the county or you will have to leave Miami.' This guy has only two agendas: to be president of Cuba for life . . . and [to] make more money."

Another casualty was Frank Calzón, CANF's esteemed executive director. José Luis Rodríguez, a former CANF vice president who resigned in 1987, said that he was asked to disseminate gossip about Calzón. "They wanted to spread rumors that the guy was gay, that the guy was no good, and this and that. I wouldn't go for that," Rodríguez said in a deposition filed when he sued the top leadership of the Foundation, charging that they cheated him out of several business deals in retribution for his resignation. Rodríguez also made the oft-repeated charge that Mas Canosa had used his CANF lobbying for his own personal aggrandizement, linking his contracting business with his CANF work. At the time of Mas Canosa's death, Miami-Dade County had given hundreds of millions of dollars' worth of business to his companies.

Mas Canosa's political and business dealings were no less controversial. In order to give Radio Martí the legitimacy he had promised his congressional supporters, he recruited Ernesto Betancourt, who had been the International Monetary Fund's governor for Cuba in the early days of the Revolution, to supervise the operation. But when it became clear that Betancourt would present news and information to the Cuban people and not the Mas Canosa agenda, his days were numbered. When Betancourt argued against starting up Televisión Martí, Mas Canosa moved aggressively against him, giving him little option but to resign. "I quit because Radio Martí was being converted into a vehicle of propaganda for Mr. Mas," said Betancourt. Martí's well-regarded research director, Ramón Mestre, also had resigned, complaining that the station "has departed significantly from its mandate" and questioning the effectiveness and integrity of its news department. Conservative columnist Georgie Anne Geyer described the showdown as "a raw battle for power," and accused the exile leader of using Radio and Televisión Martí "to advance Mas's ambitions to be president of a post-Castro Cuba," adding, "The U.S. has basically formulated no policy of its own toward Cuba because of fear of Foundation tactics."

While some were charmed by the indefatigable Cuban, others were left slack-jawed at how he preened and threw his clout around. Congressman Charles Rangel witnessed one such incident, which he felt crossed the line. "Mas came to the office, a surprise visit, and held up an imaginary jar of honey and said, 'If you cooperate with me you get the honey. Otherwise, I hit you with the jar,' " recalled an aide to Rangel. The Harlem congressman set up a meeting with the FBI and filed a complaint. When the Miami leader downplayed the threat as a rhetorical gesture, the FBI dropped its investigation. Mas Canosa then threw his money and clout behind Adam Clayton Powell IV, who sought, unsuccessfully, to unseat Rangel.

In April 1994, more than 150 exiles, representing more than a dozen exile groups, showed up for a conference in Havana despite a Miami radio blitz condemning them as "traitors" and "communists." On the eve of the conference, La Voz de la Fundación, CANF's radio station, announced unconfirmed reports that Fidel Castro had died. The rumor swept through Miami, brilliantly diverting attention away from the Havana conference. Just as the rumor peaked, Mas Canosa took to the airwaves. In what initially sounded like a Spanish language parody of Alexander Haig, he appealed for calm and assured the Cuban people that he had been in touch with senior leaders in Cuba and that CANF had everything under control. His glory, however, was short-lived. The following day, Fidel Castro let it be known that he was still very much alive.

CHAPTER 6

THE LITIGATOR

Lo que no mata engorda.
What doesn't kill you enriches you.

CUBAN PROVERB

IN THE SUMMER of 1994, I found myself on the other side of the velvet rope of journalism: participating in a news story. A month earlier, *The New Republic* had published a story of mine on Mas Canosa, which was critical but hardly the most scathing press he had known. The magazine's editor, Andrew Sullivan, deleted my title for the story, "Our Man in Miami," and substituted his own confection, "Clinton's Miami Mobster," on the cover of the magazine. Inside, Sullivan also inserted a subheading: "Mas Canosa: Mobster and Megalomaniac." When I asked Sullivan what prompted him to proceed so recklessly, he responded, "Well, he *is* a mobster." In truth, Sullivan was not alone in his thinking, but whether Mas Canosa was or was not a mobster was not the theme of the story. Intolerance and the erosion of democracy in Miami were my subjects.

Not surprisingly given his litigious past, Mas Canosa filed a lawsuit against *The New Republic*—reportedly at the urging of his friend Robert Torricelli. As the author of the story, I too was named in the lawsuit—as is the convention of such suits. As a result, I was dragged through more than two years of depositions before I was dismissed from the suit without having to apologize or retract one word of the story.

But in those two years, I would take a roller-coaster ride through the treacherous landscape of exile politics in Miami and Washington. Although I did not approve of calling Mas Canosa a mobster, which he would testify prompted his decision to sue, I supported *The New Republic*'s resolve to fight the case. I knew that the discovery process would open doors that journalists had previously only dreamed of entering. And so it would turn out to be. Even before depositions began, *The New Republic* and its Miami lawyers received all manner of unsolicited aid. It was soon apparent that Mas Canosa's enemies list was as long and broad as the Sierra Maestra mountain range in his home province of Santiago de Cuba. What was most striking was the number of close associates from CANF, his business or Radio Martí who were eager to be of assistance. In fact, the most powerful testimony came not from the left or from exile moderates and certainly not from the Cuban government, but from hard-liners not unlike himself—including former directors and members of the Foundation. What was their beef? The specific grievances varied, but all shared a belief that Mas Canosa was cut of the same cloth as Fidel Castro, and that if they did not stop him, they ran the risk of replacing one tyrant with another.

The most compelling and damning testimony came from his own brother, Ricardo Mas Canosa, who had worked for fifteen years as comptroller of Church & Tower, which installed and repaired all the cable lines for Southern Bell Telephone. Ricardo saw himself as the adoring younger brother and for most of his life, he said, he would have done anything to protect his older sibling. In 1968, while attending Miami-Dade Junior College, Ricardo, eleven years younger than Jorge, began working part-time for his brother while living with him and his family. In time, Ricardo became a shareholder of the company and the full owner of Equipment and Personal Services—to which much of the company's work was subcontracted. From 1981 on, he ran Church & Tower on a day-to-day basis, while his brother pursued his political ambitions.

In 1985 Ricardo recounted that his brother had decided that it was time to bring his eldest son, Jorge Mas Santos, who had recently graduated from college, into the company. Ricardo said he was delighted that his nephew would join them. It was, after all, a family business; their father had worked for the company as a yard manager until his retirement. But Mas Canosa had decided there was not room for both, and opted to replace his brother with his son. To achieve this, Ricardo explained, his brother began to accuse him of improprieties. When Ricardo chose to leave his brother's employ and go off on his own, the two squabbled over the value of Ricardo's stock and his contribution to the company. The feud escalated into a fistfight at Mas Canosa's home in which Ricardo claimed he had been badly beaten.

In 1986, Ricardo filed criminal charges against his brother with the State Attorney and charged him in civil court with stealing his 1983 Oldsmobile. Mas Canosa settled the case and agreed to pay $245,000 in an out-of-court settlement. Four years later, in October 1990, Ricardo sued his brother again, charging him with libel and depriving him of contracting work by writing letters to Southern Bell accusing him of extortion and fraud. Ricardo also claimed that his brother had bribed officials in Miami-Dade. This time, the case went to trial.

Mas Canosa was found liable and ordered to pay $1.2 million in compensation. But challenging a brother who is the most powerful politician in Miami has its consequences. During the trial, rocks smashed through the windows of Ricardo's lawyer's office and the tires of Ricardo's car were slashed.

In his two lawsuits against his brother, Ricardo had limited his charges to matters concerning Church & Tower and his brother's personal conduct. But in his depositions for *The New Republic*, he reviewed their entire life together, including family matters and operations, both political and financial. Ricardo arrived with an arsenal of documentation that was submitted as exhibits to the case: canceled checks, payroll accounts, bookkeeping, company files, calendars and personal letters. His allegations were more devastating than anyone had anticipated.

Ricardo testified under oath that his brother had long maintained bank accounts in Panama for bogus corporations where he laundered or hid money. Bank statements were stamped as exhibits. "It was just a front corporation," Ricardo said of one company. "The monies were funded through there and then they would be transferred to Jorge's accounts." He also stated that, at his brother's direction, he had opened accounts in 1980 at the Union Bank of Switzerland in both Zurich and Panama in the names of "Jorge, Irma, and his son . . . for him to receive those funds into his account." Asked why his brother did not set up his own accounts in Panama, Ricardo replied, "He couldn't go to Panama because he was on a list from Mr. Noriega where he was listed as a terrorist. He told me that the only person he trusted taking those big sums of money was me." Ricardo submitted as an exhibit the list of suspected terrorists dated October 25, 1976, from Panamanian military intelligence, G-2, which included the name Jorge Mas Canosa.

Ricardo stated that his brother not infrequently bribed public officials who could and would grease the wheels for his company. He cited the case of Joe Gersten, a state senator and later a county commissioner until he fled the U.S. in 1993. A year earlier, Gersten had been indicted in a raunchy sex and drugs scandal and accused of filing a false police report. In late 1984, Ricardo testified, his brother hoped to get a rate hike for Southern Bell from the Public Service Commission and believed Gersten was the man to make it happen. "Jorge told me to be around his house around 4:30," and to bring $5,000 in cash in an envelope from Jorge's desk at the office. When Ricardo arrived, he found his brother "sitting in the pool area of his house with Joe Gersten. He asked me if I had brought what he order[ed]. I said yes. I give him the envelope. He gave it to Joe Gersten [who] put it in the right pocket of his suit. And I asked Jorge if I could speak with him, [away] from Joe Gersten. I told him that I didn't feel comfortable, that I didn't want no part of it. And I left his house."

Ricardo volunteered another instance in which his brother paid for a junket for an important Miami politician. In the early 1980s, Mas Canosa treated Miami Mayor Steve Clark to a two-week trip to Spain. "He told me that they were going to talk zoning matters that were going to be coming in front of the commission and that's why they were paying for his trip," testified Ricardo. Another two-week family vacation for four in California was bought for William Palmer, "who qualif[ied] the companies to do work for Southern Bell," Ricardo Mas testified under oath. He added that his brother instructed him to purchase an old boat from Palmer for $1,500 in cash. (Palmer responded that he assumed Ricardo was buying the boat for himself and denied accepting a paid vacation from Church & Tower.) Every Christmas, Mas Canosa dispensed extravagant gifts to Miami officials, delivering crates of fine wines and scotch to their homes. The quid pro quo, according to Ricardo, was lucrative contracts; Mas even wangled a specially created freeway exit for Church & Tower.

Over three days of testimony, Ricardo outlined a company scheme masterminded by his brother to snare lucrative set-aside contracts from Miami-Dade Water and Sewer Authority that were designated for minorities. A front company called MBL Paving Company was created, whose initials stood for Mas, Banks and Lorenz. Paul Banks, an African-American who had worked for Church & Tower since 1970, qualified the company in his newly elevated position for a minority set-aside contract. But the profits from MBL were paid to and distributed by Church & Tower, and Banks was not a shareholder in the company that bore his name. "He was the front man for the company . . . just a figurehead to appear in the papers," asserted Ricardo. Given the title of president, Banks had, in fact, "no involvement with managerial decisions."

In 1986, after his second lawsuit with his brother was settled in his favor, Ricardo was told to travel to Panama to receive his $195,000 payment in cash. A month after his return to Miami, his eldest brother, Ramón, confided an unsettling conversation he had had with their brother. "Jorge said, 'I was going to have him [Ricardo] killed when he was in Panama picking up the money,'" according to Ricardo's testimony. Thereafter, as a precaution, Ricardo said he traveled with a bodyguard all the time.

Jorge Mas Canosa sat through five days of depositions. His responses were an unabashed, seamless tapestry of dissembling. Even when alluding to the most quotidian matters, easily disproved by exhibits or other testimony, he would more often than not be untruthful. He testified that he never kept a calendar, a phone book or a date book—maintaining that he was capable of keeping thirty years of international contacts and meetings in his head. But his brother had testified that he was meticulous in his record keeping. "The new calendar would be placed on top of his desk and the old one would be put in the boxes that were kept from the previous years," he explained, "and Inez [Díaz, his longtime secretary] kept her own calendar of appointments as well. And he always had a phone book with him in his briefcase."

In the course of the case, Mas Canosa claimed, among other things, that I had never attempted to contact him—despite being shown exhibits of phone bills documenting more than a dozen calls to his office and to CANF. Such incontrovertible evidence did not faze him. He steadfastly issued blanket denials, as if immune to the possibility of being held accountable for perjury in Miami. Indeed, he knew his hometown well.

Notwithstanding his claim to a superbly calibrated memory, Mas Canosa could not recall the most basic information, including the names of many of his friends and associates. His testimony was studded with the response "I cannot recall" or "I have no memory." He failed to remember his protégé, Joe García, a key figure at CANF, who became CANF's executive director after his death. When he was asked about García, his initial response was, "Who is Joe García? I don't recall who Joe García is."

Among the people he could not remember was a woman named Maribel Roig, his mistress of twenty years, who had borne a son by him in 1986. She was deposed by *The New Republic*'s attorneys and gave a riveting account. The couple had first met in 1975, when Roig worked at Southern Bell. Roig's boss was responsible for the Church & Tower account. When Mas Canosa halted financial assistance of their child, Roig reluctantly filed a paternity suit in 1994.

"I do not know her," he testified. Publicly, he attacked Roig as a Castro agent intent on "financial extortion." To assist his memory, a message tape from Roig's answering machine was played for him: a long-winded, gushy message from a speaker identifying himself as Jorge. The voice sounded unmistakably like his own with his signature cadences and pronunciation. For a moment, he appeared visibly taken aback. "It sounds like my voice, but I cannot tell you for sure," he demurred before quickly reverting to his initial position: he had never met Roig, or spoken with her or left any messages for her. "No, I do not know her," he concluded emphatically. "I never called her."

Less than a year later, Mas Canosa would settle a paternity suit with Maribel Roig, paying out several million dollars to her and her son, to whom he bore an uncanny resemblance. During two years of litigation, he refused to take a simple blood test to establish the boy's paternity with absolute certainty. He had found an exceedingly accommodating circuit judge in Judge Eugene Fierro, who threw a sweeping gag order on Roig, forbidding her from telling *anyone* her belief that Mas Canosa was the father of her son, and sealing the lawsuit at his behest. Fierro appointed a guardian for the child who was himself fighting a paternity suit. The guardian, not surprisingly, supported Mas Canosa's position unequivocally.

A bizarre and sinister twist ensued when Roig's ex-husband, Ismael Roig, a convicted drug trafficker, closed ranks with Mas Canosa after accepting a reported $9,000 cash loan from the exile leader's bodyguard, Mario Miranda, who had visited him in prison. Fierro consistently ruled for the powerful Cuban, eventually dismissing Roig's lawsuit. Mas Canosa seemed home free until the Third District Court of Appeal reversed Fierro with an unusually stern rebuke. Mas Canosa quickly forked over a multimillion-dollar settlement to Roig but went to his grave refusing to take a paternity test.

MAS CANOSA'S MANNER during his five days of deposition alternated between amused indifference, braggadocio and righteous indignation. He was, however, never out of control. Brimming with confidence, he had a natural command of the room and those in it. I chatted with him once or twice and he was pleasant enough. When I mentioned my visits to his hometown of Santiago de Cuba, he said he had no interest in Cuba while Fidel Castro was in power. On several occasions he asked for breaks in which he walked and paced about the room—sometimes gripping his back with both his hands. We would later learn that he was already battling lung cancer, which had spread to his bones.

When he was questioned about his relationships with known terrorists such as Orlando Bosch or Luis Posada, Mas grew especially foggy. He denied being acquainted with the former in spite of Bosch's letter of tribute, gratitude and friendship, which was submitted as an exhibit. There was also the curious coincidence that his attorneys, Hank Adorno and Raoul

Cantero III, ended up representing Bosch in 1988 in his fight to win release from jail and later U.S. residency, and the fact that he had he so ardently lobbied Jeb Bush and his father, President Bush, to intercede on Bosch's behalf and order his release from prison. Indeed, Bush's action would be the first presidential intercession in U.S. history for a convicted terrorist. And while Mas Canosa denied having a friendship with Bosch, he was a character witness at Bosch's parole hearing on March 3, 1988, where he stated, according to Parole Commission records, "that he has known Subject for over twenty years" and urged Bosch's immediate release.

Mas Canosa denied ever being associated with the CIA—notwithstanding his involvement in the Bay of Pigs, his training at Fort Benning and his work as a propagandist at Radio Swan, all verifiable CIA operations. Why and how the names of Guillermo and Ignacio Novo came to be published as members of CANF's Information Commission was a mystery to him. He called their inclusion "an absolute lie . . . I never hired them." Nor did he ever aid or assist the Contras or send Cuban doctors to Nicaragua. He remained clueless as to why Oliver North's notebook would have several notations concerning him. Likewise, he knew nothing about the escape of Luis Posada Carriles from prison, an event, it would turn out, in which he played a central role. He denied voicing criticism, either publicly or privately, of former CANF vice chairman José Rodríguez, CANF co-founders Raúl Masvidal and Carlos Salman or director Frank Calzón. Nor was he a factor, he testified, in Ernesto Betancourt's resignation from Radio Martí. He also made the remarkable claim that he was unaware of any ill consequences having befallen those who were denounced on Miami radio as traitors, Castro agents or communists.

Among the most damaging exhibits submitted during litigation was a typed seven-page memo dated April 5, 1993, on CANF stationery from Mas Canosa to CANF's directors and trustees. The letter, outlining the agenda of their next meeting, offered a list of enemies and their sins. Those castigated as dangerous to the Foundation included such prominent figures in the exile community as Mario Baeza, Carlos Alberto Montaner, Armando Valladares, Eloy Gutiérrez Menoyo, Roberto Solís, Frank Calzón and Huber Matos. In a style suggestive of Chairman Mao, Mas Canosa referred to himself in the third person as "Our Chairman," and on one occasion as "our Maximum Leader," the very salutation frequently adopted by Fidel Castro.

In his directive, he chastised the Clinton administration for its ingratitude. "The efforts and gestures made on behalf of Bill Clinton in the final stages of his Presidential election campaign were not properly appreciated either by him or his people," he began bitterly. "In fact, the latter have not honored the commitments they made to CANF at that time." As proof of their infamy, he cited the nomination of Mario Baeza, and the battle necessary to torpedo it, directly contradicting his deposition testimony that he played no role in Baeza's defeat. "If war is what they want," he warned, "war is what they will get." He went on to express alarm over losing National Endowment for Democracy grants and outlined his battle plan to pressure the administration into restoring them. (In his deposition, he claimed to have no interest, influence or position with the NED, which awarded its very first grant to CANF.)

The influential Cuban writer and activist Carlos Alberto Montaner was called an "opportunist and traitor," while the human rights activist Armando Valladares, the Ambassador of Human Rights to the U.N. and a political prisoner in Cuba for twenty years, was dismissed as "a similar phenomenon." He urged "a complete break" from Valladares, invoking Theocritus's warning that "If you nurture dogs they will devour you." Eloy Gutiérrez Menoyo qualified as "the highest expression of political opportunism and treason," as did all others who sought a negotiated settlement with Cuba, whom he pilloried as "vulgares dialogueros," opportunists and traitors.

He was particularly incensed by Orestes Lorenzo, the charismatic air force pilot who fled Cuba in a military plane and then won the hearts of Americans with his daring return to the island to rescue his wife and children. Lorenzo was not sufficiently anti-Castro, according to Mas Canosa, and had resisted efforts to toe the CANF line. Soon after his arrival, Lorenzo proposed sending a "Crusade of Love" to Havana—boats filled with food and provisions for their brethren as opposed to anti-Castro pickets and pamphlets. His proposal made him a pariah among hard-liners. "No more Trojan Horses in the exile community!" Mas Canosa wrote of Lorenzo and spoke of the dire imperative to adopt a strong position against "opportunists" like him.

Next he turned his attention to the fertile subject of local politics. He spoke of "recent developments in Dade County itself which give offense . . . and betrayal of the work done by the Foundation." He noted with dismay that Miguel Díaz de la Portilla had won election as a county commissioner, having run without his endorsement. These were "dangerous events that must be faced and resolved urgently," he wrote. Exile leaders Elio Muller and Frank Calzón were excoriated for allegedly seeking to discredit CANF and were identified as "the most rabid defamers of Our Chairman." The lengthy memo included a handful of threats: "Muller has yet to learn how we do politics work in this country; we should educate him," he wrote. "Calzón needs a lesson of a different kind."

He derided the war hero Huber Matos, who languished for twenty years in a Cuban prison, for his "conciliatory message" and for "his efforts against CANF and its *máximo dirigente*"—maximum leader. Francisco Aruca was blasted as "a Castro agent" and deserving of an uncertain punishment: "Now is the time to put an end to this situation which we have had to endure for years." He went on to complain of an audit of CANF's Free Cuba PAC. But he reassured his colleagues that their ally Congressman "Díaz-Balart has promised us to keep [José "Pepe"] Collado [an AFL-CIO union leader] under control."

Finally, he attacked some of CANF's own directors for doing business with companies or parties that did business in Cuba, threatening them with "expulsion from the Foundation." The CANF chairman made reference to an upcoming event at the White House "in which CANF will play its traditional leading role," and reminded the board that it "is the decision of CANF, that Congress, through its Cuban-American members, is to become the redoubt of the forces opposing compromise." He concluded by warning that "this document and the matters discussed herein must be treated with absolute discretion and confidentiality."

Mas Canosa appeared shocked that the document had ended up in the hands of opposing counsel. Following an off-the-record conference with his lawyer, he declared that "this memorandum was never written by me or any member of CANF." Later, he would attribute the memo to Cuban intelligence. His charge was easily disproved by the fax number printed at the top of the document, which was the fax number of CANF. Certainly, the source who had delivered it to the lawyers, a former director of CANF and a well-known exile, had no doubts about its authenticity.

A pattern had begun to emerge. When items of evidence clearly refuted him, he would simply challenge their authenticity. When shown a translated transcript of his comments on Radio Mambí concerning Ramón Cernuda, he contested the translation, which had been professionally prepared and certified. "But you are assuming that these transcripts came from an original tape," he said after the incriminating transcript was read into testimony. "I don't think it is fair for me to respond to a translation of something that I have not heard."

Mas Canosa was particularly cagey about his relationship with Oliver North. Asked why there were so many references to him in North's notebooks, he seemed amused. "You have to ask Ollie North," he replied. He challenged the evidence, photocopies of pages from North's notebooks: "I am not sure that this came from Ollie North's notebook or desk. I don't know," he said. "I would like to see a certification that this is a true copy or show [me] the original." When queried as to whether Jeb Bush had been his liaison with the Bush White House, Mas Canosa initially said no, then claimed not to understand the term *liaison*. "I really don't know, sir. I am not sophisticated," he demurred. Prodded on the issue, he shrugged and said, "I don't know. You have to ask him," before making a small concession: "Once he helped me in reaching the White House."

Although in many respects he had the Teflonhood of his hero, Ronald Reagan, Mas Canosa had taken a body blow in February 1994, when word seeped out that his company, Church & Tower, was poised to set up shop in China. The company had initialed letters of intent to buy 60 percent control of a major Chinese conglomerate in addition to investing $100 million in another Chinese entity. Initially, Mas Canosa saw no contradiction with his decades of vilifying any company that did business with communist Cuba. But as word of the deal leaked into the media, he went on Miami radio, where he improvised some damage control. He denied the report in the *Herald,* calling it a "fabrication," insisting that "we do not negotiate with communists," despite the fact that his son, Jorge Mas Santos, had admitted signing the letters of intent.

In deposition, Mas denied that his company or his son had ever entertained the notion of doing business with China, insisting that he would never do business with any communist country—the underlying principle of his argument for the U.S. Embargo of Cuba. In a later deposition, he reiterated that his company had never signed letters of intent to invest $200 million in China. One of *The New Republic*'s lawyers, Richard Ovelmen, then proceeded to play a videotape of Jorge Mas Santos at the signing ceremony of his joint venture with the Chinese government in 1994 as officials of the Chinese Communist Party stood around him. The signed contracts were then introduced as exhibits, as were dozens of photographs of Mas Canosa entertaining Chinese communist officials at Casa Juancho, his favorite eatery on Calle Ocho. He continued to brazenly dissemble—under oath and under penalty of perjury. "After watching the tape, I still say that it is misinformation," he said with ill-concealed scorn. "Why my son went to China, you would have to ask him."

Mas Canosa's belligerence was matched by that of his lawyer Hank Adorno, whose antagonistic behavior prompted protests from *The New Republic*'s lawyers, a reprimand from the presiding magistrate judge and action from the Florida State Bar. Adorno is Cuban-born but is not fluent in Spanish and often required translation during the proceedings. Because he lacked expertise in libel law, he recruited his former partner, Sanford Bohrer, to assist him. Bohrer's participation in the case stirred alarm in media and legal circles, as he was contracted as outside legal counsel for the *Miami Herald* and the Miami bureaus of several national publications. The standard protocol has it that media defense attorneys tend to eschew plaintiff cases, most especially a case as contentious as that of Jorge Mas Canosa, who for all intents and purposes had declared war on the media. "Suing a media entity is very problematic for a media lawyer," commented the esteemed First Amendment attorney Floyd Abrams, "especially on behalf of a controversial figure like Jorge Mas Canosa. There are inherent conflicts and I would not recommend it."

Soon after the suit was filed, I received a phone call from a colleague at *Vanity Fair,* apprising me that a prominent private investigator hired by Mas Canosa had solicited his aid in "finding some dirt" and asking his assistance in rifling through the magazine's files for information on me.

Adorno was assisted by Raoul Cantero III, an attractive young lawyer who, not incidentally, happened to be the grandson of Fulgencio Batista. While Mas Canosa relished Adorno's bulldog attack mode, he showed a genuine affection for Cantero, with whom he could chat in Spanish. (Adorno, who would later take a management position at MasTec, would have a furious falling-out with the Mas family after he filed suit, claiming millions of dollars in fees were owed to him.)

Following the conclusion of the lawsuit, Andrew Sullivan and I filed complaints against Adorno with the Florida State Bar. "Throughout my two days of being deposed," Sullivan wrote the bar, "Mr. Adorno seemed to revel in insulting and bullying those present in the room. When asked by *New Republic* lawyer Rick Ovelmen to contain his hostility, Adorno tore into a profanity-laced tirade against Ovelmen, filled with threatening innuendo. The court reporter, distressed by his behavior, fled the room."

The State Bar's designated investigator interviewed the court reporter and wrote in her report: "She said that at one point during Mr. Sullivan's deposition, someone instructed her to go off the record. Mr. Adorno then stood up, put his hands on the table to lean closer to the attorneys on the other side of the table and began screaming threats and obscenities at one of them, which included 'Fuck you' and 'I'm going to jump up your ass.' "

On at least two other occasions, Adorno tangled with another *New Republic* lawyer, an unflappable Cuban named Paul Schweip, once calling him "a disgrace" to Cuban-Americans. Schweip filed a protest with the court, which ruled that Adorno's behavior was "totally inappropriate and unnecessary, and it's not going to be tolerated."

FROM THE BEGINNING, Mas Canosa had avidly sought a settlement from *The New Republic,* notwithstanding his repeated assertions that he would "go all the way to the Supreme Court" for a verdict in his favor. In September 1996, following the arrest and indictment of Mas Canosa's close friend César Odio, Miami's City Manager, for bribery and extortion, his attorneys' pursuit of a settlement became more aggressive. According to one federal source in the Odio case, their hope was that Odio would cut a deal and implicate Mas Canosa. Odio did not name his friend but did implicate others, which won him a reduced sentence of one year in prison for obstruction of justice.

Owing to the unexpected quality and volume of evidence, it was clear that *The New Republic* stood an excellent chance of prevailing on its "mobster" headline if the case went to trial. But, lamentably, Martin Peretz, the magazine's publisher, grew weary and impatient with the case. Andrew Sullivan resigned under pressure, and arguably Peretz's close relationship with Vice President Al Gore was also a factor, in that Gore was already currying the favor of exiles for his run in 2000. Peretz is also a friend of Joe Lieberman, another longtime CANF ally, although Peretz says he never discussed the case with either man.

However, Mas Canosa had personally lobbied Peretz to settle with him. "He called me up and said, 'Let's settle this thing,' " recalled Peretz. The exile leader then flew to New York to take Peretz to lunch, which, according to magazine staffers, was held at Umberto's Clam House on Mulberry Street in Little Italy, the very same restaurant where the mobster "Crazy" Joe Gallo was mowed down in 1972. One editor at the magazine said Peretz described the lunch to him, saying, "It was like being in a scene from *The Godfather.*" Peretz recalled that Mas Canosa was "quite charming" and arrived in "a Cadillac with two other men, one of whom he said was his lawyer The men said nothing during the lunch." Although Peretz emphasized that they never discussed the option of a settlement, he said he had become convinced that he could "not let this case be tried in a Miami courtroom."

There was the additional problem that *The New Republic*'s legal team were gentlemen lawyers, not the gladiator combatants assembled by Mas Canosa. Several Miami law firms, including Steel Hector & Davis, fearful of repercussions, had refused to represent the magazine. One of *The New Republic*'s Miami attorneys, Jeffrey Crockett, while well intended, made several regrettable errors in judgment and seemed lacking in resolve.

To the consternation of the media, Peretz opted to settle. On September 12, 1996, at 7:00 P.M., the parties finalized their settlement: in its next issue, *The New Republic* would publish an apology for calling the exile titan a mobster on its cover—and fully exonerate me from any role in the wording of its headline. "The use of the word 'mobster' was the sole responsibility of *The New Republic* and not the author," the settlement language read. In the same issue, *The New Republic* reiterated its support of the article. "Although we regret our wording of the title, which was chosen without the participation of the author, Ann Louise Bardach, *The New Republic* stands fully behind the article itself. Nothing in the thought-provoking article, which addresses America's Cuba policy and the political influence of elements of the Cuban exile community in Miami, requires clarification, correction, or apology as nothing in it has been proven false or libelous." Although Mas had demanded a million-dollar settlement as well as reimbursement for his hefty attorney fees, he settled for a $100,000 graduate scholarship fund for Cuban-American students named, ironically, The New Republic Scholarship Fund.

At its request, the *Miami Herald* was the first media outlet to be notified of the settlement. But the *Herald*'s reporter, whom Adorno often referred to as his "good friend," forfeited the scoop, explaining that Adorno had told her otherwise that very evening—that there was no settlement. Documents provided to the *Herald* did not sway the reporter. Evidently, Adorno needed several days to work with his client and publicists to concoct a spin more favorable to them. The *Herald* deferred to Mas Canosa.

Four days later, Jorge Mas Canosa and Hank Adorno, flanked by key CANF officials, held a press conference at their headquarters. In an audacious performance of newspeak, they misstated the terms of the agreement and omitted any mention of my exoneration. A consummate propagandist, Mas Canosa depicted the case as his personal triumph over the perfidious Fourth Estate and continued his charade that he had been ready to fight all the way to the Supreme Court but had accepted a settlement to accommodate *The New Republic*. His comments and press release deleted the very sentences—regarding the exoneration of myself—that had made the settlement possible and indulged in his trademark red-baiting. The press release referred to me as a "frequent traveler to Cuba" and labeled an interview of mine with Fidel Castro as "sympathetic," when my coverage of Cuba had cost me my press visa to the island.

Many of those present from the media were loath to criticize CANF and had declined to publish any of the damaging material about Mas that came out during discovery. The *Herald*'s coverage of the settlement quoted Mas Canosa, Adorno and other CANF officials at length—without a single comment from *The New Republic*, its lawyers, its editors or myself. *El Nuevo Herald* went considerably further—with a blazing headline, as if Mas Canosa had just toppled Fidel Castro. The *Herald* responded to protests from *The New Republic* of its coverage by suggesting that the imbalance could be rectified by "writing a letter to the editor."

The big surprise turned out to be the Florida State Bar and its Grievance Committee. By and large, Miami legal ethics are to the law what military marches are to music. The pervasive corruption of Miami had long ago bled into the judiciary almost as thoroughly as it had eroded local journalism. No one expected the Bar, which is known for its toothless enforcement of ethics violations, to take any action against such a powerful member. But the committee voted unanimously to recommend that Adorno attend Ethics School and pay the costs of the State Bar hearing—perhaps not the most stringent punishment available to them, but certainly a black mark.

Adorno, however, would achieve some measure of revenge. I learned early on from several reporters that he was seeking to generate prejudicial stories about me that advanced his client's cause. Two years into the case, he finally succeeded in capturing a convert to his cause—an ambitious novice reporter named Elise Ackerman who wrote for a freebie weekly called *New Times*. Working exclusively from materials supplied by Mas's lawyers, without a single phone call to *The New Republic*, its editors or any of its lawyers in Miami or Washington, Ackerman delivered the hatchet job the embattled exile leader had so avidly sought.

For months, Ackerman posed as my close friend. She first contacted me by telephone, seeking assistance for a story she said she was writing on Mas Canosa's paternity lawsuit. When I returned to Miami, she invited me to dinner. My best friend had passed away a week earlier from cancer, so I was not averse to company. Arriving at my hotel in Miami Beach, Ackerman again assured me that her interests were entirely limited to research on the paternity suit. She volunteered to be my guide in Miami, urging me to come with her to her favorite nightclub. I got into the car of my newfound friend and off we went to Calle Ocho. At Café Nostalgia, she introduced me to her friends and to the club's owner. After several hours, she drove us to Wolfie's, the twenty-four-hour deli in Miami Beach. Over a late dinner, she spoke anxiously about wanting to find work at a more prestigious newspaper. She was eager for tips on sources, career advice and job references. When she dropped me back at my hotel after midnight, she invited me to visit her the next day so that I could view an apartment in her building, which she suggested I rent instead of staying in hotels.

From that point on I heard from Ackerman regularly, sometimes daily. Once, she phoned me three times in a day to nudge me to accompany her to the theater, where her former boyfriend was performing. There were numerous other invitations—for drinks, parties, nightclubs and so on. As time went by, she assured me on more than a half dozen occasions that neither she nor her paper had any interest in the *New Republic*–Mas Canosa lawsuit.

I last saw Ackerman on June 7, 1996, when the two of us went out dancing with friends from the *Miami Herald*. We had a grand time—and took turns taking photographs of each other. Two weeks later, she phoned and said she urgently needed to speak with me. She wanted me to know that the following day there would be a story she had written about me and the case in her paper. "And I hope you'll still be my friend," she said. She hastened to add that she had wanted to tell me all along, but that her editor forbade her. The editor, Jim Mullin, a bombastic Miami character, was said to regard the paper as his bully pulpit by several of his staffers. As shrewd as any Miami politician, Mullin was adept at playing both sides of the street. He saw no conflict in the fact that his newspaper's lawyer, Sanford Bohrer, was representing Jorge Mas Canosa. "I was aware of the fact that Mr. Sanford L. Bohrer, who represents this newspaper, was providing legal services for Mr. Jorge Mas Canosa . . . against *The New Republic* at the time. . . . I told Mr. Bohrer then and repeat now that *New Times* has no objection to his working on Mr. Mas Canosa's behalf," Mullin wrote the Florida State Bar on Bohrer's behalf after the story appeared. But in the *New Times* story, Ackerman and Mullin went to great pains to note that Bohrer was "erroneously recorded in federal court as one of Mas's lawyers." And so it went.

From its title to its last sentence, the piece was a model of disinformation, riddled with refutable errors. Even the photograph published with the story was intended to discredit me. Copied from a *Vanity Fair* photo, the image was blurred and framed by a jagged edge that deleted the caption "Contributing Editor Ann Louise Bardach." Instead, the article identified me as "a screenwriter and a freelance journalist." The last time I had written a screenplay was a decade earlier, and Ackerman was well aware that I had been on the masthead of *Vanity Fair* as a staff member for almost ten years.

The story had two agendas: to paint Mas Canosa as an aggrieved victim of a below-the-belt assault and to diminish me. Ackerman misinformed her readers that her story was based solely on court materials. She did not disclose that some of her material came directly out of personal confidences from me. And the truth was that she had access only to the selected, incomplete pages of depositions that had been provided to her by the office of Adorno and Zeder—as no depositions or exhibits were ever on file with the court. Incredibly, she chose to ignore the tens of thousands of pages of documents, exhibits and depositions that unequivocally supported *The New Republic*'s headline. No mention was made of Ricardo Mas Canosa's testimony about his brother's links to terrorists. Not a word was wasted on the damning depositions and exhibits provided by the former members and directors of CANF. This veritable mountain of evidence was of no interest to her.

On one occasion, Adorno took credit for the Ackerman story during a break in depositions, according to *The New Republic*'s lawyers, and warned that he would defend her if she were sued. After all, she had served Mas well. Two reporters from the *Herald* and Kerry Gruson of the *New York Times* sent letters to *New Times* contradicting Ackerman's claim that she barely knew me. Her letter, said Gruson, prompted a "furious phone call" from Ackerman accusing her of betrayal.

The simple truth was that there was no percentage in going after Mas Canosa in Miami. As the *Herald* had learned, the risks were steep: boycotts, blackballing and threats to one's family, with no assurance that local law enforcement would intervene. The rewards for positive or neutral coverage—in which Mas Canosa would have his hands ever so gently slapped for his methods while being praised for his goals—were evident to all.

In June 2001, the *Herald* quietly awarded its legal business to Adorno's firm, which had underbid all the competition. Reporters had been disconcerted several years earlier when publisher David Lawrence's son, an attorney, had been hired by Adorno. However, Lawrence had declined during his tenure to give the *Herald* account to the firm. The fact that the firm had been synonymous with Mas Canosa and many of Miami's contractors and politicians who invite press scrutiny greatly troubled some staffers. As word of the deal leaked into the *Herald* newsroom, demoralized reporters said they could hear Mas thumping and chortling from below the ground,

JORGE MAS CANOSA died in his home on November 23, 1997. He was buried with full pomp and circumstance in Woodlawn Cemetery on Calle Ocho after his cortege solemnly traveled along the streets of Little Havana. His grave, marked by a large white marble Cuban flag, is always festooned with flowers that are delivered twice a week, at the behest of his widow. An eternal flame, built into his tombstone, is often on the fritz. Soon after his passing, the elders of Miami rechristened downtown's Biscayne Boulevard "Jorge Mas Canosa Boulevard."

Mas Canosa's failing health had been rumored for almost a year but repeatedly denied by his family and CANF. On several occasions, he entered Pan American Hospital, owned by Alberto Hernández, CANF's president. A cover story was floated that he had Paget's disease, a painful skeletal condition not regarded as fatal. The *Herald*'s Jane Bussey repeatedly called CANF and MasTec for confirmation of his illness. "I called his son when Mas was dying," she said. "He said that Mas was not sick and doing fine. MasTec is a public company with shareholders who are entitled to know the truth, and CANF is a huge institution. I went to my editors and urged them to let me write the story, but someone at the *Herald* nixed running anything."

The *Herald* accorded the passing of Jorge Mas Canosa the gravity and reverence that the world press had awarded the death of Gandhi. Stories on him filled virtually the entire front section of the *Herald* and *El Nuevo Herald* for almost a week in a full-court-press beatification. "I remember when John Kennedy was killed," said Richard Ovelmen, who had served as the *Herald*'s legal counsel from 1985 to 1995. "Kennedy's death got nowhere the amount of coverage the *Herald* gave to Mas."

The *Herald* was once a newspaper with a crackerjack reputation, but its reputation and morale had dropped like a stone under the shaky rule of publisher David Lawrence, who was hired in 1989. Knight Ridder's ceaseless bottom-line pressure to generate 22 percent annual profits at the cost of its newsrooms' ambitions and standards earned it the epithet "Darth Ridder." And after its bruising battle with Mas Canosa, the paper never again took a hard look at him and committed itself only to limited forays into the pervasive corruption in Miami. Pandering trumped reporting.

On the twenty-fifth anniversary of Watergate, when the national media offered perspective on the scandal that had riven the country, Lawrence penned a folksy tribute to convicted Watergate burglar Bernard Barker. "I think it was the all-time low," said one of the paper's Pulitzer Prize–winning columnists. "I was hiding under my desk." Earlier, Lawrence had left his newsroom reeling in shock at his puff pieces on Mas Canosa and Orlando Bosch. Ricardo Mas Canosa said he contacted the *Miami Herald* in the mid-1980s offering a sensational scoop—extensive documentation of his brother's attempts to corrupt Miami officials. The *Herald* never responded.

The *Herald*'s precipitous decline engendered serial thrashings—in the

Columbia Journalism Review, The New Yorker and *The New Republic.* "The *Miami Herald,* which used to be a vigorous daily," lamented David Remnick in *The New Yorker* in 1995, "is now thin and anemic, a booster sheet." Reporters left the *Herald* in record numbers—not a few for the *New York Times* and the *Washington Post.* "Just when you think morale can't get any worse," Kevin Hall, a former *Herald* editor, told the *Columbia Journalism Review* in 1996, "it gets worse." For the dozen or so outstanding reporters and editors who soldier on—sporadically allowed to publish exceptional work—morale has plummeted with each succeeding year.

The *South Florida Sun-Sentinel,* owned by the Tribune Company, and the Miami *Daily Business Review* have often stepped into the void. The celebrated 1997 paving scandal concerning a $58 million Church & Tower contract with Miami-Dade, which turned out to be largely for phantom repairs or work improperly done, first broke in the *Miami Daily Business Review,* in a story written by columnist Tony Doris. Doris also broke the Miami airport scandal, exposing several lucrative contract awards to cronies of Mayor Alex Penelas and county commissioners, and the Port of Miami scandal, which implicated a dozen major Miami-Dade officials.

Notwithstanding some exceptional reporters, such as Gerardo Reyes and culture writer Olga Connor, *El Nuevo Herald* long ago abdicated any serious ambition to publish neutral reporting on Cuba or Miami. Some of its staff complained that the paper had become a print version of the Spanish language radio stations; others quipped that it had become the house organ of the Cuban counterrevolution. Exile Omar Martínez, whose mother spent twenty-one years in prison under Castro, joked, "I'm going to learn just as much about Cuba from *El Nuevo Herald* as I do from reading *Granma.*"

Its nadir was in July 1998, when the paper ran a front-page banner headline story claiming that Castro was mortally ill. The reporter based his story on the account of a woman living in Costa Rica named Elizabeth Trujillo Izquierdo, whom he identified as a former doctor at Havana's CIMEC hospital, a VIP medical facility. Within the week, it was discovered that the story was a hoax—that Trujillo was not a doctor and had no firsthand knowledge of Fidel Castro. Her former husband emerged and called her "a pathological liar" who did not know the difference between fiction and fact. *El Nuevo Herald* never ran an apology, and neither the reporter nor the editor was suspended for the bogus story.

Knight Ridder, in fact, promoted the paper's publisher, Alberto Ibargüen, to replace David Lawrence as chairman and publisher of both papers. Ibargüen, whose background has deeper roots in business than journalism, is a member of the Mesa Redonda, the close-knit fraternity of Miami's exile elite. It soon became apparent that nothing that could offend any prominent exile personality would appear in *El Nuevo Herald*'s pages. The *Herald* columnist Max Castro, who advocates ending the Embargo, was shut out of its Spanish language partner. Even music reviews were closely scrutinized for the slightest offense. When the *Herald*'s music critic wrote in the fall of 2000 that the new CD by Miami's patron saint of music, Gloria Estefan, was less than melodic, the offending passage was deleted from *El Nuevo Herald*.

Spirits buoyed again at the *Herald* when Ibargüen recruited *New York Times*man Martin Baron to take the helm. Baron conducted a spirited all-fronts assault on the Elián González story, which won the paper a Pulitzer, and commissioned other excellent pieces. But he was undermined by Ibargüen, who slapped an editorial he had written on page one condemning the Elián raid—in full lockstep with the González family advisers. Even more deleterious to the paper's health was Knight Ridder's mandate to slash 11 percent of the newsroom in 2001, putting out to pasture some of the *Herald*'s best people. After only eighteen months, Baron left the paper for the *Boston Globe*. Tom Fiedler, a veteran reporter and former editorial page editor, took over his job. But Fiedler, who published a hard-hitting series on the Miami school board, still had to contend with the overt politicking of Ibargüen, who wrote an editorial endorsing the embattled Bush nominee Otto Reich in 2001, according to staffers, and who has squelched or sanitized criticism of the exile leadership. In 2002, the paper's owners would find themselves lampooned by one of their own. In a thinly veiled reference to Knight Ridder, Carl Hiaasen's novel *Basket Case* savaged a newspaper chain called Maggad-Feist.

SINCE MAS CANOSA'S death, there has been contentious debate over his role and loss to the exile world. Certainly, no one has filled his shoes. His old friend Luis Posada Carriles lamented his passing and fretted that the anti-Castro movement was rudderless and drifting. "Right now is a bad time," said Posada, a year after his friend's death. "Too many years. Everybody is very old." Posada said he had last spoken with Mas Canosa about a month before his death. "He was very sick then," he said. "It was very sad. He was in terrible pain. He knew he was dying. He was a very powerful man." Posada paused and shook his head ruefully. "Now is nothing."

In his abbreviated life, from the founding of CANF in 1981, Mas Canosa set the tone and the agenda for America's foreign policy with Cuba:

no compromise, no negotiation—a policy of slow strangulation. But toward the end, he showed a willingness to confront his enemy. In September 1996, a year before he died, Mas Canosa took a dangerous gamble and went on live Spanish language television to debate Ricardo Alarcón, the president of Cuba's National Assembly. For years, Mas had railed against *dialogueros*. Now he would be dialoguing with the man who was number two in the Cuban government. Although there was no definitive winner, he was uncharacteristically restrained. He comported himself well and made his points succinctly, surprising both his critics and supporters.

An adroit strategist, Mas Canosa was a pragmatist who eschewed battles he could not win. One former CANF board member believes that he would have sized up the odds on the Elián González case and taken a pass. "Mas would have known that no one can sell the American people on keeping a son from a father who wants him back," the board member said. "Mas was very, very smart and he wouldn't have picked a turkey like Elián."

CHAPTER 7

AN ASSASSIN'S TALE IN THREE ACTS

Un bicho malo nunca muere.
A bad bug never dies.

I

Two years after the Bay of Pigs invasion ended in ignominious failure on the beaches of Cuba, two young Cuban exiles stood next to each other in the spring sun at Fort Benning, Georgia, training for the next march on Havana. The year was 1963, a time of feverish American plotting against Fidel Castro's rule. The two men had survived the bungled Bay of Pigs operation, in which 1,500 anti-Castro exiles trained by the CIA invaded Cuba. More than a hundred were killed; the rest were taken prisoner and later swapped for $53 million in medical and food assistance. The two men, Jorge Mas Canosa and Luis Posada Carriles, had enlisted in the United States Army, confident that President Kennedy would mount another attack to banish communism from the hemisphere. They vowed that this time they would succeed. They could not have been more wrong.

In April 1959, Castro and his inner circle had traveled to Washington and New York for an unofficial visit—having been invited to address the Association of Newspaper Editors in Washington, D.C. However, Castro was accorded an inhospitable and inauspicious welcome from the White House. President Eisenhower opted to play golf rather than meet with him. Vice President Richard Nixon did meet with him for about three hours and took an instant and famous dislike to the bearded revolutionary. A month earlier, Castro had seized control of the U.S.-owned Cuban Telephone Company, a gesture of nationalism that played splendidly in Cuba and disastrously in Washington. By the time Castro finished his U.S. tour—with no pledges of assistance or loans—the Eisenhower administration had decided he had to go.

On March 17, 1960, Eisenhower ordered CIA Director Allen Dulles to begin training Cuban exiles for a planned invasion of Cuba. Seven months later, in October, he imposed the original trade embargo against Cuba, initially with exemptions for food and medicine. The rarely used sanction of an embargo was slapped on the island in retaliation for Castro's having nationalized all U.S. properties during the summer of 1960. In January 1961, just prior to leaving office, Eisenhower broke off diplomatic relations with Cuba. America's most celebrated World War II general would leave office champing at the bit to invade Cuba, a sentiment that he conveyed in no uncertain terms to Kennedy at his hand-off briefing. "In his last hours as president," writes James Bamford in *Body of Secrets,* the seminal work on the National Security Agency, "Eisenhower issued what sounded to his successor like an order. 'The United States cannot allow the Castro Government to continue to exist in Cuba,' " he bluntly told the new President.

To ensure just such a conclusion, Eisenhower, in his final months as President, appointed General Lyman L. Lemnitzer, a bellicose Cold Warrior, to chair the Joint Chiefs of Staff. Lemnitzer lobbied ardently for a full-scale invasion of Cuba—similar in commitment to the U.S.-backed coup in Guatemala in 1954, which toppled its democratically elected president, Jacobo Arbenz, and installed a military dictatorship, laying the groundwork for a forty-year civil war. To his dismay, Lemnitzer would learn that JFK did not share the enthusiasm for military adventurism of his predecessor. In fact, Kennedy was quite certain that he would be unable to justify an invasion of Cuba to either the United Nations or the Organization of American States. While he was keen to displace Castro, he would commit himself only to covert actions.

Faced with Kennedy's disdain for a boilerplate coup d'état, the CIA and Pentagon began their long, colorful and often loony campaign to topple Fidel Castro: assassination attempts, covert raids and all manner of sabotage. However, Castro, who had an excellent intelligence service from the beginning, was rarely caught unawares. Ever mindful of the fate of Guatemala's Arbenz, Fidel Castro sought to hedge his bets from his earliest days in power. In February 1960, he met with high-level Soviet officials and signed a five-year trade deal for sugar and a $100 million extension of credit. Six months later, he threw down the gauntlet and nationalized all foreign properties, prompting the U.S. to demand Cuba's expulsion from the Organization of American States.

On April 17, 1961, three months into his term, the young President signed off on the CIA's plan for an exile force to invade Cuba from its southern shore at Bahía de Cochinos—the Bay of Pigs. Almost every element of the planning and execution of the operation guaranteed its failure, beginning with its grievous underestimation of the depth of popular support for the Cuban Revolution and the preparedness of Fidel Castro. The U.S. was also hoist on its own petard. Having revoked diplomatic relations with Cuba in a huff—thereby closing its embassy in Havana and consulate in Santiago de Cuba—it lost its CIA bases and staff, depriving itself of vitally needed intelligence. Worse, the invasion was arguably one of the worst-kept secrets in history. In the ten days prior to the assault, U-2 surveillance planes had buzzed over the island fifteen times. And expecting that thousands of giddily expectant exiles would keep the matter under wraps bordered on madness.

Lemnitzer and the Pentagon had multiple misgivings about the plan, based on their own secret internal analysis. According to Bamford, Lemnitzer wrote in his own unpublished account of the Bay of Pigs, entitled *The Cuban Debacle*, that the invasion was doomed due to *"the lack of predictable future mass discontent"* (Lemnitzer's emphasis). Lemnitzer backed the plan in the belief that the military would be summoned to the rescue when the attack foundered. But it turned out that Kennedy meant what he had said about no overt U.S. action. As the CIA-backed exiles fell to Castro's dedicated troops, JFK nixed using airpower and a U.S. military rescue.

In the wake of the humiliation of the Bay of Pigs, Kennedy made the removal of Castro's revolutionary government a top priority. To that end, he ordered his brother Robert Kennedy, the Attorney General, to fund Operation Mongoose, a plan to train thousands of exiles in the Florida Keys in paramilitary exercises and sabotage. Soon Miami had the largest CIA substation in its history, generously contributing to the employment and prosperity of the city. Its staff feverishly threw themselves into plotting all manner of inventive, often hilarious, schemes to remove Fidel Castro. There would be exploding cigars, beard defoliants intended to emasculate the Cuban leader, and a succession of Mata Hari sirens trained to transmit the kiss of death. However, in a breathtaking slap at the CIA, the Kennedys turned responsibility for Mongoose over to Lemnitzer's crowd at the Pentagon.

Finally, the Cold Warriors had the upper hand. Soon they produced their masterwork—a diabolical plot code-named Operation Northwoods. It would be the "most corrupt plan ever created by the U.S. government," according to Bamford, who disclosed the plots in 2001. "The plan called for innocent people to be shot on American streets; for boats fleeing Cuba to be sunk on the high seas; for a wave of violent terrorism to be launched in Washington, D.C., Miami, and elsewhere. People would be framed for bombings they did not commit, planes would be hijacked. Using phony evidence, all of it would be blamed on Fidel Castro, thus giving Lemnitzer and his cabal the excuse to launch their war."

One scenario could well have been a sequel to the "Remember the Maine" campaign that triggered the Spanish-American War. The plan called for blowing up an empty U.S. Navy ship, indignantly issuing a bogus list of casualties and then blaming the heinous deed on Fidel Castro. "Sabotage ship in harbor; large fires, naphthalene. Sink ship near harbor entrance. Conduct funeral for mock victims," read one memo from the Joint Chiefs.

"We could develop a Communist Cuban terror campaign in the Miami area, in other Florida cities and even in Washington," stated another memo. "The terror campaign could be pointed at Cuban refugees seeking haven in the United States. We could blow up a U.S. ship in Guantanamo Bay [the American military base in Cuba] and blame Cuba," which Bamford noted was similar to what was done in Vietnam a few years later at the Gulf of Tonkin. "Casualty lists in U.S. newspapers would cause a helpful wave of national indignation," the generals wrote encouragingly. Guantánamo Bay, or Gitmo, a forty-five-square-mile dusty, arid patch on Cuba's southeastern coast, was seized by the U.S. in 1898 and established as a base as a victory spoil in the Spanish-American War. It had long been a symbol in Cuba of American imperialism and perfidy. From 1952 onward, Castro rarely made a speech in which he did not fulminate about the presence of U.S. soldiers on the Cuban fatherland.

Other scenarios, worthy of Dr. Strangelove, submitted to Kennedy included accusing the Cubans of using electronic interference to sabotage the February 1962 mission of astronaut John Glenn if his launch were to fail; downing a remote-controlled unmanned plane over Cuba and blaming Castro; and persuading anti-communist islanders to stage riots and attacks on the U.S. base in Guantánamo. Later the Joint Chiefs suggested attacking Jamaica or Trinidad and Tobago and making it look as if the Cubans were responsible, hoping this might incite Britain into a war with Castro. Another plan called for using biological warfare against Cuba—in the belief that it would lessen U.S. casualties during an invasion. Despite estimates that biological agents would kill roughly one percent of those affected, the Pentagon urged its implementation.

One particularly nefarious plot suggested killing fleeing Cuban exiles for a quick propaganda bonanza. "We could sink a boatload of Cubans en route to Florida (real or simulated)," read the memo. "We could foster attempts on lives of Cuban refugees in the United States even to the extent of wounding in instances to be widely publicized." The Joint Chiefs even contemplated hijacking American civilian airplanes, which "could appear to continue as harassing measures condoned by the Government of Cuba."

To execute and follow up on these maneuvers, the CIA summoned its very best exile recruits to Fort Benning. Nearby was the notorious School of the Americas, which trained its pupils in torture and sabotage. Among the 212 exiles chosen by the CIA for its elite Cuba mission were Luis Posada Carriles and Jorge Mas Canosa. The spirits of the two men would soar and then deflate with each scheme and plot, as they anxiously waited for their marching orders. But the orders for a second invasion never came. Unbeknownst to them, Robert Kennedy had become increasingly wary and distrustful of the efforts of the Joint Chiefs and the CIA. By mid-1962, JFK had shipped Lemnitzer off to Europe to head up NATO. Frustrated and enraged by the government's inaction, the two Cubans quit the army in March of 1964 and began their own three-decade war against Castro.

Jorge Mas Canosa, the younger of the two, eventually emerged as the public face of the movement, a successful businessman who, as chairman of the Cuban American National Foundation, courted presidents and politicians, raised money and relentlessly lobbied the White House and Congress to hew to a tough line on Cuba. The older recruit, Luis Posada Carriles, a former sugar chemist and engineering student, became the most daring and effective leader of the exiles' clandestine military wing, ceaselessly plotting to kill Castro and topple his government. Posada remained in the shadows, consorting with intelligence operatives, anti-Castro militants, mercenary assassins and, according to declassified documents, reputed mobsters.

In June 1998, I spent several days with Luis Posada, who spoke at length for the first time about his lifelong career as Fidel Castro's would-be assassin and the key commando in the exile military underground. In six hours of tape-recorded interviews, he detailed his thirty-seven-year relationship with exile leaders in the United States and with the American authorities. At his safe house in the Caribbean, Posada was by turns proud, bawdy, boastful and evasive about his work as a self-proclaimed freedom fighter. He described, sometimes selectively, the role of his sponsors in the exile community and his moody, complex relationship with American officials who originally trained him and often assisted him but, since Iran-Contra, have distanced themselves from his activities.

"The CIA taught us everything—everything," Posada said. "They taught us explosives, how to kill, bomb, trained us in acts of sabotage. When the Cubans were working for the CIA they were called patriots. *'Acciones de sabotaje'* [acts of sabotage] was the term they used to classify this type of operation," he said, adding ruefully, "Now they call it terrorism. The times have changed."

Our meeting came about through a happenstance conversation with a colleague at *Vanity Fair,* who put me in touch with a Cuban businessman living in Caracas with ties to Posada. Although I anticipated a fruitless exercise, I met with the businessman and his companion, a handsome Venezuelan, in New York City. In the first week of June 1998, I made my case for an interview with Posada. The businessman, Miguel (not his real name), was a slight man in his late forties with sandy-colored hair, partial to black leather jackets. Miguel told me that he had first met Posada in Caracas in 1964, when Posada was running Venezuelan intelligence.

Miguel clearly revered Posada and was one of his cadre of eclectic patrons. In the early 1970s, he had invested heavily in Posada's detective agency, which specialized in corporate and marital espionage; fifteen years later, he would play a key role in springing Posada from a Venezuelan prison. Miguel spoke of his friend's "humanness and charm," and related the story of two misguided robbers who accosted Posada in his car in Caracas, stole his money and asked for his watch. "Luis grabbed his pistol really fast and stuck it to the guy's skull and told him, 'Give me back my wallet and my watch and start running.' He didn't kill them." And did I know, he asked, that Posada had been a legendary Lothario, even as he stepped into his eighth decade? "Luis was very handsome. Women love him. Even in prison, they were always coming to see him. It's his only vice. He doesn't smoke. He doesn't drink. Twice a week he could have private visits with women in his cell. He was always busy."

Miguel said proudly that there was no greater marksman than Luis Posada. "Luis likes to hunt with a revolver because he says that anyone can shoot with a rifle," he said. "Luis likes to be very close to the animal and he puts the revolver right up to their head. This is how he keeps up his marksmanship. He practices all the time on deer."

Two weeks later, I was checking my messages on my phone machine when I came across a gravelly male voice speaking somewhat slurred Spanish who identified himself as Ramón Medina. He left a phone number and asked that I call him back. His tone was friendly, almost jocular. I knew that Ramón Medina was a nom de guerre of Luis Posada and I knew that I was onto one of the most important interviews of my career. At the time, I was working for the *New York Times* on an investigative series on exile terrorism. I phoned my editor, Steve Engleberg, played Posada's message and offered a translation. Engleberg sighed in amazement. "Call him back, get on a plane and go," he said.

Posada's conditions for the interview were that I not divulge the exact location of our meeting in the *Times* series except to say "somewhere in the Caribbean" and that I not disclose any of his residences or phone numbers. While agreeing to allow the interviews to be tape-recorded, he declined to be photographed, saying that he did not want to aid Cuban intelligence agents in their hunt for him. "Nobody knows what I look like," he explained. "Not having pictures of my pretty face has kept me alive a long time." Another ground rule was that I would have to come alone. But both the *Times* and I had reservations about my meeting a self-confessed terrorist alone. It was decided that my writing partner, Larry Rohter, the *Times*'s Caribbean bureau chief, would accompany me on the trip, although Posada was unaware of the fact. Rohter was not present for the interviews. He did meet with Posada on one occasion in our hotel lobby, and the two chatted amiably.

Posada picked me up at the small, tidy airport in Aruba on June 18, 1998. Rohter stayed long enough to observe Posada's entrance, then scurried off to a taxi to the hotel. Posada greeted me warmly, but bore little resemblance to the one and only photo of him, taken in 1976, which showed a chiseled-featured *guapo* (handsome man) with a mass of wavy black hair. He still had an impressive head of hair, but it was silver now. His eyebrows, dense and unruly, slanted diagonally over his watery gray-blue eyes. He was seventy years old but had the spryness of a much younger man, notwithstanding a certain thickening around the middle. He wore shorts, sandals and a polo shirt and seemed as carefree as a tourist.

He carried my bags outside to a waiting van and off we went to the residential neighborhood where he was staying. The house he took me to was a pleasant, airy two-level home, hidden from view by a high stucco wall and a security gate. The home belonged to longtime friends; copies of his memoir, *Los Caminos del Guerrero—The Paths of the Warrior*—privately published in 1994, were on the bookshelf. Posada served me some iced tea, while a maid fussed about in the kitchen. For an internationally renowned fugitive, Posada was remarkably breezy. I switched on my tape recorder and we talked for several hours.

Barely half an hour into our first conversation, Posada yanked his shirt over his head to display a torso ribboned with the scars of twelve bullets, the legacy of an attempt on his life in Guatemala in 1990. Both his arms showed holes where slugs had entered and exited. Across his upper left chest was a ten-inch gash where bullets had grazed his heart. "Let me have your hand," he said, maneuvering my wrist to the right side of his jaw, shattered by the same bullet that had also damaged his tongue and nerves, leaving him with a crushed, gravelly voice. "One bullet entered here, and it exited on the left side. My chin used to be an inch longer, very nice. I was very handsome once." Posada blamed Cuban operatives for his maiming. A long period of recuperation followed the attack. Then, at sixty-four, he resumed his life's mission, doggedly determined to eliminate Fidel Castro. "It's a war, a bad war," he said.

More often than not, Posada spoke in English, which he learned early in life and which has served him well in his career. He reminded me that during the Contra support operations he had doubled as a translator for American servicemen, including Eugene Hasenfus, whose capture by the Nicaraguan Sandinistas exposed the illegal operation and led to scandal and investigation.

At the end of our first session, Posada showed me his paintings—many done in prison—which hung on the walls of the house. He is a painter of some accomplishment, partial to pastoral scenes of old Cuba. After I admired one of his canvases of two *bohíos*—shacks—by the sea, he promptly flipped it over, inscribed it and handed it to me. For three days he would pick me up at my hotel and drive us somewhere on the island for our interview sessions, always stopping for a long, pleasant lunch. At dinnertime, he would change into a crisp white long-sleeved *guayabera,* the traditional shirt of Cuba.

Posada, who had dodged the limelight his entire life, had several motives for breaking his silence. In part, he was emboldened by several near-miss assassination attempts on his life. He told a close friend he was afraid that he would not live long enough to tell his version of events. He said he was also annoyed by a *Miami Herald* article on his failed attempts to assassinate Castro in Honduras (Castro was a no-show) and Colombia and wanted to set the record straight. "The *Miami Herald* is no friend of Cuba," he huffed. And he admitted frankly that he was motivated in large part by his desire to generate publicity for his bombing campaigns in Cuba. His 1997 operations had targeted hotels and tourist areas, wreaking havoc and alarm throughout the island and in the highest levels of the government. His intention was to soldier on, he said, hoping to garner the maximum attention afforded by a *New York Times* profile. That would frighten tourists away from visiting Cuba, he reasoned aloud.

During our conversations, Posada often joked about his outlaw activities and lamented that he had devoted his entire adult life to an unrealized goal.

His lifelong nemesis, Fidel Castro, remained in power, with no sign of losing his grip. No anti-communist opposition in the world has been more fervent or well financed than the Cuban exiles living in the States. And yet, as Posada conceded, they have little to show for their efforts. He said that he was especially troubled by the vacuum of leadership and disarray within the exile world since the death of Mas Canosa.

To outsiders, the struggle between the aging Cuban dictator and the graying commando vowing to displace him may seem geriatric, an absurd relic of the Cold War, not unlike the vintage American cars that still cruise the streets of Havana. But, as Posada emphasized, the hatred of the men on the losing side of Castro's Revolution has not been dimmed by the passing of the years. "Castro will never change, never," Posada said, repeating himself with disgust. "Our job is to provide inspiration and explosives to the Cuban people."

Posada acknowledged with a smile that he has at least four different passports from different countries and in bogus names. He regards himself as a Venezuelan citizen, but has a Salvadoran passport bearing the name of Ramón Medina Rodríguez, the nom de guerre he assumed during the Contra operations, and a Guatemalan passport issued in the name of Juan José Rivas López, the alias he uses in that country. He admitted that he has an American passport but would not say how he obtained it or disclose the name. I asked when he last visited the United States and he answered with a laugh and a question of his own: "Officially or unofficially?" He added coyly that he had occasionally used his fake American passport to visit the States "unofficially." Once, he said, he used it to gain refuge in the American embassy when he was caught in the middle of a revolution in the West African nation of Sierra Leone. His friend Miguel said he had purchased the passport from a corrupt passport officer in Miami, and it bore "a gringo name from Atlanta, Georgia." "I have a lot of passports," Posada said with a laugh. "If I want to go to Miami, I have different ways to go. No problem." But he was cagey about the operational details of his raids and deflected my queries with a quip: "I take the Fifth Amendment."

Luis Clemente Posada Carriles was born on February 15, 1928, in the elegant coastal city of Cienfuegos, the eldest son in a family of four children that he described as upper-middle-class. His father owned a bookstore and printing press, and moved the family to the capital when Luis was seventeen and about to enter the University of Havana. Also at the university was an intense law student named Fidel Castro. "He was three years ahead of me," Posada recalled, describing him as tall and handsome but outfitted "like a crazy guy, dressed like a gangster." He said his most vivid memory of Castro was "his gangster style of student politics" and his intimidation of opponents, one of them being a good friend of his, a student leader named Rafael Prats.

After studying medicine and chemistry for three years, Posada worked as a sugar chemist, then as a bug exterminator, before finding employment with the Firestone Tire and Rubber Company in Havana, which later transferred him to Akron, Ohio, after the Revolution. His entire family, including his parents, two brothers and a sister, remained behind, committed to the Revolution. "The family hated him because they are all *fidelistas*," explained his friend Miguel. A younger sister, María Conchita Posada de Pérez, joined the Cuban army after the Revolution and reached the rank of colonel. "She is married to a colonel in the intelligence department," Posada said, savoring the irony. "I help her with money now and then"—a claim that was impossible to corroborate. His brother Raúl works for the electric company, he said, and another brother, Roberto, who also worked for the Cuban government, had passed away. Like the Castros, the Díaz-Balarts and the Mas Canosas, the Posada Carriles are another Cuban family sundered by politics and the Florida Straits.

Posada said he opposed the dictatorship of Fulgencio Batista, but admitted, "To be frank, I was never interested in politics when I was young. Not until the Revolution." Posada married in 1955 and within five years he had moved into open opposition against Castro. His efforts landed him in a military prison. Upon his release, he found his way to Mexico, where he sought political asylum at the Argentine embassy in February 1961. Within weeks he was in the U.S. and soon training for the CIA's Bay of Pigs invasion.

Posada was vague about what prompted him to take up arms against the Revolution so ardently supported by his own family and, initially, by the overwhelming majority of his countrymen. He said simply: "All communists are the same. All are bad, a form of evil." At one point, he handed me three sheets of yellow note paper with his credo written out—printed in block letters in Spanish. The oppression, suffering and poverty Castro has propagated, he wrote, has caused 5,000 deaths, 1,500,000 political exiles, 150,000 political prisoners and 4,000 Cubans who have "disappeared in the waters of the Caribbean while trying to flee in flimsy boats," which, he argued, "gives the right to all free Cubans to rebel in arms against the tyrant, using violence and any method within our reach that contributes to the toppling of the nefarious system and leads to the freedom of our fatherland."

Posada was sent to Guatemala to take part in a second wave of landings in the Bay of Pigs invasion, but did not see action because the initial invading force foundered and his operation was called off. In March 1963, at the CIA's behest, he enrolled in officer candidate school at Fort Benning and received instruction in demolition, propaganda and intelligence. Posada and Mas Canosa served in the 2nd Platoon, Company B, 1st Battalion of the 29th Infantry Brigade. Posada, who rose to the rank of second lieutenant, said he was certain that fate brought him together with Mas Canosa. "Jorge stood next to me every day for seven months in the line," recalled Posada. "We were very close friends."

Both men left the army one year later, when it became clear that the United States had no intention of invading Cuba again. They settled in Miami, the epicenter of anti-Castro activity, where Posada supported himself by freelancing as an exterminator. "I knew Jorge when he was poor," Posada chuckled. "I knew Jorge Jr. [Mas Santos] when he was little and blond-haired. Jorge was very excitable. He was not perfect but he was a very smart guy. He had a lot of trouble with different people, even with his own brother. But do you know anyone who made more than a $100 million and doesn't have a problem with anybody? You have to step on a lot of toes." But, all told, he said, "I trusted him."

While Mas was making his mark in business, Posada was building close ties to the CIA, which was using Miami as a base of operations against Castro. Posada joined a militant anti-Castro group called JURE (Junta Revolucionaria Cubana) and became their chief instructor of trainees in their camps in Central Florida. It was a dizzying time of conspiracies and plots, some worthy of James Bond, some deadly serious. Miami's organized crime figures, who had been well rewarded by the Batista regime, were also eager to bankroll the Cuban opposition and use them for their own ends. CIA files offer intriguing references to Posada's dealings with Frank (Lefty) Rosenthal, described as a "well-known gangster," who became the model for the fictional crime figure at the center of Martin Scorsese's film *Casino*. During the summer of 1965, Posada was "involved in passing silencers, C-4 explosives, detonators" and hand grenades to Rosenthal, according to a Defense Department intelligence report. A year later, he supplied 150 small bombs and some fuses to Rosenthal "under threat of bodily harm." The 1967 report dryly states that "station was only recently advised of this transaction," adding that its timing "suggests Posada may have been moonlighting for Rosenthal and only reported transactions to Agency when it got hotter." Rosenthal left Miami for Las Vegas soon after being questioned by police about a series of unsolved bombings.

Posada spoke obliquely about this period and provided even fewer details in his autobiography, wary of incriminating himself or his associates. Declassified documents from the National Security Archive, a nonprofit research group in Washington, made clear why: for much of that time, the CIA was directing his activities, involving itself even in such minutiae as whether he should buy a boat. (His handlers thought that it was a bad idea and that his cover would be better without it.) The documents are part of voluminous files amassed by the 1978 House Select Committee on Assassinations as part of its investigation into the killing of President John F. Kennedy. Seeking to ascertain whether anti-Castro Cubans had any links to the 1963 assassination, House investigators were permitted to read and summarize a trove of CIA and FBI cablegrams and documents, many of which were redacted and all of which remain classified.

According to the summaries, Posada provided the agency and the FBI with a steady stream of valuable information about Cuban exile activity in Miami. It was the CIA that directed Posada to "establish a training camp for guerrilla ops against Castro," and who pressed him to recruit his own brother Roberto as a spy when he went to London on business for the Cuban government—an attempt that failed. Interviewed in the late 1970s by House investigators, Posada said he had been trained as a CIA operative in the Florida Keys and had quickly become a "principal agent." He said his anti-Castro group had "worked with the Company direct" and had had arms, boats and a network of safe houses. One CIA evaluation in 1965 deemed Posada "of good character, very reliable, security-conscious." Another, a year later, said his "performance in all assigned tasks has been excellent."

At the same time, Posada and Mas Canosa were doing operations for RECE (Cuban Representation in Exile), which received some of its funding from the CIA. Additionally, Posada was the CIA's contact and informer on a host of exile paramilitary groups including RECE, Comandos L, the November 30th Movement and the 2506 Brigade, a fraternity of Bay of Pigs veterans. A series of July 1965 declassified cablegrams asserts that Posada and Mas Canosa were plotting to attack Soviet and Cuban installations abroad. One document quotes Posada as saying that "Jorge Mas Canosa of RECE had paid assassin $5,000 to cover expenses of a demolition operation in Mexico" and that Posada was "planning to place limpet mines on a Cuban or Soviet vessel in the harbor of Veracruz, and had 100 lbs. of C-4 explosives and detonators." Another document reported that Mas "had in his possession 125 lbs. of Pentol to be placed as charges on the vessels" and had "proposed to demolitions expert [that] he travel to Spain, Mexico at expense of RECE and place bombs in Communist installations in those countries."

By July 24, 1965, Posada had "completed two 10-lb. bombs for RECE, working directly with Mas Canosa." At that point, the cablegrams cryptically report, Posada was "instructed to disengage from activities," and there is no indication that the operation went forward. Posada continued in his dual roles as "Coordinator of Forces" for RECE and a CIA informer.

By the late 1960s, Posada's ties with the Agency had begun to fray. Perhaps sensing that he had fallen out of favor, Posada abruptly left Miami in 1967. A CIA memo notes that "Posada terminated 7/11/67 because he resigned from position as military coordinator for RECE. JMWAVE does not have current need. Plans to seek employment in Caracas through old friend." Another report in February 1968 complained of his "tendency" to become involved in "clandestine sabotage activities." A few months later, in June 1968, Posada was questioned about his "unreported association with gangster elements" and "thefts from CIA, plus other items."

Posada relocated to Caracas, where he had several friends in the Venezuelan intelligence service, who promptly hired him. It marked the beginning of his years as an operative for a succession of Latin American governments, although he never ceased his work as a CIA informer. His second wife, Nieves, whom he married in 1963 in Columbus, Georgia, while stationed at Fort Benning, and their son, Jorge, accompanied him to Venezuela. A daughter, Janet, was born there several years later. Posada said he never again lived in the United States, although he traveled in and out of Miami as need be. With his move to Venezuela, Posada gave up his U.S. residency, a decision he would later regret.

During this period, Posada and Mas Canosa worked closely with Orlando Bosch, a former governor of the province of Las Villas who left Cuba in 1960. From 1960 to 1968, Bosch, a pediatrician turned anti-Castro fanatic, headed up Cuban Power and MIRR (Insurrectional Movement of Revolutionary Recovery), among the most fearless and effective anti-Castro commando groups, linked by investigators to dozens of bombings and assassination attempts. Any company, individual or country that did business with or was seen as sympathetic to Cuba was regarded as fair game. In September 1968, Bosch was arrested for firing a 57-millimeter cannon into a Polish ship docked at the Port of Miami. Two months later, Bosch was convicted of the attack and further charged, according to his indictment, with "using the telegraph to convey threats: 1) to the President of Mexico to damage and destroy

Mexican ships and planes; 2) to General Francisco Franco of Spain to damage and destroy Spanish ships and planes; and 3) to Prime Minister Harold Wilson of Great Britain to damage and destroy British ships."

Bosch was sentenced to ten years in federal prison, served four years and was paroled in 1972. Meanwhile, Posada was climbing the ladder in the intelligence world: in 1969 he was made head of DIGEPOL, Venezuelan intelligence. A few years later, he convinced Bosch to join him—"to come to Venezuela to make sabotage," as he put it, against the Castro government. Bosch found Posada's offer impossible to refuse and, in 1974, fled the States to work with Posada, thereby violating the terms of his parole. It was as a fugitive that Bosch founded CORU (Commandos of the United Revolutionary Organizations) in 1976 with Posada, the Novo brothers and another militant named Frank Castro. Within ten months of its inception, CORU would take credit for another fifty bombings in Miami, Mexico, Venezuela, Panama, Argentina and New York. That same year, Bosch was arrested by the Costa Rican police on charges of plotting the assassination of Andrés Pascal Allende, one of the leaders of MIR, a Chilean guerrilla group.

Posada ascended to chief of operations for DISIP, the successor to DIGEPOL, with the help of CIA recommendations and immediately went to war against the leftist guerrilla movements supported by Castro in Venezuela. To Posada, the work was a dream job, and by all accounts he carried it out with gusto. "I persecuted them very, very hard. Many, many people got killed," he said of the guerrillas (some of whom later abandoned armed struggle and went on to play significant political roles in Venezuela under Hugo Chávez, who swept into the presidency in 2000). A falling-out with Venezuela's newly elected President, Carlos Andrés Pérez, led to Posada's dismissal as head of DISIP in 1974 and prompted him to establish his own private security and detective agency, which, he boasted, was "the largest in Venezuela."

Around the same time, Posada's relationship with the American authorities went further on the skids. An intelligence memo reported that "Posada may be involved in smuggling cocaine from Colombia through Venezuela to Miami, also in counterfeit U.S. money in Venezuela." By April 1979, the Agency seemed certain that Posada was involved with narcotic trafficking, and noted in a memo that he was "seen with known big-time drug trafficker." According to the memo, the CIA decided "not to directly confront Posada with allegation so as not to compromise an ongoing investigation." Subsequent cablegrams called Posada a "serious potential liability" whom the Agency would likely "terminate association [with] promptly if allegations prove true." Posada was questioned and "found guilty only of having the wrong kind of friends," the report concluded.

Even so, on February 13, 1976, the Agency decided to formally break its ties with Posada in what the documents cryptically described as concerns about "outstanding tax matters." Jack Devine, who ran CIA operations in Latin America for twenty years, said that by the time Posada was terminated "he was not in good odor." Matters deteriorated even more in the wake of the Church hearings in 1975, which had been triggered by a fear in Congress that the CIA was running too many rogue operations. The hearings led to a ban on CIA assassinations. Devine said that the CIA told Posada in no uncertain terms that his quest to assassinate Fidel Castro was now strictly his own.

Over the next few months, Posada sought to reingratiate himself with the CIA, in the hopes of obtaining American visas for himself and his family. To this end, he stepped up his informer activities, even volunteering information against his close friend and cohort Orlando Bosch. The memos state that in February 1976 Posada warned the CIA that Bosch and another exile were plotting to kill Allende's nephew in Venezuela. Posada's whistle-blowing prompted his comrades' arrest. He also informed on a plot by Bosch to assassinate Henry Kissinger, conceivably in retaliation for his backdoor diplomacy with the Cuban government. "Attempt against Kissinger allegedly planned for Costa Rica," the memo states. "Posada informing agency that he must go through with attempt to contact Bosch as though he did not know that Bosch had been arrested. Posada concerned that Bosch will blame him for leak of plans." On June 22, 1976, Posada again called the CIA seeking help with his U.S. visa and, according to an internal memorandum, offered the Agency a stunning and alarming piece of information: "Possible exile plans to blow up a Cubana airliner leaving Panama."

II

ON OCTOBER 1, 1976, María González, a graceful twelve-year-old, unusually tall for her age, fidgeted with excitement in the waiting lounge of the José Martí Airport in Havana. With her were nineteen teammates and their coaches, all members of Cuba's national fencing team. Outside on the tarmac, their bags were being loaded into the hull of a Cubana de Aviación DC-8 jet bound for Venezuela. It would be María's first time on an airplane, her first time leaving Cuba and her first international competition at the prestigious Caribbean Games in Caracas, the capital of Venezuela.

As the noisy jet engines revved to a thunderous din, the group was led outside to board the plane. Suddenly, María saw one of her coaches running breathlessly toward her. "He came over to me and told me, 'María, you cannot come with us. We just saw in your passport that you are not yet thirteen and all competing members must be at least thirteen. I am so sorry.' " He explained how they had always assumed that María—owing to her height and physical maturity—was well into her teen years. María gasped and then began to cry. Her teammates huddled around her and murmured consolation. "I told him that I'd be thirteen soon—in February," she recalled emotionally twenty-five years later in the beauty salon she runs on Miami Beach's Collins Avenue. "He was trying to be nice to me, but he said no, it was impossible for me to go. He said soon I would compete with the team at the Olympics."

María burst into sobs as she was led inside the terminal. Her teammates grasped her arm in solidarity as she walked by. Another teammate, Nancy Uranga, who was twenty-two, was summoned to the airport to replace her. Uranga was a tall, slender blonde, well liked by her teammates. María and Nancy were good friends, but María felt she was the better fencer. "It isn't fair," she complained bitterly to her coach. She ran home to her family's small apartment in La Víbora in central Havana, where she curled up on her narrow bed and wept. "For three days," she said, "I cried all day and all night."

It was a crushing disappointment in many ways. Athletes in Cuba are accorded the respect and treatment of movie stars. Modeled on the Soviet sports prototype of early selection, champion trainers and unstinting budgets, Cuban athletic programs rival the finest in the world. Their school, the Superior Pedagógica Atletas (SPA), enrolled more than three thousand students and was located in the central Havana neighborhood of El Cerro. Although fencing hardly had the cachet of baseball, the national obsession of Cuba, it was highly esteemed by the Soviets. To further ingratiate himself with his patrons, Fidel Castro, a dedicated sportsman, had added judo, volleyball and fencing, sports cherished by the Russians, to Cuba's curriculum.

Word soon traveled back to Havana that the fencing team had trounced the competition and would be coming home with gold, silver and bronze medals. María heard the news with mixed feelings. She could not help but feel cheated. Now the team would be coming home to a triumphant reception at the school. There would be more medals and speeches—all of which only augmented her disappointment.

On Thursday, October 6, 1976, the fencing team boarded a flight early in the morning for their return journey home. With their gold medals dangling over their clothes and their coaches in high spirits, the athletes settled into their seats, still swapping stories about their string of victories. There would be two stops for Cubana 455—one in Trinidad at 11:03 A.M. and a second in Barbados at 12:25 P.M.—before they touched down in Havana. In Barbados, eighteen passengers disembarked. Among them were two Venezuelan men who had boarded in Trinidad.

The jet took off again at 1:15. They had been in the air less than ten minutes—some twenty-eight miles south of Barbados—when an explosion thundered through the plane. At 1:24 P.M., the pilot of the plane, thirty-six-year-old Wilfredo Pérez, frantically contacted the air traffic control tower in Seawell, Barbados. "We have an explosion aboard, we are descending immediately!" Pérez hollered into the radio speaker system. "Seawell, CU-455, we are requesting immediate landing. . . . We have a total emergency!" Moments later a second explosion sundered the plane as it dove into the dark waters of the Caribbean, its hulk splintering apart on impact, then floating downward six hundred meters to the ocean floor.

Later that same day, the students of SPA were hastily called to a general assembly in the plaza outside the school grounds where announcements and assemblies were often held. The school's director walked silently past the students to the front of the outdoor plaza. Her tightly knit features and dour expression betrayed that there would be bad news—maybe another invasion of the island, no one knew. "There's been a terrible accident," she said haltingly. "The fencing team's airplane has crashed. Everyone is dead." The school held a solemn memorial days later. The students were asked to participate in the memorial. "Each of us represented a student who had been killed," said María. "I represented my friend Nancy Uranga because she had gone in my place."

When a plane tumbles from the sky it is always horrific and incomprehensible. But compounding this particular tragedy was the fact that the plane had crashed not because of engine failure, pilot error or any form of mechanical breakdown. The plane had been blown out of the sky by two time-released bombs packed into the baggage compartment. The Cubana downing would be the first time a civilian airline was blown up by terrorists—and, up until September 11, 2001, it was the single worst act of air terrorism in the hemisphere.

Among the seventy-three killed aboard the Cubana jet were the twenty prize-winning athletes in their teens and early twenties who made up Cuba's national fencing team, their five coaches, and twenty-five Cubana and government employees. There were also five North Korean passengers and eleven residents of Guyana. Everyone aboard the passenger jet had family, loved ones and a story. Among those on board was Lázaro Serrano, the suavely handsome thirty-two-year-old fiancé of Moraima Secada of the famed Cuban group the Quartet Aida; she was the aunt of a future young pop star, Jon Secada. Lázaro Serrano juggled two careers, one as a Cubana de Aviación flight attendant, and the second, the passion of his life, as a songwriter and singer. His stage name was Channy Chelacy and he wrote songs for Moraima and the Quartet Aida. Omara Portuondo, who sang with the Quartet and would have a stunning comeback with the Buena Vista Social Club twenty-five years later, remembered her friend's grief and despair. Moraima Secada would never recover from her lover's death, said Rosario Moreno, a performer at the Tropicana nightclub, who watched her friend spiral downward into depression and alcohol.

Nine days later, on October 15, a memorial was held in Havana for those who had lost their lives in the bombing. More than a million Cubans massed in the Plaza of the Revolution to pay tribute. Fidel Castro gave a thunderous speech of fury and outrage: "We can say that the pain is not divided among us. It is multiplied among us," Castro intoned. Every year thereafter, on October 6, Castro would mark the day—railing accusingly at the U.S., and repeating his charge, unsubstantiated, that the CIA had had a hand in the bombing. On the twenty-fifth anniversary of the tragedy, in 2001, just weeks after the World Trade Center airplane attacks, Castro invoked the precedent in air terrorism of the Cubana bombing. He also read off a litany of "terrorist acts" against Cuba, including fifty-one hijackings of Cuban airplanes since 1959. "On a day like today, we have the right to ask what will be done about Posada Carriles and Orlando Bosch, the perpetrators of that monstrous terrorist act," Castro railed, "and about those who planned and financed the bombs that were placed in the hotels in [Cuba], and the assassination attempts against Cuban leaders, which haven't stopped for a minute in more than forty years."

Based on the pooled intelligence of Venezuela, Cuba and the United States, investigators in Venezuela traced the bombs to the plane's luggage compartment and a restroom. The two Venezuelans, Hernán Ricardo and Freddy Lugo, who had boarded in Trinidad and disembarked in Barbados, were picked up immediately. Ricardo had checked his bag through to Havana and Lugo had brought a bag aboard. It was not long before one of the men confessed to planting the explosives. Both men were employed by Posada at his detective agency and frequently did operations with Bosch and

Posada. The police also found what they regarded as incriminating evidence at Posada's home, including a schedule of Cubana flights. A week later, Venezuelan authorities arrested Orlando Bosch and Luis Posada Carriles in Caracas and charged them with masterminding the tragedy.

The bombing of the Cubana passenger jet torpedoed Posada's career and fortunes. The day following the downing, the CIA made what its records termed "unsuccessful attempts" to reach Posada. Posada proclaimed his innocence and would later blame a Cuban colleague known as Ricardo Morales, aka El Mono, or the Monkey, calling the action "stupid." Morales died, rather conveniently, under circumstances never fully explained in a brawl in a Key Biscayne bar in 1982.

CIA memoranda, however, tell a different story. One page stamped SECRET, replete with numerous typos and whited-out portions, notes Posada's arrest for the bombing. "Posada suspected of working with Orlando Bosch and others in plot," it reads. "Persons suspected in Letelier killing [Guillermo and Ignacio Novo and José Dionisio Suárez] also mentioned. CIA did trace on them for FBI." A later notation reports: "as of yet, no hard evidence linking Ricardo Morales in bombing."

The most incriminating passage on the same page tells of an eyewitness to the plot. "Cable indicates Dominican Air Force Colonel Juan Armand Montes attended meeting of anti-Castro exiles in DR [Dominican Republic] in early November 1976 [sic] at home of former senator of Batista govt. Meeting took place when Orlando Bosch and others discussed terrorist acts such as placing bombs on Cuban aircraft. Participants of meeting included Colonel Abreu; Luis Posada and others." The date was clearly a mistake, as the men were in prison then, and Bosch and Posada's organization, CORU, first met in the Dominican Republic in June 1976 to lay out plans for more than fifty bombing attacks over the next year.

Another CIA memorandum, based on the report of a Miami informer, seems to corroborate Posada's and Bosch's involvement in the bombing. The informer, a restaurant proprietor in Hialeah, told the intelligence agency, "Posada responsible for plane bombing with Aldo Vera. Bosch went to Venezuela to settle differences between Vera's group and Bosch's group."

Another memorandum concerned Frank Castro, identified as "the behind the scenes leader of CORU," who approached Venezuelan authorities in 1978 with a threat and an offer. "In return for the release of Posada, and perhaps Bosch," reads the memo prepared for the House Select Committee on Assassinations, "[Frank] Castro will promise there will be no Cuban terrorist acts in Venezuela or against Venezuelan properties." The memo states that in the previous year, "in protest against Posada's and Bosch's imprisonment, a Venezuelan airline plane was bombed in Miami."

Secretary of State Henry Kissinger, who authored a classified memo entitled "US Position on Investigation of Cubana Airline Crash" immediately after the bombing, expressed little doubt as to his belief in Bosch's role in the attack. "U.S. government had been planning to suggest Bosch deportation before Cubana Airlines crash took place for his suspected involvement in other terrorist acts and violation of his parole," wrote Kissinger. "Suspicion that Bosch involved in planning of Cubana Airlines Crash led us to suggest his deportation urgently."

"Bosch and Posada were the primary suspects," a retired CIA official familiar with the case confirmed in an interview with the *New York Times*. He went on to emphasize that "there were no other suspects." Another source with knowledge of the bombing attacks of that period said, "It was a screwup. It was supposed to be an empty plane."

In prison, both men learned to paint, and through Cuban-American intermediaries and visitors sold their paintings in Miami and Union City, New Jersey. They also ceaselessly plotted to escape. After a year of meticulous planning, Posada escaped with Freddy Lugo in 1977. Convinced that they had allies within Pinochet's government, they turned themselves in to the Chilean embassy in Caracas, expecting a warm welcome. After all, two of their closest comrades, Guillermo and Ignacio Novo, had been charged with the killing of Chilean ambassador Orlando Letelier, one of Pinochet's targets. But they had not calculated on the backlash against the murder of a diplomat on Washington's Embassy Row. To their amazement, the Chileans wanted nothing to do with them and turned them back to Venezuela. A second failed escape landed Posada twelve days in solitary confinement. Nevertheless, Posada told me he felt that "Pinochet was the greatest dictator Latin America ever had."

While his friends were languishing in prison, Jorge Mas Canosa was flourishing. By the mid-1980s his business was booming and his political influence growing. According to a high-level CIA official, Mas would maintain friendly contacts with the Agency throughout his life, but he was no longer an asset. He was more intent and focused now on honing his relationships within the executive branch.

In 1985, Mas Canosa quietly spearheaded a movement to get his old friends out of jail. In a sworn deposition, Ricardo Mas Canosa testified that his brother had told him that Posada was "breaking down. . . . And they had to get him out of jail." Ricardo went on to recount how he had traveled to Panama to obtain the cash needed to pay for Posada's escape. "[Jorge] said that he needed me to go down and bring back $50,000 . . . to get Luis Posada Carriles out of jail, that Carriles wanted out, that he might start talking."

On April 2, 1985, Ricardo Mas Canosa said that he and another Church & Tower employee, Agustín Rey, went to a bank in Panama and withdrew $50,000. Dividing the cash in half, each man put $25,000 in his briefcase and flew back to Miami. "I gave it to Jorge," Ricardo recounted under oath, adding that he covered the withdrawal with a deposit of "three checks that amounted to close to $246,000. . . . We would never make the check the same amount because it would be obvious, it would be easy to track." Ricardo produced the Panamanian bank statement itemizing the three checks that he deposited and the withdrawal. After Ricardo handed his brother the cash, he said that "Félix Rodríguez came into his office and they went behind closed doors. . . . They were going to try to spring [Posada] out. Jorge made some comments about some glitches in the operation that it didn't take place right away." It would take four more months before Posada would "escape" from prison—this time for good.

In our conversations, Posada pointed out that he had yet to be convicted of the Cubana bombing except in Cuba, as he had escaped just prior to his trial. Only Freddy Lugo and Hernán Ricardo were convicted of placing the actual bombs. (The two were sentenced to twenty years and were released in 1993.) Posada blamed political influence peddling in the Venezuelan justice system for his and Bosch's long prison stints. Their critics argue the opposite: that because of Venezuelan corruption, Posada's and Bosch's supporters were able to buy them superb accommodations in prison, a courtroom acquittal for Bosch and, ultimately, Posada's escape.

Posada acknowledged that he might well still be in jail if friends like Jorge Mas Canosa had not come to his rescue. But his version of how the money was raised for the escape was somewhat different from Ricardo's. He said that a $28,000 bribe for the warden had come from the sale of his house in Venezuela and that the money from Mas and other friends in Miami had paid for other expenses. A third version, from José Luis Rodríguez, CANF's former vice chairman, has it that each board member was asked to contribute $2,000 in cash per person to facilitate Posada's escape. It is probable that all three versions are true: that all three sources of cash were needed to cover the expenses of bribing the requisite officials to facilitate such a high-profile escape.

During a changing of the guard at midnight on August 18, 1985,

Posada, dressed in a black jacket with a collar turned up like a priest's, crossed the courtyard of the prison. He carried an oversize Bible close to his chest and a satchel containing food and a lamp. A farmer saw him and ran to his side seeking solace, he recalled with a laugh. " 'Father, I have a son who is ill. Could you please pray for him?' I said, 'Okay, friend, walk with me and pray,' " and together the two men strolled out of the prison. "It was perfect," Posada told me, relishing his tale. Perfect except that Posada's two accomplices plus the warden, Andrés Araña Méndez, went to prison for three years. "He made a hole in the wall and put the money right there," Posada related with amusement. "And then he painted the wall like no one would see it." Worse, the warden went on a shopping spree, and took to sporting a fancy new watch and new shoes. He confessed the day after the escape. "It was stupid," said Posada, who said he had warned the warden about what not to do, reminding him that he knew what he was talking about. "*I was* the police," Posada chuckled. "But he didn't listen to me."

After fifteen days in Caracas, Posada was taken aboard a shrimp boat to Aruba, where he spent a week. From there, a private plane flew him to Costa Rica and then on to El Salvador, where Félix Rodríguez, his comrade from his early CIA days, was waiting for him. Rodríguez would later testify that he had harbored Luis Posada "at the request of a wealthy Miami benefactor who . . . financed Posada's prison escape. . . . I got a call from an old friend in Miami who has helped me financially and who wanted me to hide him."

Rodríguez had a very special job offer for Posada: to be his deputy in the covert Contra resupply operation directed by Lieutenant Colonel Oliver L. North, the NSC staffer who had been charged with providing military assistance to the Contras against the Nicaraguan government. Rodríguez had been hired for the assignment by an old friend from the CIA, Donald Gregg, who worked closely with Vice President George Bush as his National Security Adviser. Posada would very quickly undergo a spectacular reversal of fortune—from a prisoner charged with the worst act of air terrorism in history to a high-level operative running a secret operation directed from the White House.

Posada was delighted. He was not only back in favor—he was on the payroll. Posada noted with a certain pride that George Bush had headed the CIA as Director of Central Intelligence from November 1975 to January 1977, the period of the most violent years of exile activity. On November 8, 1976, a month after the Cubana attack, Bush flew to Miami for a "walking tour of Little Havana." He also met with Miami FBI special agent Julius Matson, chief of the anti-Castro terrorism division, reportedly out of concern over exile involvement in the Letelier/Ronnie Moffitt murders and the Cubana bombing. Five years later, Bush was Vice President of the United States.

The Reagan-Bush presidencies (1981–1993) were the glory years for Luis Posada. In contrast to Jimmy Carter's dogged efforts to reopen the diplomatic door with Cuba, the Reagan administration all but extinguished diplomacy with Cuba. In the unlikely event that Castro had not heard the message, the 1983 invasion of Grenada, a Cuban ally, sent an unmistakable signal. Indeed, several cabinet members in the Reagan administration were not shy about seeking a direct confrontation with Cuba. Secretary of State Alexander Haig, according to Reagan biographer Lou Cannon, gave Reagan's inner circle a fright one day when he declared, "Give me the word and I'll make that island a fucking parking lot." On another occasion, Haig fired off an order to National Security Adviser Robert McFarlane. "Get a bunch of brothers from CIA, Defense and the White House and you put together a strategy for toppling Castro," he barked. "And in the meantime, we're going to eliminate this lodgment in Nicaragua from the mainland." When word came back that such a venture was simply not going to fly, Haig went ballistic. "This is just trash, limp-wristed, traditional cookie-pushing bullshit," he boomed. But Haig, along with CIA chief Bill Casey, was undeterred. Haig wanted a naval blockade of Cuba and persisted in advocating it, according to Cannon, until the Joint Chiefs of Staff and Defense Secretary Caspar Weinberger finally put the brakes on him.

Even after that, Haig would make two public threats against Cuba, declaring his plans "to go to the source" of the Nicaraguan problem—meaning Cuba. Leslie Gelb, then a diplomatic correspondent for the *New York Times*, recalled the effect that Haig's pronouncements had on the Cuban military brass. "They were really worried about what he was saying," said Gelb, who met with Haig to discuss the matter, and later with one of Cuba's top generals. Haig gave no indication that he was bluffing, or that he had no support behind him. "He didn't say he *wouldn't* intervene in Cuba," Gelb said. Five years later, Gelb met with Rosales del Toro, the chief of staff of the Cuban military. "He began the session with this impassioned speech about how if the United States attacks Cuba," Gelb recalled, "how 'we'll fight, and we'll lose, but we'll spill a lot of American blood.' And he was thumping the table, but in a way that you could see that he assigned some real probability. Then I said to him, 'I don't think that there is any chance we'll invade Cuba, I just don't think it will happen. I don't think there is any support in the United States for it.' He got up from his seat at the table, with tears coming out of his eyes, and embraced me and thanked me for this."

But if the Reagan administration was not prepared to invade Cuba, it was certainly ready to intervene in Central America. And in its eagerness to find middlemen to carry out its ambitious new program of covert operations, it was willing to overlook a few unsavory details. Posada's new handlers seemed unruffled by his checkered past and outfitted him with a Salvadoran passport and driver's license in the name of Ramón Medina Rodríguez. Almost immediately he was put in charge of organizing the flights that ferried supplies for the Contras from the Salvadoran air base at Ilopango to the battlefront in Nicaragua. Among his duties was to coordinate the efforts of the Contras and their secret American advisers, pilots and soldiers, with their allies in the Salvadoran military. Posada had cultivated numerous friendships within the right-wing Salvadoran government, its military and its notorious death squads. Given their mutual loathing of communism and Fidel Castro, it was a marriage that served both parties well. Posada, working closely with Félix Rodríguez, directed the drops of military supplies to the Contras in the Nicaraguan jungle. With his good command of English, he served as the primary translator for the operation.

In a six-and-a-half-hour interview on behalf of the Office of Independent Counsel (OIC) with two FBI special agents conducted at the American embassy in Honduras, Posada was both revealing and cagey. The interview, conducted on February 7, 1992, was declassified three years later, although large portions were deleted or blacked out. It described Posada as the "field manager" of the Contra operations and the liaison between Juan Rafael Bustillo, a Salvadoran general with close ties to his country's paramilitary death squads, and American pilots. Posada said he set up the various safe houses in El Salvador where American personnel worked and lived and kept their sophisticated surveillance and communication encryption systems. He was also entrusted with a great deal of money, "$3,000 a month plus housing, a car, maid service, food and all other expenses." He also earned $750 for every flight he took as part of the resupply operation, often averaging $7,000 a month for flights in addition to his salary.

"Posada took care of all the matters concerning housing arrangements," the OIC report states. "He paid the leases, the maids and all utilities and phone bills for each house . . . including keeping [them] stocked with food and beer. . . . Posada recalls that the re-supply project was always looking for people to carry cash from the United States into El Salvador for Posada to dispense . . . always worried about the restriction on only taking $10,000 out of the U.S. at one time." The primary source of money was Richard Secord, who was directing the operation for Oliver North, and Southern Air Transport flew weekly into Ilopango with supplies, personnel and cash as needed.

When questioned about visitors from Miami, Posada was evasive. He told investigators he "didn't meet these Cuban visitors because he didn't want to meet any Cubans," according to the report. "He made it a point not to let the Miami Cuban community know he was there . . . because it would get out." He also sought to protect his friend Jorge Mas Canosa, saying that he "knew about the operation but was not involved. . . . Mas is too busy with his lobbying activity, that's why Posada doesn't try to contact him."

But this was not exactly the unvarnished truth. Posada told me that he had hosted Mas Canosa, who was spearheading aid for the Contras in Miami, and the late Miami congressman Claude Pepper in El Salvador. "Jorge said to me, 'Do me a favor. Take him on a tour to see the guerrillas.' This man must have been 100 years old and he could barely sit up in the helicopter," Posada related merrily. "We had to put him on top of a box and he was sleeping. Félix was flying and I manned the gun turret and Jorge and this man sat in the middle. It took six hours to get inside [the jungle] and six hours to get out." Pedro Reboredo, a Miami city commissioner, also came to visit Ilopango, although Posada claimed not to have met with him.

In his autobiography, *The Paths of the Warrior*, Posada wrote that in April 1986, Oliver North, Air Force Major General Richard Secord and Dick Gadd, a senior American military officer, flew by Learjet from Washington to Ilopango to meet with him and with their Salvadoran counterparts. Also at the meeting were Contra commander Enrique Bermúdez, El Salvador's air force commander General Juan Rafael Bustillo, and Félix Rodríguez. Posada told the FBI agent that "the Contras wanted better aircraft," but "North said don't worry about it because Americans will fly the planes." During the meeting, it was decided that all future flights to resupply the Contras with military hardware would be flown by American pilots, not Salvadoran soldiers, as had been the case up until then. Following their meeting, Posada said he gave Gadd a full tour of the Contra operation.

Posada also told the Independent Counsel investigators that Oliver North "had pressured the U.S. Ambassador Lewis Tambs to help" with the resupply operation. "Tambs then went to see [Costa Rica's] President Monge and threatened him to allow the re-supply activity to take place," using Costa Rica's air bases. He also confirmed that Edwin Corr, the U.S. ambassador to El Salvador, was fully in the loop.

The flights ended abruptly on October 8, 1986, when the Sandinista forces shot down one of the C-123 transport planes used to make drops to the Contras. Two American soldiers were killed while a third, Eugene Hasenfus, parachuted safely to the ground. Posada said he had forever teased Hasenfus, whose job was to kick the supplies out of the plane to the Contras waiting below, about his habit of wearing his parachute all the time. Posada had himself been scheduled to fly aboard the downed aircraft but had narrowly missed the flight—"by minutes." Posada said he had been especially close to Matthew Cooper, who was killed in the crash. Once he was captured by the Nicaraguan government, Hasenfus soon spilled the beans about the covert operation. He disclosed that the operation in the field was being directed by a Cuban exile known as Max Gómez, whose real name was Félix Rodríguez, and by a man he knew as Ramón Medina. It was not long before the world learned that Ramón Medina was actually Luis Posada Carriles, the international fugitive.

Hasenfus's capture was a front-page story around the world and a nightmare for the White House. The key players flew into a frantic damage control mode—with Oliver North famously instructing his secretary to shred his memoranda. Posada told the OIC investigators in 1992 that when Hasenfus's flight did not return, he immediately called Félix Rodríguez, who was in Miami. "Rodríguez told him that Radio Havana had already announced the downing of an aircraft," according to the Independent Counsel report. "Rodríguez told Posada that he would call people in Washington about the missing flight. Posada then hurried to the resupply houses and told everyone what had happened."

As reporters converged on Ilopango, a fortuitous earthquake struck El Salvador, diverting all attention from the Contra operation for several days. During the diversion, Posada said some derring-do on his part may have saved Reagan and Bush from impeachment. While El Salvador attended to a full-scale rescue, Posada raced into San Salvador and picked up some thirty American military personnel and advisers who were hiding out from reporters in safe houses. In his memoir, Posada recounted how he arrived with a truck and cleaned out all the safe houses in the country's capital, ferrying everyone to Ilopango and to Bustillo's, where he disposed of reams of incriminating documents and communication equipment.

Soon after Hasenfus's capture, Posada's point man for the operation, Robert Dutton, told him that he and other administration staffers had been debriefed by the FBI on the debacle and had informed investigators about Posada's work for the operation. He was told that "the FBI wanted to talk to him at 8:00 A.M. the next day," the report notes. "However, the FBI never called Posada. Later Dutton told Posada that it was okay, that the FBI wouldn't investigate. Dutton said that Washington had 'stopped the investigation.' "

It is clear from the OIC report that a rift had grown between Posada and his former comrade-in-arms Félix Rodríguez. Posada described his relationship with Rodríguez after Iran-Contra as frosty. "Félix was always on the phone talking with Donald Gregg," national security adviser to Vice President George Bush, Posada said to me. "He talked too much." According to the OIC report, "Posada recalls that Rodríguez was always calling Gregg. Posada knows this because he is the one who paid Rodríguez's phone bill. Posada was present at times when Rodríguez talked to Gregg.

"In Posada's opinion, Rodríguez is talkative, immature and has ego problems," the report states. "Given what Posada knows about Rodríguez's personality, Posada assumes that Rodríguez told Gregg and other friends about the re-supply project. Posada feels this way because to talk like this is 'in his nature.' Posada illustrates his point by telling the story of a scorpion who wanted to cross a stream, however, the scorpion couldn't swim. The scorpion asked a frog to take him across, and reassures the frog by saying, 'I wouldn't sting you because if I did, you would drown and I would fall in the water and also drown.' The frog agrees to take the scorpion and gets halfway across the stream when the scorpion stings him. As the frog is drowning he asks the scorpion, 'Why did you do it? Now we'll both drown.' The scorpion replied, 'I couldn't help myself, it's in my nature.' "

Matters came to a head during a contentious meeting between Donald Gregg and Rodríguez on August 12, 1986. When Rodríguez came back, he went and saw Bustillo, the Salvadoran general handling the operation. He told Bustillo that he had been called "a security risk and had to get off the project." The Salvadoran general responded genially, telling him, "Okay, then you can be the liaison between me and the resupply operation." Posada, who supplied this account, pointed out another pitfall of the illegal resupply operation in the OIC report. "It's a sensitive situation because Bustillo has been linked to the Jesuit murders," Posada noted. (Bustillo was named as one of the generals responsible for the 1989 murders of six Jesuit priests, their housekeeper and her daughter.)

ON JULY 14, 1988, FÉLIX RODRÍGUEZ was summoned to testify at the Senate's Subcommittee on Terrorism, Narcotics, and International Operations chaired by John Kerry, the Democratic senator from Massachusetts. Not only had Hasenfus mentioned him by name when he blew the whistle, he had been implicated by a notation in Oliver North's notebook, which had escaped the shredder: "Felix Rodriguez still has not got the 50G from Mas."

To the chagrin of some in the Reagan administration, Rodríguez was not a "good soldier" and did not fall on his sword. He could, after all, have disappeared for a spell in Central America and dodged a subpoena, or he could simply have taken the Fifth Amendment. Instead, he testified under oath in a closed session for several hours. In his testimony, Rodríguez confirmed that he had spoken with Mas Canosa about giving him the $50,000 noted in North's notebook, but he refused to provide further details. "I will not discuss that, Senator," Rodríguez told the committee. "It would create speculation, whatever it is, and I will not talk about it." Pressed by Kerry, Rodríguez responded almost haughtily. "Ask Oliver North, Senator," he said. But he did make one startling admission. He told the committee that he had met with George Bush, adding that he had proudly shown the Vice President a photograph of himself with his captive Che Guevara, taken hours before the famed revolutionary's execution.

Rodríguez's testimony foreclosed the possibility of plausible deniability for George Bush, who subsequently refused to answer questions about the scandal. Incensed, Senator Tom Harkin charged that the American people "deserve a full accounting of Vice President Bush and the vice president's office and its knowledge of Luis Posada's role in the secret Contra re-supply operation." He mused aloud as to "why Bush never bothered to use his good offices to investigate charges of Posada's links with the supply operation and Félix Rodríguez even after the press reported them in late 1986." Indeed, the Office of Independent Counsel decided it was a question well worth pursuing.

Four years later, Posada confirmed the connection with Vice President George Bush in his conversation with the FBI investigators from the Office of Independent Counsel. "Posada was aware of Rodríguez's contacts with the office of the Vice President (OVP)," the report states. "Rodríguez told Posada that he wanted to talk to then Vice President George Bush and that he arranged a meeting through his friend Donald Gregg." Gregg is described in the report as a "good and old friend" of Félix Rodríguez, going back to when the two served in Vietnam together. Rodríguez told Posada that he had said to "Bush that 'Salvador is very good,' " and had updated him on "the situation in El Salvador." The Vice President's response was studiously noncommittal. "What got Rodríguez very mad was that Bush said nothing at all in response," Posada told the investigators. "Bush just thanked Rodríguez. . . . This really hurt Rodríguez's ego."

When I queried Posada on Bush and Rodríguez's relationship, Posada was dismissive. Rodríguez had one meeting alone with Bush in Washington in which they discussed "the Salvador situation and the guerrillas," he said. "Félix met Bush for five minutes." Posada portrayed himself to me as the good soldier, the Iran-Contra warrior who kept his mouth shut. "They wanted me to come to Washington to testify against Oliver North. I refused to go," he told me proudly, adding disparagingly that "Félix went and testified. You see, he's like a boy, like a child. Félix was an enemy of Oliver North."

But the OIC report makes clear that Posada was in fact prepared to come to Washington and testify—albeit four years after the hearings had concluded. "Posada would be willing to come to Washington, D.C., to meet with the OIC," the report says toward the end. Of course, Posada had his own motives: he needed another operation for his bullet wounds. "Posada would like to come to the United States eventually," continued the report. "He is tired and wants to move on in his life. He also misses his family in Miami."

Posada said that he himself never met Bush but he was certain that the administration was well aware of his involvement in Iran-Contra. "Who could deny that this operation was controlled, sanctioned and run from Washington?" Posada wrote in his memoir. "Our orders in El Salvador came from the White House. . . . Coding and decoding machines—restricted to the NSA [National Security Agency]—were provided for each of our safe houses." When I pressed Posada on who in the administration knew about the operation, he made an incredulous face. "It would be very difficult for Reagan not to [have] known what was going on," he said. His gravelly voice rumbled with a deep laugh. "Everybody knew."

WHILE POSADA AND FÉLIX RODRÍGUEZ were running military operations in Central America, another Cuban exile was making an equally important contribution to the Contra effort. His name was Otto Reich. The son of an Austrian Jewish father and a Cuban Catholic mother, Reich left Cuba with his family in 1960, at the age of fifteen, and was educated in the States. After completing a bachelor's degree in international studies from the University of North Carolina in 1966, he did a two-year stint in the U.S. Army, stationed in Panama. Upon his return to the States, he attended graduate school at Georgetown University.

In 1972, Reich moved to Miami and began his career in government as an international representative for the Florida Department of Commerce. In

1980, when Ronald Reagan was elected President, Reich returned to Washington. He began his Beltway ascent as an administrator at the Agency for International Development. But it was in his capacity as director of the State Department's Office of Public Diplomacy from 1983 to 1985 that he made his mark. As chief spinner of the Iran-Contra operation, Reich supervised a staff of CIA and Pentagon specialists, and was charged with winning support for administration policies in Central America. He reported directly to Oliver North. The office wrote bogus op-eds that appeared in major newspapers under the names of Nicaraguan rebel leaders and attacked those who differed with Reagan's policies.

A bipartisan 1987 report by the U.S. Comptroller General's office entitled *White Propaganda* concluded that Reich's office "engaged in prohibited, covert propaganda activities" and had used taxpayer revenue for illegal public relations and lobbying. The office was shut down, but Reich escaped prosecution. Instead, he was dispatched to Venezuela, where he served as ambassador from 1986 to 1989, despite the Venezuelan government's objections and efforts to derail the nomination.

Reich's presence in Venezuela did much to hearten his fellow exiles Posada, Rodríguez and Jorge Mas Canosa, who viewed him as a new and powerful ally. A half dozen State Department cables suggest that Reich used his position to lobby for Orlando Bosch, a man who, the Bush Justice Department concluded, had participated in more than thirty terrorist actions. When Reich began his term as ambassador in June 1986, Bosch had served eleven years in a prison outside Caracas. He remained fiercely unrepentant about his methods and tactics. "You have to fight violence with violence," Bosch told investigators for the U.S. House Select Committee on Assassinations who interviewed him in jail in 1979. "At times you cannot avoid hurting innocent people."

On July 21, six weeks after Otto Reich presented his credentials in Caracas, a Venezuelan judge issued a surprise ruling that Bosch was innocent of the Cubana bombing. Charges of impropriety surfaced immediately, as Venezuelan justice has long been susceptible to generous *mordidas* (bribes) and extrajudicial considerations. It was noted that Bosch had been in continuous contact with the two men convicted of planting the explosives on the Cubana plane. Former Venezuelan President Carlos Andrés Pérez publicly challenged the ruling: "I am knowledgeable about this monstrous crime" he wrote, "because the initial responsibility was mine." He went on to claim that "the Bosch file had been tampered with." But Reich had no such doubts. He

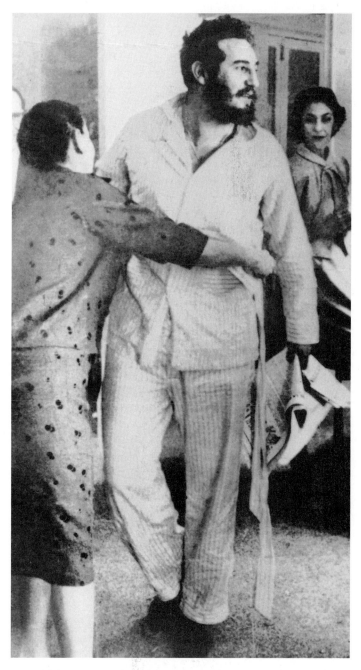

Fidel Castro with secretary Conchita Fernández tying
his pajama sash, while his confidante Celia Sánchez
looks on, Havana, 1959. (Courtesy of a family friend)

Fidel Castro and his son Fidelito at the Habana Libre Hotel, formerly the Hilton, in early 1959. (Bettmann/CORBIS)

The wedding of Fidel Castro's twenty-four-year-old sister, Enma, to Mexican engineer Victor Delgado on April 30, 1960. The service was performed by the Cuban archbishop, Monsignor Evelio Díaz, in Havana's historic cathedral. Ramón Castro is shown kneeling at center. Fidel Castro (standing, in uniform) was to give the bride away, but he arrived too late and a family friend stood in for him. (Bettmann/CORBIS)

Che Guevara, the guerrilla businessman, out of
uniform in 1966. (Bettmann/CORBIS)

Juanita Castro speaking at a
Houston news conference
eight years after her defection from Cuba, March 16,
1972. (Bettmann/CORBIS)

Party given for Fulgencio Batista and his wife, Marta Fernández, by the United Fruit Company in the mid-1940s. The couple is flanked by Eustace Walker, the manager of United Fruit's Banes division, and his wife, Bess. (Courtesy of a family friend)

Photograph from a New York newspaper of Fidelito Castro Díaz-Balart, age nine, returning to Havana with his aunt Silvia Nuñez de Glennon on January 5, 1959. (UPI)

Lina Ruz, the Castro family matriarch, on a visit to see her daughter Enma and her family in Mexico City, July 24, 1961. (Bettmann/CORBIS)

Soviet Premier Nikita S. Khrushchev (right) greets Cuban Defense Minister Raúl Castro at the Kremlin, July 3, 1962. (Bettmann/CORBIS)

THE THREE FACES OF ARMANDO PÉREZ-ROURA

Fulgencio Batista (waving) beside Armando Pérez-Roura (with mustache) celebrating the defeat of the student-led attack on Batista's palace in March 1957 in which José Antonio Echeverría and more than thirty other students were killed. (Courtesy of Bernardo Benes)

Pérez-Roura, the president of the Union of Radio Broadcasters under Fidel Castro, behind and next to Castro's Minister of Labor, Augusto Martínez, on September 13, 1960, when the radio and television station CMQ, Cuba's number one broadcaster, was confiscated and nationalized. (Courtesy of Bernardo Benes)

Pérez-Roura (third from right) aboard Air Force One with President George Bush, October 3, 1992 (Courtesy of the George Bush Presidential Library)

FIDEL CASTRO FROM THE 1945 COLEGIO DE BELÉN YEARBOOK: HIGH SCHOOL RENAISSANCE BOY

The Sportsman.

The Debater.

The Thinker.

(Photographs provided by Cindy Karp/Black Star)

Mirta Díaz-Balart sitting on the sand at a beach in Banes, Cuba, with Marjorie Skelly (in striped suit) and another friend, 1944. (Courtesy of a family friend)

Mirta Díaz-Balart (seated, third from left) on a beach in Banes, early 1940s. Standing behind her is Barbara Walker (white suit); standing next to Barbara is Mirta Batista, the daughter of Fulgencio Batista (in floral white swimsuit). (Courtesy of a family friend)

Mirta Díaz-Balart at her wedding shower on October 10, 1948 (with gardenia on dress) at the United Fruit Company American Club, Banes. (Courtesy of a family friend)

Fidel Castro gives former President Jimmy Carter a lesson in hardball, May 14, 2002, during Carter's historic trip to Havana. (Reuters NewMedia Inc./CORBIS)

Jorge Mas Canosa, the powerful exile leader, upon his return from a White House meeting with President Bill Clinton on February 26, 1996. (*Miami Herald*/David Bergman)

Portrait of the exile militant and amateur painter Orlando Bosch at his home in Miami, November 4, 1995. (*Miami Herald*/Gaston DeCardenas)

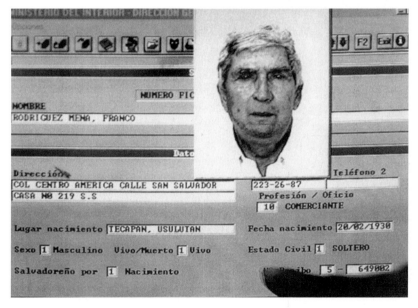

Luis Posada Carriles, Castro's would-be assassin, and the file of one of his aliases, Franco Rodríguez Mena, from El Salvador's Interior Ministry. (AFP/CORBIS)

Elizabet Brotón with her son, Elián González, Cárdenas, 1999. Inscribed on the back of the photo is "Para Rafa, de quien no los olvidan [sic]. Ely y Elián" (For Rafa, from those who have not forgotten you. Ely and Elián). (Courtesy of Jorge Munero/CORBIS)

Elizabet Brotón (far left), Lisbeth García and Zenaida Santos (third and fourth from left) on a day trip with fellow workers from the Hotel Paradiso–Punta Arenas in 1999, a few months before the doomed voyage. (Courtesy of Lisbeth García)

Protesters outside the home of Lázaro González at 2319 NW 2nd Street in Little Havana in April 2000, shortly before the raid by INS officials.
(Cindy Karp/Black Star)

Elián González upstaging Fidel Castro at his seventh birthday party at his school in Cárdenas, December 6, 2000. (Courtesy of Albert Fox Jr.)

Miami's congressional representatives Lincoln Díaz-Balart and Ileana Ros-Lehtinen with Elián González during Miami's annual Three Kings parade, January 9, 2000. (Reuters NewMedia Inc./CORBIS)

Fidel Castro, under a billboard of Elián González, with Juan Miguel González and Cuban National Assembly President Ricardo Alarcón looking on, at a ceremony to award Elián's father one of the state's highest honors, July 5, 2000, Havana. (Reuters NewMedia Inc./CORBIS)

Governor Jeb Bush greets Florida Secretary of State Katherine Harris on November 29, 2000, at a state cabinet meeting while the presidential election's recount battle rages on. (AFP/CORBIS)

Fidel Castro spends his seventy-fifth birthday with Venezuelan President Hugo Chávez at the Venezuelan jungle resort of Canaima, August 13, 2001. (Reuters NewMedia Inc./CORBIS)

Fidel Castro at a press conference during the Ninth Ibero-American Summit in Havana, November 16, 1999. (AFP/CORBIS)

Billboard in Miami, January 2000.

eagerly cabled Washington that Bosch had been "absolved" and queried Bosch's superiors about his eligibility to return to the U.S.

In some of Reich's dispatches to Washington, he argued for Bosch's innocence; in others, he fretted over his safety. In a July 1986 cable, he wrote that a contact at a cocktail party had warned him that Bosch was in physical danger. "This guy has to be taken out of the country in five seconds," the putative informant told him. "Fidel Castro would have him assassinated." Another cable reported to Washington: "The [Venezuelan] government would like to be rid of Bosch as soon as possible"—although no evidence was cited to support his claim. Reich also failed to mention in any of these cables that thirty countries had refused asylum to Bosch because of Bosch's criminal record.

On September 1, 1987, several Venezuelan newspapers reported that Bosch had sent a letter of thanks to the organizers of a conference of Cuban dissidents in Caracas for having invited him to serve as president of the conference. Reich nervously informed the State Department that Bosch's letter, which had been published, included a thank-you to his "compatriot Otto Reich" for his efforts on behalf of their common goals. Reich suggested that the letter might be "Soviet-Cuban disinformation." But Reich, a capable propagandist, seemed an unlikely dupe.

In subsequent diplomatic cables, Reich informed his superiors that Bosch's friends, with whom Reich was in contact, were ready to "whisk him out of the country on four hours' notice." Presumably this is a reference to Jorge Mas Canosa, who had been working diligently to secure Bosch's release and his return to Miami. In December 1987, Reich requested clearance to issue a visa for Bosch to travel to the U.S. This time, Reich's request was denied.

A supremely confident Orlando Bosch nonetheless flew to Miami, where he was promptly detained for a prior parole violation and for illegal entry. His rearrest became a cause célèbre among the exile leadership. As was so often the case, Mas Canosa led the charge, along with Tato Aviño, the father of Miami City Manager Joaquín Aviño, who served as Bosch's spokesman. Bosch's supporters were unapologetic about his record of violence and adopted the age-old justification for terrorism: Bosch was a freedom fighter— not a terrorist.

The campaign for Bosch's release from prison became a central focus of the 1988 congressional campaign of Ileana Ros-Lehtinen, who lauded Bosch as a hero and a patriot, and whose campaign manager at the time was the President's son, Jeb Bush. To ensure that Bosch did not endure jail for long, his more militant cohorts phoned in bomb threats to the local office of the Immigration and Naturalization Service. No bombs actually detonated, but the message was clear. Jorge Mas Canosa was one of several prominent exiles who testified at a parole hearing on Bosch's behalf, on March 22, 1988. Bosch had been a friend "of more than twenty years," Mas told the parole board, adding that he was certain Bosch would never "be involved in any violent acts again."

In January 1989, the associate attorney general rejected Bosch's application for political asylum. "For thirty years Bosch has been resolute and unwavering in his advocacy of terrorist violence," he wrote in his decision. "He has repeatedly expressed and demonstrated a willingness to cause indiscriminate injury and death." The Justice Department's decision was based in part on a letter sent by FBI special agent George Davis to Secretary of State George Shultz in 1987 in which Davis warned the Secretary of State not to allow Bosch to return to the U.S. "My colleagues and I conducted exhaustive investigations of Bosch from the time of his arrival," Davis wrote. "He was regarded by the FBI and other law enforcement agencies as Miami's number one terrorist." Bush's own Attorney General, Richard Thornburgh, described Bosch as an "unreformed terrorist," and the Justice Department concluded that Bosch should be deported from the U.S.

However, in an unusual, perhaps unprecedented, twist, President Bush rejected his own Justice Department's recommendation. In a stunning presidential intercession on behalf of a convicted terrorist, Bush expedited the release of Bosch in 1990. In 1992, he even granted Bosch U.S. residency. The *New York Times* opined that the Bush administration had "squander[ed] American credibility on issues of terrorism." Bosch was promptly hired to work for Alberto Hernández, who would succeed Mas Canosa as chairman of CANF, at his Pan American Hospital for a salary of $1,500 a month.

One high-level State Department official complained of seeing Bosch on Flagler Avenue in Miami, not long after his release from prison, rallying support and raising funds for commando operations against Cuba. "I would call the Justice Department and tell them Bosch is violating his parole again," said the official. "And they would tell me, 'Fine, we'll pick him up. But you know Jeb is going to get on the horn with his father and he'll be right back on the street again.' "

Certainly the Bush family has paid a price politically for its efforts in support of Bosch, as well as several other convicted exile terrorists. Although initially it was calculated that the exile vote in South Florida made the deals worthwhile, since September 11 the subject of Bosch has been hugely embarrassing to the Bushes. In April 2002, when *Newsweek* brought up the subject of the Marc Rich pardon with Bill Clinton, the former President snapped back, "I swore I wouldn't answer questions about Marc Rich until Bush answered about Orlando Bosch."

Orlando Bosch, on the other hand, remains confident, and defiantly unrepentant. Not long after his release, Bosch announced that he was ready to "rejoin the struggle," and called the agreement he had signed forswearing violence and setting conditions for his release "a farce." "They purchased the chain," he boasted, "but they don't have the monkey." He defended the Cubana attack, asserting that "all of Castro's airplanes are warplanes." In 1991, he told columnist Andrés Oppenheimer that the bombing of the Cubana plane was "a legitimate action of war" because "Castro's aviation has always been military." He also questioned the innocence of the deceased athletes, whom he referred to as "fencers serving the regime." Bosch argued that the young team had taken "a risk" by flying in a Cubana plane "because we are at war."

In 1993, Bosch held a showing of his paintings in Miami, the proceeds from the sale of which would buy what he termed "the ingredients for the Mix." Queried by *Herald* reporter Gerardo Reyes as to the exact meaning of "the Mix," Bosch responded, "We're not talking about flowers or meat pies," leaving the reporter to conclude that "the Mix is Bosch's euphemism for the elements that will underwrite an insurrection in Cuba."

It was crystal clear to the FBI that Bosch had no intention of retiring. In 1997, the Cuban government charged him with assisting Luis Posada's bombing campaign by sending "explosive materials" to Cuba. Bosch initially denied the charge, slyly adding, "Besides, even if we had, we would deny it because it's illegal." More recently, he admitted that the charge was true. And in late 2001, even after the terrorist attacks of September 11, he reaffirmed his support for the Cubana bombing, telling a Miami reporter, "There were no innocents on that plane."

WHILE ORLANDO BOSCH was being reincarnated in Miami as a "freedom fighter," Luis Posada found himself being pushed further underground by the Iran-Contra hearings. Well aware that he was radioactive so long as the hearings were underway, Posada stayed out of the States, ensuring that he could not be subpoenaed to appear before Congress. His home base, since his prison escape, had been El Salvador, where he was held in high regard both by the military and by well-placed officials in the government. Long estranged from his wife, Nieves, who had resettled with his children in Miami, Posada set up housekeeping with a young Salvadoran widow named Angela Bosch (no relation to Orlando Bosch), known as Titi.

At loose ends, Posada signed on as a security consultant to Vinicio Cerezo, Guatemala's first elected civilian president in a generation. Cerezo's biggest challenge was to curb the power of the Guatemalan military. Posada's shrewdness and tenacity made him an ideal choice to keep an eye on restive officers who might be planning a coup. Posada took a dim view of the Guatemalans. "It's the worst military in Latin America and the most corrupt," he said contemptuously. "They cannot be trusted. They'll kill anyone because they have no ideology." To illustrate the scope of their depravity, Posada brought up the murder of Bishop Juan Gerardi, who was bludgeoned to death in April 1998, days after the release of a report blaming the military for most of the 200,000 civilian deaths in the Guatemalan civil war. "The army killed the bishop—because he talked about [human] rights and those that disappeared. Of course they did it," he said, with an incredulous grimace. "The Guatemalan army are bandits."

While freelancing in Venezuela and Guatemala, Posada continued his campaign against the Cuban government, keeping in close touch with friends in Miami. His most crucial contact, he said, was Gaspar Jiménez, jailed for six years for the murder of a Cuban diplomat in Mexico in 1976 and later identified by investigators as the principal suspect in the bombing attack on Emilio Milián, the popular radio host who had condemned exile violence. Jiménez, known as El Gordo because of his three-hundred-pound heft, spent much of the 1990s working for Alberto Hernández, who would succeed Mas Canosa at CANF. For years, Jiménez had ferried money and messages to Posada. A knowledgeable source who has known Jiménez for forty years said the money came from contributions by exiles in Miami and that Jiménez gave Posada $15,000 "for every act of sabotage."

Posada's activities were brought to an abrupt halt on February 28, 1990, when three gunmen approached his car as it was stopped in traffic in Guatemala City and opened fire. He was hit by a dozen bullets and survived, he said, only because he was able to drive himself to a gasoline station and scratch out a note that mentioned his relationship with Cerezo and ask for an ambulance. "It took two years and three surgeries to recover," Posada said. "My last surgery was a year ago. A doctor friend from Houston came down and operated on me at an army base in El Salvador." In his memoir, Posada said his medical bills, some $22,000, were paid by friends in Miami, notably

Alberto Hernández and Feliciano Foyo of CANF. He also received a helpful check from his old colleague Richard Secord for $1,000, according to the report by the Office of Independent Counsel, after sending him one of his paintings.

Posada was certain that his attackers were Cuban operatives, citing information provided to him by an unidentified friend in the Mossad, the Israeli intelligence agency. "They were supposed to kidnap me and take me back to Cuba, interrogate me and have me confess on television," he maintained, although he acknowledged that his enemies were many and did not begin and end with Fidel Castro. Posada's longtime friend and patron Miguel recalled the vengeance with which Posada hunted leftist guerrillas in Venezuela. "He would dress as a peasant and would tell a *campesino*, 'Oh, I've lost my way,' and they would direct him to the guerrillas and he would go there and wipe them all out," Miguel explained. "Once he hunted down a guerrilla and tied a grenade to his chest, then tied it around himself and told him, 'Show me your hiding place, and if you trick me into an ambush, we die together.' "

Posada did some of his recuperation in Honduras, a country that had been a base for Contra resupply operations and whose right-wing military had always been hospitable to him. In fact, FBI investigators believe that he was behind forty-one bombings in Tegucigalpa, Honduras's capital, cases that remain unsolved but open. By 1993, he was back in action. Ever more determined to bring down Fidel Castro's government, he found a sea captain in Honduras willing to advise him of the comings and goings of Cuban ships. Posada said he only intended to use a "small mine" to destroy one freighter, but the opportunity never came. Another plot involved Colonel Guillermo Pinel Calix, then head of Honduran military intelligence, who had offered a clandestine base of operations in Honduras to a half dozen Miami exiles from which they could run operations and attacks on Cuba. The deal unraveled when Posada and his cohorts decided that they could not trust the famously corrupt Honduran military—even with more than a quarter million dollars of bribes in play.

III

WHEN BOMBS BEGAN TO RIP through some of Havana's most fashionable hotels, restaurants and discotheques in 1997, they sowed fear and speculation throughout Cuba, a police state notorious for its tight security. From one end of the island to the other, folks gossiped and speculated as to who could have been responsible. At his office in Guatemala City, a Cuban-American businessman named Tony Alvarez was certain he knew the answer. For nearly a year, he had watched with growing alarm as two of his partners—working with a mysterious gray-haired man with a Cuban accent and multiple passports—acquired explosives and detonators, congratulating one another on a job well done every time a bomb went off in Cuba.

Alvarez overheard the men talk of assassinating Fidel Castro at an upcoming conference of Latin American heads of state on Margarita Island, off the north coast of Venezuela. Alarmed, he went to Guatemalan security officials and wrote a letter that eventually found its way into the hands of Venezuelan intelligence agents and the FBI. Venezuelan authorities reacted energetically to the information, searching for explosives on the island where the meeting was to be held. But in the States, the letter elicited what Alvarez described as a surprising indifference. An FBI agent in the Miami office, Jorge Kiszinski, phoned Alvarez back and said a colleague would call soon to arrange to speak with him. In the meantime, Kiszinski urged Alvarez to leave Guatemala immediately. "He told me my life was in danger, that these were dangerous people, and urged me to get out of Guatemala," said Alvarez, then a sixty-two-year-old engineer. "But I never heard from him again." In fact, Alvarez never heard again from anyone in the FBI.

Indeed, the FBI showed a striking lack of curiosity about the bombings, a fact that did not surprise Luis Posada. "They know where I am and how to reach me," he said with a shrug. He described FBI agent Kiszinski as "a good friend" of long standing. "He's going to retire this year," Posada said with palpable feeling. "He's a very good guy. Please don't write about him. He has done not only good things for me but for many others."

Plainly embarrassed, a spokesman for the FBI explained that a friendship between the two men was implausible. "Agent Kiszinski has had two contacts with him in his entire life, the last of which was a number of years ago." Posada told a different story. He expressed confidence that the FBI was not examining his operations in Guatemala, because "the first person they would want to talk to is me, and nobody called." Nor, he said, did anyone try to interview his collaborators. "I would know," he said smoothly, adding that it was Kiszinski who interrogated him in Honduras about his role in the Iran-Contra affair for the Office of Independent Counsel in 1992. He said that the agent had confirmed to him a year earlier that an informant in Guatemala had notified the FBI about the bombing plots. Posada added that he had a second contact in the FBI. "I know a very high-up person there," Posada said, noting that his source had protected him in 1995 when the State Department asked for his whereabouts. "They wanted to know where I was," he said, "and the FBI said, 'No, we have no helpful information in this case.' "

Tony Alvarez was deeply embittered by his experiences as a whistle-blower. "I think they are all in cahoots, Posada and the FBI," he said. "I risked my life and my business, and they did nothing." In his letter alerting Guatemalan authorities to the plot, Alvarez wrote that while he opposed the Castro government and communism, "I believe that terrorism is not the way to resolve the Cuban [or any other] situation."

Had the FBI met with Alvarez, agents would have heard a remarkable tale about the anti-Castro underworld and the links between the plotters in Guatemala City and Cuban exiles living in Union City, New Jersey.

EXILE POLITICS AND PLOTTING were the last thing on Tony Alvarez's mind when he arrived in Guatemala City in 1996 with hopes of building electric power plants in rural areas. On the advice of friends, he hired a fellow Cuban exile who had lived there since 1970, José Francisco (Pepe) Alvarez, to manage a company he had set up. He recruited José Burgos, a retired veteran of the Guatemalan Army Corps of Engineers, who had worked as a bodyguard for the family of a former Guatemalan President, to run another. Both Burgos and Pepe Alvarez denied any connection to the hotel bombings, although Pepe Alvarez conceded that he had known Posada for thirty years. "He and I are old now, too old for that sort of thing," he quipped. "Hell, I'm the same age as Fidel Castro."

At first, Tony Alvarez said, things seemed to be running smoothly. But he soon noticed that his partners were spending much of their time with a peculiar visitor, a Cuban with a strangled voice "like that of a deaf-mute," giving their guest free rein to make phone calls from the office to El Salvador, Venezuela, Honduras, Spain and the United States. Eventually, Alvarez's partners confided to him that the visitor was the infamous Luis Posada Carriles, known to his friends by the ironic nickname Bambi or Lupo, Italian for wolf.

One day early in 1997, as Alvarez recalled, Posada came by the office and disbursed "a thick wad of hundred-dollar bills" to his partners. They, in turn, "were going to an electronics store and buying detonators and small calculators with timers." That was suspicious enough, Alvarez said. But his biggest surprise came when he found explosives in an office closet. "In a plastic bag," he said, "they had twenty-three tubes of stuff made by the Mexican military industry, supposedly the latest in explosive materials in the world. I saw it." In addition to Posada, two Guatemalans, whom Alvarez identified as Marlon González and Jorge Rodríguez, frequented the office. Both men were introduced to him as friends and former army buddies of Burgos. Posada said that the two worked for him as bomb makers not out of any conviction but motivated by greed, because "that was how to make the big bucks."

In April 1997, the first reports of an explosion in the discotheque of one of Havana's most popular hotels, the Melia Cohiba, were published in Miami. Those accounts were promptly denied by the Cuban government, which relies on tourism as its principal source of hard currency. Over the next five months, however, more than a half dozen explosions occurred at hotels, restaurants and discotheques in Havana and the chic beach resort of Varadero. Cuba was forced to acknowledge the attacks. Asked how the explosives had been smuggled in, Posada laughed and replied: "You know what a circus is? Inside an elephant." It was a cryptic remark, but probably, in fact, true. Raúl Ernesto Cruz León, the Salvadoran charged in several of the bombings, had worked for a private security agency in El Salvador. According to his mother, one of his assignments was protecting a Mexican circus that toured Central America and later traveled to Cuba.

Posada was vexed by the Cuban government's reluctance to acknowledge much of his handiwork. It was not until three years later that the Cubans, fearful of negatively impacting their tourism industry, finally admitted the extent of it. "On October 19, we discovered an explosive device hidden in a van owned by a Cuban tourist agency. On the 30th of that month, a similar device was found under a kiosk at a coffee shop in José Martí Airport," said a Cuban official in late 2000. He added that between April and October 1997, at least nine bombs exploded in several hotels and one restaurant, leaving one person dead and at least eleven injured, all of them foreign tourists.

Tony Alvarez said he had overheard talk about another possible smuggling route. "Posada, Pepe and José talked about the success of the bombs they sent to Cuba," he said. "They also talked about a senior mechanic who works for Aviateca who travels frequently to Cuba and who has been helping them." Aviateca, the Guatemalan airline, flies to Havana. At one point, he said, his partners offered his secretary "an all-expenses-paid trip to Cuba in a five-star hotel. In return, all she had to do was deliver a package to a certain person who would come to the hotel to meet her." Alvarez said that his secretary declined, "because she didn't want to be involved in anything that appeared dishonest or illegal." Then, in August '97, at the height of the bombing campaign in Cuba, Tony Alvarez intercepted a fax that Posada had sent from El Salvador and signed with another of his noms de guerre, Solo, after Napoleon Solo, hero of the 1960s television spy series *The Man from U.N.C.L.E.*

Posada admitted that he had written the document, a copy of which was given to me by a Venezuelan official. The fax referred to the reluctance of American news organizations to take seriously the claims of Miami exile groups that bombs were going off in Cuba. "If there is no publicity, the job is useless," Posada's message read. "The American newspapers will publish nothing that has not been confirmed. I need all the data from the discotheque in order to try to confirm it. If there is no publicity, there is no payment." The fax also discussed payments for bombings, saying that money would be "sent by Western Union from New Jersey" to "liquidate the account for the hotel." But Posada was cagey as to who was sending the money. "Somebody, a friend of a friend," provided him with the names, he said with a wink. "A priest." Then he darkened, and added with a tone of resignation, "They are going to put the finger on me."

The document instructed Pepe Alvarez to collect electronic transfers of $800 each from four Cuban exiles living in Union City. One of the men identified in the fax was Abel Hernández, the owner of Mi Bandera (My Flag), a supermarket, restaurant and Western Union office in Union City, a heavily Cuban-American town just across the Hudson River from Manhattan. At the restaurant's entrance, one of Posada's paintings was hung facing a photograph of Hernández arm in arm with Jorge Mas Canosa. Hernández denied knowing Posada and sending him money. Curiously, when I returned to the restaurant days after the series on Posada ran in the *New York Times,* the painting had disappeared from the wall.

The other three men named in the fax, Pedro Pérez, Rubén Gonzalo and José Gonzalo, also lived in Union City and belong to the Union of Former Political Prisoners, an exile group whose members have served long terms in Castro's jails and are committed to his overthrow. Posada seemed uncharacteristically troubled by the fax and asked me whether the four men in Union City "could get in trouble for this."

Tony Alvarez recounted that Posada's fax so alarmed him that he wrote a letter to Guatemalan intelligence, apprising them of "this horrendous matter." Alvarez also recalled overhearing plans for an attack on Castro during a scheduled visit to Guatemala in December 1996 and again at the Ibero-American Summit on Margarita Island in November 1997. Prior to Castro's arrival, more than 250 Venezuelan and Cuban agents combed the exclusive Isla Bonita Hotel, where the gathering was to be held. Cuban exiles who had flocked to the island to protest Castro's visit were expelled before his arrival. Still, Castro took precautions and flew to the island with a protective convoy of three jets.

IN SEPTEMBER 1997 THE Cuban government arrested a twenty-five-year-old Salvadoran named Raúl Ernesto Cruz León and charged him with carrying out a half dozen bombing attacks on tourist hotels and restaurants in Cuba. One person, an Italian tourist, was killed in the attacks. Cruz León, said Posada, was "a mercenary" who worked for him. With a rueful chuckle, he described the death of the tourist as a freak accident but said he nonetheless "sleeps with a clean conscience. It is sad that someone is dead, but we can't stop," he said. "That Italian was sitting in the wrong place at the wrong time, *pobrecito.*

"That was an inside operation in Cuba," Posada said, referring to Cruz León's bombing spree. "It is the only way to create an uprising there." He reflected a moment and added, "There are several ways to make a revolution, and I have been working on some. We didn't want to hurt anybody, we just wanted to make a big scandal so that the tourists don't come anymore." He fixed my eyes and wagged his forefinger in front of his face, Cuban style. "We don't want any more foreign investment in Cuba."

The bombs were also intended, Posada said, to sow doubts abroad about the stability of Castro's regime and to encourage internal opposition. "People are not afraid anymore, they talk openly in the street," he said. "But they need something to start the fire, and that's my goal."

"Everything is compartmentalized," Posada explained about his bombings, couriers and operators. "I know everybody but they don't know me." Posada said he was able to carry out his life's work because of the support of exiles in the States. He acknowledged his considerable debt to his old friend Jorge Mas Canosa. "Everything went through Jorge. Jorge is the one who managed everything. . . . All my contact was through Jorge. Jorge controlled everything . . . Whenever I needed money, Jorge said [to them], 'Give me $5,000, give me $10,000, give me $15,000,' and they sent it to me." Over the years, Posada estimated, Mas sent him more than $200,000. "He never said this is from the Foundation," Posada recalled, with a chuckle. He would deliver the money with the message "This is for the church."

Posada's remarks suggested that the Foundation's public advocacy of purely nonviolent opposition to Castro was a carefully crafted fiction. I asked whether he functioned in reality as the Foundation's military wing, much as the Irish Republican Army served the Sinn Fein party. "It looks like that," he replied, and laughed again.

Posada said that Mas was well aware that he was behind the 1997 bombing campaign but that the two men agreed never to discuss the details of operations. "He never met operators, never," Posada said, explaining their relationship. "[Mas] said, 'I don't want to know anything.' Nothing specific, because he was intelligent enough to know who knows how to do things and who doesn't." There was also the fact that Mas "was afraid of the telephone. You don't talk like that on the telephone." Posada said he had received another important assist from his friends at the Foundation in August 1997, when CANF issued a statement saying it did not condemn the bombing campaign in Cuba.

Posada bemoaned the fact that Cuba was not the burning issue to the Clinton White House that it had been to earlier administrations. "It's been a long time since I've done anything for them," he said, referring to the CIA. "The problem is that they think the money which helped me in the operation came from the States," a violation of American law, one that could generate a RICO indictment. When it was suggested that that was indeed the case, he replied, "Yes, it's obvious." Still, he fretted about how seriously the Clinton Justice Department and the CIA were going to pursue the matter.

Augmenting Posada's sadness over the death of Mas Canosa, who had died six months prior to our meeting, was the knowledge that Cuba today is a very different country from the one he left four decades ago. And no matter who takes power next, it will never be the country of his youth. "When I left Cuba, it was 20 percent black," Posada said, citing one example. "Now it's 70 percent black." There was also the nagging thought that his nemesis, Fidel Castro, might outlive him. "Maybe I pass away before Castro," he said. "Nobody knows." I reminded him that the Castro family tends to be long-lived and that one relative had celebrated her 105th birthday. Posada groaned, "Oh my God." Then, wagging his finger Cuban style in front of his face, he quoted a popular proverb, derived from the Cuban tradition of slaughtering a hog for a holiday meal: *"A cada lechón se le llega su Nochebuena"*—"Every pig gets its Christmas Eve."

ON OCTOBER 27, 1997, FOUR men were stopped by the U.S. Coast Guard in a forty-six-foot-long cabin cruiser off Puerto Rico. Almost immediately, one of the men, Ángel Alfonso Alemán, blurted out that he was on a mission to kill Castro. American law enforcement quickly determined that the boat was registered and owned by a member of the executive board of the Cuban American National Foundation, José Antonio Llamas, while one of the sniper rifles aboard was traced back to CANF's president, Francisco "Pepe" Hernández.

Llamas and six other men were indicted in August 1998 on charges of conspiring to assassinate Fidel Castro during his visit to Margarita Island. According to the indictment, Llamas "obtained a .50-caliber rifle" and bought a boat for his fellow conspirators and "other persons known and unknown . . . to kill, with malice aforethought, Fidel Castro at a place outside the United States." Investigators soon discovered that Llamas's boat, aptly named *La Esperanza* (Hope), had left from a private dock in Coral Gables, Florida, owned by the business partner of Feliciano Foyo, another Foundation official. A second rifle was registered to Juan Evelio Pou, another CANF member and old comrade of Posada.

Although the indictment did not mention CANF, the Foundation took it as an attack on itself, denouncing the charges as a witch hunt. According to lawyers for Pepe Hernández and Tony Llamas, both were notified that they were targets of a federal investigation, a formal step prosecutors take when they are seriously considering an indictment. Indeed, Hernández's attorney held a news conference saying he expected his client to be indicted and denouncing the prosecution as a politically motivated attack on CANF. But, to the surprise of many, Hernández was never indicted. A Justice Department official had called him "not a minor player" in the affair, but the rumor mill in Miami had it that Senator Joe Lieberman, the staunch Democratic ally of CANF, had lobbied Attorney General Janet Reno to rethink Hernández's indictment.

The others named in the indictment were José Rodríguez Sosa, Alfredo Otero, Ángel Alfonso Alemán, Ángel Hernández Rojo, Juan Bautista Márquez and Francisco Secundino Córdova. According to the charges, the would-be assassins traveled to Margarita Island, Venezuela, to scout a location for killing Castro and picked a hilltop overlooking the airport there.

Ángel Alfonso Alemán, the ostensible leader of the failed expedition, is an intense, wiry, voluble Cuban with a childlike smile. A man of courtly manners, Alfonso was a political prisoner of twenty years for his anti-Castro activities, and is an unabashed supporter of Posada Carriles. He told me that he deeply resented his forced release from prison in 1980, the result of the Carter-initiated Dialogue that freed 3,600 political prisoners. Had he had his druthers, he said he would still be a prisoner of conscience locked up in his prison cell in Cuba. Since his release, Alfonso had married, divorced, sired two children and worked as a salesman at Mi Tienda, a clothing store in Union City owned by Arnaldo Monzón, the former president of CANF's local chapter and a dedicated militant.

I had first met Alfonso at his cramped basement apartment off Bergenline Avenue in Union City, the gritty mecca of Cuban exiles in the Northeast. Later, I connected with him at Newark Airport and flew to San Juan with him, where he was to be arraigned. "I was, am and consider myself a revolutionary," Alfonso told me. "We do whatever we can. The main thing is to take Castro out, by any means necessary." He had fought as a teenager against the dictatorship of Fulgencio Batista. "I was a revolutionary, and I am a revolutionary," he explained. "But I was not a *fidelista*. I am a Cuban patriot. All the people who know me know that I only do things I believe in and I am prepared to accept the consequences." Alfonso held up a copy of Posada's memoir, *The Paths of the Warrior,* which he intended to reread during the flight.

Alfonso is a past president of the Union of Former Political Prisoners, a fraternity of some three hundred veterans of Cuban jails that meets weekly in Union City. Their clubhouse is the ground floor of a modest building off Bergenline Avenue. Covering its walls like wallpaper are photographs of *"los mártires"*—the men and women who have died fighting against Fidel Castro and those who still languish in Cuba's prisons. Two members of the union told me that Alfonso was a friend of the four men whose names were listed on Posada's fax and that Alfonso had told them that "Pepe Alvarez is one of the names we use to get money to Posada."

Alfonso, who was fifty-seven at the time of his arrest, said he had visited the White House on four occasions, "once with Reagan, once with Bush, and twice with Clinton," including once a White House ceremony for the signing of the Helms-Burton Act, two years before his arrest. With pride, he produced a photograph of himself alone with Clinton, as well as other pictures of himself with Senator Robert Torricelli, Mas Canosa and Félix Rodríguez. He averred that his $50,000 bail and a $50,000 retainer for a lawyer "was paid by various exile groups and individuals," though he declined to be more specific.

Shortly after the boat's seizure, news organizations in Miami received anonymous telephone calls and letters asserting that the assassination plot against Castro had been an attempt to grant Mas Canosa a deathbed wish. But Alfonso scoffed at the notion that he was acting on behalf of Mas Canosa or anyone else. "Nobody can use me," Alfonso said. "I think for myself." He said that he first met Mas in Miami in 1980, just before CANF was founded, and last saw him about six months before his death, when Mas Canosa visited his group in Union City. He described Mas as "a true leader who dedicated his life to the struggle."

THE CASE OF *La Esperanza* began with a fluke arrest: a Coast Guard cutter was making a routine patrol off northwestern Puerto Rico, near Aguadilla, when it spotted the craft. Only after the captain gave an incorrect registration number and asserted that the boat had sailed from Miami in a single day was it decided to board the vessel. Initially, the captain, Hernández Rojo, said that their intention "was to go fishing," but that they had run into bad weather and were turning back because a pump had failed and they were taking on water. But the only fishing gear on the boat was still in plastic wrappers and the men said they had sailed the nine hundred miles from Miami that day—a nautical impossibility.

Investigators then contacted Llamas, the boat's owner, in Miami, who told them the four men were on their way to Venezuela to sell the vessel. "They were looking for drugs, frankly," one Coast Guard official said at the time. "When four men on a boat in trouble tell you a funny story, we look for drugs." Their suspicions aroused, the Coast Guard escorted the boat to shore, searched it, and discovered, hidden beneath a throw rug, a secret compartment built into the stairs leading to the cabin. Inside was an arsenal of weapons, including seven boxes of ammunition, military fatigues, six portable radios, a satellite telephone, night vision goggles, nightscopes and two high-powered sniper rifles that sell for about $7,000 apiece and can hit a target more than a mile away. Extra fuel tanks holding an additional two thousand gallons of fuel had also been built into the vessel. The ship's navigation system had been set for Margarita Island.

Once the arms cache was found, Alfonso became suddenly agitated and launched into a frantic confession. "I have a contact on Margarita," federal agents said he yelled aloud. "Look at all the entries in my passport going to Venezuela! Do you think I went there on vacation? These weapons are mine. The others know nothing about them. I placed them there myself. They are weapons for the purpose of assassinating Fidel Castro. My sole mission in life is to kill Fidel Castro." Dumbfounded, Coast Guard officials realized they had stumbled onto something far more promising than they had anticipated.

The men were promptly arrested and charged with conspiracy to commit murder, weapons smuggling and making false statements. "You don't go out on a fishing expedition with .50 caliber weapons," said Hector Pesquera, then chief of the FBI's office in San Juan. "It doesn't compute. Most likely, additional defendants and counts will be added. There could be foreign policy implications. We are not ruling anything out."

Alfonso's arrest and subsequent trial never dampened his anti-Castro ardor. "I love life, I love my children," he told me. Pressing his hand to his heart, he added: "But the most important thing are my principles, and for these I am prepared to sacrifice everything and return to jail. I am not afraid. I am at peace with my conscience."

Posada claimed to have had nothing to do with the Puerto Rico plot, which he described as amateurish. But he acknowledged a longtime friendship with Alfonso, whom he referred to by his nom de guerre, La Cota, which in the provinces of Cuba is a parrot. He warmly described Alfonso as a "very good and dedicated person . . . but hyperexcited," whom he had first met in Miami in 1991. He expressed surprise that the men had used weapons registered to CANF's Pepe Hernández. "It doesn't look too professional to do that. I was surprised that he said, 'I want to kill Castro.' " Holding an imaginary rifle aloft, Posada said that if he had been aboard the boat, he would have told American officials that "those guns were for shooting birds." And then he laughed.

But no one at the FBI believed that Posada was not involved with the Margarita Island caper. "It would have been impossible for Ángel Alfonso and his friends to have organized that attempt on Castro without Posada," said one agent who worked closely on the case. "There is no doubt that the safe house they rented on Margarita Island was arranged by Posada," the agent said, "because Posada had been the head of [the Venezuelan intelligence agency] DISIP, which runs all its operations out of Margarita Island. There's no way a guy from Union City like Ángel Alfonso, or even his boss, Arnaldo Monzón, put this together without Posada."

FBI investigators said they were "one thousand percent certain," the agent said, that Posada was the ringmaster of the attempted assassination, having summoned his loyal followers from Union City and Miami to execute his plan. Indeed, the Bureau urged the Department of Justice to issue a RICO indictment naming prominent players in the exile world in both communities. Clinton's Department of Justice denied the request and pursued a far more limited prosecution.

"They're opening a Pandora's box they're going to regret," Alfonso's attorney, Ricardo Pesquera (no relation to the FBI's Hector Pesquera), told me at the courthouse in San Juan the day of their arraignment. Pesquera vowed to demand access to every CIA and FBI document on forty years of plots, some of them government-organized, to kill Castro. "We're going to put their whole foreign policy on trial," he warned. "We will go after the government very strongly and attack their hypocrisy." Both Ángel Hernández Rojo, the captain of the vessel, and Tony Llamas, the owner of the boat, had taken part in the CIA's Bay of Pigs operation. Brandishing a sheaf of declassified CIA memoranda documenting U.S. efforts to overthrow Castro, Pesquera fumed that "for thirty years they tried to kill Castro and now they say others can't do the very same thing they were doing."

But as events unfolded, Pesquera would be required to do very little. For reasons that were inexplicable to legal experts, an arraignment judge declared Ángel Alfonso's confessional statement—which was central to the prosecution's case—inadmissible. Then another judge tossed out the conspiracy to commit murder charge. Prosecutor Miguel Pereira soldiered on, but his case had been effectively eviscerated. The defendants were found not guilty and returned to Miami and Union City as conquering heroes.

MY INTERVIEW WITH Luis Posada Carriles became the basis of a ten-thousand-word series that ran on the front page of the *New York Times* on July 12 and 13, 1998. Not surprisingly, the Cuban American National Foundation was displeased. Coming on the heels of the arrests of the four men on *La Esperanza*, the timing could not have been worse. Although Mas Canosa was by then dead, the Foundation borrowed a page from his tactical handbook. They denied all of Posada's claims and went on the counteroffensive. "The *New York Times* slandered and the *New York Times* lied," Jorge Mas Santos declaimed at a press conference at the National Press Club a few days later. "These articles are offensive, slanderous and defamatory." He demanded a retraction and threatened suit, adding they were "99 percent certain that we will sue the *Times.*"

At a press conference at CANF's Miami offices, my writing partner, Larry Rohter, was accosted by an angry crowd. Later that day, Rohter said that someone tried to drive him off the freeway. Threats poured into the *Times*, which responded by posting security guards outside its office in Miami and at Rohter's home. The *Times* covered the brouhaha in the paper and issued a press release reiterating its "complete support and confidence" in its writers. "Their articles are based on more than 100 different sources. Both reporters met Posada and were assisted by a dozen *New York Times* editors, researchers and lawyers in preparation for publication."

To press their case, Jorge Mas Santos, Alberto Hernández, Pepe Hernández and CANF attorney George Fowler III flew to New York and demanded to see the *Times*'s publisher, Arthur O. Sulzberger, and editor, Joseph Lelyveld. Their request was denied, but managing editor Bill Keller, foreign editor Andrew Rosenthal and *Times* attorney Adam Liptak did meet with them.

Litigation had long been a coveted tool in Mas's arsenal; legal demand letters sent out by his and CANF's attorneys were often enough to discourage even the most brave-hearted. Mas was particularly crafty in pursuing enemies without assets or insurance. In 1996, he had sued the veteran Cuba diplomat Wayne Smith, who has long argued for the revocation of the Embargo. The former State Department official had long been a thorn in Mas's side because of his support for negotiations with the Cuban government. When Smith appeared on a PBS documentary on Cuba speaking critically of CANF's convoluted tax-exempt revenues, Mas pounced and sued for libel. But instead of suing PBS or the film's producers, who carried insurance, CANF targeted only Smith, knowing that he did not have the means to bankroll litigation. Although the case was entirely without merit, Smith was forced to endure a trial in Miami with a judge and jury overtly sympathetic to Mas. The jury concluded that Smith had libeled Mas, with one juror describing Smith as "a known communist." Not until the case was appealed to the Third District Court of Appeal by attorney Richard Ovelmen, who worked without a fee, was the ruling reversed and Smith exonerated.

According to Liptak, the men fulminated for about half an hour but failed to point out any specific error in the series. Certainly their expectations were high. Such a show of power in the offices of any Miami media organization would guarantee all manner of journalistic backpedaling. But the three were politely told that there would be no retraction and no apology. Liptak pointed out that the *New York Times* had never settled a defamation lawsuit, nor had it lost one. CANF quickly realized that this was not going to be like dealing with the *Miami Herald* or even *The New Republic*.

Eager to be of assistance, Miami's Spanish language radio went on the offensive. Over the next week, listeners in Miami heard the *New York Times* described as "a communist front organization," and Larry Rohter as "a spy and a traitor." There was some confusion regarding me: I was alternately described as "the lover of Fidel Castro" and as *"una tortillera"*—a Cuban epithet for a lesbian.

The Foundation denied having any involvement whatsoever with Luis Posada and denied that its leaders assisted him in any way, or even had contact with him. A day later, events appeared to contradict their claim. On July 13, Rafael Orizondo, a reporter for Miami's Univisión station, Channel 23, flew to El Salvador, where he conducted a taped interview with Posada. In the unusually brief interview, Posada—who was shown in shadow—made two denials that neatly coincided with the Foundation's talking points: that members of CANF had never sent him money and that he had not spoken with Mas Canosa in many years. "I have never received from the Foundation nor its members any economic assistance for my living expenses," he said. He then made an even more implausible claim—one that was denied in his own autobiography: "I live off my work. I paint. I sell my books."

Curiously, the tape was flown directly to CANF's offices in Miami for a prearranged press conference. The following day, the Bloomberg News Service reported that a Univisión spokesperson had confirmed that "a member of the Cuban American National Foundation was present during the television network's high-profile interview with Cuban exile Luis Posada Carriles." According to the network's spokeswoman, Anne Corley, "They taped the same interview we were taping. . . . I spoke with our news operations executives at Channel 23 [Univisión] in Miami and they explained that somebody from the Foundation was there. We don't know why or how." She referred to the man present as "an unidentified Foundation member." It was also soon revealed that the reporter Orizondo was a relative of a CANF board member. CANF now had a bigger credibility problem: if it had no contact with Luis Posada, how then was it able to arrange an interview with him?

Orizondo was less than forthcoming with the details. "Did one or more people from the Foundation facilitate the interview? Accompany Orizondo to the site? Remain in a room nearby? Did Orizondo travel to the interview aboard a Foundation airplane?" asked the *Herald*. "No comment. 'I really don't want to talk about this anymore,' Orizondo said. . . . He referred questions to his news editor, who did not return phone calls." Following his brief remarks to the *Herald*, Orizondo declined comment on the subject and was said to have gone on vacation.

CANF's transparent and clumsy damage-control maneuverings only worsened matters. Its lawyers appealed to the *Times*, arguing that the paper's readers would assume that CANF leaders had footed the bill for Posada's bombing campaign, although no such comment was published in the series. Seeking to take the high road and eliminate any potential misunderstanding, the *Times* published a brief Editor's Note a week later: "A front-page article on July 12 reported a series of interviews with Luis Posada Carriles, a Cuban exile who told of having waged a campaign of violence aimed at toppling

Fidel Castro," it read. "Mr. Posada was quoted as saying his operations had been financed for years by Jorge Mas Canosa and other leaders of the influential American lobbying group, the Cuban American National Foundation. . . . The wording was not intended to mean that Mr. Posada said the foundation leaders had paid specifically for the hotel bombings. . . . As was made clear elsewhere in the article, Mr. Posada said Mr. Mas and other leaders for the foundation did not earmark money for specific operations, and asked not to be told how he used their funds."

Although the *Times* was careful not to place the Editor's Note among its daily corrections, CANF leapt upon the minor clarification and declared victory. Not surprisingly, CANF won a small assist from the *Herald,* which ran an unsigned story saying, "The *New York Times* admits error." The *Herald* not only misstated the Editor's Note, it did so without any calls made to the *Times* newsroom, lawyers or editors. *El Nuevo Herald,* continuing in its role as the pro bono publicity arm of CANF, ran the item with a front-page banner headline. The *Times*'s managing editor, Bill Keller, promptly faxed a two-page letter of complaint disputing the *Herald*'s story to managing editor Doug Clifton. Keller's letter was slashed to a third of its length and buried at the bottom of the letters column.

In the meantime, on the far-right perimeter of the exile world, some felt that the Foundation's attempt to distance itself from Posada was mistaken and foolish. One of them was Tony Calatayud, a close friend of Mas Canosa and self-proclaimed "freedom fighter" with a high profile in Miami. Calatayud declared on Miami television a week after the *Times* series ran that the Foundation was shortsighted in denying Mas Canosa's support of covert attacks. He explained at some length that he in fact had firsthand knowledge that Mas had participated in militant attacks on Cuba with Posada. "Indeed," he said, "Jorge Mas Canosa, Luis Posada Carriles and I for years worked together in the fight for the freedom of Cuba. We were and are close friends— Jorge, Luis and I. . . . Jorge Mas Canosa was a comrade of mine in clandestine work within Cuba. We were fighting for years in direct actions that could be called violent actions, but I call them direct actions. The *New York Times* wrote up that story and the exile press denied its association with Jorge Mas Canosa, but I affirm it. I affirm it. And I say that it detracts from the historical profile of Jorge Mas Canosa when all that is ascribed to him is being a Washington lobbyist, traveling in a private jet to the air-conditioned offices of presidents and foreign ministers. . . . No, that is not the truth." Miami's entire mainstream media ignored Calatayud's comments, despite his high standing among hard-line exiles.

No matter how they spun it, the Foundation was stuck with the fact that Posada's interview had been tape-recorded—and few people, if anyone, living outside of Calle Ocho believed that the *New York Times* had published anything other than an accurate transcription of Posada's account. So another approach was pursued with a reporter named María Elvira Salazar for her program *Polos Opuestos,* aired on CBS En Español. On Salazar's program, Posada offered a third version of what had occurred. No longer was he claiming that the *New York Times* had made up its story. Now, he conceded that the *Times* story was accurate but that he had lied to the *Times.* He said that he had ascribed his funding to Mas Canosa but that it was actually someone else who gave him money, whose identity he needed to protect. He reasoned that as Mas Canosa was dead, no harm was done. The story, preposterous and transparent, only served to lend more credibility to the argument that Posada was a puppet of powerful exiles in Miami.

ON NOVEMBER 17, 2000, Luis Posada and three other exiles were arrested for plotting yet another assassination of Fidel Castro at the tenth Ibero-American Summit in Panama. None other than Castro announced an imminent assassination attempt on himself, at a press conference that diverted all attention from the summit. Describing Posada as "a cowardly man totally without scruples," Castro went further, alleging that "terrorist elements organized, financed and led from the United States by the Cuban American National Foundation . . . have been sent to Panama with the aim of eliminating me." Dressed in military fatigues, Castro dramatically intoned, "They are now in this city and have brought in arms and explosives intent on my physical elimination." Castro concluded his comments with a lighthearted jest, musing that there had been "about 600" attempts on his life.

Within hours, the Panamanian police arrested Posada and his cohorts, all of whom had entered Panama with bogus passports days earlier. A Cuban intelligence and security team that had been in Panama for several months prior to the summit, which marked Castro's first visit to the country since 1959, had made the discovery. Panamanian authorities discovered two hundred pounds of C-4 explosives and charged the exile quartet with conspiring to kill Castro. The four men had been charter members of the terrorist groups CORU or Omega 7, and all four had ties to the Foundation. Ninoska Pérez-Castellón, a spokeswoman for CANF, responding almost flippantly, suggested that Castro "should get a new story. . . . He is the terrorist. They are accusations without proof," which she derided as "the ravings of an aged rock star that needs to attract attention somehow."

Among those captured with Posada was his longtime comrade Gaspar Jiménez, whose day job was working at CANF chairman Alberto Hernández's office at 2695 SW 42nd Street in Miami. Accompanying them was Guillermo Novo of the Letelier murder case, who had been arrested in Miami for possession of illegal weapons and cocaine in 1978. The fourth man, Pedro Remón Rodríguez, the youngest of the group, was a suspect in the murder of twenty-six-year-old Carlos Muñiz Varela, a pro-Dialogue exile. Remón had been sentenced to ten years in prison for a failed assassination attempt on Cuban diplomat Raúl Roa in 1980.

Agents in the Miami office of the FBI rejoiced at the news. "It was a dream come true," said one agent, "that all of them were arrested in one fell swoop." They were not the only ones cheering. "Viva Panama!" wailed an ecstatic Castro at the announcement of Posada's arrest. "The land where the most famous criminal in the hemisphere has been captured!" Not long after the arrests, Justino di Celmo, the father of the Italian tourist killed in Havana by one of Posada's bombs, appeared on Cuban television to appeal to Panamanian President Mireya Moscoso not to allow Posada to go free. Castro asked for his extradition to Cuba, which seemed entirely unlikely, but in early 2002, Hugo Chávez, Venezuela's head of state and a close Castro ally, announced that he would seek Posada's extradition from Panama. Posada was still wanted in Venezuela for his escape from prison after the Cubana bombing.

The arrests sowed despair in the hearts of hard-line exiles who had long cheered the efforts of militants. All four men were known as the most audacious and bravest of those operating in the exile paramilitary theater. Posada was said to be particularly disconsolate. The previous year, his consort of many years, Titi Bosch, died from cancer at fifty-two. Eight months after his imprisonment, while Panamanian authorities amassed a compelling and voluminous case against them, Posada released a letter declaring his innocence and renouncing terrorism. He maintained that the quartet had been the victims of an elaborate sting operation confected by Cuban intelligence. He added, almost as an afterthought, that he had "erred" by telling the *New York Times* that Mas Canosa had bankrolled him.

In the last week of November 2000, during the presidential recount, a childhood friend of Gaspar Jiménez from Camagüey told me that the only hope for the group's release from prison lay in electing George W. Bush. "We must get Bush elected. He would help us," he said, with palpable distress. Bush's father, the former President, he noted, had been very good to the militants when he headed the CIA in the late 1970s, and had turned a helpful blind eye to the internecine warfare among exiles. He said he was confident that Bush would remember all the help given to the Contra operation by Cuban exiles. His only concern, he said, was the close ties between Alberto Hernández and Jiménez and the possible political fallout should federal authorities take a careful look at the relationship of the two men.

But he need not have worried. With George W. Bush's election, won in part with the helpful assistance of exiles in Miami-Dade, there would be no further scrutiny of exile paramilitary adventures. The FBI shuttered all investigations into exile violence, to the despair of its agents. Miami once again kicked back to the laissez-faire atmosphere of the 1980s, when everyone knew someone involved in the Contra resupply effort.

By the summer of 2001, Santiago Alvarez, a Miami developer charged by the Cuban government with being part of the plot, had raised more than $200,000 on Miami radio for the legal defense fund of Posada and his cronies. Things were looking up. With the backdoor diplomacy of the Bush administration, Gaspar Jiménez's friend was hopeful that the four would win release, just as Orlando Bosch had. He recalled how Miami celebrated with Orlando Bosch Day, and how some hard-liners had roared their approval in Miami's Orange Bowl in 2000, when Bosch was called to the podium. The team was in place once again. Any day now, he said, Posada and his friends would be walking the streets of Miami.

CHAPTER 8

THE MOVIE STAR DICTATOR

No hay mal que dura cien años ni un cuerpo que lo resiste.
There is no evil that lasts a hundred years
nor a body that can resist it.

CUBAN PROVERB

"IT'S NOT MY FAULT that I haven't died yet," Fidel Castro shot back at me, with evident amusement. "It's not my fault that the CIA has failed to kill me!" I had made a cautious foray into the delicate subject of his tenure as Cuba's ruler for life. Wasn't he tired of fighting, tired of playing David and Goliath with his superpower neighbor? "Isn't it time to retire?" I asked. There was an uncomfortable silence. His smile vanished. "My vocation is the Revolution. I am a revolutionary and revolutionaries do not retire," he said solemnly, "any more than writers." And then he laughed.

It was the first week of 1994, which in Cuba translated to "Year 36 of the Revolution," as stated on all government documents. It was also the nadir of the Special Period, the official euphemism for those grim years when the country was reeling from the quicksilver disappearance of its Russian patron. Things could not have been worse.

"I feel like it all began yesterday," Castro said, beginning with a narrative flourish, one of the rhetorical trademarks of a Castro speech or conversation. "I feel the same excitement now as I felt when I was nineteen years old and got involved in this. And in spirit, I feel just like I did when I began. Some people say I am stubborn. But in reality I have been tenacious, persistent." Castro is a formal man with old-world manners, bordering on courtliness. Although he is capable of vituperative profanity with intimates and hirelings, he is fastidiously courteous with guests. He prefers to remain standing while he speaks and sat down with me only a half hour into our three-hour conversation.

While he professed to have no interest in his legacy, every sentence asserted the opposite—that he is deeply committed to writing his own history.

"You could say that from the time I was nineteen years old, I have been committed to an intense struggle. I was nineteen when I began my political struggle, twenty-six during Moncada, thirty during *Granma,* thirty-two when the Revolution was won, thirty-four during Playa Girón [the Bay of Pigs], and over sixty when the socialist camp disappeared. I faced my greatest challenge after I turned sixty," he said, summing up his life. And, lest anyone think that he has had a moment's doubt or regret, he added, "I think that if I could live my life over again, I would do things exactly the same way."

I reminded him of Thomas Jefferson's recommendation of "a revolution every twenty years." Castro frequently invokes Jefferson, but the words didn't sit well with him. He shook his head. "I think it is better to have one every three hundred years. Life needs to renew itself," he said, pleased with his improvisation. "I am not here because I have assigned myself to this job for a lengthy period of time. I am here because this job has been thrust upon me, which is not the same thing." He leaned forward, his face close to mine. "There are times when we really cannot be masters of our own destinies." Then he sees his life as a calling, a mission? "No, I've never thought that. I can say that I have enjoyed a certain privilege—like people who live to be a hundred—not because anybody planned it but because of an accident of nature." An accident? Luck perhaps—and Castro has had more than his share of it. But could he possibly view the result of decades of military rule as an "accident of nature"? Finally, I asked whether he was the devil that his enemies claim him to be. He smiled. "If that is the case," he said with evident satisfaction, "then I am a devil who has been protected by the gods."

On January 1, 2002, Fidel Castro celebrated the forty-third anniversary of his Revolution. He has reigned longer than Spain's Franco and Yugoslavia's Tito and is gaining on history's record holder, Queen Victoria. Castro shoved Cuba, previously famous as an American brothel and gambling parlor, front and center on the international map. He is the movie star dictator—his movements clocked around the world, his utterances recorded on the wire services, the ham actor who upstages everyone else on the global stage.

The conventional wisdom, according to the CIA, was that Fidel Castro would be toppled in a matter of months soon after his triumphant march on Havana on January 8, 1959. But more than four decades later, it turns out that the spy agency has been as clueless about Castro as it was about the sudden collapse of the Soviet Union. Despite a forty-year American trade embargo, an untold number of CIA plots to assassinate him—637 times, by his own inflated count—and a million furious exiles, the indomitable Castro has maintained his steely grip on his island fiefdom. He has chewed his way through nine American Presidents and has shown no hesitation about the tenth. During the presidential campaign of 2000, he dismissed both candidates as "insipid and boring" and greeted George W. Bush with an insult: "I hope he's not as dumb as he looks." A year later, he offered his theory of Bush's ascendancy: "The Democrats didn't lose the White House. They had it stolen."

Castro is among the most intensely polarizing figures of the century—lauded by some for his nationalism and anti-Americanism and despised by an equal number as a remorseless despot responsible for the destruction of his country. In 2001, he was an improbable nominee for the Nobel Peace Prize, while, at the same time, Cuban exiles were charging him with war crimes in a court in Spain. Many now wish they had paid closer heed to one State Department memo from 1959. "It would be a serious mistake to underestimate this man," read a confidential memorandum to Eisenhower after Castro's 1959 visit to the United States. "He is clearly a strong personality and a born leader of great personal courage and conviction." Another analyst that same year concluded that "Castro was not only a bad man but had a streak of lunacy in his make-up . . . like a Cuban Hitler."

Although he has been ceaselessly scrutinized, his demise forever prophesied, Castro has remained very much a riddle. The degree to which history will absolve or condemn him is not yet entirely clear: it is clear only that history cannot be written without his name any more than it could be without the name of Napoleon or Mao or Hannibal. "For most Cubans, Fidel is the devil," writes the Cuban-American novelist Achy Obejas. "This is said both in hatred and love, in derision and admiration. Fidel, like the devil himself, is an invention of necessity. He is the mirror onto which Cubans project their heroism and betrayal, their sense of righteousness and valor. Without Fidel, there would have been no golden age, no paradisical past, no lives in the subjunctive."

Cuba may be the last chapter of the Cold War, but judging from the vigor of its tenured leader as he approaches his ninth decade, it could be the longest. Over the last decade, I have seen Castro on a half dozen occasions, and always his alertness and stamina are surprising. Dressed in a crisp olive green uniform and shiny black combat boots, he looks younger than his seventy-six years. Time has marked him in the most general ways: his hair and beard have grayed, a few sun spots have blemished his surprisingly elegant hands; only his mouth, with purplish gray lips, betrays his age.

As for his own fate, Castro made the astounding claim that he didn't care how he would be remembered. "All the glory in the world can fit into a kernel of corn. More people know about Napoleon because of the brandy than because of the battle at Austerlitz," he quipped in a speech. "I feel no fear about myself personally. Glory and my place in history do not worry me." But his seeming uninterest is less than convincing.

In 1999, he referred to his brother Raúl as his *"relevo"*—Cuban for relief pitcher—thus anointing him his successor. And after a brief fainting spell in June 2001, which flew onto the wire services and put Miami into a state of command alert, Castro went out of his way to ordain his brother as the heir apparent. In mid-2000, he assembled some of his keenest advisers, including Ramón Sánchez-Parodi—his U.S. point man from the 1970s. Their mission was to create a historical legacy for Castro anchored around *fidelismo* or *castroismo* as opposed to *comunismo cubano*. The unstated ambition is to foster a legacy like that of José Martí, Cuba's sanctified national hero and patriot, who returned from exile in 1895 only to be killed by the Spanish days later. But Castro was never a poet as was Martí, any more than Martí was a military strategist or *guerrillero*. Castro is an old-school *caudillo*—a political boss—but one of unusual gifts and flaws. Born and dispatched into this world with the engine of an athlete, Castro has the discipline of a warrior, the intellect of a chess master, the obsessive mania of a paranoiac and the willfulness of an infant. But, unquestionably, he has been blessed by the luck of the gods.

"Fidel hates that cult of personality stuff," a government spokesperson said without a trace of irony. "There are no statues or public portraits of Fidel like there were of Mao." No need. Fidel Castro is the unidentified elephant in every room in Cuba, permeating the very air of his island.

A WEEK BEFORE my interview with Castro, I spent an afternoon with his old comrade turned enemy Eloy Gutiérrez Menoyo, a man whose fierce stubbornness is rivaled only by Castro's. A gangly man, his face gaunt, his hair white, the Spanish-born Menoyo moved to Cuba when he was twelve and was one of the most valiant fighters against Fulgencio Batista. "I commanded the Second National Front in Escambray," he said in his *madrileño*-tinged Spanish. "Fidel commanded the Eastern Front in the Sierra Maestra." Each had roughly 2,500 soldiers under him. "Fidel Castro talked about a revolution as Cuban as the palm trees, of 'bread without terror,' " he says, "and that is the revolution that 90 percent of the Cuban people backed. But then, Fidel separated himself from us and carried on his own *caudillista* revolution. Although I was among the triumphant elite, I could tell that something was not right, one could already foresee the arrival of functionaries from the Soviet Union."

Castro, said his former comrade, was blinded by his Napoleonic fervor. "Since the very beginning," Gutiérrez continued, "Fidel Castro planned to take on all of Latin America, not just Cuba. When he finished the Revolution, he wasn't thinking anymore about José Martí but about Simón Bolívar." But Castro's ambitions exceeded even Bolívar's dream of a united Latin America—he envisioned Cuba as a player on the global stage. From his youth, he had revered the empire building of Julius Caesar, whom he referred to in a letter as "a true revolutionary." There would be forays not only in the Caribbean, like Grenada, or in Central America but in countries as far flung as Angola, the Congo and Algeria.

Outraged by Castro's one-man rule, Menoyo and a dozen of his supporters fled to the U.S. in 1961, where he was a founder of Alpha 66, an anti-Castro commando group. Four years later, his ragtag troop was captured in Santiago de Cuba as they attempted to lead an uprising. "They captured me and put me in a plane and took me to somewhere in the center of Cuba. There was only a table and four chairs, one where Fidel was to be sat, Raúl on the other side and Ramiro Valdés [former head of the Ministry of the Interior]. Against the wall were all the high-ranking military officers of Cuba. Fidel started the interrogation with a very big smile on his face. He broke the silence saying, 'Eloy, I knew that you would come and I knew that I would capture you. Do you know that we are going to execute you?' " Menoyo related between puffs of an ever-lit cigarette. "I told him, 'I'm aware of that.' "

Menoyo reminded Castro that one brother had died fighting Franco and another had been killed during the 1957 storming of Batista's Presidential Palace. "So I think I have won the right to rest and if you would shoot me, I would thank you," he told Castro. "After that, he said, 'Well, wouldn't you want to save your own life?' I said, 'No, because I would have to pay too high of a price.' He said, 'You are imagining that.' " Castro set only two conditions to save his life: that he declare on television that the *campesinos* of Escambray (a region renowned for anti-Castro activity) had been hostile to his insurrection and that Manuel Artíme, then the CIA's choice to replace Castro, would never lead a similar insurrection. Menoyo says both statements were essentially true. "I was delighted and agreed," he said. And Castro's reaction? "Fidel said he was hungry and had to go eat."

Menoyo was sentenced to thirty years in prison, plus an additional twenty-five years for leading counterrevolutionary activity while in prison.

For twenty-two years, he languished in every jail in Cuba, until 1987, when he was released in response to pleas from the Pope, President Jimmy Carter and Felipe González, the President of Spain. "I always thought I would die in prison," he said. "I lost the sight in one eye and the hearing in one ear and had several broken ribs from the beatings," for refusing to do prison work and wear a prison uniform. Invoking his rights as a political prisoner, a *plantado,* Menoyo said he padded around prison wearing only his underwear for twenty of those years. Every two or three years, an official bearing messages from Fidel Castro would come to see him. He would "offer me freedom if I would commit to a rehabilitation plan. Always, I would give the same message, 'Tell Fidel that the one that needs to be rehabilitated is him, not me.' Five years before my release, Fidel sent his messenger, who told me, 'I'm here on behalf of Fidel Castro and I have some bad news. Your father has just died and Fidel has ordered me to give you his condolences in his name, in the name of the Politburo and in the name of the General Congress.' "

Could he imagine sitting down with Fidel Castro and hammering out solutions for Cuba and reconciliation for its nearly one million exiles? "The only way out . . . is to bring democracy to the country," he said quickly. "That is the most noble way for him to close this page in history." Perhaps there was something else he wanted to say. Menoyo pushed his cigarette into the ashtray on his desk and toyed with a pen, and began to write a note to Castro indicating his willingness to meet. "I send them best wishes," he said, speaking carefully as he wrote, "so that they know that time has passed. And it is time now to speak of peace and not of war."

MENOYO'S NOTE, AS it turned out, was the crucial bit of leverage that won me an interview with Castro. I had been in Havana three months earlier and had snared Castro into a half-hour chat but was unable to convince him to sit for an interview. Days after seeing Menoyo, I left for Havana again. I approached an aide of Castro shortly before he was to give a speech to a group of visiting Americans including a contingent of East Hampton matrons and tycoons, a handful of old Reds, and a cadre of Hollywood writers and producers. The setting was the Consejo del Estado, downstairs in the Palacio de la Revolución, one of the few buildings in Havana that doesn't look as if it might collapse at any moment. In 1959, more than a million Cubans had gathered outside this very building in the Plaza de la Revolución to cheer Castro and their conquering heroes. Inside are tropical gardens, plants brought down from the Sierra Maestra by the former First Lady of the Revolution, Celia Sánchez. "I have a note from Eloy Gutiérrez Menoyo for the President," I confided to the aide, indicating it was far weightier than it actually was. The aide flinched almost imperceptibly. "I can read it aloud during the question period, but perhaps it would embarrass him. Or I can pass it to him privately later."

Castro gave his speech that night, and it was one of his better ones. It is immediately clear that Castro, the former lawyer, can argue anything from any side at any time. He shuttled between digressions on Greek democracy, the death of Caesar, Napoleon and the betrayal of Brutus.

Castro responded to each question with a speech, gesticulating dramatically with his long fingers. There was plenty of revolutionary rhetoric: Moscow had fallen, the Eastern bloc was in ruins, his own country in economic shambles, but Castro continued to proudly trumpet socialism. That night, as always, there was the usual litany of the "triumphs of the Revolution": Cuba's success in eradicating illiteracy, its war against infant mortality, its cradle-to-grave health care, the assault on racism and on and on. "None of this would be possible under capitalism," he boomed. "I tell you that capitalism has no future. Capitalism has destroyed in a hundred years all the oil that it took millions of years to create. What would happen if every Indian, every Eskimo had a car to drive?" he asked, making a case for "underdevelopment," formerly a taboo word of the Revolution.

Although Castro is the most famous of Cubans, he is a distinctly un-Cuban man: he does not dance or sing, nor is he known for his levity. He doesn't even drink Cuban coffee, preferring English tea. He seems lacking in appreciation of Cuba's stellar accomplishments in the arts and architecture. An avid sportsman and aficionado of his country's natural splendors, Castro has been indifferent to its cities: Havana, once the most magnificent capital in the Americas, rotted into decrepitude until Castro was convinced that its restoration could be a cash cow for the economy.

But he is brilliant rhetorically and symbolically, remorselessly inventive in needling his northern nemesis. "He is almost like a performance artist," observed culture writer Constance Penley. During his visit to the United Nations in 1960, Castro upstaged all of Broadway in his quest for the right lodgings. "Fidel wanted to hang his hammock in the U.N. gardens, but regulations forbade it," remembered Carlos Franqui, the editor of *Revolución*. "Then Fidel suggested that we camp out in Central Park, maybe set up guerrilla operations there. Finally, we were offered lodging at the Hotel Theresa in Harlem. We were delighted, especially Fidel." It was at the Harlem hotel that Castro met with Egyptian President Gamal Abdel Nasser, Indian Prime

Minister Jawaharlal Nehru and Premier Nikita Khrushchev of the Soviet Union, who was immediately smitten with the young Cuban leader. "I don't know if Fidel Castro is a communist," Khrushchev enthused, "but I'm a *fidelista.*"

During the recent U.S. presidential recount, Castro offered to send "an observation team" to monitor the elections. He has created a scholarship program for minority students from America's inner cities who now study in Havana. And when terrorists attacked New York and the Pentagon on September 11, 2001, he condemned the attack, expressed solidarity with America and offered to send medical aid. "It was as if he was saying, 'Let me remind you who your *real* enemy is,' " said Penley.

While Castro's anti-Americanism runs hot and cold, it springs from a deep well. In a letter to Celia Sánchez, in 1958, Castro wrote: "When I saw the rockets they fired on Mario's [a friend] house, I swore that the Americans would pay dearly for what they are doing here. When this war is over I shall begin a longer and greater war; the war I will wage against them. I realize that this is my true destiny." Barbara Walker Gordon, who grew up with Castro's first wife, Mirta, in Banes, remembered his diatribes against the U.S. as early as 1947. "He had an anti-U.S. bias, there's no doubt about it, even though he was a good friend to lots of us Americans," she recalled. "I remember him saying, 'Well, when I get to be the head of this country, I'm gonna get rid of you Americans and the Spanish.' He was very vocal about it. Jack Skelly, one of our other neighbors, said to him, 'What about us? We've grown up here, we love it here and we certainly don't want to leave.' Fidel shot back, 'I'll let you come and visit.' We laughed among ourselves, because who would have thought he would have had anything to say about it."

The central and unchanging doctrine of Castro has been Cuban nationalism. He has embraced, discarded and/or modified a host of other philosophies, including communism, but his nationalism has never wavered. Castro came to power determined to reverse and avenge U.S. condescension to Cuba. At his first U.S. meetings with the State Department in April 1959, and later in his three-hour conversation with Vice President Richard Nixon, neither he nor any of his aides ever requested U.S. financial assistance. In fact, as exile historian Jorge Domínguez has pointed out, Castro refused to engage the topic, to the surprise of the Americans who were "almost pushing aid on Cuba." When a reporter inquired as to whether he had asked for aid, Castro answered him in English: "No. What happens is that here in the United States you are accustomed to see governments coming for money. No, I came for good relations."

For more than forty years, Castro has not cashed a single check from the U.S. for its lease of the Guantánamo base, which was established in 1903. A 1934 lease signed by Washington and Cuba for $2,000 a year has been a source of unremitting fury from Castro. The saber rattling became so fierce during the Cuban Missile Crisis that U.S. Navy family members were shipped back to the mainland. A year later, Castro snipped the flow of utilities to the base, forcing the navy to bring in its own energy and water sources. But Castro remains a work in progress with a seemingly limitless arsenal of surprises. When the U.S. shipped dozens of its Al Qaeda prisoners to Guantánamo in 2002, the world braced for the predictable Castro outcry. Instead, he reiterated his opposition to the base on "principle" but said he was untroubled by the idea of Cuba becoming the repository for some of the most dangerous terrorists in the world. His brother Raúl went further, warning that any Al Qaeda escapees would be promptly turned over to the Americans. Judiciously picking his battles, he has decided to close ranks with his enemy, at least for the time being, on the issue of terrorism.

When needed, Castro can summon a kind of withering charm. Even his enemies speak nervously about him as "a force of nature." Frank Manitzas, who covered Castro for two decades as ABC's Latin America bureau chief, says that Castro is a natural politician. "Castro has always had the politician's touch. He picks out moments that make good stories," said Manitzas. "I remember when he came to Chile and he was making this speech in the National Stadium and somebody hollered, 'How's your cold, Fidel?' And he answered, 'The cold is doing fine, but I am miserable.' He had that touch."

While he is famously and painfully long-winded, he is also a careful listener. Most of his visitors speak of his keen attention—he listens to them with a spongelike intensity. Several old friends who have recently visited with him cite his ability to recount almost verbatim conversations from fifty years before.

Questioned by an American audience in the mid-1990s about the thousands of Cubans seeking to escape, Castro deftly spun the equation around. "A large part of the Cuban migration to the United States is an economic migration, like the Mexican migration," he says. "Mexico has plenty of oil," he continued, "faces no U.S. Embargo, is not going through a 'Special Period,' " yet thousands of Mexicans cross the U.S. border illegally every day. "In comparison, we have all these problems and only a few people leave illegally." Besides, Mexico is not blasted by Radio Martí, which he trashed as "five hundred hours of psychological warfare." He omitted the obvious: that it's clearly much easier to walk across the Tijuana border than it is to sail five days through shark-infested waters in an inner tube. Finally, he reached for a sound bite: "If a Mexican goes to the U.S. illegally, he's expelled. If a Cuban enters illegally, he's given a house." And when asked how he did not foresee the collapse of his Soviet patron, he charged with both guns blazing: "If the CIA, after thirty-five years of surveillance and $10 billion in research, did not see it coming," he asked mockingly, "how were we, a tiny island nation, to have known?"

Every Castro speech builds to an impassioned denunciation of the American Embargo, always referred to as the "blockade" in Cuba. America's Cuba policy, riddled as it is with so many inconsistencies, is made-to-order fodder for a champion debater like Castro. "Those who blockade us have [had] good relations with South Africa, excellent relations with Chile, where thousands of people have been killed . . . and Argentina, where thousands of people are missing." In his litany there is the conspicuous absence of China, which happens to be Cuba's biggest trading partner. Calling demands to improve Cuba's human rights a "cynical" maneuver, he huffed and fumed. "Never does the U.S. mention the word democracy when discussing the Middle East. It discusses only one thing: oil, never democracy." He concluded his rather digressive remarks with a rhetorical question that could well have been posed about himself: "Was Cicero a great speaker, or was he a demagogue?" As Castro exited the stage, it was evident that he was wearing a bulletproof vest under his custom-tailored guerrilla-green uniform.

Long ago, Castro's speeches became rants—with a predictable litany of canned outrages. "Notice that Fidel has always won or lost his battles not fighting, but by speaking," observed the Cuban exile writer Rene Vázquez Díaz. "One of the reasons that the Revolution became stagnant is that the Comandante's discourse lost its magnetism and mystery." Still, the applause rained down after his speech as security men dressed in pale *guayabera* shirts rushed toward Castro and led him out. One of his aides caught my eye and nodded that I should follow them. The security flanks opened and I was led "backstage." Standing in the middle of the room, I began talking with Castro. It was unclear whether he was prepared to speak with me longer than a few minutes, and I could see that behind his hooded eyelids, he was taking my measure. Across the long room were his top aides at the time: Ricardo Alarcón, Roberto Robaina and Carlos Lage, who were waiting for their boss to finish his talk with me. I quickly and nervously peppered him with questions about his relationship with Menoyo, and watched as he became engaged. I put on my tape recorder and for the next three hours, Castro's inner circle were left idling and loitering on the far side of the room.

Only minutes into our chat, Raúl Castro came bounding over to us like a hyperactive teenager. He was so contrary to what I had expected that it took me a moment to recognize him. The head of the armed forces, Raúl was the only member of the ruling cadre to skip Castro's speech. Rumors, stories and myths swirl around Raúl nearly as much as they do his brother. A small, trim man, he was ebullient and garrulous. Introduced to me, he planted kisses on both my cheeks and slipped in a crack at his brother. "Kiss me. Don't bother kissing him," he said, waving irreverently toward his brother, who was decidedly unamused. One more quick joke to save face and needle his brother another minute, and Raúl bolted from the room as quickly as he had arrived.

With his brother dispatched, I read Castro the brief, conciliatory message of Menoyo. Castro said nothing for a minute, betrayed no thoughts or feelings. I prompted him for a response. Finally, he said, "I did not expect to receive this message. I feel these are positive words which require some reflection." He said he would want to discuss it with his "closest collaborators," who were then working on the upcoming summit with exiles. "I can say that there is no lack of goodwill on our part," he said, adding quickly, "nor resolve to defend our ideas and principles."

Castro's rhetoric toward the exiles has modified over the years. He has spoken of some exiles, once trashed as *gusanos* (worms), having been transformed into *mariposas* (butterflies). But the exile leadership of South Florida is always "the Miami Mafia." Of course, Castro early on had discerned that America's Cuban diplomacy was not a foreign policy issue. "It's domestic policy," he said.

Castro seemed subdued, even tired. Still, I was struck by the decorousness of this man. While he thinks like a lawyer, he lives and behaves like a soldier: spartan, disciplined and ever vigilant. He is a fastidiously private man with little sentimentality or nostalgia. And he does not engage in personal reminiscences on subjects other than the Revolution. To fill in the gaps of his story, I spoke with some fifty former and present friends of his, along with enemies, critics, admirers and family members.

A HEADSTRONG CHILD, Castro was sent to Catholic boarding school at the age of six by his parents in the hope that it would still his rebellious nature. He was a brilliant but lazy student. Nor did he socialize well: he often ended up in fistfights with other students and, on one occasion, with a priest. One former friend said that the young Castro was cruelly teased on two counts—

having been born out of wedlock and having a *gallego* father who was said to have fought for Spain, as a cavalry quartermaster, in the War of Independence.

Luis Aguilar León, a writer and the former editorial-page editor of *El Nuevo Herald,* first met Fidel Castro at the Dolores School, a Jesuit-run school for boys in Santiago de Cuba, when the two were twelve years old. "He lived in a house at the school. I lived nearby," he said. "One day posted on the school bulletin board there was a letter from the President of the United States, Franklin D. Roosevelt. And it was to Fidel Castro." The young man from Birán had written FDR a brief and audacious letter in his fractured English: *"I am a boy, but I think very much,"* he wrote. *"If you like, give me a ten dollar bill american in the letter because I have not seen a ten dollar bill american and I would like to have one of them."* "I asked the priest, 'Who is Fidel Castro?' " recalled Aguilar León. "And the priest told me, 'That kid is one of your classmates.' So I went to see him. 'Listen, are you Fidel?' And he told me that he wrote to President Roosevelt congratulating him on his election. I said to him, 'It's very impressive that he answered you.' And he said, 'No, it's not really very impressive. I asked them for $10 and they didn't send me a cent.' That made me laugh. It was the first time that we had talked. I was very impressed and the Jesuits, as well, were impressed."

Even as a child, Castro had an unusually keen curiosity about military strategy and political power. One of his childhood hobbies was collecting cracker box trading cards of Napoleonic battles—foreshadowing his lifelong fascination with Napoleon.

At age fifteen, Castro's parents moved him to Havana so that he could attend the most prestigious school in Cuba, the Colegio de Belén, another Jesuit school. José Ignacio Rasco recalled Castro's arrival at the school. "He had this sort of rustic quality from the countryside. He went to Belén because his family had money but [they were] not cultured people. Fidel's conversations tended to be solemn and grave, alien to the usual joking and teasing of Cubans. Another thing that might seem ironic now was his initial stage fright. At Belén there was a literary academy named La Avellaneda, where the distinguished Father Rubinos taught speech and debate. But to qualify as a member of the academy there was a test that involved being able to talk for ten minutes, without any notes, about a subject given to the aspiring candidate an hour before. Fidel failed it three times before he was able to pass. The professor said when he saw him suffering at the podium, 'If you put bells in his knees he could give us a concert.' Needless to say, he soon overcame this."

Castro was a formidable athlete, excelling in track and field, soccer, basketball, baseball, racquetball and tennis. The 1945 Belén yearbook memorialized him as the all-around star athlete of the year. It was in sports that Castro honed the discipline and stamina that would fortify him throughout his life. At one time, he even traveled to Miami to play basketball for Belén. One teacher recalled that Castro beseeched him to leave the lights on at night in the gym and on the fields so that he could practice all night, which he did. "Hours and whole days of his vacation would be spent practicing sports," said Rasco. "If he could not find a catcher, he would bat the ball against the walls of the Tropicana Cabaret that bordered the school fields. He would win the 400-, 800- and 1,000-meter races, sometimes all in the same afternoon. He was a racehorse."

Ángel Fernández Varela was one of Castro's teachers at Belén. "I had Fidel for the fourth and fifth year in Civics and Economics," he recalled. "Castro was popular at the school and had many friends who were not his classmates but employees. One boy even joined him eight years later in the assault on the Moncada garrison and was killed. His name was Gildo. That boy would do anything for Fidel Castro, so much so that he died for him."

Castro was renowned at Belén and at the university for his memory and his passion for history. "He could learn, word for word, any text," said Rasco. "He was a real computer. Afterward you could ask him what the sociology book said on page fifty and he would repeat it word for word, periods and commas included. He would study at the last minute, hours before an exam. In those days he was able to go with hardly any sleep." Castro's memory remains undiminished by age. In 1995, Fernández Varela had a reunion with Castro in Cuba. To his amazement, his former pupil "recited a page from a textbook from our school word for word. He has an absolute photographic memory! This was fifty years later and he remembered a page from a book just like that."

Rasco recalled that his classmate would set tests for himself that others would dismiss as impossible or insane. "One year, Fidel challenged the superintendent of Belén, Padre Larrucea, to allow him to take all the exams for French, Logic and History of the Americas. And if he passed them with a 100 percent score, he could then take the institute exam. It seemed impossible that he could do it, but he succeeded. Of course, he didn't sleep for three days and three nights. He's a pathological personality in every way," Rasco said. He offered an anecdote to bolster his argument. "We called him El Loco. I remember the $5 bet he made with Luis Juncadella daring him to throw himself headfirst from a moving bicycle, at full speed, against a wall in the school's hallway. And he did it, at the risk of breaking his head, and he ended up unconscious in the clinic. But he won the $5. I've always seen this absurd incident as a precursor to the attack he later made on Moncada in his zeal for fame."

Castro forged a particularly strong bond with one teacher, Father Amado Llorente, who, like his own father, was Spanish-born. Indeed, part of Belén's prestige was rooted in its old-world snob appeal, and a considerable number of the faculty had avowed sympathies with Spain's strongman Francisco Franco and his Falangists. Llorente sees in Castro an ancestral disposition to succeed. "He is a Galician—*un gallego*. A Cuban would already be tired of being in power. But not a *gallego,* for whom it's until death—just like Franco, who came from Galicia as well."

Father Llorente, then only twenty-four himself, would become Castro's confidant and surrogate father. He was immediately struck by his pupil's quick intelligence and bravery. "I was in charge of the age group sixteen to nineteen of about two hundred boys, living on a day-to-day basis with the students and giving classes from time to time." The young priest was so impressed with Castro that he deputized him the leader of the Explorers Club, which would hike and backpack in the countryside on weekends. "Once I went with him and about forty other boys to the mountains. We left early and we camped on the side of a winding river in the province of Pinar del Río. We left with backpacks behind, prepared to be gone all day on the other side of the river.

"And suddenly it started raining like a flood. When we came back, Fidel said to me, 'Father, the water in the river is up to my chest.' And I said, 'Well, we have to continue on because we have forty boys who are not as strong as you and me with all their clothes and food on the other side of the river.' Fidel swam across the river with this rope in his teeth so he wouldn't go under. The water was twenty-five meters wide with rough currents, but he reached the other side. Later we found out that a *campesino* had drowned trying to cross the river. I knew Fidel had the personality of one who would never give up for any reason. He tied the end of the rope to the tree and the boys went across. I went last, but I wanted to save the rope because we needed a rope. And when I reached the river, the water swelled over me. When Fidel saw me go under with the current, he threw himself in the river to rescue me and we hugged each other. So when we came out, which was the nicest part of the story, Fidel said, 'Father, this has been a miracle!' And we were very emotional and he said, 'Father, let's pray! Three Hail Marys! Let us thank God!' So indeed, at that time Fidel Castro believed in God."

But Castro's bravery was diminished by an unforgiving nature. At one point he started to carry a pistol to school. A priest who glimpsed it hidden under his clothes took the weapon from him. "He hated this professor and he never forgave him for that," said Rasco. "Fidel never forgets and he's very vengeful. He had a fistfight with Ramón Mestre. And Ramón gave him a hard punch in his face and knocked him down. I saw it. And when Fidel marched into Havana, he put Ramón in prison for twenty years."

As an adolescent, and until his early twenties, Castro was uncomfortable with women. "Fidel was very shy when he first came to Belén, especially with girls," Rasco recalled. "He had a crush on a beautiful fifteen-year-old who lived close to the school. But he could never talk to her. He was fourteen, fifteen and looked tall, handsome, with dark hair and he had nice clothes. One of our schoolmates who was a small, nerdy guy won the girl. And Fidel was furious." Llorente believed that girls threatened him. "He was aloof, very distant with girls. I think he felt they could hurt him—and he could not tolerate feeling that way. And he would never dance. All the boys at school would dance, but not Fidel." In 2001, Castro recalled enduring his youth at Jesuit schools watching American-made romantic movies while being subjected to what he jokingly called "sexual apartheid." Rasco said that by his senior year Castro had broken through his shyness and become very popular. "He had a charismatic personality. Father Barbados told him that he was 'like a diamond in the rough, but you need to polish yourself.' " His mother, Lina, attended his graduation, recalled one of his classmates, but not his father.

Francisco Aruca, who attended Belén ten years later, said that he had reviewed all the school's yearbooks and never again saw the quality of praise that was accorded Castro. "They wrote in Fidel's 1945 yearbook, *'Fidel tiene madera, no faltará artista.'* The translation is that Fidel will rise to all occasions. I am a product of a Jesuit education and the Jesuits never praised anyone." Elsewhere in the yearbook was written, "Fidel Castro Ruz always excelled in the Humanities. Excellent and popular, he was a true athlete, forever defending the school's colors with courage and pride. He has earned the love and admiration of all. He will study Law and there's no doubt that he will write brilliant pages in the book of his life. . . . He defended the Belén pennant in almost all of the school's official sports and has been proclaimed the best athlete in the school." Father Llorente said he wrote the text, because "he was my most exceptional student. It was clear that he would go on and make an impact on the world."

CASTRO COULD NOT HAVE been better positioned for his extraordinary rise than at the law school of the University of Havana. It was here, where the scions of the leisure class mingled with social revolutionaries, that he forged his political ambitions. The university's law school, a cauldron of firebrand activism, served as a finishing school for Cuba's future leaders. But side by side with the country's elite were cadres of gangsters who exerted significant power both at the university and within the country's body politic.

The novelist Guillermo Cabrera Infante maintains that Castro was one of them. "He wore the big suits they wore and carried a pistol," he said. "He was a gangster." Luis Posada Carriles, Castro's lifelong nemesis, seconds the opinion. Posada said he had vivid memories of Castro at the university. "Castro was tall, good-looking but he had a little chin. He looks better with the beard," Posada said in a backhanded swipe.

Another notorious Castro foe, Orlando Bosch, was also at school with him. Bosch, who is exactly four days older than Castro, said that he and Castro were quite close at the university, where Bosch was president of the student association at the medical school and later president of the Student Federation. "At that time, we got along very well," Bosch told columnist Andrés Oppenheimer in 1991. "We lived next to each other. The most he got to be was a class delegate from the law school—not even the [student] president of the law school—but he was a student leader and always very vehement, agitated and paranoid. He is a man of great obstinateness. The Revolution became his vengeance. But he is a great magician who pulls cards out of his sleeve."

Max Lesnik, who was two years behind Castro at school, observed that the issue of gangs and violence was a complex matter. "There were six or seven gangs at the university, but Fidel Castro wasn't a gangster," he said. "Fidel was a university student who like the rest of us had to carry a gun in defense against the gangsters. It was a very violent time and the students were very revolutionary. Fidel was impulsive, aggressive, charismatic and very popular. Of all the student leaders of that time, he had the largest following. It was said that 'he who goes with Fidel either arrives or perishes in the attempt.' " In his insightful memoir of Castro, Carlos Franqui writes of the time: "This was gang warfare disguised as revolutionary politics. Actually, it was a collective exercise in machismo, which is its own ideology."

Castro's future brother-in-law, Rafael Díaz-Balart, claims to have first-hand knowledge of Castro's involvement with student violence during his first year at the university. "This friend of ours had told us that Leonel Gómez is about to graduate from high school and then he is going to the university and then he is going to run for president of the FEU [the Student Federation] with the full support of President Grau [Ramón Grau San Martín]," Díaz-Balart explained. "Fidel then says, 'We have to kill him.' To understand this, you must understand the conditions that existed in Cuba in 1945, in which six university students would take a vote on whether to kill a person whom they had never met. It is something that is hard to believe today but this was the situation under the presidency of Grau. So a vote was taken and it was four against two not to kill Leonel. Fidel had a .45 that his father had given him as a gift. Fidel always practiced with a lamppost at night. But fifteen, twenty days after the vote—I was home and Fidel was my sister's boyfriend by then—and someone knocks on the door. It was Fidel saying, 'You have to help me. I just shot Leonel.' " Díaz-Balart said that Castro spent the next four days hiding out at his family's home in Banes. Leonel Gómez was slightly wounded and lives today in Miami—"with the lead he still carries in his body from Fidel," according to Max Lesnik.

Salvador Lew was initially quite impressed with his schoolmate at the university's law school in 1947. "He was a student leader, as was I. I ran against the people that were backing him and he came to see me at a park in the university. He talked to me for a couple of hours and he convinced me that I shouldn't run," recalled Lew. "He's very convincing, very aggressive and very smart. He wanted to be the president of the Student Federation but he was never able to win an election at the university. He always lost and that may be the reason why he has never called for elections in Cuba. I saw Fidel at the university with *Mein Kampf* under his arm and it was known that he was an admirer of Mussolini." During this period, there was a cult of Mussolini in Latin America—notably in Argentina and Chile. But unquestionably, Castro obsessively studied men of power—of all stripes—and he was wont to quote Caesar or Napoleon on military strategy. "I don't know if it was Napoleon who said that one bad general in war is worth twenty good ones," he wrote his friend Luis Conte Agüero.

By the time Castro made his mark at the university, some trademark elements of his personality were already clearly identifiable: he maintained a code of personal privacy and honed his discipline for study and strategy. No one recalls him ever discussing his family or personal matters, although it was widely known that his father had considerable wealth and had provided his son with an unlimited wallet. One former classmate recalled going shopping with Castro for a new car: "His dad wrote him, 'I'm sending you $10,000 to buy a car and buy yourself a gun,' because Fidel had told him that he was having troubles." "Fidel never talked about his parents," said Lew. "Fidel's father gave him all the money he needed, a brand-new American car every year when only a few students could afford a car. His father loved Fidel very much but Fidel never mentions that his father was his provider. He wore good clothes, good shoes. He was living in one of the best guest houses for students and later in his own apartment, which was very unusual for students."

At the law school, Castro set his sights on a political career—and exhaustively read up on history, military strategy, Marxism and political theory. He allied himself with Eddy Chibás, the charismatic founder of the Orthodox Party, who was regarded as the great white hope for democracy in Cuba. But some of their mutual friends say that Chibás was wary of the ambitious student leader from Oriente. "I remember a rally and Fidel tried to talk to Chibás," recalled Lew. "Chibás said to me, 'I don't want gangsters here.' " Nevertheless, after Chibás shot himself on live radio following a scandal that discredited him, Castro played a central role at his media-saturated funeral. Rafael Díaz-Balart claims that Castro suggested using Chibás's death as a means to oust President Carlos Prío, whose popularity was plummeting. "When Chibás died, he proposed that we take the body to the presidential palace, kill Prío and take power," he said.

In 1948, Castro married his girlfriend, Mirta Díaz-Balart, while still at the university. On March 10, 1952, a close friend of her father's, Fulgencio Batista, a native of Banes and former colonel who had been president from 1940 to 1944, seized power in a stunning military coup. Mirta's family was quickly rewarded for their loyalty to Batista with high-level positions. Her father became the Minister of Transportation and the Minister of Communications, while her brother Rafael assumed the critically important post of deputy chief of the Ministry of the Interior, which ran the country's dreaded secret police. Castro declined his brother-in-law's invitation to join Batista's government: he had far grander ambitions.

"When Batista orchestrated the military coup, Fidel saw the opportunity to become a national leader. And that's the reason he led the assault on the Moncada," said Lew. "He knew that he was not going to win but that it would give him national stature. He gambled with his life; he did not know if he was going to be killed. By attacking the Moncada, he became the most important leader in Cuba."

Castro turned his Moncada trial into a spectacular public relations campaign. Asked who was the ringleader of the assault, he replied, "the intellectual author was José Martí." And when queried as to whether his cohort Abel Santamaría was studying the works of Lenin, he countered contemptuously: "We were all reading Lenin and other socialist writers. Anyone who doesn't is an ignoramus."

Sentenced to prison with his fellow survivors, Castro used his time optimally—reading, studying, plotting his future and writing hundreds of letters. In a letter to his friend the radio commentator Luis Conte Agüero in August 1954, Castro enumerated the perils faced by a revolutionary movement: "cult of personality, group ambition and *caudillos*."

On July 17, 1954, Castro was plunged into a personal crisis, having learned that his wife, Mirta, had been taking a stipend from the Ministry of the Interior, run by her brother Rafael Díaz-Balart. Initially, an uncharacteristically wounded Castro denied the reports, but days later his sister Lidia confirmed their truth. Castro reacted to the news as if it were a mortal blow and unforgivable humiliation of him. "I am blinded by rage," he wrote his sister. "I can hardly think anymore. I am ready to challenge my brother-in-law to a duel. The prestige of my wife and my revolutionary honor are at stake." From this point on, Castro's family feud dovetailed with his national feud. Rafael Díaz-Balart, his former best friend, his brother-in-law, had not only gone over to the enemy, in Castro's mind, he had betrayed his sister and her family.

In 1955, Batista granted a general amnesty to political prisoners. The decision—which would set in place the events leading to his ouster—was made against his better instincts but under pressure from the United States, which hoped the move would quell the widespread discontent in Cuba. Castro's brother-in-law had argued strongly against the Amnesty Law. "Batista agreed with me," said Díaz-Balart, "but the American embassy asked him to approve it and it had a lot of popular support, which is what made him change his mind."

On May 15, Castro, his brother Raúl and eighteen followers walked out of the Isla de Pinos prison and immediately resumed their revolutionary work. Less than two months later, on July 7, fearing for his life, Castro left for Mexico with his closest supporters. A few days later, at the Mexico City apartment of a *moncadista*, Castro met a young Argentine physician smitten with waging revolution named Ernesto Guevara. Guevara had fled Guatemala when the elected left-wing government of Jacobo Arbenz was torpedoed by a CIA coup and headed north on his motorcycle to Mexico. "A political occurrence is having met Fidel Castro, the Cuban revolutionary," Guevara would write in his diary, "a young man, intelligent, very sure of himself and with extraordinary audacity. I think there is a mutual sympathy between us." In a matter of days, he was dubbed "Che"—meaning "hey" in Argentine Spanish—by his Cuban compatriots for his inveterate use of the word. Guevara's view of social struggle was more romantic than Castro's. "The true revolutionary is guided by strong feelings of love," he wrote.

For the next year and a half, Castro and his cohorts plotted and strategized their clandestine return to Cuba to bring down the government of Batista. Throughout his exile, Castro remained in touch with supporters in Cuba and those working with other groups, most especially with the Directorio Revolucionario, which led the resistance in Havana. On several occasions, Castro traveled to Miami and New York, and once he swam across the Rio Grande, to meet with allies and raise money for his ragtag troops. In 1955, with an eye toward his own mythmaking, Castro traveled to Miami, Tampa, New Jersey and New York, the very trail that Martí had taken prior to the War of Independence. One of Castro's most dependable backers was none other than former President Juan Prío, who had settled in Miami.

John Cabañas, who runs a charter airline in Miami that flies to Cuba, remembers Castro from those days. "Fidel came into the life of my family at midnight on the 2nd of December 1955," recalled Cabañas, whose father headed the San Carlos Institute, the Cuban-based cultural institution in Key West, Florida. "I was thirteen years old and every night from the 2nd to the 7th of December, he would come to our house around eight or nine o'clock and he'd be there until three or four o'clock in the morning." Castro was on a mission to raise support and funds to finance an invasion of Cuba. He was twenty-nine years old and didn't have a beard yet. "He had a gray suit that he wore every day, with a white shirt and a tie—and he sweated a lot," said Cabañas. "He was a very exhaustive communicator, to the point that he convinced my entire family to follow him. My mother, father and my oldest sister became founding members of the 26th of July Movement. He said he was going to invade Cuba by December 1956 and he kept his word on that."

On November 25, 1956, Castro and eighty-two of his followers climbed aboard the dangerously overloaded *Granma* and set sail for Cuba. Che Guevara called their arrival in Cuba a "shipwreck." After their crash landing, a day late and seriously off course, at Los Cayuelos on December 2, matters went from bad to worse. Three days later, most of Castro's men, because of the betrayal of a guide, were gunned down in an ambush in a sugarcane field at Alegría de Pío. It was arguably Castro's darkest hour. Undeterred, he led

Che and his surviving band up into the Sierra Maestra mountains of Oriente Province, from which he waged a guerrilla war for the next two years. The Sierra, which encircles Santiago, Cuba's second largest city, were the mountains of his youth—where he hunted, fished and hiked with his brothers. He had wisely chosen to conduct his campaign from his home turf. Meanwhile, resistance and guerrilla attacks in Havana were being valiantly waged by José Antonio Echeverría's Directorio Revolucionario, until his death, along with twenty-four other students, in the storming of the Presidential Palace on March 13, 1957.

By the time of Castro's return, Cuba was ablaze with anti-government fever, fed by disgust with decades of corruption and Batista's excesses and brutality. Fueling the outrage was resentment toward the U.S., which regarded Cuba as little more than a colony useful for its cheap sugar and easy sin. "Batista turned out to be only a part-time tyrant," quipped Cabrera Infante. "The rest of the time he was too busy being a thief and a canasta player." Castro thoughtfully gauged and exploited the sentiment.

In the Sierra, Castro imposed an austere discipline on his troops. "Errol Flynn wanted to go up in the hills and see the revolutionaries during the war but they would not give him permission," recalled Bernard Diederich, former Latin American bureau chief for *Time*. "He was drinking all night and the *barbudos* never drank. They were the most puritanical people you could ever meet."

Castro was ably supported by a young professor from Camagüey named Huber Matos. "While I was working in the underground, I had written Fidel Castro asking that he accept me in the guerrillas," related Matos, who was a close friend of Celia Sánchez. "He said that if I came with weapons, then yes. So I spent ten months in Costa Rica to get them from the President of Costa Rica. Fidel Castro met me on the day I arrived, March 30, 1958, in the Sierra with a plane full of weapons. Fidel was thrilled and hugged me, and he treated me with great affection. He said that he had been waiting fifteen months getting promises about weapons that were never delivered."

Matos, an early revolutionary hero before his dramatic split from Castro in 1960, gleaned almost immediately that Castro pivoted between two personalities: benevolent and abusive. "When, after a few days, he saw me as a fighter, he started treating me with affection and respect and I was promoted to captain," he recalled. But perhaps sensing a rival, Castro alternated praise with ridicule: "A month later, he treated me badly with foul language in front of a group. And he had an assistant he verbally abused every morning in front of others."

Agustín Alles, a thirty-two-year-old correspondent for *Bohemia,* Cuba's most popular magazine, was the first Cuban reporter to interview Fidel Castro in the Sierra. Alles had traveled with noted photographer Eduardo Hernández for nine days, mostly on foot, and arrived at Che's camp, which was named La Mesa, in March 1958. After spending a few weeks at Che's camp, Alles moved to Fidel's Camp, La Plata, where they spent a month. "He had a fondness for the magazine *Bohemia,* which was helping him a lot," said Alles.

Castro would frustrate Alles, whom he knew from their university days, with a host of conditions. "As I was jotting something down, he said, 'No, don't put that in, that's off the record.' " Even in prison Castro was ever mindful of public relations. In one letter from jail he wrote, "Never abandon propaganda even for a minute because it is the very soul of our struggle."

One of Castro's most crucial assists came in 1957 from Herbert Matthews of the *New York Times,* whose interview virtually brought Castro back from the dead. The UPI in Havana had reported—based on a press release from Batista's government—that Castro had been killed. "In the camp they were making fun of Matthews while he was waiting to see Fidel," said Alles. "Fidel would put a guerrilla in front of him and that same guerrilla would run to the next post giving the impression that there were thousands when there were only about two hundred guerrillas. Castro told me that when the Revolution triumphs, there will never be censorship again in Cuba. He promised democracy, liberty, human rights, no political prisoners, and there were not going to be any more executions."

FROM THE TIME OF HIS 1952 coup until his fall, Batista was losing support exponentially with each passing year. Even the upper classes and businessmen had become disenchanted with his tyranny, corruption and colossal thieving. Batista was reported to be pocketing more than $1 million from the gambling casinos *every month* and he maintained Swiss bank accounts with deposits in the hundreds of millions. "We didn't care who overthrew Batista," said Julio Lobo, the country's most prominent sugar tycoon, "providing someone did."

Batista's survival became entirely dependent upon American support; the U.S. view of Cuba was tragically astigmatic. To most in the Eisenhower administration, Cuba served its purposes so long as it was a reliable supplier of sugar, cigars and rum. The U.S.'s long-term goals were maintaining its base at Guantánamo and keeping the island safe for weekend sinning. "I know Batista is considered by many as a son of a bitch," William Wieland, the then Cuba hand at the State Department, famously told *Newsweek* magazine, "but American interests come first . . . at least he is our son of a bitch." The U.S. dispatched a political crony and donor of Eisenhower's named Earl Smith to serve as ambassador. In an uncanny foreshadowing of the current situation, Smith was a wealthy mover and shaker in Florida Republican politics. He spoke no Spanish and never grasped the depth of popular loathing for Batista. For much of his tenure he assured the administration that the rebels in the Sierra were only a nuisance.

By late 1958, even Smith was forced to admit otherwise. By December, Batista had lost several important cities and provinces to rebel forces. Around the same time, a key general was secretly negotiating with Fidel Castro. On December 17, Ambassador Smith finally met with Batista and gave him the bad news. According to Cuba historian Hugh Thomas, Smith conveyed the State Department's belief that he had lost control of his country and that "it would avoid a great deal of bloodshed if he were to retire. Batista replied that without him, no military junta could survive." Batista asked Smith for a U.S. military intervention and was refused. Finally accepting his new reality, he asked for permission to go to his estate in Daytona Beach, Florida. "Smith suggested Spain instead," wrote Thomas, the idea being to get Batista's disreputable odor as far away as possible from whatever new government the U.S. hoped to cobble together.

On December 31, New Year's Eve, ensconced in his luxurious Villa Kuquine, Batista made a phone call at 10:00 P.M. to his top staff. He asked that they meet him later that night at Camp Columbia. Only three hours into the new year, Batista and forty of his top aides and generals fled to the Dominican Republic, taking most of the national treasury with them. Calls were made to alert Batista's friends and key people throughout the country: thugs like Rolando Masferrer and gangsters like Meyer Lansky, who ran gambling casinos and brothels in Havana, also quietly slipped out of Cuba that night and beelined toward Florida. Batista would move to the Portuguese island of Madeira, where he died in 1973.

With Batista's ignominious flight, Cuba went into an orgy of celebration and Castro began his famous weeklong march into Havana. Although Castro had appeared to descend from the Sierra like Moses from the mount, his triumph was, in fact, a shared victory. For several years, there was a dueling rivalry and agitated jockeying for power between the urban underground—*el llano*—and the guerrillas in *la sierra*. There were many heroes—some of whom never lived to see Batista's fall, like Frank País and René Ramos Latour, who deftly ran operations in Santiago de Cuba, and Echeverría and Carlos Gutiérrez Menoyo, both of whom perished in the assault on the Presidential Palace in 1957. With País and Echeverría gone, Castro's stature grew exponentially. He consolidated his power over the varying factions, along with his status as the preeminent revolutionary leader, when a general strike on April 9, 1958, called for by *el llano,* was deemed a failure.

However, without the campaign of the students in Havana under the Directorio, the Second Front of Escambray led by Eloy Gutiérrez Menoyo, Carlos's brother, and the taking of Las Villas, the central part of the country, by Che Guevara and Camilo Cienfuegos, there would not have been a Cuban Revolution. But there was no dispute that the guerrillas of the Sierra campaign had captured the imagination of the country, and in January 1959, Castro was the man of the hour.

Upon his arrival in Havana, Castro's first stop was Camp Columbia, formerly Batista's military barracks. Bernard Diederich, reporting for *Time,* remembered his speech there on January 8, 1959. "He went to the podium and I was right next to him, taking notes furiously. He had a very hoarse voice, having talked all the damned time, and he must have been very tired. Somebody put a glass of water out for his throat. And a little way through his speech, they let out these four doves from a cage: the white dove of peace, the war is over and all that. The doves had been there for God knows how long and they didn't look very good and one settled on his shoulder. Another dove put its head in Fidel's glass of water and started to drink and wash itself and had a real bath. Fidel's guards and I were mesmerized by this crystal-clear glass of water transformed into muddy pigeon water. And suddenly, Fidel lifts the glass and as he does we all go, 'Oh! My God!' And he looks around, sort of saying 'Why are these idiots interrupting my speech?' and without noticing what happened, he drank the pigeon's bathwater."

Journalist Lee Lockwood had caught up with Castro in Santa Clara as his caravan made the victory trek back to Havana. "He made a speech that began around two in the afternoon. By this time he was really exhausted and it was very hot," recalled Lockwood. "Like Mussolini, he was delivering a speech to the multitudes from the balcony, and he fell back into the arms of a couple of people who were supporters, follow *bui buubs,* and it looked like he could hardly breathe, and at that moment Ed Sullivan arrived with a TV crew and just marched right into the room and took over. They shut off the lights and commanded Fidel to answer some questions on camera. Sullivan, of course, knew no Spanish and said, 'Fidel, I see that around your neck you wear a cross, but that cross is *católico,* but I hear rumors that you are communist and how can you be a communist if you're wearing a Catholic cross?' Castro suffered this fool gladly and said, 'I'm not a communist, and you can be a communist and wear a cross.' " Castro had shunned Cuba's Communist Party, which had long allied itself with Batista. It was not until 1972 that he publicly identified himself as a communist.

In the first months of the Revolution, revenge was quick and executions were routine. Civil liberties were suspended—many never to be reinstated. While Castro initially enjoyed the support of 90 percent of the country, thousands of upper-class and educated Cubans, fearing the worst, fled to the U.S. In March 1959, Castro convened Operation Truth to explain and justify his policies. "There were at least a half a million people there," recalled Luis Aguilar León, Castro's former classmate in Santiago, who would soon leave for the States. "Violeta Jiménez introduced the speakers, and she said, Camilo Cienfuegos the great *comandante* will speak, but the people didn't stop talking. And then Che Guevara spoke but the people in the audience kept talking, with some applause, but not much. And then Fidel came to the balcony and took the microphone and people were still talking. And he put his finger to his lips and said, 'Shhh, shhh.' And suddenly you could see the silence extended like an invisible wave, and half a million Cubans became quiet. And then like a wave coming back, you heard the roar, 'Fi-del, Fi-del, Fi-del!' And then I thought that never again can anyone approach him and say, 'You are wrong, Fidel.' You will never believe that you are wrong again."

In the early months of his ascension to power, Castro instituted a reign of terror on his enemies and those suspected of counterrevolutionary sentiment. Unquestionably, blood vengeance ran deep among the thousands who had been brutalized under Batista. Between 1953 and 1959, an estimated 25,000 Cubans were executed. Every Cuban knew that the men captured at Moncada were tortured and that two of Castro's cohorts had been mutilated: Abel Santamaría had had his eyes gouged out and Boris Santa Coloma his genitals severed. Exile Abdo Ballestar remembers as a boy seeing the body parts of students murdered by Batista's police flowing down the Mayarí River. The rallying cry of the conquerors, "*Al Paredón*—to the wall," was shrill and shameless as thousands of Batista's men and suspected sympathizers were summarily executed.

Luis Ortega, who had returned to Cuba in January 1959 in solidarity with the Revolution, was so troubled by the random violence, arrests and executions that he fled again to the States five months later. "The police were looking for me. Fidel's police," he said. "It was a period of terror. Nobody was sure of anything then." Even Castro's revered schoolmaster from Belén,

Ángel Fernández Varela, broke from his former star pupil. "The first two years of the Revolution were possibly the worst years. The lies and events—it could not have been worse," said Fernández Varela, who fled in 1960. "I saw him during the first days after his arrival in Havana. I was having lunch in a restaurant and he came in with a journalist who later died in exile. Fidel came over to me and said, 'Professor, you thought this was going to take longer, didn't you?' This journalist asked him, 'Why do you call him professor?' and then he got tense and began to speak to me familiarly [in the *tú* form]. He was uncomfortable because the previous year the revolutionaries had invited me to come to the Sierra and I didn't go. They had held a trial for the newspaper directors to judge who was good and who was bad—the good ones were invited and the bad ones were condemned. I was among the good ones invited to go to the Sierra. I asked then, 'And who judged whether I was good or bad?' Of the three, I believe two were shot by Fidel Castro."

José Ignacio Rasco, Castro's classmate from Belén and the university, also had an unsettling meeting with Castro in those early days. "He said to me, 'Rasco, I saw you on television the other day and let me tell you we are in a revolutionary mood and we don't accept any kind of criticism. We cannot.' And I told him, 'Fidel, I will applaud you when you do something that I like, but if I don't like it I will criticize you because we want democracy here.' And he told me, 'Okay, but prepare for the consequences.' He's a great personality, no doubt about that. He's a genius but he has no feelings, no heart for anyone. I saw that he was a very solitary personality. I remember when he arrived in Havana all glorious in 1959. I felt sad for him because he looked solitary, completely alone."

TO A NOT INCONSIDERABLE EXTENT, the CIA's failed invasion at the Bay of Pigs created the legend of Fidel Castro. While Cubans had learned of him after Moncada, America's defeat at the hands of Castro's forces on the southern shores of Cuba made him into an international celebrity. He would be David, the country boy from Oriente, fighting the Ugly American Goliath. Now he was a player on the world stage. Aware of his precarious position with his northern neighbor, Castro began a full court seduction of the Russians and convinced Khrushchev that sophisticated firepower was needed to deter another U.S. invasion. "The irony is that if it had not been for the Bay of Pigs," says James Bamford, "we would not have had the Cuban Missile Crisis."

In 1962, the Soviet Union installed intermediate-range nuclear missiles and medium-range bombers in the western province of Pinar del Río, provoking the most perilous crisis of the nuclear age. Kennedy moved quickly, ordering a naval blockade of Cuba to interdict Soviet ships before the missiles were battle-ready. The Cuban Missile Crisis of October 1962 became a testament to Castro's hubris and belligerence. According to one of his biographers, Carlos Franqui, it was Castro himself who impulsively activated the missile that shot down an American U-2 spy plane, killing its pilot. Then Castro turned and faced the stupefied Russian advisers and said, "Well, now we'll see if there's war or not."

Kennedy warned Castro that he would not tolerate another attack on a U.S. plane, and still Castro kept firing. Recently declassified KGB files reveal that Castro had lobbied Khrushchev to use nuclear weapons against the U.S., but in the end Khrushchev blinked and removed the missiles. The Soviets kept a contingent of troops in Cuba and established a state-of-the-art intelligence listening post called Lourdes in Havana that operated through early 2002. And up until 1990, they picked up the tab for the lion's share of Fidel Castro's social experiment—a bill estimated by some to exceed $100 billion.

In deference to the Soviets, Castro collaborated on a host of ludicrous policies. Perhaps none was so absurd and unpopular as banning Christmas as a holiday. In 1997, Castro rescinded the ban in honor of the Pope's imminent visit and softened his hostility against the Church. Later, he sought to co-opt Christ: "Jesus Christ chose the fishermen because he was a communist," he said in a speech.

Curiously, Castro has always been starstruck by JFK, notwithstanding the plethora of disclosures of the CIA's innumerable plots under Kennedy to eliminate him. "He has huge regard for Kennedy and I never understood that," said Saul Landau, a Castro documentarian. Kennedy's decision to withhold U.S. airpower in the Bay of Pigs invasion—dooming it to failure—has never been forgotten by Castro, who continues to burnish Kennedy's memory.

Castro is exceptionally generous with the dead—be it Kennedy, Camilo Cienfuegos or Che Guevara, who is the official saint of the Revolution, his bereted mug etched on T-shirts and billboards in virtually every neighborhood in Cuba. Recently, Castro pronounced that Che "probably would have been made a saint because he had all the virtues." And the martyred Che has served Castro inestimably.

But there is broad agreement that even the iconized Che was on a slippery slope with Castro at the time of his death. Lázaro Asencio, a high-ranking commander in the Escambray, recalled problems concerning method and strategy during the guerrilla war. "When Fidel saw us for the first time in Cienfuegos after the war was over, we had many complaints about Che. I said, 'Listen, the only thing Che has done here is to fight against us.' Fidel told us, 'Do you know what I'm going to do with Che? I'm sending him to Santo Domingo so Trujillo will kill him. And my brother Raúl, who wants to damage this Revolution by turning it communist, I'm sending him to Czechoslovakia as ambassador."

"If we had followed Che's methods, perhaps we would have avoided some of these problems," reflected Castro's close friend Alfredo Guevara (no relation) in 1993, alluding to Che's admonition to stay clear of Soviet-style bureaucracy. "Che was always very worried about the bureaucrats. He was very concerned about the kind of people who work in government."

Castro's biographer Tad Szulc felt certain that a showdown between the two titans was looming, notwithstanding their close friendship, molded during their years together in Mexico, the Sierra Maestra and the first years in Havana. "I think there is no one that Fidel Castro would not have sacrificed with two exceptions," said Szulc. "One was the love of his life, Celia Sánchez, and then Che Guevara, until the falling-out. Guevara was a highly intelligent man—more than Fidel. Fidel is more of a manipulator, chess master, military leader. They were useful to one another until Che decided that Castro was betraying the principles of the Revolution."

Szulc met with Che in New York in 1964, prior to Che's departure for Bolivia to organize a peasant revolution. "It was both a philosophical and personal breach because they were both so intense," he said, citing Che's speech in Algeria in 1965, when he admonished the Russians. "If Che were alive today, I think they would be enemies. But I never believed that Che Guevara ever aspired to overthrow or replace Castro. Still, he was getting in Fidel's way. Guevara talked too much to friends in Cuba and elsewhere. He didn't call Fidel names, but it was unspoken. I don't think that Castro would have been heartbroken had Che been killed in Algeria, Mozambique or the Congo. That huge mural of Che on the side of the building [the Ministry of the Interior] in the plaza tells one that a dead Che Guevara is much more valuable to Fidel Castro than a living Che would be."

Whatever his feelings or motives, Castro was deeply affected by the death of his old comrade. The writer Norberto Fuentes recalled Castro's peculiar behavior on the night of Che's memorial service in Havana. "When Che died, he left the ceremonies at the Plaza de la Revolución and went to the basketball court at Sports City and he played all night. Everyone was flabbergasted."

Nevertheless, Che Guevara went to his death seemingly well disposed toward Castro. According to Félix Rodríguez, the CIA's point man at his execution, "Che refused to speak badly about Fidel," and when asked if he had any final messages, he told Rodríguez, "Tell Fidel that he will soon see a triumphant revolution in America."

STORIES ABOUND ABOUT CASTRO'S supernatural stamina, his ability to go days without sleep. Typically, Castro goes to bed after 4:00 or 5:00 A.M.—often at dawn. It is not unusual for him to sleep from 6:00 to 10:00 A.M., then resume his duties for the next twenty hours. But it has been years since he could go days on end without any sleep. Castro assured me that he sleeps at least four hours a night, sometimes even six. "People think he doesn't sleep, but he sleeps," said Norberto Fuentes. "He sleeps at different times during the day. It's safer to move around at dawn, when there are fewer people in the streets."

Although Castro was reportedly once bitten by a shark, this did not deter his ardor for deep-sea fishing. In 1964, Lee Lockwood spent a day snorkeling with him from a yacht off Varadero Beach. "I couldn't believe that anybody could go that deep and stay under so long, snorkeling with no tank," said Lockwood. "He had bodyguards who knew how to scuba dive, but he's fearless."

Castro seems to have lived without limits until the late 1980s. For the last decade, however, he has been a bit of a health nut. He is a devotee of Cuba's anti-cholesterol drug PPG, which has a Viagra-like side effect, prompting *habaneros* to dub it *para pinga grande*.

Max Lesnik, who regularly visits with Castro, says that he enjoys extraordinary health and stamina, and not entirely by accident. "He's obsessed with health issues," said Lesnik. "He's a hypochondriac." Looking over a sumptuous luncheon table with guests recently, Castro nibbled on grapefruit and yogurt while extolling the antioxidant powers of red wine and lecturing his American visitors on the proper temperature—180 degrees—to cook lobster. "He smokes absolutely nothing since 1985. He drinks Presidentes, a cocktail created by the Cuban president General [Mario García] Menocal, which is a drink made of rum with soda, sugar and a maraschino cherry," said Lesnik. "He drinks red wine at meals. This man's physical health is incredible. I've been with him at an event that started at 9:00 P.M. and ended at 5:00 A.M. and I went home to sleep and he kept on and on and on. He's tireless and has incredible energy."

Rumors of Castro's failing health are perennial. News stories of his present or imminent death (from heart attacks, strokes, cancer and/or Parkinson's) are annual staples in the Miami media. Denials invariably follow—usually along the lines of "Castro Not Dead Yet Again." However, Castro does have his mortal share of ailments and tribulations. No one doubts that he stopped smoking his beloved *puros* on doctor's orders. In 1993, an insider told me that Castro, who suffers from high blood pressure, had had a minor stroke while working in the Consejo del Estado, the government's offices. "They kept him in the basement clinic for two weeks," he said. "No one but his doctors and three *babalaos* were there." *Babalaos* are the equivalent of bishops in Santería, the Afro-Cuban-based religion of Cuba, which far exceeds the influence of the Catholic Church. Castro's relationship with Santería is curious and complicated. Initially he sought to repress it, despite the influence of Celia Sánchez, a *santera* herself. Eventually, realizing the futility of his efforts, he declared a truce, co-opted it to a certain extent and is now said to be a believer.

Castro has a near obsessive interest in medicine, science and biotechnology and has never suffered from a dearth of medical advice. Many of his closest friends and colleagues have been doctors, beginning with Che Guevara and René Vallejo. Carlos Lage, his current economic czar, and Fernando Remírez, one of his key U.S. advisers, are both doctors. In early 2002, hell-bent on being the Maximum Leader in perpetuity, he adopted a rigid macrobiotic diet under the guidance of Conchita Campas, an accomplished medical researcher in the Ministry of Health; its goal is to stabilize his high blood pressure and head off any more strokes. Castro is also pals with Rodrigo Alvarez Cambras, Cuba's most famous surgeon, who runs the Frank País Hospital in Havana. Cambras, who told me he counted fourteen foreign leaders as patients, operated on Saddam Hussein in the late 1980s, removing an octopus-like tumor from his spinal column. It would have been fatal, Cambras said, if it had not been skillfully removed. In appreciation, the Iraqi despot rewarded him with a hospital in Baghdad and a large fee, which Cambras said he turned over to the Cuban government. Castro rewarded him with one of the lovelier homes in the Miramar section of Havana. Hussein has also been generous with Castro, to whom he shipped one hundred Mercedes-Benz sedans to accommodate visitors when Cuba hosted the Pan American Games in 1991. In the days following the Iraqi invasion of Kuwait, Castro volunteered his diplomatic wiles to try to persuade Saddam Hussein to retreat, an offer the Bush administration declined. Since the Gulf War, the two have kept a respectful distance.

In 1994, Castro paid a visit to Ted Turner, the colorful founder of the CNN network, and a half-dozen HBO network executives at a protocol house in Havana. "He arrived with this whole squadron of troops and they looked like *Mission: Impossible* and deployed themselves all over the place," recalled one HBO executive. "A doctor with a defibrillator came with him so we thought that maybe he had heart problems. When we asked about it, someone said that he'd just been scuba diving. Turner told us that he thought Fidel was an alcoholic. This is when Ted was with Jane, and for a lot of that marriage Ted had stopped drinking and he was marking the contrast between him and Castro." Certainly, Castro has an appetite for drinking, as do both of his brothers, Raúl and Ramón, who have fought the bottle for years. But unlike his brother Raúl, Castro appears to be a periodic drinker—apt to go on binges and then leap on the wagon. More to the point, whatever his tolerance for booze, no one has ever seen him drunk or out of control.

"From the time I met Ted Turner, I became friends with him very fast," Castro told me. Turner made the decision to allow the Cubans to pluck CNN off its satellite and not to block out its signal. He even produced promo spots starring Castro for CNN, before his fellow executives straightened him out. He also broadcast the Cuban World Series until he was instructed to pull the plug. "I would really like to see him become President of the United States, but I shouldn't say that or he'll never be elected," Castro mused. A moment later, he revised his thinking and, wagging his pointer finger in front of his face Cuban style, said: "It's better to be someone who elects Presidents than to be President."

CHAPTER 9

DR. NO AND UNCLE SAM

Guerra avisada, no matan soldados.
Prepare for war and no soldiers will die.

CUBAN PROVERB

"**I** CAN'T THINK of a worse loser than Fidel," said Castro's good friend Gabriel García Márquez, who recounts a telling anecdote. The two men had gone out night fishing—one of Castro's favorite hobbies, along with deep-sea diving and snorkeling—with a mutual friend. Dawn was approaching, the men were tired and ready to turn in. But because their friend had caught more fish, Castro refused to stop fishing. This went on for hours, until García Márquez quietly exhorted their friend, "Stop fishing—we'll never leave as long as you have more fish than he. It's already 4:00 A.M.!" Finally, when Fidel caught one more fish, he said, "Let's go." It was 5:00 A.M.

It is intolerable for Castro to lose or surrender—even in the most trivial matters. At a baseball game in Caracas, he quarreled with an ally, Venezuela's eccentric President, Hugo Chávez—refusing to accept that he had been struck out. "It depends upon how narrow your strike zone is," Castro quibbled in all seriousness. He is an obsessive micromanager. Whatever he deems important, such as the Elián González negotiations, whose court rulings he could recite from memory, or thwarting the dissident-sponsored Varela Project, he supervises personally, trusting no one. A virtuoso strategist, he is often two or three moves ahead of his opponent.

In a peculiar twist, even Mexican-Cuban relations would be tested harshly in 2002. Furious over Mexico's vote to condemn Cuba's human rights record at the U.N. Human Rights Commission in Geneva in April, Castro tore into the Mexican President, Vicente Fox. Calling the tie-breaking vote "a despicable betrayal," and lambasting Foreign Minister Jorge Castañeda as "diabolical" and Fox as "a liar," Castro broke with diplomatic convention and played an embarrassing tape recording of Fox urging him to keep his attendance brief at a conference on world poverty in Monterrey—a plain contradiction of the official Mexican account of Castro's sudden departure. Defending his surreptitious recording of his guests, Castro told Cuban television, "A conversation between two heads of state is not a love letter. It is a political exchange. It is not a secret of the confessional." He even lobbed a backhanded insult at the Mexican President: "I daresay that Fox is a decent man. But he has no experience in politics at all." While Castro's actions struck many as shrill and ill-timed, they were fuel for Fox's opposition.

IT IS AN ARTICLE of faith that the blame for forty-three years of failed diplomacy with Cuba lies with a succession of ten feckless American Presidents willing to pander to hard-line exile constituents in the key states of Florida and New Jersey. The corollary to this is that Castro, hat in hand, has been incessantly rebuffed by his predatory imperialist neighbor. The truth, as in the case of all things Cuban, is more complicated. Borrowing an adage often invoked about Yasir Arafat and the Palestinians, Fidel Castro has never missed an opportunity to miss an opportunity.

During the administration of Gerald Ford, a remarkable two-year diplomatic initiative was undertaken by Secretary of State Henry Kissinger and his Assistant Secretary of State for Inter-American Affairs, William Rogers, to normalize relations with Cuba. Had the talks succeeded, the U.S. Embargo would have gradually been eliminated and diplomatic relations between the two countries would have been fully restored as early as 1976. "Kissinger was intent on dealing with Cuba," said sociologist Marifeli Pérez-Stable, "and getting it out of the way like China. It was part of the Kissinger-Nixon doctrine."

The Cuba initiative began in 1974 at Kissinger's urging, hatched after the Nixon-Kissinger opening to China and the détente effort with the Soviet Union. Rogers recently recalled that Kissinger regarded Cuba as "the remaining issue of the Cold War in the Western Hemisphere." Kissinger had made several speeches in which he sent a signal saying that permanent hostility with Cuba was no longer desirous. Some at the State Department thought that creating an opening with Cuba after the China negotiations would be a walk at the beach. Rogers laughed quietly, then said, "Little did we know."

Well aware of the hazards at hand, Kissinger kept his initiative a tightly guarded secret. Rogers equivocated as to whether even President Ford knew what was going on. "I am told or I've seen evidence that Henry advised him that it was going forward," Rogers said, indicating that Ford required plausible deniability, the ability to deny knowledge of the overture, if necessary. "It did not come out, although Reagan attacked Ford for being soft on Cuba in the 1976 campaign; the fact that we were negotiating was a deep dark secret right through the campaign."

Rogers said the negotiations began after Frank Mankiewicz, 1972 presidential candidate George McGovern's campaign manager, returned from a trip to Cuba with a unique proposition: the Cubans, he said, were ready to sit down and negotiate. It was one of those periods in U.S.-Cuban relations when the decibel level of acrimony and accusation inexplicably descends to a murmur. In September 1974, Senators Jacob Javits (R–New York) and Claiborne Pell (D–Rhode Island) had flown to Havana and met with Castro. It was the first visit by elected U.S. officials since diplomatic relations had been severed in 1961. "We wrote up a letter that Frank brought back down to Cuba," said Rogers, "and step by step the two countries prepared to offer demonstrations of good faith. We thought it was a good deal, so good they couldn't resist it."

By August 1975, the Ford administration announced modifications to the Embargo, allowing subsidiaries of U.S. companies in third countries to trade with Cuba and no longer withholding aid from countries that traded with Cuba. The negotiations were held in New York and on one occasion at a coffee shop in Washington's National Airport. Castro dispatched his trusted U.S. point man, Ramón Sánchez-Parodi, who approached his task with energy and optimism. But the talks crashed in December 1975, when Castro decided to intervene in the Angolan civil war. To their amazement, the U.S. team came to the conclusion that Castro intended to sacrifice his most crucial diplomatic opening in fifteen years to pursue a bizarre military venture across the globe.

Castro saw the intervention in an African country an ocean away from Cuba as an irresistible opportunity. In Jonas Savimbi, the thuggish leader of UNITA (who was murdered in February 2002), he would be squaring off against a U.S. proxy. Castro's Angolan adventure—which cost thousands of Cuban lives (estimates range from three thousand to five thousand of the soldiers dispatched) over fourteen years—further enhanced his profile in the pantheon of Third World revolutionary outlaws. In fact, Cuba's intervention in the region did make a crucial difference. Nelson Mandela has noted often that South Africa would not have wrenched itself free of its Boer rulers when it did if Castro had not committed his troops in Angola.

Angola gave Castro an opportunity to do what he loves best: wage war. A former Cuban soldier who served as an aide to General Leopoldo Cintra Frías, the second in command in Angola, recalled Castro's micromanagement of the war. "Every day at six o'clock, Cintra Frías would communicate by telex with Fidel, who would dictate exactly what he wanted done," he said. "Cintra Frías would explain the situation on the battlefield, but Fidel would make the final decisions in exacting detail. He even needed to know the color of the uniforms. And of course we got very impatient with him. We're over there trying to stay alive, and Cintra Frías said, 'What do you care about the color of the troops?' And Fidel went nuts. '*Comemierdas,* you can't do it that way!' he screamed. He knew exactly the terrain, where the troops were going to move and he knew the foliage color was about to turn from brown to yellow, not dark green, and would not camouflage us. He said we should swap uniforms. It turned out he was right."

Gerald Ford blamed Angola in a campaign speech for the decline in U.S.-Cuba relations, but Rogers said that even then they were ready to continue talking. Kissinger was anxious to close a deal with Castro and add another diplomatic feather to his cap. "The fact was that we had left the door open even after Angola," said Rogers. But ultimately, Castro pulled the plug on the talks, having decided that establishing diplomatic relations with the U.S. was not in his best interests. Rogers spoke with Castro again in 1997 at a luncheon meeting at the Council on Foreign Relations in New York. "He indicated to me that this was perhaps a missed opportunity," said Rogers. "He said something like 'Maybe we should have given more time and consideration to the negotiations.' "

Angola was by no means Castro's sole foray on the African continent. For shorter periods, to effect more modest goals, Cuban advisers and troops were dispatched to the Congo, Algeria and Ethiopia, as well as South Yemen, on the Arabian Peninsula. Castro viewed himself as a pioneer in the art of guerrilla warfare, and he was keen to see his model exported. His most committed efforts were in Central and Latin America, where they were run by the cunning Manuel Piñeiro, known as *Barbaroja*—Redbeard. For nearly three decades, Cuban advisers, medics and soldiers sought to replicate the Cuban model of revolution in Latin America—assisting left-wing guerrilla movements in Nicaragua, Venezuela, Guatemala, Argentina, Colombia, Bolivia and El Salvador against their oligarchic and often corrupt governments. The U.S. fought back, often supporting right-wing paramilitaries and repressive governments against such guerrilla operations. Castro's engagements ended—with few successes—in 1990 when, faced with the loss of their Soviet sponsors and withering hostility from their superpower neighbor, the Cubans retreated.

IN 1976, JIMMY CARTER arrived at the White House disposed to open relations with Cuba. It was a period of rosy optimism for Cuba watchers. A year earlier, the Organization of American States had lifted its sanctions on Cuba, while a dedicated flank of exiles was committed to dialogue with the Cuban government. Over his four-year term, Carter would enact the most significant and durable modifications of the Embargo. "Carter had wanted to achieve some reconciliation with Vietnam and Cuba," said Peter Tarnoff, who was Secretary of State Cyrus Vance's right-hand man. More might have been achieved had they not confronted the skepticism of Zbigniew Brzezinski, Carter's National Security Adviser, who sought to limit any opening with Cuba, viewing the island as a surrogate for the Soviet Union. In the end, Cuba and the U.S. agreed to reestablish quasi-diplomatic relations. Interests Sections, a euphemism for embassies, were reestablished in Havana and Washington in 1977 in the very same buildings that had housed the old embassies. Fishing rights and maritime boundary accords were signed and the U.S. lifted its prohibition on travel to Cuba, allowing citizens to spend $100 on Cuban goods during their visits.

It was also during the Carter years that a highly successful nongovernmental diplomatic endeavor, El Diálogo—the Dialogue—was spearheaded by exile banker Bernardo Benes. In late 1977, while on a family vacation in Panama, Benes had been tapped by a charismatic Cuban colonel in the Ministry of the Interior, Antonio "Tony" de la Guardia, along with Amado Padrón, the Cuban consul in Panama, and José Luis Padrón (no relation), Castro's U.S. affairs specialist, to head up a rapprochement between exiles and the Cuban government. Over the next year, Benes and his business partner, Carlos Dascal, held twenty-five meetings with Castro and organized the Committee of 75, a group of exiles chosen to negotiate with the Cuban government on behalf of the estimated 1.2 million Cubans outside the island.

"Every meeting started at ten o'clock and went for ten hours until morning," said Benes, speaking in the living room of his high-rise apartment on Collins Avenue in Miami Beach. "We smoked a lot of Cohibas because Fidel had just created the Cohiba cigar," recalled Benes, who is also a bit of a showman. "He used to flick the ashes all over the floor. We smoked two boxes of Cohibas in a night. One after the other. Once I had to go to the bathroom in his office. I was shocked to see all the toiletries, dozens of little bottles, shaving creams, aftershaves, medicines all lined up in a row because he's a hypochondriac."

Benes was astonished by the amount of research that Castro had done on him prior to his visit. "He recited my curriculum vitae—many things that I had forgotten—for more than ten minutes, without notes. He knew my life: that I was born in Matanzas to Cuban Jews. That I was a member of the Directorio and that I went to Cárdenas to the funeral of Echeverría. Incredible detail."

Eventually, the State Department, in the form of Peter Tarnoff and Robert Pastor, the Latin American specialist at the National Security Council, took over at the helm and held several secret meetings with the Cubans, including a three-day visit to Havana. There they were accorded one of Castro's ten-hour meetings. Castro's most alert hours are at night—what most of the world regards as the graveyard shift—and it was then that Tarnoff and Pastor hammered out the details of a massive prison release as Castro chain-smoked his Cohibas. In December 1978, their talks produced three notable agreements: Cuba would release 3,600 prisoners, mostly political prisoners; it would help reunite separated families by granting exit visas; and Cubans abroad would be able to visit relatives at home. Later, more than a dozen American prisoners were also released.

Castro had multiple goals for initiating the exchange. One of these was undoubtedly the hope of establishing a more moderate political beachhead in the exile community, to leaven right-wing pressure on Washington. Certainly, his motives for encouraging exiles to visit Cuba were not entirely humanitarian. "The exiles, after all, returned with dollars in hand," pointed out Wayne Smith, who headed the U.S. Interests Section under Carter. "The more who visited, the greater the Cuban government's earnings." Special stores were set up where exiles could buy appliances and goods for their loved ones using U.S. dollars. Cuba netted more than $100 million from exiles in the first two years of their visits.

"Fidel knew exactly what he was doing," said Benes, who remains convinced that Castro was ready to negotiate an end to the Embargo. But Carter, prodded by a suspicious Brzezinski, saw no percentage in going further—especially after the Soviet invasion of Afghanistan. "Castro was exceptionally interested in establishing a relationship with the United States in the Carter years," said Benes. "He loved Jimmy Carter. In my opinion, the United States government blew it."

Whatever personal affection Castro may have had for Carter, it was hardly demonstrated by the catastrophic refugee crisis he would unleash on U.S. shores seven months before the next presidential election. In April 1980, twelve Cubans seeking asylum crashed a minibus through the gates of the Peruvian embassy in Havana. The Peruvian chargé d'affaires responded with an announcement that anyone who wanted to defect could enter the embassy—prompting an overflow crowd of thousands of Cubans seeking asylum. Soon after, Carter gave a speech declaring that America would open its heart to "freedom-loving Cubans." It wouldn't take long for him to rue those words. On April 22, *Granma,* the official media organ of the Cuban government, announced that anyone who wanted to could leave the country by boat from Mariel, a port twenty-five miles west of Havana, for the United States.

A flotilla of refugees, eventually numbering 125,000, headed for the U.S., including hundreds of felons released from Cuban jails. In May, Carter declared a state of emergency in Florida and demanded that the Cuban government impose an orderly departure. He also ordered a blockade, to prevent private boats from traveling to Cuba to pick up more refugees. In August, at Castro's request, Tarnoff traveled to Havana with Pastor to discuss the crisis. Castro fulminated for hours. He made it clear that Mariel was his "act of defiance"—payback for the anti-Castro rhetoric coming out of Washington. In late September, Castro halted the exodus, proving once again his reflexive ability to provoke and terminate a crisis at will for whoever occupies the White House.

As testimony to the perils involved in a foray into Cuban politics, almost all the key players involved in the negotiations met a grim fate. Tony de la Guardia and Amado Padrón were executed for their alleged part in the infamous Drug Trials held in Havana in 1989. Bernardo Benes became a pariah in Miami—derided as a traitor. And Jimmy Carter lost the election. Only Fidel Castro emerged intact from the wreckage.

Not until the 1990s did Castro find himself with his back against the wall. In 1993, his hand forced by the collapse of the Soviet Union and the ongoing U.S. Embargo, Fidel Castro legalized what had been going on for years—the use of the dollar. It could only have been a bitter pill that three decades after Cuba tossed out the imperialist Yankees, the coin of the realm was the currency of Uncle Sam.

CUBA'S MODIFIED EQUIVALENT of a Cultural Revolution had its roots in the government campaign of the New Man of the early 1960s and flourished for a decade before losing steam. Grounds for persecution were any form of perceived decadence—sexual, ideological or stylistic. "My sense was that it had more to do with public behavior or appearances than private behavior," said Sandra Levinson, who heads the Center for Cuban Studies and has worked in Cuba since 1967. "Pablo Milanés [a famous Cuban folksinger], for instance, was sent away for wearing his hair in an Afro." The late José Luis Llovio-Menéndez, a high-ranking official in the Sugar Ministry until his defection in December 1981, joked that "*El Nuevo Hombre* [the New Man] might well have been called *La Nueva Mujer* [the New Woman]. We had a Minister of Education who proposed that women not be allowed to wear miniskirts and that men be forbidden to have long hair. He wanted to ban certain documentaries because some of the women were wearing short skirts. And he banned electric guitars." The documentaries of the late Nestor Almendros and the posthumously published memoir of the brilliant anguished writer Reinaldo Arenas contend that as many as fifty thousand Cubans were singled out for persecution.

The Writers Union, UNEAC, bore much of the brunt of the demented excesses of the New Man campaign. In 1971, the noted poet Heberto Padilla, a hard-drinking bear of a man openly critical of the government in his conversation and his poetry, was arrested by state security officials and locked up for more than a month. Thirty-eight days after his arrest, an ashen Padilla was ushered into UNEAC by state security agents and confessed his sins. "He told everyone how he thought the Revolution was really beautiful," said the literary critic and essayist José Rodríguez Feo, who had abandoned his family of sugar tycoons for the Revolution. Rodríguez Feo, who founded the literary journal *Orígenes* with José Lezama Lima and the avant-garde review *Ciclón* with Virgilio Piñera, watched Padilla denounce his friends as counterrevolutionaries, compelling them to come forward and admit their subversive ways. By the time I met Rodríguez Feo in 1993, there wasn't much love left in his love-hate relationship with the Revolution and Fidel Castro. When his guests drifted out of the living room of his shabby three-room Vedado apartment, he leaned in close to me and whispered hoarsely. "He's destroyed this country because of his pride," he said, then added, "And that's a monster."

Castro has always denied that gays and intellectuals had ever been repressed in Cuba. "Really, there has never been persecution of homosexuals here," he told me, clearly unhappy at this line of questioning. But in 1966, he confided to journalist Lee Lockwood that homosexuality was really "a deviation of nature." After more reflection, he concluded, "We could never come to believe that a homosexual could embody the conditions and requirements of conduct that would enable us to consider him a true revolutionary." Around the same time, he questioned the very existence of gays in Cuba. Carlos Franqui, then editor of *Revolución,* recalled, "Fidel would say to me, 'In the country[side] there are no homosexuals.' I had to point out that this was because all the *maricones* came to the city."

In our conversation, Castro alluded to the *machista* ethic of Cuban society and the Catholic Church's view of homosexuality as a sin. He referred to several Cuban homosexuals "whom we have appreciated greatly," including René Portocarrero, a noted artist. When I mentioned the name of his good friend Alfredo Guevara, he blanched and fixed his stare on me. Alfredo Guevara is perhaps the most enigmatic and interesting figure in Cuba's political firmament. The former president of ICAIC, the prestigious Cuban Film Institute, for more than twenty-five years, Guevara has been Castro's closest friend and confidant since the death of Celia Sánchez. Schoolmates at the University of Havana, the two were baptized into revolution with their participation in anti-government protests in Bogotá, Colombia, in 1948. Guevara was an avowed Marxist years before Castro's conversion and is known for his brilliance and prickly temperament. "Alfredo Guevara has never been considered a homosexual in our country," Castro said at last. "No?" I asked. "No," he answered quietly. "In my country he is," I said, not anticipating that this would be a sticking point.

I had met with Alfredo Guevara days before my interview with Castro. Baby-faced, balding, wearing a black dress shirt and smart tortoiseshell glasses, he cuddled his Yorkshire terrier, Bacchus, on his lap. His crowning achievement has been the creation of Cuba's film festival, which each December attracts hundreds of international films, dozens of celebrities and more than a million attendees.

Guevara said that he sees less of his old friend these days, although he remains one of the few people with unfettered access to him. "Fidel used to sleep here in my office," he said. "He would come here all the time, unannounced, at strange times. We spent our youth together." Guevara is among the very few whom Castro regards as an intellectual peer. He trusts him as much as he trusts anyone. "Fidel does not have a relationship like the one he has with Alfredo with anyone else that I know of," said the late José Luis Llovio-Menéndez, a close friend of Guevara. "Fidel does not listen to anybody except Alfredito. He would never allow anything to happen to Alfredo, who is also very close with Raúl Castro. It has been like that since their university days. Everyone knows that if something went wrong, Alfredo would report it to Fidel. Alfredo is a 100 percent *fidelista*. Castro sees him when he needs companionship. He's the only one I know of who has that kind of immunity." In Guevara's closing remarks to the film festival in 1995, he dared to try out a dangerous improvisation on the traditional revolutionary closer, *"Patria o Muerte!"*—exclaiming, instead, *"Patria y la Vida!"*

This curious bond spared Guevara any hardship when thousands of homosexuals were rounded up in the mid-1960s in what were known as the Purges and marched off to work camps to be rehabilitated. Over the gates of one such camp in Camagüey was the logo "Work Makes You Men," a macho variant on the Nazi slogan "Work Makes You Free" that appeared on the gates of Auschwitz. Credit for the Purges has been attributed to Raúl Castro, who was said to have been impressed with how Bulgaria had rid itself of "undesirables." When I queried Castro about his brother's alleged involvement in the camps, he responded angrily. "It's absolutely false from beginning to end. I have never in my life heard Raúl speak about that! It's not something I can take seriously."

I asked Alfredo Guevara whether it was true that the Purges ended after he marched into Castro's office to protest. He took a moment to respond. "I played a role," he said at last, "but I hope you will be careful with what I say because I do not want to be a hero." Placing Bacchus on the floor, he leaned across his desk toward me. "There were many of us who opposed it, but I did so the most radically. I talked to Fidel, I talked to Ramiro [Valdés— former head of the Ministry of the Interior], and I told them how I felt. And Vilma [Espín] played a really important role and Celia—you can't imagine how important she was. On one occasion, I went to Fidel about a very prominent individual and he said, 'Who is responsible for this?' And I said, 'We are. Really we all are.' " Ever the loyal soldier, Guevara maintained that Castro had no idea as to what was going on, blaming overzealous Party apparatchiks.

"I will tell you that there was no persecution in three areas," he stressed: "here at the Film Institute, at Casa de las Américas [a cultural and literary redoubt founded by Haydée Santamaría, one of the original guerrillas, who committed suicide in 1980] and at the Cuban National Ballet run by Alicia [Alonso], because we were three very strong personalities." One story has it that when Alicia Alonso learned that several of her dancers were targeted for arrest, she phoned Raúl Castro and warned, "If they touch my boys, I leave."

UNQUESTIONABLY, THE "TRIUMPH OF THE REVOLUTION," as the cliché goes, has been Castro's literacy campaign. In 1960, thunderstruck by the notion of vanquishing a staggering illiteracy rate, Fidel Castro ordered thousands of educated urbanites into the countryside to teach the ABC's to any *campesino* they happened upon. The success of the Literacy Brigades is the most significant, and arguably the sole, surviving "triumph of the Revolution." Castro tackled an illiteracy rate that was 41.7 percent in the countryside, according to a 1953 census, while 52 percent of the entire population never managed to go beyond the third grade. Cuba today not only leads Latin America in literacy, it surpasses the United States.

In 2000, Castro decreed that Cubans should be trilingual and inaugurated the University for All, which daily teaches English and French, among other subjects, on television. It is one of the richer ironies of Castro's island redoubt that every Cuban seems to have a color TV but virtually nothing to read. Owing to decades of stupefying mismanagement, many of its hypereducated populace have to and scramble daily for paper and pens. The paradoxes abound.

The dramatic debut in 2000 of Pedro Juan Gutiérrez's *Dirty Havana Trilogy,* unthinkable even five years earlier, flabbergasted many for its audacious nihilism and irreverence toward the Revolution. But the rules have changed, as they are wont to do in Cuba, with the exception of one: "Inside the Revolution, anything; outside the Revolution, nothing." And Gutiérrez's portrait of magnificent Havana as a fetid ecosystem of godless desperados pushed the limits of the official mantra to the maximum.

The fact that Gutiérrez is able to live freely in Havana and is not in jail, after penning such a derisive work, speaks to one of the great mysteries of the forty-three-year-old endurance run of Fidel Castro: namely that, in the wake of the Special Period and the crumbling of the Committees for the Defense of the Revolution, complaining is okay, but doing something about it, like organizing a demonstration, is not. And Cubans have turned the complaint—the safety valve of the Revolution—into an art form.

Those who venture further typically go directly to jail. It is believed that about eighty independent journalists operate in Cuba, sending their stories abroad via e-mail, fax, phone or courier. They are carefully monitored and are subject to capricious harassment and sometimes arrest. The poet and human rights activist María Elena Cruz Varela spent two years in prison after being assaulted by an angry mob in 1991 that literally tried to get her to eat her own words by shoving her papers in her mouth. A handful of independent reporters are usually in jail at any given time. Vladimiro Roca, the son of revolutionary hero Blas Roca, was in jail from July 1997 until days before Jimmy Carter's trip to Cuba in May 2002. Roca, a member of the so-called Gang of Four, wrote a treatise called *The Homeland Belongs to Us All*, which had the temerity to advocate open elections and a free press. He and his colleagues, Félix Bonne Carcasses, René Gómez Manzano and Marta Beatriz Roque, were arrested and convicted of sedition and spent several years in prison.

Raúl Rivero serves as the dean of the independent reporters and is the editor of his own news service, Cuba Free Press. He and a dozen others write mostly for the Internet and work as stringers for the foreign press. Rivero even contributes to *El Nuevo Herald* and Radio Martí but he knows the rules. Calling for the overthrow of the government is verboten. "You can play with the leash, but not with the dog," he says, offering a Cuban proverb. Despite their grievances with the Cuban government, most dissidents backed Elián's return to Cuba and want the Embargo to end. "I don't want to go to Miami," said Rivero, "to blather into a microphone things I don't even believe."

To the consternation of his enemies, Castro is not without his backers. "There remains support for Fidel in pockets throughout the country," said a former Cuba desk officer, "especially in the eastern part of the country." Castro's biggest threat, he said, comes from "the *nomenklatura*, Cuba's yuppies and professionals, like scientists and professors, who are watching any good life they had slip away." One dissident glumly described his country as a rowdy, dysfunctional family, incapable of severing the connection with its dictator-patriarch. "It used to be that there were the rich and the poor," said Natália Bolívar, once the head of the National Museum and a former aristocrat. "Now we are all poor."

The most resounding referendum on Castro is the fact that almost one tenth of Cuba's population has fled. The demographics of this exodus are revealing. Of the more than one million Cuban exiles living in South Florida, approximately 95 percent are white, while an estimated 70 percent of Cuba's population of 11 million is black or mulatto. "That's why there's paralysis in Cuba," a State Department Cuba analyst explained. "When black Cubans look at white Miami, they're afraid. Castro has been very successful in convincing Cubans that the most extreme and racist element in Miami has a stranglehold on U.S. policy, and when and if Castro goes, they would return and evict blacks from their old homes."

Miami resident Rosario Moreno, who left Cuba in 1963, remembers being in the exclusive Havana Yacht Club with her parents when Batista, who happened to be a mixture of black, Chinese and white, came in. "They turned the lights off," recalls Moreno, "to let him know that even though he was President, he was a mulatto and not welcome in the club. And he left." An elderly Miami exile, leafing through my photographs of Cuba recently, gasped, "Aaayyy! Look, they are all black! *Dios mío!* He even changed the race of our people!"

Castro has played the race card often and skillfully. He has reached out to black Africa—Angola, South Africa and Somalia—while assiduously courting American blacks. He visited with black leaders during his last visit to New York in 1998 for the U.N. Millennium Summit and frequently entertains delegations of African-Americans.

But it is in Cuba that race has reaped its highest dividends. A case in point is Ana Fidelia Quirot, one of the greatest runners in Olympic history and Cuba's foremost female athlete. Although she is a woman known for her unassuming manner, she was fuming when I met her in early 1997. Weeks earlier, Orlando "El Duque" Hernández, the baseball superstar, had made a daring and lucrative escape—one that landed him a $6.6 million contract to pitch for the Yankees. His half-brother, Florida Marlins pitcher Livan Hernández, had previously defected, as had a dozen other Cuban ballplayers. "I can tell you that they don't value what the Revolution has done for them," Quirot says, her voice rising. "They say El Duque is a millionaire in the United States, but he is a millionaire that was created here in Cuba."

Quirot was born in Palma Soriano, outside Santiago de Cuba. Her parents' revolutionary ardor was such that they named their newborn after Fidel Castro. Her family is not atypical of Cuban black families. Her mother, at the age of nine, began "cleaning the homes of white people" and did not learn to read until after the Revolution, when she was tutored by a Literacy Brigade volunteer.

In 1993, Quirot had a kitchen accident when she was seven months pregnant, resulting in life-threatening third-degree burns over more than half her body. "I would like you to tell me what it would have cost me in the U.S. to have been hospitalized for a year and a half," she said knowingly. "I had twenty-eight operations and I need more. And it didn't cost me anything. And not because I am Ana Fidelia, because it's the same for everyone."

According to the Cuban media, Quirot's burns were the result of a stove mishap when she was bleaching diapers for the arrival of her baby. She was using alcohol, a common, and dangerous, substitute for cooking fuel, which is scarce. But some Havana wags maintained that Quirot's accident was in fact an act of suicidal despair. Although never acknowledged in the state-controlled press, Quirot was having an affair with Javier Sotomayor, the Olympic decathalon gold winner and superstar. The two made a dazzling, Olympian pairing. Sotomayor, whose child she was shortly to bear, had been estranged from his wife. However, in January 1993, Sotomayor informed Quirot that his wife was also pregnant. Nevertheless, Sotomayor, whose reputation has been recently diminished by more than one failed drug test, rushed Quirot to the hospital and into the hands of Cuba's burn specialists. He saved her life, although the baby did not survive. Fidel Castro visited Quirot the first night and often throughout her recovery. With his encouragement, she said, she decided to attempt the impossible: to compete again in the Olympics.

Cuba has one of the highest rates of suicide in Latin America, one which has risen alarmingly since the Revolution. "For women, burning is the preferred method of suicide in Cuba," said the wife of a European ambassador based in Havana, who was not surprised to learn of the high numbers. "The men hang themselves," she adds.

A 1980 report compiled by the Ministry of the Interior found 21.6 suicides per 100,000 Cubans, according to Guillermo Cabrera Infante in *Mea Cuba*. Notables who have died at their own hand include Eddy Chibás, Haydée Santamaría and the writers Calvert Casey, Reinaldo Arenas and Miguel Ángel Quevedo, editor of the journal *Bohemia*. Cabrera Infante concludes that "all this must hark back to Martí [who suicidally rushed into battle against overwhelming Spanish firepower] if one speaks of Cuba and death." Martí's call to arms was *"La Victoria o el Sepulcro!"*—a rallying cry adapted by Fidel Castro as *"Patria o Muerte!"*

Ana Fidelia Quirot's own story had several more twists and ultimately a happy ending. She not only returned from death's door but threw herself back into training. At the 1996 Olympics, she snared the silver medal in the 400 meters in Atlanta, losing the gold by a fraction of a second. She went on to win the gold for the 800 meters at the 1997 World Championships. She then retired, married an Italian, had a baby and was upgraded to one of the grand old homes in Miramar.

WHILE CASTRO STEERS conversation away from Cuba's early treatment of gays, he's eager to expound on the Revolution's advances in women's rights. He regaled me with tales of how he created the first all-female fighting troop during the Revolution. "It wasn't an easy task . . . in the face of this macho tendency, and I personally trained the first female combat unit in the war of liberation. Some people asked me why I was giving arms to the women when there were men who didn't have any. I told them, 'I'll tell you why: they're better soldiers than you.' "

Vilma Espín, founder and chief of the Women's Federation, was one of the original guerrillas. Serving as the First Lady of Cuba, she is referred to as the wife of Raúl Castro, although the couple are said to have divorced more than twenty years ago—which the government refuses to confirm or deny. Espín came from old wealth and her father worked as a lawyer for Bacardi. She did postgraduate work at MIT in 1955 before hooking up with the young revolutionary Frank País. Like many of the inner circle, she is an *oriental* from Santiago de Cuba. She met up with Raúl and Fidel Castro before they sailed back to Cuba on the *Granma*. "At the time, I was the head of the underground for the province of Oriente," she recounted.

Espín told me that after the Revolution, Castro urged her to start the Women's Federation. "That was a big surprise. I was a chemical engineer." She reported that women today make up 50 percent of university students and 60 percent of all doctors. They have access to contraception and abortion, if needed. "Women work," she says. "They do not want five or six children like before." How many kids do they have? I wondered. "One and a half," she answered, like a statistician.

She admitted her greatest challenge now is the swelling ranks of prostitutes—*putas*—that can be found at any tourist site in Cuba. "It is terrible, but with this fast development of tourism, it's a price we have to pay," she said uncomfortably. "Some of them we can save because they have some kind of respect, morals, but others we cannot." She evaded the underlying issue. Women are lured to the world's oldest profession because they can make $10 in a half hour as opposed to $10 a month. Some—the prettiest, youngest and the most clever—often wangle marriages to foreigners and, the ultimate bonus, exit visas.

As I was leaving the federation, I noticed that the mythic ballerina Alicia Alonso had arrived, escorted by an entourage. Although she was seventy at the time and completely blind, she continued to dance with the Cuban National Ballet. With legs turned completely outward in a wrenching first position, the indomitable Alonso hobbled her way into the grand mansion. She could barely walk but, like her country, she insists that she can dance.

Two days after my interview with Fidel Castro, I had a visit at my hotel from Juanita Vera, one of Castro's aides. She wanted to talk me through Castro's comments about Guevara. "At that moment in the interview, Fidel was shocked," she explained, groping for words. "Of course Fidel knows Alfredo very well but we don't talk about a person's private life here. The people of Cuba think of Alfredo Guevara as a great revolutionary hero, not a homosexual." Yes, I understood her point, but were the terms mutually exclusive? She seemed frustrated as we each repeated our positions. Finally she said, "It's just that Fidel would prefer that Alfredo be known for being a hero of the Revolution."

Castro does not apologize as a matter of policy. Like the Chinese, he believes that apologies are a form of surrender except when used rhetorically. In 1969, when Cuba failed to produce his goal of a ten-million-ton sugar harvest, Castro theatrically apologized to the nation and even offered his resignation, then promptly forgot about it. At best, he will offer words of regret such as he did at the 2001 conference in Havana on the Bay of Pigs. Alfredo Durán, a veteran of the debacle who spent eighteen months in a Cuban prison, said he felt that Castro came close to apologizing for the suffocation deaths of eight prisoners during their transfer to Havana. But he couldn't quite get there and called what was an egregious and avoidable tragedy "a regrettable incident." When Eloy Gutiérrez Menoyo finally met with Castro in 1995, there was no apology or expression of regret for imprisoning him for twenty-two years. "Fidel Castro cleaned his hands about any wrongdoing done to me," he said. "Once I spoke with him for three hours, but he never brought up the past. No 'I'm sorry.' Nothing."

Certainly, there has been no remorse for the biggest scandal of the post-Revolution years—the Drug Trials of 1989. The Cuban equivalent of Watergate, the televised Drug Trials found eleven top officials of the Ministry of the Interior (MININT) guilty of narcotics trafficking. Four were executed, including the revered and recently decorated General Arnaldo Ochoa and Colonel Tony de la Guardia. Seven others were jailed for lengthy terms, including de la Guardia's identical twin brother, Patricio, and José Abrantes, Castro's longtime aide, for related wrongdoing. Abrantes died in prison from a heart attack after not receiving proper medical attention. Tony Castell, a decorated revolutionary hero, was tossed in prison for a year simply because he had recruited the de la Guardias to work at MININT in the early 1960s.

I asked Castro about the decision to execute Ochoa, perhaps the country's most popular general, whose career trajectory began in the Sierra and ran through Angola, and de la Guardia, a Castro favorite. The two rose to the very highest ranks of MININT and enjoyed a lifestyle with attendant privileges known to very few in Cuba. Their children, known as *los hijos de Papá*, were the Havana Brat Pack, with easy access to every sector of Cuban society. There has always been scuttlebutt that Castro knew what was going on and simply used the drug charges to eliminate potential opposition. I was curious as to why the four executed men were not granted clemency or a pardon. After all, neither murder nor espionage had been alleged.

Castro was visibly unhappy that the topic had been broached. He hesitated and folded his arms across his chest. Finally, he responded. "Because the country felt truly betrayed. There is a great difference between Ochoa and Tony de la Guardia," he said, with palpable contempt for the latter. "There is no comparison between their crimes. I mean in personality, and in historical merits, there is no comparison. Tony de la Guardia was the organizer, an irresponsible individual who risked his country's security, and Ochoa because he knew everything going on and let himself be carried away by crazy ideas about converting drug money into a resource for the country," he intoned incredulously. "He sent an aide to meet with Escobar [Pablo Escobar, the drug trafficker]! Can you imagine what it meant for a captain in the Cuban army to be making that contact in Colombia?" He paused a moment for dramatic effect. "The case of Ochoa was very moving, you know. It was hard for all of us but it was an unavoidable decision. Unavoidable. That is the right word."

Castro became agitated on the subject of Ochoa, wringing his hands as he spoke. I asked whether he felt personally betrayed. "Personally, no," he snapped. "The country felt betrayed. I don't concern myself with whether someone has betrayed me but whether they have betrayed the country or the Revolution." Although Tony's twin, Patricio, was in Angola for much of the time that his brother was accused of freelancing in narcotics, he too was put on trial and sentenced to thirty years. I asked Castro whether he was concerned by the Santería admonition to its priests, the *babalaos,* never to separate twins, much less kill one. "It's very painful not because they were twins but because they are brothers," he says, offering a bizarre biological digression. "Two brothers are a lot like twins because twins can be of one type or another: monozygotic from a single egg or dizygotic from two different eggs." He caught himself and returned to the question. "Patricio's guilt was not as heavy. The most serious responsibility fell on Tony. Justice cannot be guided by the *babalaos.*"

Many believe that Raúl Castro, once a dedicated communist who revered Stalin, was the driving force behind the executions, eager to consolidate power under himself and the army. Tad Szulc disagrees. "The execution of Ochoa and Tony de la Guardia would not have happened without Castro deciding it," said Szulc. "He is the most imperial person I ever met and a micromanager of all things. Castro would never allow any decision of any importance to be decided by anyone but himself."

The primary motive of the Castro brothers may have been to purge dissident elements from the armed forces, but they clearly got more than they bargained for. In 1991, a decorated Cuban colonel stationed in the embassy in Moscow drove across the border to Finland, with his family in tow, and defected. The colonel, Jesús Renzoli, was no ordinary *apparatchik* in the Cuban military, but a trusted adviser in the narrow inner circle surrounding the Castros. He had been Raúl Castro's personal secretary for many years, was the Russian language translator for Fidel Castro and had been privy to the most critical discussions and negotiations between the brothers for two decades. "He had been deeply shaken by the Ochoa affair," said Edward Gonzalez, a RAND analyst on Cuba who had interviewed Renzoli, "and my sense was that he was fearful that the Cuban government would collapse after the Russians pulled out." Renzoli beelined to the American embassy in Helsinki and was soon ensconced at CIA headquarters in Langley, where he was extensively debriefed. He lives in Virginia.

The mystery and paradox of the Drug Trials is that when Fidel Castro boasts of having a drug-free country, he is not entirely off base. There are drugs in Cuba—marijuana and some cocaine—but the fact is that Cuba has less of a drug problem than any other country in the Americas. It does have a serious alcohol problem, as well as a troublesome number of prescription pill addicts. But there is no evidence or ancillary crime to indicate that it has a serious drug problem. Castro's personal repugnance for drugs is well known. One military source, who believes that the de la Guardias were not rogue agents but had the approval of the government, offered another explanation. "It's true that Cuba has no interest in drugs," he says. "But Fidel is always shopping for more and better weapons. And in this hemisphere, the arms business is controlled by the narcotraffickers. You cannot buy arms without dealing with the cartels or their companies."

In 1995, I visited the elderly parents of the ill-fated de la Guardia boys for the first time. Mario was then ninety-four years old and housebound but Mimi, his wife, never missed her weekly prison visits with Patricio, who, at one point, had dwindled down to 120 pounds. A third son lives in New Orleans. The de la Guardias could well have been the poster family of Cuba: one son executed, another in exile and the third in prison.

Yet even by Cuban standards, few families have sacrificed so much.

Wealthy and privileged, Mario de la Guardia met his wife, Graciela, known to all as Mimi, an elegant beauty from Cienfuegos, in 1922. In 1944 he built the Miramar home that Mimi lives in still. "Our boys could run next door and play at the Yacht Club," Mimi reminisced during our first visit. After the Revolution, Havana's exclusive club was converted into a recreation center for military brass. When their friends and families fled in the wake of Batista's fall, the de la Guardias threw their lot, and considerable fortune, behind Castro. Their dashing twin sons became the golden boys of the Revolution. Handsome and American-educated, both did stints in Angola and rose through the ranks of MININT. Seeking to shore up foreign investment in Cuba, they traveled freely about the globe, wheeling and dealing—until their abrupt catastrophic fall from grace in 1989. As I left their home, Mario pushed a tear from his face. "Try to do something to help Patricio," he implored despondently.

In 1998, Mario de la Guardia died and Patricio was allowed to attend his funeral. Soon after, he was granted home visitation rights for most weekends and permitted to attend to his mother's failing health. However, his visits were suspended whenever there was a hullabaloo in Cuba—such as during the Pope's visit in 1998. I met with Patricio several times during his home visits. He noted that there were many ears listening to our conversation. The property was entirely bugged, even the backyard, he intimated, nodding toward the trees. "I know it's wired," he said, with a dark laugh. "I installed the same system many times." In March 2002, Patricio was released from prison through the intercession of Mexican President Vicente Fox.

THE DRUG TRIALS and the fall of Ochoa and the de la Guardias have most often been attributed to a rancorous split in the late 1980s between Raúl Castro's armed forces and the more freewheeling Ministry of the Interior. But another character, in fact an American tycoon, played an unusual and critical role.

One of the most puzzling and mysterious of Castro's relationships involved the Wall Street merger artist turned fugitive Robert Vesco, who found sanctuary in Cuba in 1983. Then on May 31, 1995, Vesco peered out of the living room window of his comfortable home in the Havana suburb of Atabey, a stone's throw away from the residential compound of Fidel Castro, and saw four government cars parked in front. Moments later, sixteen men from the Ministry of the Interior spilled out of their vehicles, headed into the house and took the American fugitive away. Vesco was charged with "unlawful acts, being a provocateur and an agent for foreign special services"—meaning espionage.

In the mid-1970s, Vesco had been charged by the SEC with providing a whopping $250,000 illegal cash contribution to Richard Nixon's 1972 election campaign. A prominent contributor to the Republican Party, he was often called Nixon's bag man: many believed the actual sum was double or triple the amount reported, with the cash earmarked to finance the notorious Watergate plumbers. Dan Vesco said his father's understanding was that Ford would first pardon Nixon and then Vesco. But after the backlash against the Nixon pardon, a second pardon became unthinkable. Vesco, who had fled the country, chose not to return to the States to face charges. As a fugitive, he flitted about the Bahamas, Costa Rica and Nicaragua before settling down with his family in Havana in 1983.

Arrested with Vesco in Havana was his longtime associate Donald Nixon, the nephew of the former President, who had joined him in 1993. Moments before their arrest, Vesco handed Nixon a piece of paper filled with phone numbers and said darkly, 'If they take me away, call these numbers.' " Printed on the paper were the home and business numbers of Ramón Castro, Fidel's older brother. Other phone numbers were those of Gloria Castro, Fidel's niece and the president of Labiofam, Cuba's internationally esteemed biotechnology facility. Nixon claimed that Labiofam was developing a wonder drug idea of his that, he said, "would revolutionize health care." Another name on the list was Fraga Castro, Fidel's nephew, a biophysicist and the director of Labiofam. Then there was Vesco's eldest son, Danny, with his phone number in Paris.

Nixon spent a month under house arrest at a nearby hotel, where he was interrogated daily. Toward the end of his questioning, he was asked what he knew about Tony de la Guardia, who had arranged Vesco's entry into Cuba and had by then already been executed. Nixon had never met de la Guardia, although Vesco had told him an interesting version of his demise. "Bob indicated to me that he was the one who had put the finger on Tony because he had allowed drug flights [over Cuban airspace] and that Fidel heard about it and told him to never do that again. Tony did do it again and got taken away."

According to Nixon, the Vesco–de la Guardia split was rooted in a very personal vendetta. Vesco's second son had been plagued with an emotional illness from his teen years, eventually requiring hospitalization. But for many years Vesco denied the seriousness of his son's disorder, attributing his problems to Tony de la Guardia, who he claimed "had stolen his boat"—a sixty-four-foot yacht—while his son was aboard. "He thought it had caused his son to go off the deep end and he'd never forgiven de la Guardia or his family for doing what they did," said Nixon. "And he had gone down and put the finger on him."

Vesco's daughter, Dawn, vividly recalled the de la Guardia–Ochoa scandal, having lived through it and watched the trial on Cuban television. "My dad was involved in bringing Tony down. I know that for a fact," she said. "In 1988, Tony moved Dad out of the house in the Marina and put him under house arrest without authority and seized my father's yacht. Tony confiscated the boat and was using it for his own personal benefit, but one of the [MININT] officers didn't trust Tony. He spent three months with my dad in a protocol house. . . . That information is what took Tony away. . . . My father was giving Tony what he thought was owed him."

Tony de la Guardia's daughter, Ileana, who left Cuba in the early 1990s, tells a different story. "When Fidel gave Vesco protection, he asked my father to be the officer in charge and to prepare his homes in the Marina Hemingway and Cayo Largo, which had a communications system, radios and a big marina. Vesco was involved with drugs. . . . My father soon came to believe that Vesco was bad for Cuba. Part of Vesco's deal was to bring in equipment from the U.S. for the Cuban sugar industry. In one of these operations, he embezzled $1 million from the Cubans." Vesco blamed the losses on FBI interdiction, but Ileana says her father believed that he was swindling the Cubans. "My father had big differences with the Cuban government because he saw that Vesco wanted everything for himself. He thought Vesco was a bandit." Ileana went further, conceding that her father was involved with drugs, but with the approval of the government. And that's why Vesco is in prison now. "Vesco can attest that Fidel and other top officials approved the drug traffic," she said bitterly.

Before the split, the two families had enjoyed a warm relationship and spent days cruising on the Vesco yacht moored in the Marina Hemingway. "I liked Tony," said Vesco's wife, Pat, now living in Orlando, Florida. "He was a very good painter and he was a very good-looking guy."

Vesco's welcome mat began to fray soon after the downfall of the de la Guardias. One former government official insisted that Vesco's welcome was always ambivalent. "Fidel never liked Vesco," he said. "He used him to help circumvent the Embargo and in reaching foreign markets but he was always suspicious." With the deluge of foreign investors in the 1990s eager to do business with Cuba, Vesco's value as a middleman was undercut. Once Havana's José Martí Airport began to fill with the private jets of European investors and American tycoons, there was precious little that Vesco could bring to the table.

Cuba was by now one of the only places willing to have Vesco and billed him plenty for the privilege (initially Vesco was said to be paying nearly $50,000 a month). In exchange, he was safe from warrants and kidnappers. An empty lot across the street from his house was used as a lookout for his assigned twenty-four-hour security detail. "Dad didn't get in the car and go for lettuce at the store without them being behind him," his son Patrick explained.

Vesco continued to do in Cuba what he had always done—deal making, finessing elaborate shell companies to import critically needed goods such as technology and spare parts. "He got involved in pharmaceutical products, educational projects, computers, agricultural stuff," said Patrick. "Dad liked Fidel a lot. He [had] absolute respect for him and said he was a guy who cared a lot for his people." When he was ten, Patrick met Fidel Castro at the CIMEC hospital when he was brought in with tonsillitis. "Fidel was there," he recalled. "He saw Dad and came over and shook his hand. And Dad said, 'This is my son.' Fidel said, 'Ah, un pequeño Vesco. Un Vescita [a little Vesco]!' And he shook my hand." On another occasion, he came home to find Fidel Castro shooting the breeze with his father in the living room. "There were a couple of Mercedes out front. Fidel asked me what I was doing. I told him I was playing with my Cuban friends. He said, 'Baseball. It's a great sport.' They must have talked for an hour after that. I know Dad had at least one meeting with Raúl [Castro] about the security that was around the house and several meetings with Fidel."

Patrick said his father saw himself as a counselor to Castro, offering advice from time to time on improving the economy of the country. Vesco told his son that it was at his urging that the Cubans began loosening up economic controls and legalized the dollar. "He sent a letter to Fidel," says Patrick, "encouraging capitalistic reforms and to allow Cubans to use dollars. Whenever Fidel needed to speak to Dad, that was arranged."

Indeed, Vesco's relationship with Cuba was a long one. In 1977, five years before his move there, Vesco engineered one of his splashiest deals via Cuba when he arranged delivery of a fleet of eight military cargo planes to Libyan strongman Muammar Qaddafi. For Vesco, the Qaddafi caper offered him a unique opportunity to ingratiate himself with the cream of his enemy's enemies—Russia, Libya and Cuba.

Though Cuba lags in virtually every segment of its economy, it is internationally respected for its pioneering work in biotechnology. Knowing Cuba's capability, Vesco recognized what he thought was a golden goose in Donald Nixon's efforts to develop a "wonder drug" called TX. "Nobody else had the infrastructure capable of doing what needed to be done in rapid format," says Nixon.

One of the most enthusiastic boosters of the project was Fidel Castro's older brother, Ramón, who happened to be Vesco's neighbor. "Ramón's pet pig had a foot infection and it would have died," related Nixon. "They put TX on and the stuff got rid of the infection immediately. And the whole family started using it." With Ramón Castro as a champion, introductions were soon made to Fraga Castro, Fidel's biophysicist nephew, and Gloria Castro, his niece, who jointly ran Labiofam.

In late 1993, Vesco found a partner for his project in an old acquaintance from his Nassau days, Enrico Garzaroli, who had become the number one importer of goods to Cuba. Garzaroli was responsible for all soft drinks and non-Cuban alcohol on the island. He also brokered a deal to open a chain of Benetton stores throughout Cuba and once had the concession on PPG, the Cuban miracle pill, said to lower cholesterol while stimulating libido. Unable to travel off the island, Vesco seized the opportunity to partner with the well-placed Garzaroli. But within the year, the relationship unraveled—each accusing the other of betrayal, backstabbing and violating Cuban laws.

Garzaroli didn't wait long to exact his revenge. According to Nixon, he dispatched a letter to Fidel Castro, who saw to it that Vesco got a copy. Garzaroli says he actually sent a sheaf of incriminating documents to a high-placed official in the Ministry of the Interior, confident that a copy would land on Castro's desk. "I gave them every single piece of paper," he said. "And they went and arrested him." But Vesco had been doing the very same thing to Garzaroli, passing reports to the Cubans to discredit him. The winner would turn out to be Garzaroli—who still filled a valuable need for Cuba. Those within the government who were peeved that Vesco had been spared in the de la Guardia–Ochoa trials finally took their consolation.

Five months after Vesco's arrest, I dropped in unannounced at the Playa home of Vesco's mistress and business partner on the outskirts of Havana. It struck me as no small irony that the *amante* of a millionaire fugitive lived in a conventional Russian-built housing project. Like everyone else who had dealings with Vesco—from the cook to social acquaintances—Lidia Alonso, a former high-placed trade official, had been subjected to nearly a month of daily grillings by security officials at Villa Marista, the dreaded prison run by the Ministry of the Interior in the run-down Havana neighborhood of Víbora. Vesco was sentenced to twenty-two years in prison; Alonso would later be arrested and sentenced to ten years. About two years ago, Alonso was released from prison and Vesco won weekend furloughs. They live together in Havana, happily but on probation.

Vesco is hardly the only U.S. fugitive in Cuba. In the mid-1980s, Dawn Vesco met another who introduced himself to her as Robert Hunter. "We were drinking buddies," she says. In 1992, he told Dawn: "They're going to round up all the foreigners and arrest us all. They're going to make a deal with the U.S. and trade us and hope it opens things up." Dawn chalked it up to drunken banter until she ran across his face in an American newspaper, identified as Frank Terpil, the CIA agent turned soldier of fortune, high on America's most wanted list for selling weapons and nuclear technology to Idi Amin and the Libyans. Terpil was arrested less than three months after Vesco, accused of swindling foreign investors. Later he was released but placed under "house arrest" in his Santa María home. Terpil and Vesco are only the cream of the fugitive crop living in Cuba, which the State Department puts at ninety-two, including three former high-level Black Panthers.

The irony, of course, is that if Vesco had stayed in the States and faced the SEC charges, he may well have beaten the case or done six months in a white-collar prison like other Wall Street swindlers. Should he survive his long Cuban sojourn, his prospects remain dim. Unlike the other American fugitives, Vesco is a man who may know too much. If a fugitive exchange with the U.S. takes place in the future, Vesco could well be the one exclusion—to the relief of many on both sides of the Cold War divide.

FIDEL CASTRO MAY BE nostalgic about a few of his old comrades, but he is by nature a singularly unsentimental man. One of Castro's bodyguards who attended to him for fifteen years had a heart attack in 1999 and was compelled to retire. Two years later, he and his family were living on his $10-a-month pension and what his wife earned cleaning houses. Then there is the case of Jesús Yáñez Pelletier, a handsome black soldier who was ordered to poison Castro's food in 1953, when Castro was a prisoner in Isla de Pinos. "Fidel's life was saved because I refused to carry out the order," said Yáñez Pelletier, who was unceremoniously fired from Batista's army. After Castro's release from prison, the former guard became his personal aide-de-camp. In 1960, however, Castro had a change of heart about the man who had saved his life and tossed him in jail for pro-American activities. Upon his release ten years later, Yáñez Pelletier became a dissident and campaigned for human rights. "In 1992, I was attacked by State Security agents and beaten up in the streets," he said shortly before his death in 2000. "I was seventy-five years old at the time. He'll drop anyone if it's of use to him. If he needs to eliminate someone, he will—no matter who he is. When we were fighting the Revolution, we never imagined it would come to this; to lose our most important right: freedom."

The transition from trusted confidant to prisoner has not been uncommon. Huber Matos, one of the leaders of the Revolution, and a handful of his followers were given twenty years in jail for naively offering their resignations. Matos, who was a pilot, teacher and rice farmer, believed he had acted with honor. To Castro, it was an act of treason. "All criticism is opposition," Castro wrote Carlos Franqui. "All opposition is counterrevolutionary."

Felipe Mirabal, Batista's loyal commander, who had protected Castro in 1948 from Rolando Masferrer's paramilitary gang, Los Tigres, met a grimmer fate: he spent twenty years in prison and died there. Aramis Taboada, Castro's friend from the university, who handled his divorce from Mirta, shared the same destiny. Sentenced to life in prison after the Revolution, Aramis developed cancer in jail. "His wife was able to meet with Fidel to talk about her husband's condition," said Rafael Díaz-Balart. "She told him, 'Fidel, Aramis is in a very bad way and is going to die in prison. Let him come home so he may die in his home.' Fidel responded, 'Let him serve as much time as he possibly can and then we'll see.' He died in jail."

All challengers have been swatted away like nuisance flies. Castro demands complete unity and lockstep loyalty from his inner circle and the army. He is wont to say *te lo dije*—I told you so—about the collapse of the Soviet Union, claiming that Gorbachev's grievous mistake was *glasnost* before *perestroika*.

Over the last few years, the political tapestry of Cuba has been rewoven owing to a sex and corruption scandal of some complexity and imagination. As a result, several major players have disappeared from the inner circle. Among them are the former Foreign Minister Roberto Robaina, who was expelled from the party in May 2002, and tourism chief Osmany Cienfuegos, the brother of the revolutionary idol Camilo. Feisty, mustached and partial to black T-shirts and pastel blazers, Robaina had landed the high glamour job of Foreign Minister at the age of thirty-six. For years he was a favorite of Castro. Robaina had headed up the Union of Young Communists and had won Castro's heart with his proposal to billboard Cuba with arty propaganda. As a result, scrawled ubiquitously around the country are such revolutionary reminders as *Venceremos!* (We Shall Overcome!), *Socialismo o Muerte!* (Socialism or Death!), and *Sea Como Che!* (Be Like Che!). But in May 1999, Robaina was abruptly dismissed and sent to the Colegio Nacional de Defensa, a military facility that maintains a reeducation camp for wayward government officials. Osmany Cienfuegos, who is known for his weakness for women, booze and perks and who was protected to a large degree by his brother's posthumous halo, was "retired" and is now living at Las Terrazas, an ecotourist resort he developed in Pinar del Río. With the government maintaining its standard Kremlinesque hush on the matter, word seeped out via a few intrepid insiders.

La bola en la calle—the buzz on the streets—at the time was that both officials had been implicated in an Internet prostitution ring run by a Mexican company. "MININT agents told me that Osmany had provided the hotel for the girls through Rumbos [a Cuban travel agency]," said one source requiring anonymity, "and that Robaina's office gave the visas."

But as with all things Cuban, the truth was more elusive and complex. "In 1998 there was a Web site called Cuba Amour that was popular with women who wanted to marry foreigners," a knowledgeable official told me. "But there was also a large prostitution ring that included Cuban girls. It was a mix of both." His company investigated the Web site at the request of the Cuban government. "I don't think that Osmany lost his job over it," he said. "But Fidel may have used it as a way to leverage him out. It was a triangle of contacts. The guy who ran Rumbos was a very close friend of Osmany. And Robaina's wife worked for him at Rumbos."

The scandal was uncovered not by the government but from the bottom up—as it were. "They were using the Hotel Yagrumas [west of Havana] for these sex vacations and some of the staff knew what was up and didn't like it," one source said with some amusement. "They were *real* revolutionaries and they wrote a letter to the Central Committee." *Granma* had reported in May 1999 that Robaina was going on a trip to the Caribbean on a Friday. The following Monday, just before the Latin American Summit in Brazil, it was announced that Robaina had been replaced by Felipe Pérez Roque. "He will never be trusted again," said a high-level source. (On July 31, 2002, Robaina began a low-level job working on an environmental project at Havana's Parque Metropolitano.)

What is stunning about these two casualties was their high standing and long tenure with Castro. "Robaina was a completely dedicated propagandist who gave these fiery speeches in front of crowds and looked adoringly at Fidel," he said. "But as he became Foreign Minister he started to get ideas from meeting different people, especially foreign visitors. He started putting his own ideas together. And therein lay the problem. Independent thinking is far more dangerous for a Cuban official than getting caught with *putas*." It was also a period when Castro was favoring hard-liners in his government—and Robaina's lobbying for moderation invited Castro's suspicions.

Robaina's successor, the boyish-looking Felipe Pérez Roque, was not known for his brilliance at the university but rather for his fiery pro-government speeches as the head of the student federation. Castro hired him as his secretary—essentially his doorkeeper—after his graduation, and the two often double-dated sisters. "Felipe is so loyal to Fidel," said one former friend, "that on the day his wife gave birth to his first child, he remained at Castro's side for ten hours. Then he went to see his newborn baby."

Alfredo Guevara is another figure who now plays a reduced role but, unlike Robaina and Cienfuegos, Guevara is not *en desgracia*. In 1999 he harshly criticized the idea of outside sponsorship for the Havana Film Festival, which Castro had endorsed. He also had a spat with Castro, who did not care for the film *Guantanamera,* Tomás Gutiérrez Alea's last work, which mocked the mind-addling bureacracies of the government. At that point, Guevara was eased out of running ICAIC. When I saw him in Havana in August of 2000, he told me he had retired from ICAIC, stressing he could now devote himself to the internationally popular festival. Guevara assured me that the gay flap in my story was of no consequence to him. However, it was *"un puñal en el corazón para Fidel,"* a knife in the heart for Fidel, he said, stabbing his own chest with an imaginary knife with both hands.

In Cuba, being out of a job does not mean one is necessarily out of power, a retired army colonel pointed out to me. And Alfredo Guevara certainly remains in power.

CASTRO TODAY OFTEN SEEMS lonely or bored. A half-dozen of his old friends from the university who fled into exile now visit him periodically. Castro seems to relish these visits and lavishes his attention and amenities upon his old friends. Luis Ortega, once his ally, then his foe, has visited Castro almost annually for the last five years. "At this time of his life, he is remembering the old friends. You see, a man like Fidel, at this moment, feels alone. He wants to talk to people from long ago. He has a lot of nostalgia. For example, in his office he has a very large photograph of his father wearing a *guayabera,* looking like an old *campesino* farmer. His style of living is completely different from most Cuban presidents. In his dining room are a table and chairs. That's all." Castro lives like a soldier. With the exception of superb food and wine, Castro's tastes are simple, almost spartan.

Almost weekly, Castro dines with one of the many visiting contingents to Cuba—sometimes movie stars like Jack Nicholson or Kevin Costner or the late Jack Lemmon, or New Economy tycoons or visiting U.S. senators and congressmen, or just ordinary American tourists thumbing their noses at the Embargo. Some attribute his role as host-in-chief to his self-imposed aloofness from the Cuban people; others say it's his ongoing love-hate affair with the United States and his determination to conquer it—even if this means seducing it one American at a time.

In 1998, Salvador Lew made an approach to Castro through his sister Enma, suggesting a framework for a transition. Enma had barely gotten to broach the topic with Raúl Castro—who politely but firmly kiboshed the idea. "Enmita, *querida*," said Raúl, "we are not going anywhere. We will die here."

Despite decades of railing against the class system, Fidel Castro remains keenly interested in power and people who have it. Ted Turner has visited Cuba often to fish, hunt and carouse with him as did French President François Mitterrand, Pablo Neruda, several members of the Rockefeller clan, Lee Iacocca, Muhammad Ali and Nobel laureate Gabriel García Márquez. Castro particularly enjoys the company of diplomats working in Havana. The wife of one European ambassador hosted several dinners for Castro at their Miramar home in 1997. "Sometimes he came with Raúl—who wore lifts on his shoes to make him look taller," she said. "Before he arrives, someone calls from the Ministry of the Interior and asks a lot of questions— like who works in the kitchen and who comes and goes, et cetera," she said. "They asked that there be a bathroom off-limits to everyone but Fidel for that entire day and evening. They told me to leave the paper wrapping on the soap and the wrapping on the toilet paper sealed. They don't take any chances."

What would happen, I asked Castro, if an unforeseen accident or illness should befall him? Who would lead Cuba? "You can ask the CIA that question since it was a part of all their plans to eliminate me," he retorted. "Candidly, I don't really think anything will happen. The government would very quickly adapt. We have all the political and legal mechanisms in place. The life of the country wouldn't be halted for even a minute." He laughed. "Well, perhaps during the funeral, which might be an unpleasant time for some people. It certainly won't bother me since I won't be able to participate—except as a body. That is, if anything is left. If I don't get eaten by a shark or disappear in a plane that blows up. What happens to my remains is a matter of complete indifference to me. It will be a problem that everyone else will have to solve without my help." The thought makes Castro laugh, a deep rumble of a laugh. "No man is indispensable in this world. I have the right to enjoy a well-earned rest."

Our interview concluded, Castro requested my tapes, suggesting that he would be happy to have them transcribed for me. When I declined his offer, he asked for copies of the tapes. An assistant promptly appeared with a duplicating machine and made copies while I waited. I asked Castro if he'd heard a popular joke making the rounds in the early 1990s. It went: "What are the triumphs of the Revolution?" He nodded for me to continue. "Education, health care, and athletics," I went on. "And what are the failures of the Revolution?" He shrugged, asking for the punch line. "Breakfast, lunch and dinner!" To my surprise, Castro laughed. Then the spin machine recharged itself. "See, when you have too much breakfast, lunch and dinner," he said, "it's bad for your health."

There is another popular joke making the rounds in Cuba as Castro slides toward his ninth decade: A Galápagos turtle is given to Castro as a gift and he asks how long the animal will live. About four hundred years, he is told. Castro shakes his head darkly, then says, "That's the trouble with pets. You get attached to them and then they die on you."

CHAPTER 10

THE RAID

When you're this nice to me, there's something rotten in Cuba.

LUCY TO RICKY RICARDO, *I LOVE LUCY*

MINUTES BEFORE 5:00 A.M. on Saturday, April 22, 2000, President Clinton was awakened by a phone call from his chief of staff, John Podesta. Armed federal agents were in place and poised to take Elián González from the home of his great-uncle by force, Podesta told Clinton. Just three hours earlier, Clinton had gone to sleep thinking, and hoping, that his headache over the Cuban six-year-old was about to end. Uncharacteristically, Clinton had kept a distance from the whole affair, content to leave the decision making to his Attorney General. Not that his relationship with Janet Reno had been without contention. He had gritted his teeth through Waco and then had to endure her cooperation with Kenneth Starr's impeachment quest. On not a few occasions, he had confided to friends that he rued the day he had appointed the sui generis Floridian.

There were other reasons to pass the Elián hot potato to Reno. Clinton's would be-successor, Al Gore, had shunted Clinton to the sidelines, seeking to distance himself at every turn in his campaign. On March 30, Gore split with the administration and endorsed giving Elián González permanent U.S. residency. Clinton took note of the savage pen-lashing Gore received from editorial writers across the country, admonishing him for pandering for Cuban-American votes. Clinton often complained that he had done more for the exile lobby by signing off on Helms-Burton than any other President in forty years, and still they were not grateful. Now he no longer needed or feared them.

Three weeks earlier, Clinton had cautiously weighed in on the matter of Elián González when confronted by reporters on Air Force One. "There are a lot of people on both sides of this issue who are more concerned with what is in the best interest of the child than the larger political issues involving

Castro and Cuba," he improvised. "That gives me hope we can find a principled resolution that is not just a train wreck for the child, a train wreck for the rule of law or a train wreck for all concerned." Clinton was keenly aware of polls showing that the overwhelming majority of Americans were anxious for a prompt conclusion of the soap opera and supported returning the boy to his father. But as the weeks unfolded, very little had been accomplished in talks with the Miami family. Now Podesta was telling him that negotiations with the family lawyers in Miami had irretrievably broken down. There would have to be an armed intervention. Clinton listened, grunted his assent and put down the phone.

For five months, Janet Reno and her staff had been haggling with the lawyers representing Lázaro González. The players often changed as the family's team of advisers ballooned to more than a dozen attorneys, investigators and consultants—creating a formidable legal moat around the Little Havana family. At two o'clock that morning, Reno had laid out her final terms for the return of Elián González to his father. Hours later, the talks had ended as they always did: in hopeless stalemate.

For months, the Miami family had demanded that Juan Miguel come to the States to pick up his son and gave every indication that they would then return Elián to him. The family and its supporters had steadfastly maintained that Juan Miguel was under the thumb of Fidel Castro—and that once he was on his own in the United States, it would only be a matter of hours before he defected. In Miami, rumors were endlessly repeated as fact that he had once applied for the lottery to come to the States, despite denials from the INS, and that he had known that his ex-wife and son were leaving and had had no objection. In fact, Miami radio assured its listeners, Juan Miguel had intended to come to the States all along. Once on American soil, he would defect and begin his new life in Miami.

In the first days of April, word spread that Juan Miguel would soon be arriving. By then, the tone between the two branches of the family had turned decidedly chilly. In several interviews in early April, Marisleysis González challenged Juan Miguel to come to her home and discuss why he wanted to take his son back to Cuba. She said she had not told Elián that his father might be coming, as it could distress him. "As a precaution, I will not tell him until everything is certain," she said. She claimed that when she told Elián once before that his father might be coming to visit, the boy burst into tears, saying, "Please don't let them take me."

On April 3, Marisleysis gave an interview to a local Miami station for the 11:00 P.M. news slot. The following morning, she rose early for a 6:30 A.M.

radio interview at La Carreta, a popular Little Havana restaurant. After the interview, she suddenly turned pale, dropped her head in a friend's lap and then ran to the rest room. She was again rushed to the hospital—having made more than a dozen visits since 1996, for what was described in ambulance reports as "acute emotional anxiety" and "panic attacks." One hospital source said that Marisleysis suffered from colitis and severe anxiety. Critics of the family were quick to point out that a young woman of such fragile mental and physical health was hardly a suitable candidate for surrogate motherhood. However, her father, Lázaro González, after visiting his daughter at the hospital, blamed the government's handling of the case for his daughter's health and emotional woes. "The government is going to destroy this family," he said. "We are only trying to protect this child."

That same day, the family's lawyers made several charges against Juan Miguel, raising the ante considerably. "We're sure he loves his own son and we know Elián loves his father," Linda Osberg-Braun, an attorney for the González clan, said on a morning TV show. Then she added, "We believe Juan Miguel is completely under the gun of the Castro regime. We think they are putting him up to psychological warfare and tactics against his own son."

Later that afternoon, Manny Díaz, Kendall Coffey's partner, who had recently come onto the case, announced that he had presented the court and the Clinton administration with damning evidence challenging the fitness of Juan Miguel as a parent. Díaz seemed to be responding to the claims of legal experts that there was no basis in the law to keep the boy unless his father was deemed unfit. "A child belongs with his natural parent unless that parent's unfit," Podesta had said days earlier on the CBS news show *Face the Nation*. "We have no indication that Elián's father is an unfit parent." Gregory Craig, Juan Miguel's attorney, promptly jumped into the fray and pointed out that the family was contradicting itself after months of acknowledging that González was a loving father. Calling their claims "outrageous," Craig pointed out that the timing of the charges was suspect.

In the early part of April, Lázaro González's legal team was considerably upgraded. Carlos de la Cruz, chairman of Eagle Brands and a trustee of the University of Miami, conferred with Kendall Coffey and Díaz and suggested augmenting the brain trust. De la Cruz recruited UM President Edward T. Foote II and UM trustee Carlos Saladrigas, a prominent Miami businessman, to help break the logjam. De la Cruz and Saladrigas, both members of the Mesa Redonda, the elite power fraternity of Miami's Latino leaders, had been deeply troubled by the public relations backlash against exiles and Miami. They also brought in a power hitter, Aaron Podhurst, a topflight

Miami attorney and a longtime friend of Janet Reno, to work with them as a mediator. The four men recognized that help was urgently needed to counter the negative publicity surrounding the family—all the more so with the imminent arrival of Juan Miguel. The quartet understood that one strategy with one endgame had to be agreed upon. At the very least, they hoped for a soft landing, if not a graceful exit.

On April 6, Juan Miguel González stepped off a plane at Dulles Airport with his wife, Nersy, and their infant son, Hianny, Elián's half-brother. He made a few comments and then left with aides from the Cuban Interests Section. When he did not defect on arrival, Miami radio claimed that this was because the Cuban government had him under lock and key.

A few days later, dapper in a gray suit, Juan Miguel met with Janet Reno in her office, his wife and baby at his side, without any Cuban officials present. It was a made-to-order opportunity for a family defection, and yet somehow he resisted. Exile leaders quickly revised their story: Juan Miguel was either drugged or brainwashed, but in time he would come around. When two weeks had elapsed and Juan Miguel still had not defected, there was only one conclusion to be made: he was a traitor. Miami radio reacted with shock and outrage. The young father soon found himself the object of unremitting denunciation as the campaign to smear him as an unfit parent went into full throttle.

Some in the leadership realized that the community was not putting its best foot forward. Hialeah's mayor, Raúl Martínez, a zealous anti-Castroite who very much wanted Elián to remain in the U.S., expressed his dismay. "If Juan Miguel was thinking of coming to the U.S. and really wanted to stay here, but he heard Cuban radio in Miami [talking about] how bad he was and all the names he was being called," said Martínez, "I wouldn't want to come to Miami either. How can you call someone all those names and then say, 'Come and be with me and let's negotiate'?"

All along, Juan Miguel had insisted that he had only come to the States to retrieve his son. But the days turned to weeks and still there was no indication that his uncles would give him back his son. Anxiously, he waited at a suburban house in Bethesda, Maryland, the residence of Cuban Interests Section chief Fernando Remírez, which had temporarily been turned over to him and his family. The two-story home was roomy and comfortable, suitable for ambassadorial entertaining with a sloping front lawn and a deck and pool in the backyard. Juan Miguel spent his days conferring with his powerhouse lawyer Gregory Craig, Remírez and other Cuban officials, usually at the house. Most days he would watch Elián on television cavorting on the fenced lawn of his relatives' Miami home. Remírez would translate for him what pundits and newscasters were saying about his son. Not infrequently, he would lunch with special guests and allies like Joan Brown Campbell and Sam Ciancio, who had rescued Elián from the sea and supported returning him to his father. Occasionally he went out with his family to visit some of the capital's tourist sites, but traveling was impeded by the massive press pack that camped outside the residence and followed his every step.

One week after his arrival, Juan Miguel was treated to the spectacle of being reprimanded by his son on national television. With their legal options dwindling and public opinion mounting against them, the Miami family gambled on a dicey propaganda salvo and released a homemade video of Elián. The video was filmed in the wee hours of April 13 in the bedroom of the house Elián shared with Marisleysis. At 1:30 A.M., Armando Gutiérrez walked outside the house and gave the forty-second video to the Univisión camera crew parked in Camp Elián across the street from the house.

The video showed a revved-up Elián wagging his right index finger at the camera and telling his father he didn't want to go home. "Papá, I don't want to go to Cuba. If you want, stay here. I'm not going to Cuba," he told the camera. His eyes skittered off camera to someone who was presumably coaching him. In a second take on the video, a more animated Elián went after Janet Reno: "Dad, did you see that old woman who went to the home of that little nun?" the six-year-old said as he chewed a mouthful of gum. "She want[s] to take me to Cuba.... I told you that I don't want to go to Cuba.... If you all want, stay here—but I don't want to go to Cuba."

Loops from the videotape ran on television ad nauseam for days. The sight of a child speaking against his father unnerved many. Decrying the video as "political kiddie porn," medical ethicist Kenneth Goodman told the *Herald,* "Children are not competent to give their consent on TV. It should never have been taken. It should never have been broadcast." Instead of swaying public opinion toward them, the video further tarnished the image of the Miami González clan and ignited a furor over the ethics of its release. Columnists and editorials debated the degree of sleep deprivation and manipulation endured by the child in the service of political stagecraft.

Partisans of the family, however, viewed the video sympathetically—further dramatizing the divide between Calle Ocho and Main Street. "I don't think he would be saying those things," said Roberto Jiménez, who lived a few blocks from the house, "if he didn't mean them. It's clear he wants to stay here." To their everlasting shock, the exile political leadership and the family's advisers learned that what played in Miami, more often than not, did not play north of the county line.

According to Joan Brown Campbell, Juan Miguel burst into tears when he saw the video played on television. Worse, he told friends that two weeks had passed and still he had not touched his son. Their rare and brief conversations were strained by the eavesdropping of his relatives. "He has had only two conversations in the last eight days," said one of his friends. "He calls every day but the family has caller ID on their phone and they don't take his calls. The only way he's got through was by using a friend's Miami cell phone."

On April 16, two days after the release of the Elián video, Juan Miguel took his case to the American public and appeared on *60 Minutes,* pleading for the return of his son. Every network and prime-time television show had vied to "get" the young father. NBC's Andrea Mitchell lobbied especially hard for the interview and in the end it came down to her and Dan Rather. Diane Sawyer's three-day splurge with the Gonzálezes in Miami not only spoiled her shot, it plunged ABC into the doghouse with the Cubans for the next two years. The Cubans decided to go with Dan Rather, who had previously interviewed Castro to their satisfaction. I also appeared on the show—offering background on the case.

"This is child abuse and mistreatment what they're doing to this boy," an emotional but well-composed Juan Miguel told Rather. "And I know I'm right in saying that we have to take him back immediately because what they're doing is making this child suffer. The way they're abusing him, turning him against his father." The thirty-two-year-old father told the veteran newsman that his son had told him on the phone that he wanted to go home with him. "He's told me so," said Juan Miguel. He accused his relatives of "putting a bunch of toys in front of a six-year-old. He cannot decide for himself. The one that decides for him is me, his father."

When Dan Rather asked him his reaction to seeing his son lecturing him on the family's homemade video, Juan Miguel spoke emotionally. "Well, I can tell you that above all, despite everything I was feeling, and everything I was suffering at that moment, I saw the betrayal inside my boy—that they made him do these things," he said, speaking carefully while visibly pushing down a wellspring of feeling. "Actually, he's suffering more here amongst them than he suffered in the sea. I'm going to tell you the truth. I don't have any tears left. I've cried too much. During this whole period of time, I've cried a lot and suffered greatly and I'm still in pain. To tell you the truth, I have no tears left."

When Rather asked the young father if he was being used, as his relatives had charged, as "a puppet at the end of Fidel Castro's strings," he reacted sharply. "Why do you have to mix in Fidel Castro into all of this?" he said. "It's just me claiming my son. It's my son and not Fidel Castro's. It's a way of bringing in Fidel Castro and making it political." He also challenged Rather's description of America as a place of "freedom and opportunity." "I ask you: What's freedom?" he said, and offered what seemed like a coached defense of his country. "Well, freedom is, for example, in Cuba where education and health care is free. Or is it the way it is here? Which of the two is freedom? For example, here when parents send their children to school they have to worry about violence. A child could be shot at school. In Cuba, things like that don't happen.... Which of the two is freedom?" His tone and demeanor were serious, not threatening. Asked for a message to deliver to his son, Juan Miguel paused a moment, then spoke with palpable emotion: "Give him a big kiss and tell him not to worry—he'll be with me soon. I love him very much. He will be with me soon, and he shouldn't worry."

Unlike in his appearance months earlier on *Nightline*, where he angrily denounced his relatives, Juan Miguel came across as a likable and decent man: an Everyman exhausted by his ordeal. He made no other television appearances—in contrast to his Miami family, who seemed to have something to say on camera each day.

The saga of Elián González had fixated the attention of the entire country on the Miami exile community—to its clear detriment. Juan Miguel's performance managed to solidify this impression. Not only did most Americans now support the immediate return of Elián to his father, they were also saying in resounding numbers that they wanted the Embargo lifted on Cuba. A Gallup poll showed that 70 percent of Americans were in favor of lifting the Embargo, with only 28 percent opposed. But most of all, they wanted to move on.

Elián fatigue had taken hold throughout the country, and the pressure was mounting with each passing day to resolve the standoff. Janet Reno, however, seemed incapable of doing so. Her critics chided her for not taking action, cartoonists lampooned her as the foil of the González family, and editorials savaged her for countenancing a flagrant disregard of the law. More distressing to her personally, she now found herself an object of derision in her hometown. Friends and aides of Reno said the crisis tormented her—

even more so than the disaster at Waco. Desperately afraid of making a mistake, Reno called friends in Miami for counsel and understanding. Her paralysis and indecisiveness were in the end what defeated her. No matter what she would do, she had already put the country through five months of torment. Tom Fiedler, who headed the *Miami Herald*'s editorial board (one of the few nationwide to support the family's claim to keep Elián), wrote of her plight: "Janet Reno, born and raised on the fringes of Miami, loves two things dearly: the law and her hometown. Because of her rigid devotion to the former, she is threatened with losing the other. It is one of this community's uglier tendencies that, when we disagree with someone on an issue, we try also to vilify him or her as a person."

Publicly, Reno kept her composure in the face of a steady stream of fury and denigration from exiles in Miami. Privately, aides said she succumbed to tears. There were round-the-clock insults on Miami radio, death threats and picketing around her Miami home. "I was born and raised in that community," she said. "I love Miami. When it is hurting, it hurts me."

IN THE FIVE MONTHS since Elián's arrival in the U.S., his relatives had explored every imaginable legal loophole in their effort to keep him in Miami. In December 1999, Lázaro González had applied for asylum for his great-nephew. When Doris Meissner, the Immigration and Naturalization Service Commissioner, ruled against him in early January, deciding that Elián "belongs with his father" and must be returned to Cuba by January 14, Lázaro asked Reno to overrule Meissner and filed for temporary custody in state court. Reno announced within days that she would uphold Juan Miguel's right to custody. On January 19, 2000, lawyers for Lázaro filed a federal lawsuit challenging the INS ruling, arguing that the INS was obliged to consider a political asylum petition filed by Lázaro.

The family's lawyers claimed that Elián had a constitutional right to an asylum hearing, as he would face political persecution if he was returned to Cuba. Their brief proposed that Juan Miguel González's protestations should be ignored, as the Cuban government had pressured him to seek Elián's return. The Justice Department countered that only Elián's father could speak for him and that the relatives had no legal standing to make an asylum request.

The family's suit effectively stalled matters for almost two months. Then, on March 21, U.S. District Judge K. Michael Moore ruled that the INS and the Attorney General had not abused their powers in their decision to reunite

Elián with his father. In a devastating defeat for the family, Moore wrote that Attorney General Janet Reno had acted within her legal discretion in refusing to consider Lázaro González's asylum request. Still, the Miami family vowed to fight on, and appealed their case to the Eleventh Circuit Court. If they failed there, only the Supreme Court could save them.

While their legal options were rapidly dwindling, the family's public relations salvos were misfiring. It was plainly evident that the Miami relatives had woefully lost the war for the hearts and minds of Americans. Carl Hiaasen, the *Herald*'s flinty columnist and resident satirist, savaged the family:

> Suppose you were Juan Miguel González, and suppose you didn't need to be brainwashed into loving your own child; you always did, and you always will. One day you learn that he barely survived a smuggler's voyage to Florida, and that he saw his mother perish. You learn that he has been put in the care of Miami relatives who scarcely know him, and who are taking stage directions from a "political consultant."
>
> Next thing you know, your son is being trotted around Disney World in front of TV cameras. He has a new bike, a new dog, more toys than he can count. For the crowds he has been taught to wave on cue, and make a V-for-victory sign. . . . You want Elián back. From Miami comes more disturbing TV: The relatives holding Elián are surrounded by lawyers. The lawyers have been hired by the rich exile groups to prevent you from retrieving your son. . . . And it hits you: This isn't about Elián at all. It's about a 40-year feud.

Nevertheless, both the Democratic and Republican presidential candidates, as well as scores of network bloviators, continued to urge that the matter be resolved by a Miami family court—as if that option had not been eliminated. The strongly worded ruling of state judge Jennifer Bailey on April 14 was perhaps the least reported, and arguably the most significant, piece of substantive news to come out of Miami in months. In a virtual knockout punch against the Miami family, Bailey ruled that Elián's great-uncle Lázaro González had no right to seek custody in family court because he was too distant a relative under state and federal law. She also pointed out that the federal government's decision to reunite the child with his father superseded the authority of a family court. "Elián González's physical presence in this country is at the discretion of the federal government," Bailey wrote in her twenty-two-page ruling. "The state court cannot, by deciding with whom his custody should lie, subvert the decision to return him to his father and his home in Cuba." She voided an emergency protective order granted by Judge Rosa Rodríguez in her controversial decision requiring Elián to stay in Miami-Dade County with his relatives until the hearing on his temporary custody. Moreover, Bailey made clear her displeasure with Lázaro González: "He fails to understand the fundamental nature of his case—it is an immigration case, not a family case," she wrote with some impatience. "Holding a hearing would only have raised false hopes."

Facing a siege of hostile publicity, the Miami family and their entourage were under keen pressure. By now, several had reason to regret their hasty decisions early on; some began to fret about the political casualties in the Elián war. Most notable was Alex Penelas, the handsome thirty-eight-year-old Mayor of Miami-Dade County. Up until the Elián crisis, Penelas, a Democrat who learned politics at the knee of Jorge Mas Canosa and often campaigned for local Republican candidates, was considered a sure bet for a national political career. His name invariably made the short list for possible cabinet posts or even as a vice presidential candidate. All such speculation ended on March 29, 2000, when Penelas torpedoed his national career with a stunning performance on the steps of the federal courthouse.

Flanked by more than half a dozen other local mayors, the telegenic Mayor, wearing an Italian suit, his wavy black hair moussed in place, declared that he would block the Miami police from assisting federal agents if they attempted to remove Elián from the Little Havana home. He warned that the blame for any violence that might follow a raid would stand squarely with the President and Attorney General. His performance was promptly compared to the demagoguery of George Wallace's threats to block court-ordered integration in Alabama. "If their continued provocation, in the form of unjustified threats to revoke the boy's parole, leads to civil unrest and violence," Penelas intoned grandiloquently, "we are holding the federal government responsible, and specifically Janet Reno and the President of the United States, for anything that may occur in this community."

At best, it seemed to many observers north of the Miami-Dade County line a final act of self-mortification. The nation's editorialists responded with poison-penned fury, accusing the young Mayor of sanctioning violence and absolving those who might incite or participate in rioting. Gallows humor flourished in Miami, where residents wisecracked about their city being "the Banana Republic of the U.S." and needing passports to come and go from city limits. "If anti-Castro fanatics declare open season on federal officials,

Penelas and his confrontational cohorts should be held accountable," lectured the *Atlanta Journal-Constitution,* while the *St. Louis Post-Dispatch* thrashed Penelas as "shameless." Outrage was even stirred in the Miami-Dade police department, where an anonymous memo was circulated mocking the mayor for his comments. But dissent within the department was unwelcome: the culprits were called on the carpet and "counseled." Blindsided by the firestorm he had lit, Penelas furiously backpedaled. Blaming the media for what he called their "misinterpretation" of his remarks, he equivocated, vacillated and demurred regarding what he had actually meant.

Outside Miami, Elián fatigue was epidemic. Patience with the González family had flat run out. Referring to the Elián saga as "a psychotic episode," the *Washington Post* let loose a stream of editorial pique: "The Miami relatives have no standing in any court except the court of Cuban émigré opinion. The majority of Americans rightly believed the child should be returned to his father and supported the administration's actions to return the child to his father."

But the family and exile community seemed oblivious—even indifferent—to the message from mainstream America, which had begun at times to take on a nasty, xenophobic tinge. On more than one occasion, non-Cuban residents of Miami lobbed bananas at City Hall. Others openly battled and jeered exiles, tooting their horns from cars with American flags flying from their antennas or sporting a *"República de Miami"* flag of Miami Mayor Joe Carollo wearing a crown of bananas and flanked by palm trees festooned with more bananas. One evening, in the dead of night, a flag was hoisted over city hall depicting the official seal of Miami surrounded by still more bananas. Raúl Martínez, the Mayor of Hialeah, responded to the unrest by urging police to arrest the banana throwers for littering.

ON APRIL 12, Janet Reno undertook an unprecedented act of personal diplomacy. She flew to Miami to meet with the González clan and virtually begged the family to return Elián to his father. Nevertheless, she returned to Washington empty-handed and humiliated. Reno was particularly taken aback, according to one negotiator, by Lázaro González's scornful defiance of the power and might of the United States government. "He basically told her that he would not give up Elián and that she could send in the army if she wanted," said the INS staffer. Two weeks earlier, Lázaro had gone on Telemundo TV in Miami and had drawn a line in the sand. "I won't cooperate in anything," he declared. "The boy lives in my house and they'll have to go find him there. I'm not going to deliver him to any immigration office."

Around the same time, some exile leaders, most notably CANF's Jorge Mas Santos, began to sense that the family was on a collision course. Seeking to avert catastrophe, Mas Santos contacted CANF's powerhouse ally Senator Robert Torricelli of New Jersey, then chairman of the Democratic Senatorial Campaign Committee, to broker a peaceful resolution. Torricelli had been a close personal friend of Jorge Mas Canosa, with whom he shared certain physical and temperamental resemblances. A pallbearer and a speaker at Mas Canosa's funeral, Torricelli had excellent capital among exiles and needed no reminder as to how seriously the Elián affair had eroded their prestige.

For forty-eight hours, hopes were high for a decorous hand-off of Elián to his father in Washington. Huddling with Mas Santos and the family's lawyers, Torricelli frantically tried to broker a graceful exit. But expectations soon evaporated. Torricelli was told that Lázaro González refused to compromise. "It was clear that he was not going to turn over Elián," said one CANF member knowledgeable of the negotiations. Torricelli and Mas Santos ruefully announced that the deal was off. The senator advised the Justice Department that a peaceful settlement was improbable.

ON THE EVENING OF April 21, Janet Reno gave the González family lawyers her final offer: "By 2:30 A.M. on Saturday, April 22, Elián González will be delivered to the Miami Federal Courthouse accompanied by Lázaro González's family members.... Elián González and Lázaro González's family will drive or fly to Washington, D.C., under escort by U.S.M.S. [U. S. Marshals Service] and proceed to Airlie House. Upon Juan Miguel González's arrival at Airlie House, Attorney General will parcel Elián González into Juan Miguel González's care. During the residence at Airlie, Elián González will live with Juan Miguel González. Lázaro González's family will reside at Airlie House in separate quarters.... The parties will remain in residence for a period determined by the Attorney General, not to exceed one week. Departure control order to be issued for Elián González to assure he remains in the United States consistent with existing injunction."

At 3:00 A.M., half an hour after the initial deadline had elapsed, Reno told Aaron Podhurst, the attorney who had been serving as a go-between for Reno and the Miami lawyers, that he had one hour—until 4:00 A.M.—to get the relatives to agree to turn the boy over to his father at a location outside

Florida. Podhurst would later tell reporters that he had woefully miscalculated the degree of her seriousness, as deadline after deadline had come and gone without enforcement. In fact, the lawyers didn't even bother to wake Lázaro to discuss the situation.

Sitting in his Miami Lakes home, Podhurst intently worked the phones, with Janet Reno on one line and the family's advisers on a second line. Manny Díaz, Kendall Coffey, Carlos Saladrigas, Carlos de la Cruz and Armando Gutiérrez were sitting around a speakerphone in the small living room of the González house. Also present was Roberto Curbelo, a recent friend of the González family, and the ubiquitous Donato Dalrymple. " 'We're running out of time,' " Reno said she told Podhurst, "because we kept getting mixed signals. I told him that I need an answer at four o'clock." But the lawyers used up the time quibbling among themselves. The sticking point centered on where Elián would be transferred. Reno had said that it must occur in Washington—not Miami. Podhurst felt he had convinced the family's lawyers on the issue of the transfer. But some felt they could never wangle a commitment out of Lázaro González—who believed he could bluff his way into keeping Elián. And he was not alone: both Armando Gutiérrez and Manny Díaz also felt they could prevail against Reno and the U.S. government. "I told them you cannot oppose the Attorney General of the United States," Podhurst told the *Herald*. "If she says Washington, it's Washington. If you don't do it, I'm gone."

Reno said she made it clear that Juan Miguel was unwilling to go to Miami because of the "tension" there. She remembered Podhurst telling her "that was a deal-breaker. And so we agreed that we had done our best. And he said, 'Could I have just five more minutes?' " At 4:21 A.M., Reno gave her final deadline. " 'You've got five minutes. Not six,' " she told Podhurst, who mused: "I'll never forget, 4:21 A.M." Reno stayed on the line even after 4:26 A.M. but Podhurst had no answer for her. The family and their advisers had spent their last five minutes plotting legal strategy—never fully believing that they had reached the end of the line. Ten minutes later, Reno put Podhurst on hold.

At 5:07 A.M. on April 22, a SWAT team of armed federal agents arrived at the home of Lázaro González in four white vans with darkened windows. Six Border Patrol agents and a female INS agent rushed to the front door and demanded entry. After knocking and waiting a half minute, they forced the door open and swooped inside the house in full riot gear. Other agents dispersed the small crowd outside the house with pepper spray. "Oh my God, Aaron, it's the marshals," Díaz gasped to Podhurst, then his line went dead.

Inside, the agents shoved open three doors, tearing through the house until they discovered Elián in the small bedroom of Lázaro González, cowering behind a sliding closet, gripped in the arms of Donato Dalrymple. An agent armed with an automatic weapon—albeit with safety lock in place—ordered Dalrymple to turn over the terrified child. In that instant, photographer Alan Díaz, who had been slipped into the house by the family, snapped the shutter of his camera. Carried in the arms of Betty Mills, a bilingual INS agent, Elián was hustled out of the house and into one of the waiting vans.

In less than three minutes, the raid was over and Elián González was en route to his father. Despite the ferocious show of force, no one was hurt. When Reno picked up the phone again, her old friend Podhurst was hollering at her. She began to cry and her deputy, Eric Holder, came over and put his arms around her.

Three hours later, a jet carrying Elián González, a government psychiatrist and agent Betty Mills landed at Andrews Air Force Base, outside Washington. Juan Miguel González rushed onto the plane. Instantly, Elián ran into his father's arms. More photos were taken—these of a jubilant Elián, his arms wrapped around his glowing dad. In the high-stakes Elián propaganda war, the two photographs duked it out. There was the photograph of an ebullient Elián in the arms of his father—the Norman Rockwell shot. Then there was the "rescue from hell" snapshot of a frightened Elián locked in the arms of Dalrymple—inches away from the automatic weapon of a federal agent.

Alan Díaz, a Cuban-American photo stringer for the Associated Press, had become a close and trusted friend of the González family and their advisers, even dining with the family on Christmas Eve. As agents descended on the house, Armando Gutiérrez, the family's public relations handler, who had been conferring with the lawyers in the living room, deftly ushered Díaz inside, guiding him to the bedroom where he snapped the damning photograph. Gutiérrez and Díaz had a prearranged understanding in the event of a raid, an arrangement also known to Reno and her team. Ironically, the searing image from the raid, which won a Pulitzer Prize and instantly became the poster shot for furious exiles, existed only because Reno refused to block Díaz's movements in the house during the operation. Most of Reno's team, sensitive to the public relations battle being waged, argued that Díaz should be kept out of the house to prevent the inevitable fallout from SWAT team images. But Reno vetoed them. "We have nothing to hide," she was reported to have told one aide.

The raid was a success for several reasons. At the dawn hour there were fewer than fifty protesters outside the NW 2nd Street house. But credit was mostly due to the fact that the Miami leadership was kept out of the loop. Police Chief William O'Brien did not inform Carollo or Penelas about the raid, as he feared they would subvert the operation. O'Brien said he told only three people: the officer who traveled in uniform in the lead van to ensure that Miami police officers would not try to block the feds; his deputy, Assistant Police Chief Ray Martínez; and Major Juan García, who was commanding the barricade outside the home. O'Brien waited until the raid had begun to inform City Manager Donald Warshaw.

THE FOLLOWING DAY, Marisleysis and Lázaro González flew to Washington, along with several of their lawyers and advisers. Accompanied by Senator Robert Smith of New Hampshire, they drove to Andrews Air Force Base in Maryland, where Elián and his family stayed initially, and demanded to see the boy. The group was turned away unceremoniously. Suddenly, the tables had turned on Lázaro González and his family—and they did not like it. They seemed baffled, even indignant, that Juan Miguel did not welcome them. "We always said Juan Miguel could come to our house to see him," Lázaro complained to reporters. "And now we can't see Elián."

On April 24, Easter Sunday, the family and some of their advisers held a lengthy, disorganized and bizarre press conference in Washington. Clutching an Easter basket that she said she wanted to give to Elián, a weeping Marisleysis rambled for more than twenty minutes. "I demand to see Elián. I will not leave until I see this boy," she said. "With my truth, I'm going to get somewhere. With the truth, I'm going to get into every heart and every mind. I need to see Elián. I know he's not okay."

Then she lambasted the government and the raid. "We didn't know who they were," she said, of the federal agents. "God forbid—we thought it was the Cuban government. . . . You know what, Janet Reno? Whether it was three minutes or thirty seconds, you still don't know what a mother is." As her audience of reporters began to shift uncomfortably and drift away, she reprimanded them: "Whoever doesn't want to listen to this, or is tired of listening to this: this could be your child!"

Marisleysis held up the famous photograph of a grinning Elián reunited with his father and denounced it as a fake. "That is not Elián," she declared. As proof of the government-perpetrated fraud, she pointed to Elián's vaguely differing hairline and the fact that he was wearing a different shirt on the night of the raid. Miami radio, dutifully fulfilling its role as a Greek chorus, immediately rebroadcast and endorsed her charges. But the photographs—taken by attorney Gregory Craig—were quickly authenticated as untouched and legitimate. It was undoubtedly Marisleysis's worst performance—a sad and regrettable finale of the five-month affair.

After the raid, the breach between exiles and Main Street USA widened immeasurably. While the González family was viciously and hilariously lampooned on *Saturday Night Live,* in Miami they were beatified as martyrs and saints. At a standing-room mass of about three thousand at Our Lady of Charity in Coconut Grove, Father Francisco Santana, the González family priest, denounced the raid and asked Elián's great-aunt, Caridad González, to stand before the congregation. Attendees cheered her on and sang the Cuban national anthem, waving miniature Cuban flags. Some carried copies of a painting of Jesus on the cross with his blood dripping down over the island of Cuba. "Have faith," Santana exhorted the crowd. "Elián is staying and Fidel is leaving."

The novelist Salman Rushdie would eviscerate all the players in the Castro-exile drama in his next work, *Fury:*

> The cult, born of Miami's necessary demonology—according to which Castro the devil, Hannibal-the-Cannibal Castro, would eat the boy alive, would tear out his immortal soul and munch it down with a few fava beans and a glass of red wine—instantly developed a priesthood as well. The dreadful media-fixated uncle was anointed pope of Eliánismo, and his daughter, poor Marisleysis, with her "nervous exhaustion," was exactly the type who would, any day now, start witnessing the seven-year-old's first miracles. There was even a fisherman involved. And of course apostles, spreading the word: the photographer living in Elián's bedroom, the TV-movie people waving contracts, publishing houses doing likewise, CNN itself and all the other news crews with their uplink dishes and fuzzy mikes. Meanwhile in Cuba, the little boy was being transformed into quite another totem. A dying revolution, a revolution of the old and straggle-bearded, held the child up as proof of its renewed youth. In this version, Elián rising from the waters became an image of the revolution's immortality; a lie Fidel, that ancient infidel, made interminable speeches wearing an Elián mask.

On Easter Sunday, exiles marched in front of the Little Havana home. Some held up copies of Díaz's photo of the federal agent holding the automatic weapon on Dalrymple and Elián and chanted, "Clinton is a Nazi. Reno is a Nazi." Others carried computer-altered versions of the photo, depicting Janet Reno or Clinton wearing a helmet with a swastika on it, holding the gun on the child. Up and down Calle Ocho, honking cars streamed by, flying the Stars and Stripes upside down with black tape over the flag to signify mourning. A day before, riot police swooped into the street in front of the González house to protect news reporters under siege by angry exiles. Teenagers had torn down and stomped on the white canopy sheltering CNN's crew, venting their fury that CNN was airing a live speech by Cuban President Fidel Castro. The fact that CNN has a bureau in Havana, along with the AP, *Chicago Tribune* and *Dallas Morning News,* infuriates some exiles, who deride it as Castro News Network.

Former Broward County associate state attorney and radio host Alberto Milián observed, "We are a lot like the Irish. Cubans are brilliant and gifted and have created an incredible culture like the Irish, but we cannot get along with each other. We are sadly self-destructive." As the two sides of the Battle for Elián grew ever more shrill, the words of the Irish bard seemed ever more apt: "The best lack all conviction," wrote William Butler Yeats, "while the worst are full of passionate intensity."

Podhurst said later he understood why Reno didn't explicitly tell him a raid was minutes away. "She said it was the longest ten minutes of her life," he said. "She said, 'I tried as hard as I could. I ran out of time.' " The Miami team was furious and claimed that a deal was within reach. "Today, I feel truly ashamed of our government," Carlos de la Cruz told the *Herald,* with his harshest words reserved for Janet Reno: "She should resign in shame after what has happened in this country early today." Saladrigas was no less hyperbolic: "I felt raped, if I may use that word." "They're wrong," countered a Justice Department official. "It was clear the negotiations were not going to get anywhere real. Anything further would have been sheer delay."

The government defended its use of force on several counts, principally on the grounds that armed, militant anti-Castro groups were around the house. They cited the presence of Mario Miranda, formerly Mas Canosa's bodyguard, a fixture in the home who carried a handgun strapped to his ankle. The house had been under helicopter surveillance for some time and the FBI felt that the probability of resistance was high. Of concern was the presence of five members of the paramilitary group Alpha 66—"including three men responsible for a 1995 attack on a hotel in Cuba," according to the *Herald,* "who were seen frequently visiting the home and milling in the crowd of demonstrators outside. All five had weapons training, and some had expressed a willingness to use violence in the event of a raid. Additionally, about 15 to 20 supporters of the Miami family had taken up residence in the house directly behind, including seven identified convicted felons with records for armed robbery, burglary, firearms charges and assault as well as five bodyguards for the González family, who had concealed weapons permits." It was also widely known that the radio station La Poderosa had broadcast warnings in the past from a neighbor's house that served as a "communications center" calling on exiles to rally around the house and protest Elián's removal.

In the ensuing days, the sound booth of Armando Pérez-Roura at Radio Mambí became command headquarters for the post-raid counterattack. For the next two weeks, virtually every player in the exile pantheon trooped through Pérez-Roura's bunker to vilify the federal government. "A crime," Joe Carollo cried aloud while depicting the events as a vicious stealth attack on a hapless exile family. Pérez-Roura went further and suggested that the federal government was orchestrating a campaign of odious lies. Referring to the photograph of Elián beaming at his father, Pérez-Roura boomed, "That is not Elián. He doesn't want anything to do with his father, so how is he going to appear in that photo as if nothing happened? Let's not give any credence to this photo. Now it will begin to rain photographs." The photograph by Alan Díaz, he said, was "the only one that has any value."

Many expressed surprise that Radio Martí, the taxpayer-funded station with a mandate to beam news and information into Cuba, failed to report the raid initially. The station had been transferred from Washington to Miami at the demand of hard-liners, a move that President Bill Clinton signed off on in 1996 and that exponentially increased the politicization of its coverage. Once ensconced in Miami, Martí's new management, in a brazen display of nepotism, hired the fathers of both of Miami's two congressional representatives, Rafael Díaz-Balart and Enrique Ros, to host their own radio shows. Local sentiment that the return of Elián to his father was a defeat for exiles was said to have prompted the station to withhold the news. Radio Martí would be among the last to report the raid.

ON APRIL 25, EXILES sympathetic to the Miami Gonzálezes vented their fury in a general strike, calling the day *Martes Muerte*—Dead Tuesday. Miami radio exhorted its listeners to stay home and not report to work in a show of solidarity. Many Cubans who wanted to be at work stayed home for fear of recriminations and reprisals. Carmen, a Cuban-American who works for the city of Miami and requested anonymity, was bluntly told that if she did not honor the strike, she would not have a job. Others indulged in flag desecration and, in one case, a tow operator dragged an American flag through Miami's streets from behind his truck. Others blocked intersections, smashed the windows of a police cruiser and ignited fires in Little Havana. More than 1,300 police, in riot gear using tear gas, put out 200 trash fires, arrested 350 protesters and answered 70 minor injury calls. Some exile leaders, like José Basulto of Brothers to the Rescue, were angered by the police response. Basulto told reporters that he believed the police had attacked demonstrators as a sideshow diversion from "the real crime—Elián's seizure."

A day after the raid, two of the González family advisers, Carlos de la Cruz and Carlos Saladrigas, convened an emergency meeting of the elite Mesa Redonda. The meeting was held in the *Miami Herald* office of Alberto Ibargüen, the *Herald*'s publisher and a member of the group. It was another ill-conceived move. No one had thought of the impropriety of conducting a political meeting at the *Herald*—and, worse, no one had apprised an embarrassed Martin Baron, the paper's editor, and his staff of what was going on above the newsroom.

In a matter of weeks, Miami's city government was purged. Mayor Joe Carollo had demanded immediately that City Manager Donald Warshaw fire Police Chief William O'Brien for failing to advise them of the raid. When Warshaw refused, Carollo fired him. O'Brien would later resign, in the interests of keeping the peace. Both were promptly replaced by Cuban-Americans, further polarizing Miami, which now had virtually all of its key positions occupied by Cuban-Americans, leaving scant representation for the 50 percent non-Cuban community. Blacks and Anglos felt further alienated from exiles, as did non-Cuban Latinos. Even within the exile world, the divisions were painful: the young, the assimilated and the moderates who generally supported Elián's return were pitted against the older generation and hard-liners.

Next came that staple of Miami warfare—the lawsuits. Donato Dalrymple filed a lawsuit seeking $100 million in damages, claiming his civil rights had been violated in the raid. Dalrymple was represented by the conservative Washington, D.C.-based group Judicial Watch, the group that had waged a legal war against President Clinton and his administration. The González family filed their own suit against Janet Reno and the administration later in the year.

The city of Miami continued to be savaged in the media. Commentator Gregg Fields proposed a Miami public relations campaign with the tag line:

"Miami—where every street is safe to block," and opined that Miami was not a banana republic because "republic indicates a framework of laws. We have a Bananarchy." Sergio Bendixen, president of the public opinion research firm Hispanic Trends, was less amused. "The situation is ugly. Miami as a community is in great danger and I hope leadership at all levels— political, civic, and religious—will address it and not just hope time will heal. Because it won't."

Several businessmen, such as Armando Codina, a wealthy Miami developer with close ties to Jeb Bush, recognized that exiles were doing inestimable damage to themselves and the cause of a free Cuba and urged reform and new thinking. But Miami's elected leaders offered no deviation from their soapbox politicking—and neither did the two men vying to be the next President. Both candidates consulted their polls and continued their pandering: neither campaign wanted to cede the Miami exile vote.

TEXAS GOVERNOR GEORGE W. BUSH, who had once said that he hoped the administration could persuade Juan Miguel González to defect and rear his family in the States, didn't hesitate to exploit the bitterness of exiles. "Certainly the picture that most of America saw," he declared, "of the boy being seized by a marshal who had an automatic weapon is not what America is about." Bush wildly compared the tactics of federal agents to those of Fidel Castro. "I am profoundly saddened and troubled that the administration was not able to negotiate a resolution and instead decided to use force to take a little boy from the place he calls home in the middle of the night."

The Republican Party had been split on the issue of Elián, and the conservative, family values wing rejected Bush's position. Christian conservatives like Representative Steve Largent had been outspoken that the boy had to be reunited with his father. "If my little boy . . . was lost," said Largent, "what position does a court have to come in and start evaluating whether I'm a fit father or not?" Seeing its potential to split the party, most Republicans decided to sit out the Elián crisis. Still, Bush felt obliged to back the Republican leadership of the exiles. He also needed to act in concert with and provide some cover for his brother, Governor Jeb Bush. Curiously, the younger Bush had remained notably low-profile throughout the saga. He was one of the few Florida Republicans not to make an appearance at the Miami house, although Armando Gutiérrez said that Jeb Bush had been in phone contact with the family and their advisers. And throughout May and June and up until the election, both presidential candidates continued to harp on the need to resolve the matter in family court—blithely ignoring the fact that the family court had emphatically ruled against Lázaro González.

Even the media was drawn into opposing camps. The day after the raid, a staffer at *El Nuevo Herald* posted an office e-mail, according to several *Herald* reporters, that stated: "Now that the Feds have snatched Elián, the following pro-Castro writers should be delighted," and listed six writers and editors whose coverage he found wanting. One of the mentioned reporters referred to the memo as "the hit list." On the other side of the divide, pundits voiced outrage that a *Herald* columnist had joined a prayer vigil in front of the González house and complainted that *Herald* stories had been watered down so as not to offend hard-liners. *El Nuevo Herald* was derided by some of its staffers as "a cartoon" and "a joke." The coup de grâce was publisher Alberto Ibargüen's page-one editorial that ran in *El Nuevo Herald* the day after the raid under the headline *"Qué Vergüenza!"*—What a Disgrace!

ON APRIL 25, Elián and his family were moved to the Carmichael Farm on the outskirts of the Wye Plantation, a government conference center on the Eastern Shore of Maryland. Under the terms negotiated with Janet Reno, Elián had to remain in the States until the Eleventh Circuit Court had ruled. Not long after their arrival, they were joined by a small contingent of visitors from Cárdenas, including four of Elián's first-grade classmates, teachers and a doctor. Exiles were chagrined to see photographs of Elián and his classmates in their Pioneer uniforms of red shorts, blue kerchiefs and white shirts. All schoolchildren in Cuba wear the Pioneer uniform—not unlike children who attend private and Catholic schools here. *El Nuevo Herald* ran photos of Elián in uniform on page one with the headline "The Pioneer Elián in Washington." "We're very troubled," Kendall Coffey told reporters. "He's being paraded as a trophy in the garb of the Communist Party. It's happening even more rapidly than our worst expectations."

Once Elián was transferred to his father's care, his relatives lobbed a barrage of complaints. The family charged that Elián would be "brainwashed" by his father—the very same charge made by Cuba against the relatives during the child's five-month stay in Little Havana. Others said it was evident that Elián was being "drugged"—again the same charge made by his grandmothers when they visited him three months earlier. Representative Lincoln Díaz-Balart of Miami spoke with his customary hyperbole. "It was a monstrous crime. Clinton and Reno took Elián by force so that Castro's psychiatrists will have time to brainwash the child before the appellate court orders

Reno to grant Elián a political asylum hearing. Have you listened to Castro's speeches today?" he continued in remarks that ventured into the histrionic. "He says the U.S. was sending him encrypted faxes. Castro knew more about what was going to happen than the American citizens who were negotiating on behalf of Elián."

Some Republicans could not resist making political hay out of the raid. Representative Henry Hyde, chairman of the House Judiciary Committee and chief manager of the impeachment trial of President Clinton, announced that he would begin a preliminary investigation of the raid. House Majority Whip Tom DeLay was more emphatic. "You bet there will be congressional hearings," he told NBC's *Meet the Press*. DeLay and Hyde had rallied a faction of the GOP behind the Miami family, and DeLay was hopeful that where they had failed in their impeachment bid of Clinton, they would succeed with hearings on the Cuban refugee.

Democrats were gleeful at the prospect of a Republican investigation. Only one day after the raid, a CBS News poll found that a majority of Americans—57 percent—believed that federal agents had done the right thing. The numbers revealed that most Americans agreed with the sentiments of Miami state senator Daryl Jones. "I think it was unfortunate it happened that way," Jones said, "but we were at the point where we were approaching kidnapping and false imprisonment." Republicans got the message: they muzzled DeLay and back-burnered the idea of hearings until the fire fizzled out.

In late May, Elián and his family moved to the Rosedale Estate in the Cleveland Park section of Washington, owned by the nonprofit group Youth for Understanding International Exchange. Despite the misgivings of the U.S. Marshals Service, which preferred the more remote Eastern Shore residence, the family was eager to live in the heart of Washington. There were some outings—including a visit to Washington's National Zoo—with the media trailing behind them. Juan Miguel, the *guajiro* from Cárdenas, became the hottest ticket for dinner in Beltway circles, and even scored an invitation to the White House Washington Correspondents Dinner. He declined all, with the exception of a party held at the home of the philanthropist Smith Bagley. He struck his few visitors as a pleasant but simple man focused on one thing: getting home with his son.

On June 1, the Eleventh U.S. Circuit Court of Appeals in Atlanta ruled in favor of the Justice Department decision to reunite Elián with his father. The Miami relatives immediately appealed the ruling to the full court, which ordered Elián to remain in the States while it reviewed the decision. On

June 23, the Appeals Court reaffirmed its decision and Juan Miguel and his family packed their bags. Three days later, on June 26, the Miami relatives, desperate to stave off the departure of Elián, filed yet another appeal, their final appeal, with the U.S. Supreme Court. Juan Miguel parked his family's bags in the foyer of the Bethesda house. On June 28, the Supreme Court rejected the relatives' appeal. Hours after the Court lifted its injunction against Elián leaving the country, the family flew home to Cuba.

The grieving and embittered González clan of NW 2nd Street found solace in Miami's exile leadership. They sternly vowed never to forget Elián and to make his loss a central issue in the looming presidential race. They had four months until the November election, and they went to work.

CHAPTER 11

THE THIRD RAIL

Que morir por la patria es vivir.
To die for one's country is to live.

NATIONAL ANTHEM OF CUBA

B ETWEEN JUNE AND THE NOVEMBER ELECTION, the Miami leadership campaigned tirelessly for George W. Bush. The message to exiles was simple: go out and vote in record numbers to deliver a resounding referendum on Elián's return to Cuba. Lázaro González was to join local politicos on Spanish language radio to rally *la comunidad* to vote against Gore. "The Cubans in Miami remember Elián," said Armando Pérez-Roura, the radio czar, who urged exiles never to forget and never again to vote Democratic. Radio hosts compared the loss of Elián to their defeat at Bay of Pigs and wagged their fingers accusingly at the same perpetrators: liberal Democrats like Kennedy and Clinton. "The Democrats have never been tough enough on Cuba," Pérez-Roura said.

Florida has been a Democratic state since Reconstruction. In the Sunshine State registered Democrats outnumber registered Republicans by roughly 5 percent, but Democrats often vote Republican. But Florida has not been immune to the general Republican drift of the Sunbelt. In fact, over the last thirty years, the only Democrats to carry Florida in presidential contests have been Jimmy Carter and Bill Clinton.

In Miami-Dade County, however, Cuban-Americans make up more than a third of its population of two million. An estimated 800,000 are exiles, with about half being citizens registered to vote. Of this group, roughly 85 percent are registered as Republicans, 5 percent as Democrats. Cuban exiles are the largest single voting bloc in Miami-Dade, and with their political and financial clout, they influence *all* races, for both parties. "The clerk of Miami-Dade counts as Hispanics only foreign-born, not first-generation American-born Cuban exiles," explained Steve Zack, an exile lawyer who has represented the county and state in reapportionment cases. "So the numbers are even higher for Cubans—who have long been one of the most active voting blocs." Several key politicians, such as Joe Carollo, Lincoln Díaz-Balart and Manny Díaz (who toppled Carollo in an upset victory in the city of Miami's 2001 mayoral election), began their careers as Democrats and switched to Republican or Independent after scrutinizing the polling data.

That said, there are still more registered Democrats in Miami-Dade than Republicans—owing to the fact that most blacks, Anglos and non-Cuban Hispanics in the county tend to vote Democrat. And Democratic inroads have been made over the years. Clinton won Florida the second time in 1996 in part by winning over some exile votes, taking Miami-Dade County decisively. Al Gore had similar hopes.

But the wild card for Gore and the Democrats turned out to be one of their own. When Gore began his march to the White House in 1999, Alex Penelas was among his most stalwart backers—accompanying him to a Bal Harbour fund-raiser and serving as his all-around escort to the Cuban-American community. However, in the crucial final months of the campaign, Penelas staged a spectacular vanishing act and did not make a single appearance for Gore. He was a glaring no-show at a Gore-Lieberman rally in Hialeah two weeks before the election, opting to vacation in Spain instead. Nor was he present for Gore's celebrity-packed finale party in Miami the night before the election.

"Penelas had a brilliant strategy," said Dario Moreno, a professor of political science at Florida International University. "Clinton became more and more popular with the Cubans, and Penelas rode that. He was using that to become a national player in the Democratic Party." But when the going got tough, Penelas bailed. He looked at Dade's demographics and his core constituencies for his upcoming re-election—then disappeared from the campaign. "If you're a judge or a mayor in this town, you have no choice but to think about how this issue will play out in the Cuban community," explained Ric Katz, a veteran Miami political consultant. "You can still get elected to countywide office without the Cuban vote, but it's awfully difficult."

In the end, Gore carried Miami-Dade County—even without a recount—but only by 39,000 votes, a precipitous drop from Clinton's hefty margin of 117,000. Florida was thrown into the Democrats' column early on election night based on exit polling. Democrat Bill Nelson had handily routed Bill McCollum, a member of the House impeachment committee, for the contested Florida Senate seat. There was little reason to believe that Democrats voting for Nelson would split their ticket and not vote for Gore. But at

2:16 A.M., Fox News—whose pollster John Ellis, a cousin of the Bush brothers, had been in contact with both of them throughout the night—moved Florida from the Democrat column to the Republican column. Minutes earlier, Florida's Secretary of State, Katherine Harris, had posted returns that gave Bush more than a 50,000-vote lead. Although Harris's statistics would prove astoundingly wrong, in a matter of minutes, the other networks followed suit and awarded victory to Bush. ABC News was the last network to change its call—at 2:20 A.M. Hours later, all the networks would declare the state of Florida undecided.

By morning, no winner had been declared for Florida, although Bush appeared to have taken the lead. Indeed, Gore had called Bush to concede, against the advice of his counselors, only to call back and reverse himself. But Bush's slender lead—after the first vote count, it was 288 votes—triggered a Florida law calling for an automatic recount. Counties throughout the state were reviewing their ballots, and absentee and military ballots had yet to be fully accounted for.

Gore's campaign would retain Kendall Coffey, the former U.S. Attorney who had represented Lázaro González, to argue his case in the Florida courts. Neither Coffey nor Gore, however, foresaw the snakebit reaction their alliance would generate. Family spokesman Armando Gutiérrez, after conferring with Coffey's law partner, Manny Díaz, at Monty's, the popular seafood restaurant in Coconut Grove in which Díaz was a part owner, said Coffey's alliance with Gore was nothing less than an act of betrayal. "Kendall Coffey was repeatedly deceived by the Clinton-Gore administration," said Gutiérrez. "I find this action incomprehensible and indefensible." Lázaro González, never shy about expressing his feelings, added: "It was a rotten thing to do." Díaz split from Coffey over the matter. And in case Coffey did not get the message, the family canceled a long-planned event to honor their lawyers so as not to have to pay tribute to him. "By that time Manny knew he was going to run for Mayor in 2001," said Coffey, who described his former law partner's outrage as merely political, "and Armando was already working with him."

Miami attorney Steve Zack argued the Democrats' case for a manual recount before the three-member Miami-Dade Canvassing Board and won. The board gave assurances that the recount would proceed and that proper police security would be provided for counters. Republicans then scurried to a state judge and pleaded their case to halt the recount. They were denied. A second judge also turned them down—and the counting continued.

On November 22, 2000, fifteen days after the election, the Miami-Dade Canvassing Board suddenly flip-flopped its position, voting 2–1 to shut down the manual recount and canceling its plans to review the 10,750 ballots that had been rejected by voting machines for having no clear presidential preference. In essence, the board overruled the Florida Supreme Court's decision that recounts could go forward. The reversal came when Circuit Court Judge Myriam Lehr, an exile married to a Republican political activist, changed her vote. David Leahy, a Republican board member and the trio's supervisor, had previously voted against a recount. The third member, county Judge Lawrence King, a Democrat, had voted for one. It was amply noted that both Lehr and King had retained political consultant Armando Gutiérrez, the González family's spokesman, for their own campaigns. The *New York Times* reported that Judge Lehr had been phoned on November 15 by one of George W. Bush's lawyers. Both Lehr and King were being targeted by Spanish language radio.

The Canvassing Board claimed to have based its reversal on security concerns. Leahy offered a somewhat disingenuous explanation: "We simply can't get it done. There was this concern that we were not conducting an open, fair process." As pundits debated the relative merits of dimpled and pregnant chads, the Republicans worked feverishly to convince the public that it was impossible to establish a coherent system of standards.

On the morning of November 22, Miami's two congressional representatives, Lincoln Díaz-Balart and Ileana Ros-Lehtinen, were guests on Pérez-Roura's radio program, the number-one-rated show among exiles. "They pretty much accused Gore of stealing the election," recalled Coffey, "then urged listeners to hurry down to the Canvassing Board and stop the recount." Hours later, the board's offices were overrun by an intimidating mob of protesters who made it impossible for the staff to do their work. Television video and photographs of the angry crowd captured the faces of a dozen Republican staffers—mostly from out of state, including several operatives from the office of Tom DeLay—in the front row pounding at the doors. Behind them were furious exiles. No security or police were present to quell the disturbance. "These were out-of-town people brought in to cause as much disruption and fear as possible," said Joseph Geller, the chairman of the Democratic Party in Dade. "They were clearly under the control of the Republican operatives." Geller himself would be briefly detained by police—at the demand of local Republicans—on the charge of having a ballot box in his car. He was released when the charge proved bogus.

Joe Lieberman opined that the board had been intimidated. Others voiced more sinister scenarios. "The whole community is very suspicious of what happened surrounding the decision to close down the recount," said

Representative Carrie Meek of Miami-Dade County. "People are suspect. Wouldn't you be if there were 10,700 votes that were not counted?" Whispers grew audible that Penelas had played Iago to Gore and had pressured the board to reverse its position. Certainly, Alex Penelas was in a position to play a decisive role. "In the hours before and after Miami-Dade County's hand recount was halted, Democrats and Republicans believed that one man had the power to determine its fate: Alex Penelas," wrote the *New York Times*. "As the county's hand recount racked up dozens of new votes for Vice President Al Gore, the mayor had lunch at the Governor's Club in Tallahassee with a Republican state legislator."

Penelas conceded that he had been in continual contact with David Leahy, the Canvassing Board supervisor—often more than three times a day—but denied any role in the decision. The *Times* reported that Penelas's telephone records indicated that he was "working both sides of the political fight," dialing around the clock to chat up key players in both camps. One call was placed to the House Republican cloakroom in Washington, and Penelas stayed in close contact with top Republicans in Florida as well as top Democratic advisers. Visibly unnerved by the events of the day, Gore called Penelas and beseeched his assistance in reversing the board's decision. According to a Gore staffer, Penelas promised he would go to bat for them with a statement calling for the recount to resume. But they were betrayed again.

In his statement, Penelas washed his hands of the matter—claiming that he had "no jurisdiction over the Board's decisions." Factually, this was true enough, but his influence was immense. "Penelas could have turned the election—just like he did for Clinton," said *Herald* editor Mark Seibel. Republicans rejoiced at Penelas's statement, while Democrats fumed and licked their wounds. Why did he do it? they asked each other aloud and in private. Most likely, Penelas coolly surveyed the wreckage of his career and realized that he could never run for office outside Miami-Dade. The video of him threatening not to uphold the rule of law would forever shadow him—except in Miami. There was only one constituency that would forgive him and that was his own. An aide to Penelas told the *Times* that the young Mayor was considering becoming a Republican and running for Congress in a Hispanic-dominated district that would likely result from the reapportionment in 2002. Pundits speculated that it was only a matter of time before Penelas switched parties. In fact, Penelas would remain a Democrat in name only. On June 24, he hosted a $250-a-plate fund-raiser at a posh Miami restaurant for Republican Mario Díaz-Balart's campaign for that U.S. House seat, mortally subverting Miami's bid to host the 2004 Democratic convention. "He took a walk for whatever reason. He was going to go fishing, which he did," said Hialeah's no-holds-barred Mayor, Raúl Martínez, who talked with Penclas soon after the recount was halted. "He sounded like he was under pressure," said Martínez. "He sounded almost like he was crying. Alex cut a deal with the devil—and with the father of the devil! He double-dealed Gore."

While mysteries remain as to exactly what happened in those crucial final days, Alex Penelas was only one soldier in the army who fought to deliver a Florida victory to George W. Bush. While exiles quickly and loudly took credit for Bush's eventual victory, there were other factors of far greater impact in which they played no role. First was the fact that Ralph Nader took more than 97,000 votes in Florida—votes that overwhelmingly would have gone to Gore. Second were the scores of irregularities that marred the electoral process. There were thousands of black voters—typically Democratic—who said they either were turned away or had had their ballots discarded for irregularities. There was the infamous butterfly ballot designed by the Palm Beach Canvassing Board supervisor, Theresa Le Pore. Her ineptly designed ballot cost Gore an estimated 25,000 votes—confusing voters into voting for either Pat Buchanan or Bush. Her incompetence, on its own, awarded victory to Bush.

Other irregularities included outright violations, such as people who had voted twice. Convicted felons had been allowed to vote, while other legitimate voters, estimated at more than 57,000, had their names stripped off voter lists by Secretary of State Katherine Harris, who doubled as George W. Bush's state chairman. More than 40,000 ballots had not been counted because they had been punched more than once. The *New York Times* reported that military ballots had poured in *after* the election but were still counted.

As the nation duly noted, Florida was an electoral travesty—presided over by Jeb Bush and Katherine Harris. Former President Jimmy Carter, who often monitors elections in the Third World, said he would not have validated the results if the election had taken place in a Latin American country, owing to its egregious irregularities. "Paraguay, Sí, Miami, No!" became one *Herald* headline.

According to the exhaustive investigative postmortems into Florida's election conducted by the *Miami Herald* and the consortium organized by the *New York Times,* if every ballot intended for Gore had been counted in Florida, he would have won. "If no one had ever heard of hanging chads, if the butterfly ballot had never flown, if no voter had bungled in the booth, who would have won Florida and the presidency of the United States?" the *Herald* wrote after studying the voting patterns in each of the state's 5,885 precincts. "Florida likely would have gone to Al Gore—by a slim 23,000 votes—rather than George W. Bush, the officially certified victor by the wispy margin of 537."

In November 2001, the consortium of newspapers that included the *New York Times* and *Wall Street Journal* concluded that Gore's decision to ask for a recount of only several counties as opposed to the entire state cost him the election. A statewide recount would have given Gore not only greater legitimacy, but also a winning margin—notwithstanding the Palm Beach butterfly ballot. But this was not immediately discernible from the consortium's report. "They sort of changed the rules in the middle of the game," said Jeffrey Toobin, who chronicled the recount in *Too Close to Call.* "The consortium wimped out by finding the one scenario where they could say that Bush won Florida—which was if the Supreme Court had not halted the Florida Court–ordered recount. But if they simply reported all the undervotes and overvotes—the most obvious and complete way to proceed—Gore was the winner."

The jaundiced view of political analysts on both sides of the aisle has it that whichever party controls the governorship and state house can sway a close election. And in this regard, Florida was a godsend for George W. Bush: his "little brother," as he referred to Jeb in his phone call with Al Gore, was Governor and the Republicans controlled both houses of the Legislature for the first time in Florida's history.

John Ellis Bush, known to all as Jeb, came to Miami in 1980 at the age of twenty-seven to work on his father's unsuccessful primary bid against Ronald Reagan. When Bush Sr. joined the Reagan ticket, the cachet of being the Vice President's son quickly attracted the support of Miami exiles, who guided him into South Florida's lucrative commercial real estate market. After graduating from the University of Texas with a degree in Latin American studies, Jeb worked briefly at a Texas bank (owned, in part, by his father's friend James Baker III) in Venezuela. He would soon learn that business in Miami-Dade was not very different from business in Caracas. In several of his ventures, the young Bush and his partners attracted the scrutiny and ire of regulators and law enforcement.

Jeb Bush's first job in Miami was as a leasing agent for Cuban-American developer Armando Codina. A few years later, Bush and Codina became business partners, and in 1985 they purchased an office building in a deal partly financed by a $4.56 million loan from a savings and loan that later failed. A third party had borrowed the money from Broward Federal Savings and then re-lent it to the Bush partnership. When federal regulators closed

Broward Savings in 1988, they found the loan, which had been secured by the Bush-Codina partnership, in default. After protracted negotiations, regulators reduced the amount owed by Bush and his partner to just $500,000 and allowed them to keep their office building. The remaining $4 million was paid by taxpayers.

In 1984, Jeb Bush became Dade County's Republican Party chairman and began a close association with Camilo Padreda, Dade's GOP finance chairman and a former intelligence officer in the Batista government. Padreda hired the young Bush as his leasing agent in 1986 for his buildings, many of which were subsidized by the Department of Housing and Urban Development. Four years earlier, according to an investigative series in *Newsday*, Padreda and another exile, Hernández Cartaya, a Bay of Pigs veteran, were indicted for embezzling $500,000 from the Jefferson Savings and Loan Association in McAllen, Texas. (Cartaya was also charged with drug smuggling, money laundering and gun running.) But the case never went to trial. Soon after the indictment came down, according to an account in *Mother Jones,* FBI officials said they got a call from someone at the CIA warning them that Cartaya was one of their own. The charges against Padreda were dropped, while Cartaya's charges were reduced to a single count of tax evasion. Assistant U.S. Attorney Jerome Sanford filed a demand with the CIA, under the Freedom of Information Act, for all documents relating to the Agency's interference in his case. The CIA, citing national security reasons, denied his request.

In 1985, Padreda was again in trouble, accused of having improperly influenced the Dade County Manager, Sergio Pereira, Padreda's silent partner, in a lucrative real estate deal. The scandal forced Pereira to resign, although Padreda was not charged in the case. In 1986, Padreda's HUD-financed building scored a huge tenant: International Medical Centers, a booming health maintenance organization. IMC was the largest recipient of federal Medicare funds and later won the distinction of being responsible for the largest HMO Medicare fraud in U.S. history, garnering an estimated $1 billion in Medicare payments by some accounts. In 1989, Padreda pleaded guilty to charges that he defrauded HUD of millions of dollars during the 1980s. Padreda's attorney defended his client to *Newsday*, describing him as "a well-respected businessman." Then he added what he felt to be the necessary context: "Miami is Miami. If you are in a Cuban community in Miami, you are in the midst of intrigue, whether you want to be or not!"

However, Padreda has always had a gift for friendship and continued to hobnob with the exile leadership, acting as a behind-the-scenes kingmaker.

He was also a key witness against Raúl Martínez in his 1991 extortion trial, during which Padreda admitted to extensive firsthand experience with public corruption. In 2002, agents in the FBI's Miami bureau warned their chief, Hector Pesquera, that he would be wise to reconsider his friendship and golf dates with Padreda. To their surprise, Pesquera declined their advice. Padreda, they noted, had assisted Pesquera's predecessor, Paul Phillips, in settling into a lucrative job as an adviser to Penelas upon his retirement. Pesquera declined comment, although Phillips was forthcoming. "I don't deny my friendship with Camilo," said Phillips, who said he was introduced to Padreda by Jim Milford, the Miami bureau chief of the DEA. "Camilo saved our bacon during the Brothers to the Rescue crisis, when Miami radio was accusing the FBI of being part of a conspiracy to down those planes. He organized a meeting between exiles and us and totally defused it."

IMC was run by a colorful exile named Miguel Recarey, who kept a pistol in his suit jacket and assault rifles stashed in his Miami mansion, where the master bedroom boasted bulletproof windows and a steel door. Recarey had long been associated with Tampa's mob boss Santo Trafficante Jr., who had had extensive gambling operations in pre-Castro Cuba. Both Recarey and Trafficante had contributed to the CIA's efforts in the 1960s to assassinate Fidel Castro.

Recarey, who had been honored as Entrepreneur of the Year in 1986 by the powerful Latin Builders Association, put Jeb Bush on the payroll as a real estate consultant. He also contributed generously to the political action committees of Jeb's father and to the Republican Party. In 1985, the young Bush phoned Health and Human Services officials in Washington several times and lobbied successfully for a highly unusual waiver on behalf of IMC. The waiver permitted Recarey a full patient load paid for by Medicare—the normal limit was 50 percent. At about the same time, Bush scored a $75,000 commission for finding IMC a new home for its headquarters. There was, however, one peculiarity: IMC never relocated. "Amazing how Jeb got a $75,000 fee for a deal that never closed," snipped Raúl Martínez. Jeb Bush was unapologetic. "I want to be very wealthy," he told the *Miami News* at the time. In 1987, McClain Haddow, the former chief of staff of HHS, testified before a congressional committee that it was Jeb Bush's influence and lobbying that won Recarey's company its waiver. Haddow told *Newsday* that Jeb Bush had directly petitioned HHS Secretary Margaret Heckler, who initially took a "dim view" of IMC, on the matter, calling him and Heckler twice each.

It would turn out that IMC had another sideline: assisting the Contra resupply initiative. In 1985, Jeb Bush delivered a letter to his father at the White House from a Guatemalan doctor seeking U.S. medical aid for the Contras. The Vice President wrote back to the doctor that he should contact Lieutenant Colonel Oliver North. An entry in North's diary for January 22, 1985, reads: "Medical Support System for wounded FDN [Contras] in Miami—HMO in Miami has ok'ed to help all WIA [wounded in action] . . . Felix Rodriguez." In 1987, the *Wall Street Journal* reported that exile José Basulto had attended meetings at IMC headquarters in Miami along with Contra leader Adolfo Calero and Félix Rodríguez. Basulto stated that he had personally brought wounded Contras to IMC hospitals in Miami, where they received free medical treatment.

Despite the influence of the Vice President's son, IMC caught the attention of an indefatigable and incorruptible HHS special agent in Miami named Leon Weinstein, who had been tracking Recarey since 1977. Uncovering evidence of Medicare fraud, Weinstein wanted to bring charges as early as 1983 but was rebuffed by his superiors at HHS, who he said threatened him if he pursued his inquiry. In 1986, Weinstein solicited the aid of Congressmen Barney Frank and Pete Stark—which led to congressional hearings into the billion-dollar scandal. "My investigation led me to conclude that there may have been a deliberate attempt to obstruct justice," Weinstein told *Mother Jones,* "because Recarey, his hospital, and his clinics were treating wounded Contras from Nicaragua . . . and part of the $30 million a month he was given by the government to treat Medicare patients was used to set up field hospitals for the Contras."

Recarey was indicted for a host of crimes, but prior to his trial, he fled the country with a $2.2 million IRS income tax refund that had been specially expedited on his behalf. Since 1987, Recarey, an FBI fugitive, has been living in Caracas and Madrid.

In 1987, Jeb Bush became Florida's Secretary of Commerce under Governor Bob Martinez. His detractors claimed that he improperly rewarded Republican backers such as nursery owner Manuel Díaz (no relation to the Miami lawyer of the same name who is now Mayor). Before filing for personal bankruptcy, Charles Keating of the notorious savings and loan debacle transferred his $2 million mansion on the island of Cat Cay in the Bahamas to Díaz. Jeb arranged a private meeting between Díaz and Governor Martinez, who awarded him a $1.72 million government contract to landscape Florida's highways. Díaz's critics charged that he had virtually no experience with landscaping work of this nature.

By the late 1980s Jeb Bush had assured his place in the exile firmament as an influential and reliable player. In 1989, he became the campaign manager for Ileana Ros-Lehtinen in her bid for a congressional seat. Jeb nimbly orchestrated appearances in Miami with his father, the President, and his candidate sailed to victory. Exiles believed that it was at Jeb Bush's prodding that his father declared, "I am certain in my heart that I will be the first American President to step foot on the soil of a free and independent Cuba." They also felt that it was Jeb's lobbying that convinced his father to overrule his own Justice Department and to release convicted exile terrorist Orlando Bosch from prison and grant him U.S. residency.

Jeb Bush speaks fluent Spanish and Florida's large Hispanic population has always been impressed that his wife, Columba, is Mexican. The marriage, however, has been a turbulent one and the two are rarely seen together, with Columba reported to spend extended periods in Miami. Jeb Bush has been linked romantically in the media with several women—all of whom have gone on to work with him. During the recount, Miami was awash with rumors tying Jeb to his Secretary of State, Katherine Harris—originating with reports from Tallahassee lobbyists who said that they had seen the two together socially throughout 2000 and that Columba had confronted Harris. Both Harris and Bush denied having a liaison. Still, he was dogged by stories of his alleged philandering. Several Florida newspapers reported rumors that he was having an affair with Cynthia Henderson, a former Playboy Bunny, whom he hired to head up Florida's Department of Management Services in early 1999.

Columnist Carl Hiaasen wrote that he didn't mind having an alleged skirt-chaser as Governor, but he questioned Henderson's qualifications and track record: "As the state's chief business regulator, Henderson once flew to the Kentucky Derby on a jet owned by Outback Steakhouse. Another restaurant patronized by Henderson saw a $185,000 state-tax bill transformed to a refund of $6,263. Then there was the time she got a government job for her nanny." Others noted that the sister of Sally Bradshaw, Bush's former chief of staff and currently a key figure in his re-election campaign, had been awarded a high-paying government job, while Bradshaw's husband is among the state's most influential lobbyists. Seeking to silence the rumors, Bush held a press conference in May 2001 at which he tried to set the record straight and volunteered that he had never slept with anyone other than his wife. "I love my wife dearly. I've been married to her for twenty-seven years," Bush proclaimed. "I've been faithful to her. There is nothing to these rumors. It is an outright lie."

Katherine Harris, who had been demonized by some of her detractors as Cruella De Vil during the recount, faced more criticism in early 2001. During the recount, she lobbied unsuccessfully to attend Mexican President Vicente

Fox's inauguration, as if a Republican victory was a certainty. And e-mails on her computer revealed that she had been in regular contact with Jeb Bush during the recount, contrary to both of their accounts. *Herald* reporters discovered that e-mails she had sent to Jeb Bush had been deleted from her hard drive after the recount. Not long after an interview with the *Herald*'s Meg Laughlin, Harris had the operating system of her computer changed—a procedure that erased all its data. "What was odd about what she did," said *Herald* managing editor Mark Seibel, "was that they installed an old operating system—not a new one—which makes you wonder why they did it."

In the summer of 2001, Harris announced that she would run for Congress. She settled on an eminently safe seat, in the district that includes her hometown of Sarasota, an affluent resort area that has long been in Republican hands.

"GOD BROUGHT ELIÁN with a purpose because he knew what would come in the future," Delfín González told *Herald* columnist Robert Steinback. The two men were sitting outside the old house at 2319 NW 2nd Street, which Delfín had bought and converted into Casa Elián, an Elián museum. "If it wasn't for Elián," González insisted, "George Bush would not have won the presidency."

Certainly Miami's political leadership had done its part to secure a victory for George W. Bush. And in the days and weeks after the inauguration, they saw to it that the country, and the new administration, took note and remembered their contribution. Ramón Saúl Sánchez, leader of the group Democracy Movement, laid out what would become a well-worn refrain: "If the Elián González case had been handled differently, Mr. Gore would've been President," said Sánchez. Al Cárdenas, chairman of the Florida Republican Party, expanded on the reasons for Bush's win, offering a litany of exile grievances: "Clinton's handshake with Cuban dictator Fidel Castro at the United Nations in September; his response to the downing of two Brothers to the Rescue planes over the Florida Straits in 1996; and the Elián case."

Now payment was in order. At the top of the hard-liners' wish list was an immediate halt to what they viewed as the new détente with Cuba. Next was leadership roles in matters concerning Latin America and, of course, Cuba. Even local politics, some felt, should have their seal of approval. When Donna Shalala, a Clinton cabinet member, was appointed president of the University of Miami, two Republican state legislators voiced their ire and raised the possibility of withholding funds to the university. State Representative Mario Díaz-Balart, Lincoln's brother, in an overheated conversation with a university board member on a flight to Miami, repeatedly called Sha- lala's appointment "offensive." His colleague State Representative Carlos La- casa said he was "ready to reevaluate UM's claim on state dollars."

Mario Díaz-Balart was more successful with Miami's other institution of higher learning, Florida International University. In 2001, he convinced a colleague in the Florida legislature to propose funding a new law school building at FIU that would be named after his grandfather, Rafael Díaz- Balart, a name shared by both his father and his brother. The decision was not a popular one at the university, which is home to the esteemed Cuban Re- search Institute. Rafael Díaz-Balart had been the lead lawyer of the United Fruit Company and later served as a cabinet minister for Batista, both associ- ated with human rights abuses. Moreover, he had never had a license to prac- tice law in Florida and had never lived in the state for any period of time, preferring to settle down in Madrid after Castro seized power. "Why don't they just call it the Fulgencio Batista Law School?" quipped columnist Max Castro. Raúl Martínez, Hialeah's Mayor, shook his head in consternation about the proposal. "We call that *una falta de respeto*," he said—a lack of re- spect.

In appreciation for the exiles' loyalty, the Bush administration rewarded Cuban-Americans with several choice jobs, including their first cabinet posi- tion. Mel Martínez, the Orlando Republican who hosted Elián's trip to Dis- ney World, got the nod as Bush's Housing Secretary. More locally, the U.S. Attorney in South Florida, Guy Lewis, a highly regarded prosecutor, was asked to step down in favor of Marcos Jiménez, a partner in the Miami branch of the law firm White & Case who worked on the GOP legal team that represented Bush in the 2000 recount battle. Jiménez's brother Frank, Jeb Bush's deputy chief of staff, was also promoted in June 2002: he was awarded the number two slot—under Martínez—in the Department of Hous- ing and Urban Development. Jiménez had been attacked by Democrats for having taken a leave from his job as counsel to Governor Jeb Bush to assist George W. Bush's campaign during the recount. Jiménez defended his pres- ence at a Thanksgiving dinner with Jeb Bush—claiming that neither he nor the governor discussed politics.

But it was in foreign policy that the exile leadership made its strongest imprint. While Democrats, moderates and free trade Republicans assumed that Bush's dicey victory would force him to govern from the middle, quite the opposite proved to be the case. As the new President began to announce his appointments, it quickly became apparent that Iran-Contra Cold War- riors were being brought back into service in droves. Miami wags cracked that the administration was staging "Iran-Contra: The Sequel," as a cattle call of Iran-Contra principal and bit players was summoned for a reprise. A conscious decision seemed to have been made to rehabilitate the old warhorses and, implicitly, the role of Bush Sr. in the scandal that almost torpedoed his career.

The appointment of Elliott Abrams to the National Security Council generated more criticism. Abrams, the Assistant Secretary of State for Latin American Affairs under Reagan, had been convicted on two counts of lying to Congress for his dealings in Iran-Contra. He had also been accused of indifference to the human rights violations of both the Contras and the Salvadoran right-wing death squads. Abrams was well remembered for his testimony before Congress, when he famously snarled: "I never said I had no idea about most of the things you said I had no idea about." Owing to his conviction (he was later pardoned by the elder Bush), a job was found that did not require congressional confirmation: senior director for democracy, human rights and international operations on the National Security Council. Referring to Abrams as "the pit bull for the administration's 'better dead than red' policy on Central America," the *Washington Post*'s Mary McGrory savaged the appointment as an act of remarkable political cynicism.

One of Abrams's Iran-Contra colleagues, John D. Negroponte, was appointed U.S. ambassador to the United Nations. Although a capable career diplomat, Negroponte had been tarnished by his tenure as ambassador to Honduras in the 1980s, when Honduras was used as a staging ground for Contra operations. While posted to Honduras, Negroponte had worked closely with the military government, which had been implicated in the murder and disappearance of dozens of political opponents. Human rights groups suggested that he was knowledgeable of and possibly complicit with the military's activities. Negroponte benefited from the chaos in the wake of the World Trade Center attacks, when Republicans pushed forward his nomination as a "high priority."

Other reprises included the appointment of Richard Armitage as Deputy Secretary of State, which quietly passed through the Senate on a voice vote. Armitage had served as Assistant Secretary of Defense for International Security Affairs in the Reagan years. His nomination for a post in the first Bush administration had been withdrawn before hearings because of controversy over Iran-Contra. Bush Sr.'s confidant Donald Gregg, who had worked with Félix Rodríguez, was also called back as an adviser to the President. Filling out the phalanx of hard-liners on Cuba were exile Roger Noriega, a longtime aide to Jesse Helms, who was named ambassador to the

Organization of American States; Emilio González, an exile army colonel from Miami, who was appointed to head the Cuba Desk at the White House's National Security Council; and José Cárdenas, who ran the Cuban American National Foundation office in D.C. for many years and became the top Republican staffer for the State Department's Western Hemisphere Affairs office.

In February 2002, another Iran-Contra player reemerged. Retired Admiral John M. Poindexter, who was convicted with Oliver North but whose conviction was later reversed on appeal, was quietly appointed by President Bush the chief of the new Information Awareness Office, in which he will monitor e-mail traffic for "terrorist messages." In the Reagan administration, Poindexter was both the President's National Security Adviser and the point man charged with financing the clandestine Contra operation.

AS THE ADMINISTRATION of George W. Bush has stockpiled Cuba hard-liners, the country has drifted in the opposite direction. Since the mid-1990s an unusual coalition has made considerable strides in reframing U.S.-Cuba policy. The group is made up of farmers from the Midwest, leading members in the U.S. Chamber of Commerce, assorted tycoons and a plethora of free traders, all of whom have only two things in common: they are all Republicans and they all are anxious to resume trade with Cuba. In concert with the traditional liberal anti-Embargo faction, they have become a force that cannot be ignored. In 2000 and 2001, the Republican-controlled House of Representatives passed bills to open up travel to Cuba, allow limited trade, and authorize medicine and food supplies, while voting to cut off funding for the Treasury Department to prosecute those who travel to Cuba illegally.

Republicans like Henry Kissinger and William Rogers have argued for some time that it is very much in America's interest to prepare a "soft landing" for a post-Castro Cuba. After all, as Rogers has noted, much of the Eastern bloc and Russia crumbled into chaos and gangsterism after the fall of communism. Should the Mafia return to Cuba, the U.S. would face immeasurable risks. Should Cuba become complicit with the *narcogobiernos* of Latin America to supply the drug lust of Americans, the U.S. would find the drug war even closer to home.

Yet despite these warnings and despite the evolution of key elements within his own party, George W. Bush has not been particularly interested in thinking long-term on Cuba. The focus of Bush's Cuba policy appears not to be just domestic policy but Florida Republican politics. In the summer of 2001, I asked one senior Bush official what the administration's agenda was toward Cuba. "Our number one priority is to do nothing that could adversely effect the re-election of Jeb Bush as Governor of Florida," he responded with unabashed candor. "It's a tactical situation. We will react when necessary but we intend to stay fairly passive in terms of changing policy. We will read the political tea leaves and we will look at the politics more than anything else." Evidently, those tea leaves have suggested a progressively more bellicose and defiant stand. "Nobody's saying that if we have a Republican administration in Washington, the Marines are going to be storming the ports of Cuba tomorrow," said Ileana Ros-Lehtinen after the election was settled by the U.S. Supreme Court, seeking to put a lid on expectations. She proceeded to accurately forecast the new hard line on U.S.-Cuba policy: tougher restrictions on American business travel and fewer contacts between Americans and Cubans, to turn back the tide of what she called "a trickling, weakening of the U.S. Embargo day by day" during the Clinton years.

The administration has kept the anti-Cuba rhetoric steamy and has backed it up with some action. Bowing to U.S. pressure, in 2002 Russia finally agreed to shut down Lourdes, its listening post in Cuba since 1964. "This decision is another indication that the Cold War is over," Bush said when Russia's decision was made public. The facility, which housed 1,500 Russian military personnel and their families, cost the Russians some $200 million annually in rent, a valued source of income for the Cuban government. A year earlier, the U.S. House of Representatives had passed a bill that sought to prevent the United States from rescheduling hundreds of millions of dollars in Russian debt unless Moscow closed the surveillance station. Lourdes provided Havana with an estimated 75 percent of its intelligence. Its loss was a humiliating blow to Castro.

The administration has acceded to hard-liners' demands that Cuba remain on the State Department list of countries supporting terrorists, although there is scant to nil evidence to back up their claim. At the same time, countries such as Saudi Arabia and Pakistan, which have had direct links to terrorist attacks on Americans, receive favored treatment. However, in one or two areas Bush has offered some modest concessions. In response to the devastation wreaked upon Cuba by Hurricane Michelle in November 2001—as well as to the vigorous lobbying of Archer Daniels Midland—the Bush team permitted a deal that finally took a small bite out of the Embargo. In a carefully calibrated negotiation, Cuba was given the green light to purchase $35 million of food products, the bulk of it from ADM and Cargill, its agribusiness rival. Free trade boosters had prevailed—allowing the Cuban government to purchase goods directly from the United States for the first time since 1962.

Ironically, the only issue upon which all sides of the Cuba debate—right, left and center—agree is that the U.S. Embargo has failed miserably to meet its stated goals. In forty-two years, the Embargo has not brought democracy, elections or free markets to Cuba—nor has it toppled Fidel Castro. The argument that the U.S. cannot engage a communist or totalitarian regime has crumbled, as trade with China, Vietnam and even North Korea has ballooned with each passing year. Even some of the most hardcore Cuban hawks have begun to mumble their doubts. "The Embargo makes Castro a kind of countercultural celebrity," said Mark Falcoff, a supporter of Reagan's Latin American policies. "If the Embargo didn't exist and the U.S. people were free to travel to Cuba . . . it would shrink Castro to being someone's sidekick." Joaquín Roy of the University of Miami said that he has been told by members of Castro's inner circle that they see the Embargo as "a gift from heaven," an all-purpose scapegoat to which Castro can reasonably ascribe all his country's woes. A 2001 poll concluded that three out of four exiles admitted that the Embargo has been a failure.

Free traders have long argued that the Embargo costs U.S. businesses billions of dollars a year and point out that a majority of Cuban-Americans are now in favor of lifting it. They also note that scores of countries around the globe, including such U.S. allies as Canada, England, France and even Israel, now trade with and invest in Cuba. One recent study concluded that American farmers alone lose an estimated $1.24 billion annually because of sanctions against Cuba. The study prompted two former U.S. Secretaries of Agriculture, John Block, who served under Reagan, and Dan Glickman, one of Clinton's most able cabinet members, to write to President Bush. "Current U.S. policy has not given relief to the Cuban people," they wrote. "And now it's just as clear: Our policy is also harming American farmers during these tough economic times. Mr. President, the sooner we lift this failed Embargo, the better." But while Bush appears to be a sincere free trader, his chief political adviser, Karl Rove, has urged him to fully accommodate exile hard-liners in return for electoral victories for both his brother and himself.

IN JULY 2001, the Cuban American National Foundation was pitched into a meltdown. On the eve of CANF's annual meeting retreat, several of its most prominent board members announced that they would not be attending. Three weeks later, a press conference was held at the Biltmore Hotel in Coral Gables in which eighteen longtime members announced they were resigning in protest over CANF's new policies. Only a few days earlier, Ninoska Pérez-Castellón and her husband, Roberto Martín Pérez, had also stepped down, bringing the number of resignees to 20 of its 150 directors.

While few were known outside the exile world, Ninoska was famous all over Miami for her fiery and sometimes hilarious radio shows. The star of *Ninoska a la Una,* she also headed up *La Voz,* the Foundation radio show that was beamed into Cuba. Stoking her fury was the fact that CANF had decided to cancel *La Voz,* claiming that it was not cost-effective and that Radio Martí made it redundant. To her fans, Ninoska was akin to La Pasionara, the fearless broadcaster of the Spanish Civil War. To her critics, she was Madame Defarge—the epitome of exile intolerance and stridency. "Since the son took the reins of the Foundation, it has been going down," board member Tony Llamas, who was among the first to resign, told the *Herald.* "There has been a huge discontent and, little by little, some of us have jumped ship. We are all dispensable, but not Ninoska."

The group's various factions were quick to hurl blame at one another, but CANF's problems actually began with the death of Jorge Mas Canosa, when the exile lobby entered into a protracted and tortured midlife crisis. The decision of Mas Canosa's son and successor, Jorge Mas Santos, to bet the house on Elián had not helped the organization. A businessman, Mas Santos approached CANF as a CEO would a new company. But there was nothing businesslike about exile politics. And, for better and for worse, Mas Santos was not his father.

For one thing, he saw more clearly than his father that CANF had positioned itself too far to the right—and he understood that with each passing year, there was less and less public and political support for its hard-line policies. Among his moves to modernize and moderate CANF was his decision to hire Dennis Hays, who had run the Cuba Desk at the State Department under Clinton, to be its executive vice president and chief lobbyist. Hays had won exile kudos when he resigned over Clinton's decision to repatriate rafters to Cuba. Mas Santos also added his father's American-born protégé, Joe García, to the board as executive director.

The new team purchased a historic 1850s town house off Embassy Row for CANF's Washington headquarters. Seeking to undermine the legitimacy of the Cuban Interests Section, the office was named the Free Cuba Embassy. But the new building, like many of Mas Santos's well-intended initiatives, bore an inauspicious history: the town house had been the former residence of Theodore Roosevelt, the only American President to have participated in an invasion of Cuba. Still, Mas Santos was astute enough to see the shifting climate and grasp the danger of CANF's being left out. He began to temper CANF's policies—using more honey than vinegar with both critics and allies. But there was one insurmountable problem: he did not have his father's stature. No one was afraid of him.

The Foundation's old guard bristled at Mas Santos's efforts toward moderation and railed at his decision not to endorse Bush in the 2000 election. Other heresies included Mas Santos's proposal to increase outreach to island dissidents and support for financial and material aid to independent businesses in Cuba. The proverbial final straw was Mas Santos's decision to woo the Latin Grammys to Miami, after the county's ban on Cuban products and performers had been struck down. (A Supreme Court ruling that overturned a similar ban in Massachusetts against Burma opened the door for the Grammys to come to Miami.) Mas Santos's bold initiative delighted most of Miami, which recognized that the city could burnish its image by hosting the awards. Taking what many considered to be the high ground, Mas Santos argued that Miami must show itself as a tolerant, world-class city. Moderates, liberals and young Cuban-Americans rejoiced at the prospect of new concerts, theater, films and gallery shows featuring artists from Cuba, who had long performed in every other major city in the U.S. Businessmen cheered as they calculated the millions of dollars that would roll into Miami with such events.

But Miami simply was not ready. Chafing over the erosion of their power, CANF's old guard vowed to keep Cuban performers out of Miami-Dade by whatever means necessary. For months, they battled quietly behind the scenes in obeisance to Mas Canosa's cardinal rule of presenting a unified front. But their differences this time were irreconcilable. Hard-liners like Alberto Hernández, CANF's former chairman and Mas Canosa's doctor, and José Antonio Llamas, who was acquitted in 1999 of plotting to assassinate Castro, were among the first to walk away. "That's an insult to the Foundation and the ideals of the Foundation," thundered Mario Miranda, Mas Canosa's former bodyguard, who joined the defectors. Miranda went on to accuse Mas Santos of "rubbing elbows with the communists. I bet you [his father] is turning in his grave."

Around the same time, CANF's very name became contested territory. At the demand of the IRS, which ruled that CANF was a lobby, and therefore could not keep its nonprofit status, the group was forced to restructure. The Jorge Mas Canosa Freedom Foundation became the nonprofit arm's new name, while the lobbying arm retained the old name, CANF. But somehow, during the restructure, the group had allowed its title to its name to lapse. On May 3, 2001, Mario Miranda filed Florida articles of incorporation in the name of "The Cuban American National Foundation Inc.," using his home address. "One of Castro's agents in Miami could've gotten this name," he explained to the *Herald*, "and tomorrow when we woke up we could've seen, Come fly with the Cuban American National Foundation to Cuba." (Miranda is being sued by the Foundation for trademark infringement and other matters.)

Through much of the summer of 2001, CANF's civil war was fodder for a spectacular food fight waged over Spanish language radio and chronicled in the Miami media. By the end of the year, two new exile groups had sprouted out of the detritus of CANF. One, headed by former CANF hard-liners, called itself the Cuban Liberty Council, and another more moderate, pragmatic organization, the Cuba Study Group, was created by businessmen Carlos Saladrigas and Carlos de la Cruz. "It couldn't have happened to a nicer crowd," quipped the Foundation's longtime critic Bernardo Benes.

There was further humiliation to come. In August, Grammys chief Michael Greene came to the conclusion that despite the assurances of Penelas and Mas Santos, there was a high probability of violence from militants if the Latin Grammy Awards were held in Miami. Joe Carollo had backed the demand of hard-liners to protest the presence of Cuban performers directly in front of the arena, a county facility, and not farther away, as had been agreed. When Greene learned that certain groups had bought hundreds of seats in the arena to stage a protest during the show, he pulled the plug eleven days before the event and returned the televised awards show to Los Angeles. Although the Latin Grammys were ultimately canceled because of the terrorist attacks on September 11, the loss of the show from Miami was a bitter setback for Mas Santos, as well as for moderate and liberal exiles.

At the same time, Mas Santos was under siege in his role as CEO of MasTec. Its stock price fell precipitously by year's end, from a combined assault of lawsuits and faulty business decisions. The year culminated with a snub by Jeb Bush, who pointedly left Mas Santos off his guest list for a dinner honoring visiting Mexican President Vicente Fox in Miami and for his brother's speech in Miami on May 20, 2002, marking Cuba's independence. "Jeb hates Jorge Jr.," said one insider. "After Jorge took Joe Lieberman over to his father's grave, after their meeting at CANF—with TV cameras—that was it!"

The clear winner to emerge from the wreckage of the swirling internecine feuding was Lincoln Díaz-Balart. The forty-eight-year-old Miami Congressman would step into the power vacuum left by Mas Canosa's passing and become the Bush administration's point man on Cuba, Miami and exile issues. A dependable and loyal partisan who proved his fealty during the election, Díaz-Balart saw his standing enhanced by the new administration's disillusionment with CANF. "Don't forget that the old Jorge Mas betrayed George Bush in 1992 with Clinton—and then Jorge Mas Santos betrayed Bush Jr.," said a key player in the Republican exile firmament. Indeed, the Bush family and exile hard-liners share a common philosophy on betrayal and loyalty. The fact that the Foundation had reached out to Clinton in 1992 to secure passage of the Torricelli bill was perceived as backstabbing in the Bush camp. In 2000, the Foundation's stock plummeted further when its leaders met with their longtime ally, vice presidential candidate Joe Lieberman, in Miami and declined to endorse either presidential candidate. The Bush camp viewed this neutrality as yet another betrayal. "The Bushes run their organization like a cult," said critic Raúl Martínez with a degree of awe and envy.

The ascension of Lincoln Díaz-Balart, whose family had been interlinked with Castro's for five decades, infused U.S.-Cuba policy with a fevered emotionality. Díaz-Balart has demanded a militant, hard-line policy on Cuba and a free hand in Miami. Like Jeb Bush, Díaz-Balart comes from a multigenerational political family. And as with the Bush sons, the expectations for Lincoln and his three brothers were high. One brother, José, is a newscaster with Telemundo; another is a Miami businessman. Lincoln's younger brother, State Senator Mario Díaz-Balart, is the chairman of the Republican House redistricting committee and has his own national ambitions. In 2002, Mario proposed a redistricting of Miami and other cities to ensure a predominantly exile congressional district. Then he announced his candidacy for the district's seat. Democrats have challenged the new district in court, with State Representative Corrine Brown charging that "the only factor they used is whether Mario could have a district." Not since 1959, when their father and grandfather were ministers in the cabinet of Batista, have the Díaz-Balarts wielded so much power. "Maybe I will not see Cuba free from Castro," said Rafael Díaz-Balart, who closely mentors his sons, "but my boys will. That is for sure."

Lincoln Díaz-Balart's career has been marred by his penchant for intemperate remarks. At an April 2001 press conference with Ileana Ros-Lehtinen and Robert Menéndez of New Jersey, he unleashed some singularly undiplomatic salvos. Speaking of his colleagues who favored relaxing the Embargo, he said, "There is another group of cretins and imbeciles in Congress," adding that "when these cretin congressmen go over there [to Cuba]," they should be asked to support him and his two Cuban-American colleagues "who struggle day by day to stop American businessmen from profiting with the apartheid economy in Cuba." The press conference was covered by Radio Martí live from Díaz-Balart's office. The station had preempted its regular programming to do so, prompting criticism that Díaz-Balart was misusing the taxpayer-funded station for his own political benefit.

In 2001, the Federal Elections Commission concluded that Díaz-Balart and his staff had collected $40,000 in unreported contributions and $114,000 in unaccounted funds during his 2000 campaign. The congressman was ordered to pay a $35,000 fine. Such a reprimand might have been fatal for any other member of Congress, but in Miami it was dismissed as politics as usual. If anyone in the Bush administration was dismayed, they certainly did not let on. As the White House looked ahead to the 2002 and 2004 elections, there was no telling how much it would need Díaz-Balart and his troops again. Word seeped through the Beltway—whatever Lincoln wants, Lincoln gets.

The night before George W. Bush's first visit with the President of Mexico, Díaz-Balart flew to the White House to brief him. Condoleezza Rice, Bush's National Security Adviser, also met with Díaz-Balart for more than an hour, and he is in frequent contact with Bush's key adviser, Karl Rove. Díaz-Balart's policy is simple: no ties to Cuba without the release of all political prisoners, free elections and the free expression of ideas. His detractors relish pointing out that the last two of these have had a less than auspicious history in Miami.

All Cuba-related appointments and matters are run by Díaz-Balart, including all business relating to Radio and Televisión Martí. Despite a series of scandals and unprecedentedly dismal ratings—dropping to an all-time low of 7 percent listenership in Cuba—Díaz-Balart had steadfastly backed Radio Martí's director, Hermenio San Román. Recognizing that San Román's leadership was blighting the prospects of the station, other exile leaders urged the congressman to find another director. CANF proposed its own candidate, attorney Alberto Mora. Finally, at the request of his father, Rafael, Díaz-Balart met with Salvador Lew. Eventually he signed off on Lew and President Bush dutifully announced his appointment.

The Cuban-born congressman had always had the ear of Jeb Bush. With his backing, Díaz-Balart and his colleague Ileana Ros-Lehtinen lobbied for and won the release from U.S. prisons of several convicted exile terrorists.

Among the most notorious were José Dionisio Suárez and Virgilio Paz Romero, both convicted for their roles in the 1976 assassination of Chilean diplomat Orlando Letelier and his American assistant Ronnie Moffitt with a car bomb in Washington, D.C. The paramilitary zealot Hector Cornillot, convicted of several bombings and murders, also walked out of jail just weeks before the September 11 attacks. A U.S. Supreme Court ruling in June 2001 found that indefinite detention of alien felons who have served prison time and are liable for deportation, but for whom no country can be found, is unconstitutional. The unstated exception is Cuba, owing to the arguments of militant exiles that their terrorists are patriots. Whereas child molesters are often prevented from leaving prison even after their terms expire, this group of convicted killers won early release. John Ashcroft's Justice Department acceded to the requests and the men resettled in the Miami area. Also on Díaz-Balart's list for release are terrorist-patriots such as Valentín Hernández, who murdered Dialogue supporter Luciano Nieves, and Eduardo Arocena, the Omega-7 bomber.

The timing of the releases proved unfortunate, coming only weeks before the attacks on the World Trade Center. A double standard on terrorism was quickly apparent: while the Justice Department announced a sweep of those "suspected" of terrorism—all Arab Muslims—it was quietly releasing men who were actually convicted of terrorism—all Cuban. But the administration correctly gambled that few Americans were paying attention to the releases of a few convicted murderers. Certainly, the mainstream press accorded them scant attention. Indeed, throughout 2001 Miami Spanish language radio continued to broadcast fund-raisers for several convicted terrorists, identifying them only as freedom fighters and patriots.

Díaz-Balart's greatest triumph has been the improbable appointment of Otto Reich as Assistant Secretary of State for Western Hemisphere Affairs, the top Latin American slot at the State Department. Reich, an anti-Castro activist and lobbyist for Bacardi Rum, guided the legislation that in 1998 stripped Cuba of trademark protection for its Havana Club rum.

Reich was among George W. Bush's most controversial nominees. Immediately, Oscar Arias, Panama's Nobel Peace Prize–winning former President, asked the administration to withdraw the nomination. Senate Foreign Relations Committee chairman Joseph Biden refused to hold a hearing on the nomination when Reich declined to submit some of the documentation that had been requested. Some Republicans on the committee privately said they would vote against him. Nor was Reich the choice of Secretary of State Colin Powell, who was reported to have voiced his reservations. For months, rumors spread that the administration would not risk losing a confirmation battle. Nonetheless, in September 2001 Reich's bruised nomination was submitted. Senator Christopher Dodd, a senior Democrat on the Foreign Relations Committee, invoked his privilege to block the nomination, putting a hold on it.

The *Wall Street Journal* responded with three withering editorials attacking Dodd and his staff, omitting to mention that Jesse Helms, the former chairman of the committee, had done the same sort of thing many times. The Reich flap became especially contentious in October, around the time of the twenty-fifth anniversary of the 1976 Cubana bombing. In his written replies to queries from the Foreign Relations Committee, Reich refused to condemn Bosch. To the question "Do you consider Orlando Bosch to be a terrorist?" Reich wrote: "I do not have sufficient knowledge of Mr. Bosch's criminal activities or record of convictions to pass judgment on his legal status." Perhaps realizing that such an evasive comment played poorly in the aftermath of September 11, Reich struggled to summon some commitment in a subsequent response: "I do consider that persons who blow up a civilian aircraft are committing an act of terrorism."

In late December, the administration leaked that it was thinking seriously of giving Reich a one-year recess appointment, thus circumventing the need for Congress to approve him. One Republican, Senator Mike Enzi of Wyoming, released a letter he wrote to Bush arguing against a recess appointment, stating that Reich could not depend upon the support of the Senate. Díaz-Balart seethed over the delay, according to one of his confidants, and raged at the resistance met by his most coveted nominee. Through Jeb Bush and the President's adviser Karl Rove, he underscored how he would not retreat from Reich, even if a recess appointment were required. In January 2002, he got his way—Reich joined Bush's foreign policy team. Reich's deputy, Lino Gutiérrez, also a Cuban exile, shares his philosophy.

EXILE HARD-LINERS HAVE set their sights on the Florida Governor's race in November 2002, hoping for a showdown between Janet Reno and Jeb Bush. In 1994, Jeb narrowly lost Florida's governorship, which derailed his long-term plans. It had been his intention to use the State House for a presidential bid in 2000—a dream he had to pass on to his older brother. Bush went on to handily win the Governor's race in 1998. Republicans have been rubbing their hands in excitement at the prospect of a Bush-Reno contest and boast that it would be a cakewalk for the President's younger brother.

They point to exiles as being the decisive factor—but not everyone agrees. "The Cubans did in 2000 what they always have done: they showed up and voted Republican," said Mark Seibel, who supervised the *Herald*'s investigation into the election. "If anyone deserves credit for the close election it is the blacks who voted for Gore 50 percent more than they did for Clinton. And if they come out like that for Janet Reno in 2002, Jeb Bush could well have a problem."

Long before the 2000 presidential election, Bush's tenure as Governor had been controversial even by the brawling standards of Florida. One generally acknowledged misstep was his "One Florida" initiative, which was heralded as "the end of affirmative action." Bush's executive order abolished racial set-asides and minority preferences in state university admissions. The initiative ignited the unremitting wrath of African-Americans, who derided the Governor, however unjustly, as racist.

Bush also aroused suspicions among Florida's well-organized environmental movement, which mistrusts his decade-long coziness with the state's developers. But as polls registered that environmental concerns were of keen interest to Floridians, Bush began to speak of his "green" side. In 2001, with his brother, the President, at his side, Jeb announced that he had added $58 million to the budget to clean up the Everglades. Next, he fought against his brother's plan to drill for oil off the coast of Florida, citing the need to protect the cash cow of the Sunshine State—its beaches. As Jeb's reelection campaign heated up, the two brothers held a press conference in the White House to announce the federal government's decision to buy back millions of dollars of oil leases for the state of Florida.

Jeb also found himself tangled and mangled by the Enron scandal. As Governor, he serves as one of three trustees of Florida's state pension plan and is responsible for its viability and safekeeping. Inexplicably, even after its precipitous drop in late 2001, the trustees continued purchasing Enron stock. When Enron finally belly-upped in 2002, Florida's state pensioners were out more than $340 million. And in the wake of Enron's collapse, Bush flew to Texas for a fund-raiser for himself hosted by Richard Kinder, a former president of Enron. There is also the pesky issue of his twenty-four-year-old daughter's drug and alcohol problems. For years, Noelle Bush was seen in Tallahassee and Miami nightspots plainly and sadly inebriated. Then on January 27, 2002, the very day of her uncle's State of the Union address, Noelle was arrested at a Tallahassee pharmacy for fraud, having falsely identified herself as a doctor while trying to obtain a prescription for tranquilizers.

The Bush campaign was further embarrassed in mid-June by the contents of a computer disk found in a park near the White House by a Democratic staffer. The disk's data, which analyzed the upcoming midterm elections, were compiled by the President's political guru, Karl Rove. Among the states judged to be vulnerable to a "possible D[emocratic] pickup" was Florida, prompting Jeb Bush to remark, "Anything can happen in Florida."

But whatever his liabilities, Jeb Bush possesses a seemingly insurmountable advantage: he is the President's brother, a President basking in high (albeit declining) poll numbers. Moreover, as the favorite of Florida's business class, he also has a multimillion-dollar war chest.

Jeb Bush, however, is not Janet Reno's only obstacle. She must first face a tough primary in September, when she squares off against several opponents, including a popular lawyer from Tampa named Bill McBride. Another impediment in Reno's path is a lawsuit filed by the family of Lázaro González charging her, Doris Meissner and Miami officials with using excessive force in the Elián raid. A judge dismissed much of the suit and dropped the city of Miami as defendants but ruled that Reno and Meissner could still stand trial. The decision was appealed and a ruling from the Eleventh Circuit is not expected until Labor Day—smack in the middle of the campaign.

Jeb Bush, on the other hand, continued to shore up his standing and poll numbers with exiles. In July he announced the nomination of Miami attorney Raoul Cantero III to Florida's Supreme Court. While Cantero, forty-one, has a pedigree that was appealing to certain hard-liners—he is the grandson of the dictator Fulgencio Batista and was a lawyer for both Orlando Bosch and Jorge Mas Canosa—he had no experience as a judge. He also served as Bosch's spokesman, calling him a "great Cuban patriot" on Miami radio.

On December 7, 2001, Floridians got an early taste of just how nasty the gubernatorial election is expected to be. Nine Cuban-American Republican state legislators marched out of the state's House of Representatives in a huff when Reno stopped by for a visit. "We decided that we needed to demonstrate, with absolute unity, that we did not welcome Ms. Reno to the House of Representatives," said Representative Carlos Lacasa, "when you consider the manner in which she treated Elián González." Reno used the protest to defend her handling of the case. She said it stemmed from her support for "family values," tweaking Republicans on a popular GOP theme. "I know they feel very strongly, but I made a decision based on what was right for a little boy and his daddy," Reno told reporters in a public gallery overlooking the House chamber. "And I stand by it," she said, one day after Elián González's eighth birthday. It was a refrain she would repeat throughout the campaign—as if the boy from Cárdenas had never left.

CHAPTER 12

THE OLD MAN AND THE LITTLE BOY

On a map of America when it was not yet called America in 1501,
Cuba appears twice. First as an island, then as a continent.

GUILLERMO CABRERA INFANTE

A T 4:40 P.M. ON JUNE 28, 2000, four and a half hours after the Supreme Court delivered its twenty-six-word order rejecting the petition of Lázaro González for an asylum hearing, Elián, his father and their entourage boarded a chartered jet at Washington's Dulles Airport. "I am extremely happy to be able to go back to my homeland," Juan Miguel told reporters, holding his son's hand in his. "I don't have words, really, to express what I feel." At Havana's José Martí Airport, the family arrived to a nationally televised hero's welcome of hundreds of cheering and flag-waving children chanting "Elián! Elián! Eliancito!"

Juan Miguel carried his son in his arms as they deplaned. Waiting for them on the tarmac were Elián's grandparents and great-grandmother. His paternal grandfather scooped him up as his schoolmates sang the Cuban national anthem on cue. Elián seemed subdued, smiling and waving at his friends. With his finely honed Madison Avenue instincts, Fidel Castro had decided not to greet the family at the airport. He had won—and won big—and there was no need to gloat.

Instead, the family was met by Ricardo Alarcón, the President of the National Assembly, who had been the Cuban official deputized to secure the boy's return. There were no speeches, no grandstanding, and after a ten-minute photo op, the family was whisked away. But as the government-controlled television cameras panned the family's cars leaving the airport, the voice of Elpidio Valdés, Elián's favorite cartoon creation, took over the broadcaster's narration: "Welcome, Eliancito," he chirped. "Now we have to win the battle against the Cuban Adjustment Act, the Blockade and the Foundation!"

Castro had, of course, every reason to believe that Juan Miguel González would return to Cuba. His immediate family were committed revolutionaries and Juan Miguel had never sought an exit visa. Leaving nothing to chance, Castro had met with the young father to take his measure not long after Elián was rescued off the Florida coast. The meeting went brilliantly and Juan Miguel, duly smitten, took to calling Castro "Jefe." Juan Miguel would also grow close to Ricardo Alarcón and his aide Miguel Alvarez.

As the dust began to settle on this surreal melodrama that had riveted viewers for seven months, the winners and losers were readily apparent. At the top of the winners list was Fidel Castro. The Maximum Leader would have been hard pressed to conjure up an outcome more satisfying to himself. For more than half a year, he had reveled in his most coveted role, the underdog guerrilla fighter squaring off against the merciless American imperialists.

Indeed, Castro could not have had a better summer. Elián González was back home, safely cocooned in the bosom of his family, just in time for the 26th of July, the national holiday commemorating the anniversary of the Revolution—this year would be the forty-first. Castro felt so festive that he donned an Italian suit for an event at Havana's Palacio de los Convenciones. Tall, svelte, barbered and manicured, his starched shirt set off by an uncharacteristically chic tie, he appeared at the event looking as dapper as an Argentine diplomat.

When an aide motioned him to a microphone, Castro mimed surprise, as if shocked that he would be asked to speak. Gesticulating like a ham silent film actor, he began his speech in a hoarse whisper, his eyes closing at moments in self-mesmerization. An hour passed—as he traversed the usual litany of achievements and complaints. His voice climbed louder, his expressive hands kneading the air. Another hour passed. His voice rose to a thundering crescendo and then it was full-tilt boogie. He had performed the rhetorical version of Ravel's *Bolero*. Still, the speech was mercifully short at only two hours. Castro had another event to attend, a concert at the Carlos Marx Theater, where his guest of honor was Juan Miguel González.

I had tailed the Maximum Leader for most of the day. He had been on his feet and on camera from 8:00 A.M. until midnight, assaulting the day with the energy of an adolescent as his aides and retinue wilted around him. The morning had begun with Castro leading one million Cubans down the Malecón, the five-mile coastal boulevard of Havana, in a seamless human ribbon. It was the largest march in Cuban history, and even the most jaundiced observers were surprised by the turnout. "It was quite impressive," said a veteran State Department hand in Havana. "You figure the CDRs [Committees for the Defense of the Revolution] got out around half a million people. But then the other half just showed up."

The march ended in front of the U.S. Interests Section. Castro's message was clear: we won. The protesters, waving their mini paper Cuban flags, marched past the new statue of José Martí clutching a young boy, hastily erected during the Elián crisis. Although officially designated as Martí's son, the sculpted boy's visage has an uncanny resemblance to Elián González. Martí's free arm is pointing accusingly straight ahead at the U.S. Interests Section, and anti-American epigrams from Simón Bolívar and Martí are engraved in the base of the statue. But *la bola en la calle*—the buzz on the streets—had another interpretation of Martí's gesture: *"Las visas están allí!"*—"Your visas are that way!"

Seeking to contrast himself with what he characterized as a ghoulish peepshow in Miami, Castro has, for the most part, kept the precocious boy out of view. He even waited two weeks before visiting Elián, upon whom he bestowed a copy of José Martí's verse and a large box of chocolates. Elián sightings were as rare as snow and even *Radio Bemba* (roughly Radio Big Mouth), Cuba's street gossip information system, had very little to murmur about. But it was clear to insiders that Castro was dazzled by the boy's intelligence, charm and outrageous destiny. Elián González, a child with preternatural self-confidence and a prime-time smile, has plainly come to fascinate Castro.

During the summer of 2000, Elián and his extended family went on a two-month government-sponsored vacation. At one point, I ran into them at the Du Pont Mansion, dubbed Xanadu by its former owners, a venerable old estate, now a museum and restaurant, in Varadero, Cuba's tourism mecca. Elián and his pals scuttled through the grand rooms, then stayed for dinner. At times, the González clan would meet up with Castro as they did in Santa Clara for his 26th of July speech (26th of July festivities tend to run a full week). The two entourages—Castro's and Elián's—settled in together at a grouping of private guest cottages on the outskirts of town sealed off by military security.

Under a searing early morning sun, Castro gave a relatively short prepared speech in front of the immense Che Guevara memorial in Santa Clara. At one point, a small Cuban flag flew off the podium—and he bent over to scoop it up, joking that if he did not pick up the flag, there would be reports of his failing health and imminent demise in a matter of minutes on the wire services. Standing in the front row were his brother Raúl and Raúl's estranged wife, Vilma Espín, the key players in Castro's inner circle and the military brass. Following the VIPs as they streamed out after the speech was Jerry Brown, the Mayor of Oakland and former California Governor, looking as if he had just swallowed the canary. Behind him was Philip Agee, the CIA agent turned whistle-blower who now lives in Havana running a travel agency called Cubalinda. A small, courtly man, Agee was wearing a Panama hat and khaki suit, as if scripted by Graham Greene.

Jerry Brown had been reveling in an extended visit with Castro, having come to the island to officiate Oakland's sister-cityhood with Santiago de Cuba. "We first had lunch in Havana and I mentioned that we both went to Jesuit high schools," said Brown. "He was talking a lot about how the Doctrine of Hell doesn't do anything for anybody. We were drinking *mojitos* after lunch and Castro said, 'Come out to Santa Clara. I'd like you to see the 26th of July rally and meet Elián and his father.' " Brown had driven to Santa Clara with the English-speaking Ricardo Alarcón. Upon his arrival at their guest quarters, he saw Elián playing outside with his cousin. At dinner that night, Brown met Juan Miguel González. "He was very quiet," he related. "He doesn't say much." The González clan opted to skip the rally, choosing to hang back at their lodgings, though they visited with Castro. No mention of their presence was noted in the press. "They came by and you know," said Brown, "Castro walks around and bestows *darshan* on everybody.

"Fidel's obsessed with Elián," Brown told me after the rally as the Castro entourage dispersed. "This kid is really destined to do some great stuff, that's all I can say. That's definitely the attitude and feeling on the part of Castro. We had a lot of conversation about Elián and what this meant in America and shifting public opinion against his Miami critics. It almost feels to him like Elián was providential. I think he's grooming him to be his successor."

Castro hit it off so splendidly with Brown that he offered to chauffeur him to the airport so that they would have a few more hours together. Then he dispatched aides to Brown's hotel to pack up his bags and rendezvous with him at the airport. Castro, Brown and a translator settled into the backseat of his Mercedes for the three-hour drive back to Havana, traveling as he always does in the middle car of a three-car Mercedes convoy, with two bodyguards in the front seat.

I HAD RETURNED TO Cuba for several reasons. One was to try to determine if there was any truth to the Miami family's insistent claim that Juan Miguel González was an abusive spouse and father. Months after Elián went home,

Sister Jeanne O'Laughlin had continued her attacks on the boy's father. Two producers of the Learning Channel reported that O'Laughlin's salutation, upon meeting them for an interview, was "Did you hear that they're still beating Elián?"

The family's allegations had been based primarily on the affidavit of a young exile named Orlando Rodríguez, who had fled from Cuba a year before Elián. I had always been interested in Rodríguez, as he had suffered unimaginable losses. His entire family—his mother, his father, two brothers and his sister-in-law—had all drowned when the boat carrying them and Elián flipped over in the Florida Straits. Rodríguez had left Cuba with his nineteen-year-old *marinovia* (live-in girlfriend), Carmita Brotón, who was the niece of Elián's mother.

Although the timing and purple prose of Orlando Rodríguez's affidavit struck many as transparently partisan, I knew that he had independently told an aunt in Miami the same story, which made me wonder if it might be true. Rodríguez claimed that Juan Miguel was a violent man and a wife batterer who had verbally abused Elián and beaten Elizabet Brotón so badly that she had gone to the hospital on one occasion. Spousal abuse is not entirely uncommon in Cuba, usually tied to alcohol abuse. Elián's great-uncles had been arrested several times for drunk driving. As alcoholism is a family disease, there was no reason not to believe that their nephew might also have a problem.

I had made repeated attempts to speak with Orlando and Carmita at their home and through relatives. But they declined to speak about the matter.

In Cárdenas, the Rodríguez home was still empty and locked up. I joined the neighbors on the stoop as they reminisced and grieved about the family. Six people from their block on Calle Spriu had died on Elián's boat. Lirka Guillermo's grandmother wobbled across the street to say hello—still heartsick over her loss. I asked her if she had been in touch with Lirka's mother, who had settled in Arizona. "No, no—what's the point?" she said. "I was her mother!" One neighbor reminded me how she knew "all the Gonzálezes—here and there," and how she didn't believe a word the Cuban government said. "*No tengo miedo*," she shrieked to the howls and giggles of her neighbors. "I am not afraid!"

A few blocks away, Lisbeth García, Elisa's old friend, was baby-sitting a relative. She said she was angry when she heard about Orlando's allegations. "I don't think he ever saw her but a few times in his life," she said. "Never in her life did she go to the hospital for an assault. And what bothers me most is that Carmita, Elisa's niece, allowed him to say that. She knows that it's a lie. I had a different impression of him when he lived here."

Lisbeth suggested that if I did not believe her, I could try to find Elizabet's half-sister, Carmen Brotón, who also works as a maid in Varadero. I found Carmen on her day off at her home on the outskirts of Cárdenas, one of its nicer and more commodious homes, with several bedrooms, a roomy kitchen with modern appliances and a terrace. Like most Cubans, she lives with her extended family—her common-law husband and her half-brother and his children.

As she greeted me, I was struck by her resemblance to her younger sister—the same dark, sad eyes, long shiny black hair, and broad forehead covered in bangs. But Carmen is larger and, in the tradition of Cuban women, stout below the waist. A soft-spoken woman of thirty-nine, she possessed an imposing reserve and dignity. She had been thrown into an impossibly complicated situation. Her beloved sister had drowned trying to flee the country and her only child's husband had filed the damning affidavit. Unquestionably, she had already paid a price for her son-in-law's treason. Her eyes moistened as she explained that she had yet to see Elián. "I am not yet ready," she explained. "He is my nephew but much more than a nephew."

Finally, I asked her about her son-in-law's affidavit. She looked down and said she had heard about it but not seen it. "I love Orlando like a son. He is a person *muy noble*," she began, "but there was no truth to it. Elisa was never in the hospital for such a thing. She never had any injuries. I knew nothing about there being problems of physical abuse and we were very close. My sister never said anything about that. So I was surprised and disappointed in my son-in-law, who is like a son to me. He wouldn't have said these things if he wasn't so far away from home and had not lost his family. He lost his mind. And his good sense."

She suggested that Rodríguez was under daunting pressure. "They have a deportable status," she said, explaining that her daughter and son-in-law, as she called Orlando, had yet to receive permission to stay in the U.S. Perhaps, she added, "some politicians" in Miami had offered their help in exchange for an affidavit. As she walked me to the door, she reminded me and my photographer that her daughter and Orlando had gone to the hospital to fetch Elián on the day he was rescued. "Carmita had *un argumento*—a fight—with Lázaro González in the hospital because she said that she felt that she should have Elián," said Carmen, "because she was closer to Elizabet. She's a blood relative of Elián, and Lázaro was more distant. But Lázaro got there first and wouldn't give him up." Carmen paused, then, choosing her words carefully, said, "I think that if Carmita had had custody of Elián, all this would have turned out very differently. Because she would have returned Elián to Cuba."

THE NEXT DAY, I visited Rosita Fernández, whose thoughts were not on Elián but on the other two survivors: her husband of ten years, Nivaldo, and his girlfriend, Arianne Horta. Almost a year later, Rosita, a small, exquisitely featured *mulata,* was still distraught, her voice barely audible. "About a month before they left, I found out he was seeing someone else," she said reticently and with evident wounded pride. "I kicked him out and he went to live with his father." Nevertheless, she assumed he would tire of his dalliance as he had before with others—so much so that she did not cancel plans for their tenth anniversary party.

She never heard from him again. Blistered with sunburn and delirious from dehydration, Nivaldo and Arianne had been rushed to the hospital after they came to shore. While in the hospital, Nivaldo had called his father in Cárdenas and said he wanted to speak with Rosita. If he did phone her, she was not at home and he never called again. Rosita said she had no plans of getting a divorce, grasping the little power left to her. "Only if I meet someone I want to marry," she said. She asked if I had a photograph of Arianne. "I hear she is very beautiful," she said quietly. Word would drift back a year later that the couple had split up, but that was cold comfort for Rosita.

I found Victor Herrera, Arianne's ex-husband, at his bartending job at the Hotel Internacional in Varadero. He was considerably more relaxed than at our first visit and had dropped his insistence that their daughter Estefany remain in Cuba. A friend of his confided that after the shipwreck, government security had pressured Herrera to demand Estefany's custody. We chatted about the thorny issue of race among Cubans. Herrera told me that he himself was part black, a fact, he said, that had caused him some problems with a few of Arianne's relatives, who referred to him as "El Negro." He hastened to add that neither Arianne nor her mother had a racist disposition, but ventured that Nivaldo would have a more difficult time in Miami.

In searing contrast to Elián González, Estefany, who was equally photogenic and irrepressible, received very little attention in Cuba and shared in none of the celebrity and perks awarded to Elián. In fact, it seemed that her presence prompted the sour memory of her mother's flight among the ruling apparatchiks in Cárdenas. At one point, Estefany's grandmother was told that the child had to be transferred to another school—ostensibly to keep Estefany separated from Elián at the Marcelo Salado School they both attended. The family was incensed at the decision and vowed to fight on until Estefany was allowed back in her classroom.

Before I left Cárdenas, I dropped by at Juan Miguel's house on Calle Cossio. There was no answer and the wrought iron gate in front was locked. I could hear *soneros* next door, where his parents and brother live, so I knocked there. After a few minutes, Juan Miguel's younger brother, Tony, came to the door. He was wearing shorts and was shirtless and I could see his girlfriend in the kitchen at the other end of the house.

Tony González, who is decidedly more easygoing than his brother, had only good news. He said he had given up his job as a security guard on the docks for a new one, driving a van for a photo company; he was able to keep the van at home. He took me to the garage to show off the spiffy new vehicle. He said his new job came not from the government, but through the connections of the husband of an NBC reporter working in Havana.

We chatted in the small box-size living room. Nothing had changed since I had been there six months earlier, except someone had put a photograph of Elián in the corner of the large portrait of Fidel hung on the wall. I was struck by Tony's lack of ill will toward his Miami relatives. He shared his father's philosophy that his great-uncles had been pressured into keeping Elián. Since his return, Tony said, they had not heard from any of them except Manuel, the sole relative in Miami to back them. Manuel had come for a two-week visit and had told the family that he was having a rough time in Miami, still ostracized by many of his siblings and his community. They had also been visited by Sam Ciancio, Donato Dalrymple's cousin, who had dived into the water and rescued Elián.

Juan Miguel had changed jobs—taking on the cashier duties at an Italian restaurant in Varadero. For some time, Juan Miguel has himself been a tourist attraction, with foreigners popping in to have their picture taken with him. When one of his friends asked him how he got any work done, Juan Miguel responded with revolutionary esprit that it did not bother him because "it brings so many people here," and thus is good for business and for Cuba, especially following the September 11 terrorist attacks, when tourism in Cuba plummeted. Juan Miguel bemoaned the lack of customers in April 2002—normally high season—to a visiting friend, pointing out that only five of fifteen tables were occupied that day. "My brother is very strong," Tony said. "He takes after our mother. He wants to have a normal life. He is concerned about too much attention on Elián and wants to create as normal an atmosphere as possible."

Yet despite his bid for the ordinary, no one will be surprised if Juan Miguel were to ease into a political career, representing Cárdenas, for instance, in the National Assembly. The Assembly is run by Ricardo Alarcón, who mentored Juan Miguel throughout his ordeal. "I think of him as my brother," Juan Miguel said during the Elián siege. The relationship has been a symbiotic one, with Alarcón's reputation further enhanced within the Borgia-like world of the Cuban Politburo. When I asked whether Juan Miguel would give up his day job for a spot in the National Assembly, the canny Alarcón answered with a smile, "He could do both. Why not?"

On December 6, 2000, Elián González celebrated his seventh birthday. The celebration was held in the courtyard of the Marcelo Salado School and all the children attended. Cake and ice cream were served—along with sandwiches. Among the VIP guests were the Reverend Joan Brown Campbell, Albert Fox of the Alliance for a Responsible Cuba Policy, an anti-Embargo group, and Fidel Castro. "Fidel knows how to talk to kids," said Campbell. "Then he went to the González house for lunch with the family. The other kids really do not act funny around Elián or treat him like he's Mr. Special," claimed Campbell, which strains credulity, as Elián is now almost as famous as Castro. To keep undesirables at bay, he is driven to and from school daily even though he lives within walking distance. Campbell said the family has told her that Elián often talks about his mother, Elizabet, with his grandmother Raquel. "He acknowledges that she died," she said. "Raquel keeps all the pictures of Elizabet out in her house. Elián always calls her 'my beautiful mama.' "

The boy wonder is hardly bashful around Castro, according to Campbell. "Fidel was joking around with the kids and he said, 'So, Elián, I hear you have a girlfriend? And you wrote her a letter.' Elián pipes up and says, 'I flushed it down the toilet, I don't love her anymore.' " When his stepmother was pregnant, Elián, with stunning aplomb, told visitors that they would be naming the new baby Elián II. He wasn't far off. The child was named Elianny.

Albert Fox was also struck by the brimming confidence of the seven-year-old, who didn't hesitate to upstage Castro. "The birthday party at Elián's school was like a school assembly with skits, et cetera. The program is over and they asked Elián to get up and speak. Everybody started chanting 'Elián, Elián,' but he wouldn't speak. And so Castro got up to speak. And while he was speaking, Elián walked right up to the microphone and started teasing his cousin. He didn't think twice about interrupting Fidel Castro, who was startled. All attention was focused on Elián, who nattered on to his cousin. Then Castro started to engage him in a conversation, but Elián ran to his seat. When Castro continued speaking, Elián's half-brother Hianny went walking up to him and got between Castro's legs, and everybody laughed. I don't know about him being a successor, but you can do the math—in fifteen years, in 2016, Fidel Castro will be ninety and Elián González will be twenty-two."

Elián González continued to stay largely out of view—with the exception of the occasional cameo guest appearance at ceremonies with his father and Fidel Castro, such as on May Day 2002. A few months earlier, Juan Miguel and his family were moved into a far grander and more spacious home in Cárdenas. Their one-story house on Calle Cossio had flooded during the ravages of Hurricane Michelle. Of course, so had the homes of thousands of others who did not get new lodgings.

Elián and his half-brother Hianny now have their own rooms. Their infant sibling with the peculiar hybrid of his brothers' names, Elianny, is staying close to his parents' bed for his first year but will also have his own room. Elián's teacher says her charge is an outstanding student of unusual intelligence and dazzling charm. He already has a host of ideas for a future career. "He wants to be a policeman, a TV artist or an astronaut," Juan Miguel González told Cuba's newspaper *Juventud Rebelde* (Rebel Youth). "I just tell him to keep studying and do his best."

Elián still keeps a framed photograph of his mother by his bed, and when asked about her by Joan Brown Campbell, he replied, "She's my friend." His father reports that his son rarely muses on or refers to his six-month stay in Miami, though he undoubtedly has his memories. "We don't talk about the past," Juan Miguel told a visitor.

In April, Campbell said she found Juan Miguel in a reflective mood. "He said he had been thinking about what had happened and who had really come to his aid," she recalled. "He said he wanted to contact Janet Reno and tell her how grateful he was to her. He said he wanted to invite her to come and visit him and the family." The celebrity dad had also extended an invitation to his former attorney Gregory Craig, with whom he has corresponded. The young father also feels deeply indebted to Cuba's ruler-for-life. "Fidel became a part of our family," Juan Miguel told a filmmaker with palpable emotion.

HAVANA IS EMERGING AS THE Casablanca of the Caribbean as tourists and foreign investment pour in from around the globe. Businessmen cradling cell phones are all over the city and, despite George W. Bush's harsher rhetoric and bolstered enforcement of travel penalties to Cuba, Americans arrive daily. There are now direct flights from Miami, JFK and Los Angeles for those with visas. In 2000, 176,000 Americans visited Cuba legally, while an estimated fifty thousand Americans went illegally—part of the estimated one million tourists who now visit the island annually. The most interesting statistic has it that since 1979, more than one million plane tickets have been sold for charters from Miami to Havana—mostly to exiles.

Ironically, a huge slice of Cuba's revenue, an estimated $1 billion annually, comes directly from the pockets of Miami exiles—presumably the very same who have demanded that Congress impose the Embargo on everyone else. Should travel to Cuba and cash remittances be eliminated at the demand of hard-liners, those most affected will be exiles, not American tourists. Exiles are Cuba's most cherished frequent fliers, bringing a steady source of dollars into the economy. Several times each day, charter flights leave Miami Airport packed with exiles, loaded to the gills with goods and cash for their families in Cuba. "I don't criticize them," says Juanita Castro, Fidel's younger sister. "They can do with their money and their lives whatever they want. But they talk garbage here—and then they go to Cuba and support the regime."

These days Cuba is awash in missionaries. Mostly Baptists and Methodists, they have fanned out from the western shores of Pinar del Río to Guantánamo, restoring and painting churches, conducting baptisms, weddings and funerals. Alarmed by the success of the Pope's 1998 visit, they have made Cuba a priority—not to save the country from communism, but, as one Pentecostal told me earnestly, "to save the Cubans from the Pope."

Since Fidel Castro's brief fainting spell during a speech in June of 2001, Miami, Havana and Washington have been triangulated by a cauldron of feverish speculation as to his succession. There are several scenarios for a post-Castro Cuba. Fidel Castro's designated successor is his seventy-year-old brother, Raúl. Many exiles scoff that he would not last a day in power. Others say there is a case to be made that the younger Castro, whose official roles include being First Vice President of Cuba, Minister of Defense and Second Secretary of the Cuban Communist Party, would survive the transition to power. Among his advantages is the fact that it is *his* army, the Revolutionary Armed Forces (FAR), that carries out much of the day-to-day business in Cuba—even running the farmers' markets and tourism through its company, Gaviota.

A coup is unlikely, as the Castro brothers have already assiduously weeded out any suspected dissident elements from the military and only Raúl Castro has been entrusted with the succession plan. In the event of a sudden illness or the death of Fidel Castro, according to a former key official, all members of his inner circle and the politburo have been instructed to report immediately to their homes and remain inside until contacted with further instructions from Raúl Castro. Should Raúl Castro decide to use brute force to maintain the status quo, he is well positioned to do so. In the wake of the Soviet pullout, resulting in the loss of Cuba's $5 billion annual subsidy, Raúl Castro has solidified and broadened his power base. He has retired many of the old *históricas*—hard-liners—in the FAR and replaced them with Communist Party members in their thirties, while shoring up the FAR's role as the central organ and decision maker of the government.

Nor does the younger Castro's clout stem solely from his military power base. Contrary to popular opinion, he has been an advocate within the government of freer markets and economic reforms. Clouding the looking glass for prognosticators are credible whispers that Raúl Castro is not particularly fired up to succeed his brother. Once a communist zealot, he has leavened his philosophy with pragmatism in the last decade and has told some visitors that he would prefer to spend his golden years with his grandchildren.

One possibility is a co-presidency of Ricardo Alarcón, now sixty-four, who *is* keen for the job, and Raúl Castro, who would do what he has always done—running things behind the scenes. Alarcón is a relative moderate who, unlike Fidel Castro, has long dreamed of an end to the Embargo. Other key players would certainly include Council of State Vice President Carlos Lage, forty-nine, Foreign Minister Felipe Pérez Roque, thirty-six, and Marcos Portal, forty-five, who is the Minister of Basic Industries and who comes with the additional bona fide of being married to Tania Fraga Castro, a niece of the Castro brothers. The only certainty is that the actuarial tables are finally stacked against Castro—and that sometime in the early part of the century, he will be gone.

Much depends, as has so often been the case in Cuba, on what the United States will do. As written, the Helms-Burton law precludes the U.S. from having relations with Cuba if either Castro is at the helm. A military intervention would be unlikely—notwithstanding the pleas of Miami's exile leadership—as it would precipitate international condemnation and its consequences. Exile writer Enrique Encinosa, who works at Radio Mambí, suggests that since George W. Bush's election, Castro is dancing as fast as he can to convince the U.S. that he is not a threat. "Castro's charm offensive is much more intense now," says Encinosa, who maintains that Castro remains a threat to the U.S. with regard to terrorism and narcotics. Part of that charm offensive was the appointment of General Jesús Bermúdez Cutino, head of the military's counterintelligence services, as director of the Center for Defense Information Studies soon after Bush's election. The general's mandate is to generate a favorable opinion of the FAR in the U.S. military establishment. He has done a good job and has drummed up some big-name converts.

On March 1, 2002, retired U.S. Army General Barry McCaffrey, Clinton's drug czar, had a twelve-hour chat with Fidel Castro and Raúl Castro and came away convinced that Cuba had friendly intentions toward the U.S. "They represent zero threat to the United States," he announced afterward. "Indeed, I see good evidence of the opposite. I strongly believe that Cuba is an island of resistance to drug traffic and . . . I don't believe they are harboring terrorist organizations," he said.

However, exiles such as Encinosa are heartened by the presence of Otto Reich and his old schoolmate Emilio González at the National Security Council and the ascension of Daniel Fisk, all three of whom are pitching Cuba as a dangerous rogue country. He says he is confident that the new Cuba team will influence the President to pursue Castro more aggressively, but adds, "That doesn't mean the administration will give them a free hand. They will push harder to limit trade and travel to Cuba and they'll tighten up more on human rights in Geneva." The hard-liners also have to contend with Congress's newly formed Cuba Working Group, twenty Republicans and twenty Democrats determined to open up U.S. markets and travel to Cuba.

Other Castro critics now feel that time is on their side. "For a long time, Castro didn't need us," says Dennis Hays, CANF's executive vice president, citing Cuba's significant losses in tourism and remittances in the wake of the September 11 terrorist attacks. "Now they do. They need our markets and credits and they're trying to emulate the Chinese economic model."

A few Cuba watchers have speculated that had the administration not been diverted by the war in Afghanistan and the increased tensions in the Middle East, a Bush-led military venture into Cuba—à la Panama and Grenada—was not out of the question. Since Reich and González have settled into the new roles, U.S. Cuba policy has become decidedly proactive. Newspapers around the globe questioned the depth of Reich's involvement in the failed coup against Venezuela's Hugo Chávez, a Castro ally. Reich was in contact with the coup planners before and after the event and prematurely cheered Chávez's demise. In early May, Under Secretary of State John Bolton told a conservative think tank that the administration believed Cuba was exporting deadly biochemical materials, and therefore the administration was placing the island-state on a "beyond the axis of evil" list, along with Syria and Libya. The announcement was met by general skepticism: State Department hard-liners were simply reviewing old data, countered the critics, the same data that previous administrations had deemed inconclusive, and interpreting it as they saw fit. The fact that Cuba has one of the most advanced biotechnology programs in the world was hardly news, and Bolton's claim that the program, which has won Cuba kudos for its vaccines and medical research, could also be used to do harm was also not news. Otto Reich insisted that the Bush team stood behind "every word" of Bolton's assertion, but the administration seemed to recognize that its Cuba hard-liners were straying too far off the reservation. Both Secretary of State Colin Powell and Defense Secretary Donald Rumsfeld pointedly declined to ratify Bolton's claims.

Some speculated that the administration was using Cuba as a pawn to leverage other countries in Latin America. "Demonizing Cuba will be even more useful in dealing with Venezuela, where the real issue is, and always will be, oil," reported Strategic Forecasting, a U.S. intelligence think tank, in May. "The Bush administration has learned that vague threats can be effective, especially at home, but that such threats also need a visible face. And who, after all, is more convenient—more usual—than Fidel Castro?" Others argued that the timing of the administration's announcement of its new "bogeyman" was strictly for domestic politics. "Governor Jeb Bush is running for reelection in Florida, and there is nothing like stoking the flames of anti-Castro sentiment in Dade County to secure the Cuban-American vote," opined a *Chicago Tribune* editorial. "And nothing like a new 'threat' to justify continued hostility toward Cuba."

But there was little doubt that Bolton's primary target was the imminent visit of former President Jimmy Carter to Cuba. However, the salvo badly misfired. While in Havana, Carter flatly disputed the veracity of the administration's claim, saying he had met with National Security Adviser Condoleezza Rice prior to his trip and she had made no reference to biological weapons. "If they had any evidence," observed Robert Pastor, who spearheaded the Carter trip, "they would have put it out."

The administration's decision to transport Al Qaeda terrorists halfway around the globe to the Guantánamo Naval Base in Cuba also raised a few eyebrows. Some of a conspiracist bent noted that this surreal relocation offers the military an excuse to beef up the base at Guantánamo. Equally telling, they pointed out, was the surprise decision by a Panamanian prosecutor to drop assassination charges against Luis Posada and his three cohorts, even though the case had previously been described as ironclad. The ruling came down within a month of Otto Reich's recess appointment to the State Department, bringing to mind Orlando Bosch's sudden reversal of fortune only weeks after Reich's arrival in Caracas in 1985.

The Bush administration remains split between the camp of Secretary of State Colin Powell, which would prefer setting the groundwork for an orderly transition after Castro's natural passing, backed by majorities in both houses of Congress who wish to end the Embargo, and the Reich camp, which enjoys the tacit support of Jeb Bush and Karl Rove and seeks to hasten Castro's demise through whatever means possible.

Otto Reich lost no time in reconfiguring the administration's Cuba team. Suspected moderates from the Cuba Desk at the State Department and CIA were promptly marginalized, with special attention paid to the U.S. Interests Section in Havana. Respected veterans such as Jeffrey De Laurentis were gently ushered out of Havana (their tenures had ended and they were not invited to stay, according to one former high-level State Department officer), while Vicki Huddleston, chief of the Interests Section, was transferred to Mali and was replaced by veteran Latin American hand James Cason. The new Interests Section replacements have been approved by Reich, who has instructed the office in Havana to shift its attentions away from migration issues, said a former State Department Cuba officer, "to focus on subversion of Castro's government."

Reich has always been mindful of the uses of media and of who may not be sympathetic toward him. Soon after a March 2002 editorial critical of U.S. policy ran in *La Jornada*, one of Mexico's leading newspapers, its State Department columnist was excluded from a Reich press conference and told the action was taken in response to the paper's "editorial line." The incident was reminiscent of Reich's actions when he ran the discredited Office of Public Diplomacy. In 1985, Reich informed Reuters, the veteran news service, that its reporters in Nicaragua were "communist sympathizers," according to one reporter who was cited, and requested that the reporters be replaced. After an internal review, Reuters determined that Reich's assertion was without merit.

On February 27, Radio Martí broadcast a comment by Mexico's Foreign Minister, Jorge Castañeda, that sparked rioting in Havana. Castañeda had responded to a question at a new cultural center in Miami about the Mexican embassy's role in Havana. Since its move to Miami, Radio Martí, a taxpayer-funded station, has abandoned its role as a neutral news organization and modeled itself after exile talk radio stations, serving as a bottomless fount of anti-Castro attacks. Numerous hosts and employees from Miami exile radio have been employed at the station, such as Armando Pérez-Roura, the controversial director of Radio Mambí, who seems to wield inordinate influence. "The doors of the embassy of Mexico in Havana are open to all Cuban citizens," said Castañeda, "in the same way that Mexico is open." Radio Martí rebroadcast Castañeda's comments out of context at least eight times throughout the day and night, generating a rumor that the Mexican embassy was open for those seeking to leave. Hours later, a crowd of Cuban asylum seekers hijacked a bus and smashed it into the gates of the Mexican embassy. About twenty Cubans demanded sanctuary in the embassy. The incident stirred memories of the 1980 onslaught on the Peruvian embassy in Havana—also sparked by a bus break-in—by thousands of asylum seekers, which led to the Mariel crisis, when 125,000 refugees arrived in the United States.

The Cuban government blamed the incident on Radio Martí, accusing the station of fomenting the embassy's occupation with a "gross provocation," while Mexico condemned the station for having "cynically manipulated" Castañeda's comments. Sally Grooms Cowal, president of the Cuba Policy Foundation, which advocates ending the Embargo, described Radio Martí as "running amok without any adult supervision." Martí's director, Salvador Lew, however, defended his station, pointing out that "we only broadcast exactly what Castañeda said. Not one word was changed." Seeking to avert another Mariel, Mexico asked the Cuban government to remove the twenty intruders, who, they said, did not have valid asylum claims. On February 28 at 4:30 A.M., Cuban security swooped inside the embassy and quickly removed the men. The State Department laid blame for the incident on Castro's repressive government, but privately, many around Colin Powell said they were aghast at how close they had come to a crisis.

Pérez-Roura exhorted exiles to express their outrage by boycotting Mexican products and demonstrating outside the Mexican consulate in Miami. Among the demonstrators, noted one FBI official, was José Dionisio Suárez, the convicted murderer of the former Chilean ambassador and his American aide, who had recently been released from prison at the behest of the exile leadership. "When we see someone like Suárez near a consulate," said the official, "boy, are we nervous."

But Pérez-Roura faced an unusual rebuff from two exile hard-liners, Ramón Saúl Sánchez and José Basulto, who rejected his calls for a boycott against Mexico. On his own radio program, Sánchez read a statement, which also ran in *El Nuevo Herald*, called "A Respectful Challenge to Armando

Pérez-Roura." Among other issues, Sánchez dared Pérez-Roura to leave his radio booth and sail to Cuba with a rifle to prove he was willing to put his life, not just the lives of others, on the line. "When I hear such lacerating expressions against Cubans, I realize how easy it is to sicken the souls of so many good people by distorting the truth," Sánchez wrote.

Notwithstanding the Bush administration's rhetorical salvos against Fidel Castro and sporadic local incidents of violence, the steamy climate in exile Miami has cooled by more than a few degrees. One telling sign was an anti-Embargo conference organized by prominent Cuban-Americans and held in Miami's Biltmore Hotel in March. Such a conference was previously unthinkable because of security concerns. The gathering attracted more than 250 exiles and an impressive array of speakers, including two U.S. congressmen and Alberto Coll, formerly of the Defense Department and currently dean of the Center for Naval Warfare Studies at the U.S. Naval War College. Representative Jeff Flake of Arizona, a conservative Republican and squeaky-clean Mormon, railed against the U.S. travel ban on Cuba: "There is no justification for imposing a Soviet-style bureaucracy on Americans who travel there, asking them where they are going, why they are going, who they will see, what their itinerary is, how much they will spend, et cetera. No American should be denied the right to see, firsthand, what a catastrophe socialism has wrought on that island." He also lambasted the loss of resources needed for the war on terrorism. "Our nation's top experts in antiterrorism are also in charge of hunting down travelers to Cuba," Flake said. "They are tracking down grandmothers from Iowa who are going on biking trips in Cuba."

In Cuba, the silent majority has also been speaking up louder. The fearless dissident leaders Elizardo Sánchez and Oswaldo Payá have launched the Varela Project, a five-point referendum seeking greater freedom. The grassroots project, named for Félix Varela, a nineteenth-century Catholic priest and independence activist, calls for a plebiscite on Cuba's future, as permitted by the existing Cuban constitution. By late April 2002, volunteers for the project had collected more than the ten thousand signatures needed for a plebiscite. Their timing, it would turn out, was divinely guided.

The centerpiece of Castro's recent charm offensive was an invitation to Jimmy Carter to visit Cuba; the invitation was extended by Castro himself at the beginning of the year. Ignoring the growls of the Otto Reich team and attempts by Ileana Ros-Lehtinen and Lincoln Díaz-Balart to block the visit, the Bush administration reluctantly granted approval. Weighing Carter's reputation as a humanitarian and peacemaker, the administration concluded that it was simply not worth expending the political capital needed to put the ki-bosh on the trip. After all, few suspected that the do-gooder peanut farmer from Georgia would cause much of a stir—there would be a few photo ops perhaps, the thinking went, and Carter's trip might even play into their hands. They could not have been more wrong.

Surprising his supporters as much as his detractors, Carter hit one out of the ballpark—upstaging the administration and forcing its Cuba players to scurry for cover and modify their policy. Among those greeting Carter and his entourage at the airport were pickets with placards reading, "President Carter—Tear Down This Wall!" But Carter's trip had an impact even before his jet touched down. On May 5, Vladimiro Roca, Cuba's most famous jailed dissident and a coauthor of the manifesto *The Homeland Belongs to Us All,* was released from prison after four and a half years. Carter not only met with Roca but huddled with the Varela Project's founders, Oswaldo Payá and Elizardo Sánchez, bestowing a spotlight and much-needed publicity upon them and their initiative. "Something has changed," enthused Payá after the visit. "The Cuban people have met hope."

Recognizing the changing times and the determinedly hostile tone of the Bush administration, Castro once again reinvented himself. Hanging up his guerrilla-green uniform, the Cuban septuagenarian sported a natty suit for his first visit with Carter, and later dined in a pale blue long-sleeved *guayabera.*

The finale of the historic trip—Carter was the highest-ranking U.S. offi-cial to visit Cuba since the Revolution—was a twenty-minute speech, carried live on Cuban television, which Carter delivered in Spanish in the main au-ditorium of the University of Havana. With Fidel Castro and most of the politburo seated in the front row, the Sunday Bible school teacher endorsed the Varela Project, gave a failing grade to the country's human rights record and rued its tortoise crawl toward democracy. But he also laid waste to American policy, dismissing the Embargo as a vestigial relic. "Our two na-tions have been trapped in a destructive state of belligerence for forty-two years," Carter remarked, reading from a prepared text, "and it is time for us to change our relationship and the way we think and talk about each other. Because the United States is the most powerful nation, we should take the first step."

To everyone's surprise, Castro allowed the speech to be published—unedited—in *Granma.* For the first time, millions of Cubans learned about the Varela Project and its hopes for change. Carter returned to America a con-quering hero, showered with hosannas by virtually every editorial page around the globe. The administration, blindsided and plainly upstaged, scrambled into damage-control mode. When a response was settled upon, Carter landed a two-hour debriefing visit with President Bush and the administration opted to tone down its hard-line policies—but not its rhetoric.

The administration had been planning to unveil its new Cuba policy review in Miami on May 20, 2002, when exiles would be celebrating Cuba's centenary as a republic. The event was to be staged to emulate Ronald Reagan's visit to Little Havana in 1983 and to burnish the image of the newly formed Cuban Liberty Council, the most hard-line exile organization. Its members, such as Armando Pérez-Roura, Alberto Hernández, Ninoska Pérez-Castellón and Diego Suárez, had deserted CANF to protest its moves toward moderation. Working closely and exclusively with the Cuba Liberty Council, the administration was expected to announce a new series of sanctions against Cuba. Hard-liners hoped to hear that Bush would be the first President not to waive the legal sanctions in Helms-Burton and that he would impose these new restrictions on remittances and travel to Cuba. There was also some optimism that Bush would move to indict Castro as a war criminal. Certainly, hard-liners expected that Bush would dismiss the Varela Project, as members of the Cuban Liberty Council had campaigned against the initiative since its inception, claiming it did not sufficiently repudiate the Castro government. Council members had also criticized Cuba's dissidents as, at best, pawns of the government.

The Council, in its role as host, had fussed over the question of who would be invited and, most especially, who would sit on the dais behind the President. In the seating arrangement the Council submitted to the White House, Orlando Bosch, the convicted terrorist paroled by Bush Sr., was given a seat in the front row. "Someone in the White House caught it," said a member of a rival exile group, "but it was sheer luck that they did."

Not only were militants like Bosch moved out of sight, but Bush did not deliver on anything from the hard-liners' wish list. The President offered plenty of steamy invective along with boilerplate demonization of Fidel Castro, which prompted the crowd to stand up and roar. "But there was no Helms-Burton, no indictment, no new sanctions, nothing," pointed out a longtime Cuba hand. "It was all talk, no action." Even worse for hard-liners, Bush endorsed the Varela Project. Undoubtedly, Bush's key political strategist, Karl Rove, had read the Bendixen poll taken a week earlier that showed that 54 percent of Miami-Dade's Cuban exiles supported the dissident project.

"Bush had to go down there and serve his baby brother," said a former

Reagan official. "Cuba is purely for the Calle Ocho crowd for the Bushes. I think Jimmy Carter actually did them a big favor. He took the heat off them. Where are the hard-liners gonna go? They're not signing up with the Democrats. The truth is, they have nowhere to go."

The isolation of the hard-liners—notably the Cuban Liberty Council— was underscored a week later when a letter by Domingo Moreira appeared in the *Herald*. A trusted associate of Jorge Mas Canosa and a director of the Cuban American National Foundation's executive committee, Moreira has long been known as a hawk on Cuba. But he had thrown in his lot with the more pragmatic CANF, which had embraced the Varela Project and Cuba's dissidents. After championing the Cuban initiative in his missive, Moreira did some public soul-searching. "For too many years, many of us kept quiet when the motives of our fellow citizens were questioned," Moreira wrote. "To those who suffered because of it, I ask forgiveness for not speaking out more forcefully. From now on, I'll refuse to play that game and will not diminish another person who fights for freedom." It was a new day in Miami.

"THIS WILL ALL BE OVER in the next year or two," predicted a veteran American Cuba diplomat, notwithstanding the fact that it has been fifty-four years since an election has been held in Cuba—the last being in 1948. Moreover, Castro indulged in some predictably bad behavior once Jimmy Carter was safely off his island. Thumbing his nose at the cacophony of calls to open up his country to democracy, Castro busied himself with amending Cuba's constitution to forever enshrine its one-party communist system. In an announcement that left Cuba watchers slackjawed, he also threatened to break off diplomatic relations with the U.S. Castro's overreaction was a response to the U.S. Interests Section in Havana handing out free shortwave radios so that Cubans could listen to Radio Martí. While undeniably a provocative gesture, it hardly warranted returning Cuba to the Cold War.

Clearly threatened by the swelling popularity of the Varela Project, Castro resolved to torpedo the initiative, even if it meant redrafting Cuba's constitution. In mid-June he called for mass demonstrations in support of a constitutional amendment to guarantee that Cuba's socialist system remains forever "untouchable." In a matter of days, the government claimed to have collected more than eight million signatures before summoning the National Assembly for a three-day session to do its bidding. An anguished Oswaldo Payá likened Castro's action to a coup. "This anti-civic attempt against the constitution, against the people's intelligence, is a very grave act against popular sovereignty," Payá warned. "The principal aim is to frighten, demoralize and divide Cubans so they feel incapable of claiming their rights," he added, exhorting his countrymen to "get up, hold your head high and claim your rights."

But no matter what the future holds for the Varela Project and Cuba's dissidents, the mood has shifted among the Cuban *nomenklatura*. As the island awakens from its Cold War stupor, many who had once sought to leave are now banking on their future in Cuba and setting down their markers. Cuba now has *cibercafés* and its own Internet tourism service, CubaWeb, which last year had more than 25 million hits and which offers legal credit card dollar withdrawals for visiting Americans. The island is changing in more profound ways. Tourists and Cubans are visiting Santa Clara for more than just the Che Guevara memorial: this sleepy city in the center of the island, once famous for its counterrevolutionaries, boasts the first legal gay nightclub.

For thousands of Cuban families reconciliation will come, if ever, with the next generation. Typical of the dilemma is the Medina family. When Fulgencio Batista and his inner circle fled the country in the wee hours of January 1, 1959, one of his pilots was a *batistiano* stalwart named Felipe Medina. Just before his departure, Medina had a furious showdown with his sister, Abilia, a *fidelista* revolutionary. Her parting words to her brother's wife in Havana were "If we ever capture my brother and he is guilty, I want to be the one to send him to the firing squad."

For more than thirty years, not a word was exchanged between the two siblings, who prior to the Revolution had been devoted to each other. Felipe moved to Miami with his young family; Abilia stayed behind, raising her family and becoming an important person in the Communist Party as well as the head of the Committee for the Defense of the Revolution in Guanabacoa, a strong revolutionary outpost not far from Havana.

In 1991, Felipe's daughter, Lilia, decided to visit the country she barely remembered—over the protests of her parents. Toward the end of her visit, she ventured out to Guanabacoa, where she met her relatives for the first time. Gingerly, she chatted with the aunt she had heard so much about. After a few hours, she made her goodbyes and prepared to leave. But as she stepped out the door, she heard her aunt's voice coming from behind her. "How is my brother?" Abilia Medina asked quietly. By then, Felipe was ill. But before he passed on, there would be an exchange of letters and a rapprochement with the sister who had wished him dead.

Most Cuban families have experienced a searingly tragic episode of separation and loss. Rosario Moreno, formerly a star at the Tropicana, supported the Revolution in its early years. Her mother did not and fled to Puerto Rico, leaving the family's magnificent colonial home in Vedado to Moreno's father, a *fidelista*. Following his death, a large extended black family from Santiago de Cuba moved into the house. When I visited the home in 1998, a young man in the house gave me a tour. The home still had its marble pillars and floors intact—though its exquisite furniture had long ago vanished. On its walls, however, were oil paintings of Moreno's relatives, including one of her great-grandfather in a Spanish military uniform. For forty years, no one had thought to take the canvases down. The young man offered to sell me the paintings. I handed him a twenty-dollar bill and watched as he deftly cut the canvases out of their frames and rolled them together. Days later, they were back in Moreno's Miami Beach living room.

Another friend of mine, a scientist who chose to stay in Cuba, said there are many days when she is impossibly tested. There was the time she drove out to Varadero in her ancient Russian Lada to visit the place where she had summered as a child. "I went to the hotel to have lunch and see the beach," she said. "The clerk told me I could not enter—that it was 'all-inclusive' for tourists, not Cubans. I got so upset. I pleaded with her—'I only want to see the beach from my childhood'—but they refused me. So I went into the lobby and recited as loud as I could 'Tengo' by Nicolás Guillén," the famous poem of Cuba's black bard who wrote of the rewards of the Revolution after a life of racial discrimination—when blacks were barred from beaches, hotels and restaurants. Now all Cubans are barred, she fumed.

> *I have what I have*
> *I have the land*
> *I have the sea*
> *. . . If not from beach to beach wave to wave*
> *gigantic open blue democracy . . .*

But the clerk stared at her unmoved. My friend drove back to Havana, smoldering with fury. Still, she swore she had no plans to leave. She said she is looking "beyond Fidel"—seeing her family's future ten years down the road. Yes, she says, she expects Castro to remain in power and, no doubt, die in bed with his boots on. But she knows that his time will end—maybe in five years, maybe in fifteen. And when it does, she says she "doesn't want to be in Miami cleaning hotel rooms." She will be in her home in Vedado—the house of her parents and her grandparents, overlooking the park—with her son, mother and grandchild. She will be in her homeland.

APPENDIX A: CHRONOLOGY OF THE ELIÁN GONZÁLEZ AFFAIR

NOVEMBER 25, 1999	Elián González is found on an inner tube in the Atlantic Ocean off Fort Lauderdale.
NOVEMBER 26	U.S. Immigration and Naturalization Service turns Elián over to relatives in Miami.
NOVEMBER 28	Juan Miguel González petitions U.S. government for return of his son to Cuba; exiles in Miami put boy's picture on poster as "child victim" of Fidel Castro.
DECEMBER 4	Services held for eleven victims of boat accident; Cuba renews call for return of "kidnapped" boy.
DECEMBER 6	Elián has sixth birthday with Miami relatives; Cubans march on U.S. mission in Havana.
DECEMBER 10	Miami relatives file political asylum claim for Elián; millions rally in demonstrations in Cuba.
DECEMBER 12	Elián goes to Disney World, asks if boat at "Small World" attraction is going to sink.
DECEMBER 13	Father meets with U.S. immigration agents in Havana.
JANUARY 5, 2000	U.S. Immigration and Naturalization Service rules that Elián should be returned to father in Cuba.
JANUARY 7	Exiles block Miami roads in protest of U.S. decision. Miami lawyers petition for custody of boy.
JANUARY 10	Florida Family Court Judge Rosa Rodríguez rules Elián should stay with Miami relatives until March hearing to determine if he would be harmed by going back to Cuba.
JANUARY 11	Rodríguez decision questioned in light of her connection to Miami family spokesman.
JANUARY 12	Attorney General Janet Reno rejects family court ruling, backs INS on Elián decision.
JANUARY 14	Republican members of Congress say they will seek citizenship for Elián.
JANUARY 19	Miami relatives file federal lawsuit to block Elián's return to Cuba and seek political asylum hearing.

JANUARY 21	Elián's grandmothers fly from Havana to New York to press their case for boy's return.
JANUARY 22	Grandmothers meet Reno in Washington.
JANUARY 24	Grandmothers fly to Miami but leave without seeing Elián.
JANUARY 25	U.S. officials order meeting between grandmothers and Elián.
JANUARY 26	Grandmothers take Learjet, helicopter to meeting with boy at Miami Beach estate.
JANUARY 27	Sister Jeanne O'Laughlin, nun who hosted Elián-grandmothers meeting, says boy should stay in U.S.; U.S. asks federal judge to dismiss relatives' lawsuit.
JANUARY 30	Grandmothers return to Cuba to hero's welcome.
FEBRUARY 9	U.S. government says it is reviewing reports that Elián's great-uncle and temporary caretaker, Lázaro González, has drunk driving convictions.
FEBRUARY 18	INS denies request from father to move boy to home of another relative, Manuel González, who supports the father's position.
FEBRUARY 20	U.S. District Judge William Hoeveler hospitalized after stroke.
FEBRUARY 22	U.S. District Judge Michael Moore assigned to Elián case.
MARCH 9	Lawyers for Miami relatives and U.S. government argue in court over whether he has right to political asylum hearing.
MARCH 21	Judge Moore dismisses relatives' lawsuit seeking political asylum for Elián, upholds INS decision that he should go back to Cuba.
APRIL 3	State Department approves visas for Elián's father and others.
APRIL 6	Juan Miguel González, his wife and their son arrive in the United States.
APRIL 12	Reno meets with Florida relatives and orders them to surrender Elián.
APRIL 22	Federal agents seize Elián in Miami in a predawn raid; Elián reunited with his father in Washington. Riots in Miami.
APRIL 25	Cuban-Americans conduct a general strike in Miami.
JUNE 1	The Eleventh U.S. Circuit Court of Appeals in Atlanta rules for the government and Elián's father, but orders the boy to remain in the United States pending appeal.
JUNE 23	Appeals Court reaffirms its decision, but maintains order blocking Elián's return to Cuba until June 28.
JUNE 26	Miami relatives file appeal with U.S. Supreme Court.
JUNE 28	Supreme Court rejects appeal; Elián returns home to Cuba.

Compiled from Associated Press, Reuters, PBS and other media sources.

APPENDIX B:
CUBA–UNITED STATES TIMELINE

JANUARY 1, 1959 — Under the command of Che Guevara, Fidel Castro's forces overtake General Fulgencio Batista's troops near Santa Clara in central Cuba. It's the last battleground in the revolution against Batista, who had ruled Cuba since seizing power in a military coup on March 10, 1952. Batista flees to the Dominican Republic and later Portugal.

MAY 17, 1959 — The Cuban government enacts the Agrarian Reform Law, which limits land ownership to 1,000 acres and expropriates all other land.

MARCH 17, 1960 — President Dwight D. Eisenhower orders CIA Director Allen Dulles to train Cuban exiles for a covert invasion of Cuba.

JULY 5, 1960 — All U.S. businesses and commercial property in Cuba are nationalized at the direction of the Cuban government. By the end of October 1960, all other American-owned property in Cuba is nationalized.

OCTOBER 19, 1960 — U.S. imposes an economic embargo prohibiting all exports to Cuba except foodstuffs, medicines, medical supplies.

JANUARY 3, 1961 — U.S. closes its embassy in Havana and breaks off diplomatic relations with Cuba.

APRIL 16, 1961 — For the first time, Fidel Castro defines Cuba as a socialist state: "We have made a revolution, a socialist revolution, right here under the very nose of the United States."

APRIL 17, 1961 — 1,300 U.S.-supported Cuban exiles invade Cuba at the Bay of Pigs. Immediately after they land, Castro calls a national alert. Two U.S.-provided ships are sunk by Cuban planes. The invasion fails to generate the internal support predicted by the CIA. Two days later, Castro claims victory.

JANUARY 22, 1962 — Cuba suspended from Organization of American States; Cuba responds with call for armed revolt across Latin America.

FEBRUARY 7, 1962 — The U.S. government bans all Cuban imports and re-export of

U.S. products to Cuba from other countries, and cuts off aid to any country that "furnishes assistance" to Cuba.

SEPTEMBER 26, 1962   Congress passes a joint resolution granting the President the right to intervene militarily in Cuba if U.S. interests are threatened.

OCTOBER 2, 1962   The U.S. again tightens the Embargo. All ports are closed to nations that allow their ships to carry arms to Cuba, and ships that have docked in a socialist country are prohibited from docking in the United States during that voyage.

OCTOBER 22, 1962   The Cuban Missile Crisis—President John F. Kennedy speaks on national television and announces that there are nuclear missile sites in Cuba and orders a naval blockade of the island.

OCTOBER 26, 1962   In a secret communication, Soviet Premier Nikita Khrushchev agrees not to break the U.S. blockade and offers to withdraw Soviet missiles from Cuba if the United States pledges not to invade Cuba and agrees to remove its Jupiter missiles from Turkey. The next day at noon, Cuba downs an American U-2 spy plane, killing the pilot. That same day, President Kennedy tells Khrushchev that the U.S. will not invade Cuba if the Russian missiles are removed from Cuba.

JULY 8, 1963   The Kennedy administration again tightens the Embargo and makes most travel to Cuba illegal for U.S. citizens. All Cuban-owned assets in the United States are frozen, including an estimated $33 million in U.S. banks.

NOVEMBER 2, 1966   President Lyndon B. Johnson signs into law the Cuban Adjustment Act. All Cubans who have reached U.S. territory since January 1, 1959, will be eligible for permanent residency after two years of residency. Nearly 123,000 Cubans apply immediately.

SEPTEMBER 8, 1969   Cuba expels Associated Press correspondent Fenton Wheeler. In retaliation, Washington prohibits Cuban news bureaus in the U.S., except those on U.N. property.

FEBRUARY 15, 1973   U.S. and Cuba sign anti-hijacking agreement, the only formal agreement between the two countries. But Cuba revokes the agreement four years later.

SEPTEMBER 28, 1974   Senators Jacob Javits (R–New York) and Claiborne Pell (D–Rhode Island) travel to Havana to meet with Castro. It's the first visit to Cuba by elected officials of the U.S. government since diplomatic relations were severed in 1961.

NOVEMBER 1974   Assistant Secretary of State William Rogers and Assistant
                   Secretary of State Lawrence Eagleburger conduct secret talks
                   with Cuban officials in Washington and New York. The talks
                   end over Cuba's intervention in Angola.

MARCH–MAY 1977   U.S. government lifts prohibition on travel to Cuba and allows
                   U.S. citizens to spend $100 on Cuban goods during their
                   visit. The United States and Cuba sign agreements on fishing
                   rights and maritime boundaries. The two countries also agree
                   to open Interests Sections in each other's capitals.

NOVEMBER–   The Committee of 75, a group of Cubans chosen to
DECEMBER 1978   negotiate with the Cuban government on behalf of the
                   estimated 1.2 million Cubans outside the island, and Cuban
                   officials hold the first of two negotiating sessions in Havana
                   called *El Diálogo*—the Dialogue. Cuba releases 3,600 political
                   prisoners and agrees to help in reuniting separated families
                   and allow Cubans abroad to visit relatives.

FEBRUARY 23, 1980 The U.S. State Department releases a white paper claiming
                   that documents prove that Cuba and other socialist countries
                   are engaged in indirect armed aggression against El Salvador's
                   government.

APRIL 1980   Mariel Boat Lift—twelve Cubans seeking asylum crash a
                   minibus through the gates of the Peruvian embassy in Havana.
                   On April 22, *Granma,* the official state newspaper of the
                   Cuban government, announces that anyone who wants to
                   leave may depart by boat from Mariel, a port twenty-five miles
                   from Havana. A flotilla of refugees (eventually numbering
                   125,000) begins an exodus for the U.S., which ends in
                   September.

JUNE 7, 1980   President Jimmy Carter orders the Justice Department to
                   expel Cubans who had committed "serious crimes" in Cuba.
                   In December, the first of several meetings occurs between
                   U.S. and Cuban officials to discuss the repatriation of the
                   marielitos.

APRIL 9, 1982   Charter air links between Miami and Havana are halted by the
                   U.S. government. Ten days later, the U.S. government
                   reinstitutes the travel ban, announcing that U.S. citizens are
                   prohibited from making monetary expenditures incidental to
                   travel in Cuba.

OCTOBER 1983   The U.S. sends troops to Grenada, following a leftist coup.

MAY 20, 1985   Radio Martí, an anti-Castro station named after Cuban patriot

José Martí, begins broadcasting to Cuba. The Cuban government immediately jams the signal.

OCTOBER 1986 · Notes of Marine Lieutenant Colonel Oliver North, in the Iran-Contra affair, reveal offer of paying $5,000 to any Contra who captures a Cuban or Sandinista officer in Nicaragua, and $200,000 for every five such captives. The money to pay the bounties would come from arms sales to Iran.

MARCH 23, 1990 · The U.S. launches its first test of TV Martí. After broadcasting to Cuba for three hours, it is jammed by the Cuban government.

OCTOBER 15, 1992 · Congress passes the Cuban Democracy Act, sponsored by Representative Robert Torricelli (D–New Jersey) in the House of Representatives and Senator Bob Graham (D-Florida) in the U.S. Senate. Known as the Torricelli Bill, it prohibits foreign-based subsidiaries of U.S. companies from trading with Cuba, travel to Cuba by U.S. citizens and family remittances to Cuba.

NOVEMBER 6, 1993 · Cuba announces it is opening state enterprises to private investment.

AUGUST 1994 · Following Castro's declaration of an open migration policy, a new boat lift begins, and 35,000 refugees set sail from Cuba.

SEPTEMBER 9, 1994 · The U.S. and Cuba issue a joint communiqué agreeing to take measures to ensure that migration between the two countries is safe, legal and orderly. The U.S. agrees that total legal migration to the U.S. will be a minimum of 20,000 per year.

FEBRUARY 1996 · Cuban MiGs shoot down two civilian aircraft belonging to the Miami-based group Brothers to the Rescue in international airspace. Three U.S. citizens and one Cuban resident of the U.S. are killed.

MARCH 12, 1996 · President Bill Clinton signs the Cuban Liberty and Democratic Solidarity (Libertad) Act, known as the Helms-Burton Act.

NOVEMBER 13, 1996 · The annual vote in the U.N. General Assembly on the U.S. Embargo of Cuba takes place. Britain, Germany and the Netherlands cast their ballots against the United States—the first time its allies have voted for the U.S. to end its three-decade economic Embargo of Cuba.

FEBRUARY 12, 1997 · The Clinton administration approves licenses for U.S. news organizations to open bureaus in Cuba.

OCTOBER 1997 · Castro confirms his younger brother, Raúl, as his successor.

NOVEMBER 25, 1999   On Thanksgiving Day, six-year-old Elián González is found in the Straits of Florida clinging to an inner tube—prompting a bitter seven-month custody fight.

JUNE 23, 2001   Castro faints during televised speech, setting off speculation about his health and successor.

JANUARY 2002   President George W. Bush extends a recess appointment to Otto Reich as Assistant Secretary of State for Inter-American Affairs. Reich assembles a team of hard-liners on Cuba.

MAY 12–17, 2002   Former President Jimmy Carter visits Cuba, addresses the Cuban people on live television, meets with dissidents, endorses the Varela Project and criticizes the U.S. Embargo.

MAY 20, 2002   President George W. Bush harshly criticizes Fidel Castro in Miami but backs off from significantly tightening the Embargo.

Compiled from data assembled by PBS's Frontline, *the Associated Press, Reuters and the* Miami Herald.

NOTES

Most of the material that forms the basis of this work comes from my own research and interviews. These interviews, the majority of which were tape-recorded and transcribed, are dated except when there were multiple conversations over a period of time. Several subjects either denied or ignored requests for interviews, including Raúl Castro, Lincoln Díaz-Balart, Lázaro González, Marisleysis González, Manny Díaz, Fidel Castro Díaz-Balart, Otto Reich, Governor Jeb Bush, Katherine Harris, Alex Penelas, Orlando Rodríguez, Carmita Brotón, Armando Pérez-Roura and Alberto Ibargüen. Not listed are interviews with approximately twenty people in Cuba and a dozen in Miami who requested anonymity, citing fears of retribution. Also not listed below are interviews with some members of the FBI, the CIA, the State Department and the Miami-Dade Police Department.

CHAPTER 1: THE SHIPWRECK

Interviews/Conversations with A. L. Bardach:

IN CÁRDENAS, CUBA: FEBRUARY 1-7, 2000, AND JULY 19-25, 2000

Elsa Alfonso
Rosa Betancourt
Roberto de Armas
Ricardo Díaz
Marta Fernández and her father
Lisbeth García
Juanito González
Juan Miguel González
Tony González
Victor Herrera
Dagoberto Munero
Mariela Quintana
Raquel Rodríguez
Milagros Sanabries
Sara Sanabries

IN MIAMI:
Carlos Corredoira, February 1, 2000
María Díaz, January 6, 2000, February 5, 2000, January 9, 2002
Verne Eastwood, Border Patrol
Nivaldo Fernández, February 1 and 22, 2000
Milagros García and Ricardo Sardinas, February 15, 2002
Delfín González, July 13, 2002
Kenny Goodman, January 10, 2002
Arianne Horta, February 1 and 22, 2000
Mayra Horta, March 28, 2002
Sondra Horta, February 1, 2000
Jorge Munero, February 13, 2000, August 22, 2000, September 17, 2001
María Munero, February 13, 2000, August 22, 2000, September 17, 2001
Juan Ruiz, March 17, 2000

IN NEW YORK:
Joan Brown Campbell, February 14 and 24, 2000

Articles:
Bardach, Ann Louise. "Elián's Boat: The Untold Story." *George,* May 2000.
Chardy, Alfonso. "Autopsy Fills in Details of Fateful Ocean Voyage." *Miami Herald,*
     June 2, 2000.
"Conducida por la Amenaza y la Violencia a la Tragedia." *Granma,* February 8, 2000.
"Cubans: Elián's Mom Was Bullied." Associated Press, February 8, 2000.
De Valle, Elaine. "Survivors of Elián Trip 'Forgotten.' " *Miami Herald,* November 26,
     2000.
"Elián's Mother's Story Contradicted." Associated Press, February 23, 2000.
"Family Reveals Religious Image." *Miami Herald,* March 28, 2000.
Fineman, Mark. "Cubans' Risky New Voyage Out." *Los Angeles Times,* January 4,
     2000.
Kripalani, Jasmine. "Rafter's Daughter Missed Fatal Trip." *Miami Herald,*
     November 28, 1999.
"Thousands Rally in Cuba Again for Elián's Return." Reuters, June 3, 2000.
Wadler, Joyce. "Standing Between Elián's Two Families." *New York Times,* April 14,
     2000.

Documents:
Letter from Elizabet Brotón to Lázaro (Rafa) Munero in Miami, dated August 14,
     1998.
Letter from Mari (María Elena) Munero to Jorge Munero in Miami, dated Septem-
     ber 3, 1998.

CHAPTER 2: CASTRO FAMILY VALUES

Interviews/Conversations with A. L. Bardach:
Luis Aguilar León, December 13, 2000, Miami
Deborah Andollo, January 24, 1997, Tarara, Cuba
Lázaro Asencio, December 11, 2000, February 14, 2001, Miami
Bernardo Benes, November 20, 2000, April 8, 2002, Miami
Natalia Bolívar, 1993–2002, Havana
Fidel Castro, October 16, 1993, January 4, 1994, July 26, 2000, Havana
Juanita Castro, December 11, 2000, April 18, 2002, Miami
Rafael Díaz-Balart, October 8, 2001
Wendy Gimbel, 1999–2001, New York
Barbara Walker Gordon, March 3, 2002
Alfredo Guevara, 1993–1994, February 7, 2000
Max Lesnik, November 22, 2000, Miami
Salvador Lew, November 27 and 28, 2000
Father Amado Llorente, January 25, 2001
José Luis Llovio-Menéndez, 1994–2000, New York, Miami
Lee Lockwood, January 16, 2001
Marjorie Skelly Lord, November 4, 2001 (phone), Miami
Marita Lorenz, 1992, Queens, New York
Ricardo Mas Canosa, May 19, 1996, Miami
Huber Matos, January 22, 2001, February 14, 2001
Rosario Moreno, 1994–2002, Miami
Luis Ortega, November 28, 2000, Miami
Guillermo Pérez Calzada, October 30, 2000, Union City, New Jersey
Nancy Pérez Crespo, January 23, 2001
Jack Skelly, April 12, 2001, Fort Lauderdale
Tad Szulc, January 12, 2001
Jorge Tabio, January 3, 1998
María de los Angeles Torres, January 4, 2001

Articles:
Bardach, Ann Louise. "Cast of Characters in a Family Melodrama." *Los Angeles Times,* January 30, 2000.
———. "Castro Family Values." *Washington Post,* January 9, 2000.
———. "Elián González: The Winners and Losers." *Los Angeles Times,* April 9, 2000.
———. "For Castro, Tug of War over Boy Is All Too Personal." *Los Angeles Times,* December 26, 1999.
———. "Forever Fidel: A Life History of the Cuban Leader." *Talk,* August 2001.
———. "The Spy Who Loved Castro." *Vanity Fair,* November 1993.
Bell, Mayra. "Second Castro Daughter Living Quietly in Miami." *South Florida Sun-Sentinel,* July 12, 2001.

Books:

Conte Agüero, Luis. *Cartas del Presidio.* Havana: Editorial Lex, 1959.

Fernández, Alina. *Castro's Daughter: An Exile's Memoir of Cuba.* New York: St. Martin's, 1997.

Franqui, Carlos. *Diary of the Cuban Revolution.* New York: Viking Press, 1980.

———. *Family Portrait with Fidel.* New York: Random House, 1984.

Geyer, Georgie Anne. *Guerrilla Prince: The Untold Story of Fidel Castro.* Kansas City, Mo.: Andrews McMeel, 1993.

Gimbel, Wendy. *Havana Dreams: A Story of Cuba.* New York: Alfred A. Knopf, 1998.

Lockwood, Lee. *Castro's Cuba, Cuba's Fidel: An American Journalist's Inside Look at Today's Cuba in Text and Picture.* New York: Macmillan, 1967.

Szulc, Tad. *Fidel: A Critical Portrait.* New York: Avon Books, 1986.

Thomas, Hugh. *Cuba; or, The Pursuit of Freedom.* New York: Da Capo Press, 1998.

Film and Video:

Dear Fidel: Marita's Story (German documentary). Pegasus Film, 2001.

Fidel, directed by Estela Bravo. Bravo Films and Fort Point Entertainment, 2000.

Person to Person, Edward R. Murrow interview with Fidel Castro. CBS, 1959.

CHAPTER 3: PLANET ELIÁN

The title for this chapter comes from Carl Hiaasen's column "Planet Elián," *Miami Herald,* January 30, 2000.

Interviews/Conversations with A. L. Bardach:

Martin Baron, February 23, 2000

Bernardo Benes, February 23, 2000, November 20, 2000

Jane Bussey, 2001–2002, Miami

Joan Brown Campbell, February 14 and 24, 2000

María Cardona, INS spokesperson, April 23, 2000

Kendall Coffey, March 3, 2002

Uva de Aragón, April 29, 2002

Sister Leonor Esnard, February 25, 2000

Delfín González, July 13, 2002

Armando Gutiérrez, December 15, 1999, December 20, 2001

Meg Laughlin, 1994–2002

Raúl Martínez, April 17, 2002

Sister Jeanne O'Laughlin, February 27, 2000

Mark Seibel, October 11, 2001, Miami

Articles:

"ABC Won't Broadcast Elián Interview." Associated Press, March 29, 2000.

"Attorney General Denies Request to Meet with 6-Year-Old Cuban Boy." *Miami Herald,* February 18, 2000.

Berger, Ellis. "Reunite Elián with Dad, Most Floridians Say." *South Florida Sun-Sentinel,* April 8, 2000.

"Boy's Grandmothers Return to Cuba." Associated Press, January 31, 2000.

Bragg, Rick. "Standoff over Cuban Boy's Fate Intensifies." *Miami Herald,* March 28, 2000.

———. "Stand over Elián Highlights a Virtual Secession of Miami." *New York Times,* April 1, 2000.

Buchanan, Edna. "Playing to the Cameras in Miami." *Miami Herald,* April 27, 2000.

Bussey, Jane, and Carol Rosenberg. "Dedication Brings Dramatic Photograph Image." *Miami Herald,* April 23, 2000.

Cazares, David, and Luisa Yanez. "House Steps In, Subpoenas Elián." *South Florida Sun-Sentinel,* January 8, 2000.

Clark, Lesley. "Reprimand Suggested for Judge." *Miami Herald,* February 23, 2001.

"Congressman Visits Elián's Home." *Miami Herald,* April 18, 2000.

"Cuban Boy's Birthday Presents Will Include a Camera." Dow Jones Newswire, December 1, 2000.

"Cuba Impide la Reunificación de un Padre con su Hijo Menor," *El Nuevo Herald,* January 31, 2000.

De Valle, Elaine. "Castro Accuses Elián Uncle of Abuse." *Miami Herald,* March 5, 2000.

De Young, Karen. "Nun's Story about Elián Is Disputed." *Washington Post,* February 21, 2000.

"Editorial Roundup." Associated Press, April 5, 2000.

"Elián a Target for Indoctrination." Associated Press, April 3, 2000.

Fineman, Mark. "Family Plight of Young Elián." *Los Angeles Times,* February 19, 2000.

García Pedrosa, José. "Give Elián the Freedom His Mother Left Him." *Miami Herald,* January 6, 2000.

Golden, Tim. "Just Another Cuban Family Saga." *New York Times,* April 23, 2000.

Greene, Ronnie. "Wealthy Member of School Board Got Richer on School Funds." *Miami Herald,* April 8, 2002.

Hiaasen, Carl. "Let's Discuss Character Issues." *Miami Herald,* April 19, 2000.

———. "Planet Elián." *Miami Herald,* January 30, 2000.

———. "The Tribulations of a School-Board Candidate." *Miami Herald,* November 1, 2000.

Jackson, Terry. "Elián's Words on Going Back to Cuba Deleted from ABC Interview." *Miami Herald,* March 29, 2000.

Jelinek, Pauline. "Psychiatrist Says Elián Needs Help." Associated Press, June 29, 2000.

Kerry, Frances. "Elián's Miami Home to Become Permanent Shrine." Reuters, November 3, 2000.

Laughlin, Meg. "A Changed Boy after Miami Stay." *Miami Herald,* April 13, 2000.

———. "Sister Jeanne Says Sources to Come Out." *Miami Herald,* February 22, 2001.

"Legal Fund for Elián Tops $200,000." *Miami Herald,* March 13, 2000.

"Little Havana." *Wall Street Journal,* March 29, 2000.

Lynch, Marika. "Very Stressed Cousin of Elián Hospitalized." *Miami Herald,* March 6, 2000.

Mármol, José. "El Futuro de Elián." *El Nuevo Herald,* January 11, 2000.

———. "El Niño Milagro." *El Nuevo Herald,* April 4, 2000.

"Questions, Answers: Guide to the Elián Case." *Miami Herald,* March 30, 2000.

"Rep. Burton: Elián Wants to Stay." *New York Times,* January 29, 2000.

Rieff, David. "The Exiles' Last Hurrah." *New York Times,* April 2, 2000.

Robles, Frances. "Elián Quoted as Saying He's Eager to Go Home." *Miami Herald,* May 25, 2000.

Salas, Aurelio. "Meaning of Asylum to a Child of 6." *New York Times,* June 2, 2000.

Salazar, Carolyn, and Marika Lynch. "Journalists Swept Up by Raid Storm." *Miami Herald,* April 23, 2000.

School board series, *Miami Herald,* April 8–10, 2002.

"Street, Park Named for Elián's Mom." Associated Press, May 6, 2000.

"Text of Letter from Juan Miguel González to Senators Trent Lott, R-Miss., and Tom Daschle, D-S.D." *Granma,* April 1, 2000.

Valdez, Juan C. "Curiosas Similitudes." *El Nuevo Herald,* February 11, 2000.

Valls, Jorge. "The Revolution and the Custody Case." *New York Times,* April 7, 2000.

Viglucci, Andres. "INS, Police Authorities Expect Work Relationship to Continue." *Miami Herald,* April 1, 2000.

Viglucci, Andres, Sandra Marquez Garcia, and Ana Acle. "Elian's Relatives Won't Budge." *Miami Herald,* April 11, 2000.

Viglucci, Andres, and Jay Weaver. "Relatives Won't Give Elián to Dad." *Miami Herald,* April 1, 2000.

Weaver, Jay, and Marika Lynch. "Elián Family Summit Takes Bizarre Twist." *Miami Herald,* February 22, 2000.

Weaver, Jay, and Andres Viglucci. "Legal Sides in Elián Saga." *Miami Herald,* January 14, 2000.

Weingarten, Gene. "A Modern Play of Passions." *Washington Post,* April 7, 2000.

Documents:

Timeline from the Web site for the PBS broadcast *Frontline*—"Saving Elián" (www.pbs.org/wgbh/pages/frontline/shows/elian/etc/cron.html), February 7, 2001.

Film and Video:

Good Morning America, Diane Sawyer interview with Elián González. ABC, March 27–28, 2000.

Frontline—"Saving Elián." PBS, February 6, 2001.

CHAPTER 4: CALLE OCHO POLITICS

Interviews/Conversations with A. L. Bardach:
Francisco Aruca, November 20, 2000

Bernardo Benes, November 20, 2000
Joe Carollo, October 15, 1998
Ileana Cassanova, 1996–2002
Juanita Castro, December 11, 2000, April 18, 2002
Kendall Coffey, March 3, 2002
Jack Devine, September 17, 2000
Enrique Encinosa, March 3, 2002, May 18, 2002
Gaeton Fonzi, 1994–2001
Carl Hiaasen, June 13, 2002
Dexter Lehtinen, May 30, 2002
Max Lesnik, November 22, 2000
Salvador Lew, November 27 and 28, 2000, January 15, 2002
Lydia Martin, January 10, 2002
Omar Martínez, 1994
Raúl Martínez, April 17, 2002
Alberto Milián, April 11, 2002
Rosario Moreno, 1994–2002
Debbie Ohanian, 1998–2000
Andrés Oppenheimer, 1995–2002
Carlos Pérez, October 25, 1994, Miami
Marifeli Pérez-Stable, December 13, 2001
Paul Phillips, former head of the FBI's Miami Bureau, July 2, 2002
Jessica Reilly, July 2001
Totty and Juan Saizarbitoria, 1995–2001, Miami
Lee Tucker, Human Rights Watch, 1994
Nelson P. Valdés, February 5, 2001, January 15, 2002
Raquel Vallejo, 1998–2002
George Volsky, 1998

Articles:
Alfonso, Pablo. "Entrevista: La Cirujana Elizabeth Trujillo." *El Nuevo Herald,* July 19, 1998.
Balmaseda, Liz. "Emilio Milián, Broadcaster Who Denounced Terror, Dies." *Miami Herald,* March 16, 2001.
———. "Milián a Symbol of Courage." *Miami Herald,* March 19, 2001.
Bardach, Ann Louise. " 'The White Cloud'—The Latino/HIV Stealth Epidemic." *New Republic,* January 5, 1995.
Branch-Brioso, Karen, Tim Henderson and Alfonso Chardy. "The Real Power in Dade." *Miami Herald,* September 3, 2000.
"Broadcaster's Son Sentenced," *Miami Herald,* March 25, 1986.
Calvo, Diana. "A Secret Split among Miami's Cuban Exiles." *Los Angeles Times,* February 5, 2001.
Castro, Max J. "Affirming One's Rights vs. Trampling over Others'." *Miami Herald,* April 5, 2000.

Davies, Frank. "Residency Bill for Elián Proposed." *Miami Herald,* March 30, 2000.

De Young, Karen. "Dissidents Wage Lonely Battle in Castro's Cuba." *Washington Post,* July 16, 2000.

Dowd, Maureen. "Biological Warfare." *New York Times,* April 2, 2000.

Fernandez, Enrique. "Take a Deep Breath and Blame It All on Cuban Coffee." *Miami Herald,* May 22, 2000.

Fields, Gregg. "Miami Getting Its Bananas in a Bunch." *Miami Herald,* May 22, 2000.

Forero, Juan. "In Miami, Some Cuban-Americans Take Less Popular Views." *Miami Herald,* April 28, 2000.

Garcia, Maria C. "Florida's Fiercest Radio Warrior." *Miami Herald,* October 13, 1984.

García Márquez, Gabriel. "Shipwreck on Dry Land." *New York Times,* April 12, 2000.

Garcia-Zarza, Isabel. "Big Brother at 40: Cuba's Revolutionary Neighborhood Watch System." *South Florida Sun-Sentinel,* October 20, 2000.

Glasgow, Kathy. "Voice of a Nation." *Miami New Times,* April 19, 2001.

Henderson, Tim, and William Yardley. "Cuban Americans Lead Other Hispanics in Home Ownership." *Miami Herald,* April 24, 2002.

Jackson, Terry. "PBS Examines Power, Politics in Elián Battle." *Miami Herald,* February 6, 2001.

Johnson, Tim. "Top U.S. Analyst Admits to Spying for Cuba: Plea Deal Gives Her 25 Years in Jail." *Miami Herald,* March 20, 2002.

Kandell, Jonathan. "Miami's War of Words." *Miami Herald,* October 23, 2000.

Levin, Jordan. "Miami-Dade Threatens to Cancel Film Fest Grant." *El Nuevo Herald,* February 25, 2000.

Lynch, Marika. "Poll: Dade 'A Tale of Two Cities.' " *Miami Herald,* November 4, 2000.

Martin, Lydia. "Diva Straddles Worlds, but Her Soul's in Cuba." *Miami Herald,* November 26, 1995.

"Miami-Dade Corruption Cases Since 1990." *Miami Herald,* September 28, 2000.

Milián, Alberto. "Reno Failed as Prosecutor and Attorney General." Letter to the Editor. *Miami Herald,* June 22, 2001.

Nieves, Gail Epstein. "Castro Role in Defection Reported at Spy Trial." *Miami Herald,* January 4, 2001.

"No Regrets, Only Gratitude, for These 'Pedro Pans.' " *Miami Herald,* January 30, 2000.

Ojito, Mirta. "Best of Friends, Worlds Apart." *New York Times,* June 5, 2000.

Pressley, Sue Anne. "A Shrine to Miami's Angel Who Flew Away." *Washington Post,* November 26, 2001.

"Regalado Investigated in Elian Disturbance." *Miami Herald,* September 16, 2000.

Richey, Warren. "In Miami, Free Speech Is Selective." *Christian Science Monitor,* April 21, 2000.

Tamargo, Agustín. "Yo Soy un Sionista Cubano." *El Nuevo Herald,* April 7, 2002.

Tamayo, Juan O. "Anti-Castro Plots Seldom Lead to Jail in U.S." *Miami Herald,* July 23, 1998.

Yanez, Luisa. "Brigade 2506 Ousts 2 for Trip to Cuba." *Miami Herald,* April 23, 2000.

Books:

Aguilar León, Luis. "The Prophet." In *Cuba: A Traveler's Literary Companion,* ed. Ann Louise Bardach. Berkeley: Whereabouts Press, 2002.

Allman, T. D. *Miami: City of the Future.* New York: Atlantic Monthly Press, 1987.

Didion, Joan. *Miami.* New York: Pocket Books, 1987.

Interview with René Vásquez Díaz from *Bridges to Cuba: Cuban and Cuban-American Artists, Writers, and Scholars Explore Identity, Nationality, and Homeland,* ed. Ruth Behar. Ann Arbor: University of Michigan Press, 1995.

Levine, Robert M. *Secret Missions to Cuba.* New York: Palgrave, 2001.

Obejas, Achy. *Days of Awe.* New York: Ballantine Books, 2001.

Pérez-Roura, Armando. *Tome Nota.* Self-published, 1993.

Rieff, David. *The Exile: Cuba in the Heart of Miami.* New York: Simon & Schuster, 1993.

Torres, María de los Angeles. *In the Land of Mirrors.* Ann Arbor: University of Michigan Press, 1999.

Vargas Llosa, Alvaro. *El Exilio Indomable.* Madrid: Editorial Espasa, 1998.

Documents:

Albright, Madeline K. "Statement on Cuba Family Reunification and Migrations Issues." U.S. Department of State, August 28, 2000.

City of Miami, Oath of Allegiance, Form No. 238, rev. June 1997.

"Cuban Anti-Castro Terrorism." Posted at the Cuban Information Archives, http://cuban-exile.com/doc_001-025/doc0021.htm

Human Rights Watch Report on Miami, 1994 (coordinator: Lee Tucker).

Landau, Anya K., and Wayne S. Smith. "Keeping Things in Perspective: Cuba and the Question of International Terrorism." Center for International Policy report, November 20, 2001.

Transcript of *Frontline*—"Saving Elián," PBS, February 6, 2001.

CHAPTER 5: THE MAN WHO WOULD BE KING

Interviews/Conversations with A. L. Bardach:

Cresencio Arcos, October 15, 2001, May 28, 2002

Francisco Aruca, November 20, 2000

José Basulto, March 12, 1996

Bernardo Benes, November 20, 2000

Medea Benjamín

Juan Antonio Blanco, Havana

Frank Calzón, March 6, 1996

José Cárdenas, April 1994, Washington D.C.

Joe Carollo, June 19, 2002

Ramón Cernuda, November 25, 1994, December 6, 1994

Marcelino del Frade, September 30, 1995, Havana
Alfredo Durán, November 25, 1994, December 6, 1994, April 27, 2002
Jeff Eller, January 5 and 22, 2002
Jay Fernandez, 1996
Gaeton Fonzi, 1994–2001
Joe García, April 1994
Alberto González, October 20, 1994
Mercedes González, June 20, 2001
Dennis Hays, October 8, 2001, June 4, 2002
Carlos Manuel Ibarra, September 30, 1995, Havana
Gary Jarmin, 1998
Saul Landau, January 14, 2001
Eddie Levy, 1995
Salvador Lew, November 27–28, 2000
Myra MacPherson, 1998
Ricardo Mas Canosa, May 19, 1996, May 23 and 24, 1996
Raúl Masvidal, November 25, 1994, December 6, 1994
Mac Melvin, 1996
Emile Milne, aide to Charles Rangel
John Nichols, 1994
Richard Nuccio, 1994, 2000
Luis Ortega, 1994, 2002
Marifeli Pérez-Stable, December 13, 2001
Moraima Rivas, June 27, 2001
Maribel Roig, 1996
Wayne Smith, August 7, 1993, November 25, 1994, December 6, 1994, April 5,
    2001
Peter Tarnoff, 2000–2002
Robert G. Torricelli, 1994
Rosa Townsend, 1998
Nelson Valdés, 2001, 2002
Armando Valladares, 1996
George Volsky
Gordon Winslow, 1994–1996

Articles:
Bardach, Ann Louise. "Our Man in Miami." *The New Republic,* October 3, 1994.
Boadle, Anthony. "Lieberman a Close Ally of Miami's Cuban Exiles," Reuters,
    August 11, 2000.
Brinkley-Rogers, Paul. "After Verdict, Families of Dead Fliers Still at Odds." *Miami
    Herald,* June 9, 2001.
Cawthorne, Andrew. "Castro Blasts U.S.-Based Cuban-American Group." Reuters,
    July 27, 1998.
Fiedler, Tom. "Clinton Backs Torricelli Bill." *Miami Herald,* April 24, 1992.
Fonzi, Gaeton. "Jorge Who?" *Esquire,* January 1993.

Franklin, Jane. "The Cuba Obsession." *The Progressive,* July 1993.

MacPherson, Myra. "The Cuban Museum War." *Washington Post,* June 29, 1988.

———. "The Great Cuban Art Bust." *Washington Post*, August 24, 1989.

Reyes, Gerardo. "Exile's Suit Exposes Rift in Ani-Castro Group." *Miami Herald*, November 24, 1991.

Slevin, Peter. "Jorge Mas Canosa: The Road to Havana." *Miami Herald,* October 11, 1992.

Documents:

Court exhibit—letter from Orlando Bosch to Jorge Mas Canosa.

Jorge Mas Canosa Chronology, compiled by Scott Armstrong and Saul Landau. Institute for Policy Studies, 1995.

Memo from Jorge Mas Canosa to CANF's board of directors and trustees, April 1993.

Memo—Jorge Mas Canosa/CANF, "On behalf of the Cubans enslaved in the island and the two million Cuban exiles, I wish to inform you that your investments or commercial negotiations in Cuba are considered an act of collaboration with a totalitarian system." November 15, 1994.

Tape transcript—Jorge Mas Canosa on WQBA Radio program, August 21, 1994.

Transcript of Jorge Mas Canosa on Ramón Cernuda, *Mesa Redonda,* Radio Mambí, May 8, 1989.

Court Depositions:

UNITED STATES DISTRICT COURT FOR THE SOUTHERN DISTRICT OF FLORIDA. CASE NUMBER: 94-2681-CIV: *JORGE MAS CANOSA* V. *THE NEW REPUBLIC, INC., ET AL. (TNR).*

Mas Canosa, Jorge
January 10, 1996: A.M.
February 20, 1996: A.M./P.M.
February 21, 1996: A.M./P.M.
April 10, 1996: 9:00 A.M.–4:00 P.M.
April 11, 1996: 9:00 A.M.–3:00 P.M.
June 6, 1996: A.M./P.M.

Mas Canosa, Ricardo
April 16, 1996: 10:00 A.M.–5:00 P.M.
May 20, 1996
June 6, 1996: 2:00 P.M.–5:00 P.M.

CHAPTER 6: THE LITIGATOR

Interviews/Conversations with A. L. Bardach:
Floyd Abrams, June 13, 2002
Gigi Anders, 1994
Francisco Aruca, November 20, 2000, January 20, 2001
Liz Balmaseda, 1994

Jane Bussey
Doug Clifton, February 19, 1997
Mario Diament
Miguel Díaz de la Portilla, June 5, 1998
Alfredo Duran, November 25, 1994, December 6, 1994
Gaeton Fonzi, 1994–2001
Bob Guilmartin
Dennis Hays, October 8, 2001, June 4, 2002
Pat Jordan, 1996
Saul Landau, January 14, 2001
Meg Laughlin
David Lawrence, February 19, 1997
Jordan Levin, 1998
Sandra Levinson, January 3, 1994
Omar Martínez, February 27, 1994
Ricardo Mas Canosa, May 19, 1996, May 23–24, 1996
Raúl Masvidal, November 25, 1994, December 6, 1994
Mack Melvin, 1996, 1998
Richard Ovelmen
Martin Peretz, January 20, 2002
Luis Posada Carriles, June 15–18, 1998
Maribel Roig, 1996
Karl Ross
Wayne Smith, August 7, 1993, November 25, 1994, December 6, 1994, April 5, 2001
Roberto Suárez
Andrew Sullivan, March–December 1994
Sam Terrelli, February 19, 1997
Rosa Townsend, 1998
Lee Tucker, Human Rights Watch, March 5, 1994
Armando Valladares, 1996
George Volsky, 1998–2002
Gordon Winslow

Articles:
Arthur, Lisa. "Contractor Convicted in Striping Overbilling; Church and Tower Hired Contractor." *Miami Herald,* March 14, 2002.
Birger, Larry. "Mas Canosa Family Considering Plan to Invest Millions in China." *Miami Herald,* February 18, 1994.
"Conduct Puts Lawyer in Ethics School." Miami *Daily Business Review,* September 10, 1998.
"Crew Cracks 4-Foot Sewer Main." Associated Press, July 25, 2001.
Doris, Tony. "Miami Dade Lawyers Turn Up the Heat on Church and Tower Probe." Miami *Daily Business Review,* October 23, 2000.
Getter, Lisa, and Jeff Leen. "Suit Prompts Tough Look at Mas Canosa." *Miami Herald,* August 2, 1996.

Marquis, Christopher. "Jorge Mas Canosa—Dead at 58." *Miami Herald,* November 24, 1997.

O'Connor, Anne-Marie. "Trying to Set the Agenda in Miami." *Columbia Journalism Review,* May/June 1992.

Ross, Karl. "Grand Jury: Firm Failed to Supervise Dade Contract." *Miami Herald,* July 10, 2001.

Swartz, Mimi. "The Herald's Cuban Revolution." *The New Yorker,* June 7, 1999.

Villano, David. "Has Knight Ridder's Flagship Gone Adrift?" *Columbia Journalism Review,* January/February 1996.

Wyman, Scott. "MasTec Bid for Contract Draws Fire." *South Florida Sun-Sentinel,* May 25, 2001.

Documents:

Declaration of Jonell Easton, court reporter, December 20, 1995.

Grievance Committee of Supreme Court of Florida Recommendation in the Case of Hank Adorno, August 11, 1998, File No. 98-70, 557 (11N).

Letter from Ann Louise Bardach to Florida State Bar, September 12, 1997.

Letter from Robert Burlington to Hank Adorno, December 19, 1995.

Letter from Pat Jordan to Ann Louise Bardach, October 10, 1996.

Letter from Jim Mullin to Florida State Bar, April 30, 1998.

Letter from State Bar Grievance Committee to Florida State Bar, August 3, 1998.

Memo from Aragon, Burlington, Weil & Crockett, October 1, 1996. U.S. District Court Civil Docket: *Jorge Mas Canosa* v. *The New Republic, Inc., et al.,* filed December, 19, 1994, by attorneys Mitchell Reid Bloomberg and Sanford Lewis Bohrer.

Memo—Jorge Mas Canosa/CANF, April 5, 1993.

Memo—Jorge Mas Canosa/CANF, February 8, 1994.

Memo by Paul J. Schweid re *Mas* v. *The New Republic* press release language, October 1, 1996.

Panamanian Military Intelligence, List on Terrorism, October 25, 1976 (Exhibit #130, *Jorge Mas Canosa* v. *The New Republic, Inc., et al.*).

Parole hearing of Orlando Bosch, Miami, March 22, 1988.

Signed letter of intent for joint venture between Church & Tower and the Chengdu Thermoelectrical Company of China for seven power plants, January 14, 1994.

Andrew Sullivan Statement to Florida State Bar, January 2, 1998.

U.S. District Court, Miami Division, Hearing on Motion to Compel, February 22, 1996, Barry L. Garber, U.S. Magistrate Judge.

Court Depositions:

UNITED STATES DISTRICT COURT FOR THE SOUTHERN DISTRICT OF FLORIDA. CASE NUMBER: 94-2681-CIV: *JORGE MAS CANOSA* V. *THE NEW REPUBLIC, INC., ET AL. (TNR).*

Cárdenas, José
March 28, 1996
March 29, 1996

Mas Canosa, Jorge
January 10, 1996: A.M.
February 20, 1996: A.M./P.M.
February 21, 1996: A.M./P.M.
April 10, 1996: 9:00 A.M.–4:00 P.M.
April 11, 1996: 9:00 A.M.–3:00 P.M.
June 6, 1996: A.M./P.M.

Peretz, Martin
November 16, 1995

Roig, Maribel
January 26, 1996: 10:05 A.M.–11:37 A.M.

Sullivan, Andrew
November 14, 1995
November 15, 1995

THE 11TH JUDICIAL CIRCUIT COURT IN AND FOR DADE COUNTY, FLORIDA. CASE NUMBER: 94-25998 FC-38: *MARIBEL ROIG V. A.B.C. JORGE MAS CANOSA AND ISMAEL ROIG.*

Mas Canosa, Jorge
July 5, 1995: 8:00 A.M.–11:00 A.M.

Roig, Maribel
October 25, 1995: 2:00 P.M.–4:00 P.M.

THE 15TH JUDICIAL CIRCUIT COURT IN AND FOR PALM BEACH COUNTY, FLORIDA. CASE NUMBER: CL 90-5064 AO: *JOSÉ LUIS RODRÍGUEZ V. JDL PARTNERS.*

Rodríguez, José Luis
November 2, 1991: 10:30 A.M.–12:05 P.M.
July 28, 1993: 8:45 A.M.–8:50 A.M.

THE 11TH JUDICIAL CIRCUIT COURT IN AND FOR DADE COUNTY, FLORIDA. CASE NUMBER: 87-52895(17): *RICARDO MAS ET AL. V. JORGE MAS CANOSA, CHURCH AND TOWER OF FLORIDA, INC., ET AL.*

Mas Canosa, Jorge
October 19, 1988
May 10, 1989
November 21, 1989

Mas Canosa, Ricardo
April 16, 1996: 10:00 A.M.–5:00 P.M.
May 20, 1996
June 6, 1996: 2:00 P.M.–5:00 P.M.
September 9, 1988: 10:20 A.M.

Video:
Video of celebration of Church & Tower signing ceremony at Casa Juancho Restaurant, Miami, with Chinese officials, 1994 (Exhibit #130).

CHAPTER 7: AN ASSASSIN'S TALE IN THREE ACTS

Interviews/Conversations with A. L. Bardach:
Ángel Alfonso Alemán, April 27, 1998
Tony Alvarez, May 5, 13 and 24, 1998
James Bamford, December 17, 2001
Jack Devine, September 17, 2000, New York
Enrique Encinosa, March 3, 2002, Miami
Gaeton Fonzi, 1994–2001
Robert Gelbard, October 1995
María González, June 27, 2001, October 11, 2001, Miami
José Alfredo Gutiérrez Solana, May 1998, Union City, New Jersey
Howard Hunt, June 1, 1998, Miami
Bill Keller, February 8, 2000, August 2, 2001
José Luis Llovio-Menéndez, October 30, 2000, New York
Mario Martínez Malo, June 13, 1998, Miami
Raúl Masvidal, 1994
Alberto Milián, April 11, 2002, Miami
Miguel Pereira, federal prosecutor, April 26, 1998, San Juan
Hector Pesquera, FBI special agent in charge, Puerto Rico, later Miami, April 28, 1998
Ricardo Pesquera, April 27, 1998, San Juan
Luis Posada Carriles, June 15–18, 1998, Aruba
Colonel Manuel Rodríguez-Madrid, May 5, 1998, Margarita Island, Venezuela
Nestor Sánchez, April 26, 1998
Frank Sturgis, March 20, 1993, Miami
George Volsky, Miami
Johnathan Winer, October 1995

Alfonso, Pablo. "Orlando Bosch Denies Blame." *Miami Herald,* September 13, 1997.

Alter, Jonathan. "Clinton's New Life." *Newsweek,* April 8, 2002.

Anderson, James. "In Barbados, Castro Honors Victims of '76 Bombing." *Miami Herald,* August 2, 1998.

"Anti-Castro Exile Renounces Terrorism." Associated Press, July 24, 2001.

Bardach, Ann Louise, and Larry Rohter. "A Bomber's Tale." *New York Times,* July 12, July 13, 1998.

———. "A Cuban Exile Details Horrendous Matter of Bombing." *New York Times,* July 13, 1998.

———. "Cuban Exile Leader Accused in Plot on Castro." *New York Times,* August 26, 1998.

———. "Life in the Shadows, Trying to Bring Down Castro." *New York Times,* July 13, 1998.

———. "A Plot on Castro Spotlights Exiles." *New York Times,* May 1, 1998.

Barry, John. "CIA's Man at the Bay of Pigs." *Miami Herald,* July 16, 1998.

Branch, Karen. "Help Bosch, Shun Ties to Castro." *Miami Herald,* June 30, 1988.

Bussey, Jane. "The Remaking of Venezuela's Justice System." *Miami Herald,* March 6, 1998.

Campbell, Duncan. "Bush's Decision to Bring Back Otto Reich Exposes the Hypocrisy of the War against Terror." *The Guardian* (U.K.), February 7, 2002.

"CANF and Luis Posada Carriles." *Miami Herald,* July 16, 1998.

Cawthorne, Andrew. "Cuba Puts Elderly Exiles on Trial for 'Invasion.' " Reuters, September 21, 2000.

Chardy, Alfonso. "Successor to Mas at Foundation Helm Mirrors His Views." *Miami Herald,* November 27, 1997.

"Cuba Accuses Salvador of Harboring Potential Killer." Reuters, November 18, 2000.

"Cuban Exile Group Holds Memorial for Victims of 1976 Plane Bombing." *Miami Herald,* October 7, 1996.

"Cuban Exile Says He Lied about Link to Bombings." *South Florida Sun-Sentinel,* August 3, 1998.

"Cuban Exile Says He Lied to Times about Financial Support." *New York Times,* August 4, 1998.

"Cuban Exile's Lawyer Accuses Castro of Framing His Client." Dow Jones Newswire, December 14, 2000.

De Valle, Elaine. "Cuba Again Links Dade Man to Plot." *Miami Herald,* June 22, 2001.

Dillon, Sam. "Cuban Exile Waging 'War' under New Identity." *Miami Herald,* October 21, 1986.

Ducassi, Jay, and Ana Veciana Suarez. "Miami Votes to Let Bosch Have His Day." *Miami Herald,* March 25, 1983.

"Editor's Note." *New York Times,* August 16, 1998.

Epstein Nieves, Gail. "Bosch's Alleged Role in Havana Bombing." *Miami Herald,* April 13, 2001.

Garcia, Luciano. "Ch. 23 Survey Upsets Bosch." *Miami Herald,* July 8, 1988.

Garvin, Glenn. "Cuba Seeks Custody of Anti-Castro Plotter." *Miami Herald,*
November 21, 2000.

———. "Panama: Exile Says Aim Was Castro Hit." *Miami Herald,* January 13, 2001.

Garvin, Glenn, and Frances Robles. "Panama Suspect Has Ties to Dade." *Miami
Herald,* November 21, 2000.

Gaynor, Tim. "Castro Talks of Murder Plot at Panama Summit." Reuters,
November 17, 2000.

Gemoules, Jack. "County's New Boss: Avino." *Miami Herald,* June 3, 1988.

Ho, David. "Kennedy Wanted More Cuba Sabotage." Associated Press, March 21, 2001.

James, Ian. "Castro Foe Denies Financial Backing." *New York Times,* July 14, 1998.

Keller, Bill. "No Error, Just Clarification, Times Says." *Miami Herald,* August 18,
1998.

"Key Cuban Exile in Alleged Plot to Kill Castro Renounces Terrorism." Associated
Press, July 24, 2001.

Kleinnecht, William, and Juan Forero. "Cuba Implicates N.J. Businessman." *New
Jersey Star Ledger,* November 8, 1998.

Lacey, Marc. "Political Memo: Resurrecting Ghosts of Pardons Past." *New York
Times,* March 4, 2001.

Landau, Saul. "Investigate Posada's Statements." *Miami Herald,* August 3, 1998.

Marquis, Christopher. "Foundation Flexes Clout in Fighting Off Allegations." *Miami
Herald,* July 31, 1998.

Morales, Maria A. "Miami-Dade Politics." *Miami Herald,* April 13, 1998.

Nielsen, Kirk. "Terrorists, but Our Terrorists." *Miami New Times,* December 20,
2001.

Powell, Robert Andrew. "A CANF-Do Attitude." *New York Times,* May 23, 1996.

"Priest Helped Cuban Exile Get False Salvadoran ID." *Miami Herald,* June 6, 2001.

Reyes, Gerardo. "Bosch's 'Mix': Ingredient for Trouble?" *Miami Herald,* June 12,
1993.

———. "CANF Leaders Subpoenaed in Castro Assassination Plot." *Miami Herald,*
December 3, 1997.

———. "FBI to Pursue Alleged Castro Death Plot." *Miami Herald,* November 11,
1997.

Reyes, Janice. "Auction Nets $18,000 for Anti-Castro Efforts." *Miami Herald,*
March 2, 1992.

Rice, John. "Castro Steals Show with Death Plot." Associated Press, November 18,
2000.

———. "Cuba, Venezuela Seek an Extradition." Associated Press, November 19, 2000.

———. "Flores, Castro Dispute Terrorism." Associated Press, November 18, 2000.

Robles, Frances. "Exiles Deny Plot on Castro." *Miami Herald,* December 15, 2000.

Tamayo, Juan O. "Exile Fighter Accused Again of Bomb Plots against Cuba." *Miami
Herald,* January 30, 2000.

Tamayo, Juan O., and Gerardo Reyes. "The Man behind Anti-Castro Plots." *Miami
Herald,* June 7, 1998.

Tamayo, Juan O., and Glenn Garvin. "U.S. Urges Clampdown on Exile's Terrorist
Acts." *Miami Herald,* September 30, 1998.

"Trail of the Bombing Conspirators." *Miami Herald,* November 16, 1997.

"Univisión." Bloomberg News Service, July 14, 2000.

"Univisión Says Exile Group Was Present during Bomber Interview." Bloomberg News Service, July 15, 1998.

Van Natta, Don, Jr. "Cuban Exile Group Plans Lawsuit against Times." *New York Times,* July 17, 1998.

"Venezuela to Ask Panama to Extradite Cuban Exile." Reuters, December 21, 2001.

Wilson, Catherine. "Convicted Terrorist Bosch Sent Bombs to Cuba." Associated Press, April 12, 2001.

Books:

Bamford, James. *Body of Secrets: Anatomy of the Ultra-Secret National Security Agency.* New York: Doubleday, 2001.

Cannon, Lou. *President Reagan: The Role of a Lifetime.* New York: Simon & Schuster, 1991.

Dinges, John, and Saul Landau. *Assassination on Embassy Row.* New York: Pantheon, 1980.

Franklin, Jane. "Addendum to Panama: Ex-Presidents Demand Extradition of Cuban Terrorists." In *The U.S. Invasion of Panama: The Truth Behind Operation "Just Cause,"* prepared by the Independent Commission of Inquiry on the U.S. Invasion of Panama. Boston: South End Press, 1991.

Gómez Estrada, Alejándro. *¡La Bestia Roja de Cuba!* Self-published, 1990.

Matthews, Herbert. *Revolution in Cuba: An Essay in Understanding.* New York: Scribner's, 1975.

Posada Carriles, Luis. *Los Caminos del Guerrero.* Self-published, 1994.

Documents:

Cable from Secretary of State Henry Kissinger, subject: US Position on Investigation of Cubana Airlines Crash, October 1976.

Committee on Foreign Affairs, U.S. House of Representatives, Staff Report, State Department and Intelligence Community Involvement in Domestic Activities Related to the Iran/Contra Affair, September 7, 1988.

Deposition of Otto J. Reich before the Senate Select Committee on Secret Military Assistance to Iran and the Nicaraguan Opposition, July 15, 1987.

"Examples of Controversial Pardons by Previous Presidents." A report prepared by Minority staff, Committee on Government Reform, U.S. House of Representatives, April 20, 2001.

Exclusion Proceedings for Orlando Bosch Avila. U.S. Department of Justice, Office of the Associate Attorney General, Washington, D.C., January 23, 1989.

Fax from Luis Posada from El Salvador, signed "Solo," August 1997.

FBI interview of Orlando Bosch on August 22, 1963, re: MIRR bombing attack on a Cuban sugar mill.

Handwritten notes (three pages) from Luis Posada Carriles, given to Ann Louise Bardach at interview, June 18, 1998.

House Select Committee on Assassinations documents:
   CIA, anti-Castro activities, Luis Posada, June 18, 1995.
   CIA, anti-Castro activities, Luis Posada, August 16, 1995.
   CIA, documents on Roland Otero, October 14, 1977.
   CIA signature sheet on Luis Posada, September 26, 1970.
   DEA outside contact report, January 25, 1978.
   Interview with Luis Posada, during Caracas incarceration, June 17, 1978.
   Interview with General Orlando García Vásquez, June 12, 1978.
   Letter to HSCA from Robert L. Keach re: Luis Posada et al., December 20, 1977.
   Meeting with Informant re: Orlando Bosch and Luis Posada, May 31, 1978.
   Periodic file summary on Luis Posada and Cesario Diosdado, March 3, 1978.
   Review (1996) of FBI files on Luis Posada, June 22, 1978.
   Review (1997) notes on Luis Posada, anti-Castro activities, June 28, 1978.
Interview with Orlando Bosch by Andrés Oppenheimer, October 18, 1991.
Interview with Jorge Mas Canosa by Andrés Oppenheimer, September 20, 1991.
Interview with Luis Posada Carriles, Office of the Independent Counsel, February 3,
   1992, conducted by the FBI in Honduras.
Jorge Mas Canosa Chronology, compiled by Scott Armstrong and Saul Landau.
   Institute for Policy Studies, 1995.
"Public Diplomacy and Covert Propaganda: The Declassified Record of Ambassador
   Otto J. Reich." A National Security Archive Electronic Briefing Book, edited by
   Thomas Blanton. Posted at www.gwu.edu/~nsarchiv/NSAEBB/March 2, 2001.
Report of the Congressional Committees Investigating the Iran-Contra Affair,
   November 13, 1987, excerpt.
State Department cables from Ambassador Otto Reich in Caracas, Venezuela:
   Subject: Bosch's Exoneration, July 1986.
   Subject: Bosch's Friends Poised to Whisk Him Away, August 1986.
   Subject: Judge Absolves Orlando Bosch, July 1986.
   Subject: Orlando Bosch Innocence Confirmed, November 1987.
   Subject: Possible Soviet-Cuban Disinformation, September 1987.
   Subject: Request for Deportation of Orlando Bosch, October 9, 1986.
   Subject: Visa Questions for Bosch, September 1987.
State Department memo from Melvyn Levitsky to Donald P. Gregg, subject:
   Responses by Vice President Bush to Telegrams Regarding Orlando Bosch,
   June 8, 1988.
Transcript of interview by Peter R. Bernal with Antonio "Tony" Calatayud,
   "Entrevista con Tony Calatayud," WRLN-TV, August 9, 1998.
U.S. Comptroller General Office report, "White Propaganda."
U.S. District Court for the District of Puerto Rico Court Transcript, *United States of
   America* v. *Ángel Manuel Alfonso et al.,* October 30, 1997.
U.S. District Court for the District of Puerto Rico Court Transcript, *United States of
   America* v. *Ángel Manuel Alfonso et al.,* April 29, 1998.
United States General Accounting Office. Report to Congressional Requesters, State's
   Administration of Certain Public Diplomacy Contracts, October 1987.

Court Depositions:

UNITED STATES DISTRICT COURT FOR THE SOUTHERN DISTRICT OF FLORIDA. CASE NUMBER: 94-2681-CIV: *JORGE MAS CANOSA* V. *THE NEW REPUBLIC, INC., ET AL. (TNR).*

Mas Canosa, Ricardo
April 16, 1996: 10:00 A.M.–5:00 P.M.
May 20, 1996
June 6, 1996: 2:00 P.M.–5:00 P.M.

CHAPTER 8: THE MOVIE STAR DICTATOR

Interviews/Conversations with A. L. Bardach:
Luis Aguilar León, December 13, 2000
Ricardo Alarcón, October 14, 1993, December 28, 1993, February 8, 2000
Agustín Alles, January 22, 2001
Rodrigo Alvarez Cambras, January 3, 1996, November 5, 2001, Havana
Francisco Aruca, November 20, 2000
Lázaro Asencio, February 14, 2001, December 11, 2000
James Bamford, December 17, 2001, January 5, 2002
Miguel Barnett, January 5, 1994
Medea Benjamín, May 20, 1996
Porter Bibb, December 23, 1993, New York
Lorna Burdsall, January 1994
John Cabañas, November 24, 2000
Guillermo Cabrera Infante, July 20, 1996, London
Fidel Castro, October 16, 1993, January 3 and 4, 1994, July 26, 2000, Havana
Juanita Castro, December 11, 2000, April 18, 2002
Rafael Díaz-Balart, October 8, 2001
Bernard Diederich, November 23, 2000
Vilma Espín, December 22, 1993
Ángel Fernández Varela, November 22, 2000
Albert J. Fox Jr., April 5, 2001
Michael Fuchs, December 22, 2000
Norberto Fuentes, November 22, 2000
Leslie Gelb, October 15, 2001
Barbara Walker Gordon, March 3, 2002
Tomás Gutiérrez Alea, 1995
Eloy Gutiérrez Menoyo, February 28, 1993, November 25, 2000
Mike Krinsky, October 1993
Saul Landau, January 14, 2001
Max Lesnik, November 22, 2000, Miami
Salvador Lew, November 27 and 28, 2000
Father Amado Llorente, January 25, 2001
José Luis Llovio-Menéndez, October 30, 2000
Lee Lockwood, January 16, 2001

Marjorie Skelly Lord, April 8, 2002
Frank Manitzas, November 21, 2000
Huber Matos, January 22, 2001, February 14, 2001
Achy Obejas, October 11, 2001
Luis Ortega, November 28, 2000
Constance Penley, November 20, 2001
José Ponce, September 1993, Washington, D.C.
Luis Posada Carriles, June 15–18, 1998
Ana Fidelia Quirot, January 24, 1997
José Ignacio Rasco, November 28, 2000
Fernando Remírez
Jack Skelly, April 12, 2001
Tad Szulc, January 12, 2001
Jorge Tabio, October 29, 1995, Havana

Articles:
Bardach, Ann Louise. "Conversations with Fidel Castro." *Vanity Fair,* March 1994.
———. "Forever Fidel: A Life History of the Cuban Leader." *Talk,* August 2001.
Calvo, Dana. "Castro Assails South Florida Group." *South Florida Sun-Sentinel,*
    July 27, 1998.
Cartier-Bresson, Henri. "This Is Castro's Cuba Seen Face to Face." *Life,* March 15,
    1963.
"Castro Attacks Foreign Press." Associated Press, January 18, 2001.
Cawthorne, Andrew. "Cuba Aims Jibes at U.S. Candidates, Vows No Surrender."
    Reuters, November 3, 2000.
———. "Cuba Detains Dissidents to Stop Shootdown Protests." Reuters, February 24,
    2001.
———. "Cuba Incommunicado to U.S. as More Phones Cut." Reuters, March 21,
    2001.
Chardy, Alfonso. "Effort to Warn JFK Turned into Nightmare." *Miami Herald,*
    March 19, 2001.
"Exiles' Elián Protests Backfired in Cuba Community." *Miami Herald,* July 3, 2000.
"Flight from Cuba Timeline." *South Florida Sun-Sentinel,* September 20, 2000.
Geyer, Georgie Anne. "Why Guevara Failed." *Saturday Review,* August 24, 1968.
"Life History of Jesse Helms." *Talk,* November 2001.
McGeary, Johanna, and Cathy Booth. "Cuba Alone." *Time,* December 6, 1993.
Mestre, Ramon. "Reverence Misdirected." *Miami Herald,* August 19, 1998.
St. George, Andrew. "The Menacing Push of Castroism." *Life,* June 2, 1961.

Books:
Anderson, Jon Lee. *Che Guevara: A Revolutionary Life.* New York: Grove Press,
    1997.
Bamford, James. *Body of Secrets: Anatomy of the Ultra-Secret National Security Agency.*
    New York: Doubleday, 2001.
Behar, Ruth, ed. *Bridges to Cuba: Cuban and Cuban-American Artists, Writers, and*

    Scholars Explore Identity, Nationality, and Homeland. Ann Arbor: University of
    Michigan Press, 1995.

Bonachea, Ramón L., and Marta San Martín. *The Cuban Insurrection, 1952–1959*.
    New Brunswick, N.J.: Transaction Books, 1974.

Bonachea, Rolando E., and Nelson P. Valdés, eds. *The Selected Works of Fidel Castro*.
    Vol. I: *Revolutionary Struggle, 1947–1958*. Cambridge: MIT Press, 1972.

Cabrera Infante, Guillermo. *Mea Cuba*. New York: Farrar, Straus & Giroux, 1994.

Conte Agüero, Luis. *Cartas del Presidio*. Havana: Editorial Lex, 1959.

———. *Fidel Castro: Psiquiatria y Política*. Mexico City: Editorial Jus, 1968.

Domínguez, Jorge I. *Cuba: Order and Revolution*. Cambridge: Belknap Press, 1978.

———. *To Make a World Safe for Revolution: Cuba's Foreign Policy*. Cambridge:
    Harvard University Press, 1989.

Edwards, Jorge. *Persona Non Grata*. New York: Paragon, 1993.

Franqui, Carlos. *Diary of the Cuban Revolution*. New York: Viking Press, 1980.

———. *Family Portrait with Fidel*. New York: Random House, 1984.

Llovio-Menéndez, José Luis. *Insider: My Hidden Life as a Revolutionary in Cuba*.
    New York: Bantam Books, 1988.

Lockwood, Lee. *Castro's Cuba, Cuba's Fidel: An American Journalist's Inside Look at
    Today's Cuba in Text and Picture*. New York: Macmillan, 1967.

Matthews, Herbert. *Revolution in Cuba: An Essay in Understanding*. New York:
    Scribner's, 1975.

Obejas, Achy. *Days of Awe*. New York: Ballantine Books, 2001.

Smith, Earl E. T. *The Fourth Floor: An Account of the Castro Communist Revolution*.
    New York: Random House, 1962.

Suchlicki, Jaime. *Cuba: From Columbus to Castro*. New York: Scribner's, 1974.

Thomas, Hugh. *Cuba; or, The Pursuit of Freedom*. New York: Da Capo Press, 1998.

Valdés, Nelson P. "The Radical Transformation of Cuban Education." In Rolando E.
    Bonachea and Nelson P. Valdés, eds., *Cuba in Revolution*. Garden City, N.Y.:
    Doubleday, 1972.

Documents:
Interview with Orlando Bosch by Andrés Oppenheimer, September 20, 1991.

CHAPTER 9: DR. NO AND UNCLE SAM

Interviews/Conversations with A. L. Bardach:
Ricardo Alarcón, October 14, 1993, December 28, 1993, February 8, 2000, Havana
Lidia Alonso, October 3, 1995, Playa, Havana
José Basulto, March 12, 1996
Bernardo Benes, November 20, 2000, April 8, 2002, Miami
Natália Bolívar, October 20, 1993, December 28, 1995, Havana
Tom Brokaw, April 12, 2001
Carey Cameron, January 5, 1998, Havana
Fidel Castro, October 16, 1993, January 3 and 4, 1994, July 26, 2000, Havana
Juanita Castro, December 11, 2001, Miami

Graciela de la Guardia, October 8, 1995, January 4, 1998, Havana
Ileana de la Guardia, October 1995, Miami
Mario de la Guardia, October 8, 1995, Havana
Patricio de la Guardia, October 20, 1997, July 2000, Havana
Jack Devine, August 3, 2001, New York
Rafael Díaz-Balart, October 8, 2001, Miami
Sam Dryden, October 25, 1993
Alfredo Durán, November 25, 1994, Miami
Vilma Espín, December 22, 1993, January 2, 1994, Havana
Enrico Garzaroli, November 20, 1995, Nassau
Reynaldo González, October 1993
Alfredo Guevara, January 3, 1994, July 22, 2000
Michael Hepburn, November 21, 1995, Nassau
Max Lesnik, November 22, 2000, Miami
Sandy Levinson, October 1993, January 1994
Salvador Lew, November 27 and 28, 2000, Miami
José Luis Llovio-Menéndez, October 30, 2000, New York
Lee Lockwood, January 16, 2001
Frank Mankiewicz, September 15, 1997
Andrés Montés, October 29, 1995, February 2, 2000, Havana
Rosario Moreno, Miami
Donald Nixon, October 20, 1995
Luis Ortega, November 28, 2000, Miami
Marifeli Pérez-Stable, December 11, 2001
Ana Fidelia Quirot, January 24, 1997, January 25, 1998, Havana
Manuel Rocha, U.S. Interests Section, Havana, October 2, 1995
José Rodríguez Feo, October 30, 1993, Havana
William D. Rogers, former Assistant Secretary of State for Inter-American Affairs, January 22, 2001
Assata Shakur, December 28, 1995, Havana
Wayne Smith, August 7, 1993, November 25, 1994, December 6, 1994, April 5, 2001
Peter Tarnoff, 2000–2002
Juanita Vera, January 5, 1994, Havana
Barbara Vesco, October 15, 1995, Orlando, Florida
Dan Vesco, October 9, 1995, New York
Dawn Vesco, December 20, 1995
Patricia Vesco, October 15, 1995, Orlando, Florida
Patrick Vesco, October 9, 1995, New York

Articles:
Bardach, Ann Louise. " 'Casablanca on the Caribbean': Cuba in Transition." *Vanity Fair*, March 1995.
———. " 'Vesco's Last Gamble': The Final Years and Capture of Robert Vesco." *Vanity Fair*, March 1996.

Brinkley-Rogers, Paul. "People on Run Finding Selves at Home Abroad with Castro." *Miami Herald,* March 10, 2001.

Díaz, Jesús. "Cuba Rota." *El País,* January 31, 2000.

Frank, Marc. "Cuban Bureaucracy Resists Castro Cleanup Drive." Reuters, March 1, 2001.

Garcia-Zarza, Isabel. "Anti-Castro Dissident Tried for 'Enemy Propaganda.' " Reuters, May 4, 2000.

Kornbluh, Peter, and James G. Blight. "Dialogue with Castro: A Hidden History." *New York Review of Books,* October 6, 1994.

"Veteran Cuban Dissident Yáñez Pelletier Dies at 83." Reuters, September 18, 2000.

Books:

Cabrera Infante, Guillermo. *Mea Cuba.* New York: Farrar, Straus & Giroux, 1994.

Levin, Robert M. *Secret Missions to Cuba.* New York: Palgrave, 2001.

Szulc, Tad. *Fidel: A Critical Portrait.* New York: Avon Books, 1986.

Thomas, Hugh. *Cuba; or, The Pursuit of Freedom.* New York: Da Capo Press, 1998.

Film:

Dear Fidel: Marita's Story (German documentary). Pegasus Film, 2001.

Fidel, directed by Estela Bravo. Bravo Films and Fort Point Entertainment, 2000.

CHAPTER 10: THE RAID

Interviews/Conversations with A. L. Bardach:
Bernardo Benes, November 20, 2000
Mayor Jerry Brown, August 14, 2000, May 25, 2001
Joan Brown Campbell, February 14 and 24, 2000
María Cardona, INS spokesperson, April 23, 2000
Kendall Coffey, March 3, 2002
Jack Devine, September 17, 2000
Luis Mariano Fernández, April 10, 2000
Armando Gutiérrez, 2000–2002
Raúl Martínez, April 17, 2002
Fernando Remírez, April 2000, Washington, D.C.

Articles:
Acle, Ana. "Raid Leaves Family Dazed and in Shock." *Miami Herald,* April 23, 2000.

Alvarez, Lizette. "Lawyers for Boy's Miami Relatives Rule Out Directly Releasing Him to His Father." *New York Times,* April 1, 2000.

Bragg, Rick. "Fight over Cuban Boy Leaves Scars in Miami." *New York Times,* June 30, 2000.

Bridges, Tyler. "New Miami Fight Looms over Picking Police Chief." *Miami Herald,* May 1, 2000.

Brinkley-Rogers, Paul. "People on Run Finding Selves at Home Abroad with Castro." *Miami Herald,* March 10, 2001.

Buchanan, Edna. "Playing to the Cameras in Miami." *Miami Herald*, April 27, 2000.

Carter, Bill. "Home Videotape Becomes Networks' News of the Day." *Miami Herald*, April 14, 2000.

"Castro Says Boy Won't Be Used as 'Trophy.'" *Miami Herald*, April 23, 2000.

Cazares, David. "Elián, Dad Poised to Return Home." *South Florida Sun-Sentinel*, June 28, 2000.

Chardy, Alfonso. "Questionable U.S. Choices Steered Saga." *Miami Herald*, June 29, 2000.

———."Questions Linger in Elián Rescue." *Miami Herald*, May 26, 2000.

Clymer, Adam. "Debate on Miami Raid Rides on Whether Deal Was Near." *New York Times*, April 25, 2000.

Davies, Frank. "Family Refusal to Give Up Boy Ended D.C. Deal." *Miami Herald*, April 13, 2000.

De Young, Karen. "Cuba Triumphant over Elián." *Washington Post*, June 29, 2000.

———. "Dissidents Wage Lonely Battle in Castro's Cuba." *Washington Post*, July 16, 2000.

Diaz, Madeline Baro. "Mayor Launches Financial Investigation of City Manager." *Miami Herald*, May 1, 2000.

Dowd, Maureen. "Biological Warfare." *New York Times*, April 2, 2000.

"Elián Case Concerns Protesters." Associated Press, April 21, 2000.

"An Elián Chronology: Chronology of Saturday Events." *Miami Herald*, April 23, 2000.

"Elian May Return Without Fanfare." Associated Press, May 29, 2000.

"Elián's Kin Won't Give Boy to Dad." Associated Press, April 1, 2000.

"Elián's Miami Kin Say Dad Is Unfit." Associated Press, April 3, 2000.

"Elián y Bahía de Cochinos: La Traición." *El Nuevo Herald*, April 17, 2000.

"Excerpts from Ruling on Hearing." *New York Times*, June 2, 2000.

"Exiles' Elián Protests Backfired in Cuba Community." *Miami Herald*, July 3, 2000.

Friedman, Thomas L. "Elián and the Panderers." *New York Times*, April 7, 2000.

Garcia, Manny. "Lázaro vs. U.S.: Blunt and Defiant." *Miami Herald*, April 16, 2000.

Garcia, Manny, Carolyn Salazar, and Andres Viglucci. "Raid Returns Elián to Father." *Miami Herald*, April 23, 2000.

Gonzalez, David. "Cuba Sees Fervor over Elián Useful in Other Battles." *New York Times*, July 5, 2000.

Hagel, Chuck. "Leave Elián Alone." *New York Times*, April 28, 2000.

Hart, Gary. "Elián Needed an Embassy." *New York Times*, April 2, 2000.

Herrera, Jose Dante Perra. "Exile Groups Divided over Elián Case." *South Florida Sun-Sentinel*, April 10, 2000.

Hiaasen, Carl. "A Father and His Son: Twigs on a Bitter Tide." *Miami Herald*, April 9, 2000.

———."Joe Carollo—'The King of Crazies.'" *Miami Herald*, May 3, 2000.

———."Penelas Had Better Pray for Peace and Sanity in Miami." *Miami Herald*, April 5, 2000.

Jackson, Terry. "Nightline Shines Bright Light on Elián Debate." *Miami Herald*, April 8, 2000.

———. "PBS Examines Power, Politics in Elián Battle." *Miami Herald,* February 6, 2001.

Kidwell, David. "Police Experts Defend Raid as Textbook Tactics." *Miami Herald,* May 1, 2000.

———. "U.S.: At Least One Gun Had Been Seen at House." *Miami Herald,* April 24, 2000.

Kilborn, Peter T. "Custody Change Could Affect Boy's Asylum Case." *New York Times,* April 25, 2000.

"Legal Fund for Elián Tops $200,000." *Miami Herald,* March 13, 2000.

Mac Swan, Angus. "Loss of Elián a Blow to Hard-Line Exiles in Miami." Reuters, June 2000.

Marquis, Christopher. "Relatives Pressured Boy to Seek Asylum." *New York Times,* May 2, 2000.

"Miami Police Criticized for Creating Obstacles in Elián Raid." Associated Press, June 7, 2000.

Ponce, Eunice. "Elián Supporters Consider Protest Options." *Miami Herald,* March 25, 2000.

"President Clinton's Remarks Saturday on the Elián González Case." *Miami Herald,* April 16, 2000.

Pressley, Sue Anne. "A Shrine to Miami's Angel Who Flew Away." *Washington Post,* November 26, 2001.

Ramo, Joshua Cooper. "A Big Battle for a Little Boy." *Time,* January 17, 2000.

Raspberry, William. "We've All Gone Boy Crazy." *Washington Post,* April 3, 2000.

"Reno Faces Challenge in Elián Case." Associated Press, April 20, 2000.

"Reno Meets Again with Elián's Dad." Associated Press, April 21, 2000.

"Reno Meets with Senators on Seizing of Cuban Boy." Associated Press, April 25, 2000.

Rieff, David. "The Exiles' Last Hurrah." *New York Times,* April 2, 2000.

Robles, Frances. "Miami Relatives Demand to See Boy." *Miami Herald,* April 24, 2000.

Robles, Frances, and Jack Wheat. "Reunion Photo Stirs Controversy." *Miami Herald,* April 24, 2000.

Rosenbaum, David E. "Congressional Republicans to Investigate Miami Raid." *New York Times,* April 25, 2000.

Rosenberg, Carol. "Poll: Most Americans Favor Removing Elián from Home." *Miami Herald,* April 19, 2000.

———. "Video of Elián Draws Passionate Reactions." *Miami Herald,* April 14, 2000.

Sniffen, Michael J. "Agent in Elián Raid Explains Role." *New York Times,* June 6, 2000.

"Statements by Father and the President." *New York Times,* April 21, 2000.

Steinback, Robert. "Elián Poll Signals Wake-up Call." *Miami Herald,* April 12, 2000.

———. "Elián Still Hovers over City Politics." *Miami Herald,* November 11, 2001.

"Text of Final Justice Department Offer for Deal on Moving Boy." *New York Times,* April 25, 2000.

Viglucci, Andres, and Jay Weaver. "Relatives Won't Give Elián to Dad." *Miami Herald*, April 1, 2000.

Weaver, Jay. "Great-Uncle's Lawyers to Rush to Court Today." *Miami Herald*, April 11, 2000.

Weaver, Jay, and Andres Viglucci. "Legal Sides in Elián Saga Fine-Tuning Next Moves." *Miami Herald*, January 14, 2000.

Weil, Martin, and Arthur Santana. "Elián, Father Emerge for D.C. Celebration." *Washington Post*, May 7, 2000.

Yanez, Luisa. "Carollo Vows to Investigate Role of Police in Elián Raid." *South Florida Sun-Sentinel*, May 6, 2000.

———. "NBC Cameraman Says INS Agents on Elián Raid Were Physically and Verbally Abusive." *South Florida Sun-Sentinel*, June 10, 2000.

Books:

Rushdie, Salman. *Fury.* New York: Random House, 2001.

Video:

60 Minutes, Dan Rather interview, CBS, April 16, 2000.
60 Minutes II, Dan Rather interview, CBS, April 20, 2000.

CHAPTER 11: THE THIRD RAIL

The epigraph for this chapter comes from the Cuban national anthem, which is based on "El Himno de Bayamo" by Perucho Figueredo.

Interviews/Conversations with A. L. Bardach:
Cresencio Arcos
Jane Bussey, April 17, 2002
Max Castro
Kendall Coffey, March 3, 2002
Edward Gonzalez, June 12, 2002
Michael Greene, president of the Grammys, May 21, 2001
Armando Gutiérrez
Dennis Hays, October 8, 2001, June 4, 2002
Meg Laughlin
Salvador Lew, November 27 and 28, 2000
Raúl Martínez, April 17, 2002
Andrés Oppenheimer, 1995–2002
Carlos Pérez, October 1994
Mark Preiss, June 10, 2002
William D. Rogers
Mark Seibel, October 11, 2001
Wayne Smith, August 7, 1993, November 25, 1994, December 6, 1994, April 5, 2001, January 10, 2002
Dean Leonard Strickman, Florida International University Law School, June 13, 2002

Peter Tarnoff
Jeffrey Toobin, January 27, 2002
Steve Zack

Articles:

Alvarez, Lizette. "Republican Leaders in House Agree to Food Sales to Cuba." *New York Times,* June 28, 2000.

———. "Senate Kills Plan for Panel to Review Cuban Embargo." *New York Times,* June 21, 2000.

Balmaseda, Liz. "Exile Dynasty Not Carbon Copy." *Miami Herald,* March 1, 2001.

———. "Milián a Symbol of Courage." *Miami Herald,* March 19, 2001.

———. "Repentant Bomber Protests Detention." *Miami Herald,* May 17, 2001.

Boadle, Anthony. "Anti-Castro Cubans Open 'Embassy' in Washington." Reuters, February 6, 2001.

Brinkley-Rogers, Paul. "New Direction Is Planned for Troubled Radio Martí." *Miami Herald,* July 16, 2001.

Bussey, Jane. "Ex-Secretary Files Lawsuit against MasTec." *Miami Herald,* May 8, 2001.

Castro, Max J. "Form over Substance at CANF." *Miami Herald,* July 24, 2001.

Cazares, David. "Mas Canosa's Son Joins Legacy." *South Florida Sun-Sentinel,* July 27, 1998.

Chardy, Alfonso. "Authorities Keep Watch on Exile Groups." *Miami Herald,* March 29, 2000.

Christensen, Dan. "Big-Name Floridians Help Defend Jersey Senator." Miami *Daily Business Review,* May 3, 2001.

———. "Campaign Contributions Refunded by Congressman." Miami *Daily Business Review,* November 13, 2000.

———. "Díaz-Balart Campaign Runs Afoul of Finance Rules, Again." Miami *Daily Business Review,* October 30, 2000.

———. "Díaz-Balart Fined for Late Campaign Reports." Miami *Daily Business Review,* February 16, 2001.

———. "Díaz-Balart's Audit Woes." Miami *Daily Business Review,* November 6, 2000.

Clark, Leslie. "Governor Bush Denounces Rumors of Affair." *Miami Herald,* May 15, 2001.

"Congressman's Campaign Pays Fines for Excessive Contribution." Associated Press, July 20, 2001.

Corzo, Cynthia, Elaine De Valle, and Tim Johnson. "Foundation Driven by Dissent among Miami Cubans." *Miami Herald,* July 21, 2001.

"Cubans Welcome Trade Ban Lift." Associated Press, June 27, 2000.

Davies, Frank. "Congressman's Campaign Pays Out Fine of $30,000." *Miami Herald,* July 20, 2001.

De Valle, Elaine. "Radio Host Disavows CANF." *Miami Herald,* July 23, 2001.

De Valle, Elaine, and Carol Rosenberg. "Ex-CANF Member Explains Resignation." *Miami Herald,* July 24, 2001.

Diaz, Madeline Baro, and David Cazares. "Latin Grammys in Miami Cause Rift in Anti-Castro Group." *South Florida Sun-Sentinel,* July 20, 2001.

———. "New Focus Dividing Members of CANF," *South Florida Sun-Sentinel,* July 22, 2001.

Driscoll, Amy, Jordan Levin, and Frank Davies. "Court Ruling Ends Dade's Cuba Policy." *Miami Herald,* June 13, 2000.

"Elián Relatives Angry as Lawyer Helps Gore." Reuters, November 10, 2000.

"Exile Group to End Broadcasts to Cuba." *South Florida Sun-Sentinel,* July 23, 2001.

Filkins, Dexter. "Miami-Dade County—A Mayor, Once Vocal for Gore, Is Silent." *New York Times,* November 25, 2000.

Fleischman, Joan. "Mas Canosa's Widow Writes Letter on Flap." *Miami Herald,* July 29, 2001.

Forero, Juan. "In Miami, Some Cuban-Americans Take Less Popular Views." *Miami Herald,* April 28, 2000.

Hiaasen, Carl. "Commentary." *Miami Herald,* May 16, 2001.

"House Votes to Lift Restrictions on Travel to Cuba." Associated Press, July 25, 2001.

Isla, Wilfredo Cancio. "Elián Relatives Cancel Ceremony." *El Nuevo Herald,* November 10, 2000.

Jackson, Terry. "Competitors Blast Univisión." *Miami Herald,* April 14, 2000.

"Kiss from Castro for Elián at Rare Cuba Appearance." Reuters, July 10, 2001.

Lynch, Marika. "Poll: Dade 'A Tale of Two Cities': Views on Elián Still Split on Ethnic Lines." *Miami Herald,* November 4, 2000.

Mann, Judy. "Gore Is Pandering Away the Presidency." *Washington Post,* May 17, 2000.

Margolick, David. "Brother Dearest." *Vanity Fair,* July 2001.

Morley, Jefferson. "The Bush Legacy." *Spin,* March 1991.

McGrory, Mary. "Contra-Intuitive." *Washington Post,* July 8, 2001.

Paterniti, Michael. "Florida: America in Extremis." *New York Times,* April 21, 2002.

Pizzo, Stephen. "Bush Family Value$." *Mother Jones,* September/October 1992.

Rabin, Charles, Jay Weaver, and Oscar Corral. "Recount Fails to Change Outcome of Close Election." *Miami Herald,* November 7, 2001.

Rosenberg, Carol. "Exiles See Reno as the Enemy: Elián Crisis the Detonator." *Miami Herald,* March 30, 2000.

———. "Foundation Pursues Goal: The Prosecution of Castro: Head-of-State Immunity Issue an Obstacle for Expensive Effort." *Miami Herald,* July 10, 2001.

Royce, Knut. "Padreda's Brush with the Law." *Newsday,* October 3, 1988.

Royce, Knut, and Gaylord Shaw. "The Jeb Bush Connection." *Newsday,* October 3, 1988.

Saladrigas, Carlos. "Cubans Need a Vision." *Miami Herald,* May 12, 2000.

Santiago, Fabiola. "Two Worlds, Two Cultures." *Miami Herald,* July 29, 2001.

Silva, Mark. "Florida Voting Too Flawed, Former President Embarrassed." *Miami Herald,* January 10, 2001.

Steinback, Robert. "CANF Rift May Open New Doors." *Miami Herald,* July 29, 2001.

Van Natta, Don, Jr., and Dexter Filkins. "To Vote in Florida Miami-Dade." *New York Times,* December 1, 2000.

Wallstein, Peter. "Aide to Gov. Bush Tapped for White House Job." *Miami Herald,*
May 31, 2002.

Wyman, Scott. "MasTec Bid for Contract Draws Fire." *South Florida Sun-Sentinel,*
May 25, 2001.

Yanez, Luisa, and Mark Silva. "Lieberman Salutes Founder of CANF." *Miami Herald,*
October 24, 2000.

CHAPTER 12: THE OLD MAN AND THE LITTLE BOY

Interviews/Conversations with A. L. Bardach:

Ricardo Alarcón, October 14, 1993, December 28, 1993, February 8, 2000, Havana
Cresencio Arcos, May 27, 2002
Sonia Baez, July 25, 2000, Havana
Natália Bolívar, 1994–2000
Carmen Brotón, July 22, 2000, Cárdenas
Mayor Jerry Brown, August 14, 2000, Havana/phone; May 25, 2001
Lieutenant Colonel Brennan T. Byrne, U.S. Southern Command, March 1, 2002
Joan Brown Campbell, February 14, 2000, April 30, 2002
Juanita Castro, December 11, 2001, April 18, 2002, Miami
Carolyn Chapman, September 10, 2000
Sally Grooms Cowal, March 4, 2002
Rafael Díaz-Balart, October 8, 2001, Miami
Enrique Encinosa, March 3, 2002, Miami
Rosita Fernández, July 23, 2000
Albert J. Fox Jr., April 5, 2001
Lisbeth García, February 5–6, 2000, July 19–22, 2000, Cárdenas
Tony González, July 19–22, 2000, Cárdenas
Alfredo Guevara, July 25, 2000, Havana
Dennis Hays, March 4, 2002, June 3, 2002
Victor Herrera, July 22, 2000, Cárdenas
John Kavulich, 1996–2001
Lochy Le Riverend, July 15, 2000, Havana
Salvador Lew, November 27–28, 2000, Miami
Dagoberto Munero, February 7, 2000, Cárdenas
Richard Nuccio, February 27, 2002
Robert Pastor, May 31, 2002
Ana Fidelia Quirot, January 5, 1998, Havana
Enzo Roberto, July 20, 2000
William D. Rogers, January 22, 2002
Julia Swoig

Articles:

Adams, David. "Bush Renews '96 Ban on U.S. Boats Going to Cuba." *St. Petersburg Times,* March 13, 2002.

"America's Cuban Independent Journalists Find Audiences Abroad, but Not at Home." Associated Press, October 3, 2000.

Arzua, Lila. "Gathering Remembers Dead in 13 de Marzo Ship Sinking." *Miami Herald,* July 14, 2001.

Bardach, Ann Louise. "Cuba: No Longer the Same." *Condé Nast Traveler,* November 1995.

Bauza, Vanessa. "Cuban-Americans Holding More Moderate Views on Relations with Homeland." *South Florida Sun-Sentinel,* October 20, 2000.

———. "In Fox Flap, Castro Flaunts Convention," *South Florida Sun-Sentinel,* April 28, 2002.

Bohning, Don. "U.S. Rebukes Cuba on Denial of Exit Permits." *Miami Herald,* August 29, 2000.

Brecher, Elinor J. "Veteran of Bay of Pigs Now Fights for Dialogue." *Miami Herald,* March 31, 2001.

Buckley, Cara. "Miami-Havana Air Traffic Hits Record High." Reuters, August 18, 2000.

"Castro's Brother Sees No Changes." Associated Press, May 13, 2001.

Cawthorne, Andrew. "Cuba Jails Anti-Castro Dissident for Three Years." Reuters, February 25, 2000.

———. "Cuba Jails Exile." Reuters, October 10, 2000.

———. "Cuban Dissidents Urge Release of Colleague Roca." Reuters, July 15, 2001.

———. "U.S. Senators Meet Castro, Dissidents in Cuba." Reuters, July 15, 2000.

Cazares, David. "Black Americans Look Past Castro to Support Cuba's Black Majority." *South Florida Sun-Sentinel,* February 18, 2001.

"Cuban Dissidents Challenge Castro to Allow Debate." Reuters, November 1, 2000.

"Cuba's Elián Wants to Be a Policeman." Reuters, April 4, 2002.

"Dissidents Seek Popular Referendum for Cuban Changes." Reuters, March 6, 2001.

Echerri, Vicente. "Antes que Anochezca." *El Nuevo Herald,* February 17, 2001.

"Elián Begins New Chapter at Home." Associated Press, June 29, 2000.

"Elián Disappears into Private Life." Associated Press, June 24, 2001.

"Elián Wishes Fidel Castro 'Happy Father's Day.' " Reuters, June 17, 2000.

"Excluyen a *La Jornada* de una Conferencia en Embajada de EU—Editorial." *La Jornada de Mexico,* March 7, 2002.

Frank, Marc. "Castro Calls Fox a Liar." Reuters, April 23, 2002.

Garcia-Zarza, Isabel. "Cuban Dissidents Demand Release of Activist Biscet." Reuters, November 3, 2000.

Kasperowicz, Pete. "Showdown over U.S. Cuba Policy Nears." *Washington Times,* March 19, 2002.

Levin, Jordan. "Dade Letting Some Companies Sign a Less Stringent 'Cuba Affidavit.' " *Miami Herald,* June 12, 2000.

Moreira, Domingo. "Commentary: Project Varela Leads Cuba to Freedom." *Miami Herald,* June 5, 2002.

Pain, John. "Authors Say U.S. Gains Little from Trade Embargo on Cuba." Associated Press, January 28, 2002.

Perez, Miguel. "Petition Urges Prosecution of Castro." *The Record,* March 16, 2001.

Sequera, Vivian. "Cuba Opposition—Three Years Sentence for Biscet." Associated Press, February 25, 2000.

———. "Raúl Castro to U.S.: Normalize Ties." Associated Press, January 5, 2001.

Slevin, Peter. "Cuba Urges Cooperation on Drug Interdiction." *Washington Post,* March 19, 2002.

Viglucci, Andres. "Winners and Losers in the Elián Saga." *Miami Herald,* July 2, 2000.

Books:

Bardach, Ann Louise, ed. *Cuba: A Traveler's Literary Companion.* Berkeley, Calif.: Whereabouts Press, 2002.

Gutiérrez, Pedro Juan. *Dirty Havana Trilogy.* New York: Farrar, Straus & Giroux, 1998.

Documents:

Strategic Forecasting, L.L.C. "Cuba's 'Axis' Listing a Cover for Other U.S. Goals." Posted at www.stratfor.com May 7, 2002.

———. "Succession Plan in Place for a Post-Castro Cuba." Posted at www.stratfor.com January 28, 2002.

BIBLIOGRAPHY

Allman, T. D. *Miami: City of the Future.* New York: Atlantic Monthly Press, 1987.
Anderson, Jon Lee. *Che Guevara: A Revolutionary Life.* New York: Grove Press, 1997.
Arenas, Reinaldo. *Before Night Falls: A Memoir.* New York: Viking Penguin, 1993.
Bamford, James. *Body of Secrets: Anatomy of the Ultra-Secret National Security Agency.* New York: Doubleday, 2001.
Bardach, Ann Louise, ed. *Cuba: A Traveler's Literary Companion.* Berkeley, Calif.: Whereabouts Press, 2002.
Behar, Ruth, ed. *Bridges to Cuba: Cuban and Cuban-American Artists, Writers, and Scholars Explore Identity, Nationality, and Homeland.* Ann Arbor: University of Michigan Press, 1995.
Betto, Frei. *Fidel Castro y la Religión.* Havana: Editorial Si-Mar, 1994.
Bolívar Arostegui, Natalia. *Los Orishas en Cuba.* Havana: Ediciones Unión, 1990.
Bonachea, Ramón L., and Marta San Martín. *The Cuban Insurrection, 1952–1959.* New Brunswick, N.J.: Transaction Books, 1974.
Bonachea, Rolando E., and Nelson P. Valdés. *Cuba in Revolution.* Garden City, N.Y.: Anchor Books, 1972.
———, eds. *The Selected Works of Fidel Castro.* Vol. I: *Revolutionary Struggle, 1947–1958.* Cambridge: MIT Press, 1972.
Cabrera Infante, Guillermo. *Mea Cuba.* New York: Farrar, Straus & Giroux, 1994.
Cannon, Lou. *President Reagan: The Role of a Lifetime.* New York: Simon & Schuster, 1991.
Castro, Fidel. *In Defense of Socialism.* New York: Pathfinder Press, 1989.
Codrescu, Andrei. *Ay, Cuba!* New York: St. Martin's Press, 1999.
Conte Agüero, Luis. *Cartas del Presidio.* Havana: Editorial Lex, 1959.
———. *Fidel Castro: Psiquiatría y Política.* Mexico City: Editorial Jus, 1968.
———. *Paredón.* Miami: Colonial Press, 1962.
Didion, Joan. *Miami.* New York: Pocket Books, 1987.
Domínguez, Jorge I. *Cuba: Order and Revolution.* Cambridge: Belknap Press, 1978.
———. "The Secrets of Castro's Staying Power." *Foreign Affairs,* Spring 1993.
———. *To Make a World Safe for Revolution: Cuba's Foreign Policy.* Cambridge: Harvard University Press, 1989.
Edwards, Jorge. *Persona Non Grata.* New York: Paragon, 1993.
Fainaru, Steve, and Ray Sánchez. *The Duke of Havana.* New York: Villard Books, 2001.
Falcoff, Mark. *The Cuban Revolution and the United States: A History in Documents 1958–1960.* Washington, D.C.: U.S. Cuba Press, 2001.

Fernández, Alina. *Castro's Daughter: An Exile's Memoir of Cuba.* New York: St. Martin's Press, 1997.

Franklin, Jane. *Cuba and the United States: A Chronological History.* Melbourne: Ocean Press, 1997.

Franqui, Carlos. *Diary of the Cuban Revolution.* New York: Viking Press, 1980.

———. *Family Portrait with Fidel.* New York: Random House, 1984.

Fuentes, Norberto. *Dulces Guerreros Cubanos.* Barcelona: Editorial Seix Barral, 1999.

Geldof, Lynn. *Cubans: Voices of Change.* New York: St. Martin's Press, 1991.

Geyer, Georgie Anne. *Guerrilla Prince: The Untold Story of Fidel Castro.* Kansas City, Mo.: Andrews McMeel, 1993.

Gimbel, Wendy. *Havana Dreams: A Story of Cuba.* New York: Alfred A. Knopf, 1998.

Gómez Estrada, Alejandro. *La Bestia Roja de Cuba!* Self-published, 1990.

González, Olympia B. *Leyendas Cubanas: A Collection of Cuban Legends.* Lincolnwood, Ill.: National Textbook Company, 1997.

Harnecker, Marta. *From Moncada to Victory.* New York: Pathfinder, 1987.

Hiaasen, Carl. *Basket Case.* New York: Alfred A. Knopf, 2002.

The Journal of Decorative and Propaganda Arts: Cuba Theme Issue. Miami: Wolfson Foundation, 1996.

Kissinger, Henry. *Years of Renewal.* New York: Simon & Schuster, 1999.

Kornbluh, Peter, ed. *Bay of Pigs Declassified.* New York: New Press, 1998.

Landau, Saul. *The Guerrilla Wars of Central America.* New York: St. Martin's Press, 1993.

Leiner, Marvin. *Sexual Politics in Cuba.* Boulder, Colo.: Westview Press, 1994.

Levine, Robert M. *Secret Missions to Cuba.* New York: Palgrave, 2001.

———. *Tropical Diaspora.* Gainesville: University Press of Florida, 1993.

Linares, María Teresa. *La Música y el Pueblo.* Havana: Editorial Pueblo y Educación, 1979.

Llovio-Menéndez, José Luis. *Insider: My Hidden Life as a Revolutionary in Cuba.* New York: Bantam Books, 1988.

Lockwood, Lee. *Castro's Cuba, Cuba's Fidel: An American Journalist's Inside Look at Today's Cuba in Text and Picture.* New York: Macmillan, 1967.

Lorenzo, Orestes. *Wings of the Morning.* New York: St. Martin's Press, 1994.

Mallin, Jay. *History of the Cuban Armed Forces.* Reston, Va.: Ancient Mariners Press, 2000.

Mallin, Jay, and Bob Smith. *Betrayal in April.* Reston, Va.: Ancient Mariners Press, 2000.

Martí, José. *Selected Writings.* Ed. and trans. Esther Allen. New York: Penguin, 2002.

———. *Veros Sencillos/Simple Verses.* Houston: Arte Público Press, 1997.

Martin, Lionel. *The Early Fidel: Roots of Castro's Communism.* Secaucus, N.J.: Lyle Stuart, 1978.

Matthews, Herbert L. *Revolution in Cuba: An Essay in Understanding.* New York: Scribner's, 1975.

Medina, Pablo. *Exiled Memories: A Cuban Childhood.* Austin: University of Texas Press, 1990.

Miller, Tom. *Trading with the Enemy.* New York: Atheneum, 1992.

Mina, Gianni. *An Encounter with Fidel*. Melbourne: Ocean Press, 1991.

Moses, Catherine. *Real Life in Castro's Cuba*. Wilmington, Del.: Scholarly Resources, 2000.

Núñez Jiménez, A., and L. Núñez Velis. *La Comida en el Monte*. Havana: Mec Graphic, 1998.

Obejas, Achy. *Days of Awe*. New York: Ballantine Books, 2001.

Oppenheimer, Andrés. *Castro's Final Hour*. New York: Simon & Schuster, 1992.

Pérez, Louis A. *On Becoming Cuban*. Chapel Hill: University of North Carolina Press, 1999.

Pérez-Roura, Armando. *Tome Nota*. Self-published, 1993.

Pérez-Stable, Marifeli. *The Cuban Revolution: Origins, Course, and Legacy*. New York: Oxford University Press, 1993.

Phillips, David Atlee. *The Night Watch*. New York: Atheneum, 1977.

Posada Carriles, Luis. *Los Caminos del Guerrero*. Self-published, August 1994.

Price, S. L. *Pitching Around Fidel*. New York: HarperCollins, 2000.

Quirk, Robert E. *Fidel Castro*. New York: W. W. Norton, 1993.

Rieff, David. *The Exile: Cuba in the Heart of Miami*. New York: Simon & Schuster, 1993.

Rodríguez, Ana. *Diary of a Survivor: Nineteen Years in a Cuban Women's Prison*. New York: St. Martin's Press, 1995.

Seers, Dudley, ed. *Cuba: The Economic and Social Revolution*. Chapel Hill: University of North Carolina Press, 1964.

Smith, Earl E. T. *The Fourth Floor: An Account of the Castro Communist Revolution*. New York: Random House, 1962.

Smith, Wayne S. *The Closest of Enemies*. New York: W. W. Norton, 1987.

Suchlicki, Jaime. *Cuba: From Columbus to Castro*. New York: Scribner's, 1974.

Sweig, Julia. *Inside the Cuban Revolution*. Cambridge: Harvard University Press, 2002.

Szulc, Tad. *Fidel: A Critical Portrait*. New York: Avon Books, 1986.

Taladrid, R., and L. Barredo. *El Chairman Soy Yo*. Havana: Trébol Ediciones, 1994.

Tattlin, Isabel. *Cuban Diaries*. Chapel Hill, N.C.: Algonquin, 2002.

Thomas, Evan. *The Very Best Men*. New York: Simon & Schuster, 1995.

Thomas, Hugh. *Cuba; or, The Pursuit of Freedom*. New York: Da Capo Press, 1998.

Timerman, Jacobo. *Cuba: A Journey*. New York: Vintage Books, 1992.

Toobin, Jeffrey. *Too Close to Call: The Thirty-Six-Day Battle to Decide the 2000 Election*. New York: Random House, 2001.

Torres, María de los Angeles. *In the Land of Mirrors*. Ann Arbor: University of Michigan Press, 1999.

U.S.-Cuban Relations in the 21st Century: A Follow-on Chairman's Report of an Independent Task Force Sponsored by the Council on Foreign Relations. New York: Council on Foreign Relations, 2001.

U.S.-Cuban Relations in the 21st Century: Report of an Independent Task Force Sponsored by the Council on Foreign Relations, Bernard W. Aronson and William D. Rogers, co-chairs. New York: Council on Foreign Relations, 1999.

Vargas Llosa, Álvaro. *El Exilio Indomable*. Madrid: Editorial Espasa, 1998.

Zito, Miriam. *Asalto*. Havana: Ediciones Abril, 1998.

Additional Suggested Readings on Cuba:

Arenas, Reinaldo. *Before Night Falls*. New York: Viking, 1993.

———. *The Doorman*. New York: Grove Press, 1987.

Avenas, Thomas. *Life Sentences: Writers, Artists, and AIDS*. San Francisco: Mercury House, 1994.

Baker, Christopher P. *The Cuba Handbook*. San Francisco: Moon Publications, 1997.

Bernardo, José Raúl. *The Secret of the Bulls*. New York: Simon & Schuster, 1996.

Blanco, Richard. *City of a Hundred Fires*. Pittsburgh: University of Pittsburgh Press, 1998.

Cabrera Infante, Guillermo. *Three Trapped Tigers*. Boston: Faber & Faber, 1982.

———. *View of Dawn in the Tropics*. Boston: Faber & Faber, 1988.

Carpentier, Alejo. *The Chase*. New York: Farrar, Straus & Giroux, 1989.

Cruz Smith, Martin. *Havana Bay*. New York: Random House, 1999.

de Aragón, Uva. *Caimán Ante el Espejo: Un Ensayo de Interpretación de lo Cubano*. Miami: Ediciones Universal, 2000.

Estevez, Abilio. *Thine Is the Kingdom*. New York: Arcade Publishing, 1999.

García, Cristina. *Dreaming in Cuban*. New York: Ballantine Books, 1992.

Greene, Graham. *Our Man in Havana*. Harmondsworth, England: Penguin Books, 1958.

Gutiérrez, Pedro Juan. *El Rey de la Habana*. Barcelona: Editorial Anagrama, 1999.

Hospital, Carolina, and Jorge Cantera, eds. *A Century of Cuban Writers in Florida*. Sarasota: Pineapple Press, 1996.

Hunt, Christopher. *Waiting for Fidel*. New York: Houghton Mifflin, 1998.

Iyer, Pico. *Falling Off the Map: Some Lonely Places in the World*. New York: Knopf, 1993.

Lamazares, Ivonne. *The Sugar Island*. New York: Houghton Mifflin, 2000.

Lezama Lima, José. *Paradiso*. Trans. Gregory Rabassa. Normal, Ill.: Dalkey Archive Press, 2000.

Medina, Pablo. *The Return of Felix Nogara*. New York: Persea Books, 2000.

Menéndez, Ana. *In Cuba I Was a German Shepherd*. New York: Grove Press, 2001.

Mestre, Ernesto. *The Lazarus Rumba*. New York: Picador USA, 1999.

Montero, Mayra. *The Messenger*. New York: HarperCollins, 1999.

Novas Calvo, Lino, "The Long Night of Ramón Yendia," in *Spanish Stories and Tales*. Ed. Harriet de Onis. New York: Pocket Library, 1954.

Obejas, Achy. *We Came All the Way from Cuba So You Could Dress Like This?* San Francisco: Cleis Press, 1994.

Padilla, Heberto. *Self-Portrait of the Other*. New York: Farrar, Straus & Giroux, 1990.

Ponte, Antonio José. *In the Cold of the Malecón*. San Francisco: City Lights Books, 2000.

Rodríguez Feo, José. *Mi Correspondencia con Lezama Lima*. Havana: Ediciones Unión, 1989.

Valdés, Zoe. *Yocandra in the Paradise of Nada.* New York: Arcade Publishing, 1995.

Yáñez, Mirta, ed. *Cubana: Contemporary Fiction by Cuban Women.* Boston: Beacon Press, 1998.

Yáñez, Mirta, and Marilyn Bobes. *Estatuas de Sal: Cuentistas Cubanas Contemporáneas.* Havana: Ediciones Unión, 1996.

INDEX

ANN LOUISE BARDACH is an award-winning investigative journalist who has been covering Cuba for ten years for the *New York Times, Vanity Fair* and other national publications. She has appeared on *60 Minutes, Today, Dateline,* CNN, *The O'Reilly Factor, Charlie Rose* and NPR. She is coauthor of the bestseller *Vicki* and edited the anthology *Cuba: A Traveler's Literary Companion,* and is visiting professor of international journalism at the University of California at Santa Barbara.

A B O U T   T H E   T Y P E

This book was set in Bulmer, a typeface designed in the late eighteenth century by the London type-cutter William Martin. The typeface was created especially for the Shakespeare Press, directed by William Bulmer; hence, the font's name. Bulmer is considered to be a transitional typeface, containing characteristics of old-style and modern designs. It is recognized for its elegantly proportioned letters, with their long ascenders and descenders.